URKEY

CYPRUS

TURKEY

Aleppo
Latakia
SYRIA
Mosul
Kirkuk
TEHERAN

BEIRUT
LEBANON
DAMASCUS
Homs

Haifa
ISRAEL
Tel Aviv
JERUSALEM
AMMAN
JORDAN
IRAQ
BAGHDAD

Port Said
Ismailia
Sinai
Ma'an
Suez
Aqaba
Eilat

Sharm e-Sheikh

EGYPT

Aswan

Lake Nasser

Port Sudan

SUDAN

Omdurman
KHARTOUM

Tigris

Euphrates

Basra

KUWAIT

Medina

Mecca

Jidda

SAUDI

ARABIA

Red Sea

Dhahran
BAHRAIN
QATAR
DAWHAH
RIYADH

Persian Gulf

TRUCIAL
STATES

MUSCAT

MUSCAT AND OMAN

SOUTHERN YEMEN

SAN'A

YEMEN

Ta'iz

ADEN

Gulf of Aden

Nile

ETHIOPIA

ADDIS ABABA

SOMALIA

MOGADISHO

Indian

Ocean

0	200	400	600	800 miles
0	400	800	1200 Km.	

CARTA, Jerusalem

THE FOREIGN POLICY SYSTEM
OF ISRAEL

Setting, Images, Process

Books by Michael Brecher

THE STRUGGLE FOR KASHMIR
1953

NEHRU
A Political Biography 1959
(Abridged Edition 1961)

THE NEW STATES OF ASIA
A Political Analysis
1963

SUCCESSION IN INDIA
A Study in Decision-Making
1966

INDIA AND WORLD POLITICS
Krishna Menon's View of the World
1968

POLITICAL LEADERSHIP IN INDIA
An Analysis of Élite Attitudes
1969

THE FOREIGN POLICY SYSTEM OF ISRAEL
Setting, Images, Process
1972

THE FOREIGN POLICY SYSTEM OF ISRAEL

Setting, Images, Process

MICHAEL BRECHER

NEW HAVEN
YALE UNIVERSITY PRESS
1972

Library of Congress catalog card number: 73–179469
International standard book number: 0–300–01549–6
Printed in the United States of America by
The Murray Printing Co., Forge Village, Mass.

TO EVA

PREFACE

The significance of foreign policy in the 1970s and beyond is, or should be, self-evident. The 'classical' system of international politics under European hegemony was shattered by forces culminating in the Second World War; and a Global System emerged in which decisions of actors anywhere have consequences elsewhere—often multiple and far-reaching. This is true for middle and small powers as well as for great and super powers. During this period, too, there were notable advances in the study of international political behaviour. Yet the proliferation of models and methods has not been an unmixed blessing. By and large the gap between deductive and inductive techniques of analysis has not been narrowed appreciably. The 'great debate' between 'science' and 'neo-traditionalism' has generated more heat than light, while the task of creating rigorous—and operational—research frameworks has barely begun. The conviction that we must move beyond a debate on methodologies to substantive theory-oriented research on state behaviour has guided this project from its inception.

This book is the result of a decade of grappling with questions of theory and methods in foreign policy analysis. The choice of 'micro-level' research—the behaviour of a single actor—arose from dissatisfaction with two trends in the study of International Politics: an excessive concentration on the system as a whole, that is, 'macro-analysis'; and traditional historical methods of surveying *foreign relations*, rather than analysing *foreign policy*. The approach used in this project is elaborated in Chapter 1. Suffice it to note that each of the components of a Foreign Policy System (the Operational Environment, the Communication Network, the Decision-Making Élite, their Psychological Environment, and the processes of Formulation and Implementation of foreign policy) will be explored autonomously within a system framework.

The focus on Israel in this inquiry into a foreign policy system in motion arises from her strategic position in the configuration of world politics during the past quarter century. Among the fundamental changes in the International System none has been more dramatic than the Retreat from Empire: since the Second World War more than seventy peoples in Asia and Africa acquired political independence, some by means of a peaceful transfer of power, others as the culmination of a long and, often, violent struggle. Among the latter is the State of Israel, proclaimed on the eve of the British withdrawal from Mandatory Palestine, on 14 May 1948.

Few international actors have been the source or the object of as much attention as the revived Jewish State. Thus a careful survey has revealed that, from mid-1967 to the end of 1969, Israel ranked third among all states—after the two super powers—as a producer of recorded international action, and in some periods, second; further, that Israel was the recipient of almost half the total flow of actions initiated from outside the Middle East and directed to that region. (See McClelland and Ancoli in the Bibliography.) There has been a flood of published materials about Israel in many languages. However, apart from peripheral attention in books and articles on 'the Middle East' or 'the Arab–Israel conflict', the stimuli, content, decision-making processes, and consequences of Israeli foreign policy have been almost totally neglected. A second purpose of this project, then, is to contribute to the understanding of a profound international conflict and of the foreign policy of a new state.

The data in this volume refer to the first two decades of Israel's independence. There are, however, exceptions, where the academic right of 'hot pursuit' was exercised; for example, the views advocated by Israeli dissenters in 1970 about 'whither Israel?'. Post-1968 developments in Israeli foreign policy will be analysed in a related book on high-policy decisions now in preparation. The object of this volume, therefore, is to give content to a universally-applicable Research Design for foreign policy analysis, drawn from the experience of one state during a twenty-year period of permanent crisis. The decisions to be explored in depth in the related volume will permit the testing of many of the hypotheses that have been generated in the literature of international politics during the past decade. These deal with the decision-making process; perceptions and misperceptions; the links between images and decisions; the impact of crises on decision-makers' perceptions and their ensuing choices among alternative options, etc.[1]

Substantial details on the Setting of Israel's foreign policy are presented in Part I. Their relevance will, it is hoped, become evident in later sections of this volume. The rationale for their inclusion may be stated thus: the dynamics, processes, and decisions of foreign policy can, I believe, be explored most rewardingly within the context of a total Foreign Policy System; and that framework requires careful attention to the Setting or Operational Environment of policy comprising, among others, military capability, the economy, the polity, interest groups, and competing élites, as well as the external dimension.

My inquiry proceeded in a dual milieu: the erroneously defined

[1] Charles Hermann; Ole Holsti; Robert Jervis; Lester Milbraith; Robert North, et al. (Stanford Studies); Glen Paige; Dean Pruitt; James Rosenau; Sydney Verba; Dina Zinnes; and the McGill Group—my colleagues, Blema Steinberg, Janice Stein, and myself.

'ivory-tower', in this case a seminar on the comparative analysis of foreign policy at McGill University since 1961, and continuous field work in Israel during the 1960s. The ideas generated in the former were tested in the latter, and the findings from my empirical research led to revised formulations of earlier ideas.

During the course of that decade I received generous support from many institutions and persons in the preparation of this book and the companion volume on high-policy decisions:

the Canada Council, an invaluable support for independent inquiry, which made available generous research grants in 1965–6, 1968, and 1969–70, as well as a Killam Award in 1970 for further research in the field of foreign policy;

McGill University, which provided extended leaves of absence for research in 1964–6 and again from 1969;

the John Simon Guggenheim Foundation, whose Fellowship in 1965–6 enabled me to spend the year in Israel gathering primary data;

my students in Political Science 774 at McGill, who challenged every concept, construct, hypothesis, and proposed method of exploring foreign policy, in a continuing action-reaction stimulus through the 1960s;

the many Israelis who gave generously of their knowledge and time in interviews held over the years about one or another aspect of Israel's foreign policy (a list of persons interviewed is included in the Bibliography);

two persons whose comments on every chapter contributed greatly to the final work, especially by emphasizing the need to link theory with empirical data and the importance of clarity of expression: my McGill colleague, Professor Janice Stein, and Sheldon Schreter, a former student and research assistant;

two persons in Israel who through meticulous attention to a massive typescript ensured its highest possible accuracy: Ya'acov Shimoni, a scholar-diplomat and Assistant Director-General in the Foreign Ministry, who has been associated with the Israel Foreign Service since its inception, and Dr. Haim Yahil, Director-General of the Foreign Office from 1960 to 1964, and later Chairman of the Israel Broadcasting Authority;

eight other Israelis who made helpful comments on particular chapters: Dr. Meron Medzini, Hanan Aynor, Mordekhai Gazit, Benyamin Geist, Dr. Emanuel Gutmann, Dr. Meir Merhav, Dr. Nissan Oren, and Elad Peled;

three members of the Israel Foreign Ministry staff, whose kind assistance in locating diverse empirical data over the years is appreciated: Mrs. Sarah Arbel of the International Organizations Department, Mrs. Miriam Doryon, custodian of the Ministry's personnel files, and Miss Liora Grynbaum, Librarian of the Foreign Office;

Mrs. Sheila Moser and Mrs. Daphne Nahmias for helpful research
   assistance in the later stages of the writing of this book;
John Bell and Miss Ena Sheen of Oxford University Press, London, for
   valuable editorial advice.

My wife Eva, as always, gave me continuous encouragement in this
intellectual endeavour and contributed to the outcome in many helpful
ways. None of these persons is responsible, however, for interpretations
contained in the book.

If there is bias scattered through the following pages, as undoubtedly
there is, I regard this as both human and inevitable. I began the project
with a fundamental affinity for Israel and her people. That empathy
remains undiminished a decade later. It has not, however, prevented
me from attempting a clinical dissection of Israel's foreign policy nor
from exercising a scholar's right—and obligation—to engage in critical
evaluation.

Jerusalem   MICHAEL BRECHER
November 1970

CONTENTS

DETAILED TABLE OF CONTENTS

PART II PSYCHOLOGICAL ENVIRONMENT

PART III PROCESS

FIGURES

TABLES

APPENDIX TABLES

CHAPTER 1

Framework of Analysis

The study of foreign policy is under-developed: its theory content is inadequate; and analysis for the most part lacks rigour. Some preparatory work has been done. State behaviour is no longer seen exclusively as a reaction to external stimuli; internal pressures, too, are now widely recognized as affecting foreign policy decisions. Yet, as Professor Rosenau has cogently observed, 'to identify factors is not to trace their influence. To uncover processes that affect external behavior is not to explain how and why they are operative under certain circumstances and not under others. To recognize that foreign policy is shaped by internal as well as external factors is not to comprehend how the two intermix or indicate the conditions under which one predominates over the other.'[1]

There have been two major orientations in this field—single-country studies and general systems theory. The former amass empirical data but are usually devoid of theoretical value. The general systems approach, on the other hand, denigrates factual detail and posits a high level of mechanistic response in state behaviour. Theory-oriented studies of foreign policy, moreover, are rather scarce. And they are essentially of the taxonomic type, that is, they develop categories for a mass of undifferentiated data. They do not, for the most part, distinguish the crucial variables of the foreign policy process nor do they establish relationships among them. Their categories are descriptive and their major concern is a narrative of events which form the cumulative flow of *foreign relations*, especially among the 'great powers'. Indeed, the analysis of *foreign policy* remains in an infant state relative to the volume and quality of international relations as a whole.[2]

The task of a new approach to foreign policy is to overcome these deficiencies. More precisely it is to guide systematic inquiry into cause-effect relations, as well as the search for patterns of regularity in state behaviour. To attempt prediction of probable choices among foreign

[1] J. N. Rosenau, 'Pre-Theories and Theories of Foreign Policy', in R. Barry Farrell (ed.), *Approaches to Comparative and International Politics*, Northwestern University Press, Evanston, Ill., 1966, p. 31.

[2] Three schools have emerged during the first stage on the long road to foreign policy theory: power, decision-making, and input-output analysis. For a critique of these theoretical approaches see M. Brecher, B. Steinberg and J. Stein, 'A Framework for Research on Foreign Policy Behavior', *The Journal of Conflict Resolution*, xiii, 1, March 1969, pp. 75–101.

policy options requires a framework in which the interplay of different pressures can be observed and measured. Such is the aim of the research design presented here. It derives in part from the input-output approach and in part from recent contributions of systems analysis in political science.[1] The core unit of analysis is the state as it functions within an international system at any point in time and space.

(a) A RESEARCH DESIGN[2]

The research design for this inquiry into Israel's foreign policy is based upon a simple proposition: the concept of system is no less valid in foreign policy analysis than in the study of domestic politics. Like all systems of action, the foreign policy system comprises an environment or setting, a group of actors, structures through which they initiate decisions and respond to challenges, and processes which sustain or alter the flow of demands and products of the system as a whole. The boundaries of this system are vertical, that is, they encompass all inputs and outputs which affect decisions whose content and scope lie essentially in the realm of inter-state relations. As such, the boundaries fluctuate from one issue to another. It is necessary, therefore, to explore the content and interrelations of these key variables—environment, actors, structures, and processes—all placed within a framework of demands on policy or inputs, and products of policy or outputs.

A foreign policy system may be likened to a flow into and out of a network of structures or institutions which perform certain functions and thereby produce decisions. These in turn feed back into the system as inputs in a continuous flow of demands on policy, policy process, and products of policy. All foreign policy systems, then, comprise a set of components which can be classified in three general categories: inputs, process, and outputs. The notion of flow and dynamic movement in a system which is constantly absorbing demands and channelling them into a policy machine which transforms these inputs into decisions or outputs is portrayed in Figures 1 and 2.

All data regarding foreign policy can be classified in one of these categories. Before Israeli content can be introduced into the research design, however, the categories must be carefully defined and the inter-relationships of inputs process, and outputs explained.

The *operational environment* defines the setting in which foreign policy decisions are taken. The concept of setting refers to a set of potentially

[1] See especially David Easton's pioneering paper, 'An Approach to the Analysis of Political Systems', in *World Politics*, ix, 3, 1957, pp. 383–400. This view was elaborated in his *A Framework for Political Analysis*, Prentice-Hall, Englewood Cliffs, New Jersey, 1965, and *A Systems Analysis of Political Life*, John Wiley, New York, 1965.

[2] This section was published initially as part of a joint paper with B. Steinberg and J. Stein, 'A Framework for Research on Foreign Policy Behavior', loc. cit.

FIGURE I

THE RESEARCH DESIGN (1)

INPUTS

OPERATIONAL ENVIRONMENT

EXTERNAL	—Global	(G)
	Subordinate	(S)
	Subordinate Other	(SO)
	Dominant Bilateral	(DB)
	Bilateral	(B)
INTERNAL	—Military Capability	(M)
	Economic Capability	(E)
	Political Structure	(PS)
	Interest Groups	(IG)
	Competing Élites	(CE)
COMMUNICATION	—The transmission of data about the operational environment by mass media, internal bureaucratic reports, face-to-face contact, etc.	

PSYCHOLOGICAL ENVIRONMENT

ATTITUDINAL PRISM	—Ideology, Historical Legacy, Personality Predispositions
ÉLITE IMAGES	—of the operational environment, including competing élites' advocacy and pressure potential

PROCESS

FORMULATION	—of Strategic and Tactical decisions in 4 ISSUE AREAS:	
	Military-Security	(M–S)
	Political-Diplomatic	(P–D)
	Economic-Developmental	(E–D)
	Cultural-Status	(C–S)
IMPLEMENTATION	—of decisions by various structures: Head of State, Head of Government, Foreign Office, etc.	

OUTPUTS   —The substance of acts or decisions

FIGURE 2

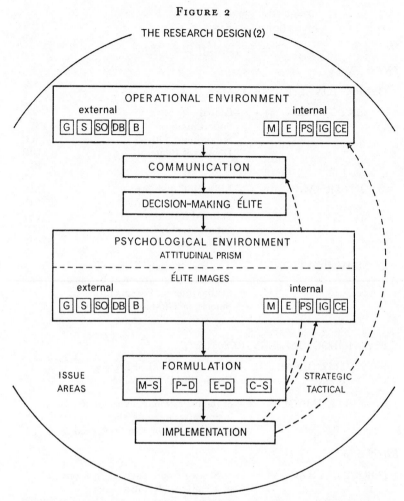

THE RESEARCH DESIGN (2)

relevant factors and conditions which may affect a state's external behaviour. The operational environment thus sets the parameters or boundaries within which decision-makers must act. The raw data of that environment are grouped into ten taxonomic variables and exist outside the decision-makers' minds as part of the natural world in which national actors operate.

Underlying this research design is the view that the operational environment affects the results or outcomes of decisions directly but influences the choice among policy options, that is, the decisions themselves, only as it is filtered through the images of decision-makers. The link between Image and Decisions is indeed the master key to a valuable framework of foreign policy analysis. This relationship of the two environments—operational and psychological—also provides a technique for measuring 'success' in foreign policy decisions. To the extent that decision-makers perceive the operational environment accurately, their foreign policy acts may be said to be rooted in reality and are thus likely to be 'successful'.[1] To the extent that their images are inaccurate, policy choices will be 'unsuccessful', that is, there will be a gap between élite-defined objectives and policy outcomes.[2]

An 'unsuccessful' decision may arise from one of two gaps in the psychological environment: first, the inaccurate perception of the operational environment by the élite; and secondly, the intrusion of new or changed data in the operational environment. Thus it is possible to distinguish the unknowable from the unknown about the reality pertinent to foreign policy. The research design clearly envisages the possibility of inputs after the formulation stage of a decision and before the implementation stage, as well as in the implementation stage itself. Such inputs change the operational environment (feedback) and thus affect both compliance and subsequent formulation.

The operational environment comprises two general types of variable, external and internal. The former refers to conditions and relationships which exist beyond the territorial boundaries of states and operate at three distinct levels: Global; Subordinate and Subordinate Other; and Bilateral, including Dominant Bilateral. The internal segment of the environment consists of five variables: Military Capability; Economic Capability; Political Structure; the specific demands on foreign policy made by Interest Groups; and the general demands advocated by Competing Élites.[3]

The total web of relationships among all actors within the international system (states, blocs, organizations) constitutes the *global system*. Not all actors, however, and not all interactions are equally important in shaping the external behaviour of an individual state; key patterns of interaction must be uncovered and explored. To illustrate, in the mid-twentieth century three types of interaction at the global level provide the most important parameters for state behaviour: the

[1] 'Reality' is a term which may be applied to the analyst's observations of the operational environment. It can be questioned whether the social scientist is capable of more accurate perceptions of that environment than is the participant decision-maker. This will vary in degree with the analyst and the decision-maker. Generally the decision-maker has superior access to sources of information which can enhance his insight into reality. The social scientist is, however, normally less involved and therefore likely to be more objective. Moreover, he possesses skills which enhance his objectivity and accuracy.

[2] Precise measurement of the gap is very difficult. One can offer only qualitative statements about that congruence, i.e. 'greater-than-lesser-than' statements.

[3] Everything in the operational environment that can affect decisions can be classified in the categories specified in Figures 1 and 2.

relations between the two power-ideology blocs, especially between the
bloc leaders, the United States and the Soviet Union; the behaviour of
the universal organization—the United Nations—and its affiliated
agencies; and the relations between the super powers and the 'Third
World'.

These patterns of interaction serve as the most important dimension
of the contemporary global system; there are others. As with all international systems the myriad of data concerning the global system can be
classified into twelve features, eight of the structural variety and four of
the textural type:

Structural: level of power; power stratification; political organization;
   military organization; economic organization; intensity of interaction; penetration *of* subordinate systems; penetration *by* subordinate systems;
Textural: level of communications; homogeneity of values; commonality
   of political systems; units' domestic stability.[1]

The content of these categories taken together constitutes an overview
of the global system. To illustrate the nature of the research exercise the
following questions may be asked. How large is the capability gap
between the most powerful states in the global system and the next order
of states, or between the most powerful and the least powerful; that is,
what is the configuration (level and distribution) of power? Is the
system bi-polar or multi-power? How can the existing level of power
—nuclear or conventional—affect the behaviour of a given state? In
short, the analyst of foreign policy must assess the impact of these and
other features of the global system on policy outcomes. Not all features
of that system impinge directly or with equal weight on the results of
foreign policy acts. Nor do decision-makers perceive all features with
equal intensity. The input role of the global system as a whole varies
greatly from one issue to another and as among different actors.[2]

A *subordinate system* represents an intermediate level of interaction
between the global system and the relations between any two states.

---

[1] These features and a partial coding of seven international systems are examined
in Michael Brecher, 'International Relations and Asian Studies: The Subordinate
State System of Southern Asia', *World Politics*, xv, 2, Jan. 1963, pp. 213–35 (reprinted
in M. Brecher, *The New States of Asia*, Oxford University Press, London, 1963, ch. 3).

[2] The dynamics of the global system in motion from 1948 to 1968, viewed as the
broadest external setting for Israel's foreign policy, are sketched in ch. 2 (*a*) below.

Some hypotheses about the impact of the global system upon state behaviour at
various periods in history are to be found in John Herz, *International Politics in the
Atomic Age*, Columbia University Press, New York, 1959, ch. 7 and 8, and his 'The
Territorial State Revisited: Reflections on the Future of the Nation-State', *Polity*, I,
1, 1968, pp. 12–34; Morton Kaplan, *System and Process in International Politics*, John
Wiley, New York, 1957, ch. 2; and Richard N. Rosecrance, *Action and Reaction in
World Politics*, Little, Brown, Boston, 1963, ch. 11 and 12.

Theoretically there may be as many subordinate systems as there are foreign policy issues, but logically they can be grouped into four categories: (1) geographic, with contiguous membership; (2) geographic, with non-contiguous members; (3) organizational, with contiguous membership; and (4) organizational, with non-contiguous members. The term 'subordinate system' in this book refers mainly to the first type, that is, to the Middle East Subordinate System; the term 'subordinate other' encompasses the second, third, and fourth types.

A subordinate system (type 1) is characterized by six conditions: (1) delimited scope, with primary stress on a geographic region; (2) at least three actors; (3) objective recognition by most other actors as constituting a distinctive community, region, or segment of the global system; (4) self-identification as such; (5) units of power relatively inferior to units in the dominant system, using a sliding scale of power in both; and (6) greater effect on the subordinate system by penetration from the dominant system than the reverse.[1] In the present international system there are six subordinate systems of that first type—American, East European, Middle East, Southern Asian, Sub-Saharan African, and West European; others may emerge.

Subordinate systems can be fruitfully analysed in the same way as the global system; that is, by grouping the relevant data into the same twelve structural and textural categories.[2] States may be members of one subordinate system, more than one, or none at all. Moreover, foreign policy choices may be influenced by pressures emanating from other systems, as well as from one's own. This distinction is described by the terms 'subordinate' and 'subordinate other'.

A *bilateral system* refers to the total pattern of interactions between any two states except for relations involving super powers or pre-eminent powers within the global system.

A *dominant bilateral system* refers to the total pattern of interactions between any state and a super power or pre-eminent actor in the global system; at present this refers to relations with the United States or the Soviet Union.[3]

International systems—global, subordinate and subordinate other, bilateral and dominant bilateral—constitute the five external variables of the operational environment for state behaviour. They create one of the two basic types of objective boundary for the policy options open to foreign policy decision-makers. The other is set by internal variables of

[1] Michael Brecher, 'The Subordinate State System . . .', op. cit., pp. 219–20.

[2] The Middle East System, as it pertains to Israel's foreign policy during the first two decades of independence, is examined through this lens in ch. 3 below.

[3] The high points of Israel's relations with the two super powers are noted in ch. 2 (*b*) below.

the operational environment, but it must be reiterated that the boundary limits to choice are operationalized only through the filtering of those data in decision-makers' perceptions.

Two of the internal variables may be dealt with briefly, for their meaning and content have been elaborated at length in the literature.

Military capability can be defined as the ability to wage war or to deter other states from attacking. Crucial tangible indices are geography, the general level of technology, military manpower, financial resources available for defence, and weaponry. To these must be added such intangibles as leadership, training, and morale.[1]

Economic capability can be defined as the total of all material and human resources available to the state for external behaviour. These range from natural resources like food and raw materials through industrial plant to scientific and technical skills, etc. Important indices include demography, gross national product, balance-of-payments position, and level of production and employment.[2]

Methods of classifying the data of military and economic capability are available.[3] The task in terms of this research design is to explore the real and potential capacity of the state under investigation, Israel, over time and in specific foreign policy situations. Crucial to this kind of analysis is the recognition that neither military nor economic capability can be defined in absolute terms for the entire range of foreign policy decisions. They must be assessed in relation to the capability of super powers, of other states in its own subordinate system, and of specific rivals—and all this with reference to the issue being examined.

Political structure denotes in part the political institutions and constitutional matrix in which authoritative decisions are made. It refers as well to various traits of the political system which may influence the decision process in foreign policy: the type of political régime (authoritarian or consensual); the character of the party system (two-party or multi-party); civil-military relations of control; and the extent of continuity and stability of the authority structures in the system. It is

---

[1] Israel's military capability is analysed in ch. 4 below.

[2] Israel's economic capability is analysed in ch. 5 below. This sequence of analysis of capability—military and, then, economic—reverses the usual order in the literature of international relations. The reason lies in one of Israel's special characteristics: her military capability is not primarily a product of economic resources and skills; rather, it is the military component which has shaped the direction, emphasis, and pace of economic development, especially since the 1967 War. This relationship will be clarified in the analysis of Israel's military and economic capability, in ch. 4 and 5 below.

[3] The most carefully integrated analysis is to be found in Klaus Knorr, *The War Potential of Nations*, Princeton University Press, Princeton, 1956.

necessary to assess the influence of these characteristics in the specific issues under analysis.[1]

Various *interest groups* exist within the internal sector of the operational environment. These perform two distinct functions in a foreign policy system: they communicate information about the environment to the decision-making élite and they may also advocate policies to those who wield authority in the system.[2] Viewed from the decision-makers' perspective, this advocacy role serves as real or potential pressure upon them to act or to refrain from acting in a particular way. The pressure exerted by these groups flows from their advocacy which, in turn, derives from their images of the environment and their goal preferences. There may be a multiplicity of interest groups in a foreign policy system. On any issue, however, there will be a limited number generating pressure for action or inaction.

As in domestic political systems, there are four types of interest advocacy concerning foreign policy—institutional, associational, non-associational, and anomic.[3]

Institutional interest groups comprise military establishments, bureaucratic organizations, and religious institutions. Not all have constituencies with interests pertaining to foreign policy. Most important are the military, especially the officer corps, the segment of the bureaucracy whose jurisdiction relates to external issues—Foreign Ministry, Finance, Trade and Commerce, etc.—and those religious institutions with transnational members and claims.

Associational interest groups are those which exist specifically to advocate interests—trade unions, business organizations, peasant associations, ethnic and civic groups, etc. In some foreign policy systems these groups do not perform either a communication or advocacy function; in

[1] The principal components of Israel's political structure which are relevant to her foreign policy system are discussed in ch. 6 below.

[2] These two functions are analytically distinct, though they frequently overlap. Interest groups communicate information about the operational environment to the élite, in addition to advocating policies. Perception by the élite of both manifest content and advocacy will vary among political systems and interest groups. The determining factors will be the strength of the interest group, real or potential, and élite predispositions.

[3] This classification was first suggested by Gabriel Almond in G. A. Almond and J. Coleman (eds.), *The Politics of the Developing Areas*, Princeton University Press, Princeton, 1960, pp. 3–64. This approach to interest groups was more fully elaborated in G. A. Almond and G. Powell, *Comparative Politics: A Developmental Approach*, Little, Brown, New York, 1966, ch. III and v.

Professor Almond's term to describe the function of interest groups is 'articulation', which he distinguishes from 'aggregation' by political parties. The distinction may be valid in a domestic political system but it obscures more than it reveals in a foreign policy system—in the light of empirical research. The term 'advocacy' is more precise to describe a function performed by both interest groups and competing élites.

others they range from relevant to crucial. The task is to uncover those associational groups in Israel which participate in the foreign policy system and to indicate the issues and issue areas in which they operate.

Non-associational interest groups refer to kinship and lineage groups, regional, status and class groups, and others of this genre, which advocate their interests intermittently through individuals, cliques, family, and religious leaders. Most of these are marginal to foreign policy analysis. There are, however, other non-associational elements which influence the foreign policy decision process. These include commentators and journalists of the mass media, and academicians who advocate specific and general foreign policy goals.[1]

Anomic outbursts are the more or less spontaneous penetrations by unorganized parts of society into the political system in the form of riots, demonstrations, assassinations, etc., where these are not simply the use of unconventional or violent means by organized groups. As in the domestic political system, latent discontent may be sparked by an incident and impinge upon the foreign policy system in the form of unpredictable and uncontrollable demands.[2]

Closely linked to interest groups, both structurally and functionally, are those *competing élites* which vie for authority to make political decisions in the system. Interest groups tend to advocate specific foreign policy demands; competing élites also propose alternative general sets of foreign policy demands. In a competitive party system competing élites may play a significant role in the foreign policy process. Their images of the operational environment, the content of their policy demands, and their capacity to generate pressure are likely to enter the incumbent élite image and thus help to shape decisions. In a single-party authoritarian system pressures on policy will be channelled through competing political factions within the monopoly party or through various interest groups.[3]

While the operational environment exists independent of its perception by decision-makers, it can have an impact on the foreign policy process only to the extent that it is communicated to the élite. Information may be communicated in a variety of ways: the mass media—press,

[1] Almond and Powell, op. cit., do not treat commentators, etc., as non-associational interest groups but essentially as part of the communications network. While they do communicate information, their significance for decision-making lies in their advocacy of policies, based upon their perceptions of the operational environment.

[2] Israeli interest groups which advocate foreign policy goals are discussed in ch. 7 below.

[3] In the Israeli political system competing élites take the form of highly centralized political parties. Their images of the operational environment and the content of their foreign policy demands are explored in ch. 8 below.

books, radio, TV; face-to-face contact; internal bureaucratic reports—cables, intelligence estimates, etc.; and direct observation of the environment. Decision-makers may also receive information from competing élites and institutional, associational, and non-associational interest groups, who process their information about the environment through the prism of their own perceptions.

In the analysis of a foreign policy issue it is necessary to examine the *communication* network within the political system and to assess the adequacy, accuracy, degree of completeness, and objectivity of the flow of information about the operational environment to the incumbent élite. In this way the degree of congruence between reality and élite images can be given first approximation.[1]

In foreign policy analysis it is also essential to identify the person(s) and/or group(s) whose images of the operational environment shape decisions. Stated generally, the *decision-making élite* consists of those individuals who perform the function of political authorization in the foreign policy arena. Political authorization may be defined as authorization sanctioned by the conventions of the system; this may or may not coincide with legal authorization.

The core decision-making group in any foreign policy system consists of the Head of Government and Foreign Minister; its size and composition will vary with the issue. The scope, nevertheless, will of necessity be narrow: many may influence decisions but they are operationalized in this research design as interest groups and competing élites. Moreover, a narrow-gauge definition of the foreign policy élite permits more fruitful comparison.[2]

The *psychological environment* for decision-makers comprises two closely-related sets of data. One may be designated as the 'attitudinal prism', the other as 'élite images'.

Every decision-maker in foreign policy operates within a context of psychological predispositions. These comprise: (*a*) societal factors, such as ideology and tradition, which derive from the cumulative historical legacy; and (*b*) personality factors—the idiosyncratic qualities of decision-makers—that is, those aspects of élite attitudes which are not generated by their role occupancy. Together, these influences constitute the screen or prism through which élite perceptions of the operational environment are filtered.

Élite image is the decisive input of a foreign policy system, in the research design presented here. The reason for this pivotal role is that

[1] The Israeli communication network as it relates to foreign policy is analysed in ch. 9 below.

[2] The composition of Israel's high policy makers and of her foreign policy technical élite is examined, respectively, in ch. 10 and 17 below.

decision-makers act in accordance with their perception of reality, not in response to reality itself.[1] Image and reality may coincide or may diverge. To the extent that they differ, as noted, policy acts will be unsuccessful—in the measure that decision-makers misconstrue, distort, or deviate from the reality of the environment within which they must act. Their images may be partial or general. They may be subconscious or may be consciously stated. They may be based on carefully thought-out assumptions about the world or they may flow from instinctive perceptions and judgements. In any event all decision-makers may be said to possess a set of images and to be conditioned by them in their behaviour on foreign policy (as well as on domestic) issues. Indeed élite images are not less real than the reality of their environment and are much more relevant to an analysis of the foreign policy flow.

The term 'élite image' is a creation of scholars—and few practitioners of foreign policy think and act as scholars do. They have neither the time nor the inclination to formulate an elaborate and integrated 'world view'. The task of the foreign policy analyst is to construct from words and deeds the operative élite perceptions of their environment, along with their views of the desirable (or proper) roles for their state at the three levels of foreign policy interaction—global, subordinate, and bilateral. Thus the élite image comprises a number of closely-related perceptions: (1) of the external environment—global, subordinate, and bilateral; and (2) of the internal environment—military capability, economic capability, political structure, interest groups, and competing élites. From these perceptions flow the élites' definition of their state's desirable role in foreign policy. These images taken together constitute a world view; and this, in turn, creates a general psychological framework for decision-making.[2]

The link between élite image and foreign policy decisions was admirably summed up by Professor Kenneth Boulding in a pioneering paper on this topic:[3]

---

[1] 'Cognitive behaviorism' is the term that Harold and Margaret Sprout use to 'designate the simple and familiar principle that a person reacts to his milieu as he apperceives it—that is, as he perceives and interprets it in the light of past experience. . . . It simply draws a sharp distinction between the psychological environment (with reference to which an individual defines choices and takes decisions) and the operational environment (which sets limits to what can happen when the decision is executed).' 'Environmental Factors in the Study of International Politics', in James N. Rosenau (ed.), *International Politics and Foreign Policy*, Free Press of Glencoe, 1961, p. 109.

[2] For explorations in depth of two prominent decision-makers' images and their effect on foreign policy decisions, see the author's *India and World Politics: Krishna Menon's View of the World*, Oxford University Press, London, 1968, and Ole R. Holsti, 'Cognitive Dynamics and Images of the Enemy: Dulles and Russia', in David J. Finlay, Ole R. Holsti, and Richard R. Fagen, *Enemies in Politics*, Rand McNally & Co., Chicago, 1967, pp. 25–96.

[3] 'National Images and International Systems', *The Journal of Conflict Resolution*, iii, 2, June 1959, pp. 120–1.

... we must recognize that the people whose decisions determine the policies and actions of nations do not respond to the 'objective' facts of the situation. It is what we think the world is like, not what it is really like that determines our behavior. . . . The 'image' must be thought of as the total cognitive, affective, and evaluative structure of the behavior unit, or its internal view of itself and its universe. . . . A decision involves the selection of the most preferred position in a contemplated field of choice. Both the field of choice and the ordering of this field, by which the preferred position is identified, lie in the image of the decision-maker.[1]

The systematic analysis of state behaviour in international relations has been retarded by an undifferentiated concept of foreign policy issues. The sheer volume of decisions requires more careful demarcation of the boundaries between types of issues, a task rendered easier by the concept of *'issue area'*.[2]

All foreign policy issues may be allocated to four issue areas, though empirical probings indicate that overlapping does exist. The criterion adopted in this research design for classifying issues within issue areas is substantive content, not motivations of decision-makers. The choice of content derives from the fact that it is self-evident, whereas motivation emerges after the analysis has been completed. To attempt prior designation by motives would be speculation without analytical value. For example, a decision by State A to conclude a trade agreement with State B may have been motivated primarily by political considerations —that is, the need of State A for State B's diplomatic support in the attainment of other goals. The substance or content of the decision is clearly economic, however, and it is therefore placed in the economic-developmental issue area—even though, in terms of the significance of input variables in shaping this decision, economic considerations (desire to enhance the economic capacity of State A) may well be far down the list of factors.

The *Military-Security* issue area comprises all issues which focus on questions pertaining to violence, including alliances and weaponry, and those which are perceived by the foreign policy élite as constituting a security threat.

The *Political-Diplomatic* issue area covers the spectrum of foreign policy interaction at each of the three levels of the external environment— global, subordinate, and bilateral—except for those dealing with violence, material resources, and cultural and status relations.

[1] The psychological environment for Israeli foreign policy decisions from 1948 to 1968 is examined in Part II of this book.

[2] The concept of issue area was introduced by Professor Rosenau in his paper on 'Pre-Theories and Theories of Foreign Policy', in Farrell, op. cit., pp. 27–92. It was further examined by him in 'Foreign Policy as an Issue Area', in James N. Rosenau (ed.), *Domestic Sources of Foreign Policy*, The Free Press, New York, 1967, pp. 11–50.

The *Economic-Developmental* issue area comprises all those issues which involve the acquisition and allocation of resources, such as trade, aid, and foreign investment.

The *Cultural-Status* issue area consists of those foreign policy issues involving cultural, educational, and scientific exchanges. It also contains status issues which relate primarily to self-image, namely, the decision-makers' perception of their state's legitimate place in the global and/or subordinate systems.

The allocation of a decision to an issue area has the merit of assisting comparative analysis and hypotheses. It is insufficient, however, to explain the process by which an élite formulates decisions, just as a general image, i.e. a world view, is inadequate for this purpose. Foreign policy issues are usually specific in content; a world view therefore provides essentially the predilection for choice among alternatives. Only some of the ten variables of the operational environment may be relevant for a specific decision, and the content of these variables will itself vary from one decision to another within a cluster of decisions.

It is not suggested in this approach that the link between élite images and all decisions is rigid. Rather, decisions may be divided into two analytic types—*strategic* and *tactical*. Strategic decisions may be defined as broad policy acts, measured by significance for the state's foreign policy system as a whole, duration of impact, and the presence of a subsidiary cluster of decisions to operationalize that policy. Those subsidiary clusters constitute tactical decisions.

It is at the level of tactical decision-making that strategic decisions undergo constant change and re-formulation, in response to the myriad of competing demands within the political system. Implementation of strategic policy acts through tactical decisions will affect the entire foreign policy system by changing in varying degrees the operational environment and élite images. This will produce new strategic decisions, which, in turn, lead to new tactical decisions. In short, there is a continuous flow effect, from operational environment to élite images to decisions. . . .[1]

(b) INITIATION AND RESPONSE IN ISRAEL'S FOREIGN POLICY

An inquiry into foreign policy may be said to have two interrelated goals. The first is to explain the *sources of decision*, that is, the pressures flowing from the real and perceived environments leading to a choice

---

[1] The processes of formulation and implementation in Israeli foreign policy during the first twenty years of statehood are examined, respectively, in ch. 15 and 16, and in ch. 19 and 20 below.

among policy options. The second is to explain the *outcomes of decision*, that is, the consequences of choice, both for the particular issue and for the foreign policy system as a whole. This is merely a formalistic way of expressing two concerns. One is to avoid the pitfalls of analysing decisions in a vacuum. The other is to put flesh on the skeletal concept of feedback, which is central to an approach aspiring to prediction of probable behaviour. Both concerns require a study in depth of the individual variables of the operational and psychological environments: these must be examined in the context of the total foreign policy system and as they impinge on the particular decisions under investigation.

A conventional work on foreign policy would ignore the total system —and perhaps even deny its existence: the focus would be on a series of randomly-selected decisions, which might be related (haphazardly) to setting, images, and decision-making process. The analysis may be illuminating about a specific choice or decision about a specific issue. But the cumulative contribution to knowledge about the behaviour of that state or that type of state in a cluster of related issues—an issue area —is minimal. It is only through an integrated framework of a foreign policy system that the foundations of cumulative insights into this branch of social science are well established. And only thus is it possible to amass sufficient knowledge about state behaviour in the past to permit tentative predictions of probable responses to similar challenges in the future. For this reason, apart from the wealth of factual detail that can be uncovered, the real and perceived environments, and the process, of Israel's foreign policy system from 1948 to 1968 will be explored at length before major decisions are analysed. Hypotheses can then be tested with care and guidelines indicated about future Israeli behaviour. Such is the rationale of this unconventional treatise on foreign policy.[1]

The behaviour of most states reveals both *initiating* and *reactive* elements. One relevant factor is clearly *status in the global power configuration*. To take an extreme example, the United States and the Soviet Union have a greater capacity for consequential initiatives in foreign policy than Paraguay or Upper Volta, Brazil or Canada, France or Japan, to cite small, middle, and great powers. Yet power is not the sole criterion of potential initiative, nor is it a mechanical one-one relationship. Even a super power does not possess an equal initiating capability in all situations within the global system or at lesser levels of interaction. And even where they can initiate policy they cannot always persist to the desired outcome, for example, Soviet behaviour in Cuba, 1962, and American behaviour in Vietnam, 1964 ff.

---

[1] There are few studies on the foreign policy of small states. The most suggestive is Annette Baker Fox, *The Power of Small States*, University of Chicago Press, Chicago, 1959. Another book of this genre draws heavily on Israeli foreign policy—David Vital, *The Inequality of States*, Clarendon Press, Oxford, 1967.

There are half a dozen other conditions which help to shape the initiating-reactive 'mix' in foreign policy.

— One is *geo-political position in the global system*. Thus a state which is located within a super-power hegemonial zone, for example, Belgium or Poland, is more restricted than a state in a competitive zone on the periphery, like North Vietnam or Indonesia.

— Another is *power configuration within a subordinate system*. If the general power level is low and its distribution equal, any member will have wide latitude in initiating foreign policy acts. If there is a hierarchical distribution of power confined to conventional weapons, the initiating potential will be influenced by the state's position on that power scale: for example, it will be low for Lebanon, Uruguay, and Chad, high for Israel, Argentine, and Nigeria, in the Middle East, American, and African Subordinate Systems respectively.

— A third condition is the *importance of the subordinate system* and its resources *to the dominant conflict* between the super powers—as perceived by their decision-making élites.

— Related to this is the *image of competitive access* held by all. The Latin American states are less constrained by this two-edged factor than those in the Middle East: the latter's resources, oil and strategic location, are considered far more important and it is a recognized 'open' zone of competition; Mexico and Chile are restricted by the US hegemonial position in the American system, while Israel and the UAR[1] are restrained by vital super-power interests in the region.

— A fifth condition is the set of *pressures* on an initiation-oriented élite which derive *from the internal balance of social, economic, and political forces*. These may propel a decision-making group to take the lead in reshaping the system or its relations with immediate neighbours, as with the UAR. They may also restrain a régime from certain courses of action, for example, Jordan's halting efforts at a political settlement with Israel in 1967–70.

— Finally, there is the factor of *relative stability or turmoil within the system and élite goals vis-à-vis other actors*. The extreme opposites are Latin America, where the doctrine of non-intervention is enshrined in law and custom—and interest—and the Middle East, where the Arab states deny Israel's right to exist and frequently undermine one another's régimes.

[1] The term UAR (United Arab Republic) was introduced in 1958 to designate the union of Egypt and Syria. The union was dissolved in 1961, but Egypt retained the name, United Arab Republic. Thus the term UAR connotes Egypt and Syria combined in references to the period 1958–61. It is also used interchangeably with Egypt for references to the years 1962 ff.

When applied to Israel's foreign policy this construct suggests a genuine 'mix' of initiating potential and reactive stimuli.

1.   Although Israel would qualify for no more than middle-power status in global terms, her *geo-political position* within a highly competitive zone greatly enhances her manœuvrability in global interaction. There is striking evidence of this: her diplomatic presence in Africa, which ranks fourth or fifth in involvement after the US, Germany, UK, and, perhaps, France; and the capacity, despite her lack of any formal alignments, to frustrate all attempts by an Arab–Soviet–Asian coalition at the United Nations to impose sanctions of any kind on Israel.

2.   Within the *Middle East power configuration* Israel has a *high status*, the legacy of military triumph in three rounds of open warfare since 1948. The result has been exceptional freedom to act within the subordinate system, as evidenced in her persistent reprisal policy, despite admonitions from the UN and some major powers.

3.   Initiative in foreign policy is permitted to Israel as well by the *relationship of the Near East to the inter-bloc conflict*. Both the US and the USSR place a high value on its resources and both deny to each other a hegemonial position in the region. This enables all Near East actors, especially Israel and the UAR, to pursue their own objectives while, at the same time, maintaining a viable client–patron relationship with one of the super powers. The coincidence of the image and the reality of competitive access to that region heightens the initiating potential in the foreign policy of Middle East states.

These three conditions—geo-political position, high status in the Middle East power configuration, and the importance of this subordinate system to the global bloc conflict—tend to emphasize the initiating potential in Israeli foreign policy. Other factors emphasize the reactive trait.

4.   The presence of a hostile super power capable of obliterating the state is a permanent source of restraint: on some occasions it has been important, as in the decision of 8 November 1956 to agree in principle to withdraw from Sinai. The obverse is no less a restriction on free choice in foreign policy, that is, the dependence on the other super power for modern weapons, as well as for diplomatic and economic assistance. In short it has been necessary to react to the *global constellation of forces*.

5.   Internal pressures can also be discerned in many issues: the demands of border settlements have influenced the timing, size, and place of reprisals; the need for more water, pressed with special vigour by *kibbutzim* and *moshavim* through their spokesmen in high

places, led to the cluster of decisions concerning the distribution of the Jordan Waters; and the demands of the citrus growers, among other economic interests, were absorbed by those who decided to seek entry into the European Common Market. In these and other issues the decision-makers were reacting to internal stimuli. The inability to formulate a clear policy on the occupied territories after the 1967 War—to return them to the Arab states, to integrate them into Israel in whole or in part, politically, strategically, economically, or all three, to support an autonomous or independent Palestine entity—all this reflected the massive counterbalancing *pressures from within the society*.

6.   It is the turmoil within the Near East and, especially, the relentless hostility of the Arab states towards Israel, which create the image and reality of a predominant reactive strain in Israeli behaviour. Whether in the Security Council or the General Assembly, or in other international forums, or in the perennial search for arms, aid, and friendship, Israel appears to be—and is—reacting to the unconcealed *Arab goal of politicide*. Certainly the Sinai Campaign and the Six Day War[1] were responses to that perceived threat; so too was the unwritten alliance with France in the 1950s and the continuing quest for a United States guarantee. The request for membership in the Common Market is not unrelated to this intra-system struggle for survival, nor was the acceptance of diplomatic relations with West Germany. Indeed, almost all Israeli foreign policy decisions can be linked to this core fact of non-acceptance by her neighbours; and in that sense Israeli behaviour may be described as overwhelmingly reactive in character. Most Israelis interviewed in the course of this inquiry so interpreted their country's external acts. Yet this is accurate only in the sense that all foreign policy is an action–reaction–interaction nexus; and Israel's policy, because of her extraordinary—and unique—existence in a permanent state of siege dramatizes the appearance of reactive behaviour.

The construct of an *initiating-reactive 'mix'* is one method of drawing attention to the major issues in Israeli foreign policy during the first twenty years. Another is to delineate these in a *challenge-response continuum*, relating these to the principal environmental source in each case. Not only is this analytically sound, in so far as Israel's continued existence is a response to a ubiquitous and multi-dimensional challenge, global and regional, internal and external, material and non-material: it has the further merit of demonstrating the link between environment and decision, the pivot of the framework used in this inquiry. The continuum can be readily portrayed in the following schematic terms:

[1] Israelis refer to the third round of the Arab–Israel War as 'the Six Day War'. The Arabs and most foreign commentators use the terms 'the June War' or 'the June 1967 War'. These terms will be used interchangeably throughout the book.

Challenge	Environmental Source	Response (Decision)
Historic Continuity of Zion	Global and Subordinate Systems; Advocacy by Competing Élites and Interest Groups	Proclaiming Jerusalem the Capital
Diplomatic Assault	Global and Subordinate Systems	Presence in Africa Diplomatic Relations with Germany Policy on Korean War
Permanent Military Siege	Subordinate System	Sinai Campaign Six Day War
Economic Blockade	Subordinate System and Economic Capacity	German Reparations European Common Market
Water	Economic Capacity and Interest Groups	Jordan Waters
Demographic Growth	Military and Economic Capacity	Ties with Diaspora Jewry

All these challenges persisted throughout the period of independence. They are, indeed, the six multi-faceted problems which required a response day by day year by year. The reactions varied in form and effectiveness, but all policy radiated from these core issues. They will recur throughout this analysis, and the major responses will be explored in depth in a later volume. There the pertinent variables from the real and psychological environments will be examined in a narrow-gauge context—the specific challenge and the decision response; similarly, the process of decision-making and implementation will be examined in detail. In short, each of the major decisions in Israel's foreign policy will be filtered through the entire framework as outlined in this chapter.

These may be termed *vertical* studies. They will be preceded by *horizontal* studies, that is, an analysis of each of the variables of the real and psychological environments and the policy process, all within a time span of twenty years, from 1948 to 1968. We shall begin with the external setting of Israel's policy, first at the global, then at the subordinate system level. Thereafter we shall explore the five internal variables, beginning with military capability, then economic capability, the political structure, and the demands advocated by interest groups and competing parties in Israeli society. How the facts of that environment are communicated to the decision-makers will lead to an examination of the policy élite and their political culture, followed by the images held by key decision-makers during Israel's first two decades. And then to the policy process—formulation and implementation.

Each of these horizontal studies may be perceived as a self-contained room in a large building. The integrating thread is the concept of a foreign policy flow—from the environment to élite images to the formulation and implementation of policy to outcomes and to their re-entry into the environment. The concept of flow derives, in turn, from the more basic idea of a foreign policy system, which provides the foundation for the building. This volume will explore the horizontal or macrodimension of Israel's foreign policy. Thereafter we shall proceed to the major decisions, each revealing the dynamics of the system as a whole, from sources of pressure to choice and the outcomes of decisions.

PART I

OPERATIONAL ENVIRONMENT

CHAPTER 2

External Setting

The external setting of Israel's foreign policy was characterized by frequent change during the first twenty years of statehood: this was so at all three levels of the environment—global, subordinate, and bilateral. Variations did not coincide in time, however. Nor did they have identical influence on the outcome of Israeli policy choices. Thus the changing configurations of reality must be examined separately, at each level of the environment. Only the broad contours will be sketched here, for the purpose is to indicate the parameters of Israel's foreign policy system through time. A detailed analysis of the relevant external variables will be included in the major studies of decision-making.

(a) GLOBAL SYSTEM[1]

An element of arbitrariness is inherent in the attempt to periodize international politics. Yet it is useful to break down a system's evolution in terms of structural and textural features,[2] with a focus on the qualitative or nodal points of time change. For the contemporary global system the break points are 1948, 1956, and 1962.

On the eve of Israel's independence the global system was in a state of transition. The Grand Alliance of the Second World War had been sundered, but bipolarity and bloc conflict had not yet crystallized. In appearance, if not wholly in reality, there existed a three-power system, with the United Kingdom and her Commonwealth-Empire the third quasi-super power. The level of power remained essentially of the order of 1939–45, with the notable difference of an embryonic atomic capability confined to the United States. As for power stratification, the gap between 'the three' and all other members of the system was great, but much less awesome than that between the two super powers and the other members a decade later. The defeated states, Germany, Japan, and Italy, lay prostrate, the first divided, and the first and second occupied. France and China, nominally victors, were weak and exhausted, the latter torn by civil war. And the Third World was yet to emerge:

[1] The following analysis is designed as a skeletal outline of the global setting of Israel's foreign policy. It is consciously brief and takes the form of an interpretative essay. For this reason there is no reference to the wealth of bibliographical materials on world politics since 1945.

[2] The twelve features of an international system which provide the categories for analysis of the global and subordinate systems were noted in ch. 1. They are presented in a more schematic form in Tables 1 and 2 on pp. 36 and 63 below.

the process of decolonization had barely begun. In system terms there was one 'universal' political organization, the United Nations, no formal structures of military organization, either for the system as a whole or for any group of states, and a number of functional economic organizations with partial membership linked to the UN, notably the ILO, the FAO, the IMF, and the IBRD. Interaction was intense, in men, goods, and services, among the states of Western Europe and North America, of lesser intensity in Latin America, severely restricted among the East European states under Soviet hegemony, and of marginal volume between East Europe and the rest of the world. There were no subordinate systems before 1948 except for Latin America, the members of which interacted mainly with the United States and, to a lesser extent, with three West European actors, France, Spain, and Italy. Elsewhere, in Asia, the Middle East, and Africa, retreat from Empire was not yet in full sweep. There was an increasing polarization of values in the system, most sharply expressed in American and Soviet societies, and much less diversity of polities or domestic instability than in subsequent periods in the evolution of the global system.

The post-war phase of transition was drawing to a close by 1948, and the next eight years witnessed profound change in the global system. The level of power had escalated with the revolution in nuclear technology, both in the quantum of destructive potential in atomic weapons and in the qualitative change created by the hydrogen bomb. The United States enjoyed a monopoly in nuclear weaponry until 1949 and overwhelming superiority until the mid-fifties, though the gap narrowed with Soviet development of the H-Bomb and a medium-range delivery system. In conventional forces the USSR maintained vast superiority. Measured by economic capability, the US was clearly the pre-eminent global actor, with a 3 to 1 margin over the Soviet Union in GNP.

The nuclear capability of these two states had not yet reached 'unit veto' proportions[1] but it set them apart from all others, giving rise to the apt designation, 'super powers'. In no other historic international system did any unit possess a military capability greater than the total of all others except the rival super power; such was the stratification of the global system by 1956. It was this which created a two-power system. And it was their conflicting ideologies and strategic objectives which gave the system the character of rather tight polarization: two clusters of states formed around the super powers, and both the US and the USSR enjoyed hegemonial status within their bloc.

[1] Professor Morton Kaplan includes a 'unit veto' system among his six theoretically possible types of international system. He defines it as being possible under one prerequisite condition: 'the possession by all actors of weapons of such a character that any actor is capable of destroying any other actor that attacks it even though it cannot prevent its own destruction'. *System and Process in International Politics*, John Wiley, New York, 1957, p. 50.

The universal actor in the system, the UN, remained impotent in the security field throughout this period. This was due partly to acute military or quasi-military bloc confrontation, first in Europe (Berlin) and then in Asia (Korea and Indo-China). It was also partly the result of the symbolic use of the organization by one bloc leader to achieve its objective (the US in Korea) and the persistent assertion by that super power of its political majority in the General Assembly, a majority which did not correspond to the distribution of power in the system. Thus the Military Staff Committee and all efforts at arms control remained stillborn. The composition of the UN, too, remained almost static, because of the Soviet–American impasse over the admission of new members. Only at the end of 1955 was this deadlock broken, in the 'package deal' which saw the influx of fifteen states; this was one of the indices of approaching change in the global system. Functional economic organizations grew in number but could not escape the consequences of systemic polarization. The significant organizational changes occurred, rather, within the blocs of the system: military (NATO and Warsaw Pact), economic (OEEC, Schuman Plan, Council for Economic Mutual Assistance), and political (Council of Europe, Communist Party Congresses), along with a host of related institutions, bilateral and multilateral, all pointing to a high degree of bloc integration. Interaction became more intense and freer within the West; it remained confined to party and government representatives in the East, and it was drastically curtailed, almost to the zero point, between the blocs.

The link between dominant and subordinate systems came to the fore during that period. One subordinate system, Latin America, received a new and refined institutional recognition in 1948, with the formation of the OAS. Two others, the Middle East and Southern Asia, emerged as the aftermath of retreat from Empire: four states acquired independence in the former region between 1946 and 1948 (Lebanon, Syria, Jordan, and Israel), and another six in the latter from 1946 to 1949 (Philippines, India, Pakistan, Ceylon, Burma, and Indonesia).[1] By the mid-fifties they had both acquired many of the requisite features of a system.

---

[1] The significance of the global anti-colonial revolution for Israel's emergence as an independent state cannot be overestimated—though few Israelis have acknowledged the link and its logical policy consequence, identification with the Third World. One who did so was Ze'ev Sharef, a prominent civil servant and, later, cabinet minister:

'The British Government would not have left Palestine with such dispatch had departure not been part of a *much broader pattern of action* or, rather, of contraction— the withdrawal of the British *raj* from India, Burma and Ceylon, and the suspension of British military and economic aid to Greece and Turkey. *It was a year of retreat and retirement in the British Empire. . . . The surrender of the Palestine Mandate was only one page in a chapter of immense historic significance which changed the face of the world in ten or fifteen years,* and the consequences of which are still today incalculable.'
Three Days, W. H. Allen, London, 1962, p. 19. (Emphasis added, M.B.)

The direction and intensity of penetration varied between the dominant two-power system and each of the three subordinate systems. There was no penetration of Latin America as a result of inter-bloc conflict; US hegemony was secure. Yet the states of Latin America exerted considerable influence on developments outside their system through their strategic control of 40 per cent of the votes in the UN General Assembly at the time. More specifically, their electoral influence was vital in the Partition Resolution of 29 November 1947, which sanctioned the establishment of the State of Israel. The members of one subordinate system in this instance helped to shape the character of another through their role·in the global political organization.

The Middle East, by contrast, was the object of continuous penetration without any reverse flow of influence. It was (rare) agreement between the US and USSR that ensured United Nations approval and support for the establishment of the Jewish State. It was Soviet bloc weapons that enabled Israel to withstand the initial Arab assault in 1948; and it was Soviet bloc weapons to Egypt and Syria (since 1955) that catalysed an inflationary spiral in the arms race within that subordinate system. The French supply of arms to Israel from 1954 and the American provision of arms to various Middle East states accentuated this type of penetration. The Tripartite Declaration (US, UK, and France) of 1950 was a restraining act but penetrative nonetheless. The evidence is conclusive. And the impact of this penetration was magnified by the absence of any feedback in that period. Nasser had come to power in 1954 following the ouster of Neguib, and Egypt had not yet emerged as a major non-aligned state. Similarly, Israel had not yet established her 'presence' in Africa. The other Arab states were weaker. And Turkey and Iran were integral parts of the US-led bloc.

Southern Asia fell between Latin America and the Middle East in terms of penetration by, and of, the dominant system from 1948 to 1956. The main thrust came from the dominant system, notably in the Korean War, and the involvement of one bloc leader, the US, and the second-ranking power of the other bloc, China, in Indo-China, though neither with its own armed forces. Anglo-American prominence in UN actions on Kashmir represented political penetration of South Asia, as did US arms aid to Pakistan (from 1953). Yet evidence of a reverse flow of influence is apparent. In 1950 India took the lead in forming the Asian–Arab Group at the UN, a pressure group on global system decisions. In 1952 India succeeded in breaking the impasse over the Korean War negotiations, thus easing inter-bloc conflict on a fundamental issue. And through her central role in the Neutral Nations Repatriation Commission, she exercised a tranquillizing role in one dangerous military confrontation. The role of India and smaller Asian states was not inconsequential at the Geneva Conference on Indo-China, despite the presence of members of both blocs, including most great powers and one super power. And in the historic decision to admit fifteen states to the UN, India's role was, perhaps, decisive. There were not many non-aligned states in the early fifties and they did not loom large in the perspectives of the super powers, though India was recognized as leader of this group and in its own right important. The Soviet Union was hostile to non-alignment until 1955, as was the United States for an even longer period.

Among the textural features, the global pattern of values became much more heterogeneous, with the Third World of Non-Alignment and the diversity of cultures within it (Hindu, Buddhist, Muslim) added to the conflict between communist and democratic worlds, with all of the variegated value systems of the latter. The existing spectrum of political systems was broadened, with authoritarian monarchies, as in Jordan and Iraq, military régimes of a modernizing élan, as in Egypt, and charismatic dictatorships, as in Indonesia. Instability reached its apogee during that period in Syria, though elsewhere, as in Pakistan and Indonesia, there were frequent changes in government. Greater than in the pre-1948 phase, political instability was conspicuously less than the plethora of change to follow in the 1960s, as the global system came to encompass all territory and people on the planet.

Most features of the contemporary global system witnessed a qualitative change during the period 1956 to late 1962. The level of power escalated sharply with the development of a Soviet inter-continental delivery capability and a rapid accumulation of nuclear megatonnage by the two super powers. The result was a 'balance of terror' in an authentic two-unit veto system. The redress of nuclear imbalance was accompanied by a shift in the balance of conventional military power in the West's favour: the Soviets reduced the size of their conventional forces, while the Americans increased theirs; and the growth of West German forces added significantly to Western bloc strength in Europe. Thus, even before the Kennedy–Khrushchev summit meeting in Vienna, in 1961, a relatively stable equilibrium of super-power capability had become a reality. The US was still superior in economic strength, but the gap had narrowed to a 2 to 1 ratio in GNP.

The system remained essentially bipolar, but there were four major changes in its power configuration. One was growing diffusion of capability—an embryonic French *force de frappe*, a formidable West German army, and impressive conventional military power in main-land China. In perspective, it was the logic of an antagonistic two-power system that was responsible to some extent for this diffusion: prolonged struggle between the super powers led them to build up the strength of their principal allies. A second modification was the assertion of independence within the blocs, notably by China and France. The

Sino-Soviet rift began in 1956 and reached near-breaking point at the end of this phase over the simultaneous crises of Cuba and the Sino-Indian border. French differences with the US reached a climax later but they were already discernible after the Anglo-American rejection of de Gaulle's proposed triumvirate within the West in 1958.

A third change was in the geographic scope and techniques of conflict between the super powers. The area of conflict widened from Europe and Asia to the Middle East, with the infusion of massive Soviet bloc arms aid to Egypt from the end of 1955, then to Africa, beginning with the Congo imbroglio in 1960, and thereafter to Latin America, through Soviet patronage of Cuba. This expansion of the areas of competition and conflict was due partly to a conscious extension of the USSR sphere of interest in the global system, hitherto confined to Eurasia, and partly to the creation of régimes willing or eager to accept Soviet assistance. The military form of confrontation diminished in frequency and importance, with the striking exception of Cuba in October 1962; other techniques became more prominent—economic, diplomatic, ideological, and political. Finally, the system moved perceptibly from 'tight' to 'loose' bipolarity, a structural change created by the vast and sweeping process of decolonization.

The new states made their first collective appearance at Bandung in 1955. The conference was organized on a geographic (Afro-Asian) basis —with exceptions, including Israel—but the sponsoring Colombo Powers, notably India and Indonesia, sought a consensus on ideological lines (non-alignment). The distinction would be blurred, it was hoped, and the result would be an active third world which would tranquillize inter-bloc conflict. That hope was never fulfilled, as Asia–Africa became increasingly sundered into aligned and non-aligned segments. And at best non-alignment was operational only in *ad hoc* conflict issues, not as a global policy. Yet Bandung achieved, in large measure, the goal of legitimacy for non-alignment. Ironically, perhaps, the first self-proclaimed Conference of Non-Aligned States, in Belgrade in 1961, took place as the global system was moving away from strict bipolarity, which gave non-alignment both legitimacy and systemic utility. And yet the third world of underdeveloped, newly-independent, non-white and, for the most part, politically unstable states reached its zenith during that period. The retreat from Empire spilled over from Asia to North Africa in the early fifties (Libya, Tunisia, Morocco) and thereafter to sub-Saharan Africa: in 1950 there were only four independent units throughout that continent; by 1962 there were more than thirty. The global system had become universal.

Nowhere was this proliferation of actors more evident and more acutely felt than in the institutional fabric of the system. The UN had a membership of 51 at its inception in 1945. This remained, with but a few additions, until 1955, when the 'package deal' brought 15 new members. The next qualitative change occurred in 1960, 'Africa Year' at the UN, when 18 states joined the world body. The impact was immediate and far-reaching, in style and tone, foci of interest, and distribution of influence. The personal rapport and informality which characterized the General Assembly with 50 or even 60 members was no longer possible as it moved towards 100 and beyond. The fact of bigness now asserted itself, making the deliberations more cumbersome and time-consuming. The direct US–USSR confrontation, which had long dominated the Assembly and had led to politically unreal but numerically decisive majorities for the West, now became diverted to a new and large constituency with different interests. Development and decolonization replaced security as the preoccupations of UN debate and decision.

Most important was the change in the pyramid of influence in Assembly decisions and in alignment patterns. The Latin American Group, which for a decade or more had controlled 40 per cent of the Assembly's votes, was now reduced to 20 per cent of the membership. Its position as pre-eminent interest group was taken by the amorphous Asian–African Group, which had grown from a dozen votes in 1955 to almost fifty at the end of this period.[1] Aligned and non-aligned, some affiliated· to the West, others to the Soviet bloc, they rarely voted in unison; but on the issues of development and decolonization they shaped UN policy. Neither the US nor the USSR was prepared to offend the new states on what the latter regarded as vital interests. Indeed the bloc leaders courted them at every opportunity, for they held a clear balance of voting strength in the Assembly. The West needed the support of Afro-Asian moderates to achieve a two-thirds majority—or at least to deny this strategic figure to the rival bloc. The Soviets gained even more from this new UN component, for they escaped from the near-permanent status of isolated minority in Assembly votes during the first decade. The price for both blocs was greater flexibility in goals and tactics to meet the wishes of moderate and revolutionary new states.

The same changes quickly extended to the specialized agencies of the UN, now growing in response to the vociferous demands for aid to the developing states. A system-wide military organization to enforce peace and security was still foundering on inter-bloc mistrust, as were the protracted negotiations for a measure of arms control. There were, however, two *ad hoc* experiments of significance, UNEF in the Middle

[1] The consequence of this change for Israel's image in the world was dramatically revealed by the General Assembly's approval, in November 1970, of the pro-Arab Afro-Asian-sponsored resolution on the Arab–Israel conflict: it gave UN General Assembly legitimacy to the Arab demand that Israel return to the Jarring Talks—without any reference to Egypt's violations of the Cease-fire Agreement of August 1970; the competing resolution sponsored by the Latin American Group failed to secure a two-thirds majority.

East and ONUC in the Congo, the former successful for a decade (1957–67), the latter an attempt (1960–4) to prevent chaos in central Africa.

There were important changes within the blocs as well. Western unity was subjected to severe strain, first by the Anglo-French assault on Suez in 1956, accompanied by the spectacle of American and Soviet parallel pressures leading to withdrawal, then by French disaffection with NATO, and third, by growing doubt about the character of the Soviet threat in the sixties. As compensation there was the inauguration of the Common Market in 1959, a process of economic integration with profound implications for the bloc, for Europe, and for the global system as a whole. In Eastern Europe the Polish 'October' and the Hungarian Revolt, along with the denigration of Stalin and the Sino-Soviet rift, marked the end of rigid centralization and the opening of a new phase of intra-bloc autonomy. The hegemony of the USSR in East European security matters remained unchallenged but her control over internal party questions, economic planning, cultural expression—and even foreign policy—was now curtailed by national pressures within the bloc.

Centrifugal tendencies in both blocs, combined with the 'balance of terror', led to a renewed dialogue between the super powers. There were visits by Mikoyan and Kozlov to America and Nixon to the Soviet Union in 1958, the historic Eisenhower–Khrushchev Camp David Talks in 1959, the abortive Paris summit conference in 1960, and the Kennedy–Khrushchev summit in 1961. The thaw extended to cultural relations, personal travel in each other's orbit, an increase in trade, and more realistic negotiation on arms control. Yet all this was accompanied by intense competition in the new states and in some old ones as well; one incident, Cuba in 1962, could have destroyed the system and all its members.

Penetration of subordinate systems was indeed intense and wide-spread during that phase. It began with the Suez Crisis—the Anglo-French invasion of Egypt and then decisive intervention by the US and the USSR. It ended with direct confrontation and near-collision over Cuba. There were many other cases of penetration by the dominant system: in Lebanon and Jordan (1958), by a US and UK military presence, respectively; in the Congo (1960), where the Soviets were ousted; in South Vietnam from 1961 onwards; through competitive aid programmes in many states of Africa, the Middle East, and Southern Asia; through relentless propaganda and large-scale intelligence networks; and through an escalating supply of military assistance to areas beyond direct bloc control, notably South Asia and the Middle East. In the latter the Soviets equipped the armed forces of Egypt and Syria, while France provided the bulk of Israel's air power; the UK continued her special ties with Jordan and gave marginal assistance to Israel; and the US extended hardware to Saudi Arabia, Jordan, and Israel. It was penetration of an extreme and sustained kind in a system characterized by acute conflict and turmoil.

The Soviets displayed more flexibility towards the non-aligned states than did the US during the late 1950s. The latter, under Dulles' guidance, dubbed non-alignment immoral or, at best, amoral, and pursued a policy of 'pactitis'. The USSR, by contrast, perceived non-alignment as a means of detaching states from the West: the Bulganin–Khrushchev visit to Afghanistan, India, and Burma at the turn of 1955–6 symbolized this new policy and led to an ambitious economic and military aid programme to select non-aligned states. Only under Kennedy did the United States accept non-alignment as a legitimate basis of foreign policy, among new and old states alike.

There was a substantial reverse flow of influence, that is, penetration *by* subordinate systems and their members, during this period. Continuous pressure by the non-aligned for relaxation of tension contributed to more frequent interaction between the bloc leaders and led to the Paris and Vienna summits. The presence of Nehru, Tito, Nasser, Nkrumah, and Soekarno at the 1960 General Assembly session had a salutary effect, despite the rejection of their call for Big Two talks; so too did the Belgrade Conference in 1961. Perhaps the most important source of reverse penetration was the very existence of the third world, some of whose members possessed a potential nuclear capability. It was this, along with the prodding of the non-aligned, which helped induce the move of the nuclear powers towards a partial test ban and, later, control over proliferation. The further function of providing a large zone for peaceful competition between the super powers also contributed to greater flexibility in the global system as a whole.

All the textural features underwent substantial but non-qualitative extension from 1956 to 1962. Thus the heterogeneity of values was enlarged with the entry of politically-organized African cultures into the system, representing a kaleidoscope of tribal value- and belief-systems hitherto outside the global framework. The diversity of polities was broadened as well—the new states of Africa exhibiting a concentration of one-party systems of the radical and gradualist modernizing types. Internal instability in the new African units was yet to appear, for the first phase of exuberant independence had not run its course. And in the global system as a whole the onrush of technology raised the level of communications to a point where men became aware of remote occurrences almost instantly.

Just as the change from transition to tight bipolarity had been dramatized by specific events, so too was the next global change, from loose bipolarity to polycentrism.[1] It was the Czech coup and the Berlin

---

[1] The term 'tight bipolarity' was introduced by Kaplan (*System and Process . . .*) but its use in this discussion is different. For him, a 'tight bipolar' international system has

blockade, both in 1948, which had catalysed the move to a cold-war type of two-power system. Similarly it was the Cuban missile crisis and the Sino-Indian border war in October 1962 which began to ease the rigid confrontation. The US and USSR recoiled from the prospect of nuclear holocaust and began to acquire awareness of a shared interest in the Himalayas—the containment of Chinese influence in South Asia and tranquillity in the Indo-Pakistani sub-continent. Other developments contributed to the new transition; these were crucial because of their impact on the super powers.

The level of power in the post-1962 period remained very high, despite the Nuclear Test Ban Treaty of 1963. The US and USSR continued to refine and to expand their armoury of nuclear weapons and their delivery capacity. The age of 'overkill' had arrived, with sober estimates in 1968 of power sufficient to destroy the planet and all its inhabitants six times over. Yet this was uni-linear change, a quantitative increase in military strength within the context of a 'balance of terror' already existing and recognized as such by the decision-making élite in Moscow and Washington; that, indeed, was the long-term significance of the near-collision over Cuba.

The effect of this reality and its accurate perception was a lessening of overt conflict between the super powers. The ideological differences persisted but without the emotional intensity of an earlier era. The new technocratic leadership in the USSR remained committed to communism but not at the risk of nuclear war. And while the US remained anti-communist, this perceived threat and policy objective was redirected to the Peking régime. The result and the expression of this more stable equilibrium was greater caution in areas of competition. Three examples will suffice: Soviet intervention in the Vietnam War remained limited and indirect; the US gave *de facto* support to Soviet efforts to mediate the Indo-Pakistani dispute over Kashmir following their 1965 war; and Moscow exercised *military* restraint in the (third)

---

no historical counterpart and is characterized by the disappearance or utter insignificance of non-bloc actors and the universal actor (the UN). Yet 'tight bipolarity' seems an appropriate designation in this context because of the increasing rigidity between the two blocs during the period 1948–56. 'Polycentrism', in this analysis, has many of the features of Kaplan's modified version of 'loose bipolarity'—what he calls a 'Very Loose Bipolar System'; this is a theorist's semantic accommodation to changing reality. See his 'Some Problems of International Systems Research', in *International Political Communities: An Anthology*, Doubleday & Co., New York, 1966, pp. 469–501.

Among other interpretations of the impact of different types of global system on international stability, three are noteworthy: Kenneth N. Waltz, 'The Stability of a Bipolar World', *Daedalus*, vol. xciii, Summer 1964, pp. 881–909; Karl W. Deutsch and J. David Singer, 'Multipolar Power Systems and International Stability', *World Politics*, xvi, 3, April 1964, pp. 390–406; and Richard N. Rosecrance, 'Bipolarity, Multipolarity, and the Future', *The Journal of Conflict Resolution*, x, 3, September 1966, pp. 314–27.

Arab–Israel War of 1967, that is, she refused to intervene directly, despite the cost of overwhelming defeat for her clients and the resulting loss of prestige.

A counterweight to this stabilizing tendency was the growing diffusion of nuclear capability. France achieved a burgeoning and protected missile complex, a delivery system of manned bombers, and membership in the H-Bomb club. More dramatically and more quickly China became the fifth nuclear power—from a primitive atomic device to an H-Bomb explosion in thirty months. And neither of these states participated in the discussions or decisions concerning arms control, France by choice, China by exclusion. There are at least six other states with the reputation for a potential nuclear capability—Canada, Sweden, West Germany, India, Japan, and Israel. Some expressed a determination, in the great debate over a non-proliferation treaty during 1967–8, to retain an option to embark on a nuclear weapons programme. Thus a multi-unit veto system—in the form of five to ten states capable of destroying the global system—seems a probable next stage during the 1970s. What remains unknown is the duration of the current transitional phase toward that variant of the historical 'multi-power' system. In the interim the US and USSR retain nuclear pre-eminence almost to the point of hegemony.

If the post-1962 transition has not yet achieved multi-unit veto dimensions, it has nonetheless given rise to a polycentric system, that is, a system with multiple centres of independent decision-making. This basic structural change was foreshadowed by the behaviour of China and France in the late fifties: it was consummated by their persistent dissent in the sixties. China not only challenged the Soviet Union for leadership of the communist bloc but hurled at Moscow every epithet in the lexicon of Maoist–Leninism, including the ultimate charge of collusion with imperialist America to encircle and throttle the Peking régime. She also disputed the legitimacy of the seizure of vast territories in Inner Asia by Czarist Russia in the preceding three centuries and terminated all but the most formal diplomatic relations. In short, China opted out of the Soviet-led bloc. France did not adopt such an extreme posture. But her assertion of independence during this phase has been unmistakable: the rejection of British application for membership in the Common Market, in 1963 and 1967–8; the aloofness from all formal discussions on arms control and all agreements on nuclear weapons; withdrawal from the integrated NATO military command; the assault on the dollar-based international monetary standard; the relentless critique of everything 'Anglo-Saxon' and the United States policy in particular; and the assertion of France's right to super-power status.

Certainly by the mid-1960s China and France constituted two autonomous units of decision-making, removed from their bloc affiliation. Indeed, viewed in systemic terms, their policies revealed some striking parallels. Each opposed a US–USSR global condominium, which would freeze the *status quo* in Asia and Europe. Each sought to enlarge its stockpile of nuclear weapons, partly as a symbol of super-power status and partly to achieve greater autonomy in international politics. Each encouraged the other's assertion of independence from its bloc leader. And each mounted a major offensive in the new states, offering alternatives to dependence upon America or the Soviet Union. To China and France may be added, as autonomous units, Roumania and, to a lesser extent, West Germany. Thus the stratification of states in the late 1960s indicates a polycentric system with at least six centres of decision-making. In reality there are more independent actors—or fewer—depending upon the foreign policy issue and the issue area. The process of decentralization will probably continue in the coming decade.[1]

There was less significant change in other structural features during the post-1962 transition. UN membership increased steadily and approached the theoretical maximum of 135, as the final stage of decolonization drew to a close. Enlargement of the principal UN organs followed, to reflect the change in size and geographic com-position since 1946—but the legal veto of the five permanent members of the Security Council remained. The impact on style and tone and on the distribution of influence, noted earlier, continued in an even more conspicuous form with the entry of more African states. And the pre-occupation with development became institutionalized in the 'Com-mittee of 77', along with a number of new specialized agencies, notably UNCTAD and UNEDO. No progress was made towards a system-wide security organization, but the role of peacekeeping, begun with UNEF in 1956, found further expression in Cyprus, while UN observation was widespread—in Palestine, Kashmir, Lebanon, Yemen, West Irian, and elsewhere. The patterns of organization set in the past for the UN continued into the period of polycentrism. Inter-state interaction, too, followed the earlier trend, with an even greater intensity.

The super powers penetrated deeply into subordinate systems during this period; so too did the aspiring great powers, China and France. The Vietnam War was the most dramatic illustration, with US involve-ment escalating from an Advisory Group in 1961 to full-scale conven-tional war with half a million troops in 1968. There was also direct American intervention in the Dominican Republic—and penetration of every subordinate system through a vast aid and/or military assistance programme embracing 73 states. The USSR, too, intervened in Viet-nam but only with military supplies. She penetrated the Indo-Pakistani

---

[1] The occupation of Czechoslovakia by Soviet bloc forces in 1968 indicated a reversion to centralization and rigidity *within* that single bloc. Yet that is only one component, however important, of the *global system*. And the adverse reaction, within the Soviet camp as well as elsewhere, suggests that the long-term trend to polycentrism in the global system *as a whole* was not basically altered by that event.

sub-continent through the Tashkent Agreement of 1966, along with military and economic aid to India and Pakistan. Both super powers were enmeshed with Middle East system conflicts, the Soviets through massive arms shipments to Egypt and, to a lesser extent, Syria, Iraq, Yemen, Algeria, and South Yemen, along with such projects as the Aswan Dam; the US through a balanced allocation of military and economic aid. The Soviet role in precipitating the 1967 Arab–Israel War and the influence of both in the prolonged political battles that followed testified to their crucial position in Middle East conflicts.

China cast her net very widely as well: military aid to the Viet Cong and North Vietnam; collaboration in the abortive Indonesian coup of 1965; open support for the Arabs in their conflict with Israel; a diplomatic and aid offensive among the revolutionary states of Africa and the Middle East; and, through Cuba, penetration of Latin America. France under de Gaulle also pressed her influence vigorously. She repeatedly called for American withdrawal from Vietnam and the neutralization of South-East Asia. She supported the Arabs in the 1967 Middle East war. She called for the dismemberment of Canada and sought the re-establishment of historic French influence in North America, through Quebec. She attempted, without success, a revival of French influence in Latin America. And she welded her former African colonies into a tightly-knit economic-security community.

The feedback from subordinate systems was drastically reduced by the mid-1960s. Nehru was dead and India was preoccupied with internal problems. Nkrumah and Soekarno were ousted, and their states were confronted with economic chaos. Only Tito and Nasser were left among the non-aligned leaders, and the latter's image had been undermined by the shattering defeat of his army in the Six Day War of 1967. No other charismatic figures had arisen to take their place. More important, the structure of the global system had been transformed: the kind of role induced, and permitted, by bipolarity was less necessary in a polycentric phase. And the growing gap in capability between dominant and subordinate system actors made this reverse penetration less effective. Little need be said of the textural features, for these remained basically unchanged after 1962—apart from ubiquitous political instability in the new states, especially in Africa.

The global system during the first twenty years of Israel's independence is presented in schematic form in Table 1. That four-phase system served as the broadest level of the external environment in which Israeli decision-makers had to formulate and implement foreign policy.

(b) DOMINANT BILATERAL RELATIONS

The systemic parameters of Israel's foreign policy, as for any state, are important: they define the limits of freedom of choice among the theoretically-possible options available to decision-makers. There is another external dimension, however—bilateral relationships. Their influence varies with the issue and the issue area; it may derive from one actor or more than one, that is, the source of pressure may be bilateral or multilateral as distinct from systemic. Yet for most states in the global system there is a small number of other units with which a special relationship exists.[1] Interaction with these units is more intense, continuous, and significant in terms of a state's external behaviour as a whole. A few examples will suffice: for Canada the principal units are the United States and the United Kingdom, with France added to this group in the 1960s; for West Germany the key states are France, the US, and the USSR; for India they are Pakistan, China, the USSR, and the US; for Kenya they are Tanzania, Uganda, and Somalia; and so on.

TABLE I

THE CONTEMPORARY GLOBAL SYSTEM

Features	Transition 1945–1948	Tight Bipolarity 1948–1956	Loose Bipolarity 1956–1962	Polycentrism 1962–
Structural				
Level of Power	2	3	5	5
Power Stratification	3	5	5	3
Political Organization	2	3	4	4
Military Organization	1	1	2	2
Economic Organization	2	2	3	3
Intensity of Interaction	2	1	3	3
Penetration of Subordinate Systems	1	4	4	5
Penetration by Subordinate Systems	1	4	4	1
Textural				
Level of Communications	3	4	5	5
Homogeneity of Values	3	2	1	1
Commonality of Political Systems	3	2	1	1
Units' Domestic Stability	4	3	2	1

Key: Very High 5   High 4   Medium 3   Low 2   Very Low 1

Israel's relationships within the global system have multiplied over the years. Indeed she has more diplomatic missions abroad than any

[1] Notable exceptions are the super powers, whose range of commitments and interests involves them in a larger number of special relationships.

other state of her size and more than most of any size, a result of the incessant conflict within the Near East core, her isolation there, and the need for support in the UN and elsewhere.[1] Yet during the first twenty years the coterie of states with a significant impact on Israel's policy has remained constant—the US, the USSR, and France (and since 1952, West Germany), apart, of course, from the core Arab states and the UN, with which Israel was permanently involved.[2]

Of the four key state relationships little need be said at this point about France and Germany, for these will be explored in depth later.[3] Suffice it to note that France was less than friendly in the formative UN debates of 1947, that a vital *de facto* alliance was forged in the years 1954-6, that France was the principal arms supplier for a dozen years, and that in 1967 de Gaulle accused Israel of aggression in the Six Day War, labelling the Jews 'at all times an élite people, sure of itself and domineering'.[4] France remained important to Israel, but the 'special tie' was terminated.

The link with West Germany has been of a different order, charged with emotion, and ambivalent. The searing memory of the Holocaust remains embedded in the national consciousness and conscience of Israel; throughout the first seventeen years it was an insuperable barrier to 'normal' relations. Yet with time and Israel's exposed position, economically and militarily, the importance of West Germany became accepted among the decision-making élite. There were four notable events in the Israeli–German association on the painful road to accommodation: the Reparations Agreement of 1952, at a time of economic travail; the Ben Gurion–Adenauer meeting in 1960, an historic confrontation between the leaders of the 'new Germany' and the resurrected Jewish state; the secret arms agreement of 1960; and

[1] The growth of Israel's diplomatic and consular presence is evident in the number and location of her missions:

	1955	1966–7
Asia	7	9
Africa	2	29
Eastern Europe	7	7
Western Europe	20	21
North America	6	13
Latin America	13	15
Australia and New Zealand	2	2
	57	96

These figures are taken from the State of Israel, *Government Year-Book, 5716* (1955–6) and *5727* (1966–7). For further details see ch. 20 (*d*) below.

[2] The UK was a member of this group of key states in Israel's policy until 1957.

[3] In a companion volume on high-policy decisions. See also ch. 16 (*b*) and (*c*) below on Israel and Germany.

[4] As quoted in the *New York Times*, 30 Nov. 1967.

the establishment of diplomatic relations in 1965. The drastic shift of France in 1967 further enhanced the significance of West Germany for Israel's foreign policy. Whereas the French–Israeli relationship turned full circle—from unfriendliness to warm embrace to public rupture of an alliance—the link with Germany, deriving from a unique historical experience, has been a slow path to the reconstruction of a dialogue. In the process the material benefits to Israel have accumulated.

Israel's involvement with the super powers has been of extraordinary intensity since the creation of the state. It was American and Soviet parallel support at the UN that was decisive in securing international sanction for independence in 1947–8. But there were other, no less compelling, reasons for Israel's quest for friendship with both the US and the USSR. The two largest Jewish communities in the world reside in these pre-eminent states of the global system—and Zionist ideology dictated a concern for the welfare of Jews everywhere. To the moral commitment was added the need for *aliya*—immigration—in order to furnish the manpower and skills, and to some extent capital, without which the new state could not grow, perhaps not even survive, in the face of permanent hostility from its Arab neighbours. The demographic component of Israel's links to the super powers became more pronounced by 1960, when the major active sources of *aliya*—North Africa and the Middle East—had almost dried up. The two remaining reservoirs were American and Russian Jewry: the former was free to migrate but was unwilling to do so in large numbers, yet it provided a substantial part of the essential foreign capital in the form of gifts and loans; the latter was assumed to be desirous of migration but was denied the right.

The importance of world Jewry in Israel's foreign policy system can hardly be exaggerated. There is indeed a unique relationship, deriving from the unique experience of the Jewish People. There is only one Jewish State—and this is consciously perceived as a restoration of a political entity which flourished in antiquity. The links between Diaspora Jews and *Eretz Yisrael* (the Land of Israel) are powerful and deep-rooted—in history, culture, religion, and emotional attachment. Jews everywhere identify themselves as members of a People. And, while only those residing in Israel constitute an Israeli nation, the sense of kinship has no parallel in international politics. Only 17 per cent of world Jewry resided in Israel in 1966, 2·3 million of 13·4 million (it was only 5·7 per cent when the state was proclaimed in 1948, and only 0·5 per cent in 1900).[1] Yet Israel is a homeland in a pervasive intangible sense for millions who live in the Diaspora. The result has been a special link between world Jewry (or any one of its parts) and Israeli foreign

[1] Central Bureau of Statistics, *Statistical Abstract of Israel* (henceforth also cited as CBI, SAI), no. 18, 1967, Jerusalem, Table B/3, p. 21.

policy—a link which has been multiple and continuous. It may indeed be argued that world Jewry is the *most important* component of the global system for Israel: David Ben Gurion, Israel's Prime Minister for most of the period from 1948 to 1963, frequently declared, 'Israel's only absolutely reliable ally is world Jewry'. More specifically, it impinged on Israel's foreign policy in many segments and in many of her major decisions, as will become apparent throughout this book.[1]

The presence of large Jewish communities in the US and the USSR —and everything that this entails—accentuates the importance of the super powers to Israel. There was the additional factor of Israel's location in a region where oil and strategy were powerful stakes in the global conflict, with consequences for her most vital interests. Thus a closely-knit set of pressures created an Israeli preoccupation with the US and the USSR: ideology; demography; economics; security. Friendship and support from both super powers would ensure survival and prosperity; hostility from both, combined with the proclaimed Arab goal of politicide, would place the state in grave jeopardy.

The policy imperative was clear and was recognized as such at the outset. In the days, perhaps weeks, before independence, Ben Gurion and Sharett asked themselves what kind of foreign policy Israel should adopt. They decided that it had to be *ee-hizdahut* (non-identification) and made it known informally in the early summer. Then, on 27 September 1948, in the midst of a war for survival, Prime Minister Ben Gurion declared before the Provisional State Council: 'We have friends both in the East and in the West. We could not have conducted the war without the important help we received from several States of East and West . . . the interests of the Jewish people are not identical with those of any State or any bloc in the world. . . . There is no identification between a small and a big nation, except if the small nation completely subordinates itself, or if the big nation is composed entirely of angels. We do not want to subordinate ourselves to anyone, and we do not

---

[1]Of special interest are the following: the population factor in military capability (ch. 4 (*b*)); the demographic aspect of economic capability (ch. 5 (*a*)); the import surplus and foreign aid (ch. 5 (*d*)), and the significance of that aid for the crucial defence burden (ch. 4 (*e*) and (*f*)); the foreign policy content of Government Programmes (Appendix A); Diaspora Jewry as an interest group advocating policy, as in the Eichmann Case, the South African Question, Soviet Jewry, etc. (ch. 7 (*a*) ii and 11 (*b*)); competing élite images of Diaspora Jewry and its ties to Israel (ch. 8); the images of Jewry held by the principal decision-makers (in ch. 11 (*a*) and (*b*), 12, and 13 (*c*), (*g*), and (*j*)); the role of Jewry in the implementation of Israel's foreign policy by lobbying on Israel's behalf (ch. 19 (*d*)); and its relevance to some of the major decisions, notably German Reparations, the Korean War, diplomatic relations with Germany, and the Six Day War, all to be explored in a companion volume on high-policy decisions. In short, this pervasive aspect of Israel's foreign policy will be examined at each relevant part of the inquiry.

believe that angels rule anywhere.'[1] This theme was given formal status in the Basic Principles of the Government Programme announced on 8 March 1949: the first of five principles of foreign policy read: 'Loyalty to the principles of the United Nations Charter and friendship with all freedom-loving states, and in particular with the United States and the Soviet Union.'[2]

The (semi-official) newspaper of the *Histadrut* (General Federation of Jewish Labour) had already referred to 'Israel's firm policy of neutrality'.[3] It elaborated on its meaning soon after the Government Programme was given formal approval: 'Neutrality for Israel must therefore mean dependence on both of the world's large groupings, without favouring either' (because Israel depends on the US for capital and on the USSR for immigration). 'We cannot therefore hope to terminate this double dependence within the foreseeable future.'[4]

In the hands of Foreign Minister Sharett the policy of neutrality became 'the principle of non-identification with either of the contending blocs', a position which he elucidated on numerous occasions in the early years.[5] Indeed Sharett was the first statesman in the new states of Asia–Africa to use this notion of non-alignment, though Israel was not regarded as non-identified or non-aligned.[6] Nor was she admitted to the councils of the Third World.

One Israeli Foreign Ministry official attributed this policy to five determinants: considerations of national defence against hostile neighbours, that is, access to arms; the concept of Jewish solidarity and mutual responsibility by and for all segments of Jewry; the need to bring about Diaspora Jewry's involvement in the enormous task of absorbing large masses of immigrants; the necessity of world peace, for Jewish as well as for general human survival; and domestic party pressures.[7] The last of these variables—the balance of domestic

---

[1] *Records of the Provisional State Council* (in Hebrew), Government Printer, Tel Aviv, 1948–9, 20th Session, p. 22, as quoted in *Israel and the United Nations* (Report of a Study Group of the Hebrew University), Manhattan Publishing Co., New York, 1956, p. 184.

[2] State of Israel, *Government Year-Book 5711* (1950), Government Printer, Jerusalem, 1950, p. 50.

[3] *Davar* (Tel Aviv), 4 Feb. 1949 (editorial).

[4] Ibid., 13 April 1949.

[5] The original text is in *Divrei Ha-Knesset* (Official Records of the Knesset, in Hebrew), Government Printer, Jerusalem/Tel Aviv, 1949–54, 1st Knesset, 2nd Session (1950), vol. vi, p. 2057. The most important of Sharett's statements on this theme was delivered to the Israeli parliament on 4 July 1950 soon after the outbreak of the Korean War. An English translation was issued the same day by the Israel Office of Information in New York.

[6] According to V. K. Krishna Menon, the term 'non-alignment' was not used by him or by Nehru until the early 1950s. See Michael Brecher, *India and World Politics*, Oxford University Press, London, 1968, p. 3.

[7] Shabtai Rosenne (Legal Adviser, Israel Ministry for Foreign Affairs from 1948 to 1967), 'Basic Elements of Israel's Foreign Policy' ,*India Quarterly*, xvii, no. 4, Oct.–Dec. 1961, pp. 328–58.

political forces—referred to the outcome of the first general election in 1949. *Mapam*, a Marxist–Zionist party with a strong commitment to pro-Soviet non-alignment, emerged as the second strongest party, with 19 of the 120 *Knesset* seats and 14·7 per cent of the votes, compared with 46 seats and 35·7 per cent of the votes for the leading *Mapai* party. There were also many in *Mapai* who were inclined to non-alignment and a widely-shared belief across the political spectrum that this policy was 'in the national interest': this meant, in essence, the opportunity to receive aid from the two blocs. One newspaper summed up the feeling with the apt remark, 'both goodwill and necessity . . . make for the choice of the middle road in Israel's foreign policy'.[1]

The total commitment to non-alignment lasted less than two years, for this policy was perceived as feasible only under certain conditions: first, permission by the super powers to remain aloof from their conflict; and secondly, either Arab acceptance of Israel or an external (bloc or global system) guarantee of Israel's security. The first condition appeared to have vanished with the Korean War, when the US insisted that friendly states 'stand up and be counted'. Within a year of the Armistice Agreements, certainly by 1951, it became clear that Arab hostility would not abate. A vague, informal guarantee of Israel's frontiers was in fact given by the three Western powers in the Tripartite Declaration of May 1950. Israel acquiesced in the Declaration and was harshly criticized by the Soviet Union for 'selling out to the West' by allegedly trying to join an abortive Western-sponsored Middle East bloc (MEDO) in 1951. Earlier the Soviets castigated the Israeli request for US arms to counter British weapons to the Arabs.

The Korean War marked the great divide in Israel's policy towards the blocs. 'We had to make up our mind', one Israeli diplomat told this writer, resignedly. 'The Israeli economy was at its lowest point. Ben Gurion had asked the Soviets for economic aid; it was a feasible expectation at the time, but Moscow's reply was negative. And American Jews were saying, "playing with Moscow will diminish aid from US Jewry". We had to cut off from one side in order to continue getting aid from America.'[2] From her initial support of the UN Security Council resolutions in June–July 1950 through the General Assembly's actions in the autumn and winter of 1950–1, Israel gradually moved towards the Western camp—to the limited extent that the US would permit.[3] The choice was perceived as natural, given the affinity of régimes, the strong ties with American Jewry, the availability of economic aid, public and private, and the apparent hostility of the

---

[1] *Davar* (Tel Aviv), 1 Feb. 1949.
[2] Interview in Jerusalem, July 1960. That, in perspective, this perception did not accord with reality will be elaborated in the concluding chapter.
[3] Israel's policy towards the Korean War will be explored in a related volume on high-policy decisions.

USSR after her brief support in 1947–8. Nonetheless it marked the erosion of non-alignment, despite the claims of some Israeli leaders in the sixties that Israel had always pursued an 'independent' course in international politics.[1]

Relations between Israel and the Soviet Union deteriorated steadily after 1950. The nadir was reached in the summer of 1967, with Soviet Premier Kosygin and UN Delegate Federenko hurling abuse and invective, including the offensive charge that Israeli behaviour during and after the Six Day War was akin to that of the Nazis in Europe.[2] Only the intervening highlights of this relationship need be noted in this brief survey of Israel and the super powers; the details will unfold in subsequent analyses of major foreign policy decisions.

A dramatic break in diplomatic relations occurred in February 1953 following an explosion in the grounds of the Soviet Mission in Tel Aviv. Official apologies and the disclaimer of *mala fides* were swept aside.[3] Relations were restored five months later, but tension continued. In the autumn of 1955 the Soviet bloc made a deep penetration into the Middle East through the sale of arms on a large scale to Egypt and Syria; this act ranged the USSR and her allies on the Arab side in the Near East conflict. Whenever necessary the Soviets used their veto to prevent any Security Council action injurious to their client Arab states, as with the Council's admonition to Egypt in 1954 to discontinue the denial of passage through the Suez Canal to Israeli ships and cargo.

[1] Mrs. Golda Meir, then Foreign Minister of Israel, told a press conference in Jerusalem on 3 November 1960 that Israel belonged to a fourth category of states—other than capitalist, socialist, and neutralist—namely, non-aligned, that is, one which judged each issue on its merits. The fact that Israel was not a member of NATO or the Warsaw Pact, she said, was further proof that Israel was 'non-aligned'. *The Israel Digest*, New York, 11 November 1960.

Israel has been *formally* non-aligned throughout the period of her independence—pactless, without guarantees, and without foreign troops or bases on her soil; but she has been dependent upon the West for crucial elements of her military and economic capability, as will be elaborated in ch. 4 (*e*) and (*f*) and ch. 5 (*d*) and (*e*) below. At the same time, as a formally non-aligned small state she has had much greater flexibility of manœuvre in policy acts than other—larger—states which are formally attached to a bloc or a bloc leader. Her persistent border retaliation policy is one expression of this greater freedom. Her initiative in the Sinai Campaign is another. And her creation of a presence in Africa from 1958 onwards is a third illustration.

Indeed Israel's *de facto* influence in international politics is extraordinary relative to her size, population, economy, etc. This role operates in both the global system and in the Middle East. And in another subordinate system, namely Africa, Israel's diplomatic presence, as noted, ranks fourth or fifth after the US, Germany, UK, and, perhaps, France. Israel also has a substantial technical assistance presence, with a disproportionate impact on Africa.

[2] *New York Times*, 20 June 1967. Soviet policy in that period will be examined in the companion volume.

[3] Former Prime Minister Ben Gurion analysed in great detail this incident and the attitudes expressed in the *Knesset*, in his memoirs, *The State of Israel Reborn*, Number 55, 'USSR Broke Diplomatic Relations With Israel', *Davar* (Tel Aviv), 25 March 1966.

Early in November 1956 Moscow used dire threats of direct bombing and the dispatch of 'volunteers' to deny Israel the fruits of victory in the Sinai Campaign.

During the 'quiet decade', 1957–67, the USSR became increasingly the sole patron of Syria and the principal source of foreign aid for Egypt. Indeed the Soviets poured about $3 billion[1] worth of arms into these two Middle East states, knowing that they were directed at Israel's destruction. There were rare intrusions of conciliation, for example, Soviet press comments that the 1966 Tashkent Agreement between India and Pakistan might be a model for mediation in the Near East. More significant for Israel was the flexibility in Soviet policy on emigration of Russian Jews, highlighted by Premier Kosygin's pledge in a Paris statement late in 1966; the 'reunion of families' scheme led to a migration of several thousand Jews to Israel in 1965–7. But even this was halted after the Six Day War. And in the years following that war the USSR replenished Egyptian and Syrian armouries to the pre-war level.[2]

The posture of the United States was very different. America's long-term importance for Israel lies in two facts: it is a super power basically friendly to Israel, and it contains the largest bloc of world Jewry. As one former Director-General of the Ministry for Foreign Affairs remarked: 'All other considerations—economic aid, military aid, a security commitment, etc.—flow from these facts; they are but elaborations, however important they may be in themselves. [Further], the American factor is constantly in the calculations of Israeli decision-makers—even though some people naively thought they could diminish the American factor, by counterposing a French–German orientation; these are not options, but, rather, complementary relationships.'[3]

The US presence looms large across the whole range of Israel's foreign policy, from the initial act of recognition in May 1948 to the political struggle following the third Arab–Israel War in 1967. Throughout, 'the stakes in relationship to America have been tremendous. She has the capacity to keep us afloat, to give us victory or to prevent defeat. It is crucial—[Government economic] aid, Jewish aid, military aid if necessary.'[4] America's role and influence will be examined in detail in subsequent studies of major Israeli decisions, notably the Jerusalem Question, German Reparations and Diplomatic Relations, the Korean War and China, the Sinai Campaign, the Jordan Waters issue, and the Six Day War of 1967. Related aspects of this connection, such as the influence of American Jewry, will be explored, as

---

[1] The word 'billion' is used throughout this volume in the North American meaning, that is, one thousand million (1,000,000,000).

[2] This arms build-up will be examined in ch. 4 (f) below.

[3] Dr. Haim Yahil, Director-General from 1960 to 1964, to the author in an interview in Jerusalem, July 1966.

[4] Interview with a Foreign Ministry official, Jerusalem, Aug. 1968.

noted, in discussion of other segments of the Israel Foreign Policy System at work. All that need be done in this probe of the external setting is to sketch some high points in the relationship.[1]

If 1948–50 can be described as the phase of Israel's non-identification, the period 1951–5 witnessed her American orientation *par excellence*. One Israeli academic critic termed it 'a conscious effort to become a US satellite, to win America's friendship and support'.[2] There were some successes, notably the beginning of economic aid and permission to float a $500 million State of Israel Bonds campaign. But the returns were meagre on the arms front, and all efforts to secure a formal security guarantee met with failure. By 1955 it had become apparent that the US Government did not want a public image in the Middle East as Israel's ally or protector. Israel responded by seeking—and finding— military aid elsewhere; the result was the French alliance, consummated in the Sinai Campaign.

Yet America remained vital in Israel's foreign policy. It had sponsored the Johnston Plan for the Jordan Waters in 1953–5. It pursued an ambivalent policy during the Sinai Campaign, which proved to be crucial—pressure for Israeli withdrawal and a pledge for safeguards against a recurrence of Egyptian security threats. It continued to extend aid in multiple forms: direct grants and loans (more than a billion dollars by 1968); permission to American Jewry to make donations as partially tax-exempt charity ($1½ billion before the 1967 War and a further $250 million during that crisis);[3] preliminary co-operation for a future desalination project, the key to irrigation of the Negev Desert; and technical assistance for special needs.

The immediate post-Sinai phase was relatively quiescent. In the first half of the 1960s, however, several important developments occurred.[4] One was a *de facto* American commitment to Israel's independence and security. 'The US had opposed the Sinai Campaign and any forcible change of the relations laid down in the Armistice Agreements; but, having forced Israel back, it began to recognize Israel's legitimate concerns, and Dulles began to recognize Israel in its existing boundaries. This was further developed by President Kennedy, with his thesis about "the special relationship" between the US and Israel: a written assurance from Kennedy to Eshkol in the autumn of 1963 contained a

---

[1] For an informative survey of Israel's relationship with the United States and the Soviet Union until 1962 see Nadav Safran, *The United States and Israel*, Harvard University Press, Cambridge, Mass., 1963, ch. XIII–XV.

[2] Dr. Benjamin Akzin, Professor of Political Science and Constitutional Law at the Hebrew University, in an interview in Jerusalem, July 1960.

[3] The US Department of Commerce reported at the end of 1967 that, from the beginning of June to the end of September 1967, American private remittances to Israel increased by $210 million. Reported in *Jerusalem Post Weekly*, 1 Jan. 1968, p. 4.

[4] The following account is derived from the interview with Dr. Yahil in July 1966, noted on the preceding page.

de facto guarantee of Israel's territorial integrity. President Johnson adhered to "the special relationship" concept and went even further during his discussions with Prime Minister Eshkol in June 1964 [and again in January 1968]. It was not an absolute guarantee, but machinery was created for joint consultation on political and military levels.'[1]

A second important development was the US departure from a position of not supplying arms directly to Israel. It began quietly in the late 1950s when Washington let it be known that, if Israel could prove an *imbalance in weapons* of some type and, further, that they were unavailable elsewhere, the US would, reluctantly, restore the balance— but not as Israel's *principal* arms supplier. This continued with Hawk missiles in 1962 (Ben Gurion's initial request for missiles in 1960 had been rejected), with tanks in 1964, Skyhawk planes in 1966, and Phantom jet bombers in 1968. Still another change related to the Jordan Waters: the US accepted Israel's drawing of her share of water under the Johnston Plan; and formal sanction was given to the project in an explicit assurance from Kennedy to Ben Gurion in 1962.

On the Arab refugee problem, too, there was movement. The Joseph Johnson Plan was shelved by mutual consent, and bilateral negotiations followed. There was an understanding, informally, that the great majority of refugees must be settled in Arab states, that an unspecified minority should be repatriated, and that the US would negotiate directly with the Arabs. Since they failed to reach agreement, the pressure on Israel eased—though the US formally continued to adhere to Article 11 of the 1948 UN Resolution which provides 'that the refugees *wishing to return* to their homes *and live in peace with their neighbours* should be permitted to do so at the earliest practicable date'.[2] Finally, while the US continued to withhold recognition of Jerusalem as Israel's capital, she agreed to cease applying pressure on states which wished to establish their diplomatic missions in that city.

The supreme test of America's commitment to Israel came in May 1967, following the massing of Egyptian troops in Sinai and the proclaimed blockade of the Tiran Straits. The record will be assessed later. But in the vital debates at the United Nations during the rest of 1967 and 1968—and again in the Rogers' Proposals of 1970—the US insisted that decisions about Israel's withdrawal from occupied territory must

[1] On this point Shimon Peres, then Deputy Defence Minister, wrote later that Eshkol told him in Washington, after a 'four-eyes' discussion in the President's office, that Johnson had said, 'The United States stands four-square behind Israel', that America would 'not be idle if Israel is attacked', and that this commitment, given by both his predecessor and himself, was a 'solemn and serious commitment'. Peres, *David's Sling*, Weidenfeld and Nicolson, London, 1970, p. 103.

[2] Para. 11 of Resolution 194 (III), adopted by the General Assembly on 11 December 1948 (186th Plenary Meeting). *Official Record of the Third Session of the General Assembly, Part I, 21 September–12 December 1948, Resolutions*, United Nations, New York, 1948, pp. 21–5. (Emphasis added, M.B.)

be linked to Arab acceptance of Israel's right to exist as an independent state within secure boundaries.

The two most significant aspects of the global system for Israeli policy have been the UN and inter-bloc conflict. The former has been closely linked to Israel since her inception. The latter, extending to the Near East, accentuated the crucial role of dominant bilateral relationships in Israel's behaviour. Moreover, super-power conflict within the Middle East added a dimension of turmoil and insecurity in the region with which Israel was indissolubly linked. And all this occurred as the Middle East crystallized into a subordinate international system, with well-defined structural and textural features. That system, to which we now turn, impinged massively on Israel's foreign policy, no less than the other two levels of her external environment.

CHAPTER 3

The Middle East Subordinate System[1]

A subordinate state system, as noted earlier, requires six conditions for its existence: (1) delimited scope, with primary stress on a geographic region; (2) at least three actors; (3) objective recognition by most other actors as constituting a distinctive community, region, or segment of the global system; (4) self-identification as such; (5) units of power relatively inferior to units in the dominant system, using a sliding scale of power in both; and (6) more intensive and influential penetration of the subordinate system by the dominant system than the reverse. Measured by these criteria the Middle East is certainly one of the few developed subordinate systems in contemporary international politics.[2]

[1] An earlier version of this chapter was published as 'The Middle East Subordinate System and its Impact on Israel's Foreign Policy', *International Studies Quarterly*, 13, 2, 1969, pp. 117–39.

[2] The author's concept of subordinate system was first set out in his 'International Relations and Asian Studies: The Subordinate State System of Southern Asia', in *World Politics*, loc. cit. The following analysis takes that framework as the point of departure but offers major revisions: (1) a dynamic rather than a static analysis, that is, an exploration of the changes through time in each of the key features; (2) an exploration of the Middle East Subordinate System in depth, that is, a more systematic comparison of each of the twelve structural and textural features within three designated time phases from 1948 to 1968 (a schematic comparison is offered in Table 2); and (3) a direct link between a subordinate system and the foreign policy of a specific state.

The literature on subordinate systems is relatively sparse. A preliminary effort to define the Middle East in subordinate-system terms is found in Leonard Binder, 'The Middle East as a Subordinate International System', *World Politics*, x, 3, 1958, pp. 408–29. Other regional applications include: Michael Banks, 'Systems Analysis and the Study of Regions', *International Studies Quarterly*, 13, 4, Dec. 1969, pp. 335–60; Peter Berton (ed.), 'The East Asian International System in Historical Perspective' (mimeo, 46 pp.), School of International Relations, University of Southern California, April 1966; Larry W. Bowman, 'The Subordinate State System of Southern Africa', *International Studies Quarterly*, 12, 3, Sept. 1968, pp. 231–61; Louis J. Cantori and Steven L. Spiegel, 'International Regions: A Comparative Approach to Five Subordinate Systems', *International Studies Quarterly*, 13, 4, Dec. 1969, pp. 361–80; Donald C. Hellman, 'The Emergence of an East Asian International Subsystem', *International Studies Quarterly*, 13, 4, Dec. 1969, pp. 421–34; Thomas Hodgkin, 'The New West Africa State System', *The University of Toronto Quarterly*, xxxi, Oct. 1961, pp. 74–82; Stanley Hoffmann, 'Discord in Community: The North Atlantic Area as a Partial International System', *International Organization*, xvii, 3, Summer 1963, pp. 521–49; Karl Kaiser, 'The Interaction of Regional Subsystems: Some Preliminary Notes on Recurrent Patterns and the Role of Superpowers', *World Politics*, xxi, 1, Oct. 1968, pp. 84–107; George Modelski, 'International Relations and Area Studies: The Case of South-East Asia', *International Relations*, ii, April 1961, pp. 143–55; Jack M. Schick, 'Conflict and Integration in the Near East: Regionalism and the Study of Crises', a paper delivered to

(a) COMPOSITION

Viewed in terms of Israel's foreign policy, the Middle East system comprises three concentric circles of states (see Figure 3):

an Arab–Israeli *Core* of six units—Iraq, Jordan, Lebanon, Syria, Egypt (UAR), and Israel herself;

a *Periphery* of eight units—four Arab states, Algeria, Kuwait, Saudi Arabia, and Tunisia, two Muslim non-Arab states, Iran and Turkey, and two Christian states, Cyprus and Ethiopia;[1] and

an *Outer Ring* of six states—Libya, Morocco, non-Arab Somalia, South Yemen, Sudan, and Yemen.[2]

The four non-Arab units on the Periphery have maintained relations with Israel ranging from cordiality to friendship; the fourteen Arab states have been unremittingly hostile.[3]

The Middle East has been characterized by permanent Arab–Israeli conflict, with three major outbursts of violence during the first twenty years: 1948 involved all five core Arab states and Saudi Arabia; 1956 was confined to Egypt; and 1967 involved all core Arab states once more, with Lebanon (and Algeria) in marginal active roles. The system had its organizational antecedents at the end of the Second World War, with the formation of the League of Arab States. It crystallized in 1948, the year Israel emerged as an independent entity; the next two decades were dominated by the Arab response to that reality. The breakpoints in the evolution of the system were 1948, 1955–6, and 1967.

Two of the systemic features have already been sketched in the analysis of the global system, namely, penetration of the subordinate system and the reverse flow of influence. These linkages, together with the level

---

the American Political Science Association, Los Angeles, September 1970; and I. William Zartman, 'Africa as a Subordinate State System in International Relations', *International Organization*, xxi, 3, 1967, pp. 545–64. For assessments of the concept 'subordinate system', see Kathryn Doherty Boals, 'The Concept "Subordinate International System"': A Critique', in Richard A. Falk and Saul H. Mendlovitz (eds.), *The Strategy of World Order*, Vol. V, *Regionalism* (forthcoming), and Michael Haas, *International Conflict*, ch. 9 (forthcoming).

[1] The analytic term 'Periphery', as used here, denotes an intermediate zone of impact on the Arab–Israel conflict and comprises states both hostile and friendly to Israel. By contrast, the 'Periphery Doctrine' in Israeli foreign policy refers only to friendly Middle East states beyond 'the Arab fence', notably Ethiopia, Iran, and Turkey.

[2] At the time of writing (1970), Libya and Sudan belong to the Periphery, indeed very close to the Core. However, the above construct applies to the period, 1948 to 1968.

[3] The newly-independent Democratic Republic of South Yemen became the 14th member of the League of Arab States at the beginning of 1968. The Palestine Liberation Organization (PLO) participated in the Arab summit conferences of the 1960s and the Arab League Council sessions as had other recognized Palestine Arab representatives since 1945. But it did not, until the close of the period under inquiry, constitute an autonomous unit within the Middle East system.

FIGURE 3
THE MIDDLE EAST SUBORDINATE SYSTEM
Composition 1968

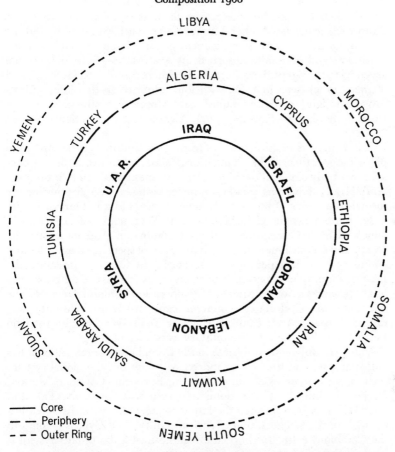

—— Core
— — Periphery
- - - Outer Ring

of power and power stratification, illuminate the Arab–Israeli pattern
of conflict through time and will be noted again briefly in that context.
The other eight features experienced little *qualitative* change during the
twenty years. Another prefatory remark relates to the focus: it is in the
Core that the system-shaping conflict was germinated and sustained;
apart from Saudi Arabia and, spasmodically, one or more other Arab
states, the units on the Periphery and in the Outer Ring did not
directly affect the outcome of the conflict. With these distinctions in
mind one may proceed to a subordinate system analysis relevant to
Israel's foreign policy, beginning with those features that have undergone *quantitative* change.

(b) SOME LESSER STRUCTURAL FEATURES

The Middle East has never achieved total *organizational integration*; this was due primarily to the decision of Arab states to limit their institutional links within the region to units of ethnic affinity.[1] The Arab League excluded other Muslim states, Turkey and Iran, and the geographically contiguous permanent enemy, Israel. Yet it remained consistent and gradually absorbed all Arab states—from the original seven in 1945 (Egypt, Iraq, Jordan, Lebanon, Saudi Arabia, Syria, and Yemen) to fourteen in 1968, with four admitted in the fifties—Libya (1953), Sudan (1956), and Tunisia and Morocco (1958)—and another three in the sixties—Kuwait (1961), Algeria (1962), and South Yemen (1968).

The League is multi-functional in the UN tradition. It has an organ of decision in theory, the Council or *Majlis*, but this is, in fact, a consultative body since all decisions must be unanimous. In addition, the Arab Heads of State have held summit meetings since 1964, outside the formal framework of the Arab League. It also has a military structure based upon a League Collective Security Pact, with Defence Council, Chiefs of Staff Committee, and joint command. And for economic, social, and cultural matters there is an array of specialized agencies and committees, with a permanent secretariat in Cairo to integrate the League's multiple activities. The structure is impressive on paper but its effectiveness as an instrument of co-operation is minimal, even on the one issue of self-declared common concern—Israel. Disunity was rampant in the Arab camp during the 1948 War, and in 1956 no League member came to the military assistance of Egypt.

Israel, the only non-Arab state in the Core, has no organizational ties with the system as a whole or indeed with any but the global system, apart from a loose association with the European Common Market. Turkey is linked to the dominant system through NATO and CENTO, as is Iran through the latter's security network. Ethiopia is a member of the Organization of African Unity. And Cyprus belongs to the Commonwealth. In short, the Middle East Subordinate System is organizationally fractured and incomplete.

The Arab League has two significant implications for Israel; one is symbolic, the other substantive. The League claims sole regional legitimacy within the Middle East, certainly in the Core. That claim spills over to demographic exclusiveness and, with it, the right to exclude or expel a non-Arab nation from 'the Arab heartland'. The League serves as the visible institutional expression of this constant

[1] That decision did not prevent certain Arab states from joining organizations of other systems—Algeria, Libya, Morocco, Sudan, Tunisia, and the UAR are members of the Organization of African Unity—or organizations dominated by non-Middle East states, for example, Iraq and the Baghdad Pact from 1955 to 1958.

Arab appeal in its total war against Israel. More concretely, the League facilitates—and induces—concerted acts, military, economic, political, and psychological, by a group of states that share an oft-proclaimed goal to extirpate Israel from the Middle East. Not always effective in integrating the Arab camp, the League nonetheless acts as a cohesive focus and as a barrier to the introduction of other (system-wide) organizations for functional co-operation, for example, an Economic Commission for the region or a Jordan Valley Development Authority.[1] Both the symbolic and substantive challenges have confronted Israeli decision-makers since 1948. These challenges have been accentuated by various efforts to achieve more formal Arab organizational unity, such as the union between Egypt and Syria in 1958 and a number of abortive federal schemes; but their impact can best be noted in terms of the changing configuration of power.

Closely related to system integration is the character of *interaction* among its members. Relations among the core Arab states are intense and multilateral. They are in constant contact at every level and use every form of interaction—diplomatic, political, social, economic, cultural, and personal. The process is so intense that developments in the domestic politics of one state have spill-over effects on the internal (and, frequently, on the external) affairs of others, as well as on the power and psychological equilibria of the Core of the system. Thus a basic change in Jordan's domestic politics, which would place it under Cairo's *de facto* control, has long been considered a *casus belli* by Israel.

No formal relations exist between the five core Arab states and Israel, but intense hostile interaction takes place at three levels—military, diplomatic, and psychological. Three wars, along with persistent Arab guerrilla tactics and Israeli reprisals, reflect a condition of permanent conflict. The annual confrontations at the UN General Assembly and at the myriad of other international conferences have provided an array of forums for interaction, despite Arab non-recognition. And the

---

[1] There is an ample literature on the Arab League which includes the following: *The Arab League* and *Basic Documents of the Arab League*, Arab Information Center, New York, 1955; P. Beyssade, *La Ligue Arabe*, Éditions Planète, Paris, 1948; Asher Goren, *The Arab League 1945–1954*, Ayanot, Tel Aviv, 1954 (in Hebrew); Muhammad Khalil (ed.), *The Arab States and the Arab League*, 2 vols., Khayat, Beirut, 1963; Michel Laissy, *Du Panarabisme à la Ligue Arabe*, Libraire Orientale et Américaine, Paris, 1948; Robert W. Macdonald, *The League of Arab States: a study in the dynamics of regional organization*, Princeton University Press, Princeton, New Jersey, 1965.

Among the many articles the following may be noted: M. S. Agwani, 'The Arab League', *India Quarterly*, vol. ix, no. 4, Oct.–Dec. 1953, pp. 355–66; B. Y. Boutros-Ghali, 'The Arab League 1945–1955', *International Conciliation*, no. 498, May 1955; Cecil Hourani, 'The Arab League in Perspective', *Middle East Journal*, vol. i, no. 2, Apr 1947, pp. 125–36; T. R. Little, 'The Arab League: A Re-assessment', *Middle Ea Journal*, vol. x, no. 2, Spring 1956, pp. 138–50; and J. S. Raleigh, 'Ten Years of t Arab League', *Middle Eastern Affairs*, vol. vi, no. 3, March 1955, pp. 65–77.

struggle for the minds of men has generated daily intercommunication through the press, radio, and television.

Interaction between states in the Core and on the Periphery—these terms as perceived by Israel—is fundamentally different, apart from Saudi Arabia and Kuwait, which are extensions of the Core in this respect. With Turkey, Iran, Ethiopia, and Cyprus the forms of contact are 'normal', that is, diplomatic, economic, and cultural relations, with the object of winning support in the Arab–Israel conflict.[1] These four states do not participate actively in the 'war system' of the Near East nor are their economic ties significant, except for Iran's supply of the bulk of Israel's oil imports after the opening of the Straits of Tiran in 1956. Yet their value in the diplomatic battle is considerable—Turkey and Iran because they are Muslim states in the Middle East that are prepared to have friendly ties with Israel, and Ethiopia because of her prominence in the African subordinate system and her geo-political location vis-à-vis the Horn of Africa. Israel's interaction with states on the Periphery of the Middle East system is important, especially during the inter-military war phases of the Arab–Israel conflict; but it has not been decisive to the outcome.

As for interaction with the Arab states in the Outer Ring, the same forms obtain as among the core Arab states. It is the intensity that is qualitatively different. The Arab League, with its regular Council meetings, sometimes converted to, or supplemented by, Foreign Ministers' Conferences, provides the main arena for personal contact; radio and television perform this function for the mass public. But apart from the special case of the Yemen civil war, with military participation by Egypt and Saudi Arabia and the diplomatic involvement of others from 1962 onwards, this group of states has been relatively isolated from the Arab–Israel conflict; and they have had little impact on its outcome at any time. All Arab states outside the Core have provided diplomatic and propaganda support; and through financial aid they made possible the expansion of the Arab guerrilla organizations, especially after the 1967 War.

There are, then, four levels of interaction in the Middle East Subordinate System: very high intensity and multiple forms among the core Arab states; lower intensity with the same forms between them and other Arab states; normal global system forms of interaction at even lower intensity with non-Arab units on the Periphery; and conflict forms of interaction of great intensity between Israel and the Arab states, especially those in the Core. On that last, fourth, level of inter-action there is a scale of intensity: for the twenty-year period as a whole

---

[1] Turkey was the first Muslim state to recognize Israel, in September 1949. Iran recognized Israel de facto in March 1950 but, unlike the others, has not maintained official diplomatic relations throughout. Since then, however, there have been continuous contacts and substantial relations, especially in the economic domain.

Egypt is at the apex, followed by Jordan and Syria, then by Iraq, and, very low in the scale (until 1969), Lebanon.[1] Two states on the Periphery, Saudi Arabia and, since 1962, Algeria, ranked ahead of Lebanon (until 1969); all other Arab states are clustered at the bottom of the scale with minimal contact.

(c) TEXTURAL FEATURES

The Middle East system is characterized by a highly-developed *communications* network. Members of the Core are small and territorially contiguous. Topography is not a serious barrier to land contact. Most important, there exists a common language among the fourteen Arab states; this eases communication via the press, visitors, the spoken and written word generally—and especially by radio and television. Arabic is also understood by a small section of the population in Turkey and Iran, notably the clergy, and is widely used in certain regions of those countries, the southern provinces bordering Syria, notably Hatay, and Khazistan, respectively. It is much more widely known in Israel, where, in addition to 300,000 Arabs and Druzes, more than a third of the Jewish population or their forebears migrated from Arabic-speaking lands. There is, then, a remarkably open and integrated communications system, which strengthens the interaction process. In fact this is the most effective instrument of cohesion within the Arab camp, all of whose members are linked to domestic and intra-system developments by radio, and many by TV—élite and mass public alike. The feedback is persistent and intense, often by pressure from emotionally-aroused masses on rulers with precarious control over their polities. Thus a pervasive communications network permits active participation in the conflict within the Core by geographically remote units. A dramatic example was the rapid mobilization of Arab support for Cairo's provocative acts in the events preceding the 1967 War.[2]

The continuing influence of this textural feature on the Arab–Israel conflict is also evident in the Israeli response: there was a substantial expansion of Arab language broadcasts over *Kol Yisrael* after the Sinai

---

[1] A quantitative analysis of international acts by Middle East actors, that is, 'official acts of a government directed abroad to another government', correctly notes a slightly different ranking on a scale of intensity of conflict *for the years 1966–9*: the UAR and the PLO (Palestine Liberation Organization) at the apex, followed by Jordan and Lebanon, and then Syria. Charles A. McClelland and Anne Ancoli, 'An Interaction Survey of the Middle East', University of Southern California, Los Angeles, March 1970 (mimeo.), p. 19. Yet the PLO operates almost entirely from Jordanian territory and is therefore included in 'Jordan' in the ranking above. Nor, it may be added, was the PLO a 'government' directing 'official acts' during those years.

[2] Noted in Michael Howard and Robert Hunter, 'Israel and the Arab World: The Crisis of 1967', *Adelphi Papers*, no. 41, The Institute for Strategic Studies, London, October 1967, p. 17.

Campaign of 1956 and again after the Six Day War;[1] moreover, television was introduced in 1968 well ahead of schedule, with emphasis on an Arabic programme to offset the flow of visual propaganda from Cairo, Amman, and Beirut. This had long been widely consumed by the 300,000 Arab residents of Israel and to a lesser extent by Arabic-speaking Jewish immigrants. The Israeli TV response was galvanized by the events of 1967—military victory and the acquisition of territories with more than a million Arab inhabitants. This created an urgent need to counter the barrage of hostility from neighbouring states. The battle of the airways had assumed a new dimension in the protracted conflict.[2]

The pattern of *values* in the Middle East exhibits a striking homogeneity at first glance. The Arab states share a common culture, history, language, art forms and, apart from Lebanon's diversity, a religious tradition. Along with the new states of Southern Asia and Africa they share the goals of economic development and a viable political order. They have a common experience of foreign, white domination, inducing a common response to certain global issues, notably colonialism and racialism. They are also deeply attached to nationalism and the symbols of independence. In all these important intangibles they are psychologically knit together as a community. Beyond these, however, there is a wide gulf in values.

There is a clash between secular and traditional orientations to public policy, as evident in Egypt and Saudi Arabia, respectively. There are sharp cleavages between 'revolutionary' and 'moderate' Arab states on the proper attitude to the inter-bloc struggle, with Algeria, Syria, Sudan, and Egypt ranged against Saudi Arabia, Jordan, Morocco, Tunisia, and Libya until 1969, and others vacillating in allegiance. There are rifts over domestic policy issues, for example, socialism and nationalization versus capitalism and encouragement to foreign investment. These and other schisms are superimposed on the base of shared values. Indeed the kaleidoscope of political forces among the fourteen Arab states indicates that their behaviour is shaped by the diverse aims and conceptions of society held by varied incumbent élites; the notion of shared values is but a first approximation. The evidence from 1948 to 1968 is conclusive, even in the display of disunity during the three rounds of Arab–Israeli warfare.

The heterogeneity of values is accentuated by the presence of other states—for the Middle East system is not synonymous with the Arab 'world', despite their persistent efforts to establish this claim. The other two Muslim members of the system, one Sunni, Turkey, and one Shi'ite,

[1] *Kol Yisrael*'s Arabic broadcasts will be analysed in ch. 19 (*b*) below.
[2] Prime Minister Meir emphasized this point to the *Knesset* in May 1969. Reported in *Jerusalem Post Weekly*, 26 May 1969.

Iran, and one Christian state, Ethiopia, are heirs to different and equally proud traditions. They experienced foreign rule for brief periods only; in fact, they are among the oldest independent units in the global system. They are ethnically and culturally different from the Arabs, and in the case of Ethiopia racially as well, with no particular affection for Arab civilization. Their patterns of thought and action are *sui generis*. Israel shares with the Arabs the experience of foreign rule and the goals of economic development and social progress. She also shares a commitment to nationalism but with her own distinctive vision of a national state. Her history, culture, language, and identity are unique and her values flow from that experience, adapted to the needs and aspirations of a modern twentieth-century society.

Various terms may be used to analyse Middle East politics. The distinction between 'modernizers' and 'traditionalists' had meaning in the early years, with the latter applying to all seven monarchies as of 1968, as well as Iraq before 1958 (then a monarchy), Yemen before 1962, Sudan, and Lebanon. Before the end of the second decade of the system, however, all member-states had become 'modernizers'. The significant division was between radicals and gradualists, all welcoming or yielding to the universal appeal of modernization: Algeria, Iraq, Syria, and Egypt (and Libya and Sudan since 1969) are 'radical modernizers'; all the others are 'gradualist modernizers', with different preferences as to the pace of change.[1] Structurally viewed, there are two general types of *political system* in the Middle East, democracy and authoritarianism, the latter taking various forms; there has not been a communist régime in any state from 1948 to 1968. Combining these typologies, the twenty members of the Middle East Subordinate System may be classified as follows:

Reconciliation Modernizers: Israel, Lebanon, Somalia, Turkey, and *Cyprus* ('Western' Democracy)

> Israel's political system has, from the outset, been the most akin to a continental (European) multi-party model. Lebanon's polity has, throughout, been based upon a delicate representational balance among the diverse religious communities, Christian and Muslim. Somalia (southern part) was granted independence by the UN and the UK (northern part) in 1960; a genuine multi-party system operated from the beginning—until the military coup of 1969. Turkey has functioned through a two-plus party system with a strong Kemalist authoritarian tradition and a military élite. In 1960, when independence was granted to Cyprus, a system was devised to govern the island by dyarchical or shared authority

---

[1] For an illuminating study of the process of modernization in the Middle East see Daniel Lerner, *The Passing of Traditional Society*, The Free Press, New York, 1958.

between the majority Greek Cypriots and the minority Turkish Cypriots, with communal rights safeguarded by built-in checks and balances. It worked out quite differently in fact.

Radical Modernizers: Algeria, Egypt, Iraq, South Yemen, Syria, and *Yemen* (Military Autocracy)

Algeria's political structure in the early years of independence (1962 to early 1966) was of the civilian authoritarian type, with Ben Bella as the dominant figure; since 1965 Boumédienne has held power through the army. Iraq had, under the cover of a constitutional monarchy, an authoritarian régime until the military coup of Kassem in 1958, followed by still others, led by Aref in 1963 and Bakr in 1968. One or another faction of the officer corps has ruled Syria almost continuously since 1949, usually in uneasy alliance with a civilian group. Since 1963 this has been in association with the revolutionary wing of the nationalist-socialist Arab Ba'ath Party. Army officers ousted Farouk from Egypt's throne in 1952, at first under the formal leadership of Neguib. Nasser assumed direct power in 1954 and dominated Egyptian politics until his death in 1970. A Liberation Front-type coalition, the only *civilian* group among the 'radical modernizers', assumed power in South Yemen at the end of 1967. After five years of civil war between royalists and republicans, a leftist-influenced and military-dominated régime emerged in Yemen at the end of 1967.

Gradualist Modernizers: Ethiopia, Iran, Jordan, Kuwait, Libya, Morocco, (Civilian Autocracy)   *Saudi Arabia, Sudan,* and *Tunisia*

Seven of these states had varying degrees of constitutional restraint on monarchical authority—none in Kuwait and Saudi Arabia, very little in Ethiopia and Morocco, somewhat more in Libya (until the monarchy was overthrown in 1969), and active legislatures with limited powers in Iran and Jordan. Haile Selassie has ruled Ethiopia since 1928. In Iran, the Shah has ruled since 1941. Jordan has been ruled by the Hashemite princes since the state was created by the British as an emirate in 1921. The Sheikhs of Kuwait have ruled under British protection for many years. King Idris occupied the Libyan throne since the state was formed in 1952 (until his dismissal in 1969). Morocco, too, has had continuity, from the incumbent Sultan at the end of the French colonial era to his son, King Hasan II. And in Saudi Arabia, still the most traditionalist monarchy in the world, power passed from King Saud to Feisal in 1964. In varying degrees all seven monarchies have taken the path to modernization. So too have the two republican régimes of the gradualist type. Sudan's political system has turned full circle: it began with a civilian government in 1956;

the military seized power in 1958, and a civilian régime was restored in 1965 (to be overthrown once more in 1969). In Tunisia, Bourguiba, the 'Father of the Nation', has exercised almost unchallenged authority since 1956 through the mechanism of a one-party state.

The structural norm for Middle East polities has been authoritarianism, whether military or civilian, monarchical or republican. Only five of the twenty states have had open, pluralistic, competitive political systems; and of these Turkey lapsed into *de facto* rule by the military, while Lebanon and Cyprus have formalized communal political structures and cultures. Yet all twenty are in the global stream of modernization, some reluctantly, others with enthusiasm.

The pattern of political change in the Middle East suggests acute and persistent instability; a closer examination reveals this to be exaggerated. The seven gradualist modernizing monarchical states have experienced continuity and for the most part tranquillity—with notable exceptions: the assassination of Jordan's Abdullah in 1951; a brief, dramatic challenge to Ethiopia's Haile Selassie in 1960; the Mossadegh crisis in Iran in 1951–3; and the replacement of Saud by Feisal in Saudi Arabia. Libya's King Idris was ousted and the monarchy abolished in 1969. And Jordan's Hussein has been under persistent attack. Among the Western-type reconciliation systems, Israel has held seven general elections, with a stable, *Mapai*-dominated coalition formed after each test at the polls; Lebanon had one grave crisis, the civil war in 1958, with far-reaching international repercussions; Somalia was tranquil until 1969; and Turkey had one phase of direct military rule (1960–1). Only Cyprus has been characterized by permanent turmoil.

Endemic instability has been confined to the radical modernizers; and even among those states the frequency of change has varied. Egypt underwent a military coup in 1952 and fluidity in the ruling junta for two years; but Nasser was in firm control until his death, with only occasional challenges to his authority, despite overwhelming defeat on the battlefield in 1956 and 1967. Algeria had one successful coup—the ouster of Ben Bella—and an abortive attempt to overthrow Boumédienne at the end of 1967. Iraq has had several major military coups, including one that toppled the monarchy, and others that devoured Kassem and Aref. Yemen has been the scene of protracted civil war from 1962 onwards. But it is Syria that created the image of Middle East instability—some fifteen coups from 1949 to 1965. Viewed in system terms and excluding the incessant Syrian coups, that widespread image requires amendment: twelve Middle East states can be designated as politically stable as of 1968—the seven monarchies, as well as Israel, Egypt, Lebanon, Somalia, and Tunisia; one is new—South

Yemen—and one is a special case—Cyprus; the hard core of instability comprises Syria, Iraq, and Yemen. For Israel the significant facts are that two of the most unstable Arab units—Syria and Iraq—are in the Core of the Middle East Subordinate System, that three nearby hostile states—Egypt, Syria, and Iraq (along with Sudan and Libya since 1969)—have military régimes, and that another, Jordan, is subject to great pressures from within and without.

(d) CONFIGURATION OF POWER 1948–1968[1]

The Middle East configuration of power has undergone drastic changes since the emergence of Israel. In 1948 the general power level was very low in both absolute and relative terms. No state was able to produce nuclear weapons or missiles. The armed forces were small in number and severely limited as to skills and weapons. And none possessed an industrial base to expand its military capability: dependence on arms-producing members of the global system was virtually complete. By 1968 the system's power level had been transformed: one state, Israel, was regarded as a potential member of the nuclear club; armies had reached beyond the quarter-million size; and economic development had been accompanied by the growth of arms-producing industries. Yet all members remained dependent upon external sources for decisive weapons—planes, tanks, heavy artillery, missiles, and naval equipment. It was this fact that permitted continuous penetration by super powers and great powers. And this dependent relationship points up most sharply the meaning of 'subordinate system' as applied to the Middle East.

There were very few Israeli planes or tanks in the 1948 War, and not many on the Arab side. Indeed the Near East arms level remained modest throughout Phase I (1948–55), certainly in comparison with the escalation of later years. That this was so reflected external penetration, namely, concerted action by the US, UK, and France to limit arms shipments to all states in the region in order not to upset the perceived balance in 1950. Whatever weapons did filter into the region were of Second World War vintage.

Configuration of power refers to stratification, as well as to level. Egypt was the most powerful state in 1948—in population, size of army, and weapons. The Arab coalition had a marked quantitative superiority and a self-image of certain victory, which was shared by most observers. Measured by tangible indices, the balance of power heavily favoured the Arabs. Three factors overcame Israel's inferiority in the 1948 War: high morale or psychological power, Arab disunity, and superior

[1] The military capability of Israel and the core Arab states during these twenty years will be examined in greater detail—geography, population, balance of weapons, etc., as well as intangible indices—in ch. 4 below.

leadership on the battlefield. In the spring of 1949, when the Armistice Agreements were signed, the tangible balance between Israel and her Arab adversaries had not changed basically; but intangibles had altered the pyramid of power. Victory had injected two stimuli into Israeli capability: the psychology of triumph over enormous odds; and a shift in the image held by other states—to a perception of Israel's inner strength and survival capacity. On the Arab side military defeat undermined self-confidence. Israel now appeared to be at least co-equal with Egypt, still the strongest Arab state.

This image was enhanced by the character and substance of the four separate Armistice Agreements (virtually identical in their principles) which Israel signed with Egypt, Jordan, Lebanon, and Syria in the first half of 1949. Each was a closely integrated system of mutual concessions and each represented joint and reciprocal obligations assumed to the UN Security Council and to each other. The preamble of each Armistice Agreement stated that it was designed to facilitate the transition from truce to permanent peace. Each called for the observance of the Security Council injunction against resort to military force in settlement of the 'Palestine Question', for a ban on the undertaking, planning, or threatening of aggressive action, and for recognition of the right of each party to security and freedom from attack.[1] Given the Arab (formal) commitment to a peace settlement and (formal) acceptance of Israel's right to 'security and freedom from attack', along with initial support by both super powers and military victory, Israel's position in the Near East power pyramid had been transformed before the first anniversary of independence.

A further power asset for Israel was injected in May 1950 with the Three Power Declaration: the US, UK, and France appeared to be extending a semi-formal territorial guarantee when they announced that 'should the three Governments find that any one of these states [in the Near East] contemplates violating the frontiers of armistice lines, they will . . . act both within and without the framework of the United Nations in order to prevent such a violation'.[2] As time passed, however, a peace settlement became more and more remote. And with time came two power assets for the Arabs. One was sparked by political change within the Core, namely, the ouster of a corrupt, inefficient Egyptian monarchy by a dynamic group of young officers determined to rebuild Egyptian military power. The other asset derived from the withdrawal of British troops, under the Anglo-Egyptian Agreement of 1954: this provided substantial military hardware for Cairo, an infusion

[1] For a careful study of the Armistice Agreements see Shabtai Rosenne, *Israel's Armistice Agreements with the Arab States: A Juridical Interpretation*, Blumstein, Tel Aviv, 1951.

[2] The text of the Declaration is to be found in J. C. Hurewitz (ed.), *Diplomacy in the Near and Middle East: Vol. 2, A Documentary Record—1914–56*, Van Nostrand, Princeton, 1956, pp. 308–9.

of psychological strength into the Arab camp. And while the formation of the Baghdad Pact at United States' initiative (but without full US participation) early in 1955 was not designed as an anti-Israel measure, it meant an increase of arms on the Arab side of the scale, outweighing the adverse effect on Arab military capability of their split over alignment in the Cold War.

Phase I of the power configuration came to an end in September 1955 with the beginning of a massive flow of Soviet bloc weapons into Egypt and Syria. Estimates varied, then and later, but the qualitative escalation of the arms race was beyond doubt, for it included Mig fighters, Ilyushin jet bombers, Stalin Mark III tanks, Czech T.34 tanks, and other heavy equipment—the most advanced in the Soviet armoury. By this diplomatic coup, Egypt had shattered the existing equilibrium and had set in motion a determined Israeli search for counterbalancing arms; it had begun with Peres' behind-the-scenes quest for French arms in 1954; it was given dramatic publicity by Sharett's failure to persuade the Big Four Foreign Ministers, gathered in Geneva in November 1955, and it culminated in success with France the following spring.[1] Notwithstanding, the balance was overwhelmingly in Egypt's favour.

The Sinai Campaign of 1956 restored the balance. In fact it created a new equilibrium, which was to last a decade, and a power stratification in which Israel and Egypt became the acknowledged 'Great Powers' within the Near East core. None of the other four Arab states could challenge Israel, alone or in concert; they were all dependent on Egypt's power. In the largest sense the 1956 War enhanced four components of Israeli power. Victory brought vast quantities of abandoned Soviet equipment, enough to assure a margin of military superiority for some years. Secondly, it produced a new injection of self-confidence or psychological power after two years of tension and uncertainty caused by the *Feda'iyun* terror raids. With victory came the re-establishment of freedom of shipping to the Red Sea as well, and this meant an accretion of economic power and political influence, through a growing Israeli 'presence' in Africa and Asia, to be forged soon after. And for the Arabs a second defeat, along with the decimation of Egypt's army, was a severe blow, despite the diplomatic triumph created by superpower largesse. With the presence of UNEF along the Gaza and Sinai frontiers and at Sharm-e-Sheikh, Egypt appeared to accept the *status quo*. And so it remained until May 1967.

There were other developments during Phase II (1956–67) which constituted short-term power assets for one side or another in the Near

---

[1] A revealing first-hand narrative of the lengthy 'quiet' negotiations is contained in Peres, op. cit., ch. 3. Although 'several [minor] transactions' were completed in 1954, the vital Mystère Mark IV jet planes did not reach Israel until March 1956.

East conflict. The union of Egypt and Syria early in 1958 (the UAR) was a psychological input for Arab pride and the quest for unity. It also created a 'sandwich-effect' on Israel's territory, with a formally-integrated army standing at two exposed frontiers; but the appearance of power shift was greater than reality. When in July 1958 the Iraq monarchy was overthrown, it was feared that Nasserist centralizing forces would be further strengthened. This was quickly countered, however, by the landing of American and British troops in Lebanon and Jordan, respectively. A major power asset for Israel was the secret arms agreement with West Germany in 1960; it did not influence the global or Arab image of the Near East balance of power but it did affect the real balance—to Israel's advantage. The following year Egypt and the Arab camp as a whole suffered a setback with the dissolution of the UAR, in spite of Cairo's symbolic retention of the name. An abortive plan for an Arab Federation in 1963, among Egypt, Syria, and Iraq, caused concern in Israel but with no real influence on the power relationship. More significant was the coming of independence to Algeria in 1962 under a militant left-nationalist régime. This had three consequences for the Near East equilibrium, two indirect and one direct. Arab political influence in the global system was strengthened. So too was Arab influence within the African subordinate system and in the militant segment of the non-aligned Third World. Most important was the effect on French Middle East policy.

As long as France was beset with a nationalist revolt in Algeria, Israel was perceived as a natural ally; and a *de facto* alliance was forged in the mid-fifties with considerable mutual benefit. For Israel it meant an assured arms supply, especially air power, to counter the steady flow of Soviet bloc arms to Egypt and Syria. But when the Algerian Affair was over France was free to reassert her historic interest and influence in the Arab world. The change was slow to unfold, for as late as 1964 de Gaulle reaffirmed the special French tie to Israel in the presence of his guest, Prime Minister Eshkol. Indeed, when the shift came, during the 1967 War, it seemed more like a *volte-face* than a product of long gestation. The outcome was that France moved from Israel's principal arms supplier and diplomatic ally to blunt critic and purveyor of arms to Israel's Arab enemies. It was the most conspicuous power setback for Israel since 1948, though far from decisive. This development crystallized at the beginning of Phase III.

There appeared to be a major infusion of confidence into the Arab camp during a flurry of summit conferences in 1964–5. Most important was the first gathering, at Cairo in January 1964. Three potentially important decisions were reached: (1) to establish a Palestine Liberation Organization (PLO) and a Palestine Liberation Army (PLA), as the spearhead of a reactivated, concerted campaign 'to liberate Palestine'; (2) to implement a plan to divert the waters of the sources of the Jordan

River on Syrian and Lebanese soil and thereby to frustrate the Israeli project to irrigate the Negev; and (3) to establish a Unified Arab Command. At the second summit, in Alexandria in September 1964, the image of a 'new' Arab unity had become tarnished. And the third summit, at Casablanca in October 1965, revealed the Alexandria pretensions to be a hollow shell, despite the formal allocation of substantial funds to increase Arab military capability and the proclamation of solidarity. The PLO was denied full satisfaction of its formal requests and both the Unified Command and the Jordan River diversion plan had stagnated. This setback was accompanied by still another, the first open and dramatic rift in Arab public solidarity on the issue of Israel. Beginning in the spring of 1965, Tunisia's Bourguiba publicly challenged the Arabs to alter their posture and their policy on 'the Palestine problem'; his absence from the Casablanca summit further dramatized the split over a hitherto sacred Arab commitment.

By the beginning of 1967 the eclipse of the pan-Arab organizations launched at the Cairo summit seemed complete. The most important source of declining Arab power lay elsewhere, however. From 1962 onwards Egypt's exchequer and army were being drained by the Yemen civil war, with some 50,000 troops, or one-third of the army, committed far from the Near East core. Finally, in this catalogue of power assets and liabilities, there was Israel's victory in securing diplomatic relations with West Germany in the spring of 1965, despite persistent efforts by the UAR-led group of Arab states; they not only failed to thwart this link but also revealed power weakness and disunity in the process.

Changes in the Near East balance of capability emanating from within and from outside the system can be analytically separated. Yet the two types of change are intertwined in time and in cause–effect relationships. This is particularly true of the Middle East Subordinate System because of the intense and sustained penetration from beyond its borders. The sharp escalation of the level of Middle East military capability by one super power in 1955 was already noted. This process, with multi-power involvement, continued unabated through the sixties, assuming the proportions of an inflationary arms race. The Soviet Union equipped the armed forces of Egypt and Syria; France was the principal supplier of Israel's Air Force; the UK and the US shared responsibility for Jordan, and the US fed the Saudi Arabian military machine.

The results were weapons systems far beyond the capacity of Near East states to develop by themselves—and systems maintained at an oppressive cost. One example will suffice. By the end of 1965 Israel was reported to have a mobilizable citizen army of 250,000, 450 aircraft of which 200 were jets, and 600 tanks. Egypt had an estimated armed force of 300,000, 180,000 of them regular troops, 500 operational aircraft, almost 400 of them jets, 1,200 tanks and assault guns, and 100 missiles. How different this was from 1948![1]

The 1967 War, which marks the beginning of Phase III, did not alter the overall level of power in the Core; it only affected the distribution of weapons as a result of the shattering Arab defeat. The major changes wrought by the war related to air-power and armour, much of the latter abandoned on the battlefield. Jordan lost 150 of its 250 tanks and all 21 fighter planes. Egypt lost 500 tanks (of which Israel acquired 100 intact), an array of other heavy field equipment, and 340 planes. And Syria lost 50–80 planes.[2] The immediate disparity in Arab–Israeli military capability was striking but not significant. Within days of the end of hostilities the Soviets began to rush replacement weapons to both Egypt and Syria; and by May 1968, the

TABLE 2

THE MIDDLE EAST SUBORDINATE SYSTEM:

THE CORE

Features	Phase I 1948–1955/6	Phase II 1956–1967	Phase III 1967–
Structural			
Level of Power	1	3	4
Power Stratification	2	3	4
Political Organization	2	2	2
Military Organization	1	1	1
Economic Organization	1	1	1
Intensity of Interaction	4	5	5
Penetration of Subordinate Systems	5	5	5
Penetration by Subordinate Systems	1	3	1
Textural			
Level of Communications	3	4	4
Homogeneity of Values	2	2	2
Commonality of Political Systems	2	2	2
Units' Domestic Stability	2	2	3

Key: Very High 5 High 4 Medium 3 Low 2 Very Low 1

[1] *The Military Balance 1965–1966*, The Institute for Strategic Studies, London, 1965, pp. 35 and 38–9, respectively.

[2] These figures are based upon a variety of sources during the 2½ years after the 1967 War, revealing a near-consensus. They will be detailed in the analysis of the decision attending that war, in a related volume on Israeli high-policy decisions. The figures of the Institute for Strategic Studies, just before and soon after the Six Day War, are different: Egypt—500 tanks, 300 intact acquired by Israel, and 275 planes lost; Syria—50–80 planes lost. Howard and Hunter, op. cit., pp. 50–1, and *The Military Balance 1967–1968*, London, 1967, p. 39–41.

twentieth anniversary of Israel's independence, the disparity had been eliminated.

The Six Day War did affect the power balance, in two respects. Israel acquired control over territory more than three times the size of the state when the war began and, with it, a marked improvement in defensible frontiers—the Jordan River, the Canal, and the Syrian (Golan) Heights. Secondly, as in 1948 and 1956, victory enhanced the sense of security of Israeli society as a whole. Indeed Israel was now clearly the pre-eminent power in the Core of this subordinate system. Egypt remained a potential equal, if not more, especially as long as Soviet arms were available in large quantity. In the short run, however, her prestige, morale, and her geo-strategic position had been dealt severe blows.[1]

[1] Changes in the configuration of power after the 1967 War will be examined in a related volume on Israeli high-policy decisions.

CHAPTER 4

Military Capability

The Six Day War of 1967 dramatized Israel's military superiority over her Arab adversaries. The Sinai Campaign had revealed this with equal effect. And the 1948 War of Independence had indicated an impressive survival capacity under adverse conditions. Yet tangible indices pointed to a marked Arab advantage throughout this period— in geography, military manpower, financial resources available for defence, and weapons. Indeed the material imbalance in power has been etched in the minds of Israel's decision-makers and has profoundly influenced her behaviour. That Israel triumphed in war was due to countervailing assets among these and other components of military capability.[1]

(a) GEOGRAPHY

Israel's geographic position until June 1967 was a strategist's nightmare. In the broadest sense she is the point of convergence among the three parts of Mackinder's 'World Island', namely Asia, Africa, and Europe. As such, Palestine may be likened to the Lowlands of Europe—alternately a battlefield and a buffer state. It consists mainly of a series of low mountain ranges separated by a few passes and valleys, which have long been the link between Egypt on the one hand and the Levant and Mesopotamia on the other, with a desert (the Negev) in the south, and a fertile coastal plain. Although Israel is very small in area, she possesses two outlets to the sea, west on the Mediterranean and south and south-east via the Gulf of Akaba. 'This geo-political situation has from the dawn of history impressed its stamp on the country.'[2]

Using a narrower strategic gauge, Israel comprised 7,992 square miles of territory from the 1949 Armistice Agreements until June 1967. She was surrounded by avowedly hostile states, with 600 miles of land

[1] The Arab–Israeli military confrontation is between a traditional-type standing army and a citizen-militia. This makes it difficult to gauge precisely Israel's real military strength at any point in time.

[2] Shabtai Rosenne, 'Basic Elements of Israel's Foreign Policy', *India Quarterly*, xvii, 4, Oct.–Dec. 1961, p. 336. This theme is explored at greater length in Rosenne's *Lectures on the Foreign Relations of Israel*, delivered to L'Escuela de Functionares Internationales, Madrid, in 1960: Lecture II, 'Geography' (unpublished MSS. made available to the author).

frontier and no space for defence in depth. Three-fourths of the population were settled on the coastal plain from Haifa in the north to a point just south of Tel Aviv and in the narrow salient leading to the capital, Jerusalem. No settlement was more than 20 miles from an Arab border except for a few in the Negev. The shortest distance from the Mediterranean to the frontier of the Kingdom of Jordan was 9–10 miles; and it was easy, in theory, for an Arab military thrust from the Jordan 'bulge' to split Israel at the waist. The Jerusalem Corridor was only 10 miles wide at points, and the Israeli half of the city was surrounded on three sides, well within Jordanian artillery range. Syrian guns on the Golan Heights were able to wreak havoc on the settlements in eastern Galilee. And access to Eilat, the southern gateway to Asia and Africa, could be easily severed. Indeed all the main roads were exposed to swift and continuous incursion.[1]

This geo-strategic condition created 'a security problem of unusual complexity', in the words of General Moshe Dayan. The term 'frontier security', he wrote in 1954, has little meaning in Israel's geographic context. 'The entire country is a frontier.' Further, 'the unique vulnerability which geography imposes . . . [is] aggravated by the fierce antagonism' of Israel's neighbours. And 'this is not the classic pattern of international conflict' because of the persistent Arab policy of non-recognition. Not a single state, he added, had a firm, unequivocal obligation to help defend Israel against aggression. Thus Israel 'faces formidable dangers [and] . . . faces them in unusual solitude'.[2]

This perception of Israel's geo-political environment was almost universally held among her military and political élites. Its effect on policy was a paramount concern with national security from the first hour of statehood throughout the first twenty years of independence. In foreign policy this was reflected in the ceaseless quest for modern weapons, a firm guarantee of territorial integrity, and as many friends

[1] The distribution of Israel's frontiers before June 1967 was as follows: north, 49 miles with Lebanon; north-east, 47 miles with Syria, the most sensitive of all Arab–Israeli borders; east, 332 miles with Jordan, much of it formed by the Triangle or 'bulge' on the West Bank of the Jordan River; and south and south-west, 165 miles of the former Palestine border with Egypt, inclusive of 28 miles with the Gaza Strip. The total land boundaries of Israel until June 1967, then, were 593 miles; the water boundaries totalled 158 miles. The maximum distance from north to south, from Dan to Eilat, was 260 miles. The widest point was 70 miles, in the Negev. North of Tel Aviv, near Netanya, the Jordan border was 8 miles away; and at Eilat it was 3¾ miles to the Jordanian town of Aqaba. The United Nations Partition Plan of 1947 had allotted 5,600 square miles to Israel. After the 1948 War, and under the Armistice Agreements of 1949, Israel held 8,048 square miles of territory. Oscar Kraines, *Government and Politics in Israel*, Houghton Mifflin, Boston, 1961, p. 10. For a discussion of the boundary question see Lewis M. Alexander, 'The Arab–Israeli Boundary Problem', *World Politics*, vi, 3, April 1954, pp. 322–37.

[2] Moshe Dayan, 'Israel's Border Problems', *Foreign Affairs* (New York), 33, 2, Jan. 1955, pp. 250–67. The quotations are taken from pp. 250–1 and 258.

as possible. Internally, the preoccupation with defence was manifest in the moulding of the economy, in the high proportion of the annual budget devoted to defence, in the building and maintenance of uneconomic enterprises, in the construction of defence-oriented agricultural settlements, in the attempted dispersal of population, in immigration policy, and in economic development generally.[1]

The specific impact on foreign policy was admirably summed up by a senior member of Israel's Foreign Service: 'There are four Arab acts which would constitute an automatic *casus belli* for Israel; two are on water, two on land, north, south, east, and west; one is the attempt to divert the waters of the Jordan, another the closing of the Straits of Tiran; a third is control of the Jordan 'bulge' by a state or united command more powerful than Amman; and the fourth is the concentration of Egyptian military power in the Sinai Desert.'[2] There is a fifth catalyst to Israeli military riposte—the intensification of Arab guerrilla warfare to a level which undermines 'normal' civilian life in Israel. The Sinai Campaign was in part a response to escalating *Feda'iyun* raids, as well as to the threat of Egyptian control over the Jordan 'bulge', with the formation of a tripartite Unified Arab Command in late October 1956. And the Six Day War followed the activation of three of these conditions in rapid succession—the massing of Egyptian armour in Sinai, the proclaimed blockade of the Tiran Straits and the creation of a joint Egyptian–Jordanian Command— all in the second half of May 1967 and set against the background of rising infiltration by Arab guerrilla formations, *Al-Fatah* and others.

The Arab perception of Israel's geo-strategic position is filtered through a different lens: it occupies an important place in the overall Arab élite image of Israel—and the inevitability of her destruction. Typical of that image is the comment by Hasanayn Haikal, editor of the Cairo daily, *Al-Ahram,* and the most influential journalist in the Arab world: 'There is one Arab nation which lives on a territory stretching from the Arab [Persian] Gulf to the Atlantic Ocean and numbers 100 million souls. The unity of this nation is not a subject for debate. . . . At the heart of this nation a foreign unit has been formed, in the shape of a sharp-angled triangle . . . this triangle separates the eastern Arab territory and peoples from the western Arab territory and peoples. . . . In this way, Israel's geographic location forms an artificial island . . . in the midst of the Arab ocean. This situation cannot persist no matter what extraordinary resources are supplied. The waves on both sides will continue to beat against this artificial island and in the course of time will wear it down until it breaks and falls apart and

---

[1] For an elaboration of this theme see Safran, *The United States and Israel,* pp. 188–92.
[2] Gideon Rafael, during an interview in Jerusalem, Aug. 1966. In October 1967 he was appointed to the post of Director-General, Ministry for Foreign Affairs.

is swept away in the mighty expanse of the ocean.'[1] This is not mere rhetoric. In fact it is a moderate presentation of the pervasive Arab view—which has had a pronounced 'feedback' effect on the Israeli élite image of Arab intentions.[2]

Haikal's words were written after the 1967 War and take no account of the basic changes in Israel's geo-strategic position. Her total land border was reduced by more than a third, to 375 miles. The frontier with Jordan was now a mere 50 miles and that with Egypt only 60 miles. Yitzhak Rabin, Israeli Chief of Staff during the Six Day War, put it cogently: 'The present borders run along natural barriers: Egypt—the Canal; Jordan—the Jordan River, a less impressive barrier than the Suez Canal but nevertheless a barrier; and with Syria, there will no longer be a need to climb up mountains.' But most important was the shift in distance from strategic and population centres. 'The distance from the Egyptian border to Tel Aviv was once 130 kilometres and only 80 kilometres from the Gaza Strip. But the distance from our border on the Canal today to Cairo is only 130 kilometres. The distance from our border to Cairo was once something over 400 kilometres. Today the distance from the Egyptian border on the Canal to Tel Aviv is 400 kilometres.'[3] In short, the pattern of frontiers was a marked Israeli liability prior to 1967. It became an equally-marked strategic asset following the Six Day War.

(b) POPULATION[4]

The population gap between the protagonists was a further indicator of superior Arab military power (Table 3 below). In May 1948 Israel's Jewish community totalled 650,000; the combined population of the five Arab states in the Near East core (and Saudi Arabia, which also participated in the first round) was 32·3 million, that is, a ratio of 1 to 50. By 1958 the ratio had declined to 1 to 21, but the absolute gap had increased by more than four million. And in 1967 the numerical gap had widened further, though the ratio remained unchanged.

[1] The text of this editorial in *Al-Ahram* was reproduced in English translation under the title, 'The Political Solution and Armed Conflict', in *New Outlook* (Tel Aviv), vol. 10, no. 8 (92), Nov. 1967, pp. 52–6.

[2] A comprehensive and informative study of articulated Arab images of Israel is provided by Y. Harkabi, *Emdat Ha'aravim Ba-sichsuch Yisrael-Arav* ('The Arab Position in the Israel–Arab Conflict'), Dvir, Tel Aviv, 1968 (in Hebrew). Israeli élite images of the Arabs will be explored in ch. 12–14 and Appendix D below.

[3] Speaking in Tel Aviv on 21 September 1967, on the occasion of the 15th anniversary of the death of Yitzhak Sadeh, founder of *Palmah*. The bulk of Rabin's speech appeared in an English translation under the title, 'Why We Won the War', in *Jerusalem Post Weekly*, 9 Oct. 1967, pp. 6, 7, 13.

[4] The economic capability aspect of Israel's demography is discussed in ch. 5 (a) below.

TABLE 3

POPULATION: ARAB STATES AND ISRAEL (in millions)

	Egypt	Iraq	Syria	Lebanon	Jordan	Saudi Arabia	Arab Total	Israel	Ratio of Arab to Is.
1948	19	4·8	2·9	1·1	1	3·5	32·3	·65	50 to 1
1958	22	5	4	1·5	1·5	4	38	1·78	21·3 to 1
1967	31	8·3	5·6	2	2·2	4	53·1	2·60	20·4 to 1

Sources: The 1948 data for Egypt, Iraq, Syria, and Lebanon are taken from the United Nations, Statistical Office, *Demographic Year-Book*, New York, 1949. The figure for Saudi Arabia, at best an approximation, is taken from the *Statesman's Year-Book*, Macmillan, London, 1949, p. 728. Gabriel Baer noted that the Saudi Arabian Government claimed a population of 6 million in 1947, that other estimates increase or reduce that figure by as much as a million, and that no reliable data had yet been published. *Population and Society in the Arab East*, Routledge and Kegan Paul, London, 1964, p. 3. The estimated population of the Kingdom of Jordan proper in 1948 was 340,000 (drawn from the *Statesman's Year-Book*); the figure cited above includes the population of the Jordan-occupied West Bank. The 1958 data for the Arab states are taken from Edgar O'Ballance, *The Sinai Campaign 1956*, Faber and Faber, London, 1959, ch. 5. These are only approximations but are adequate for the purpose of this table. The 1967 data for the Arab states are taken from The Institute for Strategic Studies,· *The Military Balance 1967–1968*, London, 1968, pp. 39–42. The figures for Israel are taken from Central Bureau of Statistics, *Statistical Abstract of Israel*, no. 19, 1968, Jerusalem, 1969, p. 20. The Israeli data, the most accurate, refer to the Jewish population of Israel.

A larger population is not an absolute index of superiority in military manpower. Other criteria are important: education and skills, that is, the level of modernization, and such intangible qualities as initiative, adaptability, and morale. In all of these Israel had a marked advantage during the first twenty years of statehood, as will be elaborated later. Yet it is noteworthy that even with Israel's qualitative assets and the need to reject 70 per cent of potential Arab recruits, the UAR could enrol three times as many military recruits annually, on the basis of the 1962 data. Further, the mobilization of 40,000 persons in Israel would mean the withdrawal of 7 per cent of the labour force; the mobilization of 200,000 Egyptians would constitute a marginal diminution (1·5 per cent) of the labour force. Closely related is the fact that Egypt had 2½ times as much revenue in that year to use for military expenditures.[1] Given the much higher Arab birth rate—the population of the UAR alone was rising by more than half a million annually in the mid-1960s —the quantitative gap is certain to grow, and with it Arab military potential.[2] Israel's triumph in war from 1948 to 1968 was due to

[1] Safran, op. cit., p. 185.

[2] That gap may be a military liability as well when the state in question, as with Egypt, is economically underdeveloped. Nevertheless, in the *long run* a larger population represents a *potential* military asset.

qualitative differences. The future of the qualitative gap cannot be so readily predicted.

In the war system of the Near East the Arab states had a significantly larger combined budget from which to enhance their military power. They also had a marked weapons superiority, except for brief periods following defeat in war. The ratios in military finance and weaponry will be explored in detail. Before doing so, however, it is pertinent to examine the origins and historical legacy of *Tzahal* (*Tzva Ha-Haganah Le 'Yisrael*—Israel Defence Forces).

(c) PRE-STATE ORIGINS OF *TZAHAL*

One perceptive scholar has observed that 'military conceptions and militant attitudes, as well as military functions, though not the military as a distinct group, have played a significant role in the history of Zionism and the social and political relationships of the Jewish state'.[1] Professor Halpern notes further, as have others, that the Jews have never been culturally committed to pacifism; rather, that it was their circumstance as a minority without means of military power which created the pattern of non-resistance or passive resistance during much of Jewish history. Indeed there is evidence of Jewish prowess on the battlefield during the ancient periods of independence and beyond. This little-known military tradition was admirably summed up by Major O'Ballance:

The Jewish fighting man is not nearly so well known [as the Arab], but he has a splendid tradition as a soldier going back to Biblical days when the Israelites fought against the Philistines, the Canaanites, the Moabites, the Edomites, the Ammonites, and other surrounding tribes and cities.

The Bible is full of stories of their battles.

Under King David's rule the Israelite soldier was feared and respected throughout the Middle East but in time the Jewish kingdoms declined and eventually the Romans became the masters of Palestine. But the fighting spirit of the Jews was not crushed and the Zealots, who were militant Pharisees, revolted, seizing various forts and towns, including the capital, Jerusalem. For eighteen months the Romans hammered away at the city walls and only retook it after desperate building-to-building fighting. When Titus finally overran it the only Jews who had given up the fight were those who could no longer stand.

Later, in A.D. 132, there was another Jewish revolt under Bar Kochba, which took the Romans three years to get under control. After this the Diaspora became a fact and the remnants of the Jewish nation were scattered to the four corners of the earth. With it disappeared the Jewish soldier and in the centuries that followed the world forgot him.

[1] Ben Halpern, 'The Role of the Military in Israel', in John J. Johnson (ed.), *The Role of the Military in Underdeveloped Countries*, Princeton University Press, Princeton, N.J., 1962, pp. 318–19.

It was not until 1794 that he came to the fore again in Poland, when a Jewish leader, Berek Joselowicz, formed a Jewish legion of 500 volunteers, and led them in revolt against the Russians. When regular Russian troops were sent against them the Jewish soldiers fought to the bitter end and there were only twenty survivors.

In the two World Wars large numbers of Jews served in the armed forces of the various countries that took part on both sides (except, of course, Nazi Germany). Their bravery did not go unrecognized and, to quote but one example, in the Second World War over 25,000 decorations for bravery were awarded to Jews serving in the American Forces.

The Jewish soldier has reappeared, perhaps without the world being fully conscious of it, and the war in Palestine [in 1948] merely emphasized and brought the fact into prominence.[1]

The legacy of that tradition to modern Israel is not insubstantial. One illustration will suffice. In 1941 the advancing Afrika Korps posed a grave threat of a German invasion of Palestine. The *Haganah* (Defence) High Command realized that a direct frontal engagement would be suicidal and that a victorious German Army would extend the Holocaust to the entire *Yishuv* (Palestine Jewish community). The result was a 'Massada strategy', designed, in the words of Yigal Allon, a hero of the 1948 War, 'to save as many lives as possible of the civil population; to hamper the advance of the German Army . . . and, if death was the issue, to die fighting the enemy rather than in the crematorium. . . . It was decided to turn the area consisting of the whole of Mt. Carmel, the valley of Zebulum (between Haifa and Acre), the mountain chains of the Western Galilee based on Haifa Bay on the Mediterranean, and

[1] Edgar O'Ballance, *The Arab-Israeli War 1948*, Praeger, New York, 1957, pp. 15–16. For informative general surveys of the Jewish military tradition see Ralph Nunberg, *The Fighting Jew*, Creative Age Press, New York, 1945, and *The Jewish Encyclopedia*, Funk and Wagnalls, New York and London, 1902, vol. ii, 'Army', pp. 120–9, and vol. xii, 'War', pp. 463–6. See also *The Universal Jewish Encyclopedia*, The Universal Jewish Encyclopedia, Inc., New York, 1943, vol. 10, 'War', pp. 449–52, and Cecil Roth (ed.), *The Standard Jewish Encyclopedia*, Doubleday, New York, 1959, 'Jews in Armed Forces', pp. 159–63.

Brief references to the military strand in Jewish history are scattered in standard works: H. Graetz, *History of the Jews*, Jewish Publication Society of America, Philadelphia, 1891–8 (6 volumes), esp. vol. ii, ch. IX–XII, XV–XVI; Salo W. Baron, *A Social and Religious History of the Jews*, Columbia University Press, New York, 1937, esp. vol. i, pp. 63–4, 154–5, 180–91; vol. ii, pp. 20–1, 81–2, 169–70, 181–2, 236–7, 366–8; vol. iii, pp. 46–8, 66–7, 99–100, 145–7; and Abram Leon Sachar, *A History of the Jews* (4th ed.), Knopf, New York, 1953.

Jewish military resistance during the Holocaust (1939–45) is becoming better known through the memoirs of persons who fought in the Jewish partisan and ghetto resistance organizations of Eastern Europe. Most of these writings are in Yiddish, Polish, and Hebrew. For a compelling eye-witness account see Emmanuel Ringelblum, *Notes from the Warsaw Ghetto*, McGraw-Hill, New York, 1958. A valuable collection of Jewish and German documents on the Warsaw Ghetto uprising in 1943 is to be found in Albert Nirenstein (ed.), *A Tower From the Enemy*, New York, Orion Press, 1959. For a gripping, fictional reconstruction of the Warsaw Ghetto see John Hersey, *The Wall*, Knopf, New York, 1950.

an airfield strip on the coast into a huge, escape fortress for all the Jews in Palestine, then just over half a million. *It was a kind of modern Massada, with greater force and better chances.*'[1]

The military strand in Jewish history has been dramatically revived in recent years. During the long night of dispersion, however, the pervasive image—and the reality—of Jewry had been one of passivity and non-resistance. It was this pattern and the accompanying stress on piety and patience in Jewish 'national character' which led Zionism to counter with a mystique of militancy (and military strength), in an effort to transform the Jewish nation.[2]

The fact that the State had to be defended at birth by military means 'created a predilection for an activist foreign policy. The continuous need for military defence created a permanent bias in favour of activism. And its success has tended to depreciate the value of diplomacy for most Israelis; there is also less concern with foreign reaction to Israeli deeds.'[3] At every international conference, remarked one Director-General of the Foreign Office, 'from birth control to river valley development, there is an Arab assault on Israel; given that unbridled hostility, everywhere and at all times, Israeli activism is a natural, indeed inevitable response; it has become a permanent trait of Israeli diplomacy and diplomatists.'[4] The philosophy of realism, the spirit of militancy and the emphasis on military strength were partly the product of the Mandatory régime and its policies: 'the enduring lesson of the Mandatory régime—everyone acts in terms of self-interest—penetrated deeply into the minds of *Yishuv* leaders, now Israeli leaders'. They were also the result of the struggle for statehood, which 'diluted the idealist strain in Zionism's yearning for its Homeland'.[5]

In the last phase of British rule, 1945 to 1948, the military capability of Palestine Jewry was divided among three organizations, each under separate command and each pursuing different tactics, which were uncoordinated for the most part and frequently in conflict:

[1] Yigal Allon, 'The Making of Israel's Army: The Development of Military Conceptions of Liberation and Defence', in Michael Howard (ed.), *The Theory and Practice of War: Essays Presented to B. H. Liddell Hart on His Seventieth Birthday*, Praeger, New York, 1965, p. 347. (Emphasis added.) For a fascinating reconstruction of the greatest symbol of bravery in the annals of Jewish history see Yigael Yadin, *Masada*, Random House, New York, and Weidenfeld & Nicolson, London, 1966. Chapter 18 contains the dramatic description of that event by the Roman historian, Josephus Flavius.

[2] This point is discussed in Ben Halpern's *The Idea of the Jewish State*, Harvard University Press, Cambridge, Mass., and Oxford University Press, London, 2nd ed., 1969, ch. III.

[3] Interview with Ya'acov Shimoni, then Director of the Asia Department in the Ministry for Foreign Affairs, in Jerusalem, July 1960.

[4] Interview with Arye Levavi in Jerusalem, April 1966.

[5] Interview with a senior Foreign Ministry official in Jerusalem, July 1960.

Haganah, founded in 1921 as the semi-official military arm of the *Yishuv*; *Irgun Tzva'i Le'umi* (National Defence Organization), better known as the *Irgun* or *Etzel, IZL,* founded by the Revisionist-Zionist Movement in 1938, in opposition to the *Haganah* policy of *Havlagah* (self-restraint); and

Lohamei Herut Yisrael (Fighters for the Freedom of Israel), better known as *Lehi, LHI,* or the Stern Group, a smaller activist group established in 1941.

There was also a semi-autonomous commando unit known as *Palmah* (*Plugot Mahatz* or striking companies), founded as a special formation within *Haganah* in 1941; it was recruited mainly from the *kibbutzim,* especially those belonging to *Ha-Kibbutz Ha-me'uhad* (the United Kibbutz Movement), the mass base of what later became the Left-socialist *Ahdut Ha'avodah* party.[1] *Palmah* members were infused with a spirit of idealism and total commitment, which spilled over into *Haganah* as a whole.

Only *Haganah* and *Palmah* had the support of a civilian organization representing the entire Jewish community—*Ha-Va'ad Ha-le'umi* (The National Council)—and only *Haganah* (and *Palmah*) were under civilian control. The two smaller dissident groups advocated and practised a strategy of terrorism, but there were differences: *Lehi* believed in indiscriminate killing of individual Britons, while *Etzel* concentrated on the Arab enemy; *Lehi* was, first and foremost, anti-imperialist and saw Britain's time of troubles during the Second World War as a unique opportunity to press the aims of the *Yishuv*; *Etzel*, by contrast, perceived the Nazi danger as the greater menace. *Haganah* concentrated on strengthening the *Yishuv* by bringing in illegal immigrants and establishing new settlements, along with military self-restraint. Gradually the latter gave way to guerrilla war tactics, and there was crystallized an overall strategy of the 'three illegals'—illegal immigration, illegal settlement, and illegal military action. Despite all these differences, however, conflict among the three military groups was limited—because of public opinion, the need of *Etzel* and *Lehi* for a

---

[1] In 1942 no less than 41 per cent of *Palmah* members came from *Ha-Kibbutz Ha-me'uhad,* which dominated *Palmah* HQ—the commander, deputy commander, and the entire General Staff except for two officers. Of 20 *Palmah* bases—*Palmah* members spent half their time training and the other half in productive labour—17 belonged to this Movement. Yehuda Bauer, *Diplomacy and Underground in Zionism 1939–1945,* Merhavia, 1963, pp. 160–1, 260–4 (in Hebrew). This book has recently appeared in English under the title *From Diplomacy to Resistance,* Jewish Publication Society, Philadelphia, 1970. The affiliation of *Tzahal*'s senior officers from 1948 to 1968 with defence structures before 1948 is documented in Amos Perlmutter, *Military and Politics in Israel,* Frank Cass & Co., London, 1969, Table 6, p. 64. Of the 8 Chiefs of Staff, 3 (Dayan, Rabin, and Bar-Lev) came from *Palmah.* Of Senior General Staff Officers, the *Palmah* proportion grew steadily over the years—from 1 out of 14 in 1948, to 5 out of 13 in 1960–1, to 8 out of 15 in 1963–5, to 10 out of 17 in 1968.

measure of public acceptance, and the common objective of independence. Viewed in the perspective of time, *Haganah* was Israel's national liberation army, with *Etzel* and *Lehi* the extremists thrown up by the turmoil of a struggle for independence, hastening through their terrorist tactics the British withdrawal.[1]

Measured by the indices of the Six Day War, Israel's military power was pitifully small on the eve of statehood. In the autumn of 1947 the manpower at the disposal of the *Yishuv* was as follows:

HAGANAH			about 42,000
HISH (Field Forces)	10,000		
HIM (Home Guard)	32,000		
PALMAH			about 3,000
JEWISH SETTLEMENT POLICE			about 1,700
ETZEL			about 2,000
LEHI			about 400

Total of all military and para-military organizations: about 50,000[2]

These figures exaggerate the real strength of Palestine Jewry at the time—because of a grave shortage of weapons. According to an authoritative Israeli account of the 1948 War, *Haganah* possessed in October

[1] There is a substantial body of literature in Hebrew on the pre-State military organizations:

on the Second World War period, Zerubavel Gilad (ed.), *Hidden Shield: The Secret Military Effort of the Yishuv During the War, 1939–1945*, Jewish Agency, Jerusalem, 1951, as well as Bauer, op. cit.

on *Haganah*, Ben Zion Dinour et al. (eds.), *History of the Haganah*, 2 vols., Ma'arakhot, Tel Aviv, 1956, 1964.

on *Palmah*, Zerubavel Gilad (ed.), *The Book of the Palmah*, 2 vols., Ha-Kibbutz Ha-me'uhad Publishing Co., Tel Aviv, 1955; and Yigal Allon, *The Campaigns of Palmah*, Tel Aviv, 1965.

on *Etzel*, David Niv, *Battle of Freedom: The Irgun Tzva'i Le'umi*, 3 vols., Klausner Institute, Tel Aviv, 1963–7; Ya'acov Banai, *Unknown Soldiers*, Hug Yedidim, Tel Aviv, 1958; and Menahem Begin, *The Revolt: Story of the Irgun*, Hadar, Tel Aviv, 1964 (English translation).

on *Lehi*, Natan Friedman-Yellin and Yisrael Eldad (eds.), *The History of Lehi*, 2 vols., Tel Aviv, 1962.

An earlier phase is well covered in Eliyahu Golomb, *The History of Jewish Self-Defence in Palestine, 1878–1921*, Tel Aviv, n.d. Brief informative accounts in English are to be found in Allon, op cit., pp. 337–56 and Halpern, in Johnson, op. cit. A more comprehensive survey is in Allon, *Shield of David*, Weidenfeld and Nicolson, Jerusalem and London, 1970, ch. 1–5. An analysis of the organizational and societal roots of *Tzahal* is to be found in Perlmutter, *Military and Politics in Israel*, ch. I–IV.

[2] These figures are drawn from three sources: Netanel Lorch, *The Edge of the Sword: Israel's War of Independence 1947–1949*, Putnam, New York, 1961, pp. 44–50; Halpern, in Johnson, op. cit.; and Shaul Ramati (Director of Public Relations of the Ministry of Defence), *The Israel Defence Forces*, Israel Today, no. 4, Jerusalem, 1958, pp. 6, 8. Lorch does not give a figure for *Hish*, and there are some minor differences: Halpern indicates 30,000 for *Him*, about 3,000 for *Palmah*, and 'less than 3,000' for *Etzel*; Ramati notes 9,500 for *Hish*, 32,500 for *Him*, 3,000 for *Palmah*, and 3,000 for *Etzel*.

1947: 8,300 rifles, 3,600 Sten guns, 700 light machine guns, 200 medium machine guns, 600 two-inch and 100 three-inch mortars, all of different types, and sufficient ammunition for three days! Even for the commando forces of *Palmah* there were weapons for only two-thirds of its active members, about 1,500 men.[1] There was not a single piece of artillery, no heavy machine guns, no anti-aircraft or anti-tank weapons, no armoured cars, no tanks, no planes, and very limited transport. Such was Israel's military capability when the United Nations passed its historic Partition Resolution.

The state of military preparedness was no more sanguine on the eve of independence but there was dramatic improvement in the course of the first Arab–Israeli War. Widely varying figures have been quoted for Israel's armed forces, but there is a consensus on substantial growth, from 30,000–35,000 in mid-May to 80,000 in mid-October 1948.[2]

[1] Lorch, op. cit., p. 49. David Ben Gurion, drawing on his voluminous diaries, notes the following arsenal for April 1947: 8,720 rifles scattered throughout the settlements and 1,353 rifles for 'state defence'—336 at the Centre, 656 in *Palmah*, and 361 for *Hish*; *Haganah* had 1,900 Sten guns, 448 light machine guns, 186 medium machine guns, 572 two-inch and 96 three-inch mortars. *The State of Israel Reborn*, no. 22, 'From Underground Organization to Regular Army', *Davar* (Tel Aviv), 9 July 1965.

[2] *Estimates of Military Manpower of Israel During the 1948 War*

	Ben Gurion[1]	Ramati[2]	Lorch[3]	Kimche[4]	O'Ballance[5]
May 14–15	29,266 28,760[1a]	50,000	50,000	35,000	35,000 60,000[5a]
June–July	41,403	—	—	60,000	60,000
mid-October	79,889	—	—	80,000	—
December	—	—	—	—	100,000

1. Ben Gurion's figures, the most precise, refer to 'the number of recruits'. In his memoirs he provides a detailed breakdown of the totals by branch of the armed forces (for May and October 1948) and by rank (for June 1948). *The State of Israel Reborn*, no. 26, 'The Plot to Destroy Jerusalem Through Thirst was Eliminated', *Davar* (Tel Aviv), 6 Aug. 1965.

1a. The figure given by Yisrael Galili, deputy to Ben Gurion in his capacity as Defence Minister. Cited in Jon and David Kimche, *A Clash of Destinies*, Praeger, New York, 1960, p. 160, footnote.

2. Ramati's figures refer to potential recruits: 'All in all, *Hagana* could call on some 45,000 men and women'; he added 3,000 for the IZL and LHI, and 2,500 volunteers from overseas (*Mahal*). Op. cit., p. 6.

3. Lorch does not indicate any figure for 15 May 1948. The figure of 50,000 noted here is that cited by him for October 1947. Surprisingly, for an 'authoritative' work, he does not offer any other figures for Israel's military manpower throughout his lengthy account of the 1948 War. Op. cit.

4. Kimche's figure for 14 May 1948 refers to 'the total number of effectives. . . . This included everything: all mobilized infantry, the Home Guard, the air force, the naval services and the special service corps.' Of these, 25,000 were actual combatants. This explains the discrepancy between the Kimche and the Ben Gurion figures for 15 May. Similarly, Kimche's figure of 60,000 refers to 8 July, the *end* of the first truce period, whereas Ben Gurion's figure refers to mid-June. Kimche, op. cit., pp. 160, 223, and 243; the quotation is from p. 160.

There is also agreement on the relative strength of Israel and her Arab adversaries during the 1948 War. At the outset there were about 50,000 combatants, almost equally divided between the two sides. The Egyptian Army was considerably larger than that of Israel—on paper, nominally 50,000, but only one-fifth were engaged in the 'Palestine War'. Jordan's Arab Legion had 5,000, Lebanon less than that, and Iraq had fewer than 10,000. As Kimche remarked, however, these figures 'do not show the rather more powerful fire-power of the Arab armies, which, despite their shortcomings, mercilessly outgunned the Israelis on every front. They also had fighter planes, and bombers of a sort. The Israelis had scarcely any artillery and no modern aircraft . . . and no armour whatsoever.'[1]

The balance of forces changed somewhat during the first truce in June–July 1948. For one thing the number of combatants increased from 50,000 to almost 100,000, with a slight majority on the Israeli side.[2] For another, Egypt acquired ammunition and modern artillery from the Canal Zone dumps of the British Army. Most important, Israel began to receive tanks, artillery, planes, and ample small arms from abroad, notably from Czechoslovakia and France. The gap continued to narrow, as Israel's capability steadily improved.[3] With all this the Arabs retained weapons superiority to the end. Their defeat in the 1948 War was due to non-quantitative factors in the military balance.[4]

---

5. O'Ballance cites 35,000 for *Haganah* on 15 May 1948 in his article, 'The Army of Israel', *Journal of the Royal United Service Institution*, vol. ciii, 1958, pp. 566–72. In his book *The Arab-Israeli War 1948*, however, he indicates a figure of 'at least 60,000 strong' for *Haganah* at the end of the Mandate (p. 70); this figure (5a above) is identical to that cited in his article for July 1948.

[1] Op. cit., p. 162. O'Ballance offers the same assessment, though he uses higher figures for the two sides: Egypt—the same, that is, nominally 50,000, with 10,000 in the initial invasion force; Jordan—6,000 (instead of 5,000), including a Mechanized Brigade of 1,500 and 17 Infantry companies of 200 each (King Hussein, many years later, cited a figure of 4,000 as Jordan's military strength in 1948, reported in the *New York Times*, 26 Jan. 1967); Syria—7,000–8,000; Lebanon—3,500, including 1 detachment of tanks and 1 of armoured cars; Iraq—21,000 (instead of 'fewer than 10,000'); and the Arab Liberation Army—2,500 Syrians, 2,500 Iraqis, and 500 Lebanese, with ample small arms; also a Palestine Home Guard of 50,000. 'Arms were very scarce on the Israeli side in May 1948,' notes O'Ballance, 'being practically limited to small arms alone.' *The Arab-Israeli War 1948*, ch. IV.

[2] Both Kimche and O'Ballance cite 60,000 for *Tzahal* when hostilities were resumed on 8 July, but Kimche notes that this included rear-echelon troops, while the figure cited for Arab soldiers in Palestine, 40,000, refers to field forces alone. Op. cit., p. 223.

Ben Gurion indicates two major sources of the increase in Israel's military manpower —2,400 volunteers from abroad (*Mahal—Mitnadvei Hutz La'aretz*) and recruits from newly-arrived immigrants (*Gahal—Giyyus Hutz La'aretz*). *The State of Israel Reborn*, no. 26, 'The Plot to Destroy Jerusalem Through Thirst was Eliminated', loc. cit.

[3] The change from Independence Day to the eve of 'Operation Ten Plagues', the strike into Sinai in mid-October, is evident in the following:

(d) INTEGRATION

More important in the long run than Israel's initial capability was the integration of her military and para-military units. The process was not without incident. The first act was the creation of *Tzahal* by Order No. 4 of the Provisional Government, on 28 May 1948: the crucial provision declared, 'The establishment or maintenance of any other armed force outside the IDF (Israel Defence Forces) is herewith prohibited.' Responsibility for the execution of this Order was assigned to the Minister of Defence.[1]

Haganah simply moved into a new, legally-sanctioned framework on 31 May as Israel's regular army. Members of *Lehi* appeared ready to join *Tzahal* as individuals but after a week of talks they were taken in as groups with their commanders receiving agreed-upon ranks. Yet *Lehi* retained some autonomy for, like *Etzel*, it refused to disband its forces in Jerusalem, then slated to become an International City.

The integration of *Etzel* was more complicated, its course marred by deep resentment over the Ben Gurion-ordered sinking of the *Altalena*,

	14 May 1948	12 Oct. 1948
Men	35,000	80,000
Guns	4	250
120-mm. mortars	none	12
6-inch mortars	none	33
3-inch mortars	105	389
2-inch mortars	682	618
Davidka mortars	16	22
PIATS and anti-tank rifles	75	675
Machine guns	1,550	7,550
Rifles	22,000	60,000
Sub-machine guns	11,000	21,300

Kimche, op. cit., p. 243.

[4] The official Israeli account of that war is contained in Historical Branch of *Tzahal*, *The History of the War of Liberation*, Tel Aviv, 1959 (in Hebrew). Another important primary source is David Ben Gurion, *In the Battle*, 5 vols., Ayanot, Tel Aviv, 1947–55 (in Hebrew). A graphic pro-*Etzel* and pro-*Lehi* journalist's reconstruction is to be found in D. Kurzman, *Genesis 1948: The First Arab–Israeli War*, World Publishing Co., Cleveland and New York, 1970, Parts II and III.

[1] The other major provisions of the *Tzahal* Establishment Order were as follows:
1. Herewith is established the Israel Defence Force (IDF), consisting of ground, air and naval forces;
2. In times of emergency conscription will be enacted for all formations and services of the IDF; ages of those liable for conscription will be determined by the Provisional Government;
3. Every person serving in the ranks of the IDF will take an oath of fidelity to the State of Israel, its constitution and its lawful authorities.

Lorch, op. cit., p. 238. For Ben Gurion's account see *The State of Israel Reborn*, no. 3, 'The Campaign for the Negev', *Davar* (Tel Aviv), 26 Feb. 1965. The proposal came from Ben Gurion at the meeting of the Provisional Government on 23 May; it was approved at a meeting on 26 May.

an *Etzel* ship carrying 900 sympathizers from Europe and a substantial quantity of small arms. The *Altalena* arrived a few miles north of Tel Aviv at a time when the new Government of Israel had assented to a cease-fire and was bound by a UN freeze on the import of new weapons and manpower. The Prime Minister was furious because *Etzel* had violated Israel's commitment to the world body and had challenged the authority of the government.[1] The situation was aggravated by the assassination of UN Mediator Count Bernadotte in Jerusalem on 17 September 1948. The Israel Government responded swiftly: *Lehi* was outlawed and its members arrested; and the *Etzel* units in Jerusalem were ordered to disband and to hand over their weapons.[2]

In line with Ben Gurion's centralizing tendencies, *Palmah* was absorbed. The task was accomplished peacefully but not without doubt—and anger—on the part of many. On 7 October the Defence Minister ordered the *Palmah* staff to disband. *Palmah* HQ appealed to the Supreme Command of *Tzahal*, citing its uniqueness as a pioneering commando force with a special élan, but to no avail.[3] Exactly a month later the last of the military formations ceased to exist. Ben Gurion the relentless centralizer had triumphed.[4]

The creation of a unified citizen army—Ben Gurion's achievement—

---

[1] The *Etzel* view of the *Altalena* incident is most forcefully presented by its commander and, later, the leader of the *Herut* (Freedom) party, Menahem Begin, in his *The Revolt* ch. xi and xii. For Ben Gurion's account see *The State of Israel Reborn*, no. 10, 'The Government Crisis After the Altalena', *Davar* (Tel Aviv), 16 April 1965. The incident is also discussed briefly in Lorch, op. cit., pp. 255–6 and in O'Ballance, *The Arab-Israeli War 1948*, pp. 130–1. A detailed account of this affair is to be found in Kurzman, op. cit., pp. 457–84.

[2] The tension with *Etzel*, leading to its enforced disbandment, is discussed in Ben Gurion's *The State of Israel Reborn*, no. 25, 'Debate on the Dissident Organizations in Jerusalem', *Davar* (Tel Aviv), 30 July 1965.

[3] The prominence of *Palmah* then and later is evident from the following data: of 12 *Aluffim* (Brigadier-Generals) on the General Staff of *Tzahal* during the War of Independence, 3 were from *Palmah*—Allon, Ratner and Sadeh; of 45 Colonels, 20 were from *Palmah*; more than 40 per cent of the Majors and Lieutenant-Colonels in *Tzahal* during the War of Independence were *Palmah* officers; since 1948, 3 *Palmah* officers became Chief of Staff of *Tzahal*—Dayan (1954–8), Rabin (1964–8), and Bar-Lev (1968–); 11 of 18 General Staff officers in the Six Day War, including the Chief of Staff and his Deputy, had served in *Palmah*; the 3 Front commanders in the Six Day War began their careers in *Palmah*—Elazar (North), Narkiss (Central), and Gavish (South).
Cited by Amos Perlmutter, 'The Israel Army in Politics: The Persistence of the Civilian over the Military', *World Politics*, xx, 4, July 1968, p. 616, footnote.

[4] The integration of *Palmah* into *Tzahal* is discussed at length in Ben Gurion's *The State of Israel Reborn*, no. 8, 'The Problem of Authority over Palmah', *Davar* (Tel Aviv), 2 April 1965; no. 22, 'From Underground Organization to Regular Army', 9 July 1965; and no. 23, 'Discussion with the Commanders of Palmah', 16 July 1965. See also Lorch, op. cit., pp. 395–7.

was completed within six months of Independence Day.[1] It was during that initial phase, too, that civilian control over the armed forces was asserted—the Chief of the General Staff exercised supreme command under the overall authority of the Minister of Defence who, in turn, acted on behalf of the Cabinet or Provisional Government. And the basic chain of command was reorganized during the second truce: thereafter Israel was divided into four territorial fronts—North, East, Central, and South—each autonomous and operating directly under GHQ; the commander of each Front was responsible for all aspects of defence in his region; and so it has remained.

The second phase began in September 1949 with the adoption of the Defence Service Law. It provided for 'National Service' for all men ($2\frac{1}{2}$ years) and women (2 years) from the age of 18 and membership in the Reserves until the age of 49. It also created the framework for a cadre of regular officers and NCOs.[2] This was the phase of mass immigration, and *Tzahal* made a significant contribution to nation-building by absorbing and educating thousands of immigrants, many of them illiterate.[3] It also increased the reservoir of military manpower in the process. The impressive military intelligence of Israel dates to that period as well. In October 1953 Ben Gurion as Defence Minister submitted a three-year military programme for a general advance in training, education, and equipment. And with the Sinai Campaign, the enormous investment in Israel's military capability—manpower,

---

[1] As to the significance of the change from *Haganah* to *Tzahal* two views are worth noting. Yigal Allon, the *Palmah* commander, remarked that it 'was, in one sense, nominal rather than substantial. . . . But, in another sense, the change was real indeed. For it symbolized the historic change of Palestine into a sovereign Jewish state, and of the Jewish community into a nation; and as such it had great spiritual significance.' 'The Making of Israel's Army . . .' in Michael Howard (ed.), op. cit., p. 361. Ben Gurion, the architect of *Tzahal*, but not of *Haganah*, accentuated the qualitative change and, as so often, drew historical analogies: 'A Turning Point in the Annals of Jewish Heroism', he termed this; 'and although Tzahal received a rich inheritance from Haganah—and without that rich heritage it is doubtful if it could have arisen—yet Tzahal is not the continuation of Haganah, as the State of Israel is not the continuation of Ha-Va'ad Ha-le'umi (the National Council) and the Zionist Executive. . . . Tzahal is not the continuation of Haganah, but a turning point in the annals of Jewish heroism, like the war of Joshua Ben Nun, the wars of King David, and Ha-shmonaim.' *The State of Israel Reborn*, no. 22, loc. cit.

[2] For the debate on the Defence Service Law of 1949 see *Divrei Ha-Knesset* (Parl. Debates) 68th meeting, 15 Aug. 1949, cols. 1336–1341.

[3] *Tzahal*'s nation-building role among the myriad of immigrant groups is discussed by Ben Gurion in his *The State of Israel Reborn*, no. 47, 'Tzahal—Educator and Integrator of the Nation', *Davar* (Tel Aviv), 28 Jan. 1966. For a descriptive summary of the structure and functions of *Tzahal* see J. C. Hurewitz, 'The Role of the Military in Society and Government in Israel', in Sydney N. Fisher (ed.), *The Military in the Middle East*, Ohio State University Press, Columbus, 1963, pp. 89–104. An expanded version of this paper appeared later as ch. 20 of Hurewitz's *Middle East Politics: The Military Dimension*, Praeger, New York, 1969.

weapons, skills, and finance—produced striking dividends. A decade later Israel's military pre-eminence in the Near East core was demonstrated once more.

(e) DEFENCE BURDEN

To achieve that position Israel allocated a large proportion of her resources to defence, larger than any of her adversaries. Yet in absolute terms the combined military budgets of the Near East Arab states were substantially greater than that of Israel during the first twenty years. The evidence of this *greater burden* and *lesser resource base* is contained in abundant statistical data.

The figures presented in Tables 4 and 5 are not exactly comparable,

TABLE 4

ISRAEL'S DEFENCE BURDEN 1950–1958

(£I Millions at Current Prices)

	1950	1951	1952	1953	1954	1955	1956	1957	1958
Total Government Consumption	94·1	123·2	192·6	244·6	340·8	428	675	625	683
Defence and Special Budgets	41·8	52·8	63·9	74·1	118·2	160	340	255	254
Gross National Product	474·8	690·4	1,063·0	1,348·7	1,823·9	2,114	2,543	3,103	3,530
Total Resources	575·5	818·8	1,325·7	1,665·6	2,196·0	2,623	3,185	3,706	4,130
Defence as Percentage of Total Government Consumption	44·4	42·9	33·2	30·3	34·7	37·4	50·4	40·8	37·2
Defence as Percentage of GNP	8·8	7·6	6·0	5·5	6·5	7·6	13·4	8·2	7·2
Defence as Percentage of Total Resources	7·3	6·4	4·8	4·5	5·4	6·1	10·7	6·9	6·1

Source: The figures are taken from Table 12, Lines 2, 2b, 6, and 7 in Don Patinkin, *The Israel Economy: The First Decade*, Jerusalem Post Press, Jerusalem, 1960, p. 45. The percentage figures for GNP and Total Resources are taken from Table 14, Lines 10 and 2b, ibid., p. 48. The percentage figure for Total Government Consumption is calculated from the above data.

for 'Total Government Expenditure' is slightly broader than 'Total Government Consumption' (it includes 'subsidies' and 'transfer payments'). Based on either calculus, however, Israel's defence burden has been (and remains) onerous. During 1950–8 her defence expenditure was less than one-third of Total Government Consumption in one year only, 1953. It exceeded 40 per cent in four years and in one of those, 1956, the year of the Sinai Campaign, defence accounted for half of all Government consumption. During the decade 1958–68, too, defence constituted less than 32 per cent of Total Government Expenditure in one year only, 1962–3; two years later it reached 40 per cent. Viewed over time, too, the massive growth and its attendant burden are apparent: between 1951 and 1966 Israel's Defence Expenditure in dollars increased fourteen times; the Defence Budget quadrupled between 1962–3 and 1967–8; and the 1967–8 Defence Budget was twice as large as originally planned.[1]

TABLE 5

ISRAEL'S DEFENCE BURDEN 1958–1968

(£I Millions at Current Prices)

	1958/9	1959/60	1960/1	1961/2	1962/3
Total Government Expenditure (Ordinary Budget)	764·9	901·4	1,048·4	1,235·6	1,397·9
Defence and Special Budgets	289·3	314·7	345·7	401·6	432·0
Defence as percentage of Total Government Expenditure	37·9	34·9	33·0	32·5	30·9

	1963/4	1964/5	1965/6	1966/7	1967/8
Total Government Expenditure (Ordinary Budget)	1,705·9	2,302·8	2,620·7	3,141·2	4,020·5
Defence and Special Budgets	575·0	922·4	858·1	1,115·3	1,772·0
Defence as percentage of Total Government Expenditure	33·6	40·1	32·8	35·5	44·1

Source: The figures for 1958–9 are taken from CBS, SAI, 1961, no. 12, Table R/2 Government Expenditure; the figures for 1959–60 and 1960–1 are from ibid., 1962, no. 13, Table R/2; the figures for 1961–2 to 1964–5 are from ibid., 1966, no. 17, Table R/6; and the figures for 1965–6 to 1967–8 are from ibid., 1970, no. 21, Table Q/7.

Viewed in global system terms, the magnitude of Israel's defence burden is evident from the data on defence expenditure in 1963–4 for 37 states (14 belonging to NATO, 7 to the Warsaw Pact, 5 to SEATO, and 11 others); Israel ranked highest in defence expenditure as a percentage of GNP, with 10·7. Only two other countries carried a comparable burden, the United States (8·9) and the United Arab Republic

[1] Statements by Finance Minister Sapir, reported in Jerusalem Post, 2 April 1967 and 7 May 1968. He termed this 'a monstrous defence burden'.

(8·6). No less than 29 states had a defence expenditure *less than half* the Israeli percentage of GNP.[1] In 1968, too, Israel's proportional defence expenditure was the *highest* among 35 states—16·1 per cent of GNP;

TABLE 6

THE BURDEN OF DEFENCE: ISRAEL AND THE ARAB STATES 1949–1966

(Percentage of Defence to Total Government Expenditure)

	1949	1950	1951	1952	1953	1954
Israel*	56·8	44·6	24·7	37·2	30·9	22·6
Egypt (UAR)	20·8	20·9	—	—	18·3	19·3
Iraq	21·1	21·9	25·5	27·0	—	—
Jordan†	66·2	62·6	24·8	27·5	—	—
Lebanon	20·8	17·2	18·9	17·4	16·5	—
Syria	27·1	—	42·4	40·8	41·5	—

	1959	1960	1961	1962	1963	1964	1965	1966
Israel	—	—	—	—	—	31·8	41·7	39·2
Egypt	32·8	—	33·2	—	24·0	24·3	23·0	21·5
Iraq	—	37·2	38·6	37·8	38·4	41·1	40·1	—
Jordan	71·2	—	—	63·9	61·3	61·3	59·5	58·1
Lebanon	—	—	17·3	19·4	16·0	16·2	16·9	19·5
Syria	—	—	—	50·6	48·7	54·6	43·7	40·3

Source: United Nations, Statistical Office, *Statistical Yearbook: Annuaire Statistique, 1953,* and *1966,* New York, pp. 471–5 and 455, and pp. 618, 640–5 and 650, respectively. The percentages in the above table have been calculated from the absolute budget figures provided in the *Statistical Yearbook.* Development Expenditures have been excluded from the total base figure.

* The percentages indicated for Israel are undervalued because the total figure for Current Government Expenditure, our base figure, includes an item, 'Other Current Expenditure', which contains an amount for 'Special Budget', sometimes rather large; this is really a defence expenditure but is not specified in the UN data and thus is not included in the figure for Defence, for purposes of calculating the percentages cited above. For example, the UN data cite one special defence item for National Security, that is included in 'Other Current Expenditure'—£134·1 million in 1953. If this is added to the 'normal' defence item the Israel defence burden for 1953 is 54·1 per cent, rather than 30·9 per cent. The UN figures for Israel's 'National Defence' in the 1960s are identical to those for 'Defence' in the *Statistical Abstract of Israel* but do not contain a separate item for 'Special Budgets', as in the latter. Thus the amounts shown for 'Special Budgets' in the official Israeli figures have been added to 'National Defence' in calculating the percentages above.

Note: The budget year for Near East states varies. Israel's budget has always been for the year ending 31 March. Jordan is the same. Iraq's budget, until 1954, ended on 30 April; thereafter, it has been 31 March. Lebanon and Syria use the calendar year. Egypt's budget, from 1949 to 1951, ended on 28 February; thereafter its budget year ended on 30 June.

† Largely financed from foreign sources, British and, later, American.

[1] The Institute for Strategic Studies, *The Military Balance 1965–1966,* London, 1965, p. 43.

only her four principal Arab adversaries—Egypt, Jordan, Iraq, and Syria—exceeded 10 per cent as well, with the US and the USSR at 9·2 and 9·3 respectively.[1] (By 1970 Israel's defence expenditures had reached an astounding 25 per cent of her GNP.)[2] Measured as a percentage of Total Central Government Expenditure, the Israeli burden in 1963–4 was exceeded by only five states, the US, Indonesia, Germany, South Korea, and Switzerland. (The spiral of Israel's defence expenditures since the Six Day War was dramatically revealed by Finance Minister Sapir three years later. The ratio of defence expenditures to the Ordinary Government Budget was, he remarked, 52 per cent in 1968 and was expected to reach 67 per cent in 1970).[3]

Within the Near East, Israel's defence burden has been persistently greater than that of her principal adversary (Table 6). In 1949 and 1950 it was more than double that of Egypt; in 1965 and 1966 it was 75 per cent higher; and in no year was the Israeli budgetary burden less. Among the other Arab states, Lebanon's defence expenditure never exceeded 20 per cent of total Government spending. Jordan's defence outlay appears much higher relatively than that of Israel but it is inflated and distorted, for it was financed largely from British and American grants. Iraq's burden was less than Israel's in the early 1950s and about the same in the mid-1960s. Only Syria's proportional defence expenditure was greater than that of Israel—and there the gap narrowed in 1965 and 1966.

A comparative analysis of defence burdens based solely on official statistics is distorted by various factors. There are 'hidden' military expenditures, notably for Israel, in the military research industry, frontier settlements, civilian defence, etc. Foreign military aid plays a vital role in the military capability of all Near East states and is not adequately conveyed by defence budget figures; for example, Soviet bloc arms deliveries and technical advisers to Egypt and Syria are only partly accounted for. No less important is the value of military hardware acquired per unit of defence outlay. In this Israel has a marked advantage because of the high Arab cost in corruption. Yet all these considerations do not alter the essential thesis that, viewed over twenty years, Israel's defence burden was heavier than that of her Arab neighbours combined: this is evident in Table 7.

The data in Table 7 suggest that the Arab states' defence burden (Defence Budget as proportion of GNP) was nearly as high as that of Israel in the earlier years, with a widening gap in 1969. Yet the absolute and relative magnitudes overstate Arab defence expenditures *directed against Israel*: for, while Israel's defence effort is concerned exclusively with the Arab states, they have allocated considerable funds, weapons,

---

[1] *The Military Balance 1969–1970*, p. 57.
[2] According to Finance Minister Sapir, *Jerusalem Post*, 3 Nov. 1970.
[3] To a Jewish Leaders' Study Mission from England, *Jerusalem Post*, 3 Nov. 1970.

TABLE 7

DEFENCE BUDGETS OF ARAB STATES AND ISRAEL:
1954, 1963, AND 1969

	1954			1963			1969		
	Million $	Ratio to Israel's Expenditure	% of GNP	Million $	Ratio to Israel's Expenditure	% of GNP	Million $	Ratio to Israel's Expenditure	% of GNP
Egypt	130	2·0	5·2	400	1·48	9·3	1,000	1·00	17·7
4 Other Arab States	120	1·85	5·6	350	1·30	9·3	675	·68	12·4
Total of five countries	250	3·85	5·4	750	2·78	9·3	1,675	1·68	15·1
Israel	65		6·7	270		10·8	1,000		21·1

Source: Dr. Eliezer Shefer (Joint Director, Research Department, Bank of Israel), 'Israel—The Economic Power of the Middle East', in *Yediot Aharonot* (Tel Aviv), 27 February 1970. The data for 1954 and 1963 are from official publications. The 1969 figures for Egypt are taken from a speech by President Nasser on 6 November 1969. Figures for other Arab states are taken from official budgets—underestimates of actual expenditures, in Shefer's view. For Israel, the 1969 data are based upon newspaper reports of speeches by ministers.

and manpower to other military ventures—Yemen, the Kurds, etc.— and have maintained large military establishments for internal security. Thus, in reality, the Israeli defence burden has been significantly higher than that of her adversaries throughout the conflict. At the same time, the economic burden of defence in the Arab states is heavy, particularly if account is taken of their low level of economic development, the growth of which is retarded by the need to allocate considerable resources to 'the military'.

If Israel's economic growth continues at the average rate of the first twenty years, her relative defence burden will decline markedly. This is borne out by the above data: in 1954, when Israel's economic base was still narrow, the combined Defence Budgets of the five Arab states were nearly four times as large as that of Israel; by 1969 the ratio had fallen to 1·68:1. In fact, asserts Shefer, if Israel's economic growth is maintained at 10 per cent per annum, compared with 5 per cent in the Arab economies, the disparity in defence burden will disappear in eighteen years. Stated differently, Israel's economic capability to sustain defence goals has been rising steadily relative to Arab economic capability.[1]

(f) BALANCE OF WEAPONS

The Arab states were also favoured with a quantitative superiority in weapons. The initial imbalance, discussed earlier, was corrected in large measure by the end of the 1948 War. Until the mid-fifties a modest arms level was preserved, largely through the Tripartite Declaration of 1950, which imposed a rationing system on arms deliveries to the Near East. How limited that regional power level was can be seen from a reliable assessment of Arab forces in 1950:[2]

Egypt—an army of 80,000, slowly being equipped with modern British arms; it possessed 100 Sherman tanks, 100 more for training purposes, and had just purchased 40 Centurions; it had also bought 110 jet planes; and its navy comprised 2 old British destroyers and some frigates.

Iraq—an army of slightly less than 30,000 divided into 3 not quite complete divisions; it had no tanks and no armour to speak of.

Jordan—an army of 8,000 well-equipped and fully-trained men, along with a trained reserve of 4,000; its Arab Legion was financed by an annual grant of £3 million sterling.

Lebanon—an army of 5,000 with a few planes and a few patrol vessels; French-equipped and trained, it had no experience in modern war.

Syria—an army of about 10,000, with French equipment and no battle experience, except for the limited involvement in the 1948 War.

The flow of weapons during the next five years enhanced Arab strength but did not undermine the military balance at the time of the Armistice Agreements. The first radical shift came with the Czech–Egyptian Arms Agreement of 27 September 1955. Estimates of the value of that deal vary—up to $320 million, to be paid for in Egyptian cotton; but there is general agreement that it involved a massive flow of planes, tanks, guns, and naval vessels. The most precise account was provided by Colonel Henriques: Egypt was to receive 50 Stalin III (heavy) tanks, 150 T.34 (medium) tanks, 200 armoured troop carriers, 100 self-propelled guns (S.U. tank destroyers), 120 Mig-15 fighters, 50 Ilyushin-28 twin-engined jet bombers, 20 Ilyushin-14 transport planes, 2 destroyers, 15 minesweepers, 2 submarines, 200 anti-tank guns, 50 guns of 122 mm., 100 5-ton vehicles, 50 10-ton vehicles, radar,

---

[1] A comparison of economic capability and its implications for foreign policy is offered in ch. 5 (f) below (Table 10 and the accompanying analysis).

[2] 'Defenders of the Middle East' (a series of six articles, one of them on Saudi Arabia), *The Economist*, London, vol. 158, 24 June 1950, pp. 1390–1; vol. 159, 1 July 1950, pp. 25–6; vol. 159, 8 July 1950, pp. 82–3; vol. 159, 15 July 1950, p. 128; and vol. 159, 22 July 1950, pp. 177–8.

recoilless rifles, and thousands of semi-automatic weapons; Syria was to receive 100 T.34 (medium) tanks, 100 Mig-15 fighters, troop carriers, anti-aircraft guns, howitzers, and lesser arms.[1] There were few, if any, then and later, who doubted that 'the entire military and political structure of the Middle East changed drastically, ominously'.[2]

The Soviet bloc arsenal reached its destinations by July 1956 and triggered a chain of events that was to culminate in the Sinai Campaign three months later. In the interim Israel had pressed its search for French arms successfully, and the imbalance was partly corrected once more.[3] Egypt's superiority in weapons was evident from a comparison of total armed forces in 1956. That Israel triumphed was due to factors other than raw weapons capability.[4]

The Egyptian Army was mauled in the Suez-Sinai War and its Air Force decimated. Vast quantities of equipment fell into Israeli hands. Within two years, however, the balance of military capability was restored, largely through Soviet bloc aid. An estimate for October 1958 suggests that the combined military power of the Near East Arab states was, roughly, double that of Israel in planes (800 to 400), with an even higher disparity in tanks (945 to 400). In field guns, too, the ratio was about 2 to 1, Egypt alone possessing 600 to 400 for Israel. The gap was accentuated by the Arab possession of 100 Ilyushin-28 bombers, a perennial threat to Israeli cities, notably Tel Aviv.[5] And as late as 1966 Israel was dependent on foreign sources for 80 per cent of her defence needs.[6]

On the eve of the Six Day War, as in 1948 and 1956, there was a gross imbalance in weapons in the Arabs' favour. Israel's armour comprised 800 tanks and 250 heavy guns. Egypt alone could field 800 tanks and 400 assault guns. To this must be added Jordan's 250

---

[1] Robert Henriques, *One Hundred Hours to Suez*, Collins, London, 1957, pp. 42–3.

[2] Terence Robertson, *Crisis: The Inside Story of the Suez Conspiracy*, Atheneum, New York, 1965, p. 17.

[3] For an authoritative source on the origins of Israel's arms industry see Peres, op. cit., ch. 6. A detailed account of the arms negotiations with France is to be found in Peres, ch. 3, and in Michel Bar-Zohar, *Suez: Ultra Secret*, Fayard, Paris, 1964, ch. III and IV.

[4] For an informative analysis of the Egyptian and Israeli armed forces in the autumn of 1956 see O'Ballance, *The Sinai Campaign 1956*, Faber and Faber, London, 1959, pp. 40–8 and pp. 55, 71–6, respectively. Chapter 2 also contains a thorough description of the organization and the strengths and weaknesses of the two armies.

[5] These figures are derived from O'Ballance, *The Sinai Campaign 1956*, pp. 199–207. A further, partial breakdown by types of weapons is revealing: Egypt, Israel's most formidable foe, possessed 60 Stalin III (heavy) tanks, 250 T.34 (medium) tanks, and 200 older British and French tanks; it also had 80 heavy bombers and 100 Mig-17 fighters (the most advanced Soviet plane at the time), and about 400 Soviet field guns (among a total of 600); Syria had 200 T.34 tanks, 50 S.U. self-propelled guns, and about 100 Migs, 70 of them Mig-17s.

[6] Moshe Kashti, Director-General of the Defence Ministry, in a Tel Aviv speech, 23 February 1966. *Weekly News Bulletin*, Jerusalem, 23 Feb.–1 March 1966.

tanks, Syria's 200 tanks, and Iraq's 400 tanks, all but those of Jordan supplied by the Soviet Union. Similarly, Israel possessed about 280 combat aircraft, compared to 840 for her Arab adversaries.[1] It is true that, from 1950 onwards, Israel agreed that the *quality* of *Tzahal* was relevant to any estimate of the balance of forces: she did not insist on quantitative equality of weapons with all Arab states combined. Indeed, in air power, which proved to be decisive in 1967 and, to a lesser extent, in 1956, Israel accepted—without enthusiasm—a ratio of about 1:3 for all Arab air forces together. The acceptable gap was less, but none-theless acknowledged in a concept of balance of weapons, for tanks and artillery. Yet Arab quantitative superiority posed serious dangers in a permanent conflict system of rapid escalation of violence—and miscalculation.[2]

The weapon changes caused by the third round have already been noted, especially the destruction of the UAR's Air Force and the loss of much of her armour.[3] Almost at once the Soviets began to replenish Arab arsenals. As early as October 1967 Israeli Prime Minister Eshkol declared that 80 per cent of the planes, tanks, and artillery lost by the UAR had been replaced.[4] In February 1968 Defence Minister Dayan asserted that Arab military strength was back to the level of the pre-ceding May, with slight differences in the way their forces were drawn up: Egypt, Jordan, Syria, and Iraq, he said, could mount two fronts against Israel—each consisting of 100,000 men, 1,000 tanks, and 250 aircraft.[5] And on the eve of the twentieth anniversary of Israel's independence Nasser acknowledged that the UAR had replaced the weapons lost in the Six Day War.[6] In the meantime, Jordan began to receive planes and tanks from the United States, and Iraq undertook abortive negotiations to purchase 54 Mirage fighter-bombers from France, the same type of plane sold to Israel but the delivery of which was now denied her. (Later, towards the end of 1969, Libya was to conclude an agreement to receive more than 100 Mirage planes.)

[1] Howard and Hunter, 'Israel and the Arab World: The Crisis of 1967'.

[2] The most comprehensive and illuminating analysis of Arab-Israeli defence expen-ditures from 1950 to 1965, with a few extensions to 1966 and 1967, and of the evolution of Arab and Israeli armed forces from 1949 to 1965 is to be found in Nadav Safran, *From War to War*, Pegasus, New York, 1969, ch. IV and V. Appendix B and Appendix C are also relevant and useful.

[3] See ch. 3, p. 63 above. For a detailed breakdown of the military capability of Israel and the Arab Near East states (except Lebanon) immediately after the Six Day War see *The Military Balance 1967–1968*, pp. 39–42.

[4] Interview with *New York Times* correspondent Terence Smith in Jerusalem. *New York Times*, 12 Oct. 1967.

[5] To a Jerusalem audience on 6 February 1968, reported in *Jerusalem Post Weekly*, 12 Feb. 1968. C. L. Sulzberger offered substantiating evidence from Cairo. *New York Times*, 29 March 1968.

[6] In a speech to Cairo University students on 25 April 1968. *New York Times*, 26 April 1968.

Indeed the traditional pattern of Arab quantitative superiority in military manpower and weapons was restored, according to a careful survey of the balance of forces in the Middle East core in July 1968 (see Table 8). And by the autumn senior United States officials estimated

TABLE 8

MIDDLE EAST CORE

Balance of Forces, July 1968

Armed Forces	Syria	Jordan	Iraq	UAR	Total Arab Forces	Israel
ARMY—						
Total manpower	50,000	53,000	70,000	180,000	353,000	255,000
Infantry brigades	13	9	13	26 1/3	61 1/3	21
Armoured personnel carriers	500	350		800	1,650	200
Artillery pieces	60	30		150	240	250
Armoured brigades	2	3	3	6	14	11
Tanks	430	230	575	700	1,935	800
Paratroop brigades	1/3			1	1 1/3	1
AIR FORCE—						
Total manpower	9,000	1,750	10,000	15,000	35,750	14,000
Bombers			18	50	68	15
Fighters	150	20	195	500	865	273
Transports	18	8	40	68	134	35
Helicopters	14	8	20	50	92	51
Combat-ready aircraft	150	20	215	400	785	270
NAVY—						
Total manpower	1,500	250	2,000	12,000	15,750	6,000
Destroyers				6	6	1
Submarines				13	13	3
Torpedo boats	17			46	63	9
Patrol & escort boats	9			32	41	11
Landing craft				21	21	4
Minesweepers	2			8	10	

Source: The Military Balance 1968–1969, The Institute for Strategic Studies, London, 1968, pp. 43–7.

that, in the preceding sixteen months, the Soviet Union had poured about $2·5 billion worth of weapons (equivalent cost for the US, $4 billion) into the Middle East; further, that this had replaced nearly all the jets, tanks, and artillery lost by Egypt in the Six Day War and had more than replaced Syrian and Iraqi losses. Apart from equipment, there were, according to US sources, 2,000 to 3,000 Soviet military advisers in the area (Israelis said more than 3,000), compared to 500 to 700 before June 1967. The only publicized major weapons counterbalance was the US sale to Israel of 58 Phantom F-4 jet fighter-interceptors.[1] The arms race had turned full circle.[2]

(g) COUNTERVAILING ISRAELI ASSETS

Arab superiority in the tangible indices of military power were counterbalanced by a variety of Israeli assets, some material, others intangible. Together they explain Israel's triumph in war. In the realm of *geography* there are five such advantages. One is an accurate *early warning system*. Another is an effective *intelligence network*. A third is the strategy of 'offensive defence', generally known as pre-emptive attack but in its Israeli variation the doctrine of '*interceptive warfare*'.[3] All these were dictated by her lack of a military operational terrain and the ensuing danger that her enemies would score a decisive first strike. Israel developed these capabilities very early and perfected them over time.

Her strategy, as revealed in 1956 and 1967, is based on the assumption that any Arab-Israel war except one of wider than Near East dimensions is bound to be short because of global system pressures, as well as internal economic factors; speed and a favourable military posture are therefore vital. In general, the strategy calls for an interceptive strike once there is clear evidence of enemy intent, in the form of mobilization and concentration of troops, tanks, and aircraft in forward areas with movement towards the frontier.[4] More specifically, it is designed to achieve the following: a spoiling attack, to reduce enemy capability; to gain ground for defence and manœuvre both on land and in the air; and to compel the enemy's withdrawal from forward lines. This in turn requires the destruction of enemy airpower and the displacement to the rear of enemy artillery, mortars, rockets—in short, transposing the battle on to enemy territory.

[1] *New York Times*, 22 Oct. and 7 Nov. 1968.

[2] For a carefully researched analysis of the Middle East arms race since the Second World War see Geoffrey Kemp, 'Strategy and Arms Levels, 1945–1967', in Hurewitz (ed.), *Soviet-American Rivalry in the Middle East*, pp. 21–36. See also the thoughtful analysis by Lincoln P. Bloomfield and Amelia C. Leiss in the same volume, 'Arms Transfers and Arms Control', pp. 37–54.

Developments in the Arab–Israel arms level and balance since mid-1968 will be analysed in the companion volume on high-policy decisions.

[3] A doctrine most closely associated with Yigal Allon, later Deputy Prime Minister of Israel. See his *Masakh Shel Hol (Curtain of Sand)*, Ha-Kibbutz Ha-me'uhad Publishing Co., Tel Aviv, 1960.

[4] In the 1967 case the imperatives of that strategy were blurred by a widely-shared Israeli élite image of political liabilities that would result from an *immediate* response to a blatant and massive Arab military threat.

This strategy, along with intelligence and early warning systems, proved to be major assets. The other two may be noted briefly. Israel's tiny land base is a liability in one sense. It has the compensation of *interior lines of communication* with shorter distances to the battlefields and ready access from population centres to the frontiers. And finally Israel's location keeps her principal *adversaries physically apart*. They can theoretically act in concert but on separate fronts. Thus Israel has responded to her geographic liabilities and maximized her countervailing assets.

The same is true with respect to *population*. The Near East Arab states vastly outnumber Israel, as noted. The critical indicator, however, is 'military manpower' and this depends on *mobilization capability*. Here Israel has a conspicuous superiority. In raw figures Egypt's active force is slightly more than twice as large as that of Israel, in 1967–8 about 150,000 to 70,000; the reserve force figures are 300,000 to 200,000. In operational terms, however, the balance of forces changes markedly, for Egypt's reserve organization is much less developed; she can handle only 20 per cent of the potential reserve. Moreover, Egypt lacks an emergency station system that can bring these reserves into being. Nor does she have a direct relationship between regular and reserve forces, as does Israel. In short, the mobilization capability of Egypt is severely limited and her mobilization mechanism inefficient: even if she has the reserves to mobilize she lacks the machinery to put them into the field quickly.

Syria suffers from the same disability; only about one-third of her 50,000 reserve troops can be made operational, partly due to political instability, which affects the armed forces, and partly due to an inept mobilization mechanism. Jordan by contrast has been able to activate the bulk of her 35,000-man reserve force. Israel's great strength in this regard has frequently been demonstrated, an ability to mobilize her 200,000 or more reserves within 72 hours and an almost flawless mobilization mechanism.

There are other Israeli manpower assets, among them *training* and *morale*. *Tzahal* compares with any army in the skill of its instructors and in the quality and rigour of training given to all of its citizen-soldiers. The result has been a mastery of weapons, a capacity to function in desert terrain, endurance, initiative, and an extraordinary sense of commitment. From the outset Israel created a 'nation in arms' which, at the same time, has been pre-eminently an army of civilians. In no other country have the armed forces been so thoroughly integrated with society nor have egalitarian civilian attitudes so pervaded the army. Unified yet decentralized organization has permitted rapid mobilization; and total participation has been the norm since the Defence Service Law of 1949 introduced National Service.[1] The citizen

[1] From 1949 until 1963 the period of National Service was 30 months for men and 24 months for women, starting at the age of 18. In December 1963 it was reduced to

militia thus created was an inspired community with superb élan and guided by creative *leadership* to apply the nine principles of warfare adopted by *Tzahal*: maintenance of aim; initiative; surprise; concentration; economy of force; protection; co-operation; flexibility; and (most important) consciousness of purpose or 'cause'.[1]

The emphasis has been on field combat, not on forms or appearance. Colonel Henriques, a professional soldier in the British Army for thirty years, expressed his admiring astonishment concerning this trait of *Tzahal* as follows:[2]

It is a strange spirit and not very easy to comprehend. Although Israeli units can be extremely smart on a ceremonial parade, there is very little discipline in the normal sense. Officers are often called by their first name amongst their men, as amongst their colleagues; there is very little saluting; there are a lot of unshaven chins; there are no outward signs of respect for superiors; there is no word in Hebrew for 'sir'. A soldier genuinely feels himself to be the equal of his officer—indeed of any officer—yet in battle he accepts military authority without question. I cannot explain, I cannot begin to understand, how or why it works. All my own military experience in the British and American Armies has taught me that first-class discipline in battle depends on good discipline in barracks. Israel's Army seems to refute that lesson.

This informality and the more effective inter-personal communication network among Israelis, derived from an egalitarian class system, has contributed another asset—greater initiative in night fighting; the Arab soldier repeatedly demonstrated an inability to fight well in the dark.

The army of the UAR was inferior in training, morale, and leadership. The quality of training was shoddy and inept by the standards of a modern army, as was the capacity to prepare large numbers of troops for desert warfare. The key cadres of instructing staff and sub-trainers were limited as to numbers and skills. Officers were promoted too quickly and lacked sufficient command experience. And the gap between sophisticated equipment and traditional outlook was enormous —in all Arab armies: the predisposition to modernity, with its emphasis on precision, routine, the manipulation of machines, and efficiency, was present in Israel society; it was underdeveloped in Arab societies.

---

26 months and 20 months, respectively. The original periods of compulsory service were restored in November 1966. And in January 1968, under the impact of the Six Day War and its aftermath, the period for men was extended by six months, that is, to 36 months. *Weekly News Bulletin*, Jerusalem, 9–15 Jan. 1968, p. 9. In addition, annual service in the Reserves for an average of 30 days was compulsory throughout for men to the age of 49. (In October 1969 the age of Reserve duty was extended to 54, to provide manpower for civil defence.)

[1] Allon, 'The Making of Israel's Army . . .', in Michael Howard (ed.), op. cit. note 13 on p. 371.

[2] Op. cit., pp. 23–4.

Typical of the training gap was the fact that Egyptian planes at the forward base of El Arish were in the air less than one-third of the time required to keep them—and their crews—operational; the Israel Air Force by contrast was at peak preparedness at all times.

This UAR disability was compounded by the morale problem. Soldiers were not adequately conditioned to the rigours of desert warfare. Officers and many NCOs were city dwellers chafing at the demands and discomforts of postings in Sinai or Gaza; their minds were back in Cairo or Alexandria or Ismailia. The contrast may best be stated in terms of adjustment to environment. The Israeli has always perceived himself as defending his home against mortal danger; the Egyptian has not. The Israeli's sense of commitment is unsurpassed; the Egyptian has little if any motivation to sacrifice in the desert.

There are countervailing Israeli assets with respect to *weapons*, too. One is the *superior maintenance* exhibited by *Tzahal*, a residue of the early years of scarcity and of the constant awareness of cost—the massive burden on economic resources. Another is the benefit of intense training in mobility and the live firing of weapons; frequent manœuvres and 'games' across difficult terrain *maximize the utility and efficiency* of weapons. In the largest sense Israel has the advantage of a better combination of skilled men using skilled equipment, men who are better attuned to working with machines by virtue of modern education, mental agility, and initiative. Arab possession of the most advanced Soviet planes, tanks, artillery, and missiles—and in substantially larger quantities than the Israeli armoury—has been an undoubted asset in the protracted conflict. The Israeli counterbalance has been very high standards of operational readiness.

In the realm of *defence expenditure*, too, Israel has adjusted to her environment. She has used her defence funds much more effectively than her Arab adversaries, without their attending evils of corruption and waste. She has also benefited from the willingness of an over-taxed Israel society to bear *awesome sacrifices* in the form of mounting taxes. The estimates for 1968–9 bring this into sharp focus. The initial budget proposals in January 1968 specified a total Government Expenditure of £I5,897 million ($1,684 million); and the Finance Minister told the *Knesset* that defence would 'eat up almost two-thirds of the nation's tax revenue'.[1] Three months later defence allocations were increased by £I500 million or $143 million to a total of £I2,200 million or nearly $630 million; 40 per cent of the additional sum was to come from cuts in development spending, while the rest would be raised by a defence loan; all taxpayers would invest half a month's income payable in ten monthly instalments.[2] The defence burden at that point, as noted,

[1] *Jerusalem Post Weekly*, 8 Jan. 1968, and *New York Times*, 3 Jan. 1968.
[2] *New York Times*, 25 April 1968, and *Weekly News Bulletin*, Jerusalem, 23–29 April 1968.

amounted to more than 44 per cent of all Ordinary Government Expenditure. (Even more startling, the Defence Budget for 1970-1—direct, indirect, and concealed—would exceed £15 billion, that is, more than double the figure two years earlier.)[1] It was made somewhat lighter by the sustained *financial support of world Jewry* in the form of gifts and Israel Bonds. The latter was a principal source for development spending, but the primary burden was borne by Israelis themselves.

In 1969 Chief of Staff Bar-Lev noted three advantages over the Arabs—human material, firepower, and the strategic depth of the administered areas.[2] All these Israeli assets were important. But the most important has been the pervasive and deep-rooted consciousness of *'ein breirah'*—'no alternative'; the price of defeat was universally held to be extinction. As so often, Foreign Minister Abba Eban voiced this Israeli feeling most poignantly:[3]

You may be surprised if I tell you that in our country the dominant memory is not of military triumph, but of the peril and solitude that preceded it [the Six Day War]. . . . Nobody who lived those days in Israel will ever forget the air of heavy foreboding that hovered over our land. . . . For let it be remembered that the Arab states could be defeated and still survive. For Israel there would be only one defeat. If the war had ended as those who launched it planned, there would be no discussion now of territories, populations, negotiations, agreements,˙occupied areas or boundary settlements. There would be a ghastly sequel, leaving nothing to be discussed—an ending with no renewal and no consolation.

[1] Finance Minister Sapir on the Israeli Television programme, *Moked* (Focus), 20 Aug. 1970.

[2] In a speech on behalf of the Defence Loan drive. *Weekly News Bulletin*, Jerusalem, 22-28 April 1969.

[3] Speech to the Jerusalem Economic Conference on 4 April 1968. *Weekly News Bulletin*, Jerusalem, 2-8 April 1968.

CHAPTER 5

Economic Capability

Writing in 1960, a distinguished Israeli economist remarked, 'Israel is a modern economy. Like most oversimplifications, this one too is not completely valid. But it is much more valid than the opposite conception of Israel as an underdeveloped economy of the genus of Egypt, India, China, and the like.' Four indices were cited by Professor Patinkin in support of this view. 'Israel does not have the basic population problems of these "classical" underdeveloped countries. Nor . . . is its problem of educating its labor force to any extent comparable in severity. . . . It is also clear . . . that the industrial distribution of Israel's labor force is quite modern—and that in particular Israel is not confronted with the fundamental problem . . . of shifting a predominantly agricultural population into other activities. . . . Finally, . . . Israel is not an underdeveloped economy from the viewpoint of both the level and the rate of growth of its per capita income and product. There is, however, one respect in which Israel differs fundamentally from both modern and underdeveloped economies. This is in its high degree of dependence on an import surplus.'[1]

This line of reasoning is persuasive, but not all concur with the conclusion. Thus David Horowitz, long-time Governor of the Bank of Israel, has written: 'Israel's listing as a developing country [by the IMF] is fully warranted by its rapid demographic growth . . . and by its adverse trade balance. Apart from all that, its geopolitical situation—involving boycott, blockade and other consequences—would justify special regard for its trade problems.' Yet Horowitz acknowledged that Israel's standard of living is high in comparison with the past (a threefold increase in the *per capita* standard since 1948) and even by comparison with developed European states.[2] It is this economic paradox which merits attention. Israel is 'developed' yet heavily dependent on foreign aid. She has a tiny area, with more than half the land a parched desert, yet she has achieved a high standard of living. Most important for an inquiry into foreign policy, Israel has a population of two and a half million with virtually no natural resources; yet she has created an economic capability to underpin and sustain formidable military power.[3]

[1] *The Israel Economy: The First Decade*, p. 43.
[2] *The Economics of Israel*, Pergamon Press, London and New York, 1967, pp. 97–8 and 107.
[3] For a succinct overview of the Israeli economy from 1948 to 1965 see Nadav Halevi and Ruth Klinov-Malul, *The Economic Development of Israel*, Praeger, New York, 1968, ch. 1.

(a) DEMOGRAPHY

A prerequisite of any society, economy, and polity is people. That need was especially acute in Israel because of the minuscule population at the time of independence, some 650,000. Rapid growth was essential to survival in the face of persistent hostility. It was also the crucial indicator of economic development, both as policy—'*kibbutz galuyot*' or 'ingathering of the exiles'—and as reality—a mass of immigrants of diverse skills and backgrounds to be absorbed into a developing economy. The legal foundations were set by two acts, the proclamation of independence on 14 May 1948 and the Law of Return in 1950, under which all Jews had a natural right to settle in Israel. The result was a massive immigration, especially in the first decade.[1]

There were three cycles of immigration during the twenty-year period under analysis. The first began in May 1948 and continued until the end of 1951. Almost 700,000 persons entered the country during those years, with a net increase or 'migration balance' of 666,000, more than the total Jewish population of Israel at the time of statehood; the two major sources were the refugee camps of Cyprus and Europe in 1948–9 and the transfer of the entire Jewish communities of Iraq and Yemen in 1951. The first plateau extended from 1952 to 1954, with a net increase of only 20,000; indeed in one of those years, 1953, there was a net *emigration* of 1·4 thousand. Another phase of substantial inflow occurred from 1955 to 1957, with a net increase of 136,000, starting with the North African communities, then the exodus from Hungary and Poland after the upheavals of 1956, and, following the Sinai Campaign, the migration from Egypt. Another plateau is evident from 1958 to 1960, with a net increase of only 47,000 in three years. The third spurt occurred in the early sixties, with a positive migration balance of 194,000 from 1961 to 1964, the bulk coming from Eastern Europe. In 1965 the net increase was almost 23,000. It dropped sharply during the next three years; indeed, to a total of only 25,000 in 1966, 1967, and 1968. (Only in 1969 did net immigration exceed 20,000 once more.)

Viewed in macro terms Israel's Jewish population increased almost fourfold from 1948 to 1968, from 650,000 to a little less than 2·5 million. Of that growth, two-thirds or 1·1 million was due to net immigration—and three-fifths of these newcomers arrived between 1948 and 1951, a larger inflow than the total increase of Jews in

---

[1] The basic source for the following demographic data is the Central Bureau of Statistics, *Statistical Abstract of Israel 1966*, no. 17, and *1970*, no. 21, Table B/2, 'Sources of Increase of the Population'. For the first decade Patinkin, op. cit., pp. 19–25, provides greater detail on an annual basis and a succinct analysis. There are slight discrepancies in the figures indicated in the two sources for 1950–8.

Palestine from all sources between 1882 and 1948.[1] This is the most rapid demographic growth of any state in the twentieth century—an annual average of about 7 per cent for Israel as a whole from 1948 to 1963, compared to a rate elsewhere varying between 0·5 and 2·5 per cent.

One result was to alter the composition of Israeli Jewry by continent of origin—from 90 per cent in Europe–America and Israel, that is, Western (for the fathers of most Israeli-born persons in 1948 had been born in Europe), and 10 per cent in Asia–Africa, to almost an equal Europe–America and Asia–Africa distribution in 1965. If the 7 per cent second-generation (or more) Israelis are placed entirely in the 'Western' category, the division would be 54 per cent Europe–America and 46 per cent Asia–Africa. Taking the population of Israel as a whole in 1968, however, the distribution by continental and cultural origins would swing the other way: the Jewish immigrants from Asia and Africa, and non-Jews, that is, the non-Westerners in a cultural sense, comprised 1·56 million of a total population of 2·81 million, or 55·5 per cent.[2]

This influx from eighty lands in all continents brought people with diverse languages, cultural traditions, and levels of development. The problems of integration and the tensions accompanying social change are not directly relevant to this inquiry, except to note that there is little evidence of interest groups emerging among these immigrant communities to articulate *foreign policy* demands; with one notable exception, the Sepharadim, they have not served as functionally-specific groups within the Israeli foreign policy system.[3] Furthermore, the gaps between the old *Yishuv* and the *Olim* (immigrants) have not created

---

[1] In 1882 there were 24,000 Jews in Palestine. This rose to 85,000 in 1914 and to 650,000 by May 1948. For a survey of Israel's population in the context of her economy see Halevi and Klinov-Malul, op. cit., pp. 15–18 and ch. 4.

[2] Data derived from CBS, *SAI 1966*, no. 17, Tables B/1, B/15 and B/16, pp. 20, 40–1 and 44–5, respectively, and ibid., *1970*, no. 21, Tables B/1, B/16 and B/17, pp. 23, 45 and 46–7, respectively. In 1948 35·4 per cent of Israeli Jews were born in Israel and 54·8 per cent in Europe or America; a shade less than 10 per cent had been born in Asia or Africa. By 1968 the Israeli-born category had risen to 43·9 per cent. More significantly, the Europe–America component had declined to 28·8 per cent, while the Asia–Africa category had increased to 27·3 per cent. Given the brevity of Israel's existence as a state, the breakdown of population by continent of origin must include place of birth of the father, as well as immigration source. In this perspective the relevant data are as follows for 1948 to 1968: of a total Jewish population of 2·43 million, Asia–Africa accounted for 494,000 (fathers of persons born in Israel) and 661,700 immigrants, that is, 1·16 million or 47·6 per cent; the comparable figures for Europe–America are almost identical, 1·10 million or 47 per cent of the total population; the remaining 5·4 per cent were second-generation (or more) Israelis.

[3] That group's advocacy will be discussed in ch. 7 (*b*) iii below. For an illuminating study of the process of immigrant absorption in Israel see S. N. Eisenstadt, *The Absorption of Immigrants: A Comparative Study based mainly on the Jewish Community in Palestine and the State of Israel*, Free Press of Glencoe, Ill., 1955. For a more general sociological analysis see his *Israeli Society*, Weidenfeld & Nicolson, London, 1967, ch. 5.

schisms within the armed forces: in the first major test of the psychological preparedness of Asian and African immigrants to fight—and die—for Israel, in the Six Day War of 1967, they responded well and earned a new dimension of respect from the 'Westerners'.[1]

Awesome gaps in education and skills have persisted, however, as the second result of the character of Israel's demographic growth. This in turn led to marked differentials in income between veteran settlers and newcomers. These socio-economic traits merit attention, for they shed some light on economic capability. Israel's Jewish population in 1948 had an enviable educational standard: more than one-third of the male adults were graduates of secondary schools and institutes of higher learning; illiteracy was virtually unknown. Economic development was at a relatively lower standard, however. Thus resources proved inadequate to raise the educational level of immigrants to that set by the *Yishuv*. The pre-independence system produced many 'over-qualified' persons who had to perform jobs requiring fewer and different skills. And there was less income inequality than in comparable European societies.

An educational downswing occurred after the first great wave of immigration, from 1948 to 1951. By 1954 the proportion with secondary and higher education had declined from 34 per cent of male veterans to 25 per cent of all Jewish men. More striking was the 50 per cent increase of persons with less than five years of primary school education. An upswing emerged in the late 1950s, and the change from 1952 to 1964 is readily apparent: the proportion of the 14–17 age group attending school rose from 43 to 57 per cent; and the proportion of the 20–24 age group attending institutions of higher learning increased from 3·0 to 10·8 per cent, more than a threefold rise.[2] It continued to increase sharply in subsequent years. Only Japan stood higher than Israel on the Asian literacy scale in 1961—97·8 to 87·9 per cent; none of the Near East Arab states except Lebanon exceeded 33 per cent.[3]

The educational gap between veteran and newcomer remains. So too does inequality in income, its natural concomitant. Thus in 1957–8 the bottom 10 per cent of Jewish urban families received 1·6 per cent of total personal income, whereas the upper tenth received 24·2 per cent of personal income, fifteen times as much. The reason, as two Israeli economists noted, is 'the fact that the various factors add up in a particular way: new immigrants are to a great extent from Asia and Africa and have less education and a lower level of professional skills'. And yet 'international comparisons of income distribution . . . show

---

[1] Related to the author by many Israelis in 1967 and 1968.
[2] Halevi and Klinov-Malul, op. cit., pp. 72–5.
[3] *Jerusalem Post*, 9 Jan. 1967, from data in the *UNESCO Statistical Handbook*. In Egypt the literacy rate was reported as 19·5 per cent, in Syria 29·5 per cent, and in Jordan 32·4 per cent. Lebanon's literacy rate was estimated at 40–50 per cent·

that Israel's income distribution is as close to equality as that of any other nation for which data are available.'[1]

The most important effect of Israel's demographic growth on foreign policy was the expansion of the manpower base for military and economic capability. As noted earlier, Israel's military manpower in May 1948 was approximately 30,000; by October it had grown to 80,000. The mobilization potential of *Tzahal* escalated sharply after the massive immigration of 1948–51, and in the Sinai Campaign it was estimated at 250,000. During the Six Day War the reservoir had increased to 300,000. Apart from all other *raisons d'être*, then, the 'ingathering of the exiles' proved to be crucial to national security for a state located in a region of pervasive hostility.

(b) ECONOMIC GROWTH

Immigration provided as well the key factor of production in a dynamic economy with an impressive record of growth. During the fifteen-year period, 1949–64, Israel experienced an average annual increase in Gross National Product of more than 10 per cent in real terms; this compared with 5·1 per cent in the European Economic Community, 3·5 per cent in the European Free Trade Area, and 3·4 per cent in the United States.[2] Further evidence of this achievement is contained in two studies in depth of Israel's economy and in various UN and other international indicators.

'The overall picture', remarked Professor Patinkin of the period 1950–8, was one 'of almost continuous growth in real GNP.' The average for those years was a compounded annual rate of 11·4 per cent; it was considerably lower in the early years, 8·7 per cent for 1950–3, and 13·1 per cent for 1953–8. More striking, 'Israel's rate of growth in real GNP during 1950–8 stands out as the highest in the non-Soviet world', a conclusion derived from the data on twenty-eight countries. Her pre-eminence did not extend to the rate of growth in *per capita* GNP but even there she ranked sixth. Professor Patinkin concludes: 'Israel's rate of growth during the period under study has been a very rapid one. More important, . . . at least one third of this growth has been due to the increased efficiency with which the economy obtained outputs from its inputs of labor and capital.'[3]

---

[1] Halevi and Klinov-Malul, op. cit., pp. 118 and 117. They rely on G. Hanoch's study, 'Income Differentials in Israel', *Fifth Report: 1959 and 1960*, Falk Project for Economic Research in Israel, Jerusalem, 1961. Hanoch had indicated four factors in the explanation of income inequality—occupation, level of education, length of residence in Israel, and continent of origin. Low ranking in the first three variables converged on immigrants from Asia and Africa.

[2] Horowitz, op. cit., pp. 35–6.

[3] Only Iceland, apart from Israel, exceeded 10 per cent in aggregate GNP annual growth, and only one other state, West Germany, exceeded 7 per cent; all but five,

Taking a somewhat longer period, Israel's GNP grew five times between 1950 and 1965, at an average annual rate of 11·4 per cent; the average *per capita* increase was 6·3 per cent.[1] And in a comparison of *per capita* GNP among the thirty most affluent states in the world from 1953 to 1965, Israel had a near-constant ranking just below the half-way mark (16th to 18th).[2]

Israel's rapid economic growth was dependent upon a massive import of capital. Before turning to that special aspect of her economy, however, it should be noted that the achievement of a *per capita* product exceeding $1,000 took place under adverse conditions. These have been admirably summed up by David Horowitz:[3]

First, a demographic growth far exceeding the rate in underdeveloped countries . . . within 15 years . . . it was more than trebled. Second, the geopolitical and military background hardly favoured development. . . . Third, the experiment was conducted in a small and largely waterless country with scarce natural resources, no coal or iron, no substantial oil wells. Fourth, part of the new population was used to European standards of living which had to be maintained within a poor and still infant economy. Fifth, the occupational structure of a section of the population and its cultural background were not adapted to local needs. . . . Sixth, people coming from eighty origins, with nearly as many

---

Iceland, West Germany, Austria, Greece, and Burma, had an annual growth rate lower than 5·7 per cent, that is to say, 21 of the other 27 countries experienced an annual *aggregate* growth rate of less than half that of Israel. Patinkin, op. cit., pp. 58–61, 69, 79. Patinkin cautions, however, that the GNP estimate for Israel 'is computed as the difference between the total resources of the economy and the import surplus. Hence its level is vitally dependent on the way in which the import surplus is evaluated. In particular, the fact that this surplus is evaluated at the official exchange rates—and that during some years these rates have frequently overvalued the Israel pound—*means that the GNP estimates of these years are also overvalued.*' p. 44 (emphasis added).

[1] Halevi and Klinov-Malul, op. cit., p. 92. Several works are available on the pre-1948 Palestine economy. In Hebrew the best known are A. Bonné, *Palestine, the Country and the Economy*, Dvir, Tel Aviv, 1936; D. Horowitz, *The Palestine Economy and its Development*, Mosad Bialik, Tel Aviv, 1944, and Horowitz, *The Israel Economy*, Masada, Tel Aviv, 1954, Part I. The best-known works in English are: D. Horowitz and R. Hinden, *Economic Survey of Palestine*, Jewish Agency, Tel Aviv, 1938; and R. R. Nathan, O. Gass, and D. Creamer, *Palestine: Problem and Promise*, Public Affairs Press, Washington, 1946.

[2] The lower limit of $200 excluded about 75 countries in the UN list for 1958 and 58 countries in the data for 1965. In 1953 Israel's average *per capita* national product was of the same order as poorer European countries like Austria, Italy, and Ireland; by 1961 the latter two fell behind. Throughout, Israel was above Latin American countries on the list and more than double, later four times as great as, the classical underdeveloped lands. Israel significantly reduced the proportionate gap between her GNP and that of the top dozen by 1965, but she remained well below the developed countries of northern and western Europe, Australia and New Zealand, and Canada, not to mention the United States. The source for Israel is CBS, *SAI 1966*, no. 17, p. 177; for other states it is United Nations, *Yearbook of National Accounts Statistics 1962* and *1966* pp. 314–17 and 725–9 respectively.

[3] *The Economics of Israel*, p. 34.

languages and sometimes centuries apart in cultural sophistication, had to be welded into an ethnic and national entity. Seventh, the restricted scope of the home market excluded the economics of scale in industrial production.

Israel's impressive growth declined in the last years of her second decade of independence, largely due to the new economic policy of *mitun* or artificial slow-down, introduced at the end of 1964. The GNP increased by only 7 per cent in 1965, dropped sharply in 1966 to a growth rate of about 1 per cent, and was restored to approximately 7 per cent in 1967, a very marked reduction from the aggregate annual average of more than 10 per cent from 1949 to 1964. The general reason for a slow-down policy was an over-heated economy with full employment, conspicuous inflation, over-consumption, and escalating imports. More specifically, it was the sharp increase in the adverse balance of payments which led to the adoption of *mitun*.[1]

There does not appear to have been any spill-over from the economic policy of *mitun* to Israel's foreign policy from 1964 onwards. The link, in so far as it may be said to have existed, was rather the reverse: the prime stimulus to a policy of economic restraint was the needs of Israel's foreign policy system. More specifically, an uncontrolled inflation and an escalating import surplus were regarded as threats to

[1] The enormous deficit in 1964 was an alarm signal, particularly as the downward trend in unilateral receipts of foreign exchange now appeared to be accelerating, with the impending termination of German Reparations and the marked decline in United States economic aid. Israel reacted with a new economic policy of forced slow-down, designed to reduce demand and inflation at home and to stimulate exports by reducing costs and re-allocating labour and investment to industries in which she had a comparative advantage.

Restraint was expressed in various measures: reduced government spending; credit restriction; subsidies to export industries; freezing of part of the capital import—mainly restitution payments from Germany; attempts to hold the wage-price line; and a curb on building activity. Policy was assisted by objective conditions: the absorption of surplus liquidity by the 1964 deficit in the balance of payments; the decline in construction, due to past accumulation of housing and the lesser demand because of a sharp drop in immigration; and the slower growth of inventories because of diminished liquidity. Together, restraint and economic reality had the desired effects—a noticeable improvement in the balance of payments during 1965, 1966, and 1967, with the deficit reduced by 30 per cent, a much lower rate of *per capita* consumption, signs of growth in personal savings, the retarding of inflation, and the strengthening of the Israel pound. (This process was undermined by the boom conditions after the 1967 War.)

The price was a precipitous decline in GNP and widespread unemployment, variously estimated from 40,000 to 100,000. Hardship was overcome, in part, by increased development projects for new settlements, agriculture, industry, water schemes, mining and chemicals, immigrant housing, and slum clearance. Nevertheless, the cost of *mitun* remained high, especially in the form of unemployment, on the eve of the Six Day War. For a succinct summary of economic developments during 1964–6 see Horowitz, *The Economics of Israel*, pp. 181–8. The background to the *mitun* and the relevant data for the period 1960–5 are analysed by Shaul Zarhi and Abraham Ahiezra, 'Israel's Economy Slows Down', *New Outlook* (Tel Aviv), vol. 9, no. 5 (80), June 1966, pp. 9–18.

economic stability and therefore to *security*; the image of Israel would suffer, and with it the capacity to attract military and diplomatic support. And this facet of Israel's economy is linked to the special characteristic of her development from the outset—dependence on an import surplus.

(c) BALANCE OF PAYMENTS

Israel has been beset by a persistent deficit in the current account of her balance of payments. Both imports and exports grew markedly throughout the period 1949–68. Yet the initial trade gap of $220 million was never reduced; on the contrary it widened steadily until 1964. Four phases are evident from the data: the import surplus ranged from $260 million to $360 million between 1950 and 1956; it stabilized around $330 million from 1957 to 1960; there was a very sharp increase in the early 1960s, to the danger point of $565 million in 1964; and then, under the impact of *mitun*, it declined somewhat. It rose sharply once more in 1967 (the spiral continuing in 1968, 1969, and 1970, largely because of massive defence imports). At the same time, the quantum of trade increased enormously, more than twenty-five times in nineteen years (1949–68) for exports and, significantly, only seven-fold for imports.[1]

The geographic pattern of imports and exports also changed markedly over time. The Middle East had supplied 15 per cent of Palestine's imports in the 1930s and more than half during the Second World War; this link was abruptly terminated in 1948. The United States quickly emerged as a major source of goods and services, providing 35 to 45 per cent of Israel's imports until 1953; this was largely due to the requisite of many American grants and loans, a key source of import finance, that the benefits be 'tied', that is, purchased in the US. The share of the United States declined after 1953; it stabilized around 33 per cent until 1961, rose to 37 per cent the next year, and then fell steadily to little more than one-fourth of all Israeli imports. With the onset of German Reparations in 1953 the importance of Western Europe increased dramatically; it jumped from 25 per cent to 45 per cent and remained almost constant until 1961. The United Kingdom share ranged from 9 to 13 per cent until 1960 and then moved swiftly to about 20 per cent of Israel's imports. By the early 1960s, then, the European Common Market and the Free Trade Area accounted for more than half of all imports, a key to Israel's efforts to secure entry into the European Economic Community. That concentration was even greater by 1968.

The states of Eastern Europe were important in the early years only,

[1] See Appendix Table 1 for further details.

largely because of the widespread use of clearing agreements in the absence of sufficient foreign exchange reserves. By 1952 their share had declined to less than 2 per cent and remained at that marginal level thereafter. Asia and Africa, too, were peripheral, hovering between 5 and 7 per cent from 1953 onwards. And Latin America has always been a negligible factor in Israel's imports. In short, Western Europe, including the United Kingdom, and North America have supplied almost 90 per cent of all Israel's imports since 1953. Using a slightly different breakdown, the OECD area supplied between 35 and 40 per cent of her imports from 1958 to 1963, the sterling area between 15 and 20 per cent, and the dollar area between 30 and 35 per cent.[1]

The pattern of export trade reveals some notable differences. The share of the United Kingdom, which had been the largest recipient of Palestine exports during the Mandate, declined precipitously in 1950 and steadily thereafter, from almost a third to less than one-eighth of Israeli exports by 1968. The United States (and Canada) filled part of that gap, especially in the early fifties, but after 1956 it accounted for barely one-sixth of those exports; and there was always a substantial import surplus. Israel's largest market by far has been Western Europe. Even before the project aid conditions of German Reparations it received a third of Israeli exports. Thereafter it rose rapidly to about 50 per cent and remained at that high level. No less striking, perhaps, has been the rapid growth of exports to the countries of Asia, Africa, and Oceania; their proportionate share almost quadrupled between 1955 and 1964—and continued to rise in the late 1960s, while their proportionate share of Israel's imports remained near-constant.[2]

Two themes stand out in the combined trade data. Israel's markets are more diversified than her sources of imports, with an increasingly important Afro-Asian component. Secondly, Israel has a large adverse trade balance with the US, and less so with the UK, while her balance is favourable with Afro-Asia, Western Europe, and Eastern Europe.

Citrus fruits and polished diamonds have been pre-eminent in Israel's export trade. In 1949 their combined share of exports exceeded 80 per cent; it remained above 60 per cent until 1958 and was still half the total in 1968. The share of diamonds has grown steadily, as with other industrial exports, notably textiles and clothing, foodstuffs, and chemicals. The services component, too, has grown over the years, from 36 per cent in 1958 to 46 per cent in 1966. The two largest items are transportation, which grew from $35 million in 1958 to $115 million in 1965, and tourism, which has escalated even more sharply—from $5.5 million in 1957 to $53 million in 1963, to an estimated $100 million in the twentieth year of independence.[3]

[1] See Appendix Table 2 for further details.
[2] See Appendix Table 3 for further details.
[3] CBS, *SAI*, various issues.

(d) IMPORT SURPLUS AND FOREIGN AID

Israel was compelled to finance her rapid economic growth by a massive import surplus of foreign exchange assets. The existence of the deficit and the ways in which it was offset impinge on Israel's foreign policy, linking economic capability to the foreign policy system as a whole. The size of her import surplus and its relative importance in the total resources at the disposal of the Israeli economy are very substantial indeed (see Table 9).

TABLE 9

TOTAL RESOURCES AVAILABLE TO THE ISRAELI ECONOMY 1950-1968

(£I million at current prices)

	Total Available Resources	GNP	Import Surplus	Import Surplus as % of Total Available Resources	Import Surplus as % of GNP
1950	576	458	118	20·5	25·7
1951	844	698	146	17·3	20·9
1952	1,344	1,044	300	22·3	28·7
1953	1,675	1,314	361	21·6	27·5
1954	2,161	1,725	436	20·2	25·3
1955	2,713	2,134	579	21·3	27·1
1956	3,287	2,553	734	22·3	28·8
1957	3,690	2,961	729	19·8	24·6
1958	4,143	3,391	752	18·2	22·2
1959	4,634	3,919	715	15·4	18·2
1960	5,143	4,364	779	15·1	17·9
1961	6,243	5,242	1,001	16·0	19·1
1962	7,914	6,358	1,556	19·7	24·5
1963	9,134	7,527	1,607	17·6	21·3
1964	10,777	8,691	2,086	19·3	23·9
1965	12,215	10,202	2,013	16·5	19·7
1966	13,141	11,500	1,641	12·5	14·3
1967	13,751	11,972	1,779	12·9	14·9
1968	16,807	13,987	2,820	16·8	20·2

Source: The data in the first three columns to 1965 are taken from Halevi and Klinov-Malul, op. cit., Appendix Table 1, pp. 284–5. These, in turn, are derived from the CBS, *SAI 1966*, no. 17, Table F/1, pp. 156–7 and other primary sources. The figures for 1966–8 are from *SAI 1970*, no. 21, Table E/1, p. 137.

Viewed in terms of current market prices, Israel's import surplus did not fall below 15 per cent of total available resources from 1950 to 1968 except for 1966 and 1967; in six of those sixteen years it exceeded 20 per cent. The most acute phase was 1952–6; thereafter, the surplus was never larger than one-fifth. Measured as a proportion of GNP, the deficit was more than 25 per cent in six years and more than 20 per cent in all but six years. For the period as a whole the aggregate data and proportions are as follows:

(£1 million at current prices)
Total Available Resources   120,192
GNP   100,040
Import Surplus   20,152
Import Surplus as Average
    Annual Percentage of Total Available Resources   18·2
Import Surplus as Average
    Annual Percentage of GNP   22·4

Professor Patinkin observed that his figures for 1950–8 are based on 'the official—and usually overvalued—rate of exchange of the [Israel] pound. If a more realistic value were to be used, the relative importance of the import surplus would appear even greater.' He suggests a revaluation of imports at 20 per cent more than the official rate for the period as a whole, while acknowledging the impossibility of getting an accurate estimate of the degree of undervaluation. Using slightly different figures—and measured at constant prices—Patinkin arrived at the following aggregates for the period 1950–8:

Total Resources   14,753 (1952 £1 million)
GNP   12,177
Import Surplus   2,576

This suggests an Average Annual Import Surplus of 17·4 per cent of Total Resources and an Average Annual Import Surplus of 20·3 per cent of GNP, both a little lower than the proportions noted.[1]

Whichever basis of calculation is used, the Israeli import surplus comprised a large part of her total resources. Thus her sustained economic growth and relatively high standard of living were heavily dependent on an assured and steady capital inflow. The external financing of that import surplus took two forms—net unilateral transfers, including governmental, institutional, and private flows, and capital transfers, governmental and private, long-term and short-term.[2]

The most striking feature is the quantum of unilateral transfers, both in absolute size and relative to the import surplus as a whole. Apart from the first three years (1949–51), they did not fall below 61 per cent of the current account deficit throughout the period under inquiry; and of the total deficit of $6 billion from 1949 to 1965 these transfers accounted for 70 per cent. The balance was covered by net capital imports

[1] Op. cit., pp. 92–3.
[2] The following analysis of foreign aid to finance the import surplus is based upon Halevi and Klinov-Malul, op. cit., pp. 154–67.

almost entirely long-term; indeed there was a net *outflow* of short-term capital from 1958 onwards and for the period as a whole.[1]

Viewed in terms of the *sources* of finance for Israel's import surplus, two themes predominate.[2] One is the extraordinary role played by a private community, world Jewry. The other is the almost total dependence of Israel for external financial aid on 'the West', comprising world Jewry, the United States and West Germany. The supporting role of Diaspora Jewry in Israel's economic development (and, thereby, in her military and foreign policy capability) is unique in modern international politics, perhaps in all world politics; it is also significant and at times dramatic. Of the $6 billion cumulative import surplus to 1965, world Jewry covered 59 per cent for the period as a whole. In the early years its share was overwhelming. Only in four years was it less than half. Indeed no less than 60 per cent of the $3·5 billion provided by world Jewry from 1949 to 1965 took the form of unilateral transfers—one indication among many of an extraordinary sense of kinship and of concern with the survival of Israel.

Jewish financial assistance to Israel is of four types: private transfers; institutional transfers; the proceeds from the sale of State of Israel Bonds; and private investment. Net *private transfers*, virtually all of them gifts in money and goods, came to $750 million; they averaged $35 million annually from 1955 to 1960 and then escalated sharply to almost $100 million a year in 1964 and 1965. *Institutional transfers* are concentrated on the United Jewish Appeal (UJA), the centralized annual fund drive of world Jewry, with lesser sums donated to the Joint Distribution Committee (JDC), *Hadassah*, the various universities, and other philanthropic and welfare organizations. Taken together, the institutional transfers amounted to $1·4 billion from 1949 to 1965, an annual average of $82 million, steadily maintained, with one major fluctuation —$117 million in 1954 as a result of a Special Campaign of the UJA. The most notable outpouring of funds, however, came in the wake of the Six Day War, when an unparalleled expression of identification led to Emergency Fund donations estimated at $300 to $500 million.[3] (And that volume of direct Jewish gifts was maintained in the years 1968–70.)

The first *State of Israel Bonds* campaign was started in the United States in May 1951 with an objective of half a billion dollars. By 1968 some $1·2 billion in bonds had been sold, the major source of funds for Israel's economic development. As a measure of its importance, world

[1] The details are to be found ibid., Table 57, p. 155: 'Financing the Import Surplus: 1949–65'.

[2] See Appendix Table 4 for further details.

[3] Various North American newspapers cited figures of this magnitude in their accounts of world Jewry's support for Israel during the 1967 conflict. As noted earlier, official remittances by Americans (alone) to Israel between June and September 1967 increased by $210 million.

Jewry accounted for 68·7 per cent of the total long-term capital transfers to Israel from 1949 to 1965—and Bond sales comprised almost 70 per cent of that inflow of Jewish funds. Long-term *private investment* has been persistently encouraged, but commercial loans to Israeli enterprises and direct investment in Israeli firms have remained an underdeveloped source of finance for the import surplus, about $750 million until 1965.

A much-publicized effort was made on the eve of Israel's twentieth anniversary to enlist the active participation of Jewish business communities throughout the world. Many pledges were made at the Jerusalem Economic Conference in April 1968, attended by almost 500 prominent Jews in industry and trade from four continents: a $100 million investment company; direct participation in management; the development of markets for Israeli products, such as food, furniture, plastics, and textiles; advice on design, packaging, and cost-reducing practices for Israel exports; assistance in the export of Israeli engineering, scientific, and technical services; the recruitment of managerial talent for Israeli enterprises; and on-the-job training for Israeli personnel.[1] All this was designed to broaden the base of co-operative endeavour between world Jewry and Israel by altering the historic emphasis on gifts and bonds.

There have been various types of US Government economic aid to Israel—grants, hard-currency loans, soft-currency loans, and technical assistance. Altogether Washington contributed $848 million from 1949 to 1965, approximately one-seventh of the cumulative Israeli import surplus. It began with *Export–Import Bank loans* in 1949, one for $100 million, another for $35 million, to finance the import of machinery and equipment for the development of agriculture, manufacturing, transportation, and housing. Apart from the direct economic benefits, these initial acts constituted an expression of confidence in the new state. Further hard-currency loans on easy repayment terms followed in 1957 ($24·2 million), 1961 ($25 million) and 1963 ($11 million). Direct *Grants-in-Aid* began in 1951 and amounted to $185 million within three years, with smaller grants continuing until 1962. Like the first hard-currency loans, their importance lay primarily in the *timing*, for the period 1949–54 was the most precarious and onerous in Israel's economic growth; they helped to fill an enormous gap before German Reparations appeared on the scene.[2]

[1] The Jerusalem Economic Conference was discussed atl ength in the entire Israeli press in April 1968. See the *Jerusalem Post Weekly* reports in the issues of 8, 15 and 22 April 1968. See also *Weekly News Bulletin*, Jerusalem, 2–8 April, 9–15 April, and 16–22 April 1968. (A follow-up Economic Conference was held in July 1969 to plan further involvement by Diaspora Jewry. The (controversial) record was assessed by David Krivine, 'The Jewish Partnership in Israel's Industry', *Jerusalem Post*, 24 Oct. 1969.)

[2] US Government aid went through four phases until the mid-sixties. From 1949 to 1951 it took the exclusive form of hard-currency loans. From 1952 to 1954 grants predominated. Then, in 1955, soft-currency loans were introduced. These included

West German payments to Israel totalled $1·73 billion from 1953 to
1965; this was the equivalent of 36 per cent of the cumulative Israeli
import surplus during that period and 28·8 per cent of the import
surplus from 1949 to 1965. It was, then, more than double the United
States' share in external Israeli finance. Those payments took two
forms, reparations, and restitution to individuals for crimes committed
by the Nazi régime against Jews and Jewry. The Reparations Agreement, a major Israeli foreign policy decision to be explored in depth
later, was signed in Luxembourg in September 1952. In essence it
provided for direct payment by the Federal German Republic to the
Government of Israel and Jewish institutions of a sum amounting to
$821 million over a twelve-year period; the funds were tied to German
products, except for fuel. Israel was to transfer $107 million to the
Jewish Claims Conference for distribution abroad and was to grant to
the Jewish Agency the Israeli pound equivalent of 18 per cent of the
remaining $714 million. An Israel Purchasing Mission in Cologne
served as the central funnel for the purchase and dispatch of goods from
Germany. Restitution payments, by contrast, were made by German
State Governments to individual residents of Israel in the form of
pensions or lump-sum grants for maltreatment. The flow of reparations
stabilized at about $80 million a year from 1954 to 1961, then declined
sharply and terminated with a payment of $16·7 million in 1965.
Restitution funds began modestly but rose steadily to a peak of $143
million in 1963; thereafter the flow declined somewhat but approached
that sum once more in 1968.

A great debate unfolded in Israel in 1965–6 about the manner in
which German Reparations were used, apart from the question of moral
cost that they entailed. In the context of Israel's need to finance the
deficit in her balance of payments, however, there can be no doubt
about the benefits. German unilateral transfers exceeded $100 million
every year from 1955 to 1965. The total of $1,736 million constituted
almost half of the total unilateral transfers from all sources between
1953 and 1965. Without German transfers or an adequate substitute—
which may or may not have been forthcoming—there would have been
a staggering uncovered deficit in Israel's balance of payments, with
consequences for her trade and economic development generally, as
well as for the stability of her currency; that is, for her economic
capability in the largest sense. At any rate this continuing concern led
Israel's decision-makers to try to lessen the adverse effects of the end of

PL 480 food surpluses and Development Loan Fund assistance for the purchase of
equipment, all repayable in Israeli currency and therefore no burden on Israel's
foreign exchange reserves. From 1962 onwards there was a conspicuous return to
low-interest hard-currency loans under the aegis of the Agency for International
Development (AID), the successor to the DLF. By then, too, Israel ceased to be
regarded as 'underdeveloped' in terms of the United States aid programme.

reparations by concluding an economic aid (loan) agreement with Bonn in 1966, for $37·6 million. This was renewed for similar sums in 1967 and 1968.[1]

The economic implications of Israel's persistent and large import surplus have been much debated.[2] At one extreme is Professor Patinkin, who concluded that this 'may well be considered to be the major failure of Israel economic policy during the period ... 1950–58'.[3] Much more sanguine and optimistic are Drs. Halevi and Klinov-Malul. Writing on the basis of the known data to 1965, they observed: 'the import surplus provided substantial additional resources'; further, 'it appears reasonable that Israel will be able to mobilize foreign unilateral and capital transfers for many years after the next five-year period during which some major unilateral transfers may decline drastically'.[4]

The optimism of Halevi and Klinov-Malul would seem to have been vindicated by subsequent events. Israel's foreign currency reserves stood at an all-time high of $636 million in 1965. They fell by $20 million the following year despite the improved trade balance, as more dollars were used to service the growing external debt. But in 1967 the net reserves rose by $82·4 million to almost $700 million, despite the larger defence imports accompanying the Six Day War: the reason was a massive influx of donations and the receipts from Israel Bonds sales.[5]

[1] The 1967 agreement provided for the same amount and the 1968 agreement for $35 million. *Jerusalem Post*, 22 July 1968.

[2] See D. Creamer et al., *Israel's National Income 1950–54*, Falk Project and CBS Special Series, no. 57, Jerusalem, 1957; Patinkin, op. cit., ch. 3, B, and 5; Halevi and Klinov-Malul, op. cit., pp. 167–75; and various articles in the *Economic Quarterly* (Hebrew), Jerusalem.

[3] Op. cit., p. 106.

[4] This expectation derived from their speculation about future sources of external finance. They noted the various stages in Israel's balance-of-payments position: the liquidation of reserves during 1949–51 in order to secure a minimal volume of imports; the sharp decline in the import surplus during 1952 and 1953 because of the lack of funds, and a lesser decline in 1954 with the expansion of exports; the rapid increase in the deficit from 1955 to 1957, largely under the impact of the Sinai Campaign and its aftermath; and, from 1958 to 1964, a sharp escalation of the import surplus, along with an improvement in the foreign exchange reserves of Israel. They assumed that certain unilateral transfers 'may be more or less permanent, or at least of fairly long duration', especially private gifts and institutional transfers. They acknowledged the end of United States grants and German Reparations but surmised that Israel Bonds 'will be sold for many years'. And as for private investment, they anticipated a minimum of $50 million a year 'for many years to come', perhaps up to three times that amount. Thus they foresaw a long-term inflow of $200 million to $350 million a year. The crucial point to emerge is that 'substantial import surpluses may continue to be a basic feature of the economy of Israel for many years to come' but this is no cause for alarm or even concern; the reserves and likely capital inflow would provide ample time for adjustment in the trade balance. Op. cit., pp. 172–5. (The quotation is on p. 174.) The same optimism was conveyed to the author as early as 1960 by Dr. Meir Merhav, another Israeli economist, then in the Research Department of the Bank of Israel.

[5] *Jerusalem Post*, 15 Jan. 1967, and *Jerusalem Post Weekly*, 22 Jan. 1968.

A year after the war the foreign exchange reserves reached $800 million.[1] In short, Israel entered the third decade of independence with a manageable balance-of-payments problem. (In 1970, however, grave concern was expressed by some Israeli economists and government officials as massive defence expenditures pushed the deficit in Israel's balance of payments well beyond $1 billion.)

(e) ECONOMIC AID AND FOREIGN POLICY

The consequences for her foreign policy of Israel's economic dependence on the West cannot be delineated in a mechanical one–one relationship; but they cannot be ignored. The most general formulation of the link between the economic variable and foreign policy was offered by Professor Patinkin.[2] The economic demand on Israel's foreign policy system, he declared, 'has been spasmodic and uneven in intensity. It has loomed large only *in extremis*, in the 1949–53 period, the most precarious in Israel's economic development. Once the survival problem was overcome, by 1953, it became less and less significant both in the awareness of government leaders and in the policy process. This is true of all states', he continued. 'Awareness of economic need is present only among a few and enters policy calculations only in dire circumstances. This is true for Israel, whose foreign trade represents 20 per cent of GNP. How much more true is it of other states, with a much smaller proportion.'

Patinkin specified four decisions or clusters of decisions in which Israel's economic conditions and/or aspirations constituted a demand on policy: the *General Foreign Policy Line 1949–53*; the decisions to seek and to accept *German Reparations*; the attempt to secure admission to the *Common Market*; and the policy of *barter agreements with East European states*. In the first phase, he remarked, there was a desperate need for aid to salvage a crisis economy. Israel suffered from a large adverse balance of trade and needed capital to absorb almost 700,000 immigrants, to supplement the grossly inadequate domestic food supply, and to secure raw materials for industry. During that period élite awareness of the economic factor was intense, in fact pervasive, because the survival of the state was at stake. Thus, much of Israel's foreign policy was geared to securing foreign aid, with energy being concentrated on the United States, as evident in the Export–Import Bank loans of 1949.

The German Reparations decisions of 1951 and 1952, Patinkin observed, were based on the recognition that a capital inflow was imperative, thus 'take it from the devil himself'. The Common Market decision, in his view, had mixed economic and political motives, among them the fact that Western Europe was a key market for Israeli

[1] *Jerusalem Post*, 22 Aug. 1968.   [2] Interview in Jerusalem, April 1966.

exports, especially citrus fruits; the quest for economic solvency was closely linked to the preservation of that market. And the barter agreements with Eastern Europe were made necessary by Israel's acute shortage of foreign exchange in the early fifties; as soon as conditions improved, however, this trade technique became expendable. In support of his thesis Patinkin noted that there was no evidence of an economic demand in such crucial decisions as the Sinai Campaign, the creation of an African presence, and policy towards Latin America, whose voting strength at the United Nations has always been important.

Using a narrower policy gauge, Professor Safran asserted a much more acute impact on Israel's external behaviour: dependence on foreign aid for economic development compelled Israel to shape her foreign policy with a view to maximizing external assistance; further, the dependence on UJA and other forms of aid by world Jewry has made it necessary to maintain friendly relations with states which have large aid-giving Jewish communities; and these two pressures converge on policies which avoid alienation of the United States.[1] No evidence was provided for the post-1953 period or indeed for any Israeli foreign policy decision.

Two former Directors-General of the Israel Foreign Ministry regarded the economic variable as secondary to political considerations in Israel's policy towards the United States.[2] Dr. Yahil termed aid a derivative element in the relationship. 'The importance of the United States for Israel lies in two factors', he declared. 'It is the leading world power and is basically friendly to Israel; and it has the largest bloc of world Jewry. All other considerations—economic aid, military aid, a security commitment, flow from these factors; they are elaborations, however important they may be in themselves.' A similar view was expressed by Shimon Peres, key figure in the Defence Ministry from 1953 to 1965 and later a prominent Israeli politician:[3] 'I don't think we looked upon Diaspora Jewry as an instrument [of economic aid] but as a target, that is, it was our first consideration in foreign policy calculations; whatever we did had to be based on the possible effects on local Jewry.' Furthermore, 'we want to be friendly with the United States in order to strengthen the link with American Jewry, not the other way around.'

For the early years, however, the primacy of economic aid in Israel's foreign policy was acknowledged by many. 'Aid and arms are the two main concerns of Israel in the international arena—in that order', said a Foreign Ministry official in 1960. 'The shift from non-identification to alignment with the United States in 1950 was motivated

[1] *The United States and Israel*, pp. 214–15, 221.
[2] Interviews with Dr. Haim Yahil and Arye Levavi in Jerusalem, July and May 1966, respectively.
[3] Interview in Tel Aviv, July 1966.

primarily by the fear of aid being seriously reduced, both from the US Government and from American Jews, who disliked neutralism.'[1] Another senior diplomat described Israel's alignment with the West as being motivated, until 1955, by the economic aid factor.[2]

Two of Israel's most prominent decision-makers affirmed its decisive role in blunt emotive words. Foreign Minister Moshe Sharett told a group of correspondents in London in March 1952: 'the crux of our problem is production. Our balance of trade is staggeringly adverse. . . . The inordinately wide gap between imports and exports creates a state of high economic tension characterized by acute shortages and strict rationing.'[3] Many years later David Horowitz, the perennial Governor of the Bank of Israel, recalled:[4] 'The main issue until the end of 1951 was supply; the economy was in a precarious state; every ship was important, for the reserve of bread in the country was sufficient for one week only; why—because we did not have foreign exchange.' The turning point was 1952, he added. Three vital new sources of foreign exchange were found and began to fill the gap—Israel Bonds, United States' grants, and German Reparations, all from 'the West'.

There is virtual unanimity in the *German Reparations* case. All those noted above expressed the view that economics was the pre-eminent demand in the Israeli decisions on that issue—Patinkin and Safran among the academics, Horowitz, Levavi, Shimoni, and Yahil among the civil servants, and Peres and Sharett among the politicians. So too did Prime Minister Levi Eshkol, a Director-General of the Prime Minister's Office, Ya'acov Herzog, a former Assistant Director-General of the Foreign Office in charge of economic affairs, Moshe Bartur, a large group of lesser officials, and many journalists.[5] No one termed economic pressure irrelevant. The overwhelming majority defined its role as decisive. A small number took pains to assert the existence of a 'political' factor. In Levavi's words, 'Ben Gurion, possibly others as well, had a sense that Germany would rise again and be powerful and that it would be unwise for Israel to ignore the future.' Ben Gurion's acute sense of history makes this plausible. And Dr. Yahil recalled Ben Gurion's comment to him the day the Luxembourg Agreement was signed, on 10 September 1952: 'This is a great day—a turning point for Israel's political future.'[6]

---

[1] Interview in Jerusalem.

[2] Interview with Ya'acov Shimoni in Jerusalem, Aug. 1960.

[3] *Yediot La-Netziguyot* (News to Representatives), Ministry for Foreign Affairs, Jerusalem, no. 473, 14 March 1952, p. 1.   [4] Interview in Jerusalem, June 1966.

[5] Interviews in Israel during 1960 and 1965–6.

[6] Interview in Jerusalem, March 1970. Other persons were sceptical of its importance then, though acknowledging that the political variable influenced the later decision to accept diplomatic relations with West Germany (1965). Ben Gurion's image of Germany will be noted in ch. 12 in the context of his View of the World and in ch. 16 (b) and (c), where some Israeli decisions on Germany are examined.

The second decision on which a substantial consensus exists about the primacy of the economic demand is the *Common Market*. Eshkol cited it along with German Reparations. Horowitz referred to it as 'the most striking example of direct influence by the economic factor on foreign policy decisions'. Bartur acknowledged that political and security advantages were in the minds of some, but 'the thrust, the main drive to association with the Common Market, was economic'. Some dissented, however. To Levavi, for example, there were two other stimuli: deep cultural attachments to Europe, which Israel wished to sustain; and the need to strengthen a network of reliable friendships for an exposed Israel and, hopefully, to create a feedback into the Near East, that is, to bring European pressure on the Arabs to make peace. In short, 'the economic factor was neither exclusive nor paramount'. The Market was viewed as an economic wedge for entry into 'Europe', with larger objectives in mind. Peres emphasized the *gestalt* character of important foreign policy decisions; in this issue as in most the security goal predominated.[1]

The policy of *barter agreements with East European states* was infrequently mentioned in this context. But few would disagree with Bartur, its architect, who indicated two demands: economic necessity, in the form of a scarcity of foreign exchange; and the need to create a substantive basis for Israel's ties with the Soviet bloc during the period of non-identification. In any event it belongs to the 'economic crisis' phase of Israel's foreign policy—as do the Reparations decision and the extreme sensitivity to US aid in the early 1950s. Thereafter it was American power, its friendship for Israel, and the presence of a large Jewish community which shaped Israel's policy towards that super power.

There was one noteworthy foreign economic policy decision after the Six Day War—the abrupt devaluation of the Israel pound in the wake of the devaluation of sterling on 18 November 1967. Finance Minister Sapir was candid and succinct in explaining the decision: 'to my mind, we had no choice—Israel exports to Britain constitute a sizeable part of all our exports. . . . If we had not adapted our rate of exchange, our exports would have incurred great damage, both directly . . . and indirectly.'[2] The benefits of devaluation were imperceptible, more in the nature of preventing deterioration in the trade balance than positive

---

[1] Interview in Tel Aviv, June 1966.

[2] Government Press Office, *Press Bulletin*, 2 Jan. 1968. On the day of devaluation Sapir told the *Knesset*, 'The Government's sole intention was to neutralize the effect of the British devaluation. Had we not done so, an estimated $250 million worth of exports to sterling and associated countries in 1968 would have been endangered, and the steady employment of some 25,000 workers in export industry thrown into jeopardy.' Not all Israeli parties, newspapers, or academic economists were convinced. See *Jerusalem Post Weekly*, 27 Nov. 1967, and *Weekly News Bulletin*, Jerusalem, 14–20 Nov. 1967.

improvement. In any event there was no discernible link with foreign policy acts.

All this suggests the following proposition: the economic variable has been of marginal potency in Israel's foreign policy decisions as a whole during the first two decades; it was pre-eminent only in two specific issues, Reparations and the Common Market; the crucial demands have been political–strategic, that is, security in the broadest sense. Patinkin's basic thesis appears to be correct.

The demographic imperative, by contrast, has been a major demand in Israel's foreign policy system. As scholar–diplomat Shabtai Rosenne observed:[1] 'immigration is the *raison d'être* of the State of Israel, the answer to the general problem of continued national existence and the preservation of the national cultural ideals. . . . The preservation of conditions—political and physical—which will make this immigration feasible is therefore a major factor in Israel's policy. . . . The impact of immigration on Israel's foreign policy is . . . felt at every turn.'[2]

Demography in the Israel context has several dimensions. One relates to the Jewishness of the state and will be explored later. Another, as noted, refers to 'military manpower' and the security nexus. A third impinges on economic capability, and in that sense economics may be regarded as a persistent demand in the foreign policy process, affecting decisions on the Soviet Union, South Africa, Argentine, and others.[3] In the more conventional meaning, however, the economic variable has been important only in the crisis phase of the early years, apart from the Common Market.

By the twentieth anniversary of independence the economic outlook had begun to improve. This was greatly assisted by the rallying of world Jewry to Israel's cause, in two forms: the replenishment of Israel's foreign exchange resources, and the pledge of even more active support and involvement, at the first Jerusalem Economic Conference. Israel's economic capability had been amply adequate to her foreign policy requirements until 1968.

(*f*) ECONOMIC AND MILITARY CAPABILITY: AN OVERVIEW

What was the relative capability of Israel and her Arab adversaries to supply defence needs and to sustain military strength *vis-à-vis* 'the permanent enemy'? Estimates for key indicators in 1969, as combined

---

[1] 'Basic Elements of Israel's Foreign Policy', *India Quarterly*, pp. 337–8.

[2] For an informative analysis of that interrelationship in the first five years of independence see Ernest Stock, 'Immigration as a Factor in Foreign Policy in the 1950s', unpublished paper delivered to the Fifth World Congress of Jewish Studies, Jerusalem, Aug. 1969. Attention is focused on Israeli decision-makers' images of *aliya* as the goal of security and economic needs, as well as of ideological commitment.

[3] To be discussed in ch. 11 (*b*) below.

in Table 10, facilitate an overview of economic capability at the beginning of the third decade of the conflict and provide the basis for forecasting relative economic power to achieve foreign policy and security objectives in the foreseeable future.

TABLE 10

ESTIMATES OF POPULATION, GROSS NATIONAL PRODUCT, AND
GROSS INDUSTRIAL PRODUCT FOR 1969: ISRAEL AND THE
ARAB STATES

	Population (millions)	Gross Industrial Product (millions $)	Per Capita GNP ($)	GNP (millions $)
Syria	5·98	150	210	1,250
Lebanon	2·64	190	530	1,400
Jordan*	1·72	50	230	400
Iraq	8·87	290†	280	2,500
Total, 4 States	19·21	680	290‡	5,550
Egypt	32·47	1,180	175	5,600
Total, all 5 Arab States	51·68	1,860	215	11,150
Israel	2·88	1,350	1,650	4,750
Ratio Israel:Egypt	1:11·27	1:0·87	1:0·11	1:1·18
Ratio Israel:4 Others	1: 6·67	1:0·50	1:0·18	1:1·17
Ratio Israel:5 Arab States	1:17·94	1:1·38	1:0·13	1:2·35

Sources: Dr. Eliezer Shefer, 'Israel—The Economic Power of the Middle East', Yediot Aharonot (Tel Aviv), 20 February 1970. The data are Shefer's own estimates—extrapolation from past statistics. They acquire credence from his reputation for knowledge and reliability on Middle East economics.

* Excluding Judea and Samaria (West Bank)
† Excluding oil
‡ Average

The 1969 data illuminate the relative capability of the protagonists to sustain a massive defence burden (as specified in Table 7 above). Modern war is waged mainly with industrial products, and the estimated superiority of all five Near East Core Arab states combined over Israel was only 38 per cent; Egypt alone, and the other four Arab states alone, had a smaller industrial product than Israel. Since the industrial structure of all these Arab countries is less developed (fewer sophisticated industries, lower technological level), Israel was, in 1969, probably superior to all of them combined in terms of industrial capability to sustain a war effort. Moreover, as the share of exports in Israel's economy and, particularly, her industry, is higher than in the Arab states, she was, in 1969, relatively less dependent upon foreign military aid; that is, she has an increasingly greater economic capability to supply her military needs. The more developed industrial base also enhances military capability in the strict sense, because domestic industry can produce military hardware under greater secrecy, with the consequent benefit of surprise in terms of quantity and quality.

If access to capital imports is included in the concept of 'economic capability', as it should be, then the gap between Israel and the five Arab states is reduced even further. Total 'normal' capital imports of Israel are about $600–$700 million per annum—equal to those of the five Arab countries combined. Furthermore, Israel's capital imports have fewer political strings attached than those of her adversaries. This further increases Israel's capability to pursue foreign policy and security goals. Conversely, the lower economic level of the Arab states may enable them to sustain a war burden for a long time. .

Egypt and Jordan were especially hard-hit by the Six Day War: the former lost the income from the Suez Canal, from oil in Sinai, and from tourism—together some $350 million annually; the latter lost the West Bank, which had accounted for 40 per cent of its GNP, and its main source of foreign exchange—tourism. Their economic capability was thus severely reduced; and it was only partly compensated by financial assistance from the Arab oil states—$250 million to Egypt and $100 million to Jordan. There were also direct losses due to war destruction: evacuation from the Suez Canal area of 750,000 inhabitants; and severe damage to Jordan's area of most intensive agriculture in the Jordan Valley.

One other statistical comparison is pertinent, for it reveals the limited Egyptian economic capability: while Israel was able to invest 23 per cent of her GNP ($1,100 million) in 1969, at the same time that she spent 21 per cent of her GNP on Defence, Egypt's gross investment was an estimated 20 per cent lower than her defence expenditures; and the investment of the five Arab states combined was only $1,800 million.

The assessment of relative economic capability in 1969 may be summarized as follows:

1. Economic capability to sustain *foreign policy* goals is greater in Israel, due to her lesser dependence on politically-conditioned aid from abroad.
2. Economic capability to supply *defence requirements* is about equal, if capital imports are included in the equation.
3. Economic capability to support *military capability* is higher in Israel, because of a more highly developed industrial structure and greater independence from foreign supplies.
4. Growth trends and a broader base for future Israeli economic growth tend to narrow the gap in industrial production still further.
5. In all respects Israel's economic capability is greater than that of

Egypt alone, and of all four other Arab states combined. Based upon past trends and performance, and leaving aside massive intrusions of aid from a super power, Israel's superiority in economic capability seems assured in the near future.[1]

In a pioneering effort to define military capability with precision, Professor Klaus Knorr offered the following equation: War Potential = Armed Forces+Economic Capacity+Administrative Competence+ Will to Fight.[2] As demonstrated in the last two chapters, Israel is superior to her Arab adversaries in all four components of this equation. Thus, if War Potential is equated, for Israel, with *Survival Potential*, it may be concluded that her capacity to survive in the long-term conflict with her neighbours is beyond doubt—barring massive intrusion by a super power, with air and sea power and large numbers of combat troops.[3]

---

[1] I am indebted to Dr. Meir Merhav for drawing my attention to the Shefer analysis and for his own valuable insights into the economic capability–military capability nexus.

[2] *The War Potential of Nations*, ch. 3, 4. See also his *Military Power and Potential*, Heath, Lexington, Mass., 1970.

[3] A similar conclusion was reached by Nadav Safran, in his *From War to War*, with a greater emphasis on manpower resources for the Armed Forces and on Defence Expenditures.

CHAPTER 6

Political Structure

The politics of Israel are fascinating and complex, but they have not been well served by scholars.[1] Moreover, the links between Israel's political system and her external behaviour have been all but ignored. Indeed the same is true of most empirical studies of foreign policy.[2]

A political system comprises three broad strands: political *culture*, political *socialization*, and political *structure*. In foreign policy analysis there are three pertinent aspects of *political culture*. One is the set of beliefs or ideas espoused by decision-makers; these constitute an 'attitudinal prism' which predisposes them to certain images of their environment; they will be explored in that context. Ideologies also influence the images held by interest groups and competing élites and thus their foreign policy demands; these demands will be explored in the following two chapters. The carriers of a political culture also merit attention in a study of foreign policy; in Israel they are parties *par excellence*.

Political socialization refers to the ways in which members of society learn about their political world, acquire a sense of identity, and participate in its activities, as consumer of authoritative rules, producer of demands, and supportive element for the system as a whole. Socialization provides insight into the 'World View' of decision-makers and will be analysed in the setting of Israel's foreign policy élite.[3] The most

[1] There are a few noteworthy exceptions: Nadav Safran, *The United States and Israel*, Leonard J. Fein, *Politics in Israel*, Little, Brown, Boston, 1967, and S. N. Eisenstadt, *Israeli Society*, ch. 9. There are also some instructive journal articles: Benjamin Akzin, 'The Role of Parties in Israeli Democracy', *Journal of Politics*, 17, 4, Nov. 1955, pp. 507–45, and 'The Knesset', *International Social Science Journal*, 13, 4, 1961; Amitai Etzioni, 'Alternative Ways to Democracy: The Example of Israel', *Political Science Quarterly*, 74, 2, 1959, pp. 196–214; three articles by Emanuel Gutmann: 'Citizen Participation in Political Life: Israel', *International Social Science Journal*, 12, 1, 1960, pp. 53–62; 'Some Observations on Politics and Parties in Israel', *India Quarterly*, 17, 1, Jan.–March 1961, pp. 3–29; and 'Israel', *Journal of Politics*, 25, 3, Aug. 1963, pp. 703–17; A. Arian, 'Voting and Ideology in Israel', *Midwest Journal of Political Science*, x, 1966, pp. 265–87; A. Antonovsky, 'Classifications of Forms, Political Ideologies and the Man in the Street', *The Public Opinion Quarterly* (Princeton), xxx, 1966, pp. 269ff.; and M. Seliger, 'Positions and Dispositions in Israeli Politics', *Government and Opposition*, 3, 4, Autumn 1968, pp. 465–84.

[2] For a thoughtful essay on that relationship see H. A. Kissinger, 'Domestic Structure and Foreign Policy', in *Conditions of World Order, Daedalus*, xcv, Spring 1966, pp. 503–29.

[3] See Chapter 11 below for a discussion of this facet of élite perceptions, as well as of their 'attitudinal prism'.

direct link between political system and external behaviour is the *political structure* of the state under analysis. Structure comprises the constitutional matrix in which decisions are authorized, the institutions which make and apply rules or decisions, and, in pluralist, competitive polities like Israel, the party and electoral systems.

(a) THE PARTY SYSTEM AND COALITION GOVERNMENT

'The beginning of wisdom in Israeli politics', remarked one writer, 'lies in recognizing the political party's pre-eminence.'[1] Another, Professor Safran, discerned four complementary thrusts to party dominance: multiplicity; emotional intensity of members; range of interests and control; and highly centralized leadership.[2] The line of argument is persuasive.

There were almost as many party lists for the seventh *Knesset* elections (1969) as there were for the first (1949). Multiplicity can be traced in the pre-State period to Jewish demography: a territorial constituency system was impractical because of the dispersion of the Zionist electorate. Indeed any electoral principle other than proportional representation (PR) weakened the national movement. The result was a crystallization of Zionist factions into parties, with their own leaders, vested interests, ideologies, rhetoric, oligarchy, etc. Parties, in short, preceded the State: in 1948 they merely shifted their theatre of operations to the State of Israel. It was natural to continue proportional representation in the new state. In fact it would have been unthinkable to do anything else.

The persistence of many parties was strengthened by what Safran calls the 'multi-axial' division in four spheres of policy:

 (i) the place of religion in the state, dividing the religious parties from all others, though with shades of difference in emphasis;
 (ii) socio-economic principles, separating Left and Right parties, but with interesting deviations from the European pattern because of the special position of the *Histadrut* and the *kibbutz* movement;
(iii) foreign policy, ranging from the New Communists' Moscow orthodoxy through *Maki*'s attachment to Moscow until 1965, *Mapam*'s eroding pro-Soviet neutralism, *Ahdut Ha'avodah*'s verbal commitment to non-alignment, and *Mapai*'s pro-Western neutralism, to the *Herut* and General Zionist preference for alignment with the West; and
(iv) territorial claims, ranging from *Maki*'s opposition to a *Jewish* state and *Mapam*'s espousal of a confederation with Jordan to *Herut*'s irredentism—reunion of 'both sides of the Jordan'—with varying shades of pragmatism in between.

[1] Fein, op. cit., p. 67.
[2] *The United States and Israel*; ch. VIII provides an illuminating analysis of party politics in Israel.

These policy conflicts express differences in ideology which, in turn, sustain emotional ties to a party. Zionism appeared at a time when many Jews were questioning traditional religious beliefs; the failure to assimilate led to a search for new ideas and a new focus of identity. Zionism was a superb outlet, providing a substitute faith for secularist Jews. To it were added social and economic ideas current in Europe in the late nineteenth century. The result was total, passionate, and explosive commitment to Zionist—and, later, Israeli—parties. Party conflict acquired the character of religious strife. Ideological purity became the norm. In Safran's words, passion, oratory, and zeal 'are but the burnt offerings made by the parties to their ideological deities as ritual homage. . . . And, from a more distant past, the fury and splendid invective of the prophets seem to echo again in the land.'[1]

The party's pre-eminence was strengthened by the tangible services it provided to members, sometimes indirectly, for example, through *Mapai*'s control of the *Histadrut*: these included youth clubs, newspapers, medical care, housing, agricultural co-operatives or communes, and even employment. Indeed most parties were self-contained and intricately knit communities within the larger Jewish society. The result has been a degree of party loyalty greater than in any other competitive political system. And within that system the authority of party leaders has been maintained by PR; the electorate votes for lists, not candidates, and lists are determined by the leadership group. Thus members of parliament (MKs) and those aspiring to a seat in the *Knesset* are almost entirely dependent on the party élite.

Multiplicity and party dominance led inevitably to coalition government and the appearance of structural instability: there were fifteen governments in nineteen years, all of them with three or more parties. At the centre, in terms of ideology and importance, has been *Mapai*, with a parliamentary strength ranging between 40 and 47 seats, that is, from one-third to 40 per cent of the total. Avowedly more radical have been *Ahdut Ha'avodah*, *Mapam*, and *Maki*. Another, short-lived, competitor was *Rafi*, the Israel Workers List, the Ben Gurion-led splinter from *Mapai* between 1965 and 1968. Only in the twentieth year of statehood was there a partial merger of the Left, with *Mapai*, *Ahdut Ha'avodah*, and *Rafi* uniting to form the Israel Labour Party.[2] More conservative than *Mapai* are the Progressive Party, or Independent Liberals, the General Zionists, or Liberals, *Herut*, and the religious parties, notably the National Religious Party (NRP).

The task of forming a government has always involved subtle calculations and gamesmanship of a high order. In theory, five *Mapai*-led coalitions were possible: with the NRP; with the General Zionists;

---

[1] Ibid., p. 113.
[2] Detailed accounts of the steps leading to this merger were carried in the Israeli press. See for example *Jerusalem Post Weekly*, Nov. 1967 to Jan. 1968 inclusive.

with *Mapam* and *Ahdut Ha'avodah*; with NRP and the General Zionists; and with NRP and one or both of the two Left parties, *Mapam* and *Ahdut Ha'avodah*. In reality the options have been fewer: the first would demand excessive concessions towards a theocratic state; the second and third would involve unacceptable change in the economic and welfare spheres, probably in foreign policy as well. The choice for *Mapai* (between 1949 and 1967) was confined to coalition with the NRP *and either* the Right or the Left.[1]

The results reflected these operative parameters. The NRP has been a member of every Government. As to the Right–Left orientation, 1955 was the break point: during the first two *Knessets* (1949–51 and 1951–5), the NRP was the only major partner of *Mapai* in four of the six governments; the General Zionists served in the other two; from 1955 onwards the *Mapai*-led coalition included *Ahdut Ha'avodah* and/or *Mapam*, until the 'Grand Coalition' or 'National Government', formed in May 1967. The small, middle-of-the-road Progressive Party was a persistent *Mapai* ally, balancing to some extent the NRP pressure for more religious law and the Left parties' demand for greater state control of the economy.

There was a high degree of stability in the composition of Israel's coalition governments, despite the bargaining gyrations: only 39 persons

[1] Fein, op. cit., p. 175, has portrayed these options and the arithmetic of coalition-building as follows:

'Table V.1 *Mapai's Coalition Needs and Resources in Each of Six Parliaments* [1949–65]

Knesset:	1st	2nd	3rd	4th	5th	6th
Mapai seats	46	45	40	47	42	45
Mapai+minor party support	57	57	50	58	48	60
Mapai+minor party support+NRP	73ᵃ	67	61	70	60	71
Mapai+minor party support+NRP +General Zionists	80	87ᵇ	74	78	77ᶜ	e
Mapai+minor party support+NRP +Mapam+Ahduth Avodah	92	82	80	86	68ᵈ	79ᶠ

a In the First Knesset, the NRP was, together with the Agudah parties, part of the Religious Bloc

b There were four different Governments during the Second Knesset, two based on the NRP alone option and two based on the NRP+General Zionist option

c By this time, the General Zionists had merged with the Progressives to form the Liberal Party. This removes the Progressives from the 'minor party support' category, and is the reason for the reduction in that support which is seen in the second row

d Earlier coalitions in this row had included both Mapam and Ahduth Avodah; in the Fifth Knesset, as part of the effort to create an alignment between Mapai and Ahduth Avodah, Mapam was not included in the coalition

e The General Zionists, now having merged with Herut to form Gahal, cease to be an eligible coalition partner

f The Mapai-Ahduth Avodah alignment is now a reality, so this cell reflects only the added Mapam seats

The actual coalitions are italicized.'

held ministerial posts in eleven governments from 1949 to 1964; and *Mapai* held most key portfolios during the first two decades—the Prime Ministership, Defence (except for the last half of 1967),[1] Finance, Foreign Affairs, Education and Culture, Agriculture, and Police. And just as the *Knesset* is a 'House of Parties', so the Government is a committee of parties, not of individuals.

Foreign policy is one of the variables in Israeli coalition politics. To begin with, the formation of cabinets is made easier by differences in priorities of party interest. *Mapai* has a high priority in foreign policy; the NRP does not—making it more acceptable as a role partner. The religious parties benefit most from the general 'principle' of complementarity in policy priorities and therefore have a greater probability of inclusion in *Mapai*-led governments. Yet foreign policy has never been a major obstacle to coalition-building. *Mapam* split over a foreign policy issue in 1954, but its successors, *Mapam* and *Ahdut Ha'avodah*, both joined a *Mapai*-led government the following year. Similarly, these two Left parties vehemently opposed *Mapai*'s German arms policy, leading to the fall of the Government on New Year's Eve of 1958; yet both were back in the 'new' Cabinet a week later. That episode, among others, also revealed much about the impact of a coalition-type cabinet structure on decision-making in Israel's foreign policy.[2]

Mapai has always insisted on the control of key portfolios, including defence and foreign affairs. While no one has seriously challenged this claim, its domination of the Foreign Ministry led to pressure in the early years to downgrade the Ministerial (Cabinet) Committee on Foreign Affairs and Defence, in order that these issues be decided by the full cabinet; they included diplomatic appointments, in which the smaller coalition members felt *Mapai* was exercising an unrestrained right of patronage.[3] Only two cabinets fell on foreign policy issues, both concerning West Germany (the sale and purchase of arms in 1957 and 1959, respectively). (There was another major Cabinet crisis over foreign policy—whether or not to accept the Rogers Proposals in July–August 1970. The second largest constituent in the Coalition—*Gahal*—returned to the Opposition, but the Labour Alignment-led Government was strong enough to survive that crisis.) Moreover, the technique of balancing smaller parties in the coalition has not been applied to foreign policy; it has been most conspicuous in economic matters (Progressives versus *Mapam*) and in religious questions (Progressives and *Mapam* versus the NRP). Yet the section on 'Security and Foreign

[1] Before *Rafi*, of which the newly appointed Defence Minister, Dayan, was a member, united with *Mapai* and *Ahdut Ha'avodah*.

[2] The Government fell, in part, because Ben Gurion wanted to use it as a disciplinary action. This episode and the more general link between the Cabinet as an institution and Israel's foreign policy will be explored in detail in ch. 16, especially (*a*) and (*b*), below.

[3] See ch. 16 (*a*) below for an elaboration of these points.

Policy' has always had a respectable place in the 'Basic Principles of Government Programme', even though it prompted much less discussion and bargaining than religious, economic, and educational planks in the coalition agreements.[1]

There are more striking links between foreign policy and the multi-party character of Israel's political system. Ideological commitment leads to sharp differences in policy, and parties feel the need to project these into external affairs as well, in order to sharpen the alternatives for the voting public. The result is a tendency to a we–they party syndrome on policy towards the Arab states, the Cold War, Germany, etc.[2]

There are more parties than distinctive foreign policy programmes: only *Mapam* and *Ahdut Ha'avodah* on the Left, and *Herut* and the General Zionists on the Right offered competing *general* platforms in this sphere. Yet all parties articulate foreign policy demands. And the core role of the party in the system leads to a single foreign policy posture within each party, except for the heterogeneous *Mapai*; when a conflict occurs the party splits, as with *Mapam* in 1954. The proportional representation principle, too, has an effect; the list system and the absence of territorial constituencies are conducive to centralized policy formation; as in France, there are no local counter-pressures on foreign policy.[3] For the same reason the selection of candidates to the *Knesset* does not normally reflect dissenting foreign policy views within a party.

(b) ELECTIONS AND FOREIGN POLICY

Foreign policy does not touch specific core interests in Israel, with few exceptions, notably the question of relations with Germany. Yet it has always been a major concern because of the national preoccupation with security; the two are often perceived as synonymous. Indeed, elections were profoundly influenced by the contest over the degree of chauvinism in relation to the Arabs—how much should be conceded or offered: *Mapam* was maximalist in this contest, *Herut* minimalist. This is evident from an inquiry into the role of foreign policy in Israel's general elections.

There were six elections to the *Knesset* during the first twenty years— in 1949, 1951, 1955, 1959, 1961, and 1965.[4] Foreign policy was not a

[1] Conveyed to the author by many party leaders during interviews in Israel in 1960 and 1965–6. The foreign policy content of the 'Basic Principles' is examined in Appendix A.

[2] On this point see T. M. Goodland, 'A Mathematical Presentation of Israel's Political Parties', *British Journal of Sociology*, 8, Sept. 1957, pp. 263–6, and Louis Guttman, 'Whither Israel's Political Parties?', *Jewish Frontier*, 28, 12, Dec. 1961.

[3] There is one superficial exception: Israeli Arabs comprise a 'constituency', though not as a regional influence on the foreign policy process.

[4] The election results are summarized in Table 11.

controversial campaign issue in 1949, but it influenced the outcome: the pro-Soviet *Mapam* won 19 seats, that is, almost one-sixth of the total vote, the highest ever. It benefited from the prevalent Non-Identification line, for this was still the honeymoon phase in Israel–Soviet relations, expressed in Moscow's support for the UN Partition Resolution (November 1947), recognition (May 1948), and support for Israel's admission to the United Nations (December 1948 and March 1949).

The 1951 election was dominated by the pervasive fact of economic austerity. By the mid-fifties, however, a new, more formidable challenge was perceived—a rejuvenated Egypt under Nasser's rule. Thus the election of 1955 was fought over security, especially the rising tension on the borders. This was the most openly competitive of all election contests: *Mapam* had split the previous year over the question of orientation to the Soviet bloc, and both the residual *Mapam* and *Ahdut Ha'avodah* were outside the coalition; both challenged *Mapai*'s global policy, calling for pro-Soviet neutralism and non-alignment, respectively; *Mapam* advocated a more conciliatory line towards the Arab states, while *Ahdut Ha'avodah* joined with the extremist *Herut* in demanding a militant response to the escalating *Feda'iyun* (commando) raids.

The Government fell on the last day of 1957 over the proposed visit of General Dayan to Germany, but there was no direct spill-over to the 1959 elections. Rather, as in 1949, the results demonstrated the feedback of a security–foreign policy issue into the political system. On this occasion it was the Sinai Campaign and border tranquillity, with *Mapai* the beneficiary; its parliamentary strength rose from a low of 40 to a high of 47. In the 1961 elections, by contrast, as in 1951, foreign policy and security were of no consequence.

They were much more conspicuous in 1965. Diplomatic relations with West Germany had just been concluded, and this agonizing issue was fresh in people's minds: both *Mapam* and *Herut* stressed the iniquity of the decision. Relations with France figured in the contest as well, largely as a result of her incipient *rapprochement* with the UAR. No less important was the Bourguiba episode and the larger question of policy towards the Arab states. The President of Tunisia had criticized Nasser and the general Arab policy of permanent war and non-recognition— and the goal of extirpating the State of Israel. The *Mapai*-led Government reacted quietly, welcoming the speech as a good sign, but no more. Whatever the reasons, criticism ensued: *Mapam*, the Independent Liberals (Progressives), and *Maki* advocated an equally dramatic gesture by Israel; *Herut* warned of the danger of appeasement.

The election results of 1965 revealed two important themes. First, the public opposed new departures in foreign policy: *Mapam* and the Communist factions each lost a seat; *Herut* and the General Zionists, now united as *Gahal*, lost three; and the governing 'Alignment' (*Mapai* and *Ahdut Ha'avodah*), combined with the *Mapai* splinter, *Rafi*, which

TABLE II

RESULTS OF PARLIAMENTARY ELECTIONS IN ISRAEL (PERCENTAGE OF SEATS WON AND NUMBER OF SEATS)

KNESSET

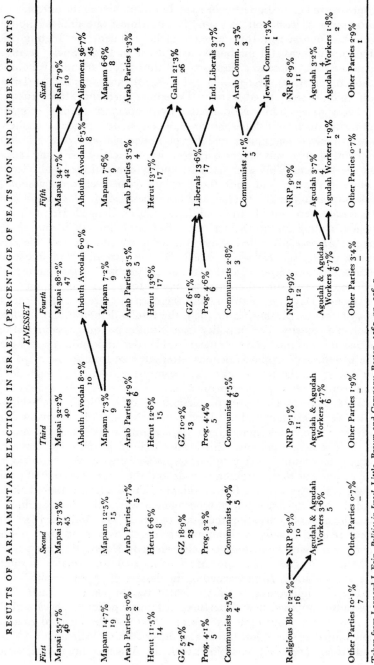

First	Second	Third	Fourth	Fifth	Sixth
Mapai 35·7% 46	Mapai 37·3% 45	Mapai 32·2% 40	Mapai 38·2% 47	Mapai 34·7% 42	Rafi 7·9% 10 / Alignment 36·7% 45
		Ahduth Avodah 8·2% 10	Ahduth Avodah 6·0% 7	Ahduth Avodah 6·5% 8	
Mapam 14·7% 19	Mapam 12·5% 15	Mapam 7·3% 9	Mapam 7·2% 9	Mapam 7·6% 9	Mapam 6·6% 8
Arab Parties 3·0% 2	Arab Parties 4·7% 5	Arab Parties 4·9% 6	Arab Parties 3·5% 5	Arab Parties 3·5% 4	Arab Parties 3·3% 4
Herut 11·5% 14	Herut 6·6% 8	Herut 12·6% 15	Herut 13·6% 17	Herut 13·7% 17	Gahal 21·3% 26
GZ 5·2% 7	GZ 18·9% 23	GZ 10·2% 13	GZ 6·1% 8	Liberals 13·6% 17	
Prog. 4·1% 5	Prog. 3·2% 4	Prog. 4·4% 5	Prog. 4·6% 6		Ind. Liberals 3·7% 5
Communists 3·5% 4	Communists 4·0% 5	Communists 4·5% 6	Communists 2·8% 3	Communists 4·1% 5	Arab Comm. 2·3% 3 / Jewish Comm. 1·3% 1
Religious Bloc 12·2% 16	NRP 8·3% 10 / Agudah & Agudah Workers 3·6% 5	NRP 9·1% 11 / Agudah & Agudah Workers 4·7% 6	NRP 9·9% 12 / Agudah & Agudah Workers 4·7% 6	NRP 9·8% 12 / Agudah 3·7% 4 / Agudah Workers 1·9% 2	NRP 8·9% 11 / Agudah 3·2% 4 / Agudah Workers 1·8% 2
Other Parties 10·1% 7	Other Parties 0·7% —	Other Parties 1·9% —	Other Parties 3·4% —	Other Parties 0·7% —	Other Parties 2·9% 1

Taken from Leonard J. Fein, *Politics in Israel*, Little, Brown and Company, Boston, 1967, pp. 226–7.

did not differ basically on foreign policy, gained five seats. The second theme relates to political change. The security feeling of the Israeli mass public had been personalized for many years in Ben Gurion and his aides, Moshe Dayan and Shimon Peres. The three men, as leaders of *Rafi*, tried to exploit this symbol but with little effect: *Rafi* had expected 20 seats but had won only 10. In terms of foreign policy and security, 'the feeling of safety was institutionalized in *Mapai*; for the first time it was depersonalized'.[1]

The role of foreign policy and security in Israel's general elections may be summarized as follows: one election (1955) was dominated by a security concern—the *Feda'iyun* raids; another (1965) was influenced by various foreign policy issues—Germany, France, and the Bourguiba episode; and in two others (1949 and 1959) the results were affected by the foreign policy–security area—Soviet friendship and the Sinai Campaign, respectively.[2]

As to the reverse impact, there is no evidence to suggest that Israel's elections influenced the content of strategic or tactical foreign policy, the decision process, or the manner of implementation. In short, this component of the political structure did not act as an environmental pressure in Israel's foreign policy system.

After each national election the new coalition government hammered out a set of 'Basic Principles' which were presented to the *Knesset*. An analysis of these articulated Government Programmes helps to uncover the changing patterns of foreign policy value orientations among Israel's multi-party (but all *Mapai*-dominated) régimes: internationalist values were pre-eminent in the Government Programmes for 1949, 1951, and 1959; nationalist values were dominant in 1955, 1961, and 1966.[3] Yet the 'Basic Principles' do not have the

---

[1] Dr. Emanuel Gutmann, interview in Jerusalem, Jan. 1966. I am indebted to Dr. Gutmann for many insights into the links between Israel's political structure and her foreign policy.

[2] A survey of reported campaign speeches in three Israeli elections (1959, 1961, 1965) reveals that few persons spoke on foreign policy and security, and that even for the party leaders with a special interest in this issue area, foreign policy was a small part of the campaign oratory. The survey was based upon the *Jerusalem Post* and *Ha'aretz* newspaper files for October 1959, July–August 1961, and October 1965. The principal spokesmen on foreign affairs and security were:

Ahdut Ha'avodah	Yigal Allon and Moshe Carmel
Herut	Arieh Ben-Eliezer, Menahem Begin, Yohanan Bader
Mapai	Abba Eban, Moshe Dayan, Golda Meir, Shimon Peres, Ben Gurion, Eshkol
Mapam	Hanan Rubin and Ya'acov Hazan
Maki	Moshe Sneh
Progressives	Izhar Harari
Rafi (1965 only)	Ben Gurion, Dayan, Peres

The content of their articulated demands will be examined in ch. 8, in the general context of party advocacy on foreign policy.

[3] See Appendix A, below, 'Foreign Policy in Government Programmes'.

force of law or of rules to be applied by governments. They are merely guidelines to behaviour. And Israeli decisions in foreign policy have other structural constraints within the political system. To these we may now turn.

(c) AUTHORIZATION

Israel is a state without a written constitution or indeed a constitution in any form. There are no 'entrenched clauses' or legislation requiring special amendment procedures: the *Knesset* (Parliament) may enact any law it wishes. An early debate on the issue of constitution-making led to a compromise *Knesset* Resolution, passed on 13 June 1950 by a vote of 50 to 38; this was to allow a constitution to develop over an unspecified period through specific acts of legislation which would be designated as 'fundamental laws'.[1] Four such laws have been adopted, dealing with the *Knesset* (1958), Israel Lands (1960), President of the State (1964), and the Government (1968).

Israel's legal system remains after twenty years a *mélange* derived from three sources—Ottoman rule, the British Mandate, and legislation passed by the *Knesset*. Ultimate authority over foreign policy continues to rest with the Government, i.e. the Cabinet; it was so granted by the *Law and Administration Ordinance No. 1*, the first legal act of the new state.[2] According to Article 14 of this Ordinance, passed on 19 May 1948,

(a) Any power vested under the law in the King of England or in any of his Secretaries of State, and any power vested under the law in the High Commissioner, the High Commissioner in Council, or the Government of Palestine, shall henceforth vest in the Provisional Government, unless such power has been vested in the Provisional Council of State by any of its Ordinances.

(b) Any power vested under the law in British consuls, British consular officers or British passport control officers, shall henceforth vest in consuls and officers to be appointed for that purpose by the Provisional Government.

The centralization of authority was complete: a declaration of war, the conclusion of peace, the making of treaties, the appointment of envoys, in fact all legal acts concerning the external world, were made exclusive prerogatives of the Government.[3] Practice over the next two decades confirmed these Executive powers.

[1] The text of that resolution is in *Divrei Ha-Knesset*, First Knesset, Second Session, 151st Meeting, June 13, 1950, III (1949–50), p. 1743, quoted in Kraines, op. cit., p. 30.

For a discussion of the early debates and the impasse on constitution-making, see Leo Kohn, 'The Constituent Assembly of Israel', *Israel and the Middle East*, i, Jan. 1949, pp. 6–7; and Emanuel Rackman, *Israel's Emerging Constitution 1948–51*, Columbia University Press, New York, 1955, esp. ch. II, III and VIII.

[2] The full text of this Ordinance is in *Sefer Ha-Hukkim* (Laws of the State of Israel), I (5708–1948), Government Printer, Jerusalem, 1949, pp. 7–11.

[3] The Foreign Minister's signature constitutes formal ratification of a decision. It is binding on the State of Israel even if his signature was not authorized by the Government as a whole.

The Israeli legislature has no direct role in foreign affairs, not even in the ratification of treaties, though some potential authority was implied in Article 6 of the 'Small Constitution', the Transition Law, enacted on 16 February 1949: 'The President of the State shall sign treaties with foreign states which have been ratified by the Knesset....'[1] The one notable case, which illuminated the competing claims, concerned the United Nations Convention on the Prevention and Punishment of the Crime of Genocide, in 1949. The proponents of legislative involvement in treaty-making urged that this was the kind of treaty which should be ratified by the *Knesset*. The guardians of exclusive Cabinet jurisdiction urged the Government to stand fast against *Knesset* intrusion lest it create a restraining precedent. Prime Minister Ben Gurion was a centralizer by temperament and conviction, and so the Government insisted on its prerogatives. Because of the special character of this treaty, however, a face-saving formula was found: the *Knesset* passed a resolution expressing gratification that the Government had approved the Convention on Genocide, but this had no constitutional significance.[2]

Unlike the British system, treaties are not 'laid before Parliament' in Israel. They are merely announced, and within twenty days are published. From time to time members of the *Knesset* have urged the emulation of this British practice—to secure involvement in the treaty process—but without success. Treaties are not self-executory in Israeli law, and so, theoretically, the *Knesset* has a role in implementation: no treaty obligation is formally binding on Israel until the legislature transforms it into domestic law. In practice, however, this is done by subsidiary legislation, that is, regulation by the relevant minister. Israeli courts, too, have no authority over foreign affairs. They have the equivalent of prerogative writs but only for administrative purposes.[3]

The President's powers are purely decorative. He signs all treaties approved by the Government. He appoints Israel's diplomatic and consular representatives, on the recommendation of the Foreign Minister. And he receives the credentials of envoys, as well as representatives

---

[1] The text of the Transition Law is in *Laws of the State of Israel*, III (5709–1949), Government Printer, Jerusalem, 1950, pp. 1–6. A series of amendments in 1951 and 1952 helped to fill many of the gaps in the original law. These are to be found ibid., V and VI.

[2] The *Knesset* resolution on the Convention on Genocide is in *Divrei Ha-Knesset*, First Knesset, Second Session, III (1949–1950), p. 313. See also *Laws and Practices Concerning the Conclusion of Treaties* (UN Legislative Series), United Nations, 1953, no. 42, p. 67. This discussion also benefited from an interview with Professor Akzin in Jerusalem, July 1960.

[3] Court involvement in foreign policy has been nil, except for extradition. There have also been cases in which lawyers have argued that an administrative act runs counter to Israel's international obligations, but to no effect.

of states and important visitors.[1] These nominal powers were picturesquely described by Dr. Chaim Weizmann, the first President of Israel. 'I am only a constitutional President and it's outside my province', he told a representative of President Truman, on the question of Arab refugees. 'My handkerchief is the only thing I can stick my nose into. Into everything else—it's Ben Gurion's nose.'[2] The dominant role of the Government in foreign policy is also apparent from an analysis of rule-making structures in Israel's political system.

(d) THE *KNESSET* AND THE *KNESSET* COMMITTEE ON FOREIGN AFFAIRS AND SECURITY

Israel's parliament is a unicameral body of 120 members, elected by proportional representation of party lists. Its formal powers are very great: governments receive their authority by a vote in the *Knesset*; it can force their resignation by a vote of no-confidence; it authorizes the state budgets; it may enact any bill whatsoever; and it cannot be dissolved except by its own decision or the expiry of its four-year mandate. In reality, however, the *Knesset* is very weak relative to the Government. The principal reason is its composition: the *Knesset* is a House of Parties, not of individual representatives of the electorate. There is only one constituency—the country as a whole. Ballots are cast for a party list. Members owe their seats to the party. And in every facet of the *Knesset*'s life, the party is pre-eminent—seating arrangements, voting procedures, the assignment of committee seats, the allocation of speakers and time in legislative debate, etc.[3]

[1] Section 6 of the *State President (Tenure) Law, 5712–1951*, enacted on 3 December 1951. *Laws of the State of Israel*, VI (5712-1951/2), Government Printer, Jerusalem, 1952, p. 4. Even these nominal powers were shared with the Minister for Foreign Affairs. Under the provisions of the Transition Law (Sections 6–7) he countersigned treaties, diplomatic appointments, acceptances of accredited foreign diplomats, and confirmations of foreign consuls. These ceremonial powers of the President were also incorporated into the *Basic Law of the President of the State*, enacted in 1964, arts. 11 & 12.

[2] Reported by the *New York Post*, 6 Sept. 1951. For a succinct discussion of the powers of the President, the Government, and the *Knesset* see H. E. Baker, *The Legal System of Israel*, Israel Universities Press, Jerusalem, 1968, pp. 12–37. For an official account of the role of the President see 'The Presidency in the First Decade of the State of Israel', State of Israel, *Government Year-Book 5719* (1958), Jerusalem, 1958, pp. 27–30.

[3] The structural antecedent of the *Knesset* was the *Asefat Ha-nivharim* (Elected Assembly), of which there were four in the pre-State period: 1920–5; 1925–31; 1931–44; and 1944–8. The later characteristics of multiplicity of factions and coalition government were already evident in the Assemblies: there were never less than 12 party lists—and in the second Assembly there were 26 factions; to the four major groups of Zionist factions—Labour, Religious, General, and Revisionist—were added communal factions like the *Sepharadim*, the Yemenites, and the Central European *Aliya Hadasha* (New Immigrants), and occupational interests. There was continuity too in individual participation: of 171 members of the fourth Assembly 55 were later members of the *Knesset*; and the seventh *Knesset* (1969–) still contained 11 persons who had served in an Elected Assembly. Samuel Sager (Editor of the Index to the *Knesset* Records), 'The Birth of Parliament in Jerusalem', *Jerusalem Post*, 25 October 1970.

The *Knesset* plays a marginal role in foreign policy. A positive act, such as the approval of a budget, is no more than a formal way of recording agreement among the coalition parties. A successful vote of no-confidence indicates the breakdown of the coalition; there has been only one case thus far. Debates on foreign affairs contribute to public education; there is always at least one a year, on the occasion of voting funds for the Foreign Office. Persistent questioning of the Foreign Minister in the House performs the same function, as do discussions on the floor arising from 'Motions for the Agenda' proposed by *Knesset* members. The *Knesset*'s primary role is to legitimate Government acts. Its substantive contribution takes place in the parliamentary committees.

The composition of *Knesset* committees and the manner of designating members are partly an extension of the concept of 'House of Parties' and partly a structural idiosyncrasy. According to the *Knesset* Standing Orders, committee 'members will be elected by the Knesset according to the principle of representation by factions (i.e. parties)'.[1] The actual procedure is conducted by the Committee on Arrangements (*Va'ada Mesaderet*), an *ad hoc* body, itself based on proportional party strength, which is reconstituted at the beginning of each *Knesset*. In arriving at the specific allocation of committee seats, the Arrangements Committee has always secured *Knesset* approval of a principle to the effect that party lists with less than a certain number of seats in the House do not have a right of choice to committee seats.

The 'number rule' was designed to deny membership in the two crucial committees, Finance, and Foreign Affairs and Security, to 'unreliable elements' in the *Knesset*. More precisely, this meant *Maki*, the Communist Party of Israel (and, since 1965, the New Communists as well), and Arab members of the *Knesset*. Communist representation, whether of one party or two, has never exceeded 6; nor has the combined representation of Arab parties affiliated to the centrist *Mapai*, the pivot of all Israeli coalition governments. Thus the 'minimum" number was fixed at 5, 6, and 8 in the First, Second, and Third *Knessets*, respectively—when *Maki* had 4, 5, and 6 MKs. The small, separate Arab lists were thus also excluded. And the Left–Socialist *Mapam*, which has always had at least one Arab among its *Knesset* members, has tacitly accepted the convention on membership of the two committees.

The Committee on Foreign Affairs and Security has broad legislative and administrative powers concerning 'foreign policy of the State, her armed forces, and her security'.[2] All bills on security and foreign affairs are dealt with by this committee, after first reading in the House. Responsibility for the Security (or Defence) Budget is shared with the

[1] *Taknon Ha-Knesset* (Regulations of the *Knesset*), Government Printer, Jerusalem, Nov. 1965, Rule 9 (a).
[2] Ibid., Rule 12 (a) (4).

Finance Committee: they meet in joint session on the all-important second reading, with the Finance Committee authorized by the *Knesset* to perform the final reading. It never comes to the House.[1] Moreover, there are special Government acts which require the approval of the Foreign Affairs Committee; for example, if mobilization of troops is not approved within ten days, and special mobilization within two months, they must be terminated.

These three functions are prescribed by *Knesset* rules. In addition, the Government may bring matters to the Committee, and the Committee itself, or one of its members, may propose topics for discussion.[2] Frequently, too, the Speaker assigns to the Committee matters that are initially raised on the floor of the House as Motions for the Agenda. And the *Knesset* sometimes transfers rule-making authority to the Committee; for example, in January 1952 it authorized the Committee to determine final implementing action on the German Reparations question 'in accordance with circumstances and conditions'.[3]

The Foreign Affairs Committee normally meets every week when the *Knesset* is in session. Special meetings are also held during the parliamentary recess as and when circumstances require. The Committee's investigative power is sweeping, in theory: it 'is permitted to demand from the relevant minister explanation and information regarding the matter under discussion or which is within its jurisdiction, and the minister is obligated, either himself or by his representative, to provide the explanation or information requested'.[4] In practice, ministers, diplomats, and military leaders exercise discretion, but testimony before this Committee is exceptionally candid. The Foreign Affairs Committee (and no other) pledges its members to secrecy (and, in contrast to other committees, including the Cabinet, secrecy is really

---

[1] The practice of a joint committee session for the Defence Budget began with the First *Knesset*. In 1964 this was extended to all aspects of the budget, that is, meetings of the Finance Committee and the relevant House Committee. However, all but the statutory Joint Committee of Finance and Foreign Affairs and Security are sub-committees of Finance.

[2] When two or more Committee factions (parties) move that a question be placed on its agenda, the chairman is obliged to do so. If only one faction so requests, the chairman has discretion; but he usually agrees, according to members interviewed in 1960 and 1965–6.

[3] A succinct account of the Committee on Foreign Affairs and Security is contained in A. Zidon, *Beit Ha-nivharim—Israel's Parliament*, Achiasaf Publishing House, Jerusalem, 3rd ed., 1964 (in Hebrew), pp. 253–4. An English translation appeared as *Knesset: The Parliament of Israel*, Herzl Press, New York, 1968. Zidon notes that, at the outset, there were those who urged the creation of two committees, but the view triumphed, he adds, that foreign affairs and security were really one policy sphere in Israel. The major reason, however, was political power: had there been two separate committees, *Mapai* would have had to concede the chairmanship of one to another party.

[4] Standing Orders (Regulations of the *Knesset*), Rule 13 (b).

kept). Moreover, this Committee and Finance are exempt from the requirement that proceedings or summaries of committee meetings be made available to each faction. As a further mark of their special status, members of the Finance and Foreign Affairs Committees are taken on periodic tours of the defence establishment.

There were four chairmen of the Committee on Foreign Affairs and Security during the period under inquiry; all have been *Mapai* stalwarts. The first was Zalman Aranne, who later became a member of the 'Old Guard'. His successor, Meir Argov, held the post for a dozen years and perceived his role as the transmitter of Government decisions to the Committee rather than the conveyor of pressures upwards to the Cabinet: 'the Committee', he remarked proudly, 'never votes against the Government'.[1] He was followed by Herzl Berger, who was more conscious of the Committee's prerogatives. And from 1965 to 1969 the Chairman was David Hacohen, an independent-minded founder of the powerful *Histadrut* construction complex, *Solel Boneh*, and the successful first Israeli envoy to Burma, 1953–5. (After the *Knesset* elections in 1969, Haim Zadok, a former *Mapai* Cabinet Minister, became Chairman of the Committee.)

The Foreign Affairs Committee has always exerted intangible influence on Israel's foreign policy: this is the consensus among participants and observers. One reason has been its formal powers and functions, noted above. Another has been the high quality of its members, a reflection of the status and importance accorded the Committee by all parties—other than *Mapai*, whose leaders were concentrated in the Government. A list of members at any time contains most prominent non-ministerial MKs (no minister can be a member of a committee): Ya'ari and Hazan for *Mapam*; Galili for *Ahdut Ha'avodah*; Dayan and Peres for *Rafi*; Harari for the Progressives (Independent Liberals); Yosef Saphir and Rimalt for the General Zionists (later Liberals); and Ya'acov Meridor and Landau, sometimes Begin, for *Herut*.

A third reason for the Committee's influence has been its role as miniature *Knesset* and the acknowledged need for a legislative forum in the foreign policy process. As former Foreign Minister Golda Meir remarked, 'because it has no gallery to speak to and no press reporting [unlike the *Knesset*], people speak much more to the point, with much less party bias. It is a good Committee and has good discussions. It also has to its credit virtually no leakages over the years.'[2]

All three Foreign Ministers, Sharett, Meir, and Eban, reportedly

---

[1] Interview in Jerusalem, July 1960.

[2] Interview in Tel Aviv, Aug. 1966. Another former minister, Dov Joseph, agreed: 'Members speak with a greater sense of responsibility in the Committee than in the House, for its deliberations are confidential; in the House they are acutely aware that they are opposition parties.' Interview in Jerusalem, July 1966. Others noted one great exception—revelations on the Lavon Affair.

maintained an excellent rapport with the Committee.[1] The attitude of Prime Minister Eshkol, too, was praised by members. And Eshkol himself showed deference: 'we look on them [Finance and Foreign Affairs] as important committees; they demand their rights; the Opposition parties are represented, and this compels us to listen to their views.' Moreover, 'it is true that the Foreign Affairs Committee is more interested and more knowledgeable than the full Cabinet, but the Ministerial [Cabinet] Committee on Defence is even more so.'[2]

On Ben Gurion's attitude and the *Knesset* Committee's influence during his years in office (1948–53, 1955–63), opinions vary. Yitzhak Navon, his Political Secretary for more than a decade, termed the Committee's functions twofold—consumer of information and provider of public support for Government policies. 'The views of its members were listened to but they had little if any effect on BG. After all, he had his Foreign Minister, his Chief of Staff, etc.'[3] Shimon Peres, also a member of the Ben Gurion inner circle, dissented: 'It was not decisive but it did exercise influence; Ben Gurion was pleased when he had the Committee's support, sensitive when he did not.'[4] Harari noted that Ben Gurion tired of the Committee in his last years in office.

'The Committee represents the pulse of the *Knesset* in foreign affairs', remarked Harari of the Progressives (later of *Mapai*), the only person with continuous membership since 1949. 'It is the only forum in which ministers can and must think seriously about a specific problem for a few hours.'[5] Rimalt of the General Zionists termed it a 'sounding board', while Rubin of *Mapam* asserted, 'it does not have great influence—but not less than the Government in foreign policy, for Ben Gurion is dominant'.[6] Peres was more positive: 'It exercised influence, in matters of Military Government, in policy toward Germany, in attitudes toward Soviet Jewry, and it united the nation around the Army.' Among the Committee chairmen, Argov denigrated its role, while Berger and Hacohen, especially the latter, perceived a moderate, restraining influence on Government policy.[7]

Two illustrations of effective restraint in the pre-1960 period may be noted. On one occasion the Government wanted to extend the law of censorship beyond security matters; the Committee was opposed, and

---

[1] In the words of veteran Progressive (later, *Mapai*) MK, Ishar Harari, 'there was no real difference in their attitude; they all appreciated its role, attended regularly, and gave full reports; there were differences in personality but not in respect for the Committee.' Interview in Tel Aviv, Aug. 1966.

[2] Interview in Jerusalem, Aug. 1966.

[3] Interview in Jerusalem, Dec. 1965.

[4] Interview in Tel Aviv, May 1966.

[5] Interview in Jerusalem, July 1960. For many years Harari was an 'Advisory Member'.

[6] Interviews in Jerusalem, Aug. 1960.

[7] Interviews in Jerusalem, Aug. 1960 (Berger) and Dec. 1965 (Hacohen).

the Government yielded. Similarly, the Government tried to extend capital punishment, which then applied only to acts of treason in time of active war, to murder committed by infiltrators; a majority in the Committee objected, and a *Knesset* vote supported its dissent; the Government yielded. A more frequent role, however, has been to legitimate Government policy choices on controversial issues: given the primacy of parties in the system, the members of coalition parties on the Foreign Affairs Committee follow their leaders, who sit in the Cabinet. In short, the Committee has not performed the role of articulating demands in foreign policy.

This concludes the inquiry into Israel's political structure as it pertains to foreign policy. There remain two other internal components of the operational environment: interest groups and competing élites. Their advocacy of policy demands will be analysed in the following two chapters.

CHAPTER 7

Advocacy: Interest Groups

There is a myriad of interest groups in Israel's foreign policy system: they range from the most formal institutional type to *ad hoc* forms of pressure. Like competing élites they perform the function of advocacy, that is, they generate and transmit demands to the wielders of decision-making authority. In the Israeli context this type of pressure on foreign policy may be classified as follows:

Institutional Defence Establishment; Diaspora Jewry; Civil Servants.

Associational *New Outlook*; *Ha'olam Hazeh*; *Ihud*; Council of the Sepharadi Community; *Matzpen*; *Siah*; Land of Israel Movement.

Non-Associational *Kena'anim*; Commentators; Academics.

Some of these groups are ephemeral and/or inconsequential. Others are enduring and vital structures. And still others are important advocates on a specific issue. There are, indeed, various degrees of durability and influence: the Magnes-Buber group, *Ihud*, which aimed at a programme designed to offer the Arabs something they could accept, for example a bi-national state, and the 'Canaanites' (*Kena'anim*) both antedate an independent Israel, and are marginal to the point of scholarly interest; *Ha'olam Hazeh* is a journalistic-parliamentary input of pressure centred on one man, Uri Avneri; and *Siah* and the Land of Israel Movement emerged from the Six Day War to advocate the withdrawal from and the retention of the 'new territories', respectively. The task is made more difficult by the paucity of hard data about some crucial interest groups, notably Defence.

(a) INSTITUTIONAL INTEREST GROUPS

i. *Defence Establishment*

Parties are the most voluble of Israel's policy advocates; the Defence Establishment is the most secretive. This gap exists in all pluralist polities, almost certainly more so in Israel, for two reasons: intense political consciousness in the society as a whole, and the permanent hostility enveloping the state since independence. It is therefore difficult to document the role of 'the Military' as an interest group in Israel's foreign policy system. Some inferences can be drawn, however, from the scanty evidence and knowledgeable assessments.

General Y. Harkabi, one of Israel's best-known writers on strategic matters, first denied the status of pressure group to the army officer corps.[1] For one thing, he remarked, the Chiefs of Staff have had different party affiliations or have been formally unaffiliated; nor are younger officers a more homogeneous group. They have been divided on issues, he added.[2] And they do not have clearly-defined views on major foreign policy questions.[3] Yet Harkabi acknowledged the essence of interest group activity by noting that *Tzahal* leaders share a single criterion for assessing foreign policy—the probable effect of a decision on Israel's security position; this has been their constant concern. More specifically, he cited the policy of retaliation from 1955 onwards as the direct result of persistent advocacy by Dayan, then Chief of Staff, with the backing of the entire senior officer group.[4] In this (important) instance, then, there was a clear causal link between army officer advocacy and decision, leading to behaviour towards Israel's neighbours.

Other discerning observers and participants concurred with Harkabi's analysis and emphasized that 'the Military' make their views known on any matter impinging on security.[5] A legitimate channel for such advocacy has long existed in the weekly meeting of the General Staff, attended, among others, by the Defence Minister.[6] There are also frequent *ad hoc* discussions, once or more daily during periods of tension, between the Chief of Staff and the Defence Minister.

A notable illustration of the army officers' advocacy role occurred in mid-November 1956. Dayan had made it known to Ben Gurion that some officers were disturbed by the decision to agree to withdraw from

[1] Interview in Tel Aviv, Oct. 1965. Dr. Harkabi, then in charge of strategic studies within the Ministry of Defence, was a former Director of Military Intelligence.

[2] Moshe Dayan, along with Ya'acov Dori, the first Chief of Staff, and Zvi Zur, campaigned actively for *Rafi* in the 1965 election. Professor Yigael Yadin, the second Chief of Staff, is non-party and remained aloof, as did the then-incumbent *Ramatkal*, Yitzhak Rabin, who was a known adherent of *Ahdut Ha'avodah*.

[3] Yadin and, even more so, Dayan are notable exceptions. There are others: Haim Laskov, another Chief of Staff, Matityahu Peled, Ezer Weizman, and Avraham Yoffe.

[4] Ben Gurion accepted this policy, partly, it was suggested, because he could not tolerate the idea of Dayan being more 'courageous' in defence policy than he was!

[5] Among them, Professor Benjamin Akzin of the Hebrew University, Yitzhak Navon, Peres, and Arye Wallenstein. Interviews in Israel during 1965–6. Navon was Political Secretary to Prime Minister Ben Gurion from 1951 to 1963. Peres was Director-General of the Ministry of Defence from 1953 to 1959 and Deputy Minister of Defence from 1959 to 1965. Wallenstein has been Reuters' resident correspondent in Israel for more than twenty years.

[6] Apart from two periods, the Prime Minister held the Defence portfolio: December 1953 to November 1955, when Sharett was Prime Minister and Lavon, followed briefly by Ben Gurion, was Defence Minister; and since May 1967, with Dayan as Defence Minister under Eshkol and, later, with Mrs. Meir as Prime Minister.

Sinai and the Gaza Strip. The Prime Minister called about twenty senior officers together at his residence, listened to their views, and explained the compelling reasons for that decision: the dissenters, led by Deputy Chief of Staff Haim Laskov, yielded to his persuasion. As related by Ben Gurion in his memoirs,

The Defence Minister saw a need to explain to the army commanders the essence of the political struggle after the Sinai Campaign. . . . While the UN's pressure was increasing [he] invited the General Staff to a meeting to convey the Government's policy. He explained that 'we need now most of all a delay so that the world would be able to think again and see that we are right'.[1]

A more dramatic confrontation occurred in the tense days preceding the Six Day War. Members of the General Staff, alarmed by the rapid mobilization of Egyptian tanks and troops in the last half of May 1967, pleaded for—some reports say, demanded—a clear decision from the Prime Minister–Defence Minister, Eshkol, at two, perhaps more, stormy sessions. Some participants in that crucial decision process termed the role of 'the Military' decisive;[2] all who probed the events leading to war cite that pressure as important.[3]

More generally, the army officer corps has been a permanent arms lobby. This inevitably spilled over to foreign policy, with the maxim, 'whichever states are prepared to furnish modern weapons are special objects of diplomatic concern'. Thus the *Government Year-Book* for 1959/60 acknowledged that 'the need to equip the Israel Defence Forces [made it] necessary for our Ministry of Defence to enter into negotiations with the German Government on both the acquisition and the sale of arms. No question has been the subject of such bitter controversy in Israel as our relations with Germany. . . .'[4] For the same reason the Defence Ministry took the initiative in 1954–5 leading to the informal alliance with France and the supply of arms vital to the Sinai Campaign.[5] 'The Military' also played a vital role in Israel's African 'presence', training the armed forces of new states, providing other forms of technical assistance, and staffing some of Israel's diplomatic missions.

In these major cases—and many minor ones—it was the Defence Establishment as a whole which operated as a foreign policy institutional interest group. More generally, it argued that, because foreign policy is, in the end, security, all foreign policy commitments must

[1] *The State of Israel Reborn*: no. 71, 'Exchange of Messages with the two Great Powers', *Davar* (Tel Aviv), 5 Aug. 1966. Mr. Ben Gurion also narrated this incident to the author during an interview at his home in Sde Boker, July 1966.

[2] Interviews in Israel, July–Aug. 1968, with Cabinet ministers, civil servants, and senior army officers.

[3] This illuminating example of an interest group role in Israel's foreign and security policy will be examined in a related volume on Israeli high-policy decisions.

[4] State of Israel, *Government Year-Book 5720* (1959/60), p. 72. For an elaboration of this illustration see ch. 16 (*b*) and (*c*) below.

[5] This will be explored in a related volume on Israeli high-policy decisions.

be subordinate to security needs and, therefore, the Foreign Office must be subservient to the Defence Ministry. Thus, *Tzahal* made known its need for weapons. But it was the Defence Ministry that directed this pressure towards larger policy horizons, especially during the tenure of Shimon Peres (1953–65). And the Ministry has had the additional interest of creating outlets for Israel's growing arms industry.

The Armament Development Authority of the Defence Ministry has expanded from the production of makeshift rifles in 1948 to the sophisticated weapons systems which have made *Tzahal* self-sufficient, except for the heaviest equipment—planes, tanks, artillery, and naval craft. Indeed its inventiveness, in rockets (the *Shavit*) and missiles among others, has placed this Armament Authority (*Reshut Le-phituah Emtsa'ey Lehima*) in the élite of military technology. One of the problems of 'Rafael', as it is called, is excess supply of small arms, made necessary to keep the arms factories fully occupied. This has led to the search for markets, readily available in an international system with many new states and a rising incidence of violence. This, in turn, caused internal political tensions over the sale of weapons, especially the famous 'Uzzi' sub-machine gun, to Germany, Belgium, Portugal, etc. In short, 'the Military' have been a major source of pressure on Israel's foreign policy decisions since independence. They have also been among the most influential decision-makers.[1]

ii. *Diaspora Jewry*

The presence of externally-based foreign policy interest groups is widespread in an age of 'penetrated political systems': no state is totally immune from group pressures stemming from beyond its territorial boundaries. None is comparable to Israel in this respect, however. Israel is a self-conscious *Jewish* state; indeed that is its *raison d'être*; and Israel is the only Jewish state, indissolubly linked to world Jewry in the minds of her leaders and of most Jews—and of most non-Jews in the Euro-American world as well.

Three other facts combine with these to create a unique institutional interest group. First, the Jews of Israel have comprised no more than almost one-fifth of the world's Jewish population at any time since independence. Yet this minority has been the only living expression of Jewish sovereignty for two thousand years. And finally, Diaspora Jewry has played a worthy part in the revival of statehood and in its sustenance since 1948. The result is an unparalleled web of emotional, spiritual, and organizational ties between the 2½ million Jews residing in Israel in 1968 and the 12 million who remained scattered in the far corners of the earth.

The relations between Israel and world Jewry is a vast and complex

[1] The Defence Ministry's role in the *formulation* of Israel's foreign policy will be analysed in ch. 15 (*c*) below.

subject, which deserves careful analysis. The place of Jewry in Israel's foreign policy, a lesser theme, will recur frequently in this inquiry.[1] In the context of advocacy, however, the focus is on Jewry as an interest group, that is, as a positive pressure on Israel's decision-makers and as a restraint on policy. Two blocs of Diaspora Jewry are significant—the 6 million in North America and the 3 million in the Soviet Union. The former is free to provide material aid to Israel, as well as to express opinions and to exert pressure; and it is free (but unwilling in large numbers) to migrate. The latter lacks affluence and freedom to participate in Jewish national development, and it survives under conditions of extreme adversity. Thus North American Jewry can (and does) perform the function of interest advocacy; Soviet Jewry is an object of concern and attention.[2]

The role of American Jews has been acknowledged not infrequently in areas other than foreign policy. A conspicuously candid example was the remark of an American reform rabbi critical of the monopoly of orthodox religion in Israel:

We are and must continue to be intimately identified with Israel and its fate and destiny. So far we have manifested this identity not only financially but by bringing influence to bear on Israel's economic policies. We have no less a right and a claim to influencing, for a time, its religious policies.[3]

Evidence of Diaspora Jewry's role as an advocate of *foreign* policy is limited but persuasive. Certainly this was true in the pre-State formulation of Zionist strategy and tactics in Palestine and the world at

---

[1] See especially the discussion of attitudinal prism and élite images (ch. 11–14) and of implementation (ch. 19 (*d*)).

[2] There is a substantial body of literature on Soviet Jewry in various languages. Apart from the large volume of polemical materials, there are some useful accounts and analyses. Some English sources may be noted: Salo W. Baron, *The Russian Jews Under Tzars and Soviets*, Macmillan, New York, 1964; Moshe Decter, 'The Status of the Jews in the Soviet Union', *Foreign Affairs*, New York, vol. 41, Jan. 1963, pp. 420–30; Nicholas Dewitt, *The Status of Jews in Soviet Education*, American Jewish Congress, New York, n.d.; Arie L. Eliav, *Between Hammer and Sickle* (new ed.), New American Library, New York, 1969; Maurice Friedberg, 'The State of Soviet Jewry', *Commentary*, New York, vol. 39, Jan. 1965, pp. 38–43; B. Z. Goldberg, *The Jewish Problem in the Soviet Union*, Crown, New York, 1961; E. Goldhagen (ed.), *Ethnic Minorities in the Soviet Union*, Praeger, New York, 1968; Maurice Hindus, *House Without a Roof*, Doubleday, New York, 1961, Lionel Kochan (ed.), *The Jews in Soviet Russia Since 1917*, Oxford University Press, London, 1970; Walter Kolarz, *Religion in the Soviet Union*, St. Martin's Press, New York, 1962; William Korey, 'The Legal Position of the Jews in the Soviet Union', *Midstream*, New York, vol. 12, May 1966, pp. 44–61; Solomon M. Schwartz, *Jews in the Soviet Union*, Syracuse University Press, Syracuse, 1951; Joseph B. Schectman, *Star in Eclipse: Russian Jewry Revisited*, Thomas Yoseloff, New York, 1961; Judd L. Teller, *The Kremlin, the Jews and the Middle East*, Yoseloff, New York, 1957; and Elie Wiesel, *The Jews of Silence*, Holt, Rinehart and Winston, New York, 1966.

[3] Rabbi David Polish of Evanston, Ill., at the Jewish Theological Seminary, New York. *New York Times*, 24 Oct. 1968.

large. The habit persisted. A continuing thread of disagreement is evident on Israel's posture towards the UN: American Jewry pressed for greater conciliation and co-operation, especially until 1956; in effect, it was supporting Sharett's soft line against Ben Gurion, who disdainfully referred to the UN (*Oumot Me'uhadot*, abbreviated to *Oum*) as 'oum shmoum'.[1]

Another source of tension was Israel's reprisal policy. Beginning with the Kibya raid in October 1953 and the Lake Kinneret raid two years later, through the 1960s, American Jewish leaders expressed their misgivings and advocated caution—almost always informally, usually quietly. Even on the territorial aspects of the Sinai Campaign, dissent was quickly conveyed. Among the massive pressures which converged on Israel's Prime Minister on 8 November 1956, leading to the decision—in principle—that night to withdraw from Sinai, 'Goldmann informed Ben Gurion that American Jewry had been most happy about the Sinai victory but would not stand behind Israel if she persisted in keeping the conquered territory. He added that collections for the national Jewish funds might be forbidden.'[2] A similar, though more subdued, cleavage existed after the Six Day War, with Goldmann and others urging Israeli concessions, including a willingness to enter into indirect talks with the Arab states.

Occasionally criticism was aired, for example by Jacques Torczyner, then President of the Zionist Organization of America, on the *al-Samua* raid of November 1966.[3] The resulting embarrassment was acknowledged by the dean of American Zionists, Dr. Emmanuel Neumann. Speaking to the Zionist General Council in Jerusalem, he decried this criticism as 'giving colour to the notion that we [Diaspora Zionists] were injecting ourselves into a painful and delicate situation in a way which most of us do not approve'. Further, the ZOA followed two rules: 'Israel military and defence matters are beyond such discussion at all times, certainly now; and we avoid personal reflection on, and certainly denigration of, people at the head of the State and Government.'[4]

Certainly the most widely-known Diaspora Jewish leader, Nahum

[1] In Yiddish and, from this, now in the Hebrew spoken by East European Jews, the addition of 'shm', or some words formed from these letters, has a derogatory, even rude inference.

[2] Michel Bar-Zohar, *Ben Gurion: The Armed Prophet*, Prentice-Hall, Englewood Cliffs, N.J., 1968, p. 235. Indeed, no less influential an American decision-maker than President Eisenhower perceived this advocacy (and communication) function by using the American Zionist leader, Rabbi Abba Hillel Silver, on two occasions during the week of the Campaign to convey combined threats and promises to Ben Gurion. Ibid., pp. 226–8.

[3] An interview reported in the *Rafi* weekly, *Mabbat Hadash* (New Look) (Tel Aviv), 5 Jan. 1967.

[4] Quoted in *Jerusalem Post*, 8 Jan. 1967. Torczyner disowned as inaccurate the interview report of his views.

Goldmann, did not adhere to these 'rules'. He took the initiative in sponsoring a drastic revision of the foreign policy platform of Israel's General Zionists and Progressives, in 1953, 1957, and 1961.[1] He has openly espoused views which are sharply at variance with official Israeli policy: on Soviet Jewry and the Soviet Union generally; on great-power involvement in the search for peace; on Israel's integration within the Near East; on the United Nations, etc.

Typical of Goldmann's fundamental dissent were his remarks to a Tel Aviv symposium in 1963 on Israel's security policy:

First of all, the State of Israel must be strong. However, this in itself is not enough. In my opinion, there can be no more fatal error [than the view] that this is the only thing which can and should be done. . . . The second task facing Israel is no less vital and decisive for survival. This is the crystallization of an Israeli political plan and the launching of a great political offensive in the world at large.

Further,

only a united Arab nation would dare to recognize Israel's existence.

Still further,

I am convinced that, under present circumstances, the Soviet Union may in fact have an interest in agreeing to joint U.S.-Soviet guarantees for the Israeli-Arab area and disarmament.

As for direct negotiations,

I am for [them] with all my heart.

But since the Arabs are not ready to agree,

this proposal is not at all realistic.

Finally, to the rejoinder that there was nothing new in his proposals— there was a great deal, in fact—Goldmann delivered a blunt criticism of the official posture:

a serious political program is not implemented by appearing at the U.N. or some other forum and announcing something in a one-time declaration.[2]

Goldmann's most dramatic (and deviationist) foreign policy proposal —the neutralization of Israel and a security guarantee by the super powers and the UN—was elaborated in his autobiography:[3]

Israel cannot exist forever as a hostile island in an Arab ocean. . . .

[1] To be elaborated in the following chapter.

[2] Reported in an interview with Nahum Goldmann, 'Military Strength is not Enough', *New Outlook* (Tel Aviv), vol. 6, no. 5 (54), June 1963, pp. 12–16. The above-noted views were reiterated by Goldmann during an interview with this writer in Jerusalem, April 1966. See also Ze'ev Katz, 'An Interview with Dr. Goldmann', *New Outlook*, vol. 9, no. 5 (80), June 1966, pp. 3–8.

[3] *The Autiobiography of Nahum Goldmann: Sixty Years of Jewish Life*, Holt, Rinehart and Winston, Inc., New York, 1969, pp. 299, 301. The extremism of Goldmann's dissent was revealed in his controversial and widely commented-upon article, 'The Future of Israel', *Foreign Affairs* (New York), vol. 48, no. 3, April 1970, pp. 443–59.

Neutralization would mean that the world

would recognize Israel's unique role of providing for its Jewish and Arab citizens, offering a haven to Jewish refugees and, at the same time, serving as the national and cultural centre that guarantees the future of the Jewish people throughout the world.

A further justification was cited. Israel,

whose mere existence requires the moral and spiritual solidarity of all the Jews of the world, must by definition be neutral if all Jews are to be able to maintain emotional and spiritual ties with it irrespective of their nationality and political orientation. Any political alignment on the part of such a state makes it difficult and sometimes impossible for Jewish citizens of certain other countries openly to profess their allegiance to it.

An equally desirable alternative, added Goldmann, is Israel's integration into a Middle East Confederation of equal states—but this will not be feasible for a long time because of profound internal divisions within the Arab world.

Goldmann took an even more extreme position in the spring of 1970. He not only advocated formal neutralization and a total withdrawal to the 4 June (1967) borders. In addition, he espoused the right of Arab refugees to return; the acceptance by Israel of something less than a peace treaty, merely a cessation of overt warfare; the acceptance of international forces on Israeli territory; and the establishment of a *de facto* 'world conscience' protectorate over Israel. To many he was advocating the dismantling of an independent Jewish state.[1]

There are two major institutional channels through which Diaspora Jewry conveys foreign policy demands to Israel's decision-makers: the World Zionist Organization and its ancillary and subordinate bodies, notably the Zionist General Council; and the Conference of Presidents of Jewish Organizations in the United States, better known as 'the Presidents' Club'. The first carried the distinctive imprint of Goldmann, President of the WZO during the first twenty-one years of Israel's independence. The second, founded by Goldmann and others in 1955, represents the collective will of pro-Zionist American Jewry, with one notable exception—the American Jewish Committee. Indeed, though

[1] Goldmann's 'radical' views, which prompted some life-long colleagues to accuse him of abandoning Zionism and of echoing the *Al-Fatah* line, were contained in a series of articles in *Ha'aretz* (Tel Aviv), 1, 3, 5, 6, 8, and 9 April, and, in English in 'The Failure of Israeli Foreign Policy' and 'Israeli Foreign Policy, Part II: What Can Be Done', *New Outlook* (Tel Aviv), vol. 13, no. 5 (115), June 1970, pp. 9–18, and vol. 13, no. 6 (116), July–Aug. 1970, pp. 22–36. He also 'stumped the country' in support of his dissenting views, which acquired world publicity as a result of the simultaneous 'Goldmann Affair', the (Goldmann) alleged invitation from Nasser to visit Cairo for talks, which the Israeli Prime Minister ineptly vetoed, with accompanying turmoil within Israel. A telling rejoinder to Goldmann's 'J'accuse'-type articles was given by Israeli Middle East expert and former Cabinet minister Eliyahu Sasson, 'The (Occupied) Territories in Exchange for a Genuine Peace', *Ha'aretz*, 26 April 1970.

much smaller in numbers than the combined weight of the 'Presidents' Club', the AJC has behaved as a self-confident interest group concerned with both the domestic and foreign policy of Israel.

The American Jewish Committee is an élite organization founded in 1890 by affluent German Jews settled in New York and other eastern seaboard cities. Its interest in Jewish welfare is humanitarian, not political. It was never in the Zionist stream; on the contrary, the AJC was anti-Zionist at the outset and, at most, ambivalently non-Zionist at the end of the Second World War. The change to greater sympathy for Jewish national aspirations was sparked by the Holocaust and was given positive form by its dominant figure before Israel's independence, Joseph Proskauer, and his successor, Jacob Blaustein, a wealthy Baltimore industrialist.

The AJC is proud of its role as an interest group in Israeli politics—in a relationship it describes as 'vigilant brotherhood'. It has continuously advocated full and equal rights for Israel's Arabs and the elimination of military government. It supported the Law of Return but opposes automatic citizenship for Jews, 'which has caused unnecessary mis-understandings'. And it has strongly opposed Orthodox control over wide areas of private life in Israel: in 1964, for example, the Committee urged Prime Minister Eshkol to resist the pressure for restrictive Sabbath Law legislation.

The foreign policy area in which the AJC has been most persistent— and most influential—has been the 'proper' relationship between Israel and Diaspora Jews. Its perception and demand were contained in a 1949 Statement of Views: 'Citizens of the United States are Americans, and citizens of Israel are Israelis . . . and just as our own government speaks only for its citizens, so Israel speaks only for its citizens. Within the framework of American interests, we shall aid in the up-building of Israel.'[1] This position was formally accepted by the Government of Israel after prolonged discussions, in the Ben Gurion–Blaustein 'Pact' of 1950.[2] Israel's Prime Minister reaffirmed:

The Jews of the United States, as a community and as individuals, have only one political attachment and that is to the United States of America. They owe no political allegiance to Israel. . . . the State of Israel represents and speaks only on behalf of its own citizens, and in no way presumes to represent or speak in the name of the Jews who are citizens of any other country.

As for the no less sensitive topic of immigration,

we should like to see American Jews come and take part in our effort. We need their technical knowledge [etc.] . . . But the decision as to whether they wish to come—permanently or temporarily—rests with the free discretion of each American Jew himself. It is entirely a matter of his own volition.

[1] The American Jewish Committee, *In Vigilant Brotherhood*, New York, 1965, p. 64.
[2] The full text of the Ben Gurion and Blaustein statements is ibid., pp. 64–6 and 66–9, respectively.

Blaustein's reply illuminated the AJC's concern and pressed its demand bluntly:

[Israel] must recognize that the matter of goodwill between its citizens and those of other countries is a two-way street: that Israel also has a responsibility in this situation—a responsibility . . . of not affecting adversely the sensibilities of Jews who are citizens of other states by what it says or does.

As for the Zionist 'exile' thesis, he was unequivocal:

American Jews vigorously repudiate any suggestion or implication that they are in exile. American Jews—young and old alike, Zionists and non-Zionists alike—are profoundly attached to America. . . . To American Jews, America is home.

This concordat was the result of grave disquiet among American Jews and others over the charge of 'dual loyalty'. It was reaffirmed in 1957 and, more formally, in 1961, following an acid comment on Diaspora Jews by Ben Gurion: 'Whoever dwells outside the land of Israel is considered to have no God, the sages said.' When Eshkol replaced Ben Gurion as Prime Minister in June 1963, Blaustein sought and received written assurances that both would abide by the 1961 State-ment. Eshkol remarked: 'You are right when you say that this under-standing enjoyed my full support. It continues to do so and will do so in the future.'[1]

No other interest group was ever granted the status of bargaining equal, apparent in the AJC–Government of Israel negotiations. In 1951 the *Knesset* did approve a law conferring special status on the World Zionist Organization, but this was diluted under pressure from various Jewish bodies. In the early years, too, the WZO tried to secure an invitation for Goldmann to Israeli Cabinet meetings: Ben Gurion refused, according to Goldmann, because of his obsession with sovereignty. 'I once told BG', he added, 'that the only two people who cared about sovereignty were de Gaulle and himself.'[2] Ben Gurion's explanation was different: 'I knew that, while having fewer members, the American Jewish Committee has greater influence in the life of American Jewry and with the American Government than does the Zionist Movement.' And to this he added his deep-rooted disdain for unfulfilled Zionists: 'American Zionists call themselves ZIONISTS, but they are not real Zionists. A Zionist is a man who comes to settle in Israel.'[3] And it was Ben Gurion's image which shaped Israel's

---

[1] Ibid., p. 59. The text of the 1961 Joint Statement is on pp. 69–70.

[2] Interview in Jerusalem, April 1966.

[3] Interview in Sde Boker, June 1966. On the status accorded to Blaustein and the American Jewish Committee, Eshkol remarked: 'I cannot tell you the reason. Perhaps it was because Ben Gurion has been in conflict with the Zionist Organization since the beginning of the State. The AJC had remained aloof and was antithetical to the Zionist Organization.' Interview in Jerusalem, Aug. 1966.

governmental receptivity to the demands generated by externally-based Jewish interest groups.

Apart from relations with non-Israeli Jews, the direct influence of Diaspora Jewry on Israel's foreign policy has been marginal. As Ya'acov Tsur, a former Acting Director-General of the Foreign Ministry and Ambassador to France, remarked: 'American Jewry tried to modify Israel's policy but they succeeded only in details.' He cited as an example American Jewry's pressure to extradite Robert Soblen, accused accomplice of the Rosenbergs in the celebrated espionage case; Soblen had fled to Israel.[1] On an earlier occasion Tsur had noted: 'The World Zionist Organization has no part in foreign policy-making; rather, it will play a role when world Jewry has to be mobilized in defence of Israel', that is, in an instrumental capacity.[2] Goldmann, too, ascribed to it little influence in the Ben Gurion era: 'I wouldn't say that Jewry tried to have influence and that Ben Gurion would not accept it; in my opinion, Jewry was too loyal to Israel.'[3]

Certainly, Israel went its own way in the major areas where dissent was apparent. All efforts to establish a UN military presence on Israel's territory failed. And United Nations' resolutions were treated in the manner of all sovereign states: those which served Israeli interests were accepted; those which were perceived as inimical were rejected. The policy of reprisal, too, was unaffected by the demands of external (and some internal) interest groups: it was a constant in the enduring conflict with Israel's neighbours.

Diaspora Jewry was a significant variable in an *objective* sense, however, for it occupied a key place in Israel's élite images and their policy consequences. This was affirmed by decision-makers with remarkable consistency.[4]

iii. *Civil Servants*

The civil servant community in Israel, as elsewhere, performs various foreign policy functions. The most important is implementation of strategic-level policy authorized by the system. Closely related is involvement in the formulation of tactical decisions. Both will be explored in depth later.[5] There is a third role which is relevant here, namely, interest group advocacy. This role is inherent in the Foreign Office and other ministries *qua* institutions: they constantly urge,

[1] Interview in Jerusalem, April 1966. Prime Minister Eshkol concurred that, in the Soblen case, American Jewry's views prevailed in an Israeli foreign policy decision. Interview in Jerusalem, Aug. 1966.

[2] Interview in Jerusalem, Aug. 1960.

[3] Interview in Jerusalem, April 1966.

[4] The central place of Diaspora Jewry and Jewishness in the attitudinal prism of Israel's foreign policy élite will be delineated in ch. 11 (a) and (b) below.

[5] See ch. 15 and 20 below.

recommend, 'demand', press for, in short, advocate specific policy acts to those with authority to make decisions.

One illustration was the pressure by a 'South African group' in the Foreign Ministry to tread softly on the *Apartheid* issue lest South African Jews suffer the backlash. 'On no issue do I remember more discussion than on *Apartheid*—among issues not directly concerning Israel's vital interests', remarked Dr. Haim Yahil, Director-General of the Foreign Ministry from 1960 to 1964. 'Since 1951 this has been so. There was intense discussion among officials in the Foreign Office. The majority pressed for a strong line on principle; a minority stressed the welfare of South African Jews.'[1]

Another important issue in which civil servant pressure was operative —far more effectively—concerned diplomatic relations with the People's Republic of China in 1954–5.[2] In the realm of foreign economic policy, a group of economists concentrated in the Finance Ministry and the Bank of Israel pressed successfully for devaluation in 1962: Sapir, then Minister of Commerce and Industry, opposed; Eshkol, then Finance Minister, yielded, perhaps knowing that the International Monetary Fund shared the Israeli economists' policy recommendations.[3]

An illuminating example of the Foreign Office Technical Élite acting as an institutional interest group is Israel's decision to vote against a US-sponsored resolution on the Arab refugees at the 1965 General Assembly. The draft incorporated the principle of repatriation or compensation, as approved in Article 11 of the 1948 Assembly resolution on this issue. Israel always accepted the *principle*, with a stress on compensation, but rejected the notion that it should be implemented by the *free choice* of *individual* refugees, preferring an overall agreement among the states concerned.

The decision process reveals the civil servant role. There was, at first, some disagreement in Israel's UN Delegation as to abstention or opposition; gradually, a consensus was reached on abstention. The Foreign Minister, Mrs. Meir, favoured explicit opposition to the US resolution.

The *Hanhalah* (Directorate) of the Ministry, comprising the Director-General, Assistant Directors-General, and Advisers, with the relevant Department Directors, invited to meetings on an *ad hoc* basis, and the Foreign Minister attending at his (her) pleasure, held at least seven 'consultations', marked by vigorous discussion. All but two persons favoured abstention, on the grounds that 'we would place ourselves in a position of isolation'; the Director-General was uncommitted; and

[1] Interview in Jerusalem, Aug. 1966.
[2] This case will be examined in depth in a later volume on Israeli high-policy decisions.
[3] Related by various persons—officials, journalists, and economists—during interviews in Israel in 1965–6.

one participant supported the Minister. Her response was: 'We must not be ashamed to be alone when our vital interests are involved.' United States pressure was considerable—directly on the Delegation in New York and through a letter from US Representative to the UN, Arthur Goldberg, to Mrs. Meir, strongly advising her, in Israel's interests, to abstain and avoid 'isolation'. Strong pressure was brought to bear from New York and within Israel, with dozens of telephone calls. Mrs. Meir, despite her personal influence on Israeli policy, found it necessary to yield to the extent of agreeing to take the issue to the Cabinet, saying, 'I will put all the objections of the *haverim* [friends] to my position as fairly as possible but I will argue strongly for my view.' The Cabinet gave her unanimous support, and Israel voted against the resolution.[1]

Other cases of a civil servant interest group role are scattered in this study. It remains to note still other institutional interest groups in Israel's foreign policy. One is the United Nations Organization, whose activities have been meshed with Israel since her independence—and even before.[2] Another is the 'foreign press', notably such newspapers and journals as the *New York Times*, the London *Times*, *Le Monde*, and the *Economist*: all are widely read by Israel's decision-making élite, both political and technical, and thereby influence images of the external environment to which Israeli policy must adjust. It is impossible to measure their influence; it would be an error to disregard them. Finally, there is evidence, to be adduced later, that foreign diplomats in Israel have 'advocated' specific acts directly to decision-makers in Israel.[3]

(b) ASSOCIATIONAL INTEREST GROUPS

There are many organized pressures in Israel's political system, apart from the parties and enduring institutions discussed earlier. Some focus primarily on domestic issues (*Histadrut*, Israel Manufacturers' Association, *kibbutz* and *moshav* organizations, etc.).[4] Others concentrate on relations with the Arabs in Israel and in the Near East as a whole. Some foreign policy interest groups emerge from special conditions and generate pressure on a specific issue, such as the Land of Israel Movement following the 1967 War. Some are persistent advocates of alter-

---

[1] Related by one of the participants during an interview in Jerusalem in April 1966. There was an interesting epilogue to this incident. A week after the vote Goldberg wrote another letter to Mrs. Meir saying that, looking back upon the events, he would have voted as she did, if he had been in her position.

[2] The UN role in various issues will be analysed in a companion volume on Israeli high-policy decisions.

[3] Ibid.

[4] The *kibbutzim* and *moshavim* performed an important advocacy role on the question of Jordan Waters. This will be explored in the companion volume.

native approaches to Israel's neighbours, for example, *New Outlook,
Ha'olam Hazeh,* the *Kena'anim* and *Ihud.* There is also a spill-over type
of interest advocacy, from economic organizations to foreign economic
policy, as with the issue of Israel's links with the European Common
Market. There is, in short, an abundance of associational pressures in
Israel's foreign policy system. The more important 'permanent' groups
will be examined in this context; *ad hoc* groups will be explored later
in the relevant case study.

i. *New Outlook*

New Outlook is an English-language monthly journal published in
Tel Aviv. Founded in 1957, in the aftermath of the Sinai Campaign,
it may be described as an organized movement of opinion directed to
Arab–Jewish reconciliation and peace in the Near East. 'A Statement
of Purpose', which appears in each issue, suggests this goal in muted
terms:

It is the desire of the sponsors and editors of NEW OUTLOOK that this publication
serve as a medium for the clarification of problems concerning peace and
cooperation among all the peoples of the Middle East . . .
  NEW OUTLOOK will strive to reflect those aspirations and accomplishments
in the economic, social and cultural fields that are common to all the peoples
and countries of the area and could, given the elimination of frictions and
animosities, flourish and produce an ever greater abundance of well-being and
happiness.

What distinguishes *New Outlook* was more sharply portrayed by Zvi
Klementynowsky, a member of its Board of Directors, as well as of the
Executive of the Liberal Party, in his opening remarks to a 1963
Symposium, one of many, on 'New Paths to Peace Between Israel and
the Arab Countries':[1]

New Outlook raises the problems of peace and of mutual relationships in the
Middle East, not as a Jewish-Arab problem alone, nor only as a regional one,
but as an international problem liable to influence, for good and evil, the
affairs of the world as a whole.
  Our fundamental assumption and constantly reiterated argument is that the
State of Israel is a fact and an inseparable part of the Middle East—both
geographically and politically. . . .
  New Outlook is an organ devoted to one aim alone—the attainment of peace
between Israel and the Arabs and improved relations in the region. It is also
one of the few journals—sometimes the only one—whose pages confront Jews
and Arabs, Israelis and members of other nations (including Africans and
Asians) interested in the problems of this region.
  The aspiration of its editors has been to seek . . . an agreement between the
liberation movement of the Jewish people returning to its homeland and
building its state and the liberation movements of the Arab peoples.

[1] *New Outlook* (Tel Aviv), vol. 6, no. 2 (51), Feb. 1963, pp. 17–18.

Many prominent Israelis—academics, journalists, politicians, and lawyers—have contributed to the dialogue of which *New Outlook* is justly proud. But in so far as it functions as an interest group in foreign policy, the image and advocacy of *New Outlook* are most acutely expressed in the writings of Simha Flapan, a member of its Editorial Board and Director of *Mapam*'s Arab Department. His voluminous articles are lucid and consistent. Basically, they articulate his party's line towards the Arab minority in Israel and the myriad of issues arising from the 'Arab–Israel conflict'. But Flapan appears to go further along the road to accommodation than *Mapam* leaders. Suffice it to select a few extracts from Flapan's writings—for the year 1963: the tone and substance were no different before or after.

But can we really continue to exist in a situation which every few years leads to greater conflict? Let me remind you: in 1936 we shot at each other with rifles, in 1948 it was tanks, in 1956 heavy tanks and jet planes, and now we have almost come to nuclear weapons. Can we really say that Israel or the Arab states can exist, and achieve their national and social aims, without a peace settlement?

But there have been contacts, there have been attempts, there have been negotiations. . . . The North African countries had always adopted a rational attitude to Israel . . . and they made offers of contacts and of mediation. But these opportunities were lost as a result of certain policies which we adopted in international affairs. . . . There have been voices, even recently. But we, in the grip of a psychosis which is partly the natural result of fear and an awareness of danger, and partly artificial, somehow no longer hear these more realistic voices—and they are there to be heard, even in the Arab States.

One of the most important [factors to be activated] are the Israeli Arabs. . . . The essential problem is the philosophy behind Military Government, the doctrine that the Arabs in Israel are a foreign body, a potential danger which must on no account be allowed to gather force. This doctrine is as dangerous as it is ill-conceived.[1]

There cannot be any peace on terms dictated by one party. There must be give and take.[2]

The main object of Israeli foreign policy must be to overcome this hostility.

Armaments have become a substitute for foreign policy and instead of being a means of defense they have become an end in themselves, to which all other aspects . . . must be subservient. This is the fundamental error of Mr. Peres' approach [that of the *Mapai* Establishment], and from that fallacy he goes on from error to error, misstating certain facts, ignoring others, in order to make reality fit his theory.

Arab hostility is not an unchanging and, even less, an unchangeable fact.

[By joining forces with Britain and France in 1956], perhaps more than the actual Israeli campaign in Sinai, it inflamed Arab hatred to an extent and an intensity hitherto unknown.[3]

[1] 'The Utter Necessity of Peace', ibid., vol. 6, no. 3 (52), March–April 1963, pp. 84–6.   [2] 'Beginnings That Bore Fruit', ibid., p. 21.
[3] 'Wonderful Logic—All Wrong', ibid., vol. 6, no. 7 (56), Sept. 1963, pp. 26–32.

The sponsors of this venture in Arab–Jewish reconciliation were a distinguished group of individuals in Israeli society. Among the fifty-seven names listed at the outset, ten were university professors, led by the venerable Martin Buber and including David Baneth (Arabic), S. N. Eisenstadt (Sociology), Shalev Ginossar (Law), and Ernst Simon (Education). There was also a representative group of ten MKs—three Progressives (Foerder, Harari, later of *Mapai*, and Shocken, the first a prominent banker and the last the publisher of *Ha'aretz*), three from *Mapam*, including Ya'ari and Hazan, two General Zionists or Liberals (Saphir and Ichilov), David Hacohen from *Mapai*, and Moshe Unna from the NRP. There were also men of letters, notably Avraham Shlonsky, businessman, and nine Arabs, headed by George Hakim, then Greek Orthodox Archbishop of Acre and Galilee. There were changes over the years but the core group remained, including members of the *Knesset* of five parties.

Shmuel Hugo Bergmann, the eminent philosopher, and Gabriel Baer, a specialist on modern Arab history, were Advisory Editors throughout the first decade. The direction of *New Outlook*, however, was shaped by five men: Flapan; Dr. Haim Darin-Drabkin, a senior economist in the Ministry of Housing for many years and author of books on the *kibbutz*, housing in Israel, etc.; Ze'ev Katz, a member of the editorial staff of *Ha'aretz*; Yitzhak Ziv-av, a former managing editor of the General Zionist newspaper *Ha-boker*, author, and Director-General of the Israel Farmers' Federation; and *Mapam* MK Abdul Aziz Zu'bi. On one occasion Flapan claimed that 'the pressure of public opinion', largely 'under the impact of *New Outlook*', was responsible for 'important relaxations in the Military Administration [and] a considerable advance in many fields of Jewish–Arab relations ...'.[1] Closer to the mark, however, was the acknowledgement by a member of its Board of Directors in 1963: 'It is, however, a matter of fact, that *New Outlook*'s influence abroad has been much greater than in Israel.'[2] Nor has the impact of this interest group grown over the years.

ii. *Ha'olam Hazeh—Ko'ah Hadash* (New Force)

Among Israel's foreign policy interest groups, perhaps the most vociferous is *Ha'olam Hazeh*, an aspiring political movement created in 1965 by Uri Avneri, the controversial editor of Israel's mass circulation weekly of the same name. For many years this magazine has combined serious comment on public policy, scandal and gossip, and sex pictorials: its readership has grown steadily. In the sixth *Knesset* elections Avneri headed a *Ha'olam Hazeh* party list and secured one seat in parliament—for himself. A new forum was now available for his

[1] 'Beginnings That Bore Fruit', p. 20.
[2] Zvi Klementynowsky, 'Five Years of New Outlook', ibid., vol. 6, no. 2 (51), Feb. 1963, p. 18.

pungent views. (In the seventh elections, 1969, the party won two seats.) Avneri's world view has been articulated in half a dozen books and pamphlets, apart from his editorials in *Ha'olam Hazeh*.[1] In the broadest sense it is secularist, Left-socialist, anti-Zionist, and committed to Semitic regionalism: the Jews of Israel, that is the Hebrews, are one of many Semitic peoples in the Near East, not a segment of a world-wide Jewish People. His goal is a Confederation of the 'Semitic Area'—from the Atlantic to Iran, including Turkey, the Arab peoples, and Israel. An offshoot of the 'Canaanite' ideology (to be noted later), Avneri's image has taken a distinctive path.

His foreign policy platform in 1965 was not unusual. It called for 'loyalty without reserve to the State of Israel, to its sovereignty, to its integrity and security. . . . [Its] independence . . . cannot be the object of bargaining.' At the global level it advocated 'restoring Israel's political independence [by] absolute non-identification with the world blocs of the East or the West'. And, as a mark of special concern, it urged 'an Israeli peace campaign in the Region'; more specifically, 'the setting up of a special ministry for Regional Affairs and Peace Headquarters which will plan and execute imaginative peace operations'.[2] This was not essentially different from *Mapam*'s conciliatory line, but the two diverge sharply on Zionism. Indeed, Avneri showed contempt for the Israel Communist Party's move towards Zionism in the mid-1960s.[3]

While urging non-identification with either of the two global blocs, Avneri favoured Israel's alignment with the Third World and, within it, as noted, membership in a Confederation of the 'Semitic Area'. He deplored Israel's rejection of Peking's offer of diplomatic relations in 1955—'we killed it'—and perceived a future link only via Israel–Arab reconciliation. Communist China, he added, will go the way of Soviet revisionism. He did not oppose diplomatic ties with Germany; in fact, he favoured relations with any existing régime. He accepted the Johnston Plan for the division of the Jordan Waters and acknowledged that Israel had to draw its allotted share pending negotiations. He was opposed to participation in the European Common Market but favoured one for the Near East; as befits his image, he rejected the idea that 'Israel is part of Europe'.

Like the Israeli Communists, Avneri contends that the relations

---

[1] Among them are: *Our Struggle* (1946); *War or Peace in the Semitic Region* (1947); *Total War* (1947); *In the Fields of the Philistines* (1949); *The Other Side of the Medal* (1950); *The Swastika* (1961); and, for a Western, English-speaking audience, in Israel's twentieth year, *Israel Without Zionists: A Plea for Peace in the Middle East*, Macmillan, New York, 1968. (All but the last were in Hebrew.) Avneri's image and advocacy pertaining to the Arab-Israel conflict are restated briefly in his 'Unofficial and Unrepresentative but . . .', *New Middle East*, London, no. 12, Sept. 1969, pp. 23–8.

[2] The text is in *New Outlook* (Tel Aviv), vol. 8, no. 7 (74), Oct. 1965, p. 56.

[3] Interview in Jerusalem, March 1966. This summary of Avneri's foreign policy demands is based on that interview.

between Israel and the Arab states are the key to everything else, internal and external, in Israel's policy. Alone among the party lists, *Ha'olam Hazeh* rejects the Law of Return—on theoretical grounds—but accepts *aliya* in practice: 'we seek to define reality as it is'. 'Israel is a state of two peoples', Avneri declared, as did Communist leader Moshe Sneh; 'one has achieved independence, the other has not; the task is to develop an Arab state in Palestine.' Avneri, in 1966, and again after the Six Day War, advocated a Federation of Israel and 'Palestine'. He has long supported the right of Palestine Arab refugees to return to their homes: 'why not; we have accepted two million Jews. . . .' The foreign policy posture is clear, and Avneri is a lucid advocate. *Ha'olam Hazeh* is highly vocal. But as an interest group its influence has been marginal.

iii. *Others*

The texture of foreign policy interest groups in Israel is further enriched by little-known or *ad hoc* associations which attempt to generate pressure on decision-makers. In the Canaanite stream is a group known as *Semitic Action*, founded in 1958 by former members of the underground *Lehi* or Stern Group. It was loosely connected with a small group of marginal and politically discontented intellectuals of the older *Yishuv*, organized as *Ha-mishtar He-hadash* (The New Régime), and emphasized the necessity of becoming integrated with all Semites. The initial aim of *Semitic Action* was a bi-national state of Israel and Arab Palestine, with full equality for all citizens. During the first stage both parts would retain sovereignty in matters of security, currency, and customs. In time, this 'League of the Jordan'—which would solve the Arab refugee problem by resettlement and rehabilitation within its territory—would participate in a federation of all Semitic peoples in the Middle East. In the global context, this federation would practise non-alignment on the Indian model. Further Jewish immigration was to be encouraged, as long as the interests of the 'League' and of the larger federation permitted.[1]

A bi-national state was also espoused by an élitist group in the pre-State *Yishuv*, the *Ihud* (Union for Jewish–Arab Rapprochement), led by the first president of the Hebrew University, Judah Magnes, and Martin Buber.[2] The coming of independence and the enduring Arab–Israel conflict reduced to the outer margin of influence this small interest group of intellectuals. The *Ihud* Association for Jewish–Arab Rapprochement, better known after independence as *Brit Shalom* (Covenant of Peace), persists as an advocate of concession, compromise, and conciliation, akin to the demands of *New Outlook*: indeed, many of the *Ihud*

---

[1] For a brief report on *Semitic Action* see *New Outlook*, vol. 2, no. 1, Sept. 1958, p. 56.

[2] For a succinct and informative survey of the origins and programme of *Ihud* see Susan Lee Hattis, *The Bi-National Idea in Palestine During Mandatory Times*, Shikmona, Haifa, 1970, pp. 258–71, 287–92, 308–11.

supporters are active contributors to its pages. Typical of the post-independence *Ihud* policy line was an 'open letter' from the editor of its organ, *Ner* (Candle), to the Deputy Minister of Defence, Peres, in 1961: '... there is no need for a peace treaty', wrote Dr. Shimon Shereshevsky, 'in order to bring about a state of co-operation and understanding between nations.' The only project which *requires* Arab–Israeli co-operation is the rehabilitation of the refugees, and 'as a basis, let us start from the United Nations resolutions', that is, the right of return: 'I consciously and out of conviction belong to those who demand that "Israel change the sequence, i.e. readmit part of the refugees before the establishment of peace, in the expectation that this readmission will pave the way for the longed-for peace".' The 'peace through deterrent strength' thesis was rejected as an illusion. And finally, 'it is the duty of every true patriot to demand insistently that the Government take the initiative in exchanging the present state of "no war and no peace" for one of understanding and closer relations.' Few in Israel have been persuaded.[1]

The Council of the *Sepharadi* (Spanish) Community in Jerusalem is the only ethnic-based Israeli associational interest group which advocates foreign policy goals.[2] Proudly tracing its descent to a body of Spanish Jews established in Jerusalem by the illustrious *Ramban*, Nahmanides, in 1267, the Council in the late 1960s comprised 62 elected members ranging across the ideological spectrum from *Maki* to *Herut*. Its activities since independence have centred on two issues: the relations between the (dominant) *Ashkenazi* or European Jews and the (subordinate) *Sepharadim*, which include all the Eastern (*Mizrahi*) or Oriental Jewish communities; and secondly, Jewish–Arab relations.[3]

The latter, foreign policy, theme is evident in the programmes of the *Sepharadi* List for the first two *Knesset* elections.[4] In 1949 it advocated 'The Saving of a Million of our Persecuted Brothers who are Trapped by the Arabs'. In 1951 it pressed for 'The Elimination of the Ishmaelic [Arabic] Dispersion', by which was meant: 'we must activate the increasing *aliya* of our brethren while there is still time'; it also demanded compensation for Jews departing from Arab lands, whose property

---

[1] The 'open letter' was reprinted as 'Peace—Without a Peace Treaty', in *New Outlook* (Tel Aviv), vol. 4, no. 7 (38), July 1961, pp. 3–9. These and related views were reiterated to the author in October 1970. A comprehensive statement of *Ihud*'s advocacy after the Six Day War appears in a special issue of *Ner*, Jerusalem, Dec. 1969.

[2] The German-speaking *Aliya Hadasha* did so before independence but then merged into the Progressive, later the Independent Liberal Party. The Yemenites, too, acted as a pressure group but without foreign policy concerns.

[3] This analysis is based upon an interview with the perennial President of the Council, Elie Eliachar, in Jerusalem in November 1970, and upon published materials provided by him.

[4] The election platforms for the first and second *Knesset* elections are to be found in *Hed Ha-mizrah* (Echo of the East), Jerusalem, no. 9, 7 Jan. 1949, p. 9, and ibid., no. 17, 8 July 1951, p. 2.

was being confiscated. By the time of the third *Knesset* elections (1955), the mass exodus of Jews from the Near East Arab states, notably Yemen and Iraq, had been completed. Thereafter, the *Sepharadim* did not contest a national election along communal lines.

From time to time the Council spoke out on other foreign policy issues as well. Its dominant figure for thirty years, Elie Eliachar, openly called for alignment with the West in May 1950, specifically urging Israel's request for Marshall Plan and Point Four aid.[1] The following year, the *Sepharadi* List was allied with the vocally pro-Western General Zionists. And in 1955 it advocated Israel's participation in defence pacts with 'the democratic countries of the West'. It also called for 'good relations with the countries of the Far and Near East' and 'peace with our neighbours', but it sternly rebuffed any efforts to reduce Israel's territory or her sovereignty.[2]

There was one foreign policy initiative of a bilateral type—pressure in favour of diplomatic relations with Spain in 1949. Eliachar played an active role, on the basis of reliable indications of an interest in Madrid: he used the *Knesset* platform to air his view that the Franco régime had saved the lives of many Jews during the Second World War and that it was certainly no more odious than the régimes of Péron, Stalin, and Tito, with whom Israel had formal relations. He also pressed Foreign Minister Sharett—but to no avail; Spain's fascist ideology was anathema to the decision-makers.[3]

After the Six Day War, Eliachar once more urged a fresh approach to Israel's neighbours. 'The order of the hour', he wrote to Prime Minister Eshkol on 18 June 1967, 'is to seek ways to liquidate [the refugee] problem . . . , the cardinal problem besetting a peaceful settlement . . .'; he also set out the idea of helping to establish a Palestine Arab entity.[4] Thereafter, he pressed his 'doveish' views through the Council's bi-monthly organ, *Bema'arakha* (In the Campaign).[5] There he castigated Israeli policy—'we missed a great and rare opportunity . . . for a final peaceful settlement with the Arabs of Palestine . . . in June 1967'. He urged the creation of a Palestine entity on the West Bank with which Israel should negotiate, and he did not reject the idea of negotiating with the *feda'iyun*: 'Is not the US negotiating with the Vietcong? Had not Paris reached an agreement with the Algerian FLN?'

---

[1] In a *Knesset* speech, reported in *Jerusalem Post*, 30 May 1950.

[2] Election Brochure, 'On What Will We Struggle in the Third Knesset?'

[3] In a letter dated 23 March 1949 the Israel Foreign Office informed Eliachar that it was not then interested in diplomatic relations with Spain. By 1953, when Israel had changed her attitude, it was too late.

[4] The above extract and those to follow are taken from Elie Eliacher, 'Israeli Jews and Palestinian Arabs: Key to Arab–Jewish Coexistence', Council of the *Sepharadi*. Community, Jerusalem, 1970.

[5] The bi-monthly successor, since 1960, of *Hed Ha-mizrah*, which appeared from 1942 to 1954; it has a circulation of about 4,000.

He called for mutual concessions but not on the fundamentals of Israel —her Jewishness, the Law of Return, and her existence as an independent state. He opposed Jewish settlement in the occupied territories. And on the most sensitive issue of all he proposed a condominium over Jerusalem, a capital city to be shared by Israel and Jordan or a Palestine Arab state, with an Israeli–Arab Municipal Government to manage local affairs.

By 1970, some of these ideas, notably that pertaining to a Palestine Arab entity, had begun to acquire legitimacy and support among the Israeli public. But, despite its very large claimed constituency (the Eastern Jewish communities comprise more than half of Israel's population), the Council of the *Sepharadi* Community has been without influence as a pressure group in Israel's foreign policy system—and with little influence on internal communal relations either.

The most extreme anti-Establishment interest groups on the Left are the small Israeli Socialist Organization, known in Israel by the name of its organ, *Matzpen* (Compass), and *Siah, Smol Israeli Hadash.* the Israeli New Left. *Matzpen* began as a (Jewish) dissident group in the still-united Communist Party of Israel (pre-1965), opposing neo-Stalinism and sympathizing with Maoist China, and rejecting the exclusively parliamentary methods of the Communist Party. Expelled in 1962, it retained an autonomous organizational existence and received growing attention *outside* Israel after the Six Day War. Its membership is perhaps five hundred.

Siah, with a membership of about two hundred, was founded at the end of 1967, as one of two splinters from *Mapam*, when that 'Old Left' party became formally associated, but did not merge, with the Alignment.[1] Unlike *Matzpen*, it is a staunch defender of a Jewish State and concentrates its foreign policy advocacy on the crucial issue of the day— 'whither Israel and Palestine'. Thus, at the height of the Jordan civil war in September 1970, it declared:[2]

The future belongs to the People of Israel and to the Palestinian Arab People, who will establish their sovereignty in our region, one beside the other. . . . [Further] the Government of Israel, which is now sabotaging the Jarring talks, is obliged to return to the bargaining table. . . . [And] in the recognition of the mutual national rights of the revived State of Israel and of the Palestinian Arab People is based . . . the possibility of security and peace.

These aims—and the related opposition to Jewish settlement in the occupied territories—are shared by a much larger community of disenchanted Jewish students abroad, the Radical Zionists.[3] But their

[1] The other was *Brit Ha-smol* (Union of the Left), headed by *Mapam* veteran, Ya'acov Riftin. It does not differ fundamentally from the parent party on ideological or foreign policy issues.   [2] *Siah* (Tel Aviv), 6, 15 Nov. 1970, p. 5.
[3] See for example the *Jewish Radical*, published bi-monthly (irregular) since 1969, by the Berkeley group of Radical Zionist students.

harsh criticism of Israeli policy does not challenge the legitimacy of Zionism as the creed of a Jewish national liberation movement. *Matzpen* goes far beyond the *Siah* critique in its foreign policy advocacy. *Matzpen's* principal thesis is that the Arabs cannot accept a state in the region which represents not only the interests of its own inhabitants but also those of Jewry throughout the world. Thus the Law of Return must be abolished. At the same time, *Matzpen* asserts the right of the Jews of Palestine to national self-determination, on the grounds that 'As a result of Zionist colonization, a Hebrew nation with its own national characteristics (common language, separate economy, etc.) has been formed in Palestine. . . . *One can therefore sum up the solution which we propose by the formula: de-Zionization of Israel and its integration in a socialist Middle Eastern union.*'[1] To this image and advocacy, which were reiterated in a series of statements during the eighteen months after the 1967 War, *Matzpen* added the broader goal—a necessity, it declared, of 'a fundamental transformation of the régimes in all the countries of the region—i.e. a socialist revolution'.

As for the Palestine Arabs, *Matzpen* recognizes their right to an independent state and the legitimacy of their resistance to 'Zionist conquest' '. . . by every means that are considered legitimate in any case of occupation', thus including terror and sabotage. They also proclaim their solidarity with *Al-Fatah* and related 'liberation' organizations, dissenting only from the formal liquidation of an independent Jewish state. And in global terms they identify themselves with the revolutionary part of the Third World. Neither of these sources of pressure—or the two larger organized political groups on the Left, *Maki* and *Rakah*—has ever been influential in Israel's foreign policy system.[2]

At the other extreme of the associational interest group spectrum is the *Ha-tenu'ah Lema'an Eretz Yisrael Ha-shlemah*, known as The Land of Israel Movement. Arising out of the Six Day War, its basic demand is direct and not unpopular—retain all of the occupied territories. Nationalist fervour and a mystical strain permeate its initial manifesto of 20 September 1967:[3]

The Six Day War has opened up a new and decisive era for the people and the State of Israel. The Jewish nation has come into the possession of its reunited

---

[1] 'The Palestine Problem and the Israeli–Arab Dispute', 2 June 1967, in The Israeli Socialist Organization (*Matzpen*), *A Collection of Political Statements 1967–69*, Tel Aviv, n.d., pp. 2–3. Subsequent extracts are taken from this source.

[2] *Maki* and *Rakah* will be analysed in the following chapter. Suffice it to note in this context that *Maki's* foreign policy advocacy for the Middle East (after 1965) is very similar to that of *Siah*; if anything, it is more conservative, for in addition to accepting the Jewish State and the Law of Return as the point of departure, it terms Israel's struggle as one of national defence and independence, with a tone less critical of the Establishment. *Rakah*, by contrast, is totally committed to the Moscow line on the Arab–Israel conflict and foreign policy generally. As such, it is more critical of Israel's policies than are *Siah* and *Maki*, but it is much less revolutionary than *Matzpen*.

[3] Reproduced in *Jerusalem Post Weekly*, 1 April 1968.

and undivided territory. We have as little right to slight the gift of victory as to abandon the State of Israel.

We hold ourselves committed to the integrity of our country. Such is our responsibility towards the generations that have gone before and towards the generations to come, and no Israeli government, however constituted, is entitled to surrender any part of this territorial integrity, which represents the inherent and inalienable right of our people from the beginnings of its history.

Our present boundaries are a guarantee of security and peace and open up unprecedented vistas of national, material and spiritual consolidation . . .

. . . only by means of a great influx of new immigrants from all parts of the Diaspora can we hope to build up and establish the Land of Israel as a unified national entity. . . .

The undersigned hereby dedicate themselves to the fulfilment of these tasks and responsibilities, and will do all within their power to bring about their active implementation by the people as a whole.

This programme echoes the oft-reiterated demand of *Herut*; and, indeed, that party has expressed its active support. But the Land of Israel Movement was sponsored by prominent men and women of many political affiliations and professions. The most distinguished men of letters are (were) among them—Nobel Laureate S. Y. Agnon, Natan Alterman, Uri Zvi Greenberg, and Moshe Shamir. So too was the widow of Israel's second president, Mrs. Rahel Ben-Zvi. There were half a dozen *Aluffim*, including the first Chief of Staff of *Tzahal*, Ya'acov Dori, a former Air Force Commander, Dan Tolkowsky, and a veteran field commander in all three Arab–Israeli wars, Avraham Yoffe. An ex-Director-General of the Foreign Ministry, Dr. Haim Yahil, was a sponsor, along with the controversial former Chief of the Security Services, Isser Harel. There were also scholars from all of Israel's universities. In fact, no other foreign policy interest group grew so quickly or had such a broad representative character. It was a variable of some influence in Israel's policy on territorial and related issues after the 1967 War, though it did not become a mass organization.[1]

There are three academic-type groups interested in foreign policy: the Israel Political Science Association; the Foreign Policy Association, established by Harari in Tel Aviv as a forum for lectures by specialists in world affairs; and the Institute for International Problems in Tel Aviv. All are marginal in terms of influence, mere forums for debate in the presence of men close to the decision-makers. A specialized economic interest group which exerted effective pressure on Israel's policy towards the Common Market is the citrus growers, acting through the Israel Farmers Federation and the Citrus Marketing

[1] There was also a short-lived counter-pressure to the Land of Israel Movement, established by younger academics and professionals in Jerusalem and Tel Aviv. This will be explored in a related volume on Israeli high-policy decisions.

Board.[1] The communal and co-operative settlements (*kibbutzim* and *moshavim*) also performed this advocacy function, especially in the Jordan Waters issue.

(c) NON-ASSOCIATIONAL INTEREST GROUPS

i. The Kena'anim (The Canaanites)

Uri Avneri's ideological roots lie in the Canaanite Movement, founded in the 1940s by a talented Hebrew poet, Yonathan Ratosh. The *Kena'anim* reject the pivotal concept of 'Am Yisrael'—the Jewish People. Rather, they perceive the modern Israeli as the descendant of the ancient Canaanite, the carrier of its language and culture in the territorial homeland. All who live in this Biblical land, whose mother tongue is Hebrew, and who identify with its traditions, belong to the *Hebrew* nation reborn. Jews elsewhere in the world are not, automatically, members of this nation; those who migrate to Israel and become absorbed in its language and culture, become 'Hebrews'; so, too, Arabs who accept the Canaanite tradition become participants in the nation. And that nation is Middle Eastern, not global. Its future is irrevocably linked to the Middle East region.

The *Kena'anim* have remained a fringe group in Israel, though they attracted attention in the forties among some *avant-garde* intellectuals: Ratosh's call for a Hebrew national renascence in the cradle of its civilization was not without appeal. His prescriptions for peace after the Six Day War provide more insight into this unusual interest group.[2] Ratosh advocates radical means to enhance the Hebrew nation, its Israeli state, and its culture: a strong army; retention of all the occupied territories; larger immigration and measures to raise the birth-rate; the replacement of Arabic by Hebrew in the minority schools; links with national and religious minorities in the adjacent states—Druzes, Kurds, etc.; and an alliance with Jordan, with the latter in a protected status. At the same time he demands steps to equalize the status of Jews and Arabs in Israel: Arabs should be admitted to Hebrew schools and the armed forces; all prerogatives of Jewish religion should be abolished; and the special links with world Jewry should be severed. The goal is to create an attachment to ISRAEL transcending all communal and religious allegiances. The radical departure from classical Zionism is glaring; and few Israelis would accept Ratosh's ideas in full. Their influence on foreign policy has not been apparent in the first twenty years.[3]

---

[1] This influence will be examined in the companion volume.

[2] *Shalom Ivri* (Pax Hebraica), Herman, Tel Aviv, 1967.

[3] Canaanite ideas have also been expressed in the publications of the Mediterranean and Levant Press, notably the monthly, *The Mediterranean and Eurafrica*, started in 1958 in New York. See also *The Levant: Behind the Arab Curtain*, Levant Press, New York, 1952.

ii. *Academics and Commentators*

University teachers in Israel are more politically active than their colleagues in most competitive polities. Many are members of parties, a few of the *Knesset* as well. Many are drawn into great national debates, as on the prolonged 'Lavon Affair', the *cause célèbre* of Israeli politics. As noted earlier, some prominent academics have been associated with *New Outlook* since its inception. There are other specific examples of this type of advocacy. In 1962 some twenty scholars, mostly from the Hebrew University, urged 'the Israeli public to act while there is still time against this terrible eventuality [nuclear weapons in the Near East], by joining in the following three demands, that:

1. The Middle Eastern countries refrain from military nuclear production, if possible by mutual agreement;
2. The UN be requested to supervise the region in order to prevent military nuclear production;
3. The countries of the Middle East avoid obtaining nuclear arms from other countries.'[1]

A similar advocacy statement, calling on Israel's Government to take the initiative to prevent the spread of nuclear weapons to the Middle East, was issued in June 1966, in Jerusalem, by the Committee for Nuclear Disarmament of the Arab–Israeli Region. Most of its fifty-five signatories were faculty members at the Hebrew University, the Haifa Technion, and the Weizmann Institute. The statement termed Israel's vulnerability to nuclear attack far greater than Egypt's and 'even if a nuclear second strike is feasible in our region, from Israel's point of view it would be a posthumous revenge'.[2]

During the economic aid negotiations with Germany in 1966, academics also made their views known: an open letter by 170 faculty members from the Hebrew University, Tel Aviv University, the Haifa Technion, and Bar-Ilan University to the Prime Minister's Office criticized the bargaining as presenting the Jewish tragedy 'in a manner lacking self-respect—in return for a $40 million loan and the prospect of conducting similar negotiations next year. . . . Ultimately, a nation's honour and uprightness are decisive to its existence.'[3]

After the Six Day War, too, university teachers pressed their views on the pervasive issue of 'whither Israel': some did so in the Buberist spirit of concessions, like the Movement for Peace and Security, an intellectual circle which, among other things, vociferously opposed Israeli settlement in the occupied territories; others participated in the

---

[1] Reproduced in *New Outlook* (Tel Aviv), vol. 5, no. 4 (44), May 1962, p. 12.

[2] Reported in *Jerusalem Post*, 30 June 1966. The Israeli mass public was not then aware of the significance of nuclear weapons stemming from an independent Israeli nuclear programme. That awareness was the contribution of this small group of academics.

[3] *Jerusalem Post*, 23 May 1966.

expansionist Land of Israel Movement. (Wide publicity to critical views of Israeli Government policy towards a peace settlement espoused by certain Israeli academics and other intellectuals was given in a *Newsweek* symposium in April 1970. Participating were economists Don Patinkin and Michael Bruno and psychologist Amos Tversky of the Hebrew University, Middle East historian Shimon Shamir of Tel Aviv University, author Yoram Ben-Porat, and Meron Benvenisti, Jerusalem municipal councillor in charge of Arab affairs.[1] In 1970 as well, a group of prominent economists, led by Patinkin, Bruno, and Michael Michaeli, took the initiative in foreign economic policy by pressing for a drastic early devaluation. They did so, *inter alia*, in direct talks with the Prime Minister. The pressure was unsuccessful.)

Journalism in Israel is largely the extension of a multi-party system and its tradition of party newspapers designed to educate the faithful. The reader is thus presented with half a dozen or more alternative policies on each issue: their influence is discounted by the knowledge of ideological and party commitment. The 'independent' newspapers are few but highly respected, notably the morning *Ha'aretz* and the evening *Ma'ariv*. The former has long enjoyed the prestige of being Israel's 'New York Times', with a reputation for quality journalism; the latter has exceptional access to the decision-making élites. They, and to a lesser extent the evening (really midday) *Yediot Aharonot*, are opinion-makers which Foreign Ministry officials, and decision-makers generally, read with attention.[2]

There are no towering individual commentators, though the satirist, Ephraim Kishon, of *Ma'ariv*, has become a national institution.[3] Other respected commentators are (were) the following, most of whom are free-lance, writing mainly in *Ha'aretz* and *Ma'ariv*: Natan Alterman, whose political poetry in *Davar* before independence was a major source of morale for the *Yishuv* and who contributed a pungent weekly prose column in *Ma'ariv* for many years, until his death in 1970; Eliezer Livneh, a former *Mapai* MK and co-founder of its daily, *Ha-dor*, later an advocate for the Land of Israel Movement; Amos Eylon; Amos Kenan; retired General Matityahu Peled; Shalom Rosenfeld; Natan Yellin-Mor, the former commander of *Lehi* and later a 'dove'; Eliyahu Salpeter, and others. Among the academics who comment on public affairs in the press the best-known are historians Jacob Talmon and Yehoshua

---

[1] The full text was reprinted in *Jerusalem Post*, 14 April 1970. This type of advocacy will be elaborated in an analysis of post-1967 foreign policy, in the companion volume noted earlier.

[2] *Ha'aretz* is viewed as one of the 40 'Great Newspapers of the World' and is assessed in J. C. Merrill, *The Elite Press*, Pitman, New York, 1968, pp. 89–92.

[3] Kishon's books in English include *Look Back, Mrs. Lot*; *Noah's Ark, Tourist Class*; *The Seasick Whale*; *Unfair to Goliath* (all published by Atheneum, New York); and the brilliant satire on the Six Day War, *So Sorry We Won* (in collaboration with Kariel Gardosh, 'Dosh'), Ma'ariv Library, Tel Aviv, 1968.

Arieli, and political scientist Shloma Avineri, all of the Hebrew University, Shimon Shamir, and Amnon Rubinstein, a law professor at Tel Aviv University.

Another type of advocacy took the form of mixed party and anomic activity—a 'movement of opinion', which conveyed specific demands. The outstanding examples relate to Germany. In both the Reparations issue (1951–2) and Diplomatic Relations (1965) various partisan organizations were actively hostile, as were certain parties—*Herut, Ahdut Ha'avodah* and *Mapam*. Their interests coalesced, and a *de facto* coalition emerged as a powerful advocate of foreign policy. More amorphous counterpressure was exerted in the Reparations issue by German Jews and other potential beneficiaries in Israeli society. The former were more vociferous and better organized; the latter had a larger base of self-interest.[1]

A 'movement of opinion' has operated in Israel's policy towards the Soviet Union as well. There is a widespread conviction in Israel that Moscow maltreats Russian Jewry. This has imposed pressure for a hard line, as compared with Goldmann's call for conciliation—with dramatically increasing intensity in the late 1960s.[2] In the treatment of Israel's Arabs, too, the predominant mood favours a strong line, but the *New Outlook–Mapam–*Independent Liberal coalition has been an influential counter-pressure, leading to the abolition of Military Government in 1967.

Public opinion, as the expression of an undifferentiated mass public, has not been a discernible policy advocate, except in the form of spasmodic clusters of 'letters to the editor'. It is through the parties and interest groups of Israel's highly-organized political system that 'the public' makes its preferences known on foreign and domestic issues. The way in which they are perceived by decision-makers was admirably conveyed by the Government of Israel in reply to a UNESCO questionnaire:[3]

Israel is blessed with a host of semi-public and private organizations which delight in giving advice to the Government. These organizations operate in every conceivable sphere of international activity. . . . Relations with them are informal. . . . As a general rule they make the first move in addressing the Ministry for Foreign Affairs . . . although it is not unusual for the Ministry to approach one or another body for advice on a specialized subject. . . . It cannot, however, be said that consultation with semi-public and private bodies works at all well. . . .

[1] These pressures will be explored in the related volume on Israeli high-policy decisions.

[2] A striking but atypical, illustration of the effective role of public opinion on Israeli foreign policy is evident in the Government of Israel's attitude to the Leningrad Hijack case, December 1970.

[3] Doc. UNESCO/SS/NIS Conf. 2/6, pp. 27–78, as quoted in *Israel and the United Nations*, Manhattan Publishing Co., New York, 1956, pp. 43–4.

CHAPTER 8

Advocacy: Competing Élites

The concept of competing élites takes various forms in foreign policy analysis—from a faction within a totalitarian régime to a formalized two-party system. Israel's multi-party system, as noted, has been characterized throughout by the necessity of a coalition government, in which the members adjust their policy preferences in the interests of inter-party co-operation. This structural imperative enhances the importance of demands advocated by lesser parties, for they are not primarily alternative claimants or competitors for power; rather, they are, with the exception of the two extremes, *Maki* and, until 1967, *Herut*, potential or actual coalition partners. Although the influence of any one party's demands is at no time decisive, all competing programmes taken together constitute a vital input into the foreign policy system. Thus it is necessary to explore the advocacy of the principal Israeli parties at the three levels of the external environment and the images giving rise to their demands, as well as their definition of Israel's proper policy *vis-à-vis* global, subordinate, and bilateral interaction.

To set the stage for this analysis a brief summary of *Mapai*'s foreign policy posture is in order, for *Mapai* has been Israel's pre-eminent party since independence. It has acted as the pivot of all coalitions and has held the three crucial portfolios dealing with foreign policy—Foreign Affairs, Defence, and Finance. Indeed most major decisions in this area have been taken within *Mapai*, not through an inter-party process. And *Mapai*'s impressive skill in absorbing ideas, policies, and factions has assured a high degree of stability in the polity as a whole.

Mapai's primacy is evident in the Basic Principles of the Government Programme.[1] Thus the 1949 five principles of foreign policy and the brief statement in the 1951 Programme were arrived at jointly by Ben Gurion and Sharett:[2] the minor coalition partners, the Religious Bloc and the Progressives, accepted their lead. The shift to nationalist values in 1955—increased military preparedness and protection of frontier settlements—reflected pressure from the militant *Ahdut Ha'avodah*, which had joined the coalition. For the most part, however, it resulted

[1] The foreign policy component of Government Programmes, from which this analysis is drawn, is examined in depth in Appendix A.
[2] Prime Minister–Defence Minister and Foreign Minister, respectively. Interview with Moshe Sharett in Jerusalem, July 1960.

from rising border tension and Ben Gurion's return to power after a self-imposed exile in the desert.

In the fourth election campaign, 1959, *Mapai* announced an eight-point foreign policy platform. All the general themes found a place in the coalition guidelines, though there were differences in phrasing; for example, a change from 'friendly relations with all the countries of the world' to 'friendly relations with each peace-loving state'. Two specific material interests noted by *Mapai* were omitted: trade relations with all countries and free passage through the Suez Canal; but these were shared by all parties in Israel. And there was one conspicuous addition to the Basic Principles of the new government—a call for general and complete disarmament in the global and Middle East systems. Its inclusion was due partly to *Mapam* pressure but also, perhaps more, to the intensive negotiations over arms control at that time.[1]

Mapai issued a similar eight-point foreign policy platform in 1961. Once more the general themes were incorporated in the Government Programme, and the reference to Suez was omitted. On this occasion, however, the *Mapai* document included the goal of global and regional disarmament. And as an obvious acknowledgement of Africa in ferment, it called for 'recognition of the right of every people to be free from foreign rule'.[2] No Israeli party dissented from this principle, which was reiterated by both *Mapai* and the coalition in 1966. Indeed all the values enunciated by the 'new' government had been espoused by *Mapai* in the election campaign for the sixth *Knesset*. By that time, however, the *Ma'arakh* (Alignment) of *Mapai* and *Ahdut Ha'avodah* had been formed; and the influence of the smaller party could be discerned in the joint platform. Of the six following points in the Alignment platform which did not appear in the Government Programme, (ii)–(v) seem to have been inspired by *Ahdut Ha'avodah*:

   (i) 'a greater measure of understanding and co-operation with the Soviet Union';
  (ii) 'normal relationships with India';
 (iii) 'ties with China';
  (iv) the suppression of infiltration;
   (v) continued parliamentary control over the defence forces through the *Knesset* Committee on Foreign Affairs and Security, and governmental control via the Ministerial Committee on Defence; and
  (vi) 'a fitting arrangement with the European Economic Community'.
The only striking addition to the coalition programme was the reference

---

[1] Details of the *Mapai* election platform for 1959 are taken from the authorized party brochure (in Hebrew). The text of the 'Basic Principles . . .' for that year is contained in the *Government Year-Book 5721* (1960).

[2] See the *Mapai* election brochure for the 1961 election (in Hebrew) and *Government Year-Book 5723* (1962).

to the danger of Nazism and the demand for the exclusion of Nazi crimes from the West German Statute of Limitations.[1]

Mapai and the Government have thus been virtually synonymous in terms of foreign policy: in general, the tone has been pragmatic—with an emphasis on strength and on 'national interests'. Yet that pre-eminence did not come by default: the Israeli electorate was deluged with competitive options and panaceas during the first twenty years. Not all the party platforms differ from *Mapai*'s or from each other. Frequently they overlap at one or more of the three levels, global, subordinate, and bilateral. Analytically, they may be grouped into three types of alternative foreign policy orientation:

(a) the Ideological Left, comprising *Mapam*, *Maki*, and, to some extent, *Ahdut Ha'avodah*;

(b) the Nationalist Right, concentrated in *Herut*; and

(c) the Pragmatists, comprising the Progressives (Independent Liberals), General Zionists, religious parties, and *Rafi*.

The policies advocated by these parties constitute the demands of 'competing élites' in Israel's foreign policy system, as distinct from the specialized demands of 'interest groups'; both served as environmental pressures on decision-makers. Party platforms will be examined over time in order to assess the degree of consistency and changes in emphasis, and at the three levels of state behaviour—global, subordinate, and bilateral. Only thus can order be brought to a myriad of demands more diverse in appearance than in reality.

(a) THE IDEOLOGICAL LEFT

i. *Mapam*

The key to *Mapam*'s foreign policy is its dual ideological origins—Marxist and Zionist. As with *Mapai*, there are socialist and nationalist strands in its world view; but their order of importance is reversed. *Mapai* was in part the product of Social Democracy, particularly as it was manifested in the Russian Revolution of 1905. Its main thrust, however, was the surge to nationalism in the late nineteenth century and its classic Jewish expression—Zionism. *Mapai*'s principal goal had long been the re-creation of a Jewish commonwealth in the Land of Israel. To achieve this it was necessary to correct the distortions in Jewish national development during the millennia of dispersion; and this in

---

[1] The extracts from the Alignment platform in 1965 are taken from the English translation in *New Outlook* (Tel Aviv), vol. 8, no. 8 (75), Nov.–Dec. 1965, pp. 63–4. This journal did not, however, reproduce the security platform, which is taken from the Alignment brochure in Hebrew. The greatest difference between the *Mapai* election platform and the Government Programme is the volume of words, with the latter growing more verbose from 1955 onwards.

turn required a 'normal' society of workers on the land and in the city. To *Mapai*, socialism meant a co-operative welfare society in which the interests of the worker would be protected and enhanced. Its socialism was pragmatic—and less doctrinaire—than for any other party in Israel espousing that creed.

Mapam or, rather, its phalanx movement, *Ha-shomer Ha-tsa'ir* (The Young Guard), had imbibed a nationalist spirit from the Zionist faith. But the core of its world view was Russian populism and Marxist-Leninism, culminating in the Revolution of 1917. There was a commitment to a Jewish renascence in the historic homeland. Yet the primary aim was the creation of an egalitarian, communal society, inspired by world socialism and realized in a national setting. National independence, as such, was dismissed as a bourgeois chimera. A Jewish nation reborn could take its rightful place only as part of a universal socialist movement in a progressive march of history.

Before independence, *Mapam* was committed to a bi-national state, and it persistently advocated a pro-Soviet line at the global level of foreign policy. Both positions were logically derived from a coherent and well-articulated image. Indeed, more than any other Israeli party, *Mapam* is ideologically oriented, some would say, dominated. And the consistency of its programme is of a high order, the result of an unchanged organizational base, leadership, and world view.[1]

The global image of *Mapam* was shaped by a Leninist dictum: 'The Soviet Union is the vanguard of world revolution.' Typical was the remark of *Mapam* MK Hanan Rubin in 1960: 'Mapam sees the Soviet bloc as the most important force for peace in the world.'[2] Hazan reaffirmed this global view in 1966, with a neat distinction: 'Mapam

---

[1] The party was formed in 1948 with two major groups: *Kibbutz Artzi*, the national organization of *Ha-shomer Ha-tsa'ir* communal settlements based upon small homogeneous social groups with an ideological identity; and the 'B' Faction of *Mapai* which had split off as *Ahdut Ha'avodah* in 1944. There were lesser elements in *Mapam*: the small urban Socialist League, the Left *Po'alei Tzyon* (Workers of Zion), a mélange group under Dr. Moshe Sneh, and the Hebrew Communists under Eliezer Preminger. By 1954, after the Slansky Affair in Czechoslovakia and the 'Doctors' Plot' in Moscow, *Mapam* was sundered: *Ahdut Ha'avodah* was reconstituted as a separate party, taking with it most of the Left *Po'alei Tzyon*; and Dr. Sneh led some younger men into *Maki*, the Communist Party of Israel. But *Ha-shomer Ha-tsa'ir* remained—to provide the bulk of *Mapam*'s members, its leaders, and its policies.

One man, Meir Ya'ari, has guided this Left-Socialist-Zionist sect throughout the half-century of its existence. Born in Galicia in 1897, Ya'ari was a co-founder of *Ha-shomer Ha-tsa'ir*. He migrated to Palestine in 1920 and was among the few who were instrumental in creating *Kibbutz Artzi* and, later, *Mapam*. In 1970 he was still General Secretary and chief ideologist of the party. His heir-apparent for decades, Ya'acov Hazan, was also a co-founder of *Ha-shomer Ha-tsa'ir* and was associated with every major event in the history of this unique social movement. It was Ya'ari, more than anyone, who produced the synthesis of Marxism-Leninism and Zionist socialism, which has persevered as the underpinning of *Mapam*'s programme.

[2] Interview in Jerusalem, July 1960.

as a party has never been neutral in the world struggle; Mapam as a member of the Government advocates non-alignment.'[1]

In the first election campaign (1949) *Mapam* called for Israel's alignment with the forces led by the Soviet Union.[2] It also echoed the general line of the international Communist movement: the danger to peace of United States 'atomic blackmail', the resurgence of Nazism in West Germany, and the like. In the euphoria of Soviet-bloc military and diplomatic aid during the War of Independence this posture was not unpopular, as noted.

Mapam's advocacy at the global level was virtually identical in 1951, except for the additional support to the Soviet bloc over the Korean War and Berlin. By 1955, however, the party had been sundered by an acute anti-Zionist campaign in the Soviet bloc, including accusations of *Mapam* espionage, in the sweeping Czech purge—the Slansky Affair. All this was reflected in the more muted *Mapam* programme for the third election. There was no attack on the Soviet camp but none on the West either; the model was now genuine non-alignment. The aim of foreign policy was 'Israel's independence and security'. 'Friendly relations' were urged 'with all the states of West and East who respect her independence'. Further, Israel 'will not join alliances or aggressive blocs and will not grant military bases to any foreign power'; and *Tzahal* 'will not be placed under foreign control and leadership'. *Mapam* also advocated a struggle against German rearmament, support for general disarmament, including the abolition of nuclear weapons, and friendly relations with Asian peoples.[3]

Mapam's 1955 global policy set the tone for the next decade. Thus the election programme for 1959 called for 'a Policy of Independence, Neutrality and Peace', citing Israel's 'security requirements' and 'the fact that the Jewish people is scattered among the different social orders'. This was made explicit with the pledge, 'Israel will not align herself with any of the big blocs and will not enter into any military or political alliances.'[4] In the sixth election campaign this policy was reiterated almost verbatim—along with the urging of an attempt to improve relations with the Soviet Union.[5]

Mapam's policy towards the Arabs appears to many Israelis to have been inconsistent: it has moved from a bi-national state to concessions, conciliation, compromise, and co-operation, along with hostility to Hussein, and then, in a full circle, after the 1967 War, to a

[1] Interview in Jerusalem, April 1966.
[2] A formal link was not urged. In any event, *Mapam*'s adherence to the Zionist creed and goals would have precluded its acceptance as a *bona fide* Communist party.
[3] Taken from the *Mapam* election brochure for the 1955 election (in Hebrew).
[4] Taken from the English translation of part of the 1959 party election platforms in *New Outlook* (Tel Aviv), vol. 3, no. 2 (24), Nov.–Dec. 1959, p. 62.
[5] Taken from the English translation of part of the 1965 party election platforms in *New Outlook* (Tel Aviv), vol. 8, no. 7 (74), Oct. 1965, pp. 58–9.

call for a confederation with Jordan. In fact, it has followed a consistent line.

In 1955 *Mapam* pledged 'to strive persistently for direct negotiations . . . to make peace and secure the just rights and free development of all the peoples of the region'.[1] The 1959 programme was more expansive: a renewed call for direct negotiations, this time 'without any pre-conditions'; 'neutralization of the Middle East and a cessation of the arms race'; a Great Power guarantee of the sovereignty and existing frontiers of all states in the area; 'constructive initiative for a practical and speedy solution to the refugee problem, within the overall framework of a peace settlement', with Israel contributing her share; and extensive regional co-operation. As in the past, *Mapam* also urged 'full equality' for Israel's Arabs and the 'immediate and complete abolition of the Military Administration'.[2]

All these points were reiterated in 1965, with one change—a more precise statement concerning the Arab refugees. The Six Day War made it possible for *Mapam* to revert to its ideological first choice—a bi-national state—though in a new garb: in 1967–8 it opposed annexation of the West Bank and advocated a confederation with the Kingdom of Jordan. The result would be a two-nation political entity in the historic area of Israel; and, though much looser than a single bi-national state, it would facilitate a solution of the refugee problem. Ideological purity and policy were more in harmony once again.

As with all other parties in Israel, *Mapam*'s election platforms contain scanty references to other states: bilateral relations are perceived as less important than the global and subordinate systems, apart from the two super powers. The only other states frequently mentioned are West Germany and China. *Mapam* opposed the acceptance of reparations in 1951–2, the arms link to Germany from the late 1950s onward, and diplomatic relations in 1965; in fact, any relations with the successor to the Nazi régime. On the China question, too, it was consistent, advocating the seating of the People's Republic of China at the UN and a 'one China' policy.[3]

ii. *Maki*

The Communist Party of Israel clearly belongs to the ideological Left but it is much less representative of that competing orientation than *Mapam*. Indeed *Maki*, until the late sixties, lacked legitimacy within

---

[1] See p. 165, n. 3 above.
[2] See p. 165, n. 4 above.
[3] *Mapam*'s ideology and foreign policy demands are communicated through a series of party publications in six languages. The authoritative party newspaper is the daily *Al-Hamishmar* (On Guard). For English-language readers an accessible source is the monthly, *New Outlook*, founded in 1957; many *Mapam* leaders and spokesmen contribute regularly.

Israel's political system: the reason was its extreme hostility to the ethos, creed, and objectives of Zionism, the ideological basis of the state. Thus its policy remained an oddity at one extreme of the party spectrum.[1]

Founded in 1919, the Communist Party of Palestine opposed the British Mandate throughout and aligned itself with Arab national aspirations. It rejected the fundamental Zionist belief in 'Am Yisrael', a world-wide Jewish people with an indissoluble link to the 'land of Zion', and aimed at an independent Palestine with an Arab majority. It fought against *aliya*, all efforts to increase Jewish autonomy, and such hybrid doctrines as *Mapam*'s Marxist-Zionism, with its goal of a bi-national state. The CPP also collaborated with the Arab Rebellion of 1936–9. Yet *Maki*, its successor, was a signatory to the Declaration of Independence on 15 May 1948, and Shmuel Mikunis, its Secretary-General, was a member of the Provisional State Council.[2]

Maki's image, global and regional, was a faithful echo of the international Communist line over the years; it need not be examined here. So too were the policy demands, certainly until the 1965 split into a *de facto* predominantly Jewish (Mikunis-Sneh) faction, the Israel Communist Party, and an overwhelmingly Arab (Toubi-Wilner) faction, the New Communists (*Rakah*).[3]

In the early post-independence honeymoon years, *Maki* advocated an alignment with the 'peace-loving forces' led by the Soviet Union. By 1955 it called for an 'independent foreign policy, of peace, independence, and national security'; essentially this meant 'liberating Israel's foreign policy from its dependence on the United States' and normal relations with all states on the basis of equality, mutual respect, non-

[1] Two small religious parties, *Agudat Yisrael* and *Po'alei Agudat Yisrael*, also rejected the Zionist *efforts* to re-establish a Jewish State. They did not, however, challenge the core Zionist belief in a Jewish *claim* to Zion, as did *Maki*; and they became legitimate members of the political system after independence. *Maki*'s anti-State posture gave way in 1965 and after, largely under the influence of Dr. Moshe Sneh.

[2] Mikunis was born in Russia in 1903. A civil engineer, he migrated to Israel in 1921. He has been a leading member of *Maki* for four decades and was a member of the *Knesset* from 1949 to 1969. A selection of his articles and speeches appeared in 1969 under the title *Besa'ar Tekufot* (In the Storm of the Times), edited by Sarah Breitstein, Communist Party, Tel Aviv.

[3] The rationale of *Maki*'s National-Communist foreign policy was conveyed to the author by Dr. Moshe Sneh in an interview in Jerusalem, Aug. 1960, almost five years before the split. An unambiguous statement of Sneh's foreign policy outlook following the Soviet invasion of Czechoslovakia is contained in *New Middle East*, London, no. 5, Feb. 1969, pp. 38–42. Dr. Sneh, one of the most intellectually impressive among Israel's politicians, has had a chequered career since his arrival in Israel from Poland in 1940. He was the '*Rama*' of the *Haganah*, i.e., Chief of the (Political) High Command, as distinct from the *Ramatkal*, Chief of the General Staff, a military post, from 1940 to 1946. He moved politically from General Zionist to *Mapam* (in 1948) and to *Maki* (in 1954), for which he served as Editor of *Kol Ha'am*, *Knesset* member, and ideological spokesman.

aggression, and co-existence.[1] Israel's national interest was defined as 'neutralism' in the 1959 and 1961 election campaigns; and this, in turn, meant friendly relations with 'the socialist countries'.[2]

Maki's policy towards the Arab–Israel conflict appears to be very similar to that of Mapam. In 1955 it urged direct negotiations 'without imperialist intervention and without preliminary conditions'. In 1959 and again in 1961 it called for a recognition of 'the just national rights of both peoples', based on the view that Palestine is the national homeland of both Arabs and Jews, and thus of the right of Arab refugees to return. At the bilateral level, too, only West Germany and the People's Republic of China were mentioned, the former in a critical vein, the latter as the rightful representative of China's 700 millions in the United Nations.

Despite the 1965 split, there were no sharp differences in foreign policy platforms. Maki urged 'an independent Israeli foreign policy . . . non-aligned with any world bloc against another'. The New Communists (Rakah) did the same without mentioning neutralism. Both also advocated the severance of links with West Germany. And even at the regional level the two factions called for efforts to achieve a settlement on the basis of mutual recognition of the legitimate rights of both peoples. Yet there was a difference—in tone, timing, and phrasing. The New Communists were blunt: 'Israel must first recognize the right of the Arab refugees to choose between returning to their homeland or receiving compensation'; this was the key to recognition of Israel by the Arab states; Maki made no such demand. Further, the New Communists referred frequently to 'Palestine' and the 'Palestine problem'; Maki did not.[3]

The difference between Mapam, Maki, and all other parties on the crucial issue of Arab refugees was revealed in a 1961 Knesset debate. A Mapai member moved a motion that 'the only solution . . . is their settlement in the Arab countries'; the vote was 63 to 11 in favour, with 13 abstentions. A Mapam motion declared: 'Israel would be willing, within the framework of peace negotiations, to discuss the return of a specified agreed number of refugees'; there were 7 in support, 60 opposed. And a

---

[1] See the Maki election brochure for the 1955 election (in Hebrew). For a succinct analysis of Maki's origins and evolution, and its policy until the mid-1950s, see Walter Z. Laqueur, Communism and Nationalism in the Middle East, Praeger, New York, 1956, pp. 73–119.

[2] See the Maki election brochures for the 1959 and 1961 elections (in Hebrew).

[3] For an English translation of the 1965 election platforms (in part) of Maki and the New Communists see New Outlook (Tel Aviv), vol. 8, no. 7 (74), Oct. 1965, p. 58, and vol. 8, no. 8 (75), Nov.–Dec. 1965, pp. 64–5, respectively. Maki published a daily newspaper in Hebrew, Kol Ha'am (Voice of the People), as well as weeklies or fortnightlies in Arabic, Bulgarian, Hungarian, Roumanian and Yiddish. These journals were split between Maki and the New Communists, the former acquiring Kol Ha'am, among others.

Maki motion calling for free choice to the refugee, to return or to receive compensation, was rejected by an even larger majority.[1]

iii. *Ahdut Ha'avodah*

Israel's Left-nationalist party opposed both *Mapam* and *Maki* motions on the Arab refugees. In fact, on this issue, and the Arab–Israel conflict generally, *Ahdut Ha'avodah* is militant and uncompromising. Its global perspective, however, has a verbal radical socialist tinge.

There are multiple roots of this dual image and the related divergence in foreign policy demands. One is the ideological make-up of *Ahdut Ha'avodah*, which combines the same strands as *Mapai* and *Mapam*— nationalism and socialism—but with a different tone and stress. Another is the personality of its leaders. A third is the role of its core movement in the pre-State growth of the *Yishuv*. All this is reflected in the ubiquitous factional behaviour of *Ahdut Ha'avodah* as a political entity: always in search of a 'home', it changed alignments with unequalled frequency.[2]

All through its chequered history *Ahdut Ha'avodah* maintained the loyalty of a hard-core membership and an organizational base—in the communal settlements of *Ha-Kibbutz Ha-me'uhad* (The United Kibbutz).[3] Yet the doctrinal differences with *Mapai* were never awesome—or

---

[1] *Weekly News Bulletin*, Jerusalem, 1–7 Nov. 1961, p. 5.

[2] The origins of *Ahdut Ha'avodah* (Unity of Labour) can be traced to the mainstream of Labour Zionism, the most powerful political current in the *Yishuv*. Two groups competed for the support of the burgeoning Jewish working class in Palestine in the early years of the century—*Ha-po'el Ha-tsa'ir* (The Young Worker) and *Po'alei Tzyon* (Workers of Zion); the first was non-Marxist in outlook, viewing productive labour and agriculture as the keys to the redemption of a Jewish nation; the latter advocated class struggle and revolutionary socialism; both were committed to practical, pioneering Zionism. The first merger occurred in 1919, between *Po'alei Tzyon* and other groups to form *Ahaut Ha'avodah*. (When *Ha-po'el Ha-tsa'ir* refused to join, a common labour organization, the *Histadrut*, was formed.) The most important merger took place in 1929–30—between *Ha-po'el Ha-tsa'ir* and *Ahdut Ha'avodah*; the result was *Mapai* (acronym for *Mifleget Po'alei Eretz Yisrael*, Party of the Workers of the Land of Israel), the pre-eminent political force since that time. A militant group of younger men, which came to be known as Faction 'B' in *Mapai*, split off in 1944 and took the old name, *Ahdut Ha'avodah*. The next year a small doctrinal group, the Left *Po'alei Tzyon*, which had refused to join the original merger in 1919—or any others—joined the new *Ahdut Ha'avodah*. In 1948 it joined with *Ha-shomer Ha-tsa'ir* to form *Mapam*; and in 1954 it split off once more. After eleven years of separate existence, *Ahdut Ha'avodah* formed the *Ma'arakh* (Alignment) with *Mapai* on the eve of the sixth *Knesset* elections; and in 1968 it merged with *Mapai* and *Rafi*, the Ben Gurion-led *Mapai* splinter, to form the Israel Labour Party. Genetically, the 1968 merger had returned to the situation before 1944, apart from Ben Gurion's aloofness.

[3] The Grand Old Man of this movement, with an intense commitment to *halutziut* (pioneering on the land), is Yitzhak Tabenkin, another of the perennial leaders of Labour Zionism. Born in Russia in 1887, a contemporary of *Mapai*'s Ben Gurion and *Ha-shomer Ha-tsa'ir*'s Ya'ari, he was the unchallenged leader of *Ha-Kibbutz Ha-me'uhad* for decades and the guardian of its ideological purity.

unbridgeable. Both were heirs to the tradition of Labour Zionism. Both were committed to a restored Jewish commonwealth. Both were dedicated to reclamation of the land and the creation of a Jewish working class. Both accepted the ideal of a socialist society. But as *Mapai* moved from the land to the city and became a 'national' party, its socialism, always secondary, became diluted. *Ahdut Ha'avodah* remained an essentially agrarian movement.

The ideological gap became blurred in time. What remained between *Mapai* and *Ahdut Ha'avodah* was a split over militancy and activism towards the British and the Arabs, a psychological attitude towards political struggle.[1] This was accentuated by a clash of personalities, at first between Ben Gurion and Tabenkin: their rivalry within the secular synagogue of Labour Zionism was an enduring conflict between two charismatic figures, proud and unyielding.[2] The clash of personalities went much deeper, however. Indeed it became interwoven with factional rivalry in the defence forces of the *Yishuv* during the War of Independence. A new generation of daring military leaders had been spawned by *Ha-Kibbutz Ha-me'uhad* during the early forties: the most notable were Yigal Allon, Moshe Carmel, and Yisrael Galili, apart from that extraordinary figure, Yitzhak Sadeh.[3] The *Palmah* became identified primarily with *Ha-Kibbutz Ha-meuhad*. And *Palmah* became the symbol of heroism and idealism. When Ben Gurion compelled it to disband in 1948, many ascribed it to party and personal rivalry. Certainly this act rankled among the young leaders of *Ahdut Ha'avodah*, and the chasm grew. Beyond that is the generation gap between these activist *Ahdut* leaders and the 'Old Guard' '*Mapainiks*', who clung to power and perceptions and policies in the face of mounting pressure from their own 'young men', of whom Moshe Dayan was the most outstanding.

In essence *Ahdut Ha'avodah* has always been a *Mapai* faction—with

---

[1] The legacy of that cleavage was later to be felt in the controversy over the disbandment of *Palmah* (1948–9). And almost twenty years later, some prominent members of *Ahdut Ha'avodah* became vociferous advocates of annexation, through settlement, of the territories acquired by Israel in the Six Day War.

[2] It was no accident that *Mapai* and *Ahdut Ha'avodah* remained apart until 1965: an alignment was regarded as treason by Tabenkin as long as Ben Gurion was Prime Minister and leader of *Mapai*; and his veto held sway. The path was eased by Ben Gurion's resignation (1963) and his sharp clash with *Mapai*'s 'Old Guard'; and the 'young men' of *Ahdut Ha'avodah* pressed forward with reconciliation and, later, merger, despite Tabenkin's dissent. (By 1970 he, too, supported reunification.)

[3] Allon became Commander of the *Palmah*, pride of the *Yishuv*, before he was thirty. Carmel served as commander of the Northern Front during the 1948 War. Galili was second in command of the *Haganah*. And Yitzhak Sadeh, founder of the *Palmah*, was described by Allon as 'a military genius of international calibre, one of the greatest commanders in Jewish history, the father of modern Jewish fighting, the teacher of most young Israeli commanders'. ('The Making of Israel's Army', in *The Theory and Practice of War*, p. 341.) There were others, less well-known at the time, like Yitzhak Rabin, who was Chief of Staff during the Six Day War.

more militant, impatient, dynamic, and younger men but a Labour Zionist faction nonetheless. It was more committed to socialist ideas than *Mapai*, less so than *Mapam*. It was more nationalist than *Mapam* and more activist than both. In schematic terms, *Mapam is left socialist, Mapai, social democrat, and Ahdut Ha'avodah, left nationalist.* This intermediate position in the left-of-centre spectrum of Israeli politics is reflected, too, in the foreign policy demands of *Ahdut Ha'avodah*.

In the first two election campaigns (1949, 1951) *Ahdut Ha'avodah* was an integral part of *Mapam*. It shared *Ha-shomer Ha-tsa'ir*'s penchant for alignment with the Soviet bloc; and in the quiet years following the War of Independence it did not press a hard line towards the Arab states. That dual perspective emerged, however, during the 1955 election, the first in which *Ahdut Ha'avodah* competed as a separate party.

At the global and bilateral levels its policy remained very similar to that of *Mapam*, despite the fact that their split had occurred over Soviet-bloc behaviour. *Ahdut Ha'avodah* opposed an alliance with the United States on various grounds: 'The USA would be able to force Israel to take part in its aggressiveness against the USSR, while the latter does not endanger Israel at all. On the other hand, the United States would not help Israel when needed. Such an alliance would divide the Jewish people all over the world . . . [And] the United States also interferes with and endangers Israel's sovereignty over the [Jordan] waters.' In more positive terms, *Ahdut Ha'avodah* demanded a 'return to the policy of independence and non-identification', opposition to German rearmament, and support for co-existence, the prohibition of nuclear weapons, the seating of Communist China at the UN and the restoration of China's territorial integrity, i.e. 'one China', as well as for the national liberation efforts of subject peoples.

The divergence from *Mapam* and the militancy noted earlier are evident in the policy advocated for the region. After acknowledging the necessity for peace, *Ahdut Ha'avodah* attacked the *Ha-shomer Ha-tsa'ir* conciliatory, compromise line: 'The borders of 29 November [set by the 1947 UN Partition Resolution] and the concept of a bi-national state are obsolete. No territorial concessions must be made. Arab refugees must be rehabilitated on the unused lands of the Arab countries, with international help'; Israel would be ready to help 'within the framework of negotiations for permanent peace'. Peace would come only through social change in the Arab world and the growth of global peace forces. 'Meanwhile we must be ready for a "second round" and we must strengthen our army and security. We must crush border incidents, by force if necessary.' The activism of the forties, repressed during the merger with *Mapam*, had been reasserted.[1]

These global and bilateral policy demands were reaffirmed in the

[1] See the *Ahdut Ha'avodah* election brochure for the 1955 election (in Hebrew).

election campaigns of 1959 and 1961, except for the removal of the explicit criticism of the United States. At the regional level, too, there was no substantive change; if anything, the tone was tougher. Thus in the 1959 programme Israel 'cannot accept the Egyptian piracy in closing the Suez Canal', and 'Nasser's criminal actions cannot be left without some defensive and deterring reply'.[1] *Ahdut Ha'avodah* also joined other coalition partners—*Mapam* and the Progressives—in demanding effective Government control of the Defence establishment. More specifically, it insisted that all ministers be 'kept fully informed of all policy decisions and operations in all spheres, particularly defence and foreign affairs'; the secret arms negotiations with Germany in 1957–8 had triggered this demand.[2] By 1965 *Ahdut Ha'avodah* was part of the *Ma'arakh* (Alignment); and *Mapai*'s greater influence in the Alignment set the (more muted) tone.[3]

(b) THE NATIONALIST RIGHT: *HERUT*

Herut has not always been regarded as a legitimate participant in Israel's political system: in the early years, until the struggle over Reparations was settled in 1952, it was suspected by many of intending to change the system by force. Unlike the Communists, however, no one doubted its commitment to the aspirations of Jewish nationalism. It differed in method—a greater stress on violence than on democratic processes—and in the intensity of attachment to the historic claim to *Eretz Yisrael*: as such, *Herut* has been the supreme exponent of Jewish irredentism.[4]

Herut has a global image but it is preoccupied with Israel and the Near East. This is evident in the many speeches made by Begin in the *Knesset* and elsewhere,[5] in the party newspaper, *Herut*, and in election

[1] See p. 165, n. 4 above, pp. 59–60.

[2] See the *Ahdut Ha'avodah* election brochure for the 1961 election (in Hebrew).

[3] *Ahdut Ha'avodah* publishes a daily Hebrew newspaper, *Lamerhav* (Into the Open), as well as a weekly in Yiddish, *Folksblatt*, and fortnightly periodicals in several languages.

[4] The *Herut* (Freedom) Movement—it was never called a party—is descended from a great split in the ranks of world Zionism. Rising discontent with the slow, patient, conciliatory diplomacy of Weizmann led to the creation of the (Revisionist) New Zionist Organization in 1935 and the call by its leader, Jabotinsky, for greater militancy in the struggle for Palestine. Coercion was extolled and, in time, a para-military force, the *Irgun Tzva'i Le'umi* or *Etzel*, emerged from a split in the *Hagonah*—during the escalating Arab-Jewish war of the late thirties. Jabotinsky died in 1940. Soon after, the leadership of *Etzel* passed to a fiery and brilliant young orator, Menahem Begin, who made his way to Palestine via the Polish Army in 1942. *Etzel*'s power was checked in the *Altalena* incident in June 1948, as noted, and it was suppressed in the autumn, after the assassination of Count Bernadotte. It was formally reconstituted as the *Herut* Movement in June 1948—and Begin has been its perennial leader.

[5] His perspective in the mid-sixties was well articulated in 'Conceptions and Problems of Foreign Policy', *Ha'uma* (Tel Aviv), March 1966, pp. 462–70 (in Hebrew).

programmes. A lucid statement was provided by Ya'acov Meridor, second-in-command of *Etzel* and a senior parliamentary leader of his party.[1] He began at the regional level, linking image to advocacy throughout the analysis.

> The present State of Israel occupies only part of the territory of historic Israel as defined in the Bible, which is broadly the area included in the Mandate, that is, both sides of the Jordan. Thus the primary goal of foreign policy is to re-create historic Israel—by liberating Trans-Jordan. Israel can never rest until this is accomplished.

Here in essence is the *Herut* perception and policy demand. Certain implications were then articulated.

First, Israel must maintain the claim to Trans-Jordan; otherwise, it would have to withdraw from any Jordan territory occupied in future wars, as in the case of Sinai in 1957.

Second, Israel must not make a formal peace settlement with Jordan, for this is unredeemed territory; *Herut* in power would accept an interim arrangement but not a treaty involving the abandonment of the territorial claim.

Third, the 'claim' comprises Jordan (including, of course, the West Bank) and Gaza, but no other Arab territory; thus peace treaties with all other Arab states are in order. On the manner of achievement, Meridor invoked the doctrine of 'hot pursuit': 'if they send marauders across the border, we will pursue them into their own territory and not come back'.

The concept of a bi-national state was treated with contempt; but all Arabs in the acquired territories could become citizens of Israel.

At the global level the *Herut* image is 'realism' *par excellence.* 'The question of alignment or non-alignment', said Meridor, 'is insignificant, for Israel cannot influence the world struggle. On each specific issue Israel must act in terms of its national interests.' A distinction was drawn between Israel and Diaspora Jewish interests; they are different but not necessarily incompatible.

Thus *Herut* supported France on the Algeria issue—'because the alliance with France is more important than idealism'.

South Africa was supported on the *Apartheid* issue—because it was friendly to Israel and because of local Jewish interests.

And despite its pronounced anti-Communism, *Herut* would favour the discontinuance of American aid to Israel if this were the price for Moscow's permission for mass emigration of Soviet Jews.

On the relations between Israel and world Jewry, he concluded, *Herut* accepts the dictum of an early Zionist leader, Max Nordau, 'either we liquidate the Diaspora or the Diaspora will liquidate us'.

All of these themes found expression in *Herut* election platforms with

[1] Interview in Jerusalem, Aug. 1960.

a remarkable degree of consistency. The 1959 programme was typical. On the crucial Arab–Israel issue, irredentist nationalism was triumphant. First, 'the right of the Jewish people to *Eretz Yisrael* (Land of Israel) in its historic entirety is an eternal and inalienable right.' Second, '*a peace treaty* . . . is possible with the realization of this right: the reunification of *Eretz Yisrael*, where all its inhabitants, regardless of origin, creed or community, will live as free and equal citizens of the Hebrew State.' Third, in the interim, 'until such a *peace treaty* is attained and signed, *peaceful conditions* are possible', i.e., an end to the state of war, blockade, etc. And fourth, 'Israel fully reserves to herself the right of national self-defence. . . .' At the bilateral level Germany was the *bête noire*: *Herut* promised to annul the arms agreement with the 'killer nation' of Germany and condemned all talk of diplomatic relations. In the broader world setting it advocated 'a policy of mutual alliances based on common interest between Israel and her allies', as well as help to prevent a third world war.[1] Most of this was reiterated in 1961—the regional demands and the attack on Israel's German policy. At the global level *Herut* declared that neutralism was unrealistic for Israel; it 'should be part of the free world'.[2]

The sixth election campaign (1965) coincided with the beginnings of basic change in Israel's party system. *Mapai* and *Ahdut Ha'avodah* had formed the Alignment. *Maki* had split. And *Herut* had joined forces with the General Zionists in *Gahal*. The effects on *Herut*'s foreign policy demands were striking. The tone was more moderate throughout the *Gahal* platform. There was no reference to the 'historic boundaries of *Eretz Yisrael*', nor to the distinction between 'peace treaty' and 'peaceful conditions'. The right of self-defence was reaffirmed, as was the rejection of pressure to repatriate Arab refugees; but there was an unqualified pledge of 'a constant striving for peace with the Arab peoples'. Germany was singled out once more for criticism, but the hostility was less strident. On global policy a pro-West posture was emphasized: 'the State of Israel is part of the free world'. And there was one novel demand, namely, that the President of Israel should be head of the armed forces.[3]

(c) THE PRAGMATISTS

Unlike the ideology-type competing élites, the pragmatists have not dissented from the fundamentals of Israel's foreign policy. The religious parties, the General Zionists, the Progressives, and *Rafi* shared *Mapai*'s

[1] See p. 165, n. 4 above, p. 60.

[2] See the *Herut* election brochure for the 1961 election (in Hebrew).

[3] See p. 165, n. 5 above, pp. 56–7. No other party has ever made this recommendation in an election platform. Apart from its daily Hebrew newspaper, *Herut*, which ceased publication in 1969, the *Herut* Movement published weeklies and/or fortnightlies in several languages.

general posture on foreign affairs.[1] The main reason, perhaps, has been *Mapai*'s behaviour as the peer pragmatist in Israeli politics. Yet there have been differences in tone and nuance in the foreign policy programmes of these parties.

i. *General Zionists*

Labour Zionism was one major stream within the Jewish national movement before independence. Revisionism was another. And, despite its pretensions, *General* Zionism was the third. Among its leaders the most illustrious was Chaim Weizmann, near-perennial President of the World Zionist Organization and first Head of State in Israel. The General Zionist Party, along with the Progressives, has been the carrier of that third tradition in the politics of Israel.[2]

The General Zionists and Progressives appear more akin than apart in outlook and policy. Both are parties of 'the Centre'. Both represent the middle class. Both support private enterprise. Both are advocates of individual rights and the separation of State and religion. Both are sympathetic to the West and its values. Yet there are differences, primarily linked to socio-economic composition, and these have prevented an enduring union.

The General Zionists are men of commerce, industry, and agriculture, entrepreneurs of the classic type. The Progressives are men of the 'free professions', notably law, medicine, teaching, and journalism, with a sprinkling in high finance. Further, the General Zionist leaders have more diverse ethnic backgrounds. Thus the General Zionists represent the bourgeois component of the middle class, from small shopkeeper to corporate executive; the Progressives speak mainly for professionals. The General Zionists have bitterly opposed *Histadrut* and other non-private enterprise (though in the early 1960s they established a faction within the *Histadrut*, as did *Herut*); the Progressives have welcomed a

---

[1] Many Israeli political figures concurred: Harari of the Progressives (interviews, Aug. 1960 and July 1966); Rimalt of the General Zionists (interviews, July 1960 and Dec. 1965); and Peres of *Rafi* (interview, July 1966).

[2] They have much in common—as do *Mapai* and *Ahdut Ha'avodah*. And the pattern of their relations—splits and mergers—is not dissimilar. The General Zionists and Progressives were originally united within the World Confederation of General Zionists. Already in the 1920s and 1930s they had split into separate parties, within the World Zionist Movement. In 1946 they formed the General Zionist Party in Palestine, with two wings—General Zionists 'A', oriented towards the Left, and General Zionists 'B', comprising industrialists, merchants, and private agricultural producers. Two years later General Zionists 'A' split off once more to form the Progressive Party, with the 'B' faction inheriting the original party name and tradition. There were various abortive efforts at reunion in the fifties, but success was not achieved until 1961, on the eve of the fifth *Knesset* elections. The merger, known as the Liberal Party, was short-lived. When the majority General Zionist wing opted for a 'bloc' with *Herut* in 1965 (as *Gahal*), the Progressives split off once more, this time as the Independent Liberals.

mixed economy and are directly represented in the *Histadrut* as *Ha'oved Ha-tzyoni*. The protection of individual rights is at the very apex of Progressive Party objectives, and it has thrown its full weight into the battle against theocracy; these values have been less crucial for the General Zionists. Set within the Anglo-Saxon tradition, the Progressives are a Left-liberal party with a welfare-state orientation; the General Zionists are Israel's 'small-c' conservatives.

Given their values and economic interests, the General Zionists were the natural exponents of a pro-Western foreign policy. They were staunch advocates of a US alliance in the early 1950s and have always proclaimed that 'Israel is part of the free world'. The global image leading to this policy demand was succinctly portrayed by party leader Yosef Saphir in 1960. 'Israel belongs to the Western concept of life', he began. 'Israel could never be aligned with the East because of profound differences in our way of life—and because the majority of Jews are in the West.' A related perception was that of contrasting attitudes to Israel: 'no Soviet régime can consider Israel a necessary part of the Middle East; it is not committed to Israel's survival.' By contrast, 'Western friends and non-friends—there are no Western enemies of Israel—will always take Israel into account, though they will not always abide by its wishes.' And 'Western public opinion is helpful to Israel; there is none in the East.' Finally, Israel's economic ties are predominantly with the West. All these factors, he concluded, require alignment with the West.[1]

During the discussions leading to the formation of Israel's first Cabinet in March 1949, the General Zionist leaders told Ben Gurion that, 'in regard to foreign policy they did not see basic differences; their main point was that the Government must not discriminate between the public and private [economic] sectors'.[2] In the 1951 and 1955 election campaigns they strongly urged a defence alliance with the United States. By 1959, however, this had become a more flexible call for 'friendly relations with peoples and states all over the world, based on mutual interests and concern for the strengthening of Israel's army'; the lessons of the Sinai Campaign had been absorbed. The only specific demand was for economic integration with the European Common Market. A volte-face took place in the fifth election (1961), largely under the influence of Nahum Goldmann, and within the framework of union with the Progressives. The line was very similar to that of *Mapam*: 'Israel's relations with the blocs should be balanced according to her

---

[1] Interview in Jerusalem, July 1960. Rimalt presented a similar perspective, adding: 'There is no real difference with *Mapai* on foreign policy, for *Mapai* shares the General Zionist Western orientation; so too on security issues.' Interview in Jerusalem, July 1960.

[2] David Ben Gurion, *The State of Israel Reborn*: no. 42, 'Birth Pangs of Coalition' *Davar* (Tel Aviv), 24 Dec. 1965.

national interests and the fact that the Jewish people is scattered all over the world.' There was also a specific reference to strengthening relations with the new nations in Asia and Africa.[1] In 1965, as noted earlier, the General Zionists, together with their *Herut* ally, reverted to the maxim that 'Israel is part of the free world', while retaining the emphasis on national interest.

At the regional level the General Zionist image was even closer to *Mapai*'s. Israel was in the Middle East by right. The Arab refugees are a responsibility of the Arab world: India and Pakistan, remarked Rimalt, do not talk about returning their fifteen million refugees, nor does West Germany claim the right of refugees to return to the east. At the same time, Israel must seek a peace settlement with her neighbours. To ease a solution, the 1959 platform urged the creation of an interim budget reserve for compensation payments to Arab refugees, to be used 'for their resettlement in the Arab states'. This demand was reiterated in 1961, along with the Goldmann-inspired proposal to neutralize the Middle East and achieve regional disarmament. In 1965 there was a harsher line, under *Herut* pressure. The only bilateral issue stressed by the General Zionists over the years was Germany: they approved the Reparations and arms agreements, as well as diplomatic relations.

ii. *Progressives*

The Progressive Party was cast in the liberal mould. Its values were those of the democratic West, and its approach to the Arab–Jewish conflict in the pre-State period was characterized by tolerance, conciliation, and concessions. This in turn created a widespread image of an anti-independence group—though no one doubted its loyalty to the *Yishuv*.[2] And concern about that image had an enduring effect on its policy orientation. 'From the outset,' remarked Professor Paltiel, 'the Progressive Party never deviated from the course pursued by the government of the day.'[3]

[1] Taken from the General Zionist election brochures for the 1951, 1955, 1959 elections, and the Liberal Party election brochure for the 1961 election (all in Hebrew).

[2] *Aliya Hadasha*, meaning New Immigration (in fact, from German-speaking Central Europe), one of the party's forerunners, adhered to Zionist aims but was shocked by Jewish terrorism. It never adopted the ideology or policy of bi-nationalism. Yet it refused to endorse the Biltmore Programme of 1942, which called for a Jewish State. An *Aliya Hadasha* Statement of Policy in March 1946 favoured the continuation of the Mandate as a UN Trusteeship, postponing independence indefinitely. One faction of the Progressives continued to support co-operation with the United Kingdom and parity with the Arabs in a Trusteeship scheme. The other, led by Pinhas Rosenbleuth (later, Rosen), secured a narrow majority in favour of partition, along the lines of the 1937 Peel Commission recommendations. And dissension on 'foreign policy' continued until the United Nations Resolution of 29 November 1947: Rosen's view carried overwhelmingly.

[3] K. Z. Paltiel, 'The Progressive Party: A Study of a Small Party in Israel' (unpublished Ph.D. thesis, The Hebrew University, Jerusalem, 1964, p. 114). This

The 1949 election platform did not dissent from the Provisional Government's foreign policy, though some, like Rosen, reserved their stand on the inclusion of Jerusalem within Israel. It also called for non-alignment in the Cold War and a quest for understanding with the Arabs. The party's members of parliament were permitted a free vote on the Reparations issue in 1951–2, but the Progressives were a loyal coalition partner in the controversy over arms sales to Germany (1957–8). And they turned down Goldmann's entreaties for a policy change, on two occasions: a proposal in 1953 that Israel seek to integrate with the Middle East, if necessary by offering to join the Arab League; and a call in 1957 for neutralization of the Middle East, along with Israel's reassertion of non-alignment.

The second Goldmann plea came after a more pronounced defence-oriented and pro-Western posture in the Progressive programme for the 1955 election. In 1959 the call for a security alliance with the United States was dropped, and greater flexibility was displayed at the global and regional levels, similar to the change in the General Zionist platform: the two parties were beginning to move closer. In the fifth election campaign (1961), as noted, the new united Liberal Party adopted Goldmann's *Mapam*-like soft line towards the Arabs and non-alignment in super-power conflicts.

The 1965 programme of the defecting Progressive wing, now known as the Independent Liberals, was very similar to that of the Alignment. At the global level it advocated merely 'an effort to improve ties with the different blocs'. The focus was on Arab–Israel issues: the Independent Liberals urged 'the reinforcement of our security forces'; 'political initiative to further peace on the basis of the status quo'; 'a . . . foreign policy aiming to widen the range of international forces prepared to help us'; the removal of 'the area from the sphere of the Cold War and of Great Power rivalry and to obtain guarantees from the Great Powers'; and 'action against the Arab boycott'. They also advocated 'closer political, economic and cultural contacts, and aid exchanges with the developing countries', and a 'struggle to ensure the right of emigration from all countries of the Diaspora . . . (especially) the rights of Soviet Jewry'.[1]

---

analysis of the Progressive Party's image and foreign policy advocacy (to 1961) draws heavily on ch. IX of Paltiel's study, 'Foreign Policy and the Attitude Towards the Arab Minority in Israel'.

[1] As in other parties, there were factional differences on foreign policy among the Progressives. There were two main groups: the traditionally moderate German Zionists, led by Rosen, who stressed the impact of Israeli deeds on world opinion, the need for friends, and the value of goodwill towards the Arabs; and the labour-radical group, represented by Harari, who echoed the Ben Gurion stress on security and military preparedness. Differences were evident on the Jerusalem question, on the readiness to accept the return of some Arab refugees, and the treatment of the Arab minority in Israel, with Rosen close to *Mapam*, and Harari to *Mapai*; so too with

iii. *Religious Parties*

In the kaleidoscope of Israel's politics there are two pairs of religious parties: *Mizrahi*, a middle-class, orthodox Zionist group, and its much larger labour counterpart, *Ha-po'el Ha-mizrahi*; the anti-Zionist, ultra group, *Agudat Yisrael*, and its labour equivalent, *Po'alei Agudat Yisrael* (PAGY). In the first election campaign all four were united as the Religious Bloc. Thereafter the two *Mizrahi* groups merged to form the National Religious Party (NRP), a permanent member of Israel's coalition governments.[1] The two *Agudah* factions became reconciled to the State of Israel, despite the absence of visible divine intervention in its creation; and PAGY has been in the government since 1960.

Neither the NRP nor the *Agudah* groups has ever displayed much interest in foreign policy. Their *raison d'être* is *Torah* (the Law) and their aim the re-creation of a theocratic society. Thus the strengthening of links with Diaspora Jewry is important, as is the encouragement of immigration. The infusion of religious values into Israel's conduct of foreign relations and into the Foreign Service is a persistent demand. Yet the focus has been extremely narrow—the Arab–Israel conflict and Jewry. At the global level they have followed *Mapai*'s lead. And rarely does a bilateral issue enter the compass of discussion by religious parties. A few selections will demonstrate their relative indifference to foreign policy.

The NRP election platform for 1955 was brief and vague—and 'realistic'. 'In this world', it began, 'the weighing of loss and gain is more important than the moral and political righteousness of people. Therefore our people must struggle alone for its existence. . . .' They also urged continued efforts to achieve support at the UN, consideration for any reasonable peace plan, and the strengthening of *Tzahal*.[2] In 1959, too, its programme was similar to *Mapai*'s, with a stress on the

---

their attitude to reprisals. And on the degree of readiness to approach the West for aid, Rosen took a position similar to the General Zionists. Yet 'these issues were of secondary interest to the party and not of a kind for which the Progressives would sacrifice their participation in the Government'. Paltiel, op. cit., p. 130.

See p. 165, n. 5 above, pp. 57–8. The difference in outlook and policy between the General Zionists and the Progressives is perhaps best illustrated in the editorials of *Ha-boker* (The Morning), official daily of the former until it merged with *Herut*, and *Ha'aretz* (The Land), the leading independent daily newspaper in Israel, whose editorial policy reflected Progressive views. Both General Zionists and Progressives also published weeklies, fortnightlies, and monthlies in English, Polish, Yiddish, and other languages.

[1] Its principal leader, from Israel's independence until his death in 1970, was Haim Moshe Shapiro, for many years Minister of the Interior. Others are Dr. Z. Warhaftig, who held the Religious Affairs portfolio for many years, and Yosef Burg, long-time Minister of Social Welfare.

[2] See the NRP election brochure for the 1955 election (in Hebrew).

region: to strive for peace, based on the recognition of Israel's sovereignty; and to seek external support. There was also, as on earlier occasions, a pledge to attempt 'to break the party monopoly of the Foreign Ministry', as well as a call for closer ties 'with the Jewish nation in the Diaspora'.[1] In the same campaign the *Agudat Yisrael* confined its demands to increased immigration and an expression of readiness 'for a just peace and real stability in the Middle East'.[2]

In the sixth election campaign (1965) the NRP reiterated all the themes mentioned in 1959. The *Agudat Yisrael* urged the quest for peace and friendly relations with all peoples; and it declaimed that '*kashrut* and *shabbat* must be the central pillars of *Tzahal*, and its moral superiority must be assured'. Political controversy, it added, should be excluded from the army.[3] The PAGY had a slightly wider ambit. It advocated a solution of the Arab refugee problem by compensation and resettlement outside of Israel; further unification of families 'only on the basis of peace negotiations'; primary concern with the cause of Diaspora Jewry; and opposition to the broadening of relations with Germany.[4] On the whole the religious parties adopted a hard line. on the path to peace, as evident in the editorials of *Ha-modi'a* (*Agudat Yisrael*), *She'arim* (*Po'alei Adudat Yisrael*), and to a lesser extent in *Ha-tzofeh*) NRP). One example will suffice to suggest a commitment to power monism, of which any practitioner of *Realpolitik* would be proud. Commenting on the Rehovoth Conference on Science and Development in the New Nations, in August 1965, *Ha-modi'a* declared that it would not add to Israel's standing among the nations:[5]

The world of our days, East and West alike, is built, perhaps more than at any other time, on the standards of physical strength, position of power and ability to manœuvre between the competing blocs. Any other consideration, even if it be the most reasonable, just, righteous and sincere, is of no value or weight in inter-state relations.

iv. *Rafi*

The last of the pragmatic groups and the most short-lived is the Ben Gurion-inspired splinter from *Mapai* in 1965, *Rafi, Reshimat Po'alei Yisrael* (Israel Workers List); three years later, with the dissent of its mentor, *Rafi* reunited with *Mapai* (and *Ahdut Ha'avodah*) to form the Israel Labour Party. Thus it functioned as a competing élite in one election only. And even then *Rafi* did not offer an alternative foreign policy platform—with good reason. Ben Gurion's image had been paramount in shaping *Mapai*'s (and the Government's) policy from

---

[1] NRP election brochure for the 1959 election (in Hebrew).
[2] See the *Agudat Yisrael* election brochure for the 1959 election (in Hebrew).
[3] *Agudat Yisrael* election brochure for the 1965 election (in Hebrew).
[4] See the *Po'alei Agudat Yisrael* election brochure for the 1965 election (in Hebrew).
[5] 11 Aug. 1965.

1948 to 1963. Dayan had been a prominent member of the foreign policy élite for a decade, and Peres, the third leader of *Rafi*, almost as long. Finally, foreign policy was not a cause of the split.

One feature of *Rafi*'s foreign policy was its insignificance in the overall programme: Peres, for example, noted seven basic election planks to a press conference—and not one was remotely concerned with foreign policy.[1] Another feature was its brevity and vagueness. Indeed there was no integrated set of provisions in this sphere. At the global level it urged 'friendship with all the peoples of the world', that is, the Germans, too. In the Near East, 'we seek peace with our neighbours' but, more important, 'diligent efforts to preserve our independence in security affairs'. And to this end *Rafi* demanded that Israel 'not accept any form of international inspection to which other countries of the world are not submitted'. Joint action between Israel and Diaspora Jewry was advocated 'to promote the demand that the Jews of the Soviet Union be permitted to emigrate'. And aid to developing countries was defined as one of Israel's 'central tasks'—a 'moral and social responsibility'.[2] It was a programme with greater emphasis on action and even less on ideology than the parent party—but one to which *Mapai* would not object.

A comparison of the foreign and defence policy programmes in the 1965 election campaign reveals that the gap between incumbent and competing élites was not great. At the global level only *Gahal* urged open alignment with the West; all others concurred with the Alignment's call for friendship with all nations, though *Mapam* specified the Soviet Union in this context, and *Rafi* stressed self-reliance. Peace with Israel's Arab neighbours was urged by all parties, with differing degrees of emphasis. Only *Mapam* differed from the widespread view that all Arab refugees be settled in Arab lands, with suitable compensation; an unspecified number should be repatriated, was the dissenting view. There was unanimity on the need for a strong *Tzahal* but disagreement on various related points; the Alignment and the NRP called for ministerial control of the Defence establishment, while *Gahal*, *Mapam*, and the Independent Liberals pressed for parliamentary control; the NRP urged the abolition of army service for girls; *Mapam* opposed nuclear arms in the Middle East; and the Independent Liberals called for the exclusion of politics from the military. *Gahal* repudiated all ties with Germany, while *Mapam* opposed any extension of relations.

These were not mere nuances; yet permanent siege had imposed

---

[1] The seven points were: electoral reform; streamlining the economy; reduction of administrative bureaucracy; national health insurance; a master science plan; free education for the age group 3–16; and promotion of sports and the preservation of Israel's natural beauty. *Jerusalem Post*, 13 Oct. 1965.

[2] See p. 165, n. 5 above, p. 57. *Rafi*'s views were communicated by its party leaders in the *Knesset* and elsewhere, and in the weekly party organ, *Mabbat Hadash* (New Look).

restraint and had narrowed the boundaries of dissent from a 'national interest-oriented' foreign policy. Only in the years following the Six Day War did the more basic cleavages in image and policy demands noted in this analysis of party advocacy come to the surface, as Israel found herself at the crossroads of political decision in relations with the Arab states.

CHAPTER 9

Communication Network:
Link Between Environments[1]

Foreign policy decision-makers derive much of their crucial information from various channels or news media. One is the written word,
which takes many forms—daily newspaper, weekly, fortnightly, monthly,
and quarterly magazine, pamphlets, books, indeed, the array of publications that pours from the printing press in the contemporary world. But
there are other image-creating sources in written form, for example,
reports from representatives abroad, intelligence assessments, and
related types of secret information. Another broad category of news
flow is the spoken word, principally in the form of radio news, but
including face-to-face contact as well. And thirdly there is the combined
audio-visual medium which is almost universally present in the global
system of 1970—television.

All these channels for communicating perceptions of reality are
present within Israel's foreign policy system; but, as elsewhere, they are
of unequal intensity and influence in shaping the View of the World
held by decision-makers. For one thing, TV did not exist during the
period under inquiry, May 1948 to May 1968: it was introduced in
the autumn of 1968 and, apart from educational programmes, was
confined to a few evenings a week during the first year. For another,
the habit of decades has sustained an extraordinary dependence upon
Kol Yisrael (Voice of Israel) news reports.[2] Finally, the press, as many
other institutions in Israeli society, developed along political party
lines: this enhances the importance of those media which are com-
monly considered to be politically unattached. All this, combined with
the tradition of learning, created a sophisticated communication network for the transmission of the raw data in image formation. These

---

[1] There are few systematic inquiries into the communication flow of 'foreign policy'
news to decision-makers (as well as to the attentive and mass publics). Noteworthy
are Bernard C. Cohen, 'Mass Communication and Foreign Policy', in J. N. Rosenau
(ed.), *Domestic Sources of Foreign Policy*, The Free Press, New York, 1967, ch. 6, and
Cohen, *The Press and Foreign Policy*, Princeton University Press, Princeton, N.J., 1963,
ch. IV; and Johan Galtung and M. H. Ruge, 'The Structure of Foreign News: The
Presentation of the Congo, Cuba, and Cyprus Cases in Four Norwegian Newspapers',
in *Journal of Peace Research*, 2, no. 1, 1965, pp. 64–91.

[2] The name was changed to *Shiddurei Yisrael* (Israel Broadcasts) in 1969, soon after
the advent of television.

are filtered through an Attitudinal Prism, that is, a lens through which the Operational Environment is defined by the recipient of news. For Israelis, as the next chapter will indicate, the pre-eminent component of that prism is Jewishness, the cumulative historical experience and culture of an old nation in a new state.

Israel's decision-makers derive their day-to-day perceptions of the contemporary world through four basic media: news bulletins of *Kol Yisrael* in Hebrew—there were 7 a day in 1950 and 13 in 1968 (further increased to 19 in 1970); the Hebrew press, notably the Big Three daily newspapers—*Ha'aretz*, *Ma'ariv*, and *Yediot Aharonot*; cables and reports from Israeli envoys around the world; and reports, often in the form of oral briefings, from Israel's intelligence agencies.[1] To these continuous image-forming media of communication must be added discussions with visitors from abroad—prominent Jews, friendly (and not so friendly) officials from other states, etc., exchanges with resident diplomats in Israel, encounters and impressions while visiting foreign lands, and some prestige newspapers, especially the *New York Herald Tribune*, *Le Monde*, *The Times*, the *Observer*, and the *Washington Post*.[2] Not all are read by all decision-makers, but they are kept informed of editorial views in these and other journals, notably *Time*, *Newsweek*, and the *Jewish Chronicle*.

Sharett, for example, read an array of foreign newspapers; so to does Eban. Ben Gurion relied less on external media of opinion. And Meir and Eshkol receive(d) a weekly survey of the foreign press, especially on items relating to Israel, the Middle East, Arabs, Jews, Soviet Russia, etc.[3] In that context, too, some high policy decision-makers attempted to influence perceptions of colleagues (and the mass public) by granting interviews in the foreign press, which were 'played back' to Israel.

This inquiry will concentrate on two important media which link the Operational and Psychological Environments of Israel's foreign policy—radio news and the daily press. Moreover, they are accessible to research, unlike the content of cables and reports by Israeli diplomats, or the intelligence materials made available to decision-makers. And

---

[1] There are five separate agencies within Israel's Intelligence community: *Sherut Bitahon*, better known by its initials, *Shin Bet*, the (General) Security Service, which is responsible for all counter-intelligence within Israel and, since 1967, in the occupied territories as well; *Ha-Mosad*, literally, The Institute, which deals with all intelligence activities abroad; *Agaf Modi'in (Aman)*, the Intelligence Bureau of *Tzahal*; *Heker*, the research and political intelligence Department of the Foreign Office; and *Anaf Tafkidim Me'uhadim (Atam)*, the Special Tasks Branch of the Police.

[2] The *New York Times* is not readily available in its full daily edition, but its major reports and editorials pertaining to the Arab–Israel conflict are transmitted via diplomatic cables, *Kol Yisrael*, and Israeli newspaper summaries or texts, especially in *Ha'aretz*. The latter, through the *New York Times* Service, also carries some feature columns, notably those of James Reston and C. L. Sulzberger.

[3] All major stories on Israel in the foreign press are prominently featured in Israeli newspapers, but foreign policy decision-makers tend to read them in the original source.

they have the further asset of being amenable to quantitative analysis.[1]
Some hard facts are known, however, about the information flow by
cables: these will be noted first.

(a) CABLES

The principal medium of communication within the Foreign Service
is the diplomatic cable. Information about the volume of perceptions
coming into the Israel Foreign Office and of out-flowing instructions
(though the division of function is not that rigid) is provided for the
mid-1960s by the annual reports of the Ministry.[2] A precise distribution of the cable flow by diplomatic mission is not available, but a
two-level classification is apparent: 'important' missions, like Washington, New York (UN), Paris, London, Brussels (since 1960), and Bonn
(since 1965); and 'other'. Knowledgeable estimates (Foreign Service
officers) suggest that the first three missions account for more than
half the volume of words flowing into the Ministry and from Jerusalem
abroad.

Not all foreign policy decision-makers receive copies of all diplomatic
cables—or even all important ones. Within the Foreign Office total
access to code cables is confined to the Minister, the Director-General,
his Deputy, the Head of the Research Department, and the Heads of
Bureaux of the Minister and the Director-General. Other members
of the Foreign Service Technical Élite—Assistant Directors-General,
Advisers, and Heads of Department—receive those cables which, in
the judgement of the DG's Head of Bureau, are pertinent to their
sphere of responsibility.[3] This unequal access to 'internal' information
may create, even within the Ministry, divergent perceptions of the
Operational Environment in which decisions must be made. Within the
High Policy Élite,[4] the only persons other than the Foreign Minister
who normally have access to all code cables are the Prime Minister
and the Defence Minister.[5]

Code cables also went to Eban, for example, when he was Deputy
Prime Minister (June 1963–January 1966) and, since the beginning
of 1966, to Yisrael Galili, Minister without Portfolio. They also went to

[1] Newspaper sources of image formation, however, suffer from certain disabilities:
(a) conflicting views, both within the same source over time and vis-à-vis other sources,
making for uncertain credibility; (b) a tendency to speculate; and (c) the urge for
'scoops'.
[2] See Appendix Table 7 for details.
[3] The Foreign Service Technical Élite is analysed in ch. 17 below.
[4] To be explored in the following chapter.
[5] During Israel's first two decades the posts of Prime Minister and Defence Minister
were held by the same person except for two brief periods, 1954–5 and 1967–8, totalling
slightly less than three years. (A qualitative change occurred on the eve of the 1967
War: these posts have been held separately since then.)

the Director-General of the Prime Minister's Office. This wider distribution among Israeli public figures arose because of a prevalent appetite for the prestige associated with 'secret matters of state'. The high value placed on access to code cables has more to do with this concern than with actual content. Indeed, over the years Foreign Ministry officials have become cynically convinced that, if their cables are not dispatched 'Secret', they are not taken seriously. And this, in turn, was due to an established practice of using 'Open' cables to transmit reviews of the foreign press and radio, including editorials, feature articles, etc. One further reason for unequal access is noteworthy: both the Foreign Office and *Ha-Mosad* have their own code. On many occasions Ben Gurion and others used the latter when they wished to avoid diffusion of certain kinds of information to the Foreign Service Technical Élite and other colleagues.

Access to Foreign Ministry telegrams, as to other sources of information, is not synonymous with exposure. Foreign Service officials with full access read all the cables. So did Sharett and so does Eban, among the Foreign Ministers. But Mrs. Meir, both as Foreign Minister and as Prime Minister, read what was prepared by her Head of Bureau: this was usually a small portion of the outgoing cables, along with about two-thirds of those arriving from Israeli missions.[1] Ben Gurion read all cables that interested him, that is, those pertaining to Security, to the Arabs, to the behaviour and posture of the super powers, France, Germany, and the UK, and to the 'Periphery' states.[2] Eshkol read even less than Meir and relied heavily on oral summaries prepared by his Head of Bureau. And Dayan, partly because of a physical disability, skims written materials and has a great deal read to him. Thus, even if this source of information is isolated from all others, the perceptions of reality created by cables have an uneven audience, with varying degrees of receptivity. This is accentuated by a scale of reliance in the judgement of different diplomat-reporters: the place of x in the scale varies among recipients, sometimes drastically. And though that scale cannot readily be given quantitative form, it exists in the minds of decision-makers. For all these reasons the images derived from diplomatic reports lack uniformity.

These are not, in any event, the crucial source about the external world for Israel's High Policy Élite. For most, including Ben Gurion, Meir, Eshkol, and Dayan, reports and briefings by the intelligence services, notably *Aman* and *Ha-Mosad*, are more authoritative. Their assessments are available to a few, Cabinet Ministers and certain Directors-General. And the unanimous view of recipients is that they are often decisive in arriving at high policy decisions.

[1] This point is elaborated in ch. 13 (*f*) below.
[2] Ben Gurion's 'Circles of Interest' in foreign policy are elaborated in ch. 15 (*b*) i below.

Cables and intelligence reports are unevenly distributed among Israeli decision-makers. By contrast, the news flow through radio and the press is accessible to all, and to the attentive and mass publics as well. Both of these media play a vital and continuous role in image formation about the Operational Environment.

(b) RADIO NEWS

Kol Yisrael has been the Israeli's principal link with the outside world since independence. Its audience is almost the entire adult Jewish population. And the credence placed in its news bulletins is very high. Indeed, 'listening to the news' is a compulsive and, for most, a compulsory habit. Nor is this confined to periods of *acute* tension on the border, as evident in the results of surveys of the extent of radio listening in Israel—conducted in June 1960, February 1961, June 1965, and January–February 1969.[1]

In 1965 no less than 89·2 per cent of the Jewish population aged eighteen and over answered affirmatively to the question, 'Do you usually listen to the radio?' This had grown from 86·4 and 86·5 per cent in 1960 and 1961. And by 1969 it had risen to an astounding 92 per cent.[2] News bulletins had the largest national audience—64 per cent at 7 p.m., slightly less at 8.30 p.m., and 50 per cent at 7 a.m., in 1965. There was a substantial increase in the size of audiences four years later: 72·5 per cent at 7 p.m., 70·5 per cent at 8 p.m., and 53·8 per cent at 7 a.m. There are two further quantitative indicators of the importance of News in the overall programmes of *Kol Yisrael*. Of the twenty-one categories of Hebrew-language broadcasts, News ranks third in volume of time on Channels A and B combined during a standard week in the six-month period 5 November 1967 to 5 May 1968, with 12·33 per cent of radio time. Moreover, as noted, news bulletins increased from 7 a day in 1950 to 19 in 1970, all on the hour.[3]

'We do not use information that has not been checked', said a veteran News Department official; 'it must be hard.' Generally, when an 'important story' comes to the attention of *Kol Yisrael* from a news

---

[1] The data are taken from Central Bureau of Statistics and Israel Broadcasting Authority, *Radio Listening and Television Watching January 1969*, Special Series no. 292, Jerusalem, 1969, pp. vii–ix, xix–xxiii; the 1961 data are taken in part from *Weekly News Bulletin*, Jerusalem, 9–15 Feb. 1966, p. 10.

[2] Surprisingly, perhaps, 78 per cent of all listeners in 1961 indicated that they listened to the radio on the Sabbath; this dropped to 71 per cent in 1965, and rose again to 73·8 per cent in 1969.

[3] An experimental daily half-hour programme (quarter-hour news, quarter-hour comment) was initiated in 1962. It was unsuccessful: Prime Minister Ben Gurion himself voted against its continuance. The programme was reintroduced in 1968 in a changed fifty-minute format as *Ha-Yom Hazeh* (Today).

agency, it waits for confirmation by another source, especially when it deals with Israel. For news about the Middle East the *Agence France Presse* (AFP) has long been regarded as the most reliable international agency source, followed by Reuters, with United Press (UP) and Associated Press (AP) on a distinctly lower level of reliability.[1] But the highest credence is placed in Israel's Monitoring Service. For external comment on the Middle East and on decisions taken by the Powers concerning the Middle East the greatest reliance is put on *Kol Yisrael*'s correspondents abroad: 'stringers' (associate correspondents) were appointed from 1959 onwards in the US, UN, UK, France and Italy, followed by residents there and elsewhere.

Among foreign press sources for Middle East news the order of reliability for *Kol Yisrael*'s News Department is the *New York Times*, the *Washington Post*, the BBC, and *Le Monde*: stories in the first two are taken as printed; those from the last two are checked and, if not confirmed, may be used with an explicit reservation. It is assumed that AFP is a mouthpiece for the *Quai d'Orsay*, Reuters for the British Government, and AP for the US Government. The decision to use news stories is taken by the editor on duty at the time: it is determined by the flow of news into the News Department as filtered through his mind. In that connection one Director of News remarked: 'I find that, very often, my staff looks at stories in terms of what they read that day in *Ha'aretz* and *Ma'ariv* [the leading morning and evening Israeli newspaper, respectively]. It becomes necessary for him to disentangle himself and go to the source.' The use of commentary material is usually determined by the *Kol Yisrael* expert on the Middle East.[2]

With few resident correspondents abroad, *Kol Yisrael* sometimes uses those from *Ma'ariv* and *Yediot Aharonot*—but only for voice coverage, not for cable reports. Moreover, it has always been more dependent upon international news agencies than are these mass-circulation dailies. Thus the images held by Israelis while listening to radio news are formed much more by foreign information sources than are the perceptions held by newspaper readers—as will be evident in a quantitative analysis to follow.

Israeli images are also partly shaped by political and military commentaries regularly carried by the national radio. Over the years these have been offered by government officials (active and retired), like

[3] In 1948 there was only one agency in Israel—Reuters. A limited UP wire service was introduced in 1950; a teleprinting service came two years later. The Associated Press and *Agence France Presse* followed soon after. *Kol Yisrael*'s correspondents abroad were not appointed until the end of the fifties.

[2] The Hebrew News Section serves all other languages except Arabic. It prepares the master news bulletins, which are then translated into the other languages. The French Section, however, has direct access to the AFP Service and may use some of its material instead of the Hebrew master draft. The Russian News Section has some autonomy as well.

Eytan of the Foreign Office, and Medzini of the Government Press Office; retired army officers, such as General Haim Herzog, Colonel Yosef Nevo, and General Meir Amit; academics such as Arieli, Avineri, and Talmon from Jerusalem's Hebrew University, and Shamir from Tel Aviv University; and journalists, like S. Rosenfeld, H. Zemer, A. Kapeliuk, and S. Segev. Although not tested by polls, there appears to be a high degree of trust in the accuracy of these political and military analyses.

Kol Yisrael was a part of the Prime Minister's Office until May 1965.[1] Since then the form and content of its operations have been controlled and directed by the Broadcasting Authority, which consists of thirty-one persons appointed by the President on the nomination of the Government. (In its first major test it displayed impressive independence—during the 1969 controversy over TV broadcasts on Friday evening, the beginning of the Jewish Sabbath: the Prime Minister tried to impose Government authority, in an inelegant display of political intrusion into the affairs of a public service corporation, in order to satisfy the demands of the religious parties in the Coalition.)[2]

As with newspaper copy, anything on the radio that deals with military subjects—and this is given wide interpretation—is subject to military censorship. There is no political censorship as such; 'but being a State institution,' remarked a senior *Kol Yisrael* official, 'we have to give the Government a right to express itself; at the same time they cannot dictate to us'. The pressures were greater, he added, when *Kol Yisrael* was in the Prime Minister's Office: as employees of that ministry they could have been—and occasionally were—instructed 'to do this or that; now the Prime Minister's Office must go through the Board of Directors of the Broadcasting Authority and the Director-General of *Kol Yisrael*'.[3] 'It took us a long time to get rid of the stigma of officialdom. But that image was bound to be', another remarked. 'I think we have now [summer 1968] broken through. We can now cross-examine officials.' As further evidence it was noted that *Kol Yisrael*'s military news was always accepted by listeners as accurate, while political news was received with some scepticism—until Israel's radio network was given quasi-independent status in 1965.[4]

[1] A bill to set up a Broadcasting Authority was tabled in the *Knesset* in June 1963, upon the recommendation of an advisory committee. It became law almost two years later.

[2] The Israeli press carried detailed accounts of the controversy in October–November 1969.

[3] Perhaps the best example of *political* censorship concerned the Lavon Affair in 1960–1: hardly a word leaked on the radio. In 1966 the Foreign Office asked that a telegram from Tunisia's President Bourguiba to the opening ceremony of the Truman Center for the Advancement of Peace, in Jerusalem, *not* be read over the radio.

[4] This analysis of *Kol Yisrael* news owes much to interviews with three senior staff members in 1968—Shmuel Almog, Director-General, Amos Gordon, Director, News and Current Events, and Yitzhak Gaulan, the latter's deputy.

(c) NEWSPAPER REPORTS

The Israeli press is a vigorous medium of communication to the news-conscious Israelis—decision-makers and public alike. It is impressively diverse and multilingual, with various shades of editorial opinion. The 1969–70 official survey lists twenty-three daily morning newspapers and two daily evening ones. Of the former, nine were in Hebrew, two in Arabic, and one each in Bulgarian, English, French, German, Hungarian, Polish, Roumanian, and Yiddish, apart from those on sports, in simple Hebrew, etc. Many are party journals, a further reflection of the dominant position of political parties in Israeli society: *Al Hamishmar (Mapam)*; *Davar (Histadrut*, really *Mapai)*; *Ha-modi'a (Agudat Yisrael)*; *Ha-tzofeh* (National Religious Party); *Ha-yom (Gahal)*, a merger of *Ha-boker* (General Zionist) and *Herut (Herut)*, which itself ceased publication at the end of 1969;[1] *Kol Ha'am (Maki)*, which became a weekly in 1969; *Lamerhav (Ahdut Ha'avodah)*; and *She'arim (Po'alei Agudat Yisrael)*. The Big Three—in circulation and influence—are independent, *Ha'aretz, Ma'ariv,* and *Yediot Aharonot,* the last two appearing at midday. There are also over twenty-five weeklies in a dozen languages, the most important being *Ha'olam Hazeh*, already discussed in the context of interest groups, and the Army magazine, *Ba-mahaneh*.[2]

Israel's foreign policy decision-makers read at least two daily Hebrew newspapers—almost all, *Ha'aretz* and *Ma'ariv*. Many also read or skim their party daily in the morning and *Yediot Aharonot* in the afternoon. *Ha'aretz* is reputed to be the most reliable Israeli newspaper, with the highest intellectual standard. This, combined with its penchant for dissent from much of Government policy—it has long been anti-Establishment and liberal non-conformist—makes it required reading. *Ma'ariv* is staffed by many ex-Revisionists and is hawkish on Israel's Arab policy and, generally, anti-Establishment from a rightist perspective. Its operative assumption appears to be that the average Israeli can satisfy his need for news through *Ma'ariv* and *Kol Yisrael. Yediot Aharonot* is the closest Israeli version of a daily tabloid but it has reliable information on domestic and party politics and on foreign policy acts. There is a sensationalist tinge in *Yediot*.

The following sales figures are claimed by the Big Three:[3]

[1] *Ha-yom,* too, ceased to exist in 1970.

[2] State of Israel, Government Press Office, *Newspapers and Periodicals Appearing in Israel 1969–1970,* Jerusalem, 1970, pp. 3–10.

[3] Response to the author's inquiry by the editorial offices of these newspapers, in May 1970. The figures for *Ma'ariv* exclude sales abroad. *Davar,* once the leading Israeli daily newspaper, reported the following circulation figures:

March	Weekdays	Fridays
1962	34,000	37,000
1964	35,000	38,000
1968	36,000	40,000

	March 1962 Weekdays	March 1962 Fridays	March 1964 Weekdays	March 1964 Fridays	March 1968 Weekdays	March 1968 Fridays
Ha'aretz	29,920	34,840	32,980	42,280	38,200	55,760
Ma'ariv	83,553	94,259	98,541	113,796	156,968	199,348
Yediot Aharonot	70,000	85,000	82,000	101,000	110,000	156,000

Israeli newspapers have accepted some limits on freedom of the press —on sensitive issues of vital interest such as immigration from the Soviet Union, the flow of oil from Iran, and *aliya* from Roumania. Self-censorship is based upon guidelines established by a committee consisting of an editor, a lawyer, and an army officer: the committee has authority to fine offending members. At the same time the press has not concealed its dissent from the expansion of the area of censorship, even in a state of war. The most outspoken critic has been *Ha'aretz*. As the leading opponent of the foreign policy pursued since the Six Day War by the Government of National Unity, it often challenged the extension of this 'secret' realm.[1]

Precise measurement of press influence is impossible, but it is certain that the bulk of image-forming news about the external setting is acquired from the daily press, supplemented by some foreign newspapers, and the news bulletins of *Kol Yisrael*.[2] For this reason the flow of news about the Operational Environment to decision-makers can be explored most effectively by a quantitative analysis of a sample of press and radio news. We shall begin with the Big Three and examine their news reporting in two fortnightly periods.

[1] Typical was an editorial on 26 April 1970 entitled 'Political Censorship'. *Ha'aretz* attacked the Censor for excising from a news story references to a clash between Eban and Begin on the issue of Jewish settlement in Hebron, Mrs. Meir's refusal to use the term 'withdrawal' in Government documents, and a letter of protest over the 'Goldmann Affair' from a group of high-school students. 'The Censor deleted this—not for reasons of security but because of inconvenience to the Government.' More generally, 'in the new Cabinet Mrs. Meir tends to bring most issues for discussion to a plenary session of the Ministerial Committee on Defence. . . . This is a dangerous trend. Soon the impression will be created that the full Government deals only with papyrus and the X-ray technicians' strike.'

Ha'aretz was here inveighing against a Government decision in July 1966 forbidding disclosure of discussions and decisions of the Ministerial Committee on Defence, as well as the *very fact that the Committee met or was scheduled to meet*, unless this was specifically authorized by the Prime Minister or the Defence Minister, or on their behalf. What prompted that stringent decision was leaks to the press of deliberations in that pivotal Cabinet committee, a widespread practice which has continued nonetheless.

There is also *military* censorship of dispatches abroad by foreign correspondents in Israel, but this aspect is outside the framework of our discussion—communication of information about the external world *to Israelis*.

[2] Since the advent of the jet plane (1961–2), foreign newspapers have increased their sale in Israel. *Time* heads the list with 14,000 in 1969; *Newsweek* follows with about 5,000; and, much lower, are European papers such as *Le Monde, Die Welt, The Times, The Guardian,* and the *Daily Telegraph*.

i. *'Foreign Policy' News, March 1962*

What news coverage about the external world is available to the Israeli decision-maker in his daily newspaper? Some hard data provide insights into the potential perceptions thus acquired.[1]

TABLE 12

'FOREIGN POLICY' NEWS REPORTING IN SELECTED ISRAELI NEWSPAPERS, 1–15 MARCH 1962*

Number of Items and Space (in square centimetres)

	Ha'aretz	Ma'ariv	Yediot Aharonot
Geneva Conference on Disarmament and East– West Relations	31 (4,030)	21 (2,170)	9 (1,617)
Algeria	21 (2,817)	15 (1,845)	6 (932)
Arab World	45 (2,132)	24 (1,204)	7 (866)
Israel Foreign Relations	37 (2,297)	24 (2,670)	12 (1,100)
Other News	84 (5,072)	16 (733)	9 (1,878)
Total	218 (16,348)	100 (8,622)	43 (6,393)

* This excludes all news concerning the internal affairs of other states.

It is immediately apparent that *Ha'aretz* devoted far more attention to 'foreign policy' news than did *Ma'ariv* or *Yediot Aharonot*—or the two combined. In number of items *Ha'aretz* coverage was more than twice as large as *Ma'ariv* and five times as large as *Yediot Aharonot*; in space, it was almost double that of *Ma'ariv* and two and a half times as much as that of *Yediot*. The gap is also evident in a comparison of the proportion of news space, including domestic and foreign news, editorials, and articles on political, economic, and social affairs, devoted to 'foreign policy' news during the fortnight as a whole: *Ha'aretz*, almost 7 per cent; *Ma'ariv*, 3·7 per cent; and *Yediot Aharonot*, 4·1 per cent. The proportion of 'foreign policy' news to extended news, for all three, would be much higher if the base were confined to hard news; but the gap would remain.

There are striking differences as well in the sources of 'foreign policy' news used by these Israeli newspapers during that period.

The 'foreign policy' news reports of *Ha'aretz* reveal the greatest variety in sources: the four principal ones were Reuters, AFP, UP, and their own correspondents. None predominates: Reuters accounts for 26·5 per cent, AFP 21·5 per cent, and UP and OC about 16 per cent

[1] The data for the quantitative analysis of news reporting in Israel's press and radio in 1962, 1964, and 1968 were assembled meticulously by Miss Jemima Levy, an MA student in International Relations at the Hebrew University of Jerusalem.

TABLE 13

'FOREIGN POLICY' NEWS REPORTING IN SELECTED ISRAELI
NEWSPAPERS, 1–15 MARCH 1962

Sources of News

	Ha'aretz	Ma'ariv	Yediot Aharono
Agence France Presse (AFP)	64	1	—
Associated Press (AP)	—	9	—
Reuters	79	3	2
United Press (UP)	50	2	3
Jewish Telegraph Agency (JTA)	8	2	—
Own Correspondents (OC)	47	45	29
Not Indicated*	34	38	10
Other†	16	—	—
Total‡	298	100	44

* Often prepared by desk men from agency, radio, and other sources.
† Comprises selections from the World Press (10), Walter Lippmann articles (4), etc.
‡ Some reports were based upon two or more sources.

each. *Ha'aretz* was sharply distinguished from both *Ma'ariv* and *Yediot Aharonot* in its frequent use of several sources for its articles: in fact, there were twenty-three stories with two sources, twenty-seven stories with three sources, and one story with four sources. *Yediot Aharonot* had the narrowest information base of 'foreign policy' news: almost two-thirds came from their own correspondents; and only five stories were taken from a news agency. *Ma'ariv*, too, relied heavily on its own correspondents: they accounted for almost half of the news items, with *Ma'ariv* desk men compiling most of the remaining stories.

Apart from the news agencies, *Ha'aretz* has, for some years, received the copy flowing from the *New York Times* and *Le Monde* world services, while *Ma'ariv* has taken the *Washington Post* material. *Ha'aretz* has resident correspondents in Washington, London, Paris, and Bonn, and many associate correspondents or 'stringers'. *Ma'ariv* has resident correspondents in New York, London, Paris, Bonn, Rome, Brussels, and Ankara, with 'stringers' in many cities. Both also have specialists in Arab and Middle East affairs, domestic politics, defence, diplomacy, etc. By all accounts they have the most varied sources of news within the Israeli press community. But *Ha'aretz* relies much more on external sources and seeks verification of news reports to a much greater extent.

There were marked contrasts, too, in the scope and follow-up of coverage of 'foreign policy' news by the three Israeli newspapers during the March 1962 period, both in the Middle East and global systems. This is abundantly clear from the treatment accorded the Arab World and the Geneva Disarmament Conference. *Ha'aretz* contained nine separate stories on the Arab World in its issue of 2 March 1962. *Ma'ariv*'s coverage of the Arab World on 1 March was nil: it appears at noon and is comparable, therefore, to the *Ha'aretz* issue of the following morning—though there is some spillover. But even if the 2 March issue is included, *Ma'ariv* reported only one item on the Arab World: a *New Statesman* article was summarized under the heading 'Future Hopes for Arab Peace Agreement with Israel'. *Yediot Aharonot* contained no news about the Arab World on either day.

A week later, on 9 March 1962, *Ha'aretz* carried four news items on the Arab World, among twenty-six 'foreign policy' news reports that day. *Ma'ariv* reported two of these stories on the 8th and 9th. *Yediot Aharonot* had no stories on the Arab World either day. On the last day of the surveyed period in 1962, 15 March, *Ha'aretz* carried ten 'foreign policy' news stories, including two on the Arab World. *Ma'ariv* carried eight 'foreign policy' news items on the 14th, with an unusually high proportion—half—on the Arab World. There was no news on the Arab World in *Yediot Aharonot* on the 14th. Indeed the paucity of news on this topic in *Yediot* is starkly evident—there were only seven news items during that fortnight. *Ma'ariv* was better—twenty-four stories; but *Ha'aretz* contained almost twice as many reports on the Arabs—forty-five. The same is true of all other major topics of 'foreign policy' news during the period—Geneva Conference (37 to 21 to 9), Algeria (27 to 15 to 6), and Israel's Foreign Relations (37 to 24 to 12).

The most widely-reported global system news item of that fortnight was the seventeen-nation Geneva Disarmament Conference. *Ha'aretz* carried thirty-one stories on this and the related issue of East–West relations, *Ma'ariv* twenty-one, and *Yediot Aharonot* nine. This accounted, respectively, for one-seventh, one-fifth, and one-fifth of all 'foreign policy' news in the three newspapers during that period. Yet their sources differed. *Ha'aretz* carried brief reports of the approaching conference on the 1st, 2nd, 4th, 5th, 6th, 7th, 9th, and 11th, always in sober terms. From the 12th to the 15th there were seven stories, in short, very wide coverage of a global and inter-bloc issue of importance to the Israeli decision-maker. *Ma'ariv* by contrast did not carry a single report on the Geneva Conference until the 11th. During the next three days there were seven items. As for *Yediot Aharonot*, the first report on Geneva appeared on 6 March. Then, from the 11th it carried six stories.

There were two basic differences in reporting the conference. *Ha'aretz* exposed its readers to the impending talks with a good deal of analysis and background material during the preceding ten days; *Ma'ariv* and *Yediot Aharonot* did not: they waited until the eve of the conference. Moreover, all *Ma'ariv* reports but one, and all *Yediot* reports came from their own correspondents, that is, they were filtered through an Israeli lens before being presented to Israeli readers; *Ha'aretz* relied entirely on international news agencies, two or three of them for most of its reports.

The greatest contrast between *Ha'aretz* and the other two leading dailies is the range and volume of 'foreign policy' news coverage. Apart from the major topics noted in Table 12, *Ha'aretz* carried eighty-four stories on other subjects of that kind during the period 1–15 March 1962; *Ma'ariv* had only sixteen, and *Yediot Aharonot* nine. Readers of *Ma'ariv* were exposed to a broader segment of the external environment than *Yediot* and to more detail about events. But the *Ha'aretz* coverage was incomparably greater than both—nine times as many items as *Yediot* and five and a half times as many as *Ma'ariv*. All of the topics reported by *Ma'ariv* were also in *Ha'aretz*—and in greater depth. In addition, it devoted considerable attention to the following regions, issues, and topics:

Africa—8 stories, including Tshombe and the Congo (4)
Asia—8, including 2 on China–Tibet relations
Dutch–Indonesian relations—7
Europe—9, many on the Common Market and on inter-European relations
Germany—4
Latin America—6, mostly on US–Cuba relations
Rhodesia—3
Sino-Soviet relations—4
Soviet'Bloc—4
US–Indian relations—2
US aid to Vietnam—2

In terms of distribution of news by system level, *Ha'aretz* devoted eighty-two stories (of 218) to the Arab World and to Israel's Foreign Relations (37·5 per cent). If Algeria is included within the Middle East System, *Ha'aretz* regional coverage rises to 47 per cent of 'foreign policy' news. The corresponding figures for *Ma'ariv* are 48 of 100 (48 per cent), and including Algeria, 63 per cent. For *Yediot Aharonot* they are 19 of 43 (45 per cent), and 59 per cent including Algeria. In short, the reader of *Ha'aretz* was given the broadest and most varied set of perceptions about the external Operational Environment—with the greatest attention to global system news. The reader of *Yediot Aharonot* alone was barely made aware of the world beyond the Middle East.

ii. 'Foreign Policy' News, March 1964

The coverage of 'foreign policy' news by the Big Three Israeli newspapers for the period 1–15 March 1964 indicates a similar pattern.

During the March 1964 period *Ha'aretz* contained almost twice as many 'foreign policy' news items as *Ma'ariv* and four times as many as *Yediot Aharonot*, a slightly lower ratio than in 1962. It also devoted more space to 'foreign policy' news than the other two dailies; but while the gap with the latter remained the same, 2·5 to 1, it was much narrower

TABLE 14

'FOREIGN POLICY' NEWS REPORTING IN SELECTED ISRAELI
NEWSPAPERS, 1–15 MARCH 1964*

Number of Items and Space (in square centimetres)

	Ha'aretz	Ma'ariv	Yediot Aharonot
Cyprus Conflict	31 (5,594)	25 (5,723)	16 (3,485)
French Foreign Policy	17 (1,906)	12 (1,167)	—
African States	13 (594)	3 (162)	—
Communist Bloc	11 (429)	4 (642)	1 (19)
East–West Relations	6 (243)	—	—
Arab World	53 (2,651)	27 (2,143)	8 (472)
Israel Foreign Relations	31 (2,478)	28 (3,721)	22 (3,258)
Other News	45 (3,354)	9 (991)	1 (104)
Total	207 (17,249)	108 (14,549)	48 (7,338)

* This excludes all news concerning the internal affairs of other states.

with *Ma'ariv* than in the comparable fortnight two years earlier. Indeed, in 1964 the average *Ma'ariv* report was longer (131 sq. cm.) than in *Ha'aretz* (83 sq. cm.). This is evident in the coverage of most major topics: Cyprus Conflict—*Ha'aretz* had six more items but less overall space; the Communist Bloc—*Ha'aretz* had almost three times as many items but devoted less space; the Arab World—*Ha'aretz* had twice as many stories but only slightly more space; and Israel's Foreign Relations—*Ha'aretz* had three more items but almost 50 per cent less space. To the last topic, *Yediot Aharonot* devoted more space than *Ha'-aretz*, though it ran nine fewer reports. The narrowing of the gap in reporting is also apparent from a comparison of the proportion of extended news space given by the Big Three to 'foreign policy' news: *Ha'aretz*—5·5 per cent; *Ma'ariv*—4·6 per cent; and *Yediot Aharonot*—3·2 per cent.

The differences in sources of news about the external setting remained unchanged (see Table 15). As in 1962 (and again in 1968) the *Ha'aretz* reports are derived from a variety of sources: the three principal ones were AFP, Reuters, and their own correspondents; together they account for 71 per cent of all sources used to report 'foreign policy' news during the 1964 fortnight surveyed. Once more there were many more sources than stories, unlike *Yediot Aharonot* and, with few exceptions, *Ma'ariv*: in fact, *Ha'aretz* carried sixteen reports with two sources, the most frequent combination being Reuters and AFP (9), five reports with three sources, and two reports with four sources each. *Yediot* again had the narrowest information base of 'foreign policy' news: all but seven of its stories came from its own correspondents, and only one from a news agency. In *Ma'ariv*, too, there were few agency-derived

TABLE 15

'FOREIGN POLICY' NEWS REPORTING IN SELECTED ISRAELI
NEWSPAPERS, 1–15 MARCH 1964

Sources of News

	Ha'aretz	Ma'ariv	Yediot Aharonot
Agence France Presse (AFP)	56	1	—
Associated Press (AP)	16	3	—
Reuters	57	1	—
United Press (UP)	10	2	1
Jewish Telegraph Agency (JTA)	10	2	—
Own Correspondents	57	71	39
Not Indicated*	17	33	6
Other†	16	—	2
Total	239‡	113‡	48

* Often prepared by desk men from agency, radio, and other sources.
† Includes 6 from *New York Times* Service (in *Ha'aretz*); others are selections from the world press.
‡ Some reports were based upon two or more sources.

stories, only nine: almost two-thirds were filed by its correspondents abroad.

In its coverage of 'foreign policy' news during the 1964 surveyed period, *Ha'aretz* accorded the greatest attention to the Arab World, in number of items, and to Cyprus, in space. The largest number of reports in both *Ma'ariv* and *Yediot Aharonot* concerned Israel's Foreign Relations, with the Arab World and the Cyprus Conflict close behind in the former, and Cyprus in the latter; Cyprus was accorded the most space in these newspapers, qualitatively so in *Ma'ariv*.

Among seventeen 'foreign policy' news items in its issue of 1 March 1964 *Ha'aretz* contained four on the Arab World. *Ma'ariv* and *Yediot Aharonot* ran two reports on the Arab World that day.[1] A week later, on 9 March 1964, *Ha'aretz* carried eight reports (of eighteen) on the Arab World. *Ma'ariv*, by contrast, had sparse coverage of the Arab World on 8 March, only two stories. The next day it carried one of the *Ha'aretz* stories—and another on Syria. In *Yediot Aharonot* there were no reports on the Arab World on the 8th or 9th. On 15 March *Ha'aretz* carried twelve 'foreign policy' news items, of which only two dealt with the Arab World. *Ma'ariv* reported one of those stories on the 13th (the 14th was a Saturday), along with a report from the *Jewish Observer* in London, headlined, 'Nasser—Six Conditions for War Against Israel'. There were no reports in *Yediot Aharonot* on the 13th or the 15th. Once

[1] The last day of February 1964 was a Saturday, when Israeli newspapers are not published. Thus the normal comparison of stories in *Ha'aretz*, *Ma'ariv*, and *Yediot*—one day apart—does not entirely apply in this case.

more, the very limited exposure of its readers to the external Operational Environment is evident.

Both *Ha'aretz* and *Ma'ariv* reported extensively on the conflict over—and within—Cyprus during the first half of March 1964, *Yediot* less so in absolute but not in relative terms: in *Ha'aretz* it occupied one-seventh of all 'foreign policy' news items and more than one-fourth of the space; in *Ma'ariv* it accounted for a fourth of the stories and more than one-half of the space, and in *Yediot* a third of the reports and almost half of the space given to 'foreign policy' news. The readers of all three Israeli newspapers were, in that instance, given thorough and essentially similar coverage. A plausible explanation for the narrower gap in the volume of reporting is the fact that, while Cyprus was a global system issue, its proximity to the Near East gave it special interest to more inward-oriented readers of *Ma'ariv* and, especially, *Yediot Aharonot*. Yet the fundamental difference in sources of news applied to Cyprus as well: unlike *Ha'aretz*, they reported mainly what their correspondents wrote about the conflict.

The contrast in range of 'foreign policy' news between *Ha'aretz* and the other two newspapers was no less apparent in March 1964 than in March 1962: it carried fifty-one items on other topics, *Ma'ariv* nine, and *Yediot* only one—a report that the German Foreign Office was trying to prevent the enactment of a law concerning German scientists abroad.[1] In terms of the distribution of 'foreign policy' news by system level, the Middle East System (the Arab World and Israel's Foreign Relations) accounted for 84 of 207 *Ha'aretz* reports, that is, 40 per cent, and almost 30 per cent of the space. *Ma'ariv* devoted 55 of 108 items to the Middle East System, almost 52 per cent, accounting for 41 per cent of the space. And *Yediot Aharonot* devoted 30 of 48 'foreign policy' news

---

[1] *Ma'ariv* reported that 'British Officers [were] to Leave East Africa', 'President Johnson Will Have to Decide Fate of War in Vietnam', 'Ambassadors of Non-Aligned States to Confer This Month in Colombo', 'MacNamara Leaves for Vietnam', 'US Ambassador to Paris on Home Leave for Consultations', 'Panama Agrees to Re-establish Relations with US', 'US, Britain and Germany Agree to Finance the Greater Part of UNEF Expenses', 'American Diplomat Who Was Spying for Soviet Union Allowed to Retire', 'Demonstrators in Cambodia Attack British and American Embassies', and 'De Gaulle to Mexico'. All were derived from their own staff. *Ha'aretz* reported on most of these topics and many more: 5 stories on Germany; 8 items on the United States; 8 reports on the Vietnam War, especially the growing US role; 4 stories on the 'confrontation' between Indonesia and Malaysia; 5 Cables in Brief, containing 'foreign policy' news; 3 Selections from the World Press; 2 items each on the Sino-Soviet conflict, on Soviet–German relations, and on the Soviet protest against renewed U2 penetration of her air space; and 1 report on each of the following: a proposal to condemn anti-Semitism, in a UN document; the 'Kennedy Talks' on tariff reductions; Chou en-lai's visit to Ceylon; a Polish proposal for a nuclear freeze in Europe; Spain and the Common Market; Soviet–Swedish relations; Italy's foreign policy; South Africa's decision to leave the International Labour Organization; a cease-fire between India and Pakistan during a border clash; a cut in British foreign aid; and a Nepali request for British military assistance.

items to the Middle East System, close to 63 per cent, comprising half of the total space.

Readers of *Ha'aretz* were thus exposed to a large and representative segment of the changing Operational Environment—at the global, regional, and bilateral levels of international politics. Those who read *Ma'ariv* alone received conspicuously less information about the global system—in both volume and proportion of 'foreign policy' news. And those whose View of the World was formed by *Yediot Aharonot* were given the skimpiest coverage, with overwhelming emphasis on the Middle East, and with large gaps in news reporting even within that region.

Another notable difference is that *Ha'aretz* coverage of 'foreign policy' news was *outer-directed*, while that of *Ma'ariv* and *Yediot* was *inner-directed*. *Ha'aretz* relied to a much greater extent on international news agencies, while the reports in the two evening newspapers were overwhelmingly from their own correspondents or news staff. Thus *Ha'aretz* readers were bombarded with image-forming 'news' about the external world as filtered through the perceptual lens of foreigners—representatives of news agencies, and often more than one. By contrast, *Ma'ariv* and *Yediot* readers acquired their perceptions—in so far as they were derived from the daily press—from the filtering of news by Israelis.

(d) NEWS REPORTING: POST-SIX DAY WAR

The data analysed thus far pertain to the relative tranquillity between the second and third rounds in the Arab–Israel conflict. Changes of emphasis occurred after the 1967 War: these will be evident in a content analysis of *Ha'aretz* and *Ma'ariv* 'foreign policy' news during the first week of March 1968. Their reports for that period also permit a comparison with the flow of news through the two leading newspapers before the Six Day War. And they make possible as well a comparative inquiry into the two major Israeli media of image formation about the Operational Environment—press and radio.

i. *'Foreign Policy' News, March 1968: The Press*

There is a conspicuous change in both the volume and range of 'foreign policy' news reports. While *Ha'aretz* continued to exceed *Ma'ariv* in the number of items, the latter devoted more space to news about the external world—both in overall terms and in three of the five specific topics of concentrated attention, Communist Bloc, East–West Relations, and Israel Foreign Relations. Moreover, the average length of 'foreign policy' news items in *Ma'ariv* was longer in all subject categories except the Arab World. And even in proportional terms there is a striking change: *Ha'aretz*, 5·7 per cent, and *Ma'ariv*, 5·8 per cent. In 1962 the comparison was 7 to 3·7 per cent in favour of *Ha'aretz*. In

TABLE 16

'FOREIGN POLICY' NEWS REPORTING IN SELECTED ISRAELI
NEWSPAPERS, 1–7 MARCH 1968*

Number of Items and Space (in square centimetres)

	Ha'aretz		Ma'ariv	
Communist Bloc	12	(991)	8	(1,293)
East–West Relations	4	(194)	3	(579)
Arab World	9	(832)	6	(429)
Israel Foreign Relations	13	(795)	14	(1,044)
Arab–Israel Conflict	46	(4,577)	32	(4,444)
Other	5	(885)	5	(1,110)
Total	89	(8,274)	68	(8,899)

* This excludes all news concerning the internal affairs of other states.

1964 it was 5·5 to 4·6 per cent. And in 1968 the proportion of 'foreign policy' news to extended news showed a slight edge for *Ma'ariv*.

Another change relates to the distribution of 'foreign policy' news by system level, especially in the case of *Ha'aretz*. Its proportion of such news items allocated to the Middle East was 37·5 per cent (47 per cent including Algeria) in March 1962, 40 per cent in March 1964, and in March 1968 76 per cent. The comparable figures for *Ma'ariv* were 48 per cent (63 per cent including Algeria), 52 per cent, and 78 per cent. The same trend is evident in the space devoted to Middle East news between 1962 and 1968.

One other noteworthy change is the emphasis on the Arab–Israel Conflict in post-1967 'foreign policy' news reporting by the press: it ranked first by far in the 1–7 March 1968 period, accounting for more than half of all such news in *Ha'aretz* and half in *Ma'ariv*, both in number of items and in space. The category Arab–Israel Conflict was not used in the 1962 and 1964 data: it was subsumed in the term Israel Foreign Relations. A comparison of attention given to the conflict, along with Israel's Foreign Relations, before and after the Six Day War, indicates a qualitative shift:

Ha'aretz 17 per cent (1962)
          15 per cent (1964)
          66 per cent (1968)
Ma'ariv 24 per cent (1962)
          26 per cent (1964)
          68 per cent (1968)

The basic differences in sources of 'foreign policy' news, evident in March 1962 and March 1964, remained four years later.

TABLE 17

'FOREIGN POLICY' NEWS REPORTING IN SELECTED ISRAELI
NEWSPAPERS, 1-7 MARCH 1968

Sources of News

	Ha'aretz	Ma'ariv
Agence France Presse (AFP)	18	3
Associated Press (AP)	5	5
Reuters	21	5
United Press (UP)	10	6
Jewish Telegraphic Agency (JPA)	9	—
Own Correspondents (OC)	42	43
Not Indicated*	13	12
Other†	5	—
Total‡	123	74

* Often prepared by desk men from agency, radio, and other sources.
† Comprises *Le Monde* (3), *Economist* (1), and *Tass* (1).
‡ Some reports were based upon two or more sources.

As in 1962 and 1964, *Ha'aretz* derived its news about the external
world from a wide variety of sources. Moreover, it continued to rely on
multiple sources—for more than a fourth of the eighty-nine items:
seventeen had two sources, four had three sources, and three items four
sources each. Yet the ranking changed drastically: its own correspondents stood first, accounting for one-third of the total number of sources
(42 of 123)—and twice as many as the second most frequently used
source, Reuters, with AFP close behind; all the news agencies contributed to *Ha'aretz* coverage. The *Ma'ariv* pattern remained unchanged:
its own correspondents accounted for 60 per cent of all 'foreign policy'
news used during the first week of March 1968. The four international
news agencies combined provided less than half of the reports prepared
by *Ma'ariv* correspondents. And there were only three items—of
sixty-eight—with multiple sources: two with two sources each, and one
with five sources. Unlike 1962 and 1964, the scope of 'foreign policy'
news in the two leading Israeli newspapers was essentially similar in
March 1968, both in the Middle East and in the global system. There
were nine reports on the Arab World in *Ha'aretz* during the first week
of March 1968 (compared with nine stories on the Arab World on a
single day, 2 March, in 1962). *Ma'ariv* carried six stories on the Arab
World during that week—but all were on different topics from the
Ha'aretz reports. There is no apparent reason for this total non-
coincidence of news reporting.

The most widely-reported global news items during that period were
the Communist Summit in Budapest and the Warsaw Pact Conference

in Sofia immediately afterwards. *Ha'aretz* carried no less than twelve stories in the six issues which appeared between 1 and 7 March 1968. *Ma'ariv* covered the same terrain in its reports on the Communist Bloc. Indeed, readers of the two newspapers were given thorough, comprehensive, and almost identical image-forming daily headlines concerning the two Communist bloc conferences in the first week of March 1968.

Ma'ariv ran only four stories on other 'foreign policy' news during that period, following its earlier pattern of concentration on a few topics or areas. *Ha'aretz*, too, reported on very few other aspects of the external Operational Environment—only five of eighty-nine items, that is, 5·6 per cent of the total—compared with 34 per cent in March 1962 and 22 per cent in March 1964. In short, there has been a steady narrowing of *Ha'aretz* coverage of 'foreign policy' news, with increasing attention to the Middle East. Stated differently, *Ha'aretz* 'foreign policy' news reporting moved in the direction of *Ma'ariv*'s unchanging pattern of news coverage and distribution between the global and regional systems.

ii. *'Foreign Policy' News, March 1968: Kol Yisrael*

An examination of *Kol Yisrael*'s Hebrew news bulletins during the period 1–7 March 1968 provided informative data on the content, volume, and range of 'foreign policy' news communicated to Israel's foreign policy decision-makers in the new phase of political struggle after the Six Day War.

TABLE 18

'FOREIGN POLICY' NEWS REPORTING ON *KOL YISRAEL*,
1–7 MARCH 1968*

	Number of Items	Space in Lines†
Communist Bloc	31	280
East–West Relations	16	130
British Foreign Policy (mainly towards Rhodesia)	29	302
Vietnam	6	36
Arab World	29	155
Israel Foreign Relations	35	314
Arab–Israel Conflict	88	858
Other	20	136
Total	254	2,211

* This excludes all news concerning the internal affairs of other states.
† Refers to the typescript from which radio news bulletins are read.

The number of items is deceptively large: of the 254 noted in Table 18, 101 were repeated in two or more bulletins. They are counted as separate reports because of the nature of radio as a news medium: each bulletin is equivalent to a story in the daily newspaper in providing image-forming words about the Operational Environment, audial and visual, respectively. Thus every time a 'foreign policy' news item is mentioned on *Kol Yisrael* it constitutes an autonomous unit of communication.

There are two noteworthy parallels in radio and press reporting of 'foreign policy' news. First, the five principal topics covered in *Ha'aretz* and *Ma'ariv* during the first week of March 1968 were also reported in *Kol Yisrael* broadcasts—and in the same order of frequency: Arab–Israel Conflict; Israel Foreign Relations; Communist Bloc; Arab World; and East–West Relations. Secondly, the coverage of the Arab–Israel Conflict is pre-eminent in all three communication flows: it claimed half or more of the total space in the two newspapers and 45 per cent of *Kol Yisrael* space (devoted to this branch of news) during the week under investigation. The differences, however, are even more striking.

1. The distribution of attention among the five major topics of 'foreign policy' news is much more sharply skewed in press reports than in radio bulletins: the Arab–Israel Conflict accounted for more items and more space than the other four topics combined in both *Ma'ariv* and *Ha'aretz*. On *Kol Yisrael*, by contrast, the Arab–Israel Conflict occupied far more space than any other *single* topic, but three of the four other major topics received a similar order of radio coverage.

2. Two topics which appeared in *Kol Yisrael*'s news bulletins, Rhodesia (and British policy) and Vietnam, the former with high frequency, were not mentioned in the two newspapers during that period. Indeed, Rhodesia (and British policy) occupied almost as much space in radio news as did Israel Foreign Relations.

3. Radio reporting of 'foreign policy' news was much more evenly distributed between the global system and the Middle East: 40 per cent to 60 per cent on *Kol Yisrael*; and 24 per cent to 76 per cent in both newspapers.

4. The proportion of *Kol Yisrael* news devoted to foreign policy issues was much greater than in the press: almost 44 per cent to 5·7 per cent each for *Ha'aretz* and *Ma'ariv*. The figures are not strictly comparable, for the base was extended news, including articles, etc. Nonetheless, the difference is stark. Stated differently, radio news bulletins report news only (apart from weather, which occupied 15 per cent of the total during the week), whereas the daily newspaper contains much more than bald news reporting.

The sources of radio news are diverse, as the following data (Table 19) reveal. The Hebrew News Section of *Kol Yisrael* communicates news about the external world received from all the principal Western and local sources. During the week surveyed, its own correspondents furn-

TABLE 19

'FOREIGN POLICY' NEWS REPORTING ON *KOL YISRAEL*,
1–7 MARCH 1968

Sources of News	
Agence France Presse (AFP)	24
Associated Press (AP)	27
Reuters	38
United Press (UP)	37
Jewish Telegraph Agency (JTA)	11
Own Correspondents (OC)	41
Not Indicated*	9
Other†	3
Total‡	190

* Often prepared by desk men from agency, radio, and other sources.
† Comprises *Itim* (2) and *France Soir* (1).
‡ Some reports were based upon two or more sources.

nished the largest number—but a much smaller proportion of the total radio 'foreign policy' news items than in the case of *Ha'aretz* or *Ma'ariv*: respectively, it was 21·5 per cent, 33 per cent, and 58 per cent of the total news sources used. In other words the distribution curve among *Kol Yisrael* sources was the flattest of the three, with all four major international news agencies well-represented, especially Reuters and United Press. Thus *Kol Yisrael* is more akin to *Ha'aretz* in that the news received by its listeners is filtered through the images of foreigners to a much greater extent than through an Israeli lens. Another similarity with *Ha'aretz* is the reliance on multiple sources—in *Kol Yisrael*'s case, 32 of the 153 separate stories: 29 with two sources, two with three sources, and one report with five sources.[1]

iii. *Radio and Press Communication: Further Comparisons*

A one-day sample of 'foreign policy' news reports on *Kol Yisrael* and in *Ha'aretz* and *Ma'ariv* provides added empirical data for comparative analysis. On 2 March 1968 radio news carried seventeen stories in the following sequence:[2]

8 a.m.   1. Question of South Africa's Participation in Olympiad to be Raised Once More Before International Olympic Committee

[1] Not all Israelis are impressed with the quality of *Kol Yisrael* news coverage. For a harsh critique, a subjective assessment of adequacy based upon a one-day personal listening survey, see Misha Louvish (former Editor, Foreign Language Publications, Government Press Office, Jerusalem), 'Radio News Bulletins Faulty', *Jerusalem Post*, 12 Sept. 1969.

[2] There are always fewer *Kol Yisrael* news bulletins on Saturday than on weekdays. On the days surveyed here for comparative analysis there were 10 bulletins on Saturday, 2 March 1968, and 12 bulletins the preceding day.

	2.	Roumanian Government Issued Official Statement Justifying its Dissent at Communist Summit Conference
1 p.m.	3.	Israel Accused Soviet Union of Anti-Semitism During UN Committee on Human Rights Debate
2 p.m.	4.	Algerian Newspaper Reports De Gaulle Invitation to Algeria's President to Make Official Visit
	5.	General Shukheiry, Iraqi Defence Minister, to Visit Paris at End of Month (Repeat of item 3)
5 p.m.	6.	Abba Eban Comments on Peace Prospects for Middle East—in Interview on French Television
	7.	Nasser Has Submitted to Gunnar Jarring a Formula for Settlement with Israel, According to *France Soir* Correspondent
6 p.m.	8.	Italian and Hungarian Delegates to Communist Conference Warn of Danger of Undermining International Communist Movement
	9.	Soviet Defence Minister Grechko Attacked Today in Peking *People's Daily*
7 p.m.	10.	According to *New York Times*, Egypt Has Agreed to Send Delegates to Cyprus to Negotiate with Israel under Jarring's Auspices
	11.	A Report on Britain's Bid to Enter Common Market
8.30 p.m.	12.	Togo and Dahomey Disassociated Themselves from Addis Ababa OAU Conference Resolution (on Arab–Israel Conflict) (Repeat of item 10)
10 p.m.	13.	U Thant Denies *New York Times* Report That UN Secretariat Aware of Arab Willingness to Open Negotiations with Israel
	14.	*Jeune Afrique* Criticizes De Gaulle Attitude Towards Arab–Israel Conflict (Repeat of item 12)
midnight	15.	British Government Requested India to Refrain from Retaliation Against British Law Restricting Immigration of Asians and Africans
	16.	Roumanian Exit From Communist Conference Supported by Mass Rallies in Roumania, according to Yugoslav Information Agency (Repeat of items 12, 13, and 14)
	17.	A Summary of the Contents of Prime Minister Eshkol's Interview with UP Correspondent

Ma'ariv carried stories on four of these items (2, 3, 10, 17) in its issue the following day, Sunday 3 March (*Ma'ariv* goes to press in the early morning—it is on the street by 10.30 a.m. and thus has access to all *Kol Yisrael* news bulletins of the previous day, as well as those at 6.00 a.m. and 7.00 a.m. the same day). In addition *Ma'ariv*, on Sunday 3 March, ran two of the fourteen separate news items that appeared in radio news bulletins the preceding Friday. *Ma'ariv* contained nine other 'foreign policy' news items that day. Some concerned a principal news item on the radio—the Jarring Mission—but most dealt with entirely different topics: Nasser's withdrawal of the allegation about US aid to Israel during the 1967 War; the status of the occupied territories; explosions at three embassies in Holland; a UN conference in India; a Vatican comment on Israel's demand for direct negotiations; and a call for patience with Israel's African friends by Ghana's Ambassador to Israel.

The spillover between *Kol Yisrael* and *Ha'aretz* reports was even less. The latter carried only three of the radio items in its issue of 3 March (*Ha'aretz* goes to press in the very early morning hours and also has access to all radio bulletins of the previous day). In addition *Ha'aretz* on Sunday 3 March ran two of the separate news items that appeared in *Kol Yisrael* news bulletins the preceding Friday. *Ha'aretz* also carried thirteen other reports on 'foreign policy' news that day as follows: US apprehension about Nasser's internal weakness and its adverse effects on the prospects for a peace settlement; Roumania's clash with Arab Communists over Israel; Soviet experts in Egypt—Nasser's denial; the Egyptian Foreign Minister's debunking of the Rhodes formula; the Israeli Interior Minister's Ordinance concerning the occupied territories (3); Rabin's presentation of credentials as Ambassador to the US; a Gaza incident; and an Arab notable's protest against Jewish settlement in East Jerusalem, etc.

Not only were few *Kol Yisrael* 'foreign policy' news items of 2 March 1968 reported in *Ma'ariv* or *Ha'aretz* the following day: there was little duplication of items in the two newspapers—except for the lead story on Jarring. The central conclusion to be drawn is that the principal media for communicating 'foreign policy' news to Israelis coincide at points but overlap only marginally: they are *essentially complementary sources of images about the changing Operational Environment.*[1] *Kol Yisrael's* news bulletins carry the widest range of hard news, directly from the agencies and their own correspondents, in a continuous flow of brief reports of events, actual and expected. Thus Israeli decision-makers (and others) perceive the external world through both an international news agency prism and an Israeli lens. More important, those who read only *Ha'aretz* or *Ma'ariv* receive a much narrower foreign policy perspective than those who read both. Similarly, persons who read one of these newspapers and listen to several *Kol Yisrael* bulletins daily secure a limited image of current international developments. Only a combination of the three provides an adequate portrait, with the inevitable biases of an Israeli filtering of the news. And since the 1967 War the range of perceptions has narrowed—because of a marked decrease in attention, in both radio and press news, to anything unrelated to Israel.

[1] It does not follow that decision-makers are conscious of the complementarity of news sources. Further, while they may—and in fact do—absorb images from radio and newspaper(s), the widely-held belief in Israel that local news sources are redundant tends, it may be surmised, to create in the decision-makers' minds the belief that by reading one newspaper they are getting access to all the news available to the public. The consequence is unequal intake and diverse images of the Operational Environment. This disparity is more striking before 1968 than after that date.

Three sample periods were selected for comparative content analysis —1–15 March 1962, 1–15 March 1964, and 1–7 March 1968. While a larger sample would have been more representative in the formal sense, it was the consensus of veteran Israeli journalists that the trends and qualitative distinctions elicited by this analysis were, in fact, characteristic of the entire period. The emphasis laid on these three media of communication should not obscure one basic point: as important as they are in forming Israeli images, they are less than the total sources available to, and used by, Israeli decision-makers. Intelligence reports are qualitatively more influential at the high policy level. Cables may be as well. Newscasts on the BBC World Service are also given attention, because of their growing number of listeners and the Israeli decision-makers' perception of marked pro-Arab bias. And the prestige international press often serves as a corrective to local sources. Finally, personal encounters and other written materials enlarge—and sometimes confuse—the information pool on the basis of which decisions are reached. Nevertheless, the cumulative weight of daily reading and absorption of news accounts from the Big Three dailies—they all read every major 'foreign policy' news item, as well as editorials on foreign policy—combined with politicians' sensitivity to the mass media, justify a conclusion that the three Israeli news media are the relied-upon source for the bulk of day-to-day image-forming reports: they are absorbed, naturally, perhaps subconsciously, by those who make Israeli foreign policy decisions. To the members of Israel's High Policy Élite and their underlying Attitudinal Prism we may now turn.

PART II
PSYCHOLOGICAL ENVIRONMENT

CHAPTER 10

The High Policy Élite

High policy in foreign affairs is made by a small group of men who are authorized by the political system to act on *strategic*-level issues. These may be broad guidelines such as alignment or non-alignment. They may be crisis decisions involving war and peace. They may be crucial but non-crisis in character, for example diplomatic recognition. And they may be initiating or responsive actions. But whatever their type, origin, and duration, strategic decisions have in common a qualitative impact on state behaviour. For this reason they are the monopoly of the very few—the *High Policy Élite*. The Technical Élite, by contrast, comprises civil servants in the foreign office and related ministries, notably those dealing with defence, finance, and trade; they implement basic decisions in day-to-day acts with other states. Membership in the two élite groups may overlap; but the analytical boundary may be drawn between high policy decision-maker and bureaucrat.

Men who make foreign policy decisions, like all men engaged in public affairs, are predisposed to view their environment through a distinctive lens or prism. This derives in part from their political culture; that is, their values and attitudes on such core questions as liberty and authority, the rights and duties of citizenship, change and the *status quo*, and legitimacy in the exercise of power. To discover this underlying belief system was one of the purposes of the earlier discussion of Israel's polity. But predisposition also depends upon the historical legacy and personality traits. Together they illuminate the Attitudinal Prism through which men filter the information acquired through the communications media. These will provide the dual focus of this and the following chapter—the analysis of Israel's High Policy Élite and the prism of its members' world view.[1] It will serve, too, as an introduction to the inquiry into Israeli élite images of their environment, the key to their choices among foreign policy options.

(a) HIGH POLICY ÉLITE: COMPOSITION

The first task is to locate Israel's High Policy Élite over time and within different issue areas. Various indicators will be used for this purpose. Some are institutional, notably membership in the Government and its Ministerial Committee on Defence. Others are informal,

[1] The Israeli Technical Élite from 1948 to 1968 will be explored in ch. 17 and 18 below.

the results of interviews with about 200 prominent and knowledgeable persons in Israel's public life—ministers, party leaders, civil servants, journalists and academics: there was a striking consensus in the assessments.[1]

We may begin with the *Government* or Cabinet: this sets the outer institutional limit of élite membership, for all ministers have an equal vote, and most strategic-level issues came before that body. In some cases a ministerial ballot had profound long-term significance, as in the decision, announced to the *Knesset* on 13 December 1949, to make Jerusalem the seat of Government. In others it was fraught with danger, as in the 9–9 split on 27 May 1967 over the question of a full-scale military response to Egypt's closing of the Tiran Straits. And in still others a Cabinet decision postponed but did not solve a critical problem, as in the rejection of Prime Minister Ben Gurion's recommendation of November 1955 to break the blockade of Eilat by force.[2] And when a major decision was taken without a Cabinet vote, as in the German arms deals, the Government fell—in December 1957 and July 1959.[3]

There were fifty-four persons who held office in the fourteen Israeli Governments from 1948 to 1968.[4] Many, however, were uninvolved in foreign policy most of the time and for most issues: three were in the Cabinet less than a year, while nine ministers from the religious parties and three non-party members accepted *Mapai*'s lead in this sphere. Others dissented from the main policy lines—the three *Mapam* ministers, their three colleagues from *Ahdut Ha'avodah*, until the Alignment of 1965, and, at the other extreme of the ideological spectrum, the seven General Zionist (later, Liberal) ministers and one from *Herut*. Thus membership in the Government did not provide automatic entry into the High Policy Élite.

A better quasi-institutional guide would seem to be the group of *Mapai* ministers, a unique club known as *Sareinu*—'our ministers'. There were twenty-five members between 1948 and 1968, and from the early years they functioned as an inner cabinet, meeting as a group before most formal Cabinet sessions. Given the *Mapai* majority in the Government, its tight party discipline, and its control over the key portfolios—Defence, Foreign Affairs, Finance, Education, Agriculture, Police, and usually Commerce and Industry, as well as the Prime

---

[1] These interviews were conducted during July–August 1960, September 1965–August 1966, July–August 1968, and the autumn of 1969. A list of persons interviewed will be found in the Bibliography.

[2] These decisions will be examined in detail in a related volume on Israeli high-policy decisions.

[3] This will be analysed in the context of the formulation of high policy. See ch. 16 (*b*) and (*c*) below.

[4] This includes the Provisional Government from 15 May 1948 to 7 March 1949. A complete list of ministers and the portfolios they held from 1948 to 1968 is to be found in Appendix C.

Ministership—the decisions of *Sareinu* were almost always final, in foreign and security policy as in other matters: in 1968, for example, it comprised all fourteen ministers from the Alignment, in a Government of twenty-two. But not all *Mapai* or Alignment ministers exerted equal influence in party or government decisions.

i. *Ministerial Committee on Defence*

There is a more pertinent guide to the High Policy Élite, namely, the *Ministerial Committee on Defence*. It was established in April 1953 as the Ministerial Committee on Foreign Affairs and Defence but remained insignificant as a decision-making organ for many years. The Prime Minister and Defence Minister, Ben Gurion, insisted that defence matters, with rare exceptions, be decided by the Government as a whole; and apart from a few months in 1955, he was not an active member of this committee. Mrs. Meir recalled its main function as the appointment of envoys—'it was really a Diplomatic Appointments Committee'.[1] Ze'ev Sharef concurred, adding that if there was a committee on foreign affairs, 'it was not important'.[2] Of the thirteen persons on the committee during its first phase (1953–61), only two were members throughout— Mrs. Meir and the NRP leader, Haim Moshe Shapira. Sharett was a member until his resignation as Foreign Minister in June 1956, while *Mapai* Education Minister Zalman Aranne and the Progressive leader, Pinhas Rosen, were members most of the time. The remaining seven members, mainly from the lesser coalition partners, were transients.

The committee was transformed in name, role and, partly, in composition in November 1961 when Ben Gurion yielded to the pressure of *Ahdut Ha'avodah* and formed a Ministerial Committee on Defence. But it was only after Levi Eshkol became Prime Minister and Defence Minister, in June 1963, and especially after the sixth general election, from January 1966 onward, that the committee became the principal decision-making body in this field. Mrs. Meir, who was Foreign Minister at the time, recalled: 'It really discussed problems. It was in effect a powerful small cabinet responsible for decisions on security.'[3] Thus its membership in the second phase provides an important key to the High Policy Élite in the sixties.

Until the beginning of 1966 there was a small, compact, inner ministerial group of six which made the basic decisions on security and foreign policy. There was very little circulation: Eban replaced Ben Gurion, who resigned as Prime Minister–Defence Minister in June 1963; and Aranne took Dayan's seat when he left the Cabinet and opted

[1] Interview in Tel Aviv, 10 Aug. 1966.
[2] Interview in Jerusalem, 20 March 1966. As Secretary to the Government from 1948 to 1957, Sharef was among the most knowledgeable Israelis on the work and importance of Cabinet committees.
[3] Interview in Tel Aviv, 10 Aug. 1966.

TABLE 20

MINISTERIAL COMMITTEE ON DEFENCE[1]

10th Government (2 November 1961)	11th Government (24 June 1963)	12th Government (22 December 1964)	13th Government (12 January 1966)	Enlarged (5 June 1967)
Eshkol	Eshkol	Eshkol	Eshkol	Eshkol
Meir	Meir	Meir		
Shapira	Shapira	Shapira	Shapira	Shapira
Allon	Allon	Allon	Allon	Allon
Ben Gurion				
Dayan	Dayan			Dayan
	Eban	Eban	Eban	Eban
		Aranne	Aranne	Aranne
			Galili	Galili
			Sapir	Sapir
			Barzilai	Barzilai
			Kol	Kol
			Warhaftig	Warhaftig
				Begin
				Y. Saphir
				Y. S. Shapiro
				Sasson

Note. The order in which names are listed is not designed to indicate relative importance. Rather, it is to show changing composition from the 11th Government onward, and the striking increase of membership in the Ministerial Committee in 1966 and 1967. (At the end of 1969 it was further enlarged—to seventeen ministers, in a Cabinet of twenty-four. Since *Gahal*'s withdrawal from the Government in August 1970—over Israel's acceptance of the Rogers' 'peace initiative'—the composition of the Ministerial Committee of Defence has been identical with the Cabinet as a whole, with a membership of eighteen.)

for *Rafi*. These eight persons clearly belong to the High Policy Élite. To them must be added from the enlarged committee *Ahdut Ha'avodah* leader Yisrael Galili and the *Mapai* Finance Minister, Pinhas Sapir. All the others may be excluded—by the consensus of those interviewed: they were either from lesser coalition parties of long standing (Barzilai—*Mapam*, Kol—Independent Liberal, Warhaftig—NRP), or from near-permanent opposition parties (Begin and Saphir—*Gahal*), or additions from *Mapai* to maintain a majority (Y. S. Shapiro and Sasson). It is noteworthy that *Mapai*, later the Alignment, held a clear majority in the Committee on Defence throughout—4 to 2 until 1966, then 6 to 4, and 8 to 7 in the enlarged committee. This, too, highlights

[1] The composition of this committee was made known to the author, in July 1968, by the Secretary to the Government, Mrs. Y. Uzay.

the importance of *Sareinu*, the inner club of *Mapai*-Alignment ministers.[1] There is another valid indicator—role performance. Thus Israel's military leaders would normally qualify for membership in the Technical Élite. Yet the consensus among those interviewed is that three of the eight men who served as Chief of Staff also merit inclusion in the High Policy Élite: Yigael Yadin, because of his crucial role in the shaping of *Tzahal* from 1948 to 1952; Moshe Dayan, included in the later years on other grounds, because of his charisma and influence with Ben Gurion from 1953 onward; and Yitzhak Rabin, upon whom Eshkol as Prime Minister–Defence Minister relied heavily in security matters, from 1964 to 1968. The criterion of role performance applies as well to Shimon Peres, Director-General of the Defence Ministry and later Deputy Minister of Defence, as well as to David Horowitz, the perennial Governor of the Bank of Israel. Drawing upon these varied indicators, institutional and functional, and testing the results in a large number of interviews, it is possible to designate Israel's High Policy Élite during the first two decades.

ii. *The Eighteen and the Inner Circle*

The data in Table 21 (see the next four pages) reveal a group of eighteen persons, almost all deriving from the mainstream party, *Mapai*, or its splinter factions.[2] Viewed over the twenty-year period, there was a near-constant at the summit with Ben Gurion as Prime Minister and Defence Minister from 1948 to 1963 except for a brief period in the mid-fifties when he withdrew to his desert retreat at Sde Boker.[3] Eshkol was Prime Minister for the remaining five years and Defence Minister

---

[1] A closely-related informal party institution is *Havereinu*—'our comrades', referring to the senior leaders of Mapai. It comprises the ministers from *Mapai* (later the Alignment, and later still the reunited Israel Labour Party), the Secretary-General of the *Histadrut*, the central party organizational leaders, and special invitees, including key branch leaders from Haifa, Tel Aviv and elsewhere. Participants and observers emphasized to the author that this group profoundly affected domestic policy but was rarely used as a forum for discussing foreign and security policy.

The role of these governmental and party institutions is related to the discussion of policy formulation and will be treated in that context (ch. 16). They were noted here to assist in uncovering the High Policy Élite.

[2] Shapira, the one exception, was the senior leader of the NRP until his death in 1970. Yadin and Rabin are non-party but the latter is generally identified with *Ahdut Ha'avodah*. Allon and Galili are leaders of *Ahdut Ha'avodah*, the earliest of the *Mapai* splinters (1944), while Dayan, Peres, and Ben Gurion himself led the later defection, *Rafi* (1965). All but Ben Gurion were formally reunited in the Israel Labour Party (1968).

Menahem Begin, leader of *Herut* and, later, of *Gahal*, belonged to the Overall High Policy Élite for the last year, 1967–8; however, as the *de facto* Leader of the Opposition in Israeli politics from 1948 to 1967, it would be analytically misleading to include him in a construct of the High Policy Élite for the first two decades of independence.

[3] Ben Gurion resigned on 7 Dec. 1953 and returned to the Defence portfolio on 21 Feb. 1955 in the Government headed by his successor, Moshe Sharett; he resumed the Prime Ministership on 3 Nov. 1955, following the third general election.

ISSUE

Phase	Overall	Military-Security
May 1948–June 1956	Ben Gurion Sharett	Ben Gurion Sharett Yadin (1948–52)[1] Dayan (1953–)[2] Lavon (1954–5)[3] Peres (1955–)[4]
June 1956–June 1963	Ben Gurion Meir[12] Dayan (–57, 59–)[13] Peres[14]	Ben Gurion Meir Dayan Peres Allon (1961–)[15]
June 1963–end 1965	Eshkol[18] Meir	Eshkol Meir Allon[19] Dayan (–64)[20] Peres (–65)[21] Rabin (1964–)[22]
January 1966–May 1967	Eshkol Eban[23] Meir[23] Galili[24] Sapir[25]	Eshkol Eban Rabin Allon Galili
May 1967–May 1968	Eshkol Eban Dayan[27] Allon[28] Galili Sapir Meir[29]	Eshkol Eban Dayan Rabin Allon Galili

1 Yigael Yadin was Chief of Operations of *Tzahal* from 1948 to November 1949 and then Chief of Staff until 1952.

2 Moshe Dayan served as Chief of Staff of *Tzahal* from December 1953 to January 1958 and was, throughout, in the inner circle of Ben Gurion.

3 Pinhas Lavon replaced Ben Gurion as Defence Minister from January 1954 to February 1955.

4 Shimon Peres was Director-General of the Defence Ministry from December 1953 to December 1959. He, too, was in Ben Gurion's inner circle of high-policy decision-makers.

5 Ben Gurion and Sharett dominated this area of policy—by all accounts. Five other persons may be noted, however. Golda Meir, Haim Moshe Shapira, and

AREAS

Political-Diplomatic	Economic-Developmental	Cultural-Status
Ben Gurion	Kaplan (1948–52)[6]	Ben Gurion
Sharett[5]	Eshkol (1949–)[7]	Sharett
	Horowitz (1954–)[8]	Shapira[10]
	Sapir (1955–)[9]	Aranne (1955–)[11]

Ben Gurion	Eshkol	Ben Gurion
Meir	Sapir	Shapira
Peres	Horowitz	Aranne (–60)[16]
		Eban (1960–3)[17]

Eshkol	Eshkol	Aranne
Meir	Sapir	Shapira
Eban	Horowitz	

Eshkol	Eshkol	Aranne
Eban	Sapir	Shapira
	Horowitz	
	Sharef[26]	

Eshkol	Eshkol	Aranne
Eban	Sapir	Shapira
Dayan	Sharef[30]	
Allon	Horowitz	
Galili		

Zalman Aranne served on the Ministerial Committee on Foreign Affairs and Defence, the first two from its formation in April 1953, the third from nine months later, throughout this period and beyond. More important, Meir and Aranne were influential figures in the leadership of *Mapai*, while Shapira, the leader of *Ha-po'el Ha-mizrahi* and, later, the NRP, carried considerable weight because of the balance-of-power position held by the religious parties in the coalition. The fourth person was Dov Joseph, Military Governor of Jerusalem during the 1948 siege and then, successively, holder of a series of portfolios: Supply and Rationing; Communications; Agriculture; Commerce and Industry; Justice; and Development. Cabinet colleagues testified to his active participation in the discussion of foreign policy issues. And David Horowitz exerted influence over political-diplomatic decisions, as Director-General of Finance and Economic Adviser to the Government.

6 Eliezer Kaplan dominated Israel's economic policy during the critical early years, as Finance Minister and the acknowledged *Mapai*, as well as Jewish Agency, leader in this sphere, the counterpart of Sharett in diplomacy. Before independence, from 1935 to 1948, he was the dominant figure in the *Yishuv*'s economic policy.

7 Levi Eshkol was the principal moulder of economic policy in Israel from 1952 onward, when he succeeded Eliezer Kaplan as Minister of Finance. And prior to that, he qualified as a member of the High Policy Élite in this issue area as Director of the Settlement Department of the Jewish Agency (1949–63) and Minister of Agriculture (1951–2).

8 David Horowitz has been the perennial Governor of the Bank of Israel—since its establishment in 1954. Prior to that, he was a member of the Technical Élite as Director-General of the Finance Ministry (1948–52) and Economic Adviser to the Government (1953).

9 Pinhas Sapir joined the High Policy Élite in November 1955 when he became Minister of Commerce and Industry. Before then he was a prominent figure in the Technical Élite as Director-General, Defence Ministry (1949–53), and Director-General, Finance Ministry (1953–5).

10 Shapira exerted great influence in this issue area as Minister of the Interior (1949–53) and, thereafter, of Religious Affairs.

11 Aranne served as Minister of Education and Culture (1955–60).

12 Meir was Foreign Minister throughout this period.

13 Dayan continued as Chief of Staff until the beginning of 1958 and then, after a period of study at the Hebrew University, he entered politics and became Minister of Agriculture, in December 1959. He also served on the powerful Ministerial Committee on Defence.

14 Peres continued as Director-General of the Defence Ministry until December 1959 and was then appointed Deputy Minister of Defence. Both were, nominally, Technical Élite posts but, as the Defence Minister was also Prime Minister throughout this period (Ben Gurion), Peres functioned as a member of the High Policy Élite. The inclusion of Dayan and Peres in the Overall High Policy Élite (Dayan was not a member in 1958 and 1959) arises primarily from their special relationship with Ben Gurion.

15 Yigal Allon joined the Government (and its Ministerial Committee on Defence) as Minister of Labour in November 1961. Although a member of *Ahdut Ha'avodah*, not the pre-eminent *Mapai*, his military record and reputation (a hero of the 1948 War of Independence) imparted considerable weight to his views on military-security issues. The other two members of the Committee on Defence in that period, Eshkol and Shapira, followed Ben Gurion's lead in this sphere.

16 Aranne was Minister of Education and Culture from 1955 to 1960 and again from June 1963 onwards.

17 Eban, after a decade at the UN and Washington, and some months as Minister without Portfolio, served as Minister of Education and Culture from 1960 to 1963.

18 Eshkol succeeded Ben Gurion as Prime Minister and Defence Minister on 24 June 1963.

19 Allon remained on the Ministerial Committee on Defence and, with the move towards an Alignment and Dayan's defection to *Rafi*, his influence grew considerably in this sphere.

20 Dayan remained a member of the High Policy Élite in this issue area until his resignation from the Government in December 1964.

21 Peres' influence declined with the departure of Ben Gurion but he remained a key figure in military-security issues as Deputy Defence Minister until his resignation in 1965.

22 Yitzhak Rabin became Chief of Staff in January 1964 and served in that capacity

for four years. Eshkol's reliance on his military judgement gave him High Policy Élite membership.

23 Eban replaced Meir as Foreign Minister in January 1966. Yet Meir remained a member of the Overall High Policy Élite through her leadership position, formally as Secretary-General of *Mapai*, as well as her continuing influence with Eshkol.

24 Yisrael Galili, a leader of *Ahdut Ha'avodah* and one of the architects of the Alignment, joined the Government in January 1966 as Minister without Portfolio in charge of Information. By all accounts he was a member of the Overall High Policy Élite thereafter.

25 Sapir, like Galili, joined the Ministerial Committee on Defence in January 1966. Long a key figure in economic policy and in party affairs, and a confidant of Eshkol, Sapir gradually broadened his influence.

26 Ze'ev Sharef became Minister of Commerce and Industry in November 1966 and joined the High Policy Élite in the sphere of foreign economic policy.

27 Dayan took over the Defence Ministry from Eshkol on 31 May 1967 and was once more a member of the High Policy Élite.

28 Allon enters the Overall Élite at the same time as Dayan, by virtue of Eshkol's increasing reliance on him as a counterweight to Dayan.

29 Meir retired from her formal position as Secretary-General of the (united) Israel Labour Party early in 1968. And while she was not involved in most foreign policy decisions, she continued to carry weight on high policy questions, thus qualifying for continued membership in the Overall Élite.

30 Sharef's influence in this issue area grew from the beginning of 1968 when he added the Finance portfolio to his responsibilities.

There were other persons who participated in high-policy decisions on specific issues; for example, Giora Josepthal and Nahum Goldmann on German Reparations, and Rabbi Maimon, among others, on the Jerusalem question. In the detailed analysis of major decisions (in a later volume) the extended policy élite for each issue will be indicated. The persons indicated here are those whose influence was exercised in one or more issue areas as a whole or in large measure.

as well until the eve of the Six Day War, when Dayan assumed that post. And there have been only three Foreign Ministers since independence, Moshe Sharett from 1948 to 1956, Golda Meir for the next decade, and Abba Eban thereafter.

Viewed in delimited time spans and issue areas, one notes marked differences among the eighteen persons in durability and influence. In the first phase (1948–56) twelve persons played a high-policy role. However, Yadin left the élite ranks in 1952 when he moved from *Tzahal* to the Hebrew University; and Lavon was a member briefly, as Defence Minister in the absence of Ben Gurion. More pointedly, all but two men were confined to a specific issue area. Those early years were dominated by Ben Gurion and Sharett to an extraordinary degree: only in economic matters did other members of the élite, namely Kaplan and Eshkol, have substantial autonomy; and even there, as with the decisions on German Reparations and Jordan Waters, the two pre-eminent figures were involved.[1]

The major change in phase 2 (1956–63) was Mrs. Meir's replacement of Sharett. The Foreign Minister's influence declined because of her

[1] This will be elaborated in a related volume on Israeli high-policy decisions.

conspicuously lower stature in this sphere: Sharett had earned his position through his pre-State role as 'diplomat of the *Yishuv*'. The change was accentuated by the rise of Dayan and Peres, competing with Mrs. Meir through a *de facto* foreign office in the Defence Ministry, as well as in the security field proper.[1] The relative autonomy of Eshkol, aided by Sapir and Horowitz, continued in economic policy. Yigal Allon acquired influence in military matters towards the end of this phase, as did Eban in the cultural-status area. Altogether eleven persons played a high-policy role, but the power of decision lay with Ben Gurion and, in the economic sphere only, with Eshkol. Indeed, the towering position of Ben Gurion is the decisive fact about Israel's High Policy Élite from 1948 to 1963.

The accession of Eshkol marks the great divide in the pattern of influence within the élite. For one thing, the difference between him and Mrs. Meir in stature, style, and outlook was less striking than that between Prime Minister and Foreign Minister at any time in the Ben Gurion era: they were near-equals. Moreover, the influence of Dayan and Peres (Ben Gurion's 'young men') declined rapidly. Eshkol, with less pretension to military expertise than Ben Gurion, relied more on Allon and the new Chief of Staff, Yitzhak Rabin. And Sapir emerged as the central figure in economic issues.

It was after the sixth general election that the most significant change became apparent—the development of a collegial decision-making group in the crucial security area, with Eshkol first among equals. Galili and Sapir were the new members. And Dayan was restored to even greater prominence on the eve of the 1967 War. The dispersion of influence spilled over to the diplomatic area thereafter, with numerous and, frequently, discordant voices speaking for Israel on the strategies and conditions of peace.

The average membership in Israel's High Policy Élite was nine years for eighteen persons. The details are as shown in Table 22.

Half of the High Policy Élite occupied that position for ten years or more: they ranged from Shapira, the perennial member, to Lavon, who was Defence Minister for a year. But durability is not the crucial indicator of influence: in fact three of the long-term members—Shapira, Horowitz, and Aranne—were never part of the core group. Viewed in time perspective, the Inner Circle consists of nine persons:

Ben Gurion: the dominant figure in foreign (as in domestic) policy from 1948 to 1963.
Sharett: the second-ranking figure in the Government, creator of the Foreign Ministry, and architect of the alternative path to Ben Gurion's hard line towards Israel's neighbours, from 1948 to 1956.

[1] The relationship between the two ministries in the formulation of policy will be examined in ch. 15 (c) below.

TABLE 22

MEMBERSHIP IN THE HIGH POLICY ÉLITE 1948–1968

	Years	Period	Issue Area
Ben Gurion	15	1948–63	Overall
Sharett	8	1948–56	Overall
Kaplan	4	1948–52	Economic
Yadin	4	1948–52	Military
Shapira	20	1948–68	Cultural
Eshkol	17	1951–68	Overall, especially Economic
Meir	12	1956–68	Overall, especially Political-Diplomatic
Dayan	10	1953–7, 1959–64, 1967–8	Overall, especially Military
Peres	10	1955–65	Overall, especially Military
Lavon	1	1954–5	Military
Horowitz	18	1948–52, 1954–68	Economic
Sapir	13	1955–68	Overall, especially Economic
Aranne	10	1955–60, 1963–8	Cultural
Eban	5	1960–3, 1966–8	Overall, especially Political-Diplomatic
Allon	7	1961–8	Overall, especially Military
Rabin	4	1964–8	Military
Galili	2½	1966–8	Overall
Sharef	2	1966–8	Economic

Meir: Foreign Minister for a decade (and, later, Prime Minister), who inspired and achieved Israel's impressive African presence, from 1956 to 1968.

Dayan: the charismatic military hero and symbol of Israel's daring, from 1953 to the beginning of 1958, in the early sixties, and again from May 1967 onwards.

Peres: the technocrat *par excellence* who forged the alliance with France and shaped the Defence establishment as Ben Gurion's deputy, from 1955 to 1965.

Eshkol: the principal decision-maker on economic policy, foreign and domestic, from 1952 to 1963, and then first among equals in the Overall High Policy Élite until his death in office.

Sapir: influential in economic policy from 1955 onwards, increasingly so from 1963.

Allon: hero of the War of Independence, whose limited influence in the military field in the early 1960s grew after the Alignment in 1965 as possible successor to the Old Guard.

Eban: at first influential in the cultural field, from 1960 to 1963, and, from the beginning of 1966, as Israel's supreme advocate once more.

(b) HIGH POLICY ÉLITE: PROFILE

A collective portrait of Israel's High Policy Élite may be drawn from some salient biographical data on the eighteen members: these deal with date of birth, place of birth, time and age of arrival in Israel, education, intellectual attainments, occupational diversity, and related themes.[1]

i. Background

TABLE 23

HIGH POLICY ÉLITE 1948–1968

Date of Birth			
Pre-1900		*1911–20*	
Ben Gurion	1886	Galili	1911
Kaplan	1891	Eban	1915
Sharett	1894	Dayan	1915
Eshkol	1895	Yadin	1917
Meir	1898	Allon	1918
Aranne	1899		
Horowitz	1899		
1901–10		*Post-1920*	
Shapira	1902	Rabin	1922
Lavon	1904	Peres	1923
Sharef	1906		
Sapir	1909		

Seven of the eighteen élite members were born in the last century. In terms of outlook and generation gap the dividing line is 1900, with those born earlier comprising the 'old guard'. But the division is not rigid, for Ben Gurion, the oldest member of the élite, was more akin to the younger group. Among the Inner Circle, four are on one side of the time barrier—Ben Gurion, Sharett, Eshkol, and Meir—and five on the other —Sapir, Eban, Dayan, Allon, and Peres. All but five of the eighteen members had entered the High Policy Élite by 1956, and those five had achieved prominence in related fields—Eban in diplomacy, Allon, Rabin and, to a lesser extent, Galili in the military sphere, and Sharef in the civil service.

[1] The primary source for the data that follow is (the incomplete) *Who's Who, Israel* (annual), Mamut Ltd., Tel Aviv. This was supplemented by periodic 'Biographical Notes' on Government Ministers published by the Government Press Office of Israel and biographical articles in the world press, notably the *New York Times*. There have been book-length biographical studies of four members of the High Policy Élite—Ben Gurion, Eshkol, Meir, and Dayan.

TABLE 24
HIGH POLICY ÉLITE 1948-1968

Place of Birth		
Poland*	*Russia*	*Israel*
Ben Gurion	Kaplan	Dayan
Horowitz	Sharett	Yadin
Shapira	Eshkol	Allon
Lavon	Meir	Rabin
Sapir	Aranne	
Galili		*South Africa*
Peres*	*Roumania†*	Eban
	Sharef	

* Peres was born in an independent Poland between the world wars; all the rest were born in a pre-First World War Poland that was part of the Czarist realm.
† Part of Austria–Hungary at the time of Sharef's birth.

No less than twelve of the eighteen persons were born in Poland or Russia, and that pervasive origin of the High Policy Élite helped shape their perceptions of the world. The four *sabras* attained eminence in warfare during their twenties and thirties—and their outlook was not unaffected. Only one person counted English as his mother tongue.

TABLE 25
HIGH POLICY ÉLITE 1948-1968

Time and Age of Arrival in Israel								
2nd Aliya 1904-14			*3rd Aliya 1919-23*			*4th Aliya 1924-31*		
Ben Gurion	1906	20	Meir	1921	23	Sharef	1925	19
Sharett	1906	12	Horowitz	1922	23	Shapira	1925	23
Eshkol	1914	18	Kaplan	1923	32	Aranne	1926	27
Galili	1914	3				Lavon	1929	25
						Sapir	1929	20
5th Aliya 1932-8						*Post-Second World War*		
Peres	1934	10				Eban	1946	31

There are only four persons from the Second *Aliya* (really three, since Galili was a small child when he arrived). But the 'Second *Aliya* mentality' or 'old guard' outlook applies to all twelve pre-1930 arrivals. Only two members of the group arrived after 1930 while four, as noted, were born in Palestine. The median age upon arrival was 21·9, apart from Galili, with two adolescents, Peres and Sharett. Among the

Inner Circle the proportions change: four of the nine persons were either born in Israel (Dayan and Allon) or arrived rather late (Eban and Peres); they are outside the 'Second *Aliya* mentality'.

ii. *Education*

TABLE 26

HIGH POLICY ÉLITE 1948–1968

Higher Education

Ben Gurion: studied in Constantinople, 1912–14.
Kaplan: held an engineering degree.
Sharett: studied law in Constantinople, 1913–14, and studied at the London School of Economics, 1920–5.
Meir: completed a teacher's course in Milwaukee, 1916–17.
Aranne: studied at the Academy of Social Sciences and the Faculty of Agriculture, Kharkov University.
Shapira: was an ordained rabbi from the Rabbinical Seminary, Berlin.
Lavon: studied at Lwow University.
Eban: was educated in Oriental Languages and Literature at Cambridge University.
Dayan: attended a senior officers' school in England and studied at the Tel Aviv School of Law and Economics and the Hebrew University.
Yadin: received a doctorate in archaeology at the Hebrew University.
Allon: studied at the London School of Economics, the Hebrew University, and St. Antony's College, Oxford.
Rabin: studied at a military staff college in England.

In terms of the level and focus of higher education, the breakdown is as follows:

High School (*Gymnasium*) or less:[1]   6   Eshkol, Horowitz, Sharef, Sapir, Galili, Peres

Partial university studies: 6   Ben Gurion, Meir, Aranne, Lavon, Dayan, Rabin

Degree & higher studies: 6   Kaplan—engineering
Sharett—law, economics
Shapira—theology
Eban—oriental languages and literature
Yadin—archaeology
Allon—political science

There is considerable diversity in terms of the country of higher education: five studied in England, four in Israel, two each in Poland, Turkey, and the United States, and one each in Germany and Russia. Some studied in two countries.

[1] Eshkol was educated at a *Gymnasium* in Vilna. There is no reference to education in *Who's Who, Israel* in the entries for Sapir, Sharef, and Galili.

The raw data on education provide only a first approximation to the intellectual standards of Israel's High Policy Élite. Three men stand apart in terms of formal education—Eban the Cambridge don, Sharett the master of languages, and Yadin the well-known archaeologist. A few received specialized training—Kaplan in engineering, Dayan and Rabin in military science, others in agriculture. Most members of the group were exposed to some higher studies. In terms of erudition, the self-educated Ben Gurion is no less impressive than Eban or Sharett. Men like Dayan, Allon, and Peres have displayed a talent for innovative ideas in the defence/foreign policy arena, while Eshkol and Sapir, neither of whom attended a university, were efficient managers of an unorthodox economy.

As a group the High Policy Élite of Israel is prolific: no less than eleven of the eighteen members—and seven of the nine persons in the Inner Circle—have published books and articles.

Ben Gurion: his Works exceed ten volumes.

Sharett: wrote one book, *Roaming Over Asia* (1957), and numerous articles in *Davar* and other newspapers and periodicals; a collection of his 1946–9 speeches appeared as *At the Gate of the Nations* (1958); and the first volume of his *Political Diary* was posthumously published in 1969.

Eshkol: published two books, *On the Way* (1958) and *In the Pangs of Settlement* (1966).

Horowitz: has written many papers and books on economics including *The Palestine Economy and its Development* (1944), *The Israel Economy* (1954), *The Economics of Israel* (1967) and *The Abolition of Poverty* (1969), as well as an account of the background to independence, *State in the Making* (1953), and a partial autobiography, *My Yesterday* (1970).

Lavon: published a collection of theoretical articles on Socialist-Zionism under the title *Yesodot* (Foundations), as well as many articles on political and labour problems.

Sharef: wrote a detailed account of the final phase preceding the declaration of independence, *Three Days* (1962).

Dayan: published his *Sinai Diary* in 1965 and has written on current military and political affairs, his post-Six Day War views being incorporated in *New Map—Other Relationships* (1969).

Eban: is among the most prolific of Israeli leaders. His publications include *Zionism and the Arab World* (1947), *Voice of Israel* (1957, 2nd enl. ed., 1969), *Tide of Nationalism* (1959), *My People: Story of the Jews* (1968), and *To Live or Perish* (forthcoming).

Yadin: is a well-known archaeologist whose works include *The Science of War in Biblical Lands in the Light of Present Archaeological Discoveries* (1963) and *Masada: Then and Now* (1966).

Allon: has written a book on the Arab–Israeli conflict, *Curtain of Sand* (1960), another on *The Campaigns of Palmah* (1965), and two accounts of Israel's armed forces, *The Making of Israel's Army* (1970) and *Shield of David* (1970).

Peres: has published many articles in the Israeli press on current problems, some of which were included in a 1965 selection, *The Next Stage*, as well as a book entitled *David's Sling* (1970).

(Most of Ben Gurion's works and the books by Sharett, Eshkol, and Lavon, along with many of their articles, appeared in Hebrew only.)

iii. *Occupational Diversity*

There is marked occupational diversity, too, in Israel's High Policy Élite.

Some members were active in institutionalized *politics* for decades, notably Ben Gurion, Sharett, Eshkol, Meir, Aranne, Shapira, and Lavon. Others came late upon the scene (Allon in 1954, Sapir in 1955, Dayan, Eban, and Peres in 1959, and Sharef in the mid-sixties). And some were never directly involved in party politics (Yadin and Rabin).

Many of the eighteen were engaged in *agriculture* at one stage of their life in Israel (Ben Gurion, Eshkol, Meir, Sapir, Galili, Dayan, Allon, Peres, and Rabin); and most of these were affiliated to *kibbutzim*.

A few members of the 'old guard' did *military* service in the First World War (Ben Gurion and Eshkol in the Jewish Legion, Sharett in the Turkish Army), while others were professional or quasi-professional soldiers for many years in *Haganah*, *Palmah*, and *Tzahal* (Galili,[1] Allon, Yadin, Dayan, and Rabin).

Most members of the 'old guard' held important positions in the *governmental*, *trade union* and/or *co-operative industrial* hierarchies of the *Yishuv*. Thus Ben Gurion was Chairman of the Jewish Agency Executive from 1935 to 1948. Sharett was Head of the Agency's Political Department—the pre-State Foreign Office—and Kaplan was Treasurer during the same period, while Shapira was Director of the Immigration Department, and Horowitz of the Economic Department. As early as 1920 Ben Gurion and Sharett were among the founders of the *Histadrut*; and they and others (Kaplan, Eshkol, Meir, Aranne, and Lavon) served on its executive over the years. Some, like Lavon, were also directors of its industrial arm, *Solel Boneh*.

There were two professional practitioners of *diplomacy* in the group— Sharett and Eban. In addition, Meir served briefly as Minister to the Soviet Union and for almost ten years as Foreign Minister. Rabin moved

[1] Galili was prominent in *Haganah* and *Palmah* and he served in 1948 as Ben Gurion's Deputy Minister of Defence.

to Israel's premier diplomatic assignment (Washington) in 1968. Eshkol, Sapir, and Horowitz acted as economic envoys of Israel with skill. And Peres did the same in the security field.

Five persons were in the state *bureaucracy* after independence: Eshkol, Sapir, and Peres each served as Director-General of the Defence Ministry in 1948–9, 1949–52 and 1953–9, respectively; Horowitz held the same post in Finance from 1948 to 1952, and Sapir from 1953 to 1955; and Sharef was Secretary to the Government from 1948 to 1957, as well as Civil Service Commissioner (1951–2) and Director of State Revenue from 1954 to 1961.

Journalism claimed the attention of Ben Gurion from 1910 onwards, and of Sharett, especially from 1925 to 1931, both primarily with *Davar*. After his resignation as Foreign Minister the latter was associated with a leading Israeli publishing house, *Am Oved*, from 1956 to 1965.

Only two members chose *teaching* as a vocation, Eban at Cambridge and Yadin at the Hebrew University; the former maintained his links with the academic community as President of the Weizmann Institute from 1958 to 1968. Meir had trained as a teacher. And Aranne was Head of the *Histadrut* Workers' College from 1936 to 1948.

There was only one *economist*, Horowitz, but two held important positions in *banking*—Kaplan as Treasurer of the Jewish Agency and Horowitz as Governor of the Bank of Israel since 1954.

There were, then, nine occupations represented in the High Policy Élite. Viewed in terms of the Inner Circle, there is also evidence of multiple interests and experience.

Politics: has been practised by all.
Agriculture: all but one of the nine (Eban) were exposed to rural life, and four members maintained close links (Ben Gurion, Eshkol, Sapir, and Allon).
Military: two qualify as professionals (Allon and Dayan).
Trade Unionism: four persons were *Histadrut* leaders (Ben Gurion, Sharett, Eshkol, and Meir).
Diplomacy: three were immersed in this field (Sharett, Eban, and Meir) and three others practised the art in their own sphere (Eshkol, Sapir, and Peres).
Bureaucracy: there were three who served as civil servants (Eshkol, Sapir, and Peres), the latter two for extended periods.
Journalism: in the earlier years Ben Gurion and Sharett were so occupied.
Teaching: only Eban fits this category in a formal sense.
Economics: none of the Inner Circle was a professional, but two of them (Eshkol and Sapir) had vast experience in applied economics.

The portrait that emerges is that of a group with many talents and many skills. In reality the Inner Circle comprises two groups which are separated by age, background, acculturation, and outlook—though the lines are not rigid. The 'old guard' of Ben Gurion, Sharett, Eshkol, and Meir dates to the late nineteenth century and East Europe, the pioneers of the Second *Aliya* with a yearning to rebuild Zion on the foundations of labour equality. The younger men, Allon, Dayan, and Peres, symbolize the new *sabra* Israel, free of the *galut* (Diaspora) mentality and assertive of the natural and national right of Israel's independence in the Middle East. Eban belongs to the 'Israel' group in generation terms only, being much closer to Sharett in outlook, while Ben Gurion has a marked kinship with the 'young guard'. And Sapir is closer to the 'Second *Aliya* mentality'.

For most specific issues of foreign policy there was a larger decision-making group, which may be designated the 'extended élite': this comprised some core members of the High Policy Élite and persons with technical skills in various ministries.[1] Yet it was the Inner Circle that framed the guidelines and made the strategic choices in Israeli foreign policy. Thus it is they whose general 'View of the World' or psychological environment proper will be explored. To set the stage for that inquiry we shall apply to the Israeli élite the pivotal concept of Attitudinal Prism.

[1] These will be specified in the analysis in a related volume of Israeli high-policy decisions.

CHAPTER 11

Attitudinal Prism of Decision-Makers

Men choose among alternative paths in accordance with their perception of the world in which they must act. The lens through which that setting is filtered may, as noted earlier, be called the *Attitudinal Prism*. The content of that which they perceive is the *Image*. Together these constitute the *Psychological Environment*, the framework of choice, decision, and action. In foreign policy, as in all politics, the prism is shaped by three interacting variables—political culture, historical legacy, and the personality traits of decision-makers.

Political culture has been 'authoritatively' defined as 'the pattern of individual attitudes and orientations toward politics among the members of a political system . . . the subjective realm which underlies and gives meaning to political actions. [These] involve several components, including cognitive, . . . affective, . . . and evaluative orientations.'[1] In more direct and simple language it is 'how people think and feel about the political world, what they believe and what they believe in, how they behave, and how all these beliefs, behaviors, and feelings are distributed among the groups in society'.[2]

(a) THE DOMINANT PRISM: JEWISHNESS

For Israel's High Policy Élite, as for the entire society, there is a primordial and pre-eminent aspect of the political culture—its *Jewishness*: this pervades thought, feeling, belief, and behaviour in the political realm. Many have commented on this dimension of Israel, none more forcefully than one of her Foreign Office intellectuals, Shabtai Rosenne:[3]

Israel is a Jewish State. The only Jewish State in the world, it was re-established deliberately by the Jewish people as a Jewish solution to the Jewish problem, which has scarred the history of mankind for over 2,000 years. This is the

---

[1] Gabriel A. Almond and G. Bingham Powell, Jr., *Comparative Politics: a developmental approach*, Little, Brown and Co., Boston and Toronto, 1966, p. 50. This definition is amplified as follows: 'Such individual orientations involve several components, including a) *cognitive orientations*, knowledge, accurate or otherwise, of political objects and beliefs; b) *affective orientations*, feelings of attachment, involvement, rejection, and the like, about political objects; and c) *evaluative orientations*, judgments and opinions about political objects, which usually involve applying value standards to political objects and events.' [2] Fein, *Politics in Israel*, p. 32.
[3] 'Basic Elements of Israel's Foreign Policy', *India Quarterly*, loc. cit., p. 328.

cardinal feature dominating all Israel's policy, domestic and foreign. This makes Israel unique. Without full appreciation of this elemental factor, it is impossible to understand Israel or any aspect of Israel's policy—domestic or foreign.

No member of the Inner Circle, the High Policy Élite, or the extended élite would demur from this pronouncement: it illuminates the Attitudinal Prism for all.

'Who is a Jew?' and 'What is Judaism?' are recurrent questions with legal and theological relevance. But almost all Israelis, apart from Arab and Druze residents, identify themselves as Jews—whether they be observant or secular, traditional or modern, radical or liberal or conservative or reactionary.[1] This consensus on Jewish identity was expressed with typical self-assurance by Ben Gurion when he was asked, 'what is your definition of a Jew?'[2]

You see, we were Jews without a definition for the last 3,000 years and we will remain so. There are several definitions but the thing existed before any definition was given and after many definitions were given to the same thing. By one definition the Jews are a religious community, and there are a number of Jews who accept that definition. There is a definition that Jews are a nation, and there are a number of Jews who accept that definition. There are Jews without any definition. They are just Jews. I am one of them. I don't need any definition. I am what I am.

The consciousness of being Jewish creates a unique Attitudinal Prism for members of the High Policy Élite, as for most Israelis. They perceive Jewry as a world people of which Israelis are an integral part—though not all would accept Ben Gurion's priorities: 'I said to the World Zionist Congress in 1957 [it was in 1956], "I am first of all a Jew and second an Israeli".'[3] Yet even those who reverse the order of identity see Israel as the bastion of world Jewry, with rights and obligations flowing from this relationship.

They emphasize Israel's link with Jewish antiquity and refer to the rebirth of Jewish sovereignty as the 'Third Commonwealth' after two millennia of dispersion. They have a searing consciousness of the Holocaust—the destruction of six million Jews in Nazi-occupied Europe—and they perceive the State of Israel as the logical, necessary, and rightful successor to the collective interests and rights of the few who survived. Israel as the voice, the representative, and the defender of Jews in distress anywhere—this is a role which flows naturally from the 'Jewish prism'. Through this lens, too, there is created an expectation

---

[1] As noted earlier (ch. 7 (b) ii and iii, and (c) i), there are some small political-intellectual sects in Israel, notably the Kena'anim, who identify themselves as 'Hebrews', a distinctively Middle Eastern nation.

[2] To foreign correspondents at a press conference in Tel Aviv, 20 Feb. 1959. Made known by the Government Press Office, Jerusalem.

[3] Recalled to the author in an interview at Sde Boker, July 1966.

that world Jewry will reciprocate with massive and continuous support for that segment of the People resettled in the Homeland. In its extreme form, with Ben Gurion, this is expressed as the 'two-camp thesis': 'It is not important what the *Goyim* [Nations] *say*, but rather what the Jews *do*.'[1] And on many occasions he has declared that world Jewry is the only certain and reliable ally of Israel.

Many of these themes are part of the Israeli élite image. At the same time they are inexorable 'spill-overs' from the Attitudinal Prism. And the impact of the Jewish aspect of Israel's political culture on her foreign policy is so great that these strands may be dealt with here. Once more Ben Gurion is the most articulate exponent. As Israel's dominant decision-maker for fifteen years he is also our most appropriate guide.

With relentless consistency Ben Gurion has declared that Israel is indissolubly bound up with Jewry. 'This is Israel's primary and principal bond, prior to all other attachments and ties, vital to her life and soul, her character and future.' The State was made by and for the Jewish people. 'That is its title to life.' And since the Jews are a world people, 'Israel is the State of and for a world people'; it is something beyond citizenship and sovereignty.[2] On the Jewish claim to nationhood he noted that Jewry had always maintained its attachment to the Homeland, to its laws and commandments—and to its language; these, he stated, are the sources of its 'national will'. And on the unbroken link to the land of Zion he referred to Israel as 'a country which had been inhabited by Arab invaders for 1,300 years'.[3]

Ben Gurion intoned a lament for the 'Six Million' less frequently than other Israeli and Jewish leaders. But that unparalleled tragedy was central to his thought: indeed it was the catalyst to his policy of reconciliation with Germany from the late 1950s onward: 'If you want the overall reason in a single sentence, it was the final injunction of the inarticulate six million, the victims of Nazism whose very murder was a

[1] Speech on Independence Day 1955 at Ramat Gan, as reported orally by three members of the audience. *Goyim*, in colloquial present-day usage, refers to non-Jews. Classically, and correctly, it means 'the Nations'.

[2] 'Achievements and Tasks of our Generation', State of Israel, *Government Year-Book 5722*, 1961/2, Jerusalem, pp. vii–lxxx.

[3] 'Israel and the Diaspora', State of Israel, *Government Year-Book 5717*, *1957*, Jerusalem, pp. 12, 13. This essay provides a powerful expression of Ben Gurion's basic views on a host of themes relating to Israel and Jewry:
(a) Source of continuity and identity of Jewry
(b) Uniqueness of Israel
(c) Forces that revived the State of Israel
(d) Ossification of Zionism
(e) Profound differences in principle between Israeli Jewry and Diaspora Jewry
(f) Basic goals of Israel
(g) Content of Jewish consciousness
(h) Tasks of achieving greater Jewish unity
It is an essay full of controversy, particularly on the secondary role of Diaspora Jewry in building the state and the 'exile' character of all Jews outside Israel.

ringing cry for Israel to rise, to be strong and prosperous, to safeguard her peace and security, and to prevent such a disaster from ever again overwhelming the Jewish people.'[1] On the relationship between Israel and the Jews of the world, and the representative and catalytic role assumed by the new state, he remarked: 'The two groups are interdependent. The future of Israel—its security, its welfare, and its capacity to fulfil its historic mission—depends on world Jewry. And the future of world Jewry depends on the survival of Israel. . . . [The State] ensures . . . a life of sovereign freedom for the entire Jewish people. . . . The State has become the pillar on which the unity of Diaspora Jewry now rests. The State is also a product of that unity.'[2]

The fortress mentality was clearly expressed by Ya'acov Herzog, Director-General of the Prime Minister's Office under Eshkol and Meir: 'The Israeli élite looks upon Israel as the bastion of the collective Jewish group and, as such, it takes into account the interests of its parts. But it places primary value on the whole and, to that end, the survival and enhancement of the bastion.'[3]

Many Israeli decision-makers spoke candidly about the place of Diaspora Jewry in their images and the foreign policy consequences. Ben Gurion, as usual, stated his position unequivocally:[4]

It was *always* my view that we have always to consider the *interests* of Diaspora Jewry—any Jewish community that was concerned. But there is one crucial distinction—not what *they* think are their interests, but what *we* regarded as their interests.

If it was a case vital for Israel, and the interests of the Jews concerned were different, the vital interests of Israel came first—because Israel is vital for world Jewry.

I cannot remember any conflict of *interests*. And their *views* I need not accept.

Eshkol was also emphatic in declaring that he was conscious of the impact of Israel's decisions on the welfare of Jews abroad. The *views* of American Jewry are given special attention, he noted, and the *effects* on Russian Jewry are important in shaping decisions—even if their views are not known. More generally, 'it is difficult to establish a formula as to where Israeli vital interests end and the interests of world Jewry prevail. They are individual decisions in each case. For example, there is a difference between one hundred thousand Jews in South Africa and three million in Russia.'[5]

[1] *Ben Gurion Looks Back in talks with Moshe Pearlman*, Weidenfeld and Nicolson, London, 1965, p. 162.
[2] Ibid., pp. 241–2.
[3] Interview in Jerusalem, March 1966.
[4] Interview in Sde Boker, July 1966.
[5] Interview in Jerusalem, Aug. 1966. On the status accorded to Blaustein and the American Jewish Committee by Ben Gurion see ch. 7 (*a*) ii above.

Peres was more precise. 'World Jewry is an Israeli national interest. But when we stand between a local Jewish interest and a basic moral problem we give up the local Jewish interest. Such was the case on *Apartheid*. If it weren't for the racist issue I would continue to abstain on UN votes and thus assist local Jewry.'[1] Ya'acov Tsur, a former Acting Director-General of the Foreign Ministry, defined the link succinctly: 'The impact of Jewry in the relevant area is always a consideration in Israel's foreign policy decisions; it is rarely decisive but frequently important.'[2] Another thoughtful Foreign Office veteran remarked in a similar vein: 'There is a general predisposition to take into account Jewish interests—as long as Israel's national interests are not sacrificed. The latter clearly have priority, though Jewish interests are sometimes so much to the fore that they dominate.'[3] Herzog concurred: 'The "Jewish factor" is always present in the minds of decision-makers. Its importance depends on the relative balance of two considerations—the degree of danger to local Jewry flowing from the act and the importance of the act in terms of Israel's national interests. If it came to a crunch, and absolutely crucial interests of Israel were at stake, the latter would obtain, this being considered the ultimate Jewish interest.'[4]

(b) IMPACT OF JEWISHNESS ON FOREIGN POLICY

Shabtai Rosenne summed up the consensus by noting a fourfold impact of Israel's *Jewishness* on her foreign policy. First, the aim of giving every Jew the freedom to settle in Israel makes the unrestricted right to immigrate to Israel a vital national interest. (This bears on Israel–Soviet relations *vis-à-vis* Russian Jewry.) Secondly, as the only Jewish state, Israel is concerned about the well-being of Jews everywhere. (This was reflected in the 1959 Swastika-daubing incidents and the Eichmann Case.) Thirdly, Israel's aim of free and continuous contact with Jewish communities elsewhere leads her to measure the friendliness of other states by their acceptance of such contact. (This is one reason for the qualitatively-different relationship with the United States and the Soviet Union.) And finally, as a self-conscious Jewish state, Israel expects the responsibility for immigration to be shared by world Jewry.[5]

Four specific issues were cited by many members of the foreign policy élites as having special relevance: (1) Israel's UN votes on South

---

[1] Interview in Tel Aviv, July 1966.
[2] Interview in Jerusalem, Aug. 1960.
[3] Interview in Jerusalem, July 1960.
[4] Interview in Jerusalem, March 1966. Subsequent extracts from interviews with Ben Gurion, Eshkol, Peres, *et al.* on the following four issues are taken from the interviews cited above.
[5] 'Basic Elements of Israel's Foreign Policy', *India Quarterly*, loc. cit., pp. 334–5.

Africa's *Apartheid*; (2) Soviet Jewry; (3) the Swastika Affair of 1959; and (4) the Eichmann Case. There were lesser instances as well.

i. *South Africa and Apartheid*

Since 1955 Israel had supported UN General Assembly resolutions 'deploring' or 'condemning' South Africa's policy of *Apartheid*. But as long as no further action was recommended to UN members and Black Africa remained overwhelmingly in a colonial state, the issue aroused very little interest among the Israeli public and competing élites. The *objective* situation changed in 1960-1, with the coming of independence to many African states—eighteen entered the UN in the autumn of 1960—and the consequent pressure for stronger action against South Africa. This, in turn, led to the General Assembly's sanctions resolution of November 1961, which Israel supported, except for (an abstention on) the paragraph recommending the expulsion of South Africa from the UN—unless she abandoned the policy of *Apartheid*. Later, Israel withdrew the head of her diplomatic mission to Pretoria—though diplomatic relations were not severed; and Israel retained her weekly *El Al* flight to South Africa, whose Jewish community was a conspicuously staunch supporter of the Zionist cause and of Israel.

It was those substantive changes in the political landscape of Africa and the UN, combined with the pressure for *visible* anti-South Africa acts, which stirred a small segment of Israeli public opinion, especially the Nationalist Right: the Government's condemnation of *Apartheid* was criticized, and even more so, any contemplated concrete acts against the Pretoria régime—which might undermine the security of Jews in South Africa. All this came to the surface in the *Knesset* debate of November 1961, the first serious discussion on *Apartheid* in Israel's parliament.

Ben Gurion remarked in reply to a question:

That was the reason for our votes at the UN [to avoid difficulties for South African Jews]. After 1960 we changed because we didn't want to alienate the new African countries. We knew the Jews there wouldn't suffer very much. The South African Government was angry but not against the Jews there—against Israel.

If there would have been *pogroms*—if their lives were in danger—then we would have abstained, but we would not have voted in favour, certainly not. A Jew can't be for discrimination.

Eshkol was brief: 'The South African Jews understood our position after we had discussions with them.' Herzog observed that Israel criticized South Africa because Israel's national interest in friendship with the newly-independent Black African states was at stake. The most revealing comments were made by Haim Yahil, Director-General of the Foreign Ministry from 1960 to 1964:[1]

[1] Interview in Jerusalem, Aug. 1966.

On no issue—among those not directly concerning Israel's vital interests—do I remember more discussion than on *Apartheid*. Since 1951 this has been so. There was intense discussion among officials in the Foreign Office. The majority pressed for a strong line on principle; a minority stressed the welfare of South African Jews. Sharett said that we must take a strong line on principle—but not to support the expulsion of South Africa. He was a strong proponent of universality in the United Nations.

Yahil doubted that Sharett, as Foreign Minister, brought such questions to the Cabinet: 'only conclusions were brought to the Government'. And the issue did not reach the *Knesset* until 1961.

By 1960 the question sharpened, as did our interests. We had to keep in step with African states on this issue because we couldn't on two other key issues—Algeria and French atomic tests. The only reason for not taking a stronger stand was South African Jewry. And so we explained to them that our opposition to *Apartheid* was a necessary stand for three reasons: moral principle; Israeli national interests; and the interests of world Jewry—if Israel took a compromise position it would bring contempt.

Apartheid became a great issue in Israel: there was heated discussion in the *Knesset* Committee on Foreign Affairs and Security and in the press. A minority favoured the Government stand; very few wanted a stronger position; the majority stressed the interests of South African Jewry. It was a difficult question. We abstained on economic sanctions—we were conscious of the implications for Israel. We abstained on the severance of diplomatic relations. And we voted for the General Assembly Resolution as a whole. Later we lowered the level of diplomatic relations to a Chargé but we did not sever the EL AL air link—the only direct air link to South African Jewry. The South African Government applied some economic sanctions, blocking the flow of Jewish funds to Israel.

Ben Gurion [then Prime Minister] was kept informed but did not intervene. He had a clear view on principle but did not take the lead.

African leaders were satisfied with Israel's policy on *Apartheid*. They never pressed Israel to sever the air link.[1]

---

[1] In November 1961, Israel again supported a UN resolution condemning *Apartheid*. Ben Gurion explained to the *Knesset* the reasons for Israel's vote: three considerations were cited. First, Israel speaks only for Israelis but she cannot disregard Jewry, 'and we cannot afford to give any excuse to our many enemies' for mistreatment of their Jewish population. Secondly, Israel could not ignore the feelings of Asian and African peoples 'who would be quite unable to understand its failure to join in this protest' And thirdly it was a matter of conscience: 'moral imperatives of Judaism were involved. . . . Was it possible for Israel . . . to remain indifferent to the deplorable régime of racial discrimination that reigns in South Africa?' Statement to the *Knesset* on 27 Nov. 1961. Cited in *Weekly News Bulletin*, Jerusalem, 22–28 Nov. 1961, pp. 2–4.

Arthur Lourie, a South African by birth, who has at different times had a supervisory responsibility for relations with South Africa in the Foreign Ministry, cited three factors in Israel's policy: the moral issue; Israel's political interests in Africa, especially after 1959; and the welfare of South African Jewry. Interview in Jerusalem, Oct. 1965. Another Foreign Ministry official remarked: 'You can assume that South African Jewry put pressure on Israel, was unhappy with our policy, and that we took it into account.' Interview in Jerusalem, Nov. 1965.

ii. *Soviet Jewry*

This is one of the most delicate aspects of Israel's foreign policy. Yet decision-makers expressed their perceptions with candour.

Ben Gurion declared: 'In our policy towards Russia the position of Russian Jews is the main concern. Of course, three million Jews are involved. We could get one million now if they were allowed to leave. The Russians know that the Jews there want to come to Israel.'

Eshkol remarked simply: 'World Jewry must take the lead; Israel must be in the rearguard of this pressure.'

Peres was more revealing: 'When it comes to Soviet Jewry the consideration of local Jewry is dominant—because of the real danger to their survival. We can't forget the Doctors' Plot, etc. We use Yevtushenko's theme—their attitude to Jews is the barometer of Soviet policy.' Furthermore, 'Russian Jews may be the greatest potential to come to Israel.' There is no doubt, he added, that the Russian origin of many members of the Israeli political élite is a further stimulus to activism regarding Russian Jewry.

Arye Levavi, who was Director-General of the Foreign Ministry from 1964 to 1967, stated: 'Certainly we would be better off in our relations with the Soviets if we did not constantly press for amelioration of the conditions of Soviet Jews. But the imperatives of the situation—the welfare of a major Jewish community—demand, in the eyes of Israeli decision-makers, a special effort by Israel.'[1]

Yahil observed that the welfare of Soviet Jewry is regarded by 'almost everybody' as an Israeli national interest, as well as a vital interest of the Jewish People. This, he added, is the reason for Israel's policy towards the Soviet Union—which alienates Moscow. Yet it is doubtful that Israel's relations with the Soviets would improve if the question of Soviet Jewry did not exist. As with most members of the decision-making Technical Élite, Yahil expressed optimism on the probable immigration of Soviet Jews. Two factors were perceived to operate—internal changes in the Soviet Union and external pressure on the Soviet régime. A détente between the super powers would assist the process.

Herzog cited four components of the Israeli élite image of Soviet Jewry: the sense of 'Am Yisrael' (the Jewish People); the sense of mission, namely, that Israel must protect 'Am Yisrael' (apropos, Yahil suggested that Pope Paul had given tacit recognition to Israel as the guardian of world Jewry by defending the actions of Pope Pius XII towards the Jews during the Second World War, as he was leaving Israel during his tour of the Holy Land in 1962); the image of a potential contribution by Soviet Jewry to the upbuilding of Israel; and the emotional link of many Israeli leaders to their Russian origin.

[1] Interview in Jerusalem, Dec. 1965.

iii. *Swastika-Daubing Incidents*

On Christmas Eve 1959 there occurred a brief but widespread resurgence of symbolic Nazism—the painting of Swastikas on synagogues and other Jewish sites in a dozen countries.[1] The Government of Israel responded by sending identical notes to the governments concerned, expressing 'the profound shock felt by Israeli public opinion' at these anti-Semitic acts. Israeli diplomats were also instructed to attend services in the desecrated synagogues and 'to keep a close watch' on that disturbing affair. This representative and protective role was expressed simply yet directly by the Minister of Justice to Parliament: 'The Government and the people of Israel are sensitive and alert to anything that affects our brethren in the lands of dispersion. . . . The Government of Israel will act on the basis of the reports that will reach it' (and it did). Moreover, the *Knesset* Foreign Affairs and Security Committee was invited to 'discuss ways and means of transmitting a grave warning to the States of the world'.[2]

Ben Gurion justified this initiative: 'Theoretically it is so: we always say we are responsible only for the Jews of Israel. But practically Israel belongs to the Jewish People. We know, in a way, that we represent the Jewish People. One cannot be "an Israeli, not a Jew". And we are the only Jews who appear internationally, in the UN, as diplomats. A Jewish Army is their army. They know that Israeli representatives are their representatives.' Most pointedly, '*we are responsible for the fate of the Jewish People; but we cannot accept the views of Diaspora Jews because they are split Jews.* They are afraid and, often, they do not tell the whole truth.' (Emphasis added.)

Tsur related that he had taken this decision himself (as Acting Director-General of the Foreign Ministry), without consulting either the Prime Minister or Foreign Minister. (Within the Foreign Office he consulted Yahil, who was already known to be the designate Director-General.) Tsur justified the dispatch of 'notes of concern' to a dozen governments in terms of a basic Government of Israel responsibility for the welfare of Jews everywhere.

Peres dissented, as did many others. 'You must be careful in using your official power. I wouldn't hesitate to use Israeli state power when

---

[1] The Swastika epidemic ended practically everywhere in the middle of February 1960. However, sporadic incidents of the same kind took place up to the end of 1960 in at least 23 countries. A report of these anti-Semitic actions was prepared by N. Robinson of the Institute of Jewish Affairs of the World Jewish Congress, New York. See Report no. 19, 2 June 1961.

[2] *Statement by Mr. Pinhas Rosen, The Minister of Justice, in the Knesset on Tuesday, 5 January 1960.* Issued by the Government Press Office, Jerusalem. It was not the first time that Israel took direct action on behalf of Jews elsewhere. As noted earlier (ch. 7 (*a*) ii), this act was cited by the American Jewish Committee in its expression of concern about the State of Israel's intervention in the affairs of Diaspora Jewry.

the physical existence of Jewry is in danger. I would make known our willingness to use our power *in such cases*—as a deterrent.'

Herzog demurred on other grounds: Israel, he said, has no right to set itself up as the guardian of Jewish rights in *democratic states*. But no foreign policy decision-maker interviewed on this point rejected totally —and in principle—a protective role for the Government of Israel towards Jews elsewhere.

iv. *Eichmann Case*

The abduction of Adolf Eichmann in Argentina by members of the Israel Security Service (the *Shin Bet*) caused a brief international incident in 1960 and some misgivings in Diaspora Jewry, especially among American Jews. Only seven or eight persons in Israel knew about Eichmann's capture and arrival in Israel on 23 May. The Foreign Office was instructed to say nothing, on the assumption that the Argentine Government would not object. It did so, however, despite official Israeli pleas for understanding—and brought the issue to the UN Security Council. An attempt was made to arrange a meeting between Ben Gurion and President Frondizi in Europe in mid-June but this failed. The Israeli ambassador was declared *persona non grata* soon after, but a new ambassador arrived in November. In the interim the rift was settled by a formula worked out by Rosenne, Legal Adviser to the Israel Foreign Ministry, and his opposite number in Buenos Aires. There were no lasting ill-effects in the relationship between the two countries.

The Eichmann Trial was the object of extraordinary attention in the world press and in the subsequent literature of contemporary history; but it is not, *per se*, within the scope of this analysis. Rather, it is the mind of the foreign policy élites and the light this incident shed on the 'Jewish prism' that compel attention. For one thing, Eichmann was tried under an Israeli law—the *Nazis and Nazi Collaborators (Punishment) Law, 5710—1950*; this stipulated that persons who, during the Nazi régime, committed crimes against the Jewish People or against humanity during the Second World War, will be liable to the death penalty (para. 1).[1] Ben Gurion's plea to Frondizi was conciliatory: 'I do not underestimate the seriousness of the formal violation of Argentine law

[1] The formal charge was that the accused, 'during the period of Nazi rule, was one of those responsible for the murder of millions of Jews in European countries under circumstances constituting offences under the above paragraph of the above Law'.

'A crime against the Jewish people is defined as the commission of any one of the following with the intent of destroying the Jewish people in whole or in part:
— killing Jews;
— causing serious bodily or mental harm to Jews;
— placing Jews in living conditions calculated to bring about their physical destruction;
— imposing measures intended to prevent births among Jews;
— forcibly transferring Jewish children to another national or religious group;

committed by those who found Eichmann, but I am convinced that very few people anywhere can fail to understand their feelings and appreciate the *supreme moral validity* of their act. These events cannot be approached from an exclusively formal point of view.'[1] Yet it was 'en famille' that the Israeli Prime Minister spoke his mind.

The American 'Presidents' Club' (comprising the leaders of the major American Jewish organizations) was split on the Eichmann Affair. Some, including Nahum Goldmann, proposed an international tribunal; others supported an Israeli trial. Ben Gurion wrote to Goldmann, the President of the World Zionist Organization and the World Jewish Congress, in words that laid bare the 'Jewish prism':[2]

The calamity that the Nazis inflicted on the Jewish people is not merely a part of the crimes they committed in the world as a whole. . . . It is a specific and unparalleled act . . . which Hitler and his collaborators did not dare to commit against any other people.

It is therefore the *duty of the State of Israel, the only sovereign authority in Jewry*, to see that the whole of the story, in all its horror, is fully exposed, without in any way ignoring the Nazi régime's other crimes against humanity, but as a unique and unexampled crime, unparalleled in the annals of mankind. . . .

It is perhaps the first act of historic justice of this kind in human history that *a small nation*, beset by many foes, should be able on its sovereign territory to try *one of its chief enemies for atrocities* against hundreds of thousands of *its sons and daughters*.

Historic justice and the honour of the Jewish people demand that this should be done *only by an Israeli court in the sovereign Jewish State*. This was the decision of the Government of Israel and the opinion of the entire Jewish people in its own land.

In the midst of the crisis Ben Gurion scathingly dismissed those who questioned Israel's right to judge Eichmann: 'Let the world understand: whatever may be the protestations and the sophisms of these so-called experts, who are immersed in inhuman formalism, Eichmann will be tried in Israel by a purely Israeli Court under the Israel law passed in 1950 for the specific case of the Nazi butchers.' As for the Argentine complaint to the Security Council, 'do the Argentinians understand *the*

— destroying or desecrating Jewish religious or cultural assets or values;
— inciting to hatred against Jews.
The above crimes were excluded from the provisions of the later law abolishing the death penalty in Israel.'
The charge is indicated in a *Press Bulletin* issued by the Government Press Office, Jerusalem, 5 June 1960. The definition of 'a crime against the Jewish people' is contained in *The Israel Digest*, Jerusalem, vol. iii, no. 12, 10 June 1960, p. 2.

[1] The full text of this letter to the Argentine President, dated 3 June 1960, was issued as a *Press Bulletin* by the Government Press Office, Jerusalem, on 11 June 1960 (emphasis added).

[2] 'Why Adolf Eichmann Must Be Tried in Israel', *Extracts from Statements by Mr. David Ben Gurion, The Prime Minister*, Government Press Office, Jerusalem (emphasis added). Much of this was reproduced in *The Israel Digest*, Jerusalem, vol. iii, no. 12 10 June 1960, p. 1.

sufferings we have endured? Have they had six million of their people murdered? . . . At that time they were neutral in a conflict that threatened the very future of humanity.'[1] Six years later he remarked: 'We always consider what may happen to local Jews—but we didn't think they would suffer.' The breach was healed, 'not only because of the position of the Jews there, but also because we didn't want to quarrel with them—one of the largest states in Latin America'.[2]

Eshkol confirmed that the possible effects on Argentine Jewry were discussed, with the conclusion that they would not suffer.

Peres concurred, adding, 'if we would have thought that there was a basic danger to Argentine Jewry, we would not have taken Eichmann. We discussed carefully the probable effects on them.'

The decisive factor seems to have been Ben Gurion's powerful urge to link the fate of Jews everywhere with the consciousness of Israeli youth, unaware of the Holocaust. As he himself wrote to Goldmann, 'it is not the penalty to be inflicted on the criminal that is the main thing—no penalty can measure up to the magnitude of the offence—but the full exposure of the Nazi régime's atrocious crimes against our people'.[3] As one member of the Technical Élite observed, 'to BG the *Goyim* had their Nuremberg, and the Jews must have their national tribunal on Nazism'.[4] Few if any Israelis dissented from this attitude.

v. *Other Illustrations*

There were other major issues in Israel's foreign policy which revealed the impact of the 'Jewish prism', notably the decisions on Jerusalem.[5] There were less-publicized issues as well. At the United Nations Israel abstained on the question of the credentials of the Hungarian delegation in 1957 and the General Assembly reports on Hungary in 1958 and 1959 because of concern about the position of Hungarian Jews. Earlier, in 1952, partly in response to expressed worry by Jews living in Libya at the time, Israel denied her support to the Bevin–Sforza plan for a UN trusteeship, which thereby failed for the lack of a two-thirds majority—and thus contributed to the hastening of Libya's independence.[6] And on one occasion Israel supported Morocco in a UN-aired dispute with Algeria—partly, it was suggested, in order not to affect adversely the position of Jews still in Morocco.[7]

A little-known precedent for Israel's *démarche* in the Swastika episode of 1959 occurred in 1950, following the arrest of some forty prominent

[1] Interview in *Le Monde* (Paris), 22 June 1960. Reprinted by the Government Press Office, Jerusalem.
[2] Interview in Sde Boker, July 1966.   [3] Loc. cit.
[4] Interview with a Foreign Ministry official in Jerusalem, July 1960.
[5] These will be explored in a related volume on Israeli high-policy decisions.
[6] Related by a Foreign Ministry official in Jerusalem in July 1960.
[7] Related by Aviad Yafeh, then Political Secretary to the Prime Minister, during the author's interview with Prime Minister Eshkol in Jerusalem, Aug. 1966.

Roumanian Zionists. Israel dispatched a strong protest—which made known her self-assumed role of guardian of the welfare of Jews everywhere: 'The Government of Israel have every reason to believe that the Roumanian Government is fully aware that the persecution of Zionists in any country is bound to impair the friendly relations between that country and Israel and to outrage the feelings of the Jewish People throughout the world.'[1] There was no outcry about 'intervention' from American Jews or others.

Such representations are, indeed, perceived as 'normal' in South America: according to Ya'acov Tsur, the Israeli ambassador is assumed to be legitimately involved in local Jewish welfare. On one occasion, as Ambassador to Argentina, he went to see President Peron about the arrest of Jewish leaders; the approach was accepted. On another, when Communists, including a few Jews, were arrested, the Minister of the Interior called in Tsur to explain that they were arrested as Communists, not as Jews.[2] Similar incidents occurred elsewhere.

The first Director-General of Israel's Foreign Ministry, Walter Eytan, claimed a dual function for Israeli envoys—a resident link between two political entities and the representative of local Jewry. 'This has come to be accepted generally—by other governments in the "free" world, by the Jews of the Diaspora, and by everyone in Israel.' Thus Turkey expressed regret to Israel over damage to Jewish property during Greek–Turkish riots. And King George VI told the Chief Rabbi of the Commonwealth that he had received 'your ambassador'. Even Communist China at one stage recognized the link by informally offering Israel, through a visiting Israeli delegation (in 1955), a compound in Peking for an embassy as compensation for Jewish property confiscated in Shanghai.[3] 'Jewish communities abroad', in Eytan's view, 'are often "colonies" in at least as real a sense as the Germans or Danes or Swiss.'[4] Many dissent from this interpretation, notably the leadership of Diaspora Jewry; but it is an important part of the 'Jewish prism' which is widely shared among Israel's foreign policy élites. Indeed, even President de Gaulle, who, in his last years, resented manifestations of solidarity by French Jews with Israel, said to the Israeli Ambassador in Montevideo during his State visit to Uruguay in October 1964, 'You must have a great deal of support in this country, you have a large community here.'[5]

[1] From a confidential Foreign Ministry source, Jerusalem.
[2] Interview in Jerusalem, Aug. 1960.
[3] Related by Daniel Lewin, a senior Foreign Ministry official who was a member of the delegation to China. Interview in Jerusalem, Dec. 1965.
[4] *The First Ten Years: A Diplomatic History of Israel*, Simon and Schuster, New York 1958, pp. 192–4.
[5] Interview with Yeshayahu Anug in December 1970. De Gaulle obviously meant the 50,000 Jews of Uruguay and not the dozen Israeli officials stationed in that country at the time.

vi. *'Light to the Nations'*

There is another dimension of Jewishness which is relevant to Israel's foreign policy, namely, the sense of messianic mission. Throughout the millennia of dispersion Jewry maintained an extraordinary bond with the Bible, a belief in the concept of Chosen People, and a vision of a unique role in the messianic era to unfold. Even among non-observant Jews of the past century this consciousness was widespread, though often concealed or denied. Certainly it was pervasive among the leaders of the *Yishuv*. And when the rebirth of Israel as a sovereign state was achieved, the age-old idea of her special role was affirmed with renewed vigour: it also became a matter of policy significance.

No one has written with such grandeur about Israel's 'national spirit' as Ben Gurion. His writings are full of references to the teachings of her prophets, the ethical norms bequeathed to mankind, and her mission. Typical are the following extracts from essays dating to his tenure as Head of Government. The 'vision of Messianic Redemption', he wrote in 1957, is 'the central feature of the uniqueness of the Jewish People'. That vision 'has prepared and fitted us to be a *light to the nations'*. It also imposed 'the duty of being a *model people* and building a *model state'*.[1] Soon after independence, in a philosophic guide to foreign policy—'Israel Among the Nations'—he declared:[2]

A universal attachment to social and international justice is . . . engraved deeply upon the nation's soul. The passion of our Prophets was launched against all violence, usurpation, oppression and lawlessness in human and in international affairs. The Prophet Isaiah was one of the first to foretell the social revolution. . . .

Ben Gurion was often criticized for the seeming arrogance of his claims—to Israel being a 'light unto the nations' and a 'model people'. On one occasion, when addressing Brandeis University, he retreated to the concept, 'every people is chosen':[3]

The Jewish people is a small one. . . . So that the claim that Israel in its Land might be a light to the Gentiles may be regarded as exaggerated and chauvinistic. To dispel this error from the minds of my listeners, I will say that I do not hold that we are a chosen people. Every people, to some extent, is a chosen people—in its own eyes, at any rate.

Yet even in that context he reaffirmed the concept of special role: '. . . recognition of the equality of peoples cannot lessen our admiration for those *few exceptional peoples* which have played a *uniquely fructifying role* in the annals of humanity.' It was made clear in other speeches that, for him, Jewry is one of these 'exceptional peoples'. Thus, 'Israel is in a unique position. Israel is not a member of any family of nations, like the

---

[1] 'Israel and the Diaspora', op. cit., pp. 17, 21 (emphasis added).

[2] State of Israel, *Government Year Book 5713*, 1952, Jerusalem, pp. 19–20.

[3] 'Science and Ethics'. Address at Brandeis University on 9 March 1960. *Brandeis University Publications*, vol. 1, no. 1, p. 2.

Scandinavians or the Arabs. Our ideals, our capacity and our achievements until now show that we ought to be—and I am confident that we shall be—a light unto the nations.'[1]

Various explanations have been offered for the themes of messianism and uniqueness. The most generous—and plausible—is that Ben Gurion has a conscious, tangible policy aim—to make Jews the world over proud of Israel and to make the Gentile world aware and interested in her survival. Hence the constant admonition to his people to make Israel 'a model state'. There is a real danger, in Ben Gurion's view, that Israel could lapse into the category of another Levantine state; and who then, Jews or Gentiles, would care about her fate?[2]

The messianic impulse to policy had roots in the teachings of the Prophets. And others expressed these ideas as well. For example, Pinhas Lavon, the arch-foe of Ben Gurion in the 1960s, wrote as Secretary-General of the *Histadrut*:[3] 'Hardly a week passes without our being given a lesson concerning our being a chosen people and our obligation to be a light to the nations. . . . We cannot rest content with being an ordinary people of two million, living its life like every other nation. . . .'

The policy consequences of this aspect of Jewishness are difficult to measure; but there are at least two areas in which participants perceived a link. 'Non-identification', as noted, was the basis of Israel's policy towards the super powers until 1950. It derived in part from self-interest, but the messianic vision was present as well, as Eytan remarked:[4]

Israel beset by Arab armies could lean on the support of the two mightiest nations on earth [in the 1948 War]. More than this—there was a feeling that Israel had somehow brought East and West together. If they could act in concert, or at least in step, on Israel, why should they not come to agree on other things. The *messianism latent in the Jewish soul*, stimulated by the miracle of Israel's rebirth, *was ready to embrace the whole world. With the fulfilment of the Biblical prophecy, a new era of peace and goodwill could be dawning for all men.*

The other area in which a sense of mission is manifest is Israel's policy towards Africa from the late 1950s onwards. There, too, vital interests were involved—political, diplomatic, economic, and security. Yet the 'spiritual' component was also present. There was sympathy for

[1] At the Annual Journalists' Luncheon in Tel Aviv, 1 Dec. 1961. The text was made available by the Government Press Office, Jerusalem.

In 1970 one acute observer, Robert Alter, noted that messianism was no longer a salient element in Israel's political culture. In that context he referred to Ben Gurion as the classic exception—an 'unreconstructed messianist'. Many Israelis would agree. 'Zionism for the 70's', in *Commentary* (New York), vol. 49, no. 2, Feb. 1970, pp. 47–57.

[2] This interpretation was given by Yitzhak Navon, who served as Ben Gurion's Political Secretary from 1952 to 1963. Interview in Tel Aviv, June 1966.

[3] 'A Chosen People and a Normal Society', in *New Outlook* (Tel Aviv), vol. 5, no. 2 (42), Feb. 1962, p. 5.

[4] *The First Ten Years* . . . , p. 139 (emphasis added).

the victims of exploitation. There was an identity with peoples who had been persecuted on racial (or ethnic) grounds. And there was a powerful thrust flowing from the prophetic teachings—to share knowledge with the less fortunate and to assist in the search for the 'good society'. To these was added the moral obligation of the contemporary rich nations to aid the process of development.

Thus Mrs. Meir, who made Africa a special object of attention during her tenure as Foreign Minister, told the *Knesset* in 1963: 'Israel has always assumed, is assuming and will continue in the future to assume, an active role in every operation and every objective meant to consummate the restoration of human and national dignity to once-downtrodden peoples in Africa and in every place on earth.'[1] The reason for Israel's policy, she declared on another occasion, was 'a conception of the world which considers it her own moral duty as well as that of the community of nations, towards the developing countries'.[2] (This may sound like empty rhetoric, but in Mrs. Meir's case it was an expression of genuine feeling.) It was Ben Gurion, however, who expressed these themes in terms of a moral—and political—imperative: 'It is now the duty of the rich and the developed—for the sake of their own peace and liberty and future—to offer their devoted assistance to the backward peoples. . .',[3] 'thus helping to solve the greatest problem of the 20th century—the problem of the dangerous gap between Asia and Africa on the one hand and Europe and America (and Australia) on the other.'[4] One cannot weigh with quantitative precision the effect of this prism and image in Israel's Africa policy, but it is not negligible.

(c) OTHER COMPONENTS

i. *Socialist Ideals*

Two other aspects of Israel's political culture have already been discussed—the East European orientation of the High Policy Élite and the predominant socialist ideology. These were largely intertwined, for Israeli policy was shaped by men who grew up in the shadow of the Russian Revolutions of 1905 and 1917—and whose world view was

[1] Budget speech to the *Knesset*, as reported in *The Israel Digest*, Jerusalem, vol. vi, no. 6, 15 March 1963, p. 3. This theme was reiterated in virtually all of her annual budget speeches to the *Knesset*.

[2] Mrs. Meir's opening article for the special issue on Israel in *Afrique Nouvelle* (Dakar), 22 Nov. 1961, as quoted in Samuel Decalo, 'Messianic Influences in Israeli Foreign Policy', *Occasional Papers in Political Science*, no. 2, University of Rhode Island, 1967, p. 8. Decalo's paper drew my attention to this aspect of Jewishness and its effect on Israel's foreign policy.

[3] 'The Vision of Isiah for Our Time', *New York Times Magazine*, vol. vi, 20 May 1962, p. 29.

[4] 'Israel's Security and Her International Position before and after the Sina Campaign', State of Israel, *Government Year-Book 5720*, 1959/60, Jerusalem, p. 69.

partly formed by those momentous events, along with the currents of thought then prevalent in German and Austrian Social Democracy. As noted in another context, this was true of both the *Mapai* 'old guard' and the leaders of the Left-socialist *Mapam*: indeed they were, in effect, the ideological offspring of the two Russian Revolutions.[1] This explains in part their preoccupation with Russian Jewry. It also illuminates their attitude towards the Soviet régime—*Mapai*'s mistrust and thinly-disguised hostility, *Mapam*'s faith and sense of kinship. Even the older leaders of the Left-nationalist *Ahdut Ha'avodah* drew their inspiration partly from the populism of Russia's *Narodniks*.

All these groups identified in some form with socialist ideas and ideals: they were committed to social and economic equality among men and nations, to freedom from class and alien rule, to co-operative enterprise and, in general, to the values of nineteenth-century socialist humanism. Those ideals were translated into action in Israel's policy towards the new nations, first in Burma, then in Ghana, and far and wide in the Third World. Two examples of decisions inspired by socialist idealism may be noted. In 1949 Spain appeared to have been prepared to establish diplomatic relations: Israel refused because of the Fascist character of the régime. And in 1952 Israel supported Libya's admission to the UN—partly because of the principle of the universal right of national self-determination.[2]

Closer to home there was a vision of Jewish–Arab friendship and co-operation in a Near East freed of Imperialism: this flowed from the fraternal and egalitarian character of the Jewish labour movement and its socialist ideology. Moreover, the anti-colonial struggle of Palestine Jewry led to the hope of a shared goal in ejecting the foreign ruler, an attitude which was widespread in the Second *Aliya* leadership of the *Yishuv*. Unlike the link between messianism and non-identification, however, this left no visible mark on Israeli foreign policy—because vital *interests* clashed with *aspirations*. From the outset the Arab states made it clear that they did not share the vision of partnership. Thus policy desires were discarded in the face of perceived reality. Nor were all members of the Israeli High Policy Élite equally committed. Yet this ideological strand is apparent in Sharett's policy of conciliation. To take but one example, Israel conveyed approval and extended the hand of friendship to Egypt in 1954 upon her reassertion of control over the Canal Zone: to Nasser, Sharett declared in effect: 'you want to get the West out of the Middle East; make peace with us, and we shall do so together'.[3] Apart from socialism, the political theory of Zionism

[1] See ch. 8 above, especially section (a) i, and Appendix B.

[2] Related to the author by Foreign Ministry officials in Jerusalem, July 1960.

[3] The link between Israel's socialist ideology and her policy of Jewish–Arab co-operation was most consistently articulated in Israel's second decade in the pages of *New Outlook*. See ch. 7 (b) i above. Sharett's image and policy will be examined in depth in the following chapter.

undoubtedly served as an autonomous force in shaping Israeli decisions.

ii. *Historical Legacy*

The impact of historical legacy is evident throughout this discussion of Attitudinal Prism. First and foremost was the Jewish presence in the Holy Land in antiquity and the expectation through the ages of a 'National Return'. Moreover, the claim was rooted in biblical sources and sustained Jewry in its times of troubles. The prophetic teachings of that golden age as well were able, through the lens of Israel's High Policy Élite, to influence image and decisions in the new state. Yet there were more recent strands of historical experience which affected perception and choice after 1948: these date to the British period.

Throughout the Mandate the conflict between Zionism and the British régime centred on two issues—the right of Jewish immigration and the right of Jewish defence in Palestine. The first reflected the long-term interests and needs of the Jewish People; the second expressed the immediate requirements of the *Yishuv*. This duality of interests, remarked Rosenne, a legacy of the Mandate, permeated Israeli foreign policy after 1948. He observed further that the first imposed a 'maximum of flexibility' and made the maintenance of world peace the primary concern—the 'real national interest of the Jewish people as a whole'. The second led 'to unavoidable opportunism in an all-out attempt to prevent (at least quantitatively) an adverse power ratio between Israel and the Arab states'; Israel's foreign policy has had to navigate between these two poles.[1]

A corollary of this dualism was the clash between the *Yishuv* and Diaspora Jewry for control over the 'foreign policy' of the Zionist Movement. The conflict was resolved after independence in favour of the State, but for most of the earlier period foreign relations in the struggle for Palestine were largely in the hands of 'outsiders'—men like Weizmann, Abba Hillel Silver, Brodetsky, and Goldmann. Friction extended over a wide range of issues, both on the substance of Zionism's posture towards the rest of the world and on the techniques of pursuing its aims. The Political Department of the Jewish Agency in Jerusalem was the *de facto* spokesman of the *Yishuv* in foreign policy.[2]

It was in the pre-independence period, too, that the sources of the later conflict between the protagonists of diplomacy and the activist school in Israeli policy began to appear. The Weizmann credo, whose most articulate exponents were Sharett and, later, Eban, continued the pre-State belief in the efficacy of moderation. By contrast, Ben Gurion and Dayan, along with Peres, Allon, and *Herut*'s Begin, emphasized the

[1] 'Basic Elements of Israel's Foreign Policy', pp. 331–4.

[2] I am indebted to Dr. Emanuel Gutmann of the Hebrew University for drawing my attention to this point. See Yehuda Bauer, *From Diplomacy to Resistance*, Jewish Publication Society of America, Philadelphia, 1970

primacy of coercion in the conduct of foreign and security policy. This disagreement cuts across the Diaspora Jewry–Israel nexus. Still another legacy of the Mandate was the triumph of realism in the foreign policy élites—the acceptance of self-interest as the supreme basis of foreign policy. And in the same spirit militancy became the norm in Israel's behaviour towards her Arab enemies: the siege mentality from the twenties and thirties became an integral part of the élite outlook. Finally, an air of cynicism became increasingly evident in the conduct of policy—a product of the 1945–8 struggle for international recognition. The Arabs used oil as a political weapon, and Zionism used American Jewry as a means of pressure: both, one senior official remarked, were 'the Almighty's gifts to the contending parties; the use of one was no less moral than the other'.

(d) PERSONALITY TRAITS

There remain the personality traits of decision-makers. These will emerge in detail during the biographical analyses to follow. Moreover, an élite group of such complex and diverse individuals cannot be readily examined *en masse*. Yet some general observations can be made about personality and Israeli foreign policy.

The most striking dichotomy in Israel's Inner Circle is between decisiveness and hesitancy. Ben Gurion was decisive. So too are Meir, Dayan, Allon, and Peres. Sharett and Eshkol were not. Nor are Eban and, except in economic matters, Sapir. Closely related are the dichotomies between extremism and compromise, ruthlessness and compassion, and rigidity and flexibility. All nine persons have displayed a capacity for compromise, compassion, and flexibility in certain situations; but there is a qualitative distinction. Ben Gurion and Meir stand at one end of this personality spectrum, Sharett and Eban at the other. Once more, Dayan, Allon, and Peres fall into the firmer, tougher, and harder syndrome on foreign and security policy, Eshkol and, especially, Sapir into the softer school.

There is, too, a conspicuous contrast between men of deeds and men of words, but in this respect the classification differs. Sharett and Eban are *par excellence* men committed to the importance of words, of formulae, of persuasion, and of diplomacy, though they are not averse to (coercive) action. Ben Gurion was also gifted in the use of words but he was, by temperament, a man of action, as are Dayan, Allon, Peres, and Meir. Eshkol and Sapir (had) have neither flair nor interest in words, but they (were) are not men of deeds in the same sense.

i. The 'BG Complex'

The members of Israel's Inner Circle have been treated thus far as equals—for analytical purposes. One person, however, Ben Gurion, held a leadership position of towering dimensions. Indeed all others suffered from what many called a 'BG Complex': 'What will the Old Man say?' was a crucial question before any act of consequence. And that pre-eminence extended back to the days of the *Yishuv*, when he was Chairman of the Jewish Agency Executive, from 1935 onwards. As Prime Minister and Defence Minister from 1948 to 1963, with only a brief interregnum, Ben Gurion's influence had added institutional authority. Thus the personality traits of others impinged on high policy to the extent that they meshed with his predispositions: in a very real sense BG was the pivot of the decision-making process.

The personal relations among the other eight were much less important than the ties between Ben Gurion and each individual—the trust and temperamental affinity, and BG's respect for their judgement. But these inter-personal relationships go far beyond a discussion of Attitudinal Prism, especially because they were affected by diverse images of the setting for Israeli policy: they will be explored in the following three chapters. It is sufficient here to illustrate the 'BG Complex' and thereby to uncover traits which coloured his policy lens.

No member of the Inner Circle was more conscious of Ben Gurion's greatness or more preoccupied with the 'BG Complex' than Sharett. And no man was better equipped to probe the personality of the 'Old Man'—for whom he felt a mixture of awe, admiration, envy, and enmity. Sharett's analysis took the form of a comparison some years after he was compelled to leave the Government: it is a luminous commentary on both men.[1]

There has been a temperamental incompatibility throughout. I am quiet, reserved, careful; BG is impulsive, impetuous, and acts on intuition, not reason.

My capital C is CAUTION, BG's is COURAGE.

I see all the implications and consequences of an act, BG sees only one side, what he wants to see, and suppresses everything else.

BG is very egocentric in every respect—and a highly complex egocentrism at that.

BG is a man of extraordinary erudition—he is very widely read in certain fields. He is typical of the self-educated man who devours books.

He has great mental, though not intellectual, faculties.

He delights in reading philosophy, has a special attraction for metaphysical speculation and abstract ideas—which he remembers. Yet with all this his knowledge is appallingly superficial and unbalanced. He has a single-track mind, which focuses intensely on a few objects.

He possesses depth in chosen fields of interest but lacks breadth—in learning, knowledge, and vision.

He has incredible drive and concentration.

BG finds time for reading, despite his various positions of responsibility. Many aspects of his work will be neglected, but he pursues his books.

He is constantly discovering the universe around him. No matter that his

[1] Interview in Jerusalem, July 1960.

'discoveries' have been uncovered by others before him. He does not read broadly in a field. Thus he suddenly 'originates' a view—which may be a well-known fact or theory. Thus much of what he writes or says is cliché.

Ben Gurion's egocentrism is threefold. As a man—he is completely pre-occupied with himself, his thoughts, deeds and emotions. The evidence is his loneliness, his apartness, for Ben Gurion is a solitary figure, without close friends. His constant stress on the uniqueness of the Jewish people is another aspect of this egocentrism (cultural egocentrism). The third aspect is his assumption of a messianic mission vis-à-vis Israel and Jewry.

BG really believes that he created the State. In large measure he is right, for without the courage to act when he did there would not have been a state at that time.

BG's speeches are declaratory, mine are explanatory. People go to see Ben Gurion; they come to my meetings to learn.

[As for his constant emphasis on the early settlers, the 'Petah Tikva complex'] Ben Gurion never recovered from the awe at his own aliya!

This assessment was made in the setting of a private interview, by an old comrade then disenchanted with Ben Gurion. Yet it is not in most essentials different from another appraisal by a friend of long-standing, Zalman Shazar, the third President of Israel:[1]

. . . your way of life has always seemed to me to lie along mountain tops. It is the atmosphere of lofty peaks that surrounds you—air that is at once rarefied and perilous. . . .

[What] made of your decisions the turning point in our people's destiny . . . was rather your unerring historical instinct and along with it the power of your will and your unshrinking courage. Like some ancient, blind seer . . . you seemed to look through dangers and past them. You were like a man overpowered by a hidden but luminous mission. . . .

Ever since you have felt to the full the enormous distinction between the 'before then' and the 'after then'. . . .

It is said that victory goes to the single-minded. . . . In every particular period you have devoted yourself exclusively to one task. That one task has invariably taken on the nature of a mission. . . .

Zionism has indeed been the essence of your life.

To these traits must be added charisma, decisiveness, and ruthlessness. And when they are combined with his Jewish prism, the consequences for Israeli foreign policy are apparent. They will be elaborated and illustrated in later studies of decision.

In summary, the Attitudinal Prism of Israel's High Policy Élite comprises the following components: Jewishness as the dominant strand; Socialist ideology and ideals; an East European perspective; a dual historical legacy—the continuity with Jewish antiquity and the realism born of the Mandate experience; and a personality predis-

[3] 'To David Ben Gurion at 70', published originally in Davar (Tel Aviv), 21 Sept. 1956, on the occasion of Ben Gurion's 70th birthday, and reprinted in the Jerusalem Post, 30 Sept. 1966, to mark his 80th birthday. The extracts are taken from the English version.

position to deeds, with corresponding decisiveness, extremism, and rigidity, epitomized by Ben Gurion. We may now proceed to explore the images held by the members of the Inner Circle, beginning with the contrasting views of the world espoused by Ben Gurion and Sharett.

CHAPTER 12

Ben Gurion and Sharett:
Contrasting Views of the World

Few high-policy decision-makers have the time or inclination to formulate a coherent view of the world. Yet all may be said to possess a set of images and to be governed by them in their response to foreign policy problems. The crucial link between images and decisions was suggested at the outset of this Work: it merits restatement here before exploring the perceptions of the Inner Circle among Israeli leaders.[1]

Images may be partial or general. They may be subconscious or consciously stated. They may be based on carefully thought-out assumptions about the world and one's own state or they may flow from instinctive perceptions and judgements. But whatever their character and source, images exist. Indeed they are no less real than the reality of the environment and they are more relevant to the analysis of a foreign policy flow. The environment, as noted earlier, comprises three levels, that is, states operate in three fields or zones of foreign policy interaction —global, subordinate, and bilateral. Thus a foreign policy image comprises six closely-related perceptions: of the external environment —global, subordinate, and bilateral—and of the desirable or proper role which a state should play in each of these fields. These image components taken together constitute a View of the World. In the precise words of Professor Kenneth Boulding,

. . . we must recognize that the people whose decisions determine the policies and actions of nations do not respond to the 'objective' facts of the situation. It is what we think the world is like, not what it is really like that determines our behavior. . . . The 'image' must be thought of as the total cognitive, affective, and evaluative structure of the behavior unit, or its internal view of itself and its universe. . . . A decision involves the selection of the most preferred position in a contemplated field of choice. Both the field of choice and the ordering of this field, by which the preferred position is identified, lie in the image of the decision-maker.[2]

[1] Ben Gurion himself acknowledged the cardinal importance of image analysis. Soon after Nasser's death in 1970 he remarked about the Egyptian President's *Philosophy of the Revolution*: 'I read it and re-read it ten times in order to understand and to grasp fully its intent.' Interview with *L'Actualité* (Paris), reproduced in *Ha'aretz* (Tel Aviv), 12 Oct. 1970.

[2] 'National Images and International Systems', *The Journal of Conflict Resolution*, vol. iii, no. 2, June 1959, pp. 120–1.

The 'image' as thus defined is all-inclusive; it is a total 'belief system' or, in more traditional terms, a 'world view', a *weltanschauung*. But most foreign policy decision-makers concentrate on the external segments of their environment, that is, they manifest a 'view of the world'. It is this part of the overall perceptions of Israel's Inner Circle that will be explored in the next three chapters. The terms 'images', 'View of the World', and 'perceptions' will be used interchangeably: they provide the key to decisions.[1]

A major problem in image analysis over time—and we shall be examining Israeli élite images during a twenty-year period—is that reality changes and new information is fed to decision-makers. Their 'attitudes' may remain stable, for they are *'predispositions* to respond in a particular way toward a specified class of objects', especially with respect to 'enemies'. But their 'perceptions', that is, the actual *content* of their response, may change in the light of new information. The tendency, as some social psychologists argue, is towards 'balance' or the reduction of 'cognitive dissonance' in perception whenever new information challenges long-held beliefs (cognition) or feelings (affect) and thereby challenges a stable attitude (predisposition).

Balance may be achieved by various strategies, as Ole Holsti observes. The source of discrepant information may be discredited. One may search for counter-information which supports the pre-existing balance. A person may stop thinking. He may indulge in wishful thinking. He may reinterpret the new information to confirm rooted attitudes. Or he may differentiate the discrepant information into disassociated categories. A person may also accept the new data or portrait of reality and alter his earlier 'attitude'. Whether he will adopt a strategy leading to balance or demonstrate flexibility in outlook will depend on the situation, that is, the Operational Environment, the content of the new information, its source, and the personality of the recipient.[2]

The first three of these factors of 'persuasibility' have been discussed in the Israeli context at the macro-level. With these introductory remarks we may turn to the View of the World espoused by Israel's two

[1] Professor Ole R. Holsti uses very similar terminology in his illuminating analysis of John Foster Dulles' image of Soviet Russia: 'Cognitive Dynamics and Images of the Enemy: Dulles and Russia', ch. ii in David J. Finlay, Ole R. Holsti, and Richard R. Fagen, *Enemies in Politics*, Rand McNally & Co., Chicago, 1967, p. 29, fn. 10. The distinction between 'world view' and 'view of the world' was introduced in the writer's 'Elite Images and Foreign Policy Choices: Krishna Menon's View of the World', *Pacific Affairs*, vol. xl, nos. 1 and 2, Spring and Summer 1967, p. 62. In short, what Boulding terms the 'image', Holsti calls the 'belief system', and this writer, a 'world view'; and what Holsti calls the 'image' is, for this writer, in foreign policy analysis, the 'view of the world'.

[2] Op. cit., pp. 29–36. Holsti draws much from the work of social psychologists in the areas of cognitive dissonance and attitude change, notably Milton J. Rosenberg *et al.*, *Attitude Organization and Change*, Yale University Press, New Haven, 1960.

pre-eminent figures during the formative years, David Ben Gurion and Moshe Sharett. The primary source materials for this analysis are their voluminous published work—books, essays, articles, speeches, statements, diary excerpts, press conference transcripts—and interviews conducted by this writer.[1]

(a) 'COURAGE' VERSUS 'CAUTION'

Ben Gurion and Sharett differed in personality, character, and View of the World. 'There has been a temperamental incompatibility throughout', said Sharett with candour, as noted. 'I am quiet, reserved, careful; Ben Gurion is impulsive, impetuous, and acts on intuition. My capital C is CAUTION, Ben Gurion's is COURAGE.' There was indeed a clash of personalities. Ben Gurion was decisive, Sharett was hesitant. Ben Gurion could not bear Sharett's procrastination but respected his technical skills. Sharett admired Ben Gurion's daring but could not tolerate his indifference to external criticism—summed up in the remark, 'it is not important what the *Goyim think*, rather, what the *Jews do*'.

Ben Gurion was here expressing his profound belief that the Jewish national renascence could be realized only through rebellion. Sharett, like Weizmann, saw this revival as a natural flow of modern history; the problem was how to harmonize its coming with the international community. This difference went deeper. Ben Gurion aspired to be a totally free Jew, contemptuous of *Galut* (Diaspora) mentality and the traditional feeling of dependence. Sharett was much more a product of the Middle East than was Ben Gurion but he was always overwhelmed by the external factor—'what will the *Goyim* think'.

Both men came to Palestine in 1906, Ben Gurion at the age of almost twenty, Sharett at twelve; Ben Gurion alone, with a passionate commitment to Labour Zionism, Sharett with his family (his father had been among the earliest pioneers, the *Biluim*, in the 1880s); Ben Gurion from

---

[1] Among the works of Ben Gurion consulted are:
(in English) *Rebirth and Destiny of Israel*, Philosophical Library, New York, 1954. *Ben Gurion Looks Back in talks with Moshe Pearlman*, Weidenfeld and Nicolson, London, 1965. Essays in various *Government Year-Books* between 1952 and 1962.
in Hebrew) *Ketavim* (Works), 4 vols., Mapai, Tel Aviv, 1949. *Be-ma'arakha* (In the Battle), 5 vols., Ayanot, Tel Aviv, 1947–55. *Medinat Yisrael Ha-mehudeshet* (The Restored State of Israel), 2 vols., Am Oved, Tel Aviv, 1969.
For both Ben Gurion and Sharett there are voluminous speeches, in the *Knesset* and elsewhere, many of them in English translation as issued by the Government Press Office in Jerusalem. Among Sharett's works consulted are speeches at the United Nations and elsewhere and articles in the Hebrew and English press. Especially valuable sources were four interviews with Sharett in July 1960, lasting eight hours, and two interviews with Ben Gurion in 1966, lasting nine hours. Detailed notes were taken throughout and, in the latter, Mr. Ben Gurion checked my accounts and affirmed their accuracy.

the Pale of Poland, Sharett from the Ukraine, the heartland of Russian Jewry. In his manner of speech, his accent, and other superficial traits Ben Gurion remained 'the man from Plonsk'. But in his activism, toughness, and ruthless determination he heralded the coming of the free Jew in Israel prepared to fight for his rights. Sharett's Hebrew was a model for a whole generation of Israelis. But in his temperament and character he displayed a greater affinity to the Diaspora Jew—hesitancy, subservience, a reliance on diplomacy, a tendency to compromise, and a preoccupation with Gentile attitudes to Jewish behaviour.

Ben Gurion spent his early Palestine years on the land, at Sejera. In 1910 he moved to Jerusalem, as editor and party official for *Po'alei Tzyon* (Workers of Zion). The Sharetts lived for two years in an Arab village, a formative influence on Moshe's later outlook. He then attended the Herzliya *Gymnasia* in Tel Aviv and stood first in the first graduating class in the first Hebrew secondary school in the country. Both men were studying law in Constantinople at the outset of the First World War. Sharett served most of the war years in the Turkish Army; Ben Gurion was active in the organization of the pro-Allied Jewish Legion, in North America as well as in Palestine.

Soon after the war Ben Gurion played a major role in two significant developments within the burgeoning *Yishuv*, the formation of *Ahdut Ha'avodah*, the United Labour Party, in 1919, and the *Histadrut* the following year. Sharett was a member of the party's executive from 1920 to 1925. In that year he began his studies at the London School of Economics, another formative influence on his View of the World. He returned in 1929 and became Assistant Editor of *Davar*. Two years later he entered the *Yishuv*'s diplomatic service as Secretary of the Jewish Agency's Political Department. He succeeded the assassinated Haim Arlosoroff as Head of that key department in 1933 and remained in this post until independence. It was regarded as natural that he should become Israel's first Foreign Minister—just as Ben Gurion was the certain choice for Prime Minister. Throughout this period BG had strengthened his political primacy in the Labour Zionist Movement—with the formation of *Mapai* in 1929/30—and in the *Yishuv* as a whole; he was Chairman of the Jewish Agency Executive in Jerusalem—Palestine Jewry's 'shadow government'—from 1935 to 1948.

Ben Gurion and Sharett were colleagues for thirty-five years. And for more than two decades, until the rupture of 1956, they worked intimately together, in the Jewish Agency and then as Prime Minister and Foreign Minister of the new state, in its formation and its time of trial. Yet they were not friends, for in Sharett's view, shared by most, Ben Gurion 'is a solitary figure preoccupied with himself, his thoughts, deeds, and emotions'.

Ben Gurion's estimate of Sharett was also ambivalent. He was capable of an effusive tribute, as on the occasion of the conferment of the 'Freedom of the City of Jerusalem' on Sharett in August 1964:[1]

One of the greatest personalities of our generation . . . , a distinguished Jewish statesman in the period of Jewish revival . . . , a blazer of the path of the renewal of Jewish independence, and . . . the architect of the policy of the sovereign State of Israel for many years. . . .

Moshe Sharett is distinguished not only for his Hebrew style and flair for language, but also for his exemplary life and his sense of civil and human responsibility, one of the few exemplary spirits of our generation, a giant of the spirit and of Jewish stalwartness in the loftiest sense of the term. . . .

Yet one year later Ben Gurion absented himself from Sharett's funeral. And to this writer he was more critical, though not hostile: 'He knew more about the details of foreign affairs than I did; but when it came to an important problem he didn't know how to distinguish words from deeds.' Further, 'he was the greatest Foreign Minister of our day in peacetime but not in time of war'. And of his personal qualities, 'he was honest—and there was great nobility about him'.[2]

No one, friend or foe, and Sharett had few of the latter, would disagree with Ben Gurion's last remark. Indeed, these qualities were stressed when he died. Eban referred to 'Moshe incarnating the public conscience. . . . He knew that no man in Israel commanded a similar affection.'[3] And Goldmann praised him as 'the greatest moral figure in Jewish life' and a man who 'became (in his later years) a kind of moral conscience of this country'.[4]

While Sharett was endowed with nobility, Ben Gurion was a greater leader of men. Sharett possessed knowledge about politics but little insight. He was enamoured of the art of persuasion but he had little understanding of the mechanics of power in domestic politics. Ben Gurion was preoccupied with power and had this understanding in abundance, along with an intuitive grasp of political forces and a vision of history. And his achievements were of a much higher order—in independence and nation-building. Sharett recognized Ben Gurion's political greatness, a further measure of his honesty. And Ben Gurion assumed this higher status without hesitation. 'Ben Gurion respected the personal qualities of Sharett, his precision and thoroughness; he thought of him as a brilliant technician; but he felt that Sharett lived in an artificial world where gestures, words, were given great importance.'[5] In short, the two men combined respect for each other with

[1] *Jerusalem Post*, 8 July 1965.
[2] Interview in Sde Boker, June 1966.
[3] 'Moshe Sharett's Life Was Like the National Saga Itself', *Jerusalem Post*, 8 July 1965.
[4] 'The Greatness of Moshe Sharett', *Jerusalem Post*, 24 June 1966.
[5] Shimon Peres, interview in Tel Aviv, June 1966.

disdain for some of the other's traits, a not uncommon ambivalence among comrades in public life.

Ben Gurion's actions were always dominated by a single-minded purpose—the rebirth and survival of a Jewish state. It is not surprising, therefore, that his View of the World changed little over the decades. He was not averse to some adjustment in the light of new knowledge and experience, especially when Jewry and Israel were not adversely affected: a notable example was his revised perception of Israel's unique pioneering achievements following a visit to the Zuider Zee project in Holland in 1960—though he never abandoned the view that Israel surpassed all other states in this creative spirit. And in its essentials Ben Gurion's View of the World reveals the pervasive influence of the Jewish prism.

Sharett was no less inspired by the Zionist ideal. But his personality and life pattern were different, with the result that other concerns affected his View of the World. There were in fact three basic threads in his image. One was an outlook rooted in the Old Testament as the sourcebook of Jewish nationhood, acquired in his father's home. Another was a feeling of awe about how the world looked at Jews, the product of his London years. And close contact with Arabs from adolescence onward created a fascination for the Canaanite idea—that the Hebrews (Jews in Palestine) were simply another Middle East nation. Sharett wavered between his sense of the Jewish People and Canaanism, as illustrated by a court incident in 1936—when he refused to take an oath on the Bible, on agnostic grounds—and his stress in the early 1960s on Judaism as essential to the survival of Israel. Ben Gurion never suffered from this duality: for him the Jews are a world people cast in a Biblical role.

There were other differences in attitude and perception. For BG Diaspora Jewry had a legitimate function, even an obligation, to assist Israel achieve her foreign policy goals; for Sharett each had to take the other's interests into account. Sharett was concerned about the impact of Israeli acts on world opinion; Ben Gurion was not. Ben Gurion had little use for diplomacy; Sharett understood its role better but exaggerated its importance. There were also contrary views about the possibility of peace with the Arab states, from the early 1950s onward.

Stated more generally, their images differed along virtually the whole spectrum: of Israel's recent past, that is, of the forces that led to independence; of the global system, notably the United Nations; of the Middle East system and the Arab mind, polity, and society; of Israel's proper place in the world and region; and of the time and proportionate role for diplomacy and force as techniques of Israeli statecraft. Thus, their choices of policy, style, and specific decisions differed markedly. Indeed, by focusing attention on the images held by Ben Gurion and

Sharett it is possible to illuminate the two broad competing strands of
Israeli perceptions and high policy in the period 1948 to 1956.

(b) TWO IMAGES OF THE ROAD TO STATEHOOD

Deep insight into the minds of Ben Gurion and Sharett is provided
by their contrasting images of the road to statehood; in fact, much of
their later thought and action flow from these perceptions. Both are
plausible and consistent, yet partial and subjective. They provide a
splendid starting point for an inquiry into their general View of the
World.

i. *Ben Gurion: 'The State is the Result of Our Daring'*

The Ben Gurion image has an attractive simplicity. It grants the role
of, and even the need for, vision, as articulated by Herzl and others, as
well as the fact of age-old emotional attachment to Zion. But the
turning point in the modern history of the Jews, for Ben Gurion, was
the *aliya* of the late nineteenth century and beyond. It is the presence
of Jews in the Land of Israel, the concrete, physical fact of Jews living
on the soil of Zion that constitutes the true beginning of the rebirth of a
Jewish commonwealth. Everything preceding this in time or parallel
to it, such as political agitation, diplomatic battles, and the raising of
funds, are distinctly secondary to the creation of a living *Yishuv*.

The conclusions are inescapable. The entire epoch of the longing for
Zion in the millennia of Dispersion does not form a part of the road to
statehood. At most it is a preface in time to the cardinal fact of settlement, of physical presence. The path to independence begins in time
and substance with the *Biluim* and the early villages of Mikve Israel,
Petah Tikva, etc. Moreover, to Ben Gurion the state 'is the result of our
daring'. Thus the diplomatic struggle, especially at the UN, was peripheral. In its most extreme form the BG interpretation would assert
that, regardless of the outcome at the United Nations in 1947–8, the
state would have or could have survived provided that courage and
will and daring were present in the *Yishuv*. Conversely, no UN resolution could have created the state if that determination were lacking.

Ben Gurion expressed these views consistently over the years. One
example will suffice. On the fifteenth anniversary of the Partition
Resolution he declared:[1]

The United Nations wiped out the credit due to i t for its decision on November
29, 1947, on May 15, 1948. If the UN had been worthy of its name it should
have defended its honour when certain countries tried to destroy the people of
Israel in its Land. But there was not a single state—not even the United States
or the Soviet Union—that lifted a finger on the 15th of May. And I am not

[1] Reply to a question at the Annual Journalists' Luncheon in Tel Aviv, Government
Press Office, Jerusalem, *Press Bulletin*, 30 Nov. 1962.

obliged as a Jew to give them credit for anything. The State of Israel exists thanks only to the people of Israel and, first and foremost, to the Israel Defence Forces.

Ben Gurion was still Prime Minister when he conveyed this unconcealed bitterness about the UN and his disdain for the 'external factor' in Israel's survival.

Ben Gurion was capable on rare occasions of rising to effusive tribute to his peers in the Movement, Herzl and Weizmann, especially the latter. 'Both were giant figures', though in his memoirs of that period he devoted much more space to Karl Netter, the founder of Mikve Israel, than to Herzl. 'Weizmann was also the greatest Jewish emissary to the gentile world. . . . There was no one quite like him. With his Jewish grandeur, his Jewish profundity, his sense of history . . . Weizmann's place in Jewish history is alongside the great rulers and kings of old, and as the foremost leader who fashioned our sovereign statehood in our own times.'[1] Yet it is difficult to accept this eulogy at face value, for in the main thrust of his image Ben Gurion denigrates their contributions —vision and diplomacy, respectively. They did not migrate to Israel, and that lacuna is crucial for BG. As Sharett remarked, and many others agreed, 'Ben Gurion never recovered from the awe at his own *aliya*.'

Was this paramount stress on the role of the *Yishuv*—where Ben Gurion dominated—a mere coincidence? Sharett termed it a further expression of BG's egocentrism: 'Only that is important which he himself contributed, and the diplomatic battle was outside his sphere of action.'[2] Others were more charitable, attributing it to Ben Gurion's genuine conviction. As for his denigrating vision (Herzl) and diplomacy (Weizmann and, it may be added, Sharett), the same conjecture is apparent. To Sharett, both personal and ideological considerations led Ben Gurion to treat their contributions as secondary. 'Deep in his heart', declared Sharett to this writer, 'Ben Gurion knows the vital role of the diplomatic battle at the United Nations but he cannot bring himself to admit this in public.' Others perceived his indifference as a function of his activist philosophy and the necessity for morale within Israel.

Whatever the Ben Gurion motivation, his single-factor image of the road to statehood has long been shared by the majority of Israelis. Moreover, this image has had profound operational significance. BG's disdain for the UN role in making history, especially in the creation of Israel, carried over into the post-1948 period of high policy: his contempt for the UN, his reliance on the *Yishuv* and, particularly, on *Tzahal*, is a logical, an inevitable, extension of his image of the events of 1947–8. 'The United Nations counted for little then in the Middle East, it counts for nothing now'—this has long been the essence of

[1] *Ben Gurion Looks Back in talks with Moshe Pearlman*, pp. 59, 61, 65.
[2] Interview in Jerusalem, July 1960.

Ben Gurion's view, with far-reaching consequences for Israeli foreign policy from 1948 onwards.

Two further observations may be made. Ben Gurion's depreciation of the UN role in the Arab–Israel conflict *after* 1948 may well have been due in part to the need to 'prove' his thesis that the UN was unimportant in the birth of the state, for personal or morale reasons, or both. Moreover, there is no logical necessity to assess the United Nations role as identical in 1947–8 and in the post-independence period—either as vital or secondary; that is to say, the objective conditions changed over time. To assert that Israel's security in the 1950s and 1960s depended upon her own armed strength, even if correct, does not prove that this was so in 1948 when Israel was much weaker, relatively and absolutely. It is more plausible to argue that the UN was crucial in 1948, when Israel needed international sanction, but not later when she was firmly established. In short, this image of an unchanging United Nations role, which is common to Ben Gurion and Sharett, though with opposite conclusions, is open to serious criticism.

ii. *Sharett: The Return as a Dialectic*

The Sharett image of the path to independence is set within a different frame of reference. The Jewish presence in the Land of Israel is, of course, important but it is not primary in time or substance.[1] To take the *aliya* of the 1880s as *the* turning point is to distort history and to abstract one concrete phenomenon from the broad and complex movement of the Return to Zion. For Sharett the novel and decisive event in modern Jewish history is the *reawakening of a national will* among various sections of the Jewish People and the capacity to translate that will into action. The reawakened national will, he declared, was the product of faith and vision, not of the Jewish presence. On the contrary, it was that faith, with the added impetus of the Russian *pogroms*, which generated *aliya*. But not only did vision operate through this channel: it was a factor in itself with influence on the Return, both by its impact on Jews to migrate and on world chancelleries to support Zionism. Finally, the reawakened national will was not confined to those who settled in Israel. It affected the whole Jewish People, and their awakening led them to contribute to the Return—in different ways.

Sharett proceeded with a dialectical reading of the Return. It was the continued presence of a small Jewish community in Palestine during the centuries and the unbroken spiritual attachment of Jewry to Zion which persuaded Gentile statesmen to accept the claim of a right to Return. These along with diplomacy secured the Balfour Declaration (1917) and the Mandate (1922). They in turn created the possibility for the Third *Aliya* and a more rapid building of the National Home.

[1] Ibid., in a lengthy exposition of the two perceptions. This account is based upon detailed notes taken during the interview.

Further, the strengthening of the *Yishuv* gave greater weight to the diplomatic and political struggles of the 1940s. Together this interplay of forces, practical (the *Yishuv*) and political (diplomatic), created the state.[1]

Sharett argued vigorously that the road to statehood could not be torn from its international and political context, for the Return was an *international* phenomenon—in the composition of *aliyot*, in the catalytic force of the Holocaust, and in the struggle for world support. On the relative importance of internal and external forces he was emphatic in giving primacy to the diplomatic battle. His reasoning was as follows: it required courage to proclaim independence (Ben Gurion's act), but that act was possible only in a political vacuum—and that vacuum was created by the termination of the Mandate and the physical withdrawal of the British, their army, police, and administration. And the termination of the Mandate was achieved by diplomacy at the UN and elsewhere, not in Israel. In support of his perception Sharett observed that the British Colonial Secretary, Creech-Jones, had publicly declared in 1947 that the approach to the UN did not have as its purpose the termination of the Mandate. Moreover, Foreign Secretary Bevin sought UN support for the *continuation* of the Mandate, after which he would seek economic and other sanctions. 'This could easily have brought us to our knees. We might have gone down fighting, but the objective was to win through to victory. Thus the great achievement at the United Nations was to terminate the Mandate and secure the British withdrawal, thereby creating the indispensable condition for independence.'

In Sharett's view the struggle both at home and abroad contributed to independence. The difference with Ben Gurion, then, is not one of emphasis. BG virtually ignores the external factor—'the state is the result of our daring'. Sharett admits both but is driven to an extreme view: 'I am not ashamed to say it—we owe our state to the United Nations.' He ridiculed the BG contention that UN assistance in 1948 was insufficient because it did not include an international army: 'This was a political impossibility at the time, for the United States would not agree to Russian troops in the Middle East, and the Russians could veto any other international force [this was before the (1950) General Assembly Uniting for Peace Resolution]; the UN did what it could, and that was vital.'

[1] The consistency of this part of Sharett's image is evident in the following extract from a speech he delivered in London on the eve of the Second World War, more than twenty years earlier:

'It is of course clear that, as in the past, the brunt of the struggle on behalf of the Jewish National Home will be borne by the Yishuv in the front-line trenches. The Yishuv is in fact the most powerful instrument. . . . [However,] this great weapon was in itself the result of two powerful political instruments, the Balfour Declaration and the Mandate. . . .' (*Zionist Review*, London, 19 May 1939.)

The contrast in perception of the past is basic. How much is due to conviction and how much to the imperatives of one's place in history is difficult to discern. One aspect is clear, however: as with Ben Gurion, the impact of Sharett's image on his foreign policy decisions was pervasive. For one thing, his image of a crucial UN role in 1948 led him to a reliance on the universal organization, at least to the maximum avoidance of acts which might alienate the UN. Secondly, his pride in the accomplishments of diplomacy in 1947–8 and his faith in the United Nations strengthened his personality predisposition to a policy of caution, antipathy to violence, and opposition to border raids; that is, diametrically opposed to the Ben Gurion line. Indeed, 'the basic specific question over which we clashed was the question of retaliation'. It was over this issue that Sharett resigned in June 1956, a few months before the Sinai Campaign.

On that momentous decision Sharett demurred. 'It was unnecessary', he said in 1960. When pressed by this writer he acknowledged that, by 1956, perhaps, there was no way of avoiding the clash—but the tension built up between 1953 and 1956 could have been drastically reduced by another policy. 'Every Arab act on the border was magnified and led to Israeli retaliation; this in turn led to continuous aggravation and escalation of the conflict.' The alternative path is implicit in this comment; it will be elaborated in the comparison of Ben Gurion–Sharett images of the Arabs.

Suffice it to note Sharett's illustration in this context. Some prize sheep were stolen from *kibbutz* Mishmar Ha-Emek in 1955. Dayan, the Chief of Staff, had plans for a retaliatory raid which, said Sharett, might involve the deaths of women and children—for sheep. Typical of his outlook was the remark, 'I could see the headlines in the world press'. As Prime Minister he refused to authorize the raid; 'Dayan was furious'. Two days later, through the intervention of UNTSO Chief, General Burns, the sheep were returned. It was this kind of reaction, concluded Sharett, which could have avoided the road to the Sinai Campaign. Most Israelis disagree. But the incident reveals the chasm between the two leading decision-makers in the early years. Two sources of the contrasting BG–Sharett images have now been exposed—personality and interpretation of the path to independence; there are others.

(c) BEN GURION'S VIEW OF WORLD POLITICS

David Ben Gurion has never concealed his World View. Indeed he has used his pen assiduously over the decades as part of the struggle for a 'Restored State of Israel'.[1] The result has been a dozen volumes of

[1] The title of his recent collection of memoirs, *Medinat Yisrael Ha-mehudeshet*, 2 vols., Am Oved, Tel Aviv, 1969.

essays, many of them polemical, speeches, interviews, letters, and memoirs. They are not equally important nor of uniform quality; but they are rich in insight into BG's 'public philosophy'. For his View of the World the most valuable—and accessible—are four essays which he contributed to the *Government Year-Book* during his tenure as Prime Minister: 'Israel Among the Nations' (1952–3); 'Israel's Security and Her International Position before and after the Sinai Campaign' (1959–60); 'Towards a New World' (1960–1); and 'Achievements and Tasks of our Generation' (1961–2). According to his closest political aides, men like Shimon Peres and Yitzhak Navon (his Political Secretary from 1952 to 1963), the first and second are the most authoritative expression of the images underlying Ben Gurion's basic foreign policy decisions. The others provide a broader intellectual framework for his view of world history, of peoples, of cultures, and of the contemporary era. They offer an illuminating introduction to Ben Gurion's (more schematically conceived) image of the global and subordinate systems and Israel's proper role within international and regional arenas.

i. *The Contemporary Era*

'Towards a New World' contains little that is new or original, but there are very few, and only marginal, errors in a sweeping historical survey. There is evidence of wide reading, a thorough grasp of essentials, an ability to place the modern world in historical perspective, an understanding of the main forces at work in contemporary world politics—and, as in much of his writings, a striking arrogance. Ben Gurion notes at the outset that we live in a new and unprecedented era in human history, with two interrelated developments—the coming of freedom to all peoples and the growing dependence of all nations on each other. There is also a dual set of psychological forces—the rising expectations of the underprivileged and the increasing acceptance of responsibility by the developed states. Asians and Africans are not innately inferior to Westerners, he observes, as the Japanese victory over Russia in 1905 revealed dramatically. Further, 'the peoples of Europe were not always in the van of culture', and the Afro-Asians are destined to exert a powerful influence on the future of mankind. These are his conclusions from a detailed and accurate survey of European expansion overseas and the reasons for its success.[1]

Set against the sweep of history, Ben Gurion's image of the contemporary era begins—and ends—with the place of Jewry: no epoch has been more appalling and heartening, more tragic and heroic, with greater suffering and havoc, yet with more hope and salvation; nor is there any parallel to Jewish tribulations and endurance. Over and over again there is reference to the uniqueness and mission of Jewry which,

[1] 'Towards A New World', in State of Israel, *Government Year-Book 5721*, 1960/1, Jerusalem, pp. 11–33.

unlike other nations, never succumbed to other faiths. But while Jewish history is unique it does not develop in a vacuum; it is part of world history.

Ben Gurion perceives an era of global wars; of totalitarian régimes—with 'no parallel among the tyrannies hitherto chronicled; they exist, they spread, they may spread further'; of a revolution in transport, communications, and technology; of continued disunity, but with narrowing gaps and falling barriers; of the liberation of peoples and continents—'the mightiest and most revolutionary development in history'; of the glaring chasm between rich and poor—'a grave and painful problem, perhaps no less so than the dominion of man over fellow-man'; of cold war, and of a necessary but weak United Nations. He emphasizes the revolution in science, noting that scientists are, legitimately, involved in everything, for pure and applied science are necessarily integrated; yet science must also be related to morality. BG is proud of the notable role of Jewry in the scientific revolution, from Spinoza to Einstein and including Marx and Freud; but their Jewish identity, he regrets, was masked—until 1948. He then closes the circle of Jewish consciousness by extolling the renascence of the Jewish state—an extraordinary phenomenon, particularly when viewed against the absolute negation posed by the Holocaust to Jewish creativity and, indeed, survival.[1] Elsewhere he elaborates on the accomplishments of Israel restored.[2]

ii. 'Israel Among the Nations' (1952)

The outlines of Ben Gurion's early post-independence image are contained in a few major speeches at the time: friendliness and aid by the two super powers; international sanction by the UN; and a natural community of Arab–Jewish interests. These were the perceptual foundations of the 'five principles' of foreign policy enunciated by Israel's first elected Government in March 1949.[3] But it was not until four years after independence that BG provided a substantive exposition of his View of the World, in his essay, 'Israel Among the Nations'. The pre-eminence of security is already apparent, but this pivotal concept was fully expounded only after the Sinai Campaign.

Few countries enjoy a security based upon geography, observes Ben Gurion at the outset; and even those which did so, like Britain and the United States, are no longer immune to assault—from the air. Yet in comparison with history, 'geography varies little or not at all'. Certainly this is true of Israel: 'Its geographico-physical definition is

---

[1] 'Achievements and Tasks of Our Generation', in State of Israel, *Government Year-Book 5722*, 1961/2, Jerusalem, pp. vii–lxxx.

[2] This is done at length in *Medinat Yisrael Ha-mehudeshet*, vol. 2, and in *Ben Gurion Looks Back . . .* , pp. 171 ff.

[3] See Appendix A, pp. 574–9 below, for a discussion of these principles.

practically unaltered, although vast and vital changes have taken place in its geopolitical surroundings.' He cautions that 'no historical situation is like the next' and that 'experience is likely to turn into a canker and a mortal risk if we pursue it blindfold . . .' In that context he notes that Israel's two ancient epochs were alike in three respects: 'the centre of gravity of the world in which the Jewish people lived . . . was the Mediterranean region'; Israel was surrounded by different peoples, whose quarrels could be exploited for her security; and the Jews 'entered the Land from the East'.

None of these conditions exists in the age of the third Jewish commonwealth. Indeed, 'only two exceptional portents of our times need be mentioned here. First, the waning hegemony of Europe and the rise of Asia, [whose three principal nations, India, China and Japan] are pregnant with a destiny no less great and fruitful than Europe once knew. The second portent is the struggle for leadership of the world between two mighty powers, the United States of America and the Soviet Union. . . .' Yet the global system is not rigidly bipolar, in Ben Gurion's image; nor are the super powers identical.

. . . it would be wrong to say that the world is divided into two parts, the Soviet bloc on the one side and the American bloc on the other. Only the Soviet bloc is uniform, cohesive, and subordinated to a single supreme authority which has its home in the Kremlin [and] which decides affairs [in all spheres, including] everyday thought and behaviour. . . . Perhaps Communist China should be excluded, for its links with the Soviet Union are those rather of friendship than of dependence. . . . The rest of the world does not make up a uniform, homogeneous body in any respect. . . .

Within that non-Communist world Ben Gurion perceives various types of actors: 'primitive states still existing under a theocratic-monarchical régime'; feudal or semi-feudal societies; capitalist-democratic countries; dictatorships; and 'progressive, socialistic' nations. A notable omission in this perceptive image of global politics is the UN; by 1952, perhaps earlier, BG had dismissed the world body as of no consequence.

There is a conspicuously softer tone in the emotive words which Ben Gurion uses to describe the West: 'Some of these countries are allied to one another for purposes of mutual defence—the countries of the Atlantic Pact, with the United States at their head.' This distinction between the blocs and the super powers is emphasized at various points in the essay. Thus Ben Gurion distinguishes three kinds of states encountered by Israel: those which refuse any links; those which permit relations with their Governments only; and those which allow contact with their people as well. 'The difference between the third and the second group', he writes, 'is hardly less important than that between the second and the first. For every nation the freedom of its contacts with other nations [at all levels] . . . is of primary, even critical, importance. With Israel these contacts have a very special and vital meaning [because of the dispersion of world Jewry].' And while he acknowledges the role of the Soviet Union, as well as that of the United States, in the 1947-8 period, 'still, from one adamantine and infinitely important fact there is no escaping, that only in the countries of democratic freedom, where America is in the van, has our State found or is it likely to find succour from the peoples themselves and the Jewish communities among them'.

Ben Gurion's image of global politics is only partly rooted in the reality of dispersion. It also derives from the *raison d'être* of Zionism: 'The State sees itself as the creation of the Jewish people and as designed for its redemption. It sees Jews throughout the world as one nation, not only in the past but in the present and future as well.' Still another conscious source is the perceived affinity of values. 'Israel is not indifferent to the ideological conflict', wrote BG. 'Its devotion to the values of human freedom, freedom of thought and spirit, freedom of choice and criticism . . . is ingrained in its character. . . .' And finally, Ben Gurion's socialism is of the democratic type, formed in the spirit and at the time of the first (1905) Russian Revolution; he has never abandoned that commitment. In short, interests and ideology—and perhaps temperament as well—created an image of the super powers favourable to the United States; and experience moulded his view of the UN.

There are few explicit advocacy references in this essay pertaining to the global system. At one point Ben Gurion acknowledges the need for passive concern: '. . . even countries which belong to neither bloc, like Israel, cannot disregard this battle of Titans, which may precipitate itself into a Third World War'. In the most general terms he expounds 'five paramount missions of Israel'; these include three impinging on external policy—immigrant absorption, military and political security, and the safeguarding of sovereignty. More narrowly conceived, he cautions that 'our Government is neither able nor entitled to boast that its weight in the scales of international politics is decisive or even particularly impressive'. Yet, 'its wishes and its capacity are not a negligible quantity. . . . In international politics, too, there are imponderable forces, and there is no doubt that, in a fair degree, Israel is one of them.' The final admonition reaffirms Ben Gurion's image of the road to statehood: 'We should prize the Charter of the United Nations and respect the [Big Three] declaration [of 1950]. . . . [But] Israel stood up by its own strength and will stand firm only if it trusts first and foremost in itself as a power of growing greatness.'[1]

iii. *'Israel's Security and Her International Position . . .' (1960)*

The behaviour of the super powers and the UN during the Sinai Campaign only strengthened Ben Gurion's image of world politics—

---

[1] The above analysis and quoted extracts are taken from 'Israel Among the Nations', State of Israel, *Government Year-Book 5713*, 1952/3, Jerusalem, pp. 1–47.

and of the path to independence. This is evident in his extensive analysis of 'Israel's Security and Her International Position before and after the Sinai Campaign'.[1] The Soviet Union's relentless hostility, which reached its peak in the dire Bulganin threats of direct intervention and air assault in the early days of November 1956, and continued with the attempts to impose UN sanctions against Israel, appeared to BG and others as total confirmation of his image: Moscow was not only the most powerful promoter of the Arab cause and the principal supplier of arms to Israel's enemies; it also resorted to vicious language and diabolical threats against a small state.

The United States was also opposed to the Sinai Campaign, though her sharpest criticism was directed to Israel's allies, Britain and France. Washington also refused to condone any Israeli territorial gains. Yet in the prolonged diplomatic crisis over Israeli rights in the Tiran Straits, during the early months of 1957, the US showed much sympathy. Indeed it was Secretary of State Dulles who produced the key pledge of 'guarantees'; and President Eisenhower, in his exchange of letters with Ben Gurion, made clear American intentions to support Israeli claims in this crucial sphere.[2] Thus the image of the United States as a friend, though critical of some aspects of Israeli policy, was solidified by her perceived behaviour.

Ben Gurion's suspicion about Secretary-General Hammarskjöld's 'objectivity' was also fortified. So too was his disdain for the UN role: it was unable to secure peace or to assist Israel to defend herself and it passed pro-Arab resolutions. Yet Ben Gurion had a marked ambivalence towards the United Nations. 'It has not the power, the authority or the will to put its principles into practice', he wrote on another occasion. 'The State of Israel felt that weakness the very day it was born. . . . All the same . . . some kind of supreme authority for mankind is taking shape. . . . The UN may yet do great things in drawing the peoples closer and building peace in the world.'[3]

Of BG's denigration of the UN role in the Arab–Israel conflict, Abba Eban remarked: 'Ben Gurion has a monistic view of history; his perspective does not encompass a plurality of factors influencing the course of events. More than de Gaulle or Churchill he identifies the nation's history with himself; whatever does not involve him he simply ignores; and since he played no role in the UN theatre he dismisses it as of no consequence.'[4] (Not without reason is Eban regarded as Sharett's successor.)

Much of 'Israel's Security and Her International Position . . .' deals

[1] The full text is in State of Israel, *Government Year-Book 5720*, 1959/60, Jerusalem, pp. 9–87.
[2] This will be explored in detail in a related volume on Israeli high-policy decisions.
[3] 'Achievements and Tasks of Our Generation', pp. ix, x.
[4] Interview in Rehovot, Dec. 1965.

with a landmark in Israeli foreign and security policy, the Sinai Campaign—its complex background, the decision, the ensuing political struggle, and the consequences of that 'second round'. But this essay also provides insight into other aspects of Ben Gurion's image, especially concerning Israel's proper role in the global system. To begin with, BG offers a precise and comprehensive definition of 'security':[1]

... just as the problem of Israel's security is different from that of other countries, so the scope of our defence is wider than that of any other country, and does not depend on our army alone.

Israel can have no security without immigration. . . .

Security means the settlement and peopling of the empty areas in north and south; the dispersal of the population and the establishment of industries throughout the country; the development of agriculture in all suitable areas; and the building of an expanding (self-sufficient) economy. . . .

Security means the conquest of the sea and the air, and the transformation of Israel into an important maritime power. . . .

Security means economic independence. . . .

Security means the fostering of research and scientific skill on the highest level in all branches of [science and] technology. . . .

Security means vocational training of a high standard for our youth. . . .

And, finally, security means a voluntary effort by the youth and the people in general for difficult and dangerous tasks in settlement, security and the integration of the immigrants. . . .

But Israel can have no security without her Defence Forces, and . . . we must meet their needs in equipment of the finest quality. . . .

This concept takes on added significance in view of the pivotal role of *security* in Ben Gurion's general world view, as emphasized by those who know his thinking.

Ben Gurion had no illusions about the impact of the Sinai Campaign. It produced respect and admiration among many Asian and African peoples, he claimed, as well as tranquillity on the borders, 'inner confidence of the nation', and 'faith in its army'. It also led to freedom of navigation in the Tiran Strait and the Gulf of Aqaba. At the same time, 'there is one illusion . . . born of the Campaign that must be destroyed without compunction . . . namely that the Sinai Campaign has completely solved the problem of our security. . . . Basically . . . the problem has not been solved. It is doubtful', he added philosophically, 'whether war can solve historical problems at all,' but he hastened to add, 'although there are unavoidable wars that have to be fought. . . .'

Ben Gurion reverted to a theme touched upon in earlier essays—the two different spheres in which Israel must operate, the 'small' sphere or Middle East, and the 'large' sphere or the global system. The importance of the latter he attributes to three factors: first, the dispersion of the majority of the Jewish People, 'from which we draw manpower, material and cultural resources, and moral and political support';

[1] Op. cit., pp. 22–4.

secondly, 'the forces at work in the wider sphere [, who] will not lightly accept all the decisions secured by the Israel forces, *if these decisions are in opposition to their true or imagined interests*'; and, thirdly, the continued dependence of Israel's armed forces '*on the good will of those who manufacture the arms*'; and, he added, only a few are prepared to make them available.[1]

Yet BG was not unaware of the impact of the new states on the global system: 'The adhesion of new countries to the United Nations has considerably altered the relationships between world forces, and to some extent has mitigated the domination of the great powers, the United States and the Soviet Union.' And 'there is no doubt', he declared, 'that Israel's international standing has improved thanks to . . . ties with the new countries'.[2]

In what sphere does Israel belong? She is not only Middle Eastern, asserts Ben Gurion, but a Mediterranean nation as well. Further, 'in effect Israel is neither . . . but a *world people*. . . . It is the attachment to the scattered Jewish people that is decisive for Israel.' In a later essay he extended Israel's regional links to 'the Red Sea region and, through it, to the Indian Ocean'.[3]

Ben Gurion observes that Israel is unaligned—but he is not pleased with this isolation:

Thᴇ little State of Israel does not belong to any alliance or bloc—and this is not ᴄ˙ its own choosing. There are indeed doctrinaires who regard Israel's isolation as a blessing. If this is a 'blessing', it is a 'blessing' forced upon us.

[And to the neutralists at home and abroad] why should Israel be prohibited from doing what is permitted to Poland, Czechoslovakia, Belgium, Turkey, Denmark and France—namely being a partner in a defensive alliance with friendly nations?

[Moreover, in the wider sense of the term,] certainly no one can demand that Israel should adopt an attitude of moral neutrality.

And in that context he bluntly differentiated the super powers: 'Israel is neither able nor obliged to admire a régime that deprives Jews of the right to Jewish education, the right to emigrate . . .; nor is Israel able and obliged to refrain from distinguishing between a régime that maintains human liberty and self-respect and one that denies them.'

Two basic foreign policy goals were specified: (1) the maintenance of an effective military deterrent—'deterrence and the prevention of war are more important and desirable than military victory'; and (2) friendly relations with the maximum number of states, for this might 'weaken the Arab wall of hatred and finally pave the way for a pact of peace'. His concluding thoughts related to the 'two basic aspirations' underlying the Return to Zion—'to be like all the nations, and to be

[1] Op. cit., pp. 57-8.
[2] Replies to questions by Joel Marcus, in *Davar* (Tel Aviv), 26 April 1961.
[3] 'Achievements and Tasks of Our Generation', p. lv.

different from all the nations', that is, free and equal, and at the same time a model Jewish society.

Many of these themes were also expressed in later speeches and writings.[1] But the most authoritative statement of Ben Gurion's image of global politics and his view of Israel's proper role in that 'sphere' is 'Israel's Security and Her International Position . . .' (1960). There were no substantive changes for the rest of his tenure as Prime Minister and Defence Minister, or even after 1963. Ben Gurion was, *par excellence*, an adherent of the 'national interest' approach to foreign policy—which was recently given academic legitimacy by Hans Morgenthau.[2]

(d) SHARETT'S VIEW OF WORLD POLITICS

Moshe Sharett was no less prolific than Ben Gurion: a compilation of his yet-to-be-collected works exceeds one thousand items.[3] All but a few are newspaper articles, speeches, and pamphlets. There is only one book, *Roaming Asia*, an account of his Goodwill Mission to twelve Asian states in 1956.[4] And the most valuable part of his literary legacy, a careful diary assiduously maintained for lengthy periods during three decades, remains inaccessible; only one volume has appeared.[5] It is possible, nonetheless, to reconstruct Sharett's View of the World during his tenure as Foreign Minister, from May 1948 to June 1956, during which time he also served briefly as Prime Minister (December 1953–November 1955), a fact that is strangely forgotten by many Israelis.

Like the mind that produced them, Sharett's speeches are lucid, logical, and of impeccable linguistic quality. Unlike those of Ben Gurion, they are free from repetition and messianic imagery. For his articulated image of the global system and his view of Israel's proper role we shall draw from four major speeches at the UN (11 May 1949, 27 September

---

[1] An excellent illustration of Ben Gurion's articulated image before an important and well-reported public forum was his address to the *Knesset* on 1 July 1959: it was devoted mainly to the controversial issue of the sale of arms to Germany, but with broader implications; and there are revealing insights into the Prime Minister's general view of the world. Issued in English translation on the same date by the Government Press Office, Jerusalem.

[2] Professor Morgenthau's 'realist' approach was authoritatively elucidated in his *In Defense of the National Interest*, Alfred A. Knopf, New York, 1951, and *Politics Among Nations*, Alfred A. Knopf, New York, 1948 (1st ed.), 1967 (4th ed.), ch. 1.

[3] Shmuel Lachower (ed.), *The Writings of Moshe Sharett, A Bibliography 1920–1965*, World Zionist Organization, Jerusalem, 1965 (in Hebrew).

[4] *Mashot B'Asia*, Davar, Tel Aviv, 1958.

[5] *Yoman Medini* (Political Diary), Am Oved, Tel Aviv, 1968. This deals with 1936. The importance of Sharett's diary was affirmed by many persons, among them Ze'ev Shek, his Political Secretary at the Foreign Office from 1953 to 1956:
'Sharett worked from his diary. He would first write an account of the day in his diary and, when abroad, he would then send a cable from that account. His diaries are thus a basic source; they will tell his whole story.' Interview in Jerusalem, June 1966.

and 4 October 1950, and 15 November 1951), as well as two before the *Knesset* (4 July 1950 and 23 January 1951) and two in the United States (19 June 1952 and 21 November 1955).[1] Both the similarities with Ben Gurion's image and the points of divergence can be discerned.

i. *Non-Identification*

Until the outbreak of the Korean War both Ben Gurion and Sharett were reluctant to recognize the bipolar character of global politics. Israel's Prime Minister, as noted elsewhere, had declared before the Provisional State Council on 27 September 1948: 'It is incorrect to state that, so far as concerns us, the world is simply divided into East and West, one side being wholly friendly and the other wholly hostile. There could be no greater misrepresentation of the facts. . . . We have friends both in the East and in the West.'[2] Sharett's image, too, was coloured by Israel's unique experience. 'Our acceptance into the family of nations', he said with pride on the occasion of Israel's admission to the UN, 'is of itself a not unhopeful omen. Both the United States and the Union of Soviet Socialist Republics were among those powers which have joined hands in welcoming Israel into the world.'[3] Even in September 1950, when the Korean War had approached a point of acute threat to world peace (the crossing of the 38th parallel by UN forces was then in the air), Sharett was still denying the dangerous bipolarity of international politics. 'To divide the world into two camps', he told the General Assembly, 'is to oversimplify the issue. Even among the countries adhering to the Soviet pattern, uniformity is by no means absolute. In other parts of the world, there prevails a wide diversity of constitutional régimes and social orders.'[4]

One reason for this view was Israel's interest in continued support by both super powers, a prospect which was, at the time, realistic. The other was ideological presupposition—and hope—that the gulf between the two blocs could be bridged: 'The question is, can rival systems coexist peacefully or must their struggle end in deadly clash? . . . Let us be honest and frank. There is no complete certainty in an optimistic answer. . . . The more determined the effort, the greater its chances of triumph.'[5] Sharett, like Ben Gurion, appeared to be infusing

---

[1] Selections from four of these eight speeches, the first and last at the United Nations and the two before American audiences, are to be found in Moshe Sharett, *Israel in a World of Transition*, Ministry for Foreign Affairs, Jerusalem, 1956. A comprehensive collection of Sharett's speeches during the critical period, 1946–9, is to be found in *B'shaar Ha'umot* (At the Gate of the Nations), Am Oved, Tel Aviv, 1958.

[2] *Records of the Provisional State Council* (in Hebrew), Government Printer, Tel Aviv, 1948–9, 20th session, p. 22, as quoted in *Israel and the United Nations*, pp. 183–4.

[3] To the General Assembly of the United Nations on 11 May 1949. *Israel in a World of Transition*, p. 4.

[4] *Statement . . . before the General Assembly of the United Nations, September 27 1950*, Israel Office of Information, New York, GA 68, same date.

[5] Ibid.

his image of the super powers with the traditional Jewish—and Zionist —desire to be friends with all peoples.

This image led both men to a logical advocacy for Israel in world politics—non-alignment with the contending blocs or, in the Israeli variant, *non-identification*. First propounded by Sharett in speeches before the Provisional State Council in 1948, it was an integral part of the foreign policy programme of Israel's first coalition Government: it suited the ideology of (the then pro-Soviet) *Mapam*, as well as the historic Zionist goal of universal friendship, as perceived by Ben Gurion, Sharett and others, and the interests of an infant state surrounded by enemies and daily threatened with extinction.

This policy and its underlying image were strengthened by a shared belief in Israel's uniqueness among modern states. That indeed was another point of similarity in their perception of world politics, though Sharett viewed the uniqueness of Israel in somewhat different terms. This he expressed clearly in a 1952 speech to the Philadelphia World Affairs Council: 'Israel's claim to distinctiveness—not to be mistaken for pretension to superiority [Ben Gurion would never have displayed that humility]—is based on four basic characteristics. First, democracy. . . . Second, social and economic progress. . . . Third, the world's help. . . . Last, the connection with the Jewish people. Of the four, this, perhaps, is by far the most basic and far-reaching consideration. In this regard Israel is indeed unique among the nations of the world.'[1] Ben Gurion would accept all of these, the third, perhaps, grudgingly. He would also stress the last point. But he would—and did—lay even greater emphasis on Israel as 'a light to the nations', on the unbroken four-thousand-year link with her homeland, the transformation of an abnormal urban commercial society into a normal nation, and related 'unique' characteristics.

The perception of Israel's link with world Jewry is the most significant common thread in their images of the global system. Sharett was no less emphatic than BG in asserting Israel's special role:[2]

It exacts no political allegiance from and imposes no constitutional obligation upon any Jew living outside its borders. Yet the spiritual attachment of Jews everywhere to Israel and the moral responsibility which Israel somehow feels for the good name, well-being and safety of Jewish communities in other lands are *cardinal facts of contemporary Jewish history which profoundly influence Israel's conception of its mission and cannot but set their stamp on its international orientation.* . . . We do not propose to divest ourselves of our universal—Jewish and general— associations. They are as much part of our life as our ancient geographic origin and present location.

Ben Gurion would say, 'much more a part of our life'. But the real difference was on the methods of maintaining this link and performing

[1] *Israel in a World of Transition*, pp. 20–1.
[2] Ibid., p. 21 (emphasis added).

Israel's 'mission'. BG assumed responsibility for the welfare of Jews everywhere—'as we define it'—but denied them any role, active or passive, in Israeli policy-making. With Sharett, too, they were outside the policy-making apparatus, but their pressure was regarded as legitimate and often heeded.

ii. *Post-Korean War Shifts*

Sharett appears to have been more committed to the doctrine and the policy of non-identification. For Ben Gurion Israeli interests narrowly conceived were the compelling motive; with Sharett the ideological dimension and the vision of a link between two contending forces also loomed large. For both, however, the trauma of the Korean War necessitated a reappraisal of Israel's basic posture in global politics. Before the year 1950 was over, a pro-Western orientation was already apparent—in word and deed. Sharett tried to retain the stance of non-alignment, partly because of his desire not to alienate, and isolate Israel from, the Third World. At the same time the growing pressure from Washington 'to stand up and be counted' eroded the commitment. Thus, in an important policy declaration to the *Knesset* on 4 July 1950, Sharett foreshadowed the change by postulating a dual meaning to non-identification:[1]

The principle of non-identification [which was reaffirmed] is Israel's way of serving world peace, of making its specific contribution towards preventing a widening of the breach and perhaps, within its restricted means, of helping in narrowing and healing the breach. But this principle . . . cannot be perverted into a repudiation of world peace, nor can it serve as a pretext for running away from responsibility towards the United Nations, nor can it be turned into a weapon which instead of preserving peace might well affect the security of Israel itself.

By the autumn there was more evidence of a pro-Western line—in two speeches at the UN. On 27 September Sharett declared: 'It is fallacious to draw the dividing line between imperialism and the true brotherhood of peoples. Imperialism is not an attribute of social philosophy but a product of physical might. Nor is it true to represent the issue as of capitalism versus socialism.' Further, 'the point at issue is . . . whether a system rightly or wrongly held to be superior by some governments should be imposed by force on other countries. . . .' And again Israel's value affinity to the West, a point often made by Ben Gurion, was stressed: 'Freedom is the very breath of Israel's existence and development. Its democracy is based upon full political and cultural liberty in its internal life and on unrestricted contact of its citizens with the world outside.' It was in this speech, not surprisingly,

[1] *Divrei Ha-Knesset*, 1st Knesset, 2nd Session (1950), vol. vi, p. 2057, as quoted in *Israel and the United Nations*, p. 185.

that Israel indicated her support for the novel Uniting for Peace idea then being mooted by the United States as a way of overcoming the paralysing veto in the Security Council. Sharett tried to maintain a semblance of non-alignment by continuing to advocate the seating of Peking China at the UN—in defiance of the US. He also evinced a lukewarm attitude to the use of force in Korea.[1]

By October Sharett's perception of the struggle over Korea had become indistinguishable from that of America: in the light of the North Korean attitude, he had concluded that 'the occupation of all Korea by the United Nations forces might be the only method to achieve effective unity and peace in Korea'.[2] In short, by September–October 1950 Sharett's image of global politics had changed in the light of the increasing bipolarization created by the Korean War. With it came a change in view about Israel's proper policy—from 'non-identification' to an 'independent' foreign policy which, in practice, meant growing alignment with the West, to the extent that the US, Britain, and France permitted Israel's attachment.

Sharett's image of the Soviet bloc never matched Ben Gurion's harsh perception, however: a difference in tone was evident all through the ensuing years of Soviet hostility to Israel, Zionism, and Jewry—the Prague Trials of 1951–2, the Doctors' Plot, the rupture of diplomatic relations with Moscow, the massive supply of arms to Egypt and Syria, and even the Soviet threats during the Sinai Campaign. His less hostile attitude to the Soviets was undoubtedly due in part to his primary role—diplomacy and the management of Israel's foreign relations: the Soviets were unfriendly, but Israel could not afford the luxury of undisguised alienation of a super power. Sharett's image also owed much to his positive view of Russia and to a lingering hope that, with patience, the Soviet line in the Middle East might change.

There is one other component of a global image which Sharett and Ben Gurion had in common, namely, a sympathetic perception of the Third World. As early as 1951 Sharett addressed himself to the ferment then sweeping Afro-Asia and its implications for international stability:[3]

What we see around us is, in the broadly historic sense of the term, a revolutionary phase, the root cause of which lies in the obsolescence of time-honoured relationships of dependence and sway. . . .

The clash between the Orient and the Occident sometimes mingles with what is usually termed the conflict between East and West. . . . Yet there is no organic unity between them. The historical coincidence of the two struggles need not lead to their political identity. It is vital that it should not. For their merger is fraught with an incalculable aggravation of the world crisis. . . .

[1] Op. cit.
[2] GAOR, 5th Session, 1st Committee, 352nd meeting, 4 Oct. 1950, p. 45, as quoted in *Israel and the United Nations*, p. 229.
[3] To the UN General Assembly on 15 Nov. 1951. *Israel in a World of Transition*, pp. 8–11.

Quite apart from that grave collision [the bloc conflict], differences of race, religion, culture and economic standards, sharpened by complexes arising from close and prolonged relationships of political and social inequality, are liable to grow into unbridgeable gulfs. . . . A synthetic and harmonious solution of the problem entails on both sides courageous forethought, freedom from prejudice and wise restraint.

Sharett did not—at that time—relate the Third World to Israel's security and her foreign policy, though he did express sympathy and support for the coming of independence throughout the non-Western world. Ben Gurion, however, to judge from his writings and speeches, began to recognize this significant aspect of global politics only *at the end* of the 1950s. Even China, which BG wrote and spoke about at length in the sixties, escaped his attention, particularly during the strange episode of embryonic—but unfulfilled—Sino-Israeli relations in 1954-5.[1] Indeed Sharett was much more sensitive to the Third World: it was he who prepared many of the intellectual and policy guidelines for Israel's far-reaching presence in Africa which Golda Meir, his successor as Foreign Minister, was to transform into a major policy initiative from 1958 onwards.

iii. *Differences with BG—the UN, legitimacy, and the 'two-camp thesis'*

The differences in image of global politics held by Ben Gurion and Sharett, while fewer than the points of affinity, had immense policy significance. The UN stood at the core of this contrast in perception. Thus Sharett's view of Israel's essential attachment to the world body in 1947-8 was given renewed expression during the Korean War. To the *Knesset* he declared on 4 July 1950:[2]

The Government of Israel regards the United Nations, first and last, as a union of nations mutually guaranteeing the preservation of peace. This bond of mutual guarantee confers rights and imposes duties. Just as Israel will not waive its rights or claims vis-à-vis the international organization, so she cannot escape her obligations towards it. The force of both claims and responsibilities must endure so long as the organization itself lasts.

But the basic divergence in attitude to the UN was contained in another Sharett speech some months later: 'As a State in the position we find ourselves, we are interested that the United Nations should be strong, not weak. . . .'[3] Ben Gurion, as a realist, perceived the United Nations as a supplementary instrument of Israeli security—as Clemenceau of France perceived the League of Nations. But he *never* attributed to the UN the degree of influence over the course of contemporary inter-

---

[1] Israel's early contacts with China will be examined in a related volume on Israeli high-policy decisions.

[2] Op. cit.

[3] To the *Knesset* on 23 Jan. 1951. *Divrei Ha-Knesset*, 1st Knesset, 3rd Session (1951), vol. viii, p. 928, as quoted in *Israel and the United Nations*, p. 223.

national politics, in the Middle East or elsewhere, that Sharett almost always did. And yet, on occasion, Sharett echoed the Ben Gurion 'self-reliance' line. Thus in November 1955, following the sharp disequilibrium in the Arab–Israel arms balance caused by Soviet bloc military aid to Egypt and Syria, he declared:[1]

Israel owes her restoration to independence . . . in no small measure to the awakening of world conscience. . . . Yet moral solidarity alone cannot be adequate. . . . As a State surrounded on all its land borders by hostile forces, Israel's primary preoccupation must be her security. . . . Israel's first and paramount need in this hour is additional arms.

As one of Ben Gurion's admirers acknowledged, 'certainly Sharett was sensitive to the security factor in foreign policy; but he believed his methods were better; he attached great importance to world opinion and the attitudes of other states'.[2]

A closely-related difference in global system perception pertains to legitimacy: this too derived from the contrasting images of the road to statehood. For Ben Gurion Israel achieved that status when she proclaimed her independence and established its *de facto* conditions— control over a defined territory, a stable government, the habitual obedience of her people, etc.; that is, self-rule, internally induced. For Sharett statehood was legitimated when Israel was formally accepted by the international community and was admitted into the United Nations. Thus he told the General Assembly on 11 May 1949 that UN admission was 'the consummation of a people's transition from political anonymity to clear identity, from inferiority to equal status, from mere *passive* protest to *active* responsibility, from exclusion to membership in the family of nations'.[3] Many Israelis were appalled by what they interpreted to be a tone of servility in these words. To the *Knesset* Sharett added: 'By our admission to the United Nations, the highest seal has been placed on our international recognition.'[4] Stated in different terms, Ben Gurion adhered to the declaratory or subjective view of recognition, while Sharett expounded the constitutive or objective view—which attributed a creative role to recognition by the international community.

There is another contrast in outlook—Sharett's greater awareness of the economic dimension in foreign policy. On many occasions, especially in the early years, he expressed concern about the large gap in Israel's

[1] To the National Press Club in Washington, 21 Nov. 1955. *Israel in a World of Transition*, p. 24.

[2] Yitzhak Navon, interview in Tel Aviv, May 1966.

[3] GAOR, 3rd Session, 2nd Part, 207th Plenary Meeting, 11 May 1949, p. 332, as quoted in *Israel and the United Nations*, p. 30. Strangely, this important passage is not included in the selection from this speech contained in Sharett's *Israel in a World of Transition*.

[4] On 15 June 1949. *Divrei Ha-Knesset*, 1st Knesset, 1st Session (1949), vol. i, p. 717, as quoted in *Israel and the United Nations*, p. 50.

balance of payments and its consequences. Typical is the following remark in 1952: 'The crux of our problem is production. Our present balance of trade is staggeringly adverse . . . [and this] creates a state of high economic tension. . . .'[1] Ben Gurion displayed an olympian indifference to economic problems though, as noted, he gave prominence to this aspect of security—verbally. When confronted with its reality he referred to will, daring, and determination, which would certainly overcome these mundane difficulties. Sharett had a more balanced image of the instruments of statecraft, with an awareness of the interplay of military, political, and economic components. Ben Gurion emphasized the first and ignored the third. Indeed during the War of Independence his perception was described by a colleague as follows: 'As far as Ben Gurion was concerned the concept of "State" in those days had no other significance than as an instrument for war.' And BG himself was recalled as having said, 'I find it difficult now to understand any other language than the language of war. . . . I feel that the wisdom of Israel *now* is the wisdom to wage war, that and nothing else, that and only that.'[2] Undoubtedly that trauma and the condition of permanent war left their mark on his perception during the next two decades.

The state of siege, superimposed on the pervasive Jewish prism, gave rise to the most distinctive element in Ben Gurion's image of the global system—the two-camp thesis. Israel and world Jewry constitute one camp, the rest of the world the other. BG acknowledged that some non-Jews and even some non-Jewish states, for example, Holland, Belgium, and the Scandinavian countries, are unselfishly friendly to Israel; but these are exceptions. More to the point, the only *completely reliable* ally of Israel is the Jewish People, as demonstrated in 1948, 1956, and 1967, and on innumerable occasions, less dramatic, during the years of independence. The two are inevitably and inextricably interlocked, members of one family who are bound together by a thousand ties of history, religion, culture, sentiment, and experience. There is a slight difference in the degree of dependence: 'The future of Israel . . . depends on world Jewry. And the future of world Jewry depends on the *survival* of Israel.' But the two-camp image is unmistakable: 'Do not forget that although Israel enjoys the friendship of many nations it is the only country which has no self-governing "relatives" from the point of view of religion, language, origin or culture. . . . The only *permanent loyal* "relatives" we have is the Jewish people.'[3] Ben Gurion expressed this view frequently.[4] Sharett, too, valued the support

[1] 'Israel and the Near East', text of Sharett address to the World Affairs Council of Philadelphia, 19 June 1952, p. 2.
[2] Ze'ev Sharef, *Three Days*, p. 191.
[3] *Ben Gurion Looks Back* . . . , pp. 241, 247 (emphasis added).
[4] To this writer, among others. Interview in Sde Boker, July 1966.

of Jewry but never subscribed to the extreme bifurcation of global politics symbolized by the notion of two camps, Jewish and non-Jewish.

(e) IMAGES OF 'THE MIDDLE EAST'

Like most states, Israel has always been more concerned with what Ben Gurion called the 'small sphere' than with global politics: in her case this is a logical consequence of an exposed location and acute permanent conflict with her neighbours. Within that sphere there are two interrelated strands of the Israeli élite's Psychological Environment, 'the Middle East' and 'the Arabs'. The first is a political, territorial, regional 'system' concept. The second is a societal, cultural, state-of-mind idea filtered through the Attitudinal Prism of Israelis. The two often overlap, especially since most decision-makers do not perceive their setting in precise schematic terms. Nevertheless, 'the Middle East' and 'the Arabs' are analytically distinct components of their View of the World.

The Middle East Subordinate System was defined earlier as comprising three concentric circles of states—designated as Core, Periphery, and Outer Ring—with changing composition and structural and textural features over a twenty-year period; three phases were noted, 1948–55/6, 1956–67, and 1967– .[1] How valid is this construct from the Operational Environment (reality) for the Psychological Environment (image) of Israeli leaders like Ben Gurion and Sharett? A few denied its validity altogether or claimed that, at most, this 'system' is ephemeral, its membership changing for each decision.[2] The majority of persons interviewed, however, including senior Israeli Foreign Ministry officials, affirmed the existence of a 'Middle East System' in the perception of Israeli decision-makers, a well-defined regional framework whose composition has changed gradually over the years; further, that there is a hierarchy of actors, their importance varying with issues. But there is a consensus view of 'the Middle East' as the durable primary setting in which Israel must operate.

Two periods were perceived in the evolution of this system—1948 to 1962, and 1962 to 1968. In the first phase 'the Middle East' comprised the six Arab neighbours or near-neighbours of Israel—Egypt, Jordan, Syria, Lebanon, Iraq, and Saudi Arabia—and Israel herself; in Ben Gurion's phrase, 'the Bible lands'.[3] Sudan was marginal to the system, even after her independence, while Turkey, Iran, and Ethiopia were

[1] See ch. 3 above.

[2] This view was stated most vigorously—and unpersuasively—by *Aluf* (Major-General) Y. Harkabi, Chief of Military Intelligence from 1955 to 1959 and later a Senior Lecturer on International Relations at the Hebrew University. Interview in Tel Aviv, Oct. 1965.

[3] 'Israel's Security and Her International Position . . .'. Ben Gurion listed the Bible lands as Israel, Egypt, Mesopotamia, Syria, and Canaan, in that order.

regarded, from the mid-1950s onwards, as 'the Periphery'. The 'Periphery doctrine' was designed to create the image, in the region and in the world at large, that 'the Middle East' is not exclusively Arab or even Islamic but rather a multi-religious, ethnic, cultural, and national area. Its initiator was Reuven Shiloah, a Foreign Office specialist, but it was Ben Gurion who gave it policy significance:[1]

The Middle East is not an exclusively Arab area; on the contrary, the majority of its inhabitants are not Arabs. The Turks, the Persians and the Jews—without taking into account the Kurds and the other non-Arab minorities in the Arab States—are more numerous than the Arabs in the Middle East, and it is possible that through contacts with the peoples of the outer zone of the area we shall achieve friendship with the peoples of the inner zone, who are our immediate neighbours.

The major perceived change was the coming of independence to Algeria in 1962: at that point all three Maghreb states joined the Middle East System, in the Israeli view, even though Morocco and Tunisia had been independent since 1956. Yet they remain in the 'outer zone'. So too did Kuwait and Libya, South Yemen and Sudan until after the 1967 War: the first two entered the system, as perceived by Israelis, when they began to subsidize Egypt and Jordan with oil-derived revenues, the latter two with the emergence of militant leftist régimes which identified more vocally with the core Arab states in the conflict with Israel. Thus the Israeli élite image of 'the Middle East' is not fundamentally different from the construct as academically designed. The phases are not identical, but the concepts of Core, Periphery, and Outer Ring (or zone) are present. To Israelis 'the Middle East' is a 'permanent' conflict system. Actors are perceived at the time and with the intensity of their alignment with Israel's enemies in the Core, notably Egypt and Syria; hence the greater importance given to Algeria and Sudan than to Morocco and Tunisia. The system has been correctly perceived in dynamic terms, changing over time—slowly—and with issues.

Members of Israel's High Policy Élite have not often articulated an image of 'the Middle East' as a state system. Ben Gurion did so on occasion. Thus in his essay, 'Israel Among the Nations', he perceived the Middle East as comprising six independent Arab states—Lebanon, Syria, Jordan, Iraq, Saudi Arabia, and the Yemen—with an area 170 times as large as Israel and a population, in 1952, 13 times as large. With the addition of Egypt the proportions increased to 215 and 27 times, respectively. Of this Arab core, all but Jordan were UN members, 'a single solid bloc'. With realism he remarked: 'Never once in the past was the State of Israel girdled at all points by a tight ring of that

[1] Ibid., p. 86. Abba Eban, before he became Israel's Foreign Minister, also enunciated the 'Periphery doctrine' in his important essay, 'Reality and Vision in the Middle East', *Foreign Affairs* (New York), vol. 43, no. 4, July 1965, pp. 632, 634–5.

kind. And it is a bloc that is likely to grow, for we may assume that Tunis, Algeria and Morocco as well will become autonomous . . . and be admitted, with Libya also, to the . . . United Nations.' And to this bloc he added most Islamic states—Pakistan, Persia, Afghanistan, and Indonesia—which support the Arabs 'as a matter of course in . . . their attitude towards Israel'. 'This, then,' concluded Ben Gurion, 'is the sweep of the problem of security and of politics which the Arab countries present to the young State of Israel', as perceived in 1952.[1] And yet, later in the same essay, he remarked about the prospects of war:[2] '. . . we may utter a word of warning against undue alarm. For all the satanic hatred of us common to the Arab States, they are themselves far from united inside or outside . . . so that the power to act is blunted and cannot quickly be tempered, although we must not therefore suppose that the Arabs are not capable of reforms and domestic progress.'

In his 'Israel Among the Nations' Ben Gurion referred to three 'domains'—world, Middle East, and Diaspora Jewry. The conception of different zones or spheres of foreign policy was made more explicit in his 'Israel's Security and Her International Position . . .': 'Ever since the foundation of the State, Israel faces a combined military and political array of forces, in two spheres; in the "small" sphere of our own area, which includes the Bible lands . . . and the large sphere, which comprises the entire globe.'[3] Long before that, in the midst of the War of Independence, Ben Gurion had a clear perception of the two spheres and their interaction. In his memoirs he recalled an important foreign policy discussion in the Provisional Government on 27 September 1948:[4]

The Prime Minister [Ben Gurion] declared that the Foreign Minister expressed the Government's stand and that there is nothing to add to his words, but that there is a need to clarify several basic assumptions upon which the foreign policy of the State of Israel must be based. One assumption: we stand in a *combined campaign, both military and political, and there is an interdependence between the two campaigns*, and it must not be thought that only one of these two factors, military or political, will be ultimately decisive. The second assumption: in this double campaign there are *two circles of interest of power relations* and of their conflicts: a *small circle of Jews and Arabs in the Middle East*, and a *large circle of world powers*—and there too there is struggle. If only the small circle had existed, then only the military factor would have determined the outcome. . . . But the small circle alone is not decisive, and in the big circle various powers clash, helpful and hostile. And it seems that in this period our superiority in the military sphere is greater than in the political, because the balance of world powers is not entirely in our favour. Therefore it seems to me that we should not rely on the political campaign alone. Yet the military campaign alone . . .

---

[1] Op. cit., pp. 14–15.   [2] Ibid., p. 25.   [3] Op. cit., p. 57.
[4] *Medinat Yisrael Ha-mehudeshet*, vol. 1, pp. 291–2 (emphasis added).

will not determine the outcome because there are forces in the world that will not permit this.

It is an error to think that the big circle is simply divided into East and West. . . .

Sharett, too, articulated an image of 'the Middle East' but as a region, not a circle or sphere or system. His focus of attention was primarily on the Core. Thus in 1953 he declared: 'If the Middle East is a region then Israel is the center of it.'[1] A year earlier, however, in a speech ostensibly devoted to 'Israel and the Near East', the only reference to 'the Middle East' was to 'the entire crescent of Arab countries encompassing it [Israel] and to the Arab hinterland beyond', which may be taken to symbolize the Core and the Outer Ring or, in Ben Gurion's terms, the 'inner zone' and the 'outer zone'.[2] Usually Sharett concentrated on Israel's immediate neighbours, but the wider grouping of Arab states was invoked to stress the injustice of the Arab claim to territory in the conflict with Israel. 'The ratio between the area of Israel and the combined territories of the Arab States is about 1 : 300', he declared in 1955. 'The idea that Israel must accept a shrinkage in order that the Arab States should expand [Anthony Eden's proposal at the time] is singular indeed.'[3]

(f) 'THE ARABS': THREE ISRAELI IMAGES

Israeli images of 'the Arabs' as a world, mind, society, people, or enemy are much more acute. In fact they are central to the View of the World held by makers of high policy. And their contrasting perceptions are crucial to the developing conflict over policy between Ben Gurion and Sharett in the period 1953–6. Their views assume added significance when related to a threefold typology of Israeli images of 'the Arabs'.[4]

'Buberism' (reconciliation through compromise), named after the distinguished philosopher, Martin Buber, who during his years in Palestine-Israel made a sustained effort at reconciliation between the two nations. In essence its line of argument is as follows: Judaism is a religion of high moral standards; injustice has been done to the Arabs; therefore Israel must expiate these immoral acts. There is no more poignant expression of this view than the following passage from Buber's writings, entitled 'The Samsonites':

[1] 'Israel and the Middle East', Address before the National Press Club, Washington, 10 April 1953. Israel Office of Information, New York, 1953, p. 6.

[2] Israel in a World of Transition, p. 17.

[3] Ibid., p. 26.

[4] The content of this typology, but not its nomenclature, was suggested by one of the most thoughtful members of Israel's Technical Élite, Mordekhai Gazit, Minister to the United States, 1960–5, later Adviser, and at the time of a series of interviews in Jerusalem, 1966, Assistant Director-General of the Ministry for Foreign Affairs, in charge of the Middle East.

When we returned to our Land after many hundreds of years, we behaved
as if it were void of inhabitants—no, worse than this, as if the population we
encountered was not our concern, as if we did not have to care for it; that is to
say, as if it did not perceive us. But it did. It saw us, not with such clarity, a
clarity with which we would have perceived them, had we been natives and
another people had come in ever greater numbers to settle [on the land];
not with this clarity, but clear enough; and, as is natural, with ever-increasing
clarity from year to year. We did not pay attention to this. We did not pay
attention to ourselves. There is only one way to behave in the light of this
increasingly conspicuous spectacle: to co-operate honourably with this population, to involve it in the development of the country, in our work and its
fruit. . . . And to those who pointed to an ever-blossoming Arab nationalist
movement, we replied that that did not have to be considered, or that we
could handle it. And from this events turned out as they did. . . .

The question—whom did [the Arabs] see in the role of Philistines infil-
trating into their country, the British or us—can possibly be left unanswered;
my own hypothesis is, 'Both as one'.[1]

This image, shared by the old *Ihud* bi-national group of Buber and
Magnes with *Mapam*, *New Outlook*, scattered voices in the universities
and muted dissent in the Foreign Ministry and elsewhere, leads logically
to a *policy of concessions*. The substance varies among groups and in
different periods, but the main thrust is towards concessions for peace.

'*Ben Gurionism*' (reconciliation resulting from superior strength). This
image, which stands at the other extreme of the spectrum, may be
defined thus: we Jews have been persecuted for two thousand years; at
last we have recovered this notch of territory in our historic homeland;
the Arabs should have received us warmly as cousins; instead they are
trying to create another ghetto by blockade, boycott, etc. First Haman,
then Eichmann, now Nasser and Shukairy—they are out to destroy us;
and we will not permit it. The core of 'Ben Gurionism' or 'the little
notch' image is the belief that 'the Arabs' are incapable of accepting
peaceful coexistence at this time. Thus Israel must show her fist and
display it often. The consequence was frequent resort to force, which
was given its classic expression in the *policy of retaliation* under Ben
Gurion and Dayan during 1955–6. In the post-Six Day War period it
takes the form, with many, 'don't yield an inch'. There is the further
component that, if Israel can maintain the image (and the reality) of
permanent invincibility, this will cause a change of heart among 'the
Arabs'.

'*Weizmannism*' (reconciliation through rational search for moderate
solutions). The basic premise of this view is that the Arab–Israel confrontation is *not* an abnormal international conflict; rather, that it is an

[1] *Te'uda V'ye'ud* (Testimony and Destiny), vol. II, *People and World*, Sifriyat Tzyonit,
Jerusalem, 1967, p. 331. A prominent publicist of the Buberist persuasion, Dr. Simon
Shereshevsky, dissented from the notion that Buber believed Israel must 'expiate
these immoral acts'—in a letter to this writer dated 4 Oct. 1970. The above extract
would suggest the contrary.

acute and prolonged dispute but within the realm of the 'normal' and should be treated as such. Further, the conflict cannot be resolved by a dramatic single act but only by a series of seemingly inconspicuous measures over time. And thirdly, its proponents contend that Israel, initially the 'David' in the region, became the 'Goliath' by the early 1960s and should have taken the initiative.

In policy terms the key is a change in atmosphere, a lowering of the general level of tension by constructive acts. One would have been to reorient the tone and substance of *Kol Yisrael*'s Arab-language broadcasts—to eliminate all degrading references to Arab culture, politics, etc. Another would have been to enlarge direct contact by gently persuading Lebanon to permit direct movement of tourists to Israel through a border gate at Rosh Hanikra. Still another would have been to establish a genuine dialogue with Arab students at North American and European universities, to attain, gradually, their acceptance of the fact of Israel and the ultimate possibilities of positive peaceful coexistence, for these are the future leaders of Arab society. A fourth step would have been to try to create, however intermittent and indirect, Israeli contact with Arab leaders so that the transmission of ideas, proposals, postures could be accomplished by mutually-trusted third parties. While some argued that such actions were feasible in the mid-sixties, when some tentative steps were actually taken, the cataclysm of the Six Day War made all efforts at reconciliation through rational discourse even more remote and impracticable.

(g) 'THE ARABS': BEN GURION'S PERCEPTION

Ben Gurion was a 'Ben Gurionist' during most of his tenure in office, and Sharett belonged, throughout, to the third school; the first has never commanded much support in Israel. Yet Ben Gurion did not always perceive 'the Arabs' in suspicious, hard-line terms. On the eve of independence and during the early years of statehood he (publicly) perceived a natural harmony of interests, which was temporarily blurred by fanaticism and hate, and he advocated 'a Jewish–Arab alliance'. This is evident in three brief extracts:[1]

(1) The historic interests and aspirations of the Jews and Arabs are . . . complementary and inter-connected. . . . Cooperation between Jews and Arabs will prove the truest blessing for both peoples. Such cooperation can rest only upon equality . . . [upon a] Jewish–Arab alliance. . . .

(4 July 1947 to UNSCOP)

(2) We extend the hand of peace and good neighbourliness to all the neighbouring states and their peoples and invite their cooperation. . . .

(Declaration of Independence, 14 May 1948)

[1] As quoted in 'On Peace and Negotiations', *New Outlook* (Tel Aviv), vol. 6, no. 1 (50), Jan. 1963, pp. 41–2.

(3) Israel wishes to see Egypt free, independent, progressing. . . . We have no
enmity against Egypt. . . . We have never sought to exploit Egypt's political
difficulties with a Great Power [England]. . . .

(To the *Knesset*, 18 August 1952)

In 1948, too, as he recalled, he welcomed the idea of a customs union
with Jordan; further, 'we can also participate in a federation, but only
as a fully independent state'.[1] By 1954, however, a deep suspicion had
taken root in Ben Gurion's image.

From his reading of the Nasser-led revolution in Egypt and the
failure of various sub-rosa efforts at negotiation—'I personally was
involved in four attempts at mediation with Nasser'—he became committed to a 'realistic' view.[2] Its essence is that Israel lives in an inherently
hostile Arab world, that the best one can work for is acceptance of
Israel, and that the only way to achieve this is to hammer away at the
Arab states whenever possible—a policy of strength, for this is all the
Arabs respect. A soft line, the argument proceeds, would weaken
Israeli security by giving hope to those Arab groups who look for signs
of weakness and an opportunity to destroy Israel. In short, one cannot
buy security with concessions. Thus Israel must persist with a strong
line until 'the Arabs' become reconciled to her existence.

The long-term goal, as with the 'Weizmannist' approach, is positive
coexistence after twenty years or more of hostile acquiescence. The
'Ben Gurionists' assert, however, that no alternative to a hard line
exists, for the Arabs do not have a compelling motive for peace. The
absence of an incentive for a settlement is attributed to three factors:
self-delusion—'the Arabs' are victims of their own propaganda about
Israel's survival potential; *idealism*—'the Arabs' genuinely feel the
obliteration of the Palestine Arab community and the alienness of
Israel, which they would like to eliminate; and *self-interest* in the perpetuation of the conflict—Israel provides an excellent focus for Arab
unity. Nasser can always negotiate with Israel—why now, the question
was posed before the 1967 War. If Israel were to offer to repatriate one

[1] *Medinat Yisrael Ha-mehudeshet*, vol. 1, p. 218.
[2] Ben Gurion elaborated on this 'secret' at an informal meeting of the Israel Institute
of International Affairs in June 1965. Two of these attempts, he said, were initiated
by Americans, one an emissary of President Eisenhower and the other 'a very high
State Department official'. The third attempt was by an English journalist who had
interviewed Nasser. The fourth, which Ben Gurion related to this writer in detail at
Sde Boker in July 1966, was through an Israeli friend of Tito who tried to establish
contact when Nasser was in Yugoslavia (in July 1956). Nothing came of these efforts
added Ben Gurion. As reported by Mark Segal in the *Jerusalem Post*, 29 June 1965.
   Shortly after Nasser's death in September 1970, Ben Gurion revealed further details
concerning some of these contacts, notably in 1956 via Robert Anderson, a former
US Secretary of Defense. And he divulged details of an abortive Nasser expression
of interest in meeting him in 1963. Indeed, added BG, eight days before his death
Nasser told someone he wanted to meet him as soon as possible. Interview in *L'Actualité*
(Paris), reproduced in *Ha'aretz* (Tel Aviv), 12 Oct. 1970.

hundred thousand refugees, why should Nasser accept this as sufficient for peace? He could take this as a starting point and wait for more; so too with territorial adjustments. Moreover, he could hope that Soviet arms and a shift in American strategic policy would enable him to destroy Israel. If not, he could always meet the Israelis at a later date. In short, as long as there is no Arab *need* for peace there will be no peace. This 'Ben Gurionist' image and its policy consequence—firmness as the key to acceptance—commanded widespread support in Israel. The perception that there were no compelling Arab motives for immediate peace was plausible *until the Six Day War of 1967*. The critical question is whether this view was valid after 'the third round'. Most Israelis appeared to think so in 1970; BG himself has not, since that War.

Ben Gurion expressed these views frequently from 1955 onwards with varying points of emphasis. A few illustrations of this image may be cited:[1]

(1) Peace and cooperation with the Arabs . . . must always be our major objective. . . . But I have no illusions about peace with the Arabs. . . . I doubt if we shall get it until there are thoroughly stable governments in the Arab States instead of cliques.

(Interview with correspondent of *The Times*, London, as reported in the *Jerusalem Post*, 29 August 1955)

(2) Peace cannot be achieved until the Arabs, or rather the Arab leaders, will be persuaded they cannot destroy Israel either by economic boycott or by political pressures or by military offensives. . . . And no foreign Government can compel the Arabs to make peace.

(Interview with Golda Zimmerman, 25 March 1958)

(3) The hope of peace depends on three factors: whether democracy will grow in the Arab countries, whether our neighbours will realize that it will not be easy to destroy Israel, and whether world tension will be less than it is now. . . .   (To foreign correspondents, 2 February 1959)

Yet his early call to Israel's neighbours to forge a co-operative relationship was reaffirmed from time to time. Thus in 1965, soon after Tunisia's President Bourguiba urged a new Arab look at Israel, Ben Gurion told the *Knesset*: 'We should not also ignore the isolated voices that emerge here and there among some of the Arab peoples, from those who adopt a sober and realistic view of Israel–Arab relations . . . those Arabs who aspire for peace.'[2] And in March 1967 he predicted that, when peace came, Israel would be able to find her place 'even in some loose form of Middle Eastern Federation'.[3] Paradoxically, BG had subjected the same idea to sharp criticism when it was mooted by Nahum Goldmann during the 1961 Israel election campaign: then,

---

[1] The last two of the following extracts were made available by the Government Press Office in Jerusalem.

[2] *Jerusalem Post*, 23 Nov. 1965.

[3] *The Israel Digest*, Jerusalem, vol. x, no. 7, 7 April 1967.

Ben Gurion had lashed out at 'the important visitor from New York', ridiculed the idea of integrating with the Arab world, and accused Goldmann of 'knowingly misleading the public'.[1]

The main thrust of Ben Gurion's image of 'the Arabs' and his related policy lay in the realm of toughness and no compromise. Only after the Six Day War did he perceive a compelling Arab need for peace—and the logical derivative, a policy of concessions. Not by accident did he advocate a virtual return to the 4 June borders, apart from Jerusalem and the Golan Heights—in exchange for a genuine peace settlement.[2] (He continued to advocate this in 1970: 'We should evacuate all territories conquered in June 1967, except Jerusalem and the Golan Heights. There is enough room in Israel, as it was before the Six Day War, to receive all future Jewish immigrants, and that is all that matters.')[3]

(h) 'THE ARABS': SHARETT'S IMAGE OF THE TWO SCHOOLS

This writer's perception of the Ben Gurion image was put to Sharett in 1960. His response was revealing: 'The summary is correct and the line is correct. However, this is not all. To demonstrate firmness and strength, yes. But one must also understand that the Arabs are proud and sensitive. The Arabs are people, not just enemies.' When pressed to elaborate, he remarked that his difference with Ben Gurion was one of 'style not substance' and 'tactics not strategy', a 'mode of approach or language based on understanding of the Arabs' character'. As an example he referred to the expectation (among 'Ben Gurionists') that the Sinai Campaign would lead to peace. For Sharett this was 'an illusion, an absurdity—because the Arabs rally to their leaders under pressure'.[4]

The most incisive comparison of the Ben Gurion and Sharett images of 'the Arabs' was provided by Sharett himself in a brilliant lecture one year after the Sinai Campaign; its contents were made public only nine years later, after his death.[5] As always his analysis was lucid and intellectually honest.

[1] See Appendix B, p. 581 below.
[2] In various statements and interviews during June–Aug. 1967 and reiterated frequently thereafter.
[3] Interview with *Le Nouvel Observateur*, 15 Nov. 1970, as reported in the *Jerusalem Post*, 16 Nov. 1970.
[4] Interview in Jerusalem, July 1960. (This would seem to be borne out by the support of Egyptians for Nasser during his hour of greatest defeat—June 1967—and again in the winter–spring of 1969/70, during Israel's 'deep penetration' raids.)
[5] The lecture was delivered in November 1957 at Beit Berl, the *Mapai* study centre. The text was published in the first issue of *Ot*, the short-lived quarterly of the *Mapai*-*Ahdut Ha'avodah* Alignment, in October 1966. A translation of the bulk of this lecture, from which the following extracts are taken, appeared in the *Jerusalem Post*, 18 Oct. 1966 (emphasis added).

There was, first, a gentle chiding at the Jewish failure to understand Arab psychology:

We were so filled with the sense of the historical justice of our claim that we did not consider how this justice looked from the other side. . . . Nor did we realize the depth of national consciousness in *the Arab world*.

On the self-satisfying belief that material gain is a substitute for nationalism:

We offered the Arabs economic advantages and social progress, but with total disregard of the national question. After all, we had never expected that two-thirds of the Arab population of this country would suddenly uproot itself and leave. We had expected to live together. . . .

We offered them a mass of economic and social pottage . . . and expected them to sell their national birthright. When I say this I am looking at it with Arab eyes. . . . [Was Ben Gurion capable of this empathy?]

On Israeli perceptions immediately after the War of Independence:

Far more significant [than Israeli achievements during the War] was that the Arab States signed this revolutionary agreement [the Armistice Agreements] with the State of Israel, explicitly . . . and that this agreement was understood as an intermediate stage to peace. We thought the Arabs had accepted it . . . even if it might take a few years still. *We all thought it, without any exception. . . . We thought the Arab world was ready for peace, and this became our greatest disappointment.*

The illusion was renewed after the Sinai Campaign, Sharett said; and

The question of peace will not be solved either by material arguments or by logic. . . . It is ultimately a matter of willingness . . . whether we create an atmosphere conducive to peace or at least remove mental obstacles to peace.

There were, said Sharett, certain basic elements in an Israeli consensus about how to approach Arab hostility:

The first basic element is *security*. The territorial integrity of the State of Israel, the lives of its citizens, their property, freedom of movement, work and develop-ment—these must be defended at all costs. *In this sphere, there can be no compromise and no withdrawal.* . . .

The second basic element is the Arab *refugee problem*. . . . I feel one can safely say that the point of view in this country generally opposes the return of the refugees; and *this view is justified*, in the short as well as the long term [but he acknowledged the need for a broadened scheme of reunion of families].

There is a third basic element on which all are agreed, including 'Herut': Israel's vision, and her eventual political objective, is not eternal warfare, but *peace* with the neighbouring Arab peoples.

But these common elements do not solve the day-to-day policy prob-lems, he added.

. . . two approaches indeed exist.

The *one approach* says that the only language the Arabs understand is force. The State of Israel is so tiny and so isolated . . . that if it does not increase its actual strength by a very high coefficient of demonstrated action, it will run into trouble. From time to time, the State of Israel must give unmistakable proof of its strength, and show that it is able and ready to use force in a crushing and highly effective manner. If it does not give such proof, it will be engulfed and may even disappear from the face of the earth.

As far as peace is concerned—says this school of thought—it is doubtful in any event; whatever happens, it is very remote. If peace comes, that will only be when the Arabs are convinced that this country cannot be brought to its knees. . . . The problem of peace, therefore, need not hamper our considerations when it comes to deciding on some large-scale show of strength to solve a problem of everyday security. . . .

If we add to these arguments the natural human inclination to react; if we add the special sensitivity characteristic of the Jew that people may perhaps suspect him of weakness; if we add the proximity in time to the Golden Age of our triumph in war . . .—we shall understand the factors behind the atmosphere fostering this approach, over and above the political and military considerations, which are very weighty in themselves.

According to the *second school of thought*, the question of peace must not be lost sight of for one single moment. This is not solely a political consideration; in the long view, it is decisive from a military point of view. Without diminishing the importance of considerations of day-to-day security, we must always bring the question of peace into our overall calculations. We have to curb our reactions. And the question always remains: has it really been proven that reprisals establish the security for which they were planned? . . .

Do people consider that when military reactions outstrip in their severity the events that caused them, grave processes are set in motion which widen the gulf and thrust our neighbours into the extremist camp? How can this deterioration be halted? . . .

Those who support the first approach say that the development of events was inevitable. Arab hatred of Israel is an immutable element of the situation. The integration of the Arab–Israel dispute into the Cold War has become a part of world realities . . . and the danger to Israel inevitably increased. In the absence of a vigorous reaction, things would have been worse . . . it was only thanks to the victories we won that our security was assured. . . . The situation is grave; we do not claim that everything is fine as it is; but in our grim circumstances this approach has won us very considerable achievements.

It is difficult, indeed, to query these achievements. None the less it is possible to argue that if we had adopted a different approach, if we had sought to minimize incidents rather than play them up, if we had not taken the course of Kibya [December 1953], Gaza [February 1955] and so forth, then the political deployment of the other side would have assumed a different pattern. Nasser might perhaps not have been *forced* into the Czech deal, and the Soviet Union might not have found such an easy opening for its penetration of the Middle East. We might have suffered a little more in the meantime, but our overall situation would have been less serious.

Always the intellectual, groping for truth, Sharett asked,

Who was right? It may be found that the two approaches should have been synthesized. It may be determined that such vacillation would have a harmful effect. . . . I cannot overlook the organic complexity of the problem.

Lest there be any doubt that he was not a 'Buberist', Sharett remarked,

I utterly reject the approach that it is permissible to ask Israel for any concessions whatsoever for the sake of peace. I refute the thesis that the peace can be purchased at the price of concessions. Peace can be bought at the price of mutual advantages (like a corridor to the Mediterranean for Jordan or a free port area in Haifa). . . . It would be a concession if we curtailed immigration for the sake of peace. Suggestions like that are not open for discussion. They will not bring peace any closer. If we start adopting that course, the Arabs will say: we were stubborn for ten years—now we are beginning to falter.

He agreed with Ben Gurion's statement *at the time* that

only the Powers are in a position to alleviate the tension now. But I do not believe we can clear Israeli policy from all responsibility. . . . *What we do is worth something. Even what we say is worth something.*
    The matter is complex. . . .

Sharett's forecast did not differ from that of Ben Gurion, namely, that it may take decades to achieve peace. Yet his analysis illuminated the fundamental divergence in their image of 'the Arabs', the cause, he acknowledged, of his resignation from the Government in June 1956.[1] That basic disagreement in perception of 'the Arabs' and the approach to peace continues in the period following the Six Day War, with Dayan and Eban as the principal exponents of the two approaches summarized by Sharett with remarkable objectivity.

In the language of image analysis Ben Gurion revealed an 'inherently bad faith' perception of 'the Arabs'; the 'Buberists' adhered to the 'inherently good faith' model; and Sharett's image was characterized by empathy and firmness—without rigidity. The commanding figure of Ben Gurion in foreign and security policy has few parallels—Adenauer, de Gaulle, Mao, Nehru, Stalin, and during the Second World War, Churchill and Roosevelt. Yet his perception of 'the Arabs' bears the most striking resemblance to the John Foster Dulles image of 'the enemy'. The influence of the US Secretary of State on American foreign policy from 1953 to 1959 is generally regarded as massive. Ben Gurion's influence on Israeli foreign policy was even greater—and for a longer period. There were some common factors—an elaborate conception of their role, frequent crises, widespread support from their publics, intellectual arrogance, and a deep-rooted, carefully rationalized image of 'the enemy'. Ben Gurion had, however, an even wider latitude, by virtue of his role as 'father of the nation', and for many years almost universally trusted Head of Government and Defence Minister.
    A recent study of Dulles's image of Soviet Russia has given rise to some general conclusions about foreign policy images which are rele-

[1] This will be examined in the discussion of policy formulation in ch. 15 (*b*) i below.

vant to this part of our inquiry.[1] One seems a truism but worth noting nonetheless: 'When decision-makers for both parties to a conflict adhere to rigid images of each other . . . meaningful communication with adversaries, much less resolution of the conflict, [is] almost impossible.' This is the burden of Sharett's plea for another approach to 'the enemy'. More substantive conclusions by Ole Holsti are the following:[2]

(1) Inherent bad faith models in effect rule out the existence of data which might challenge the model itself. . . . Under these circumstances it is unrealistic to expect that single acts, or even a short series of acts, can break down high tensions and mutual distrust. [The Arab–Israel conflict illustrates this proposition.]

(2) If decreasing hostility is assumed to arise from weakness and frustration and if the other party is defined as inherently evil, there is little cause to reciprocate. Rather, there is every reason to press further, believing that added pressure will at least insure the continued good conduct of the adversary and perhaps even cause the enemy to collapse. As a result, perceptions of low hostility are self-liquidating, and perceptions of high hostility are self-fulfilling. [Certainly this is confirmed by the pre-1967 Ben Gurion image and pattern of behaviour.]

(3) In summary. . . . If the major premise defining an enemy as implacable is *incorrect*, opportunities for peaceful resolution of differences are almost certain to be lost. . . . [This is the essence of Sharett's critique.]

While these conclusions are relevant to Arab images of Israel and Israeli images of 'the Arabs', it is necessary to reaffirm the central thesis of this chapter: Ben Gurion and Sharett articulated contrasting Views of the World, both at the global level and in the Middle East; and these images led them inescapably to different foreign policies for Israel.

In summary, there were *more* shared themes in the *global* system images of Ben Gurion and Sharett, but the points of divergence were *more serious*. The two men recognized the bipolar character of the system, at first haltingly; they advocated non-alignment with the contending blocs in the early years and then perceived greater affinity with the West after the outbreak of war in Korea; they articulated concern for Jews everywhere; they attributed uniqueness to Israel; and finally, they were sympathetic to the aspirations of the Third World. Yet even in these components there were *differences* in *tone*, *stress*, and *nuance*. And their basic difference in outlook—the place of the UN in global politics and, particularly, in the Middle East conflict, as well as in Israeli foreign policy—overshadowed all the points of convergence. For the implications of this disagreement extended to diplomacy versus force, the attitude to external factors in Israeli policy, the issue of

---

[1] Ole R. Holsti, 'Cognitive Dynamics and Images of the Enemy: Dulles and Russia', op. cit. A more succinct version of this study is to be found in *The Journal of Conflict Resolution*, vol. vi, 1962, pp. 244–52.

[2] 'Cognitive Dynamics and Images of the Enemy . . .', pp. 94–6.

legitimacy, etc. The single-mindedness of Ben Gurion also led to indifference to the economic aspect of policy and to the pivotal 'two-camp thesis'.

Their images of 'the Arabs' were even more sharply at variance, as the analysis of 'the two schools' revealed. The crux was the contrary interpretations of Arab character—'the only language the Arabs understand is force' (BG) versus 'the Arabs are proud and sensitive; they are people, not just enemies' (Sharett). In policy terms this was expressed as retaliation versus 'creating an atmosphere conducive to peace'. Not by accident were there no major acts of retaliation during Ben Gurion's retirement to Sde Boker, from January 1954 to February 1955—when Sharett was in formal control of policy.[1]

It was their contrasting images of 'the Arabs' which gave rise to this basic policy disagreement. And that, in turn, led to the irrevocable split between Ben Gurion and Sharett in June 1956. The two men represented then and later alternative approaches to the cardinal issue in Israel's foreign policy—relations with neighbouring Arab states. A successful formula eluded them, as it continues to cause turmoil among their successors.[2]

We may now turn to a parallel analysis of the images of three other members of the Inner Circle—Eshkol, Meir, and Sapir. Levi Eshkol, it will be recalled, was the most influential figure in foreign (and domestic) economic policy from 1952 to 1963 and was Prime Minister for the next six years, as well as Defence Minister much of that time. Golda Meir, as noted, was Foreign Minister for almost a decade, from June 1956 to the beginning of 1966, and later succeeded Eshkol as Head of Government. And Pinhas Sapir was a major figure in economic and party affairs as Eshkol's confidant and successor in the Finance portfolio.

[1] It was, however, during that period that there occurred the 'security mishap' in Cairo, which led to Israel's *cause célèbre*, the Lavon Affair.

[2] Ben Gurion and Sharett had clearly-articulated images of many other aspects of foreign policy, both specific issues and countries. Notable among them are Jerusalem, Germany, France, China, and Jordan Waters. Their perceptions will be explored in the relevant decision studies in a later volume.

CHAPTER 13

Élite Images II: Eshkol, Meir, Sapir

(a) ESHKOL'S ROAD TO ZION

Levi Eshkol was described by an admirer as the 'last of the first', referring to the 'founding fathers' who shaped the character of modern Israel.[1] His background was indeed typical of the men of the Second *Aliya* (1904–14): he was born (1895) and spent his formative years in a little town or *shtetl* (Oratowa, in the Kiev district of the Ukraine); a traditional *heder* education was followed by preparation for the Russian *Gymnasia*, but he had to complete his formal studies (1911–13) in distant Vilna because of the *numerus clausus* (it was not without compensation, for that historic centre of Jewish learning was then in ferment with new ideas—of revolution, socialism, and Zionism); and among the reasons for his own *aliya* was the pervasive anti-Semitism of the Czarist realm, especially that Russian variant of race hatred, the *pogrom*. Many years later Eshkol recalled that the atmosphere of *pogroms* 'hung over our heads all the time, although the storm passed our district by [in one assault, during 1905]. For weeks we sat at home with doors barred and boards nailed over the windows, expecting an attack that never came.'[2] He was not often brought face-to-face with the more brutal forms of persecution experienced by some of his colleagues. His successor as Prime Minister, Golda Meir, for example, never forgot the 'joke' played by a neighbouring peasant who came up to her and another little girl, both seven years old, knocked their heads together playfully and said, 'that's what we will do with the Jews; we'll knock their heads together and we'll be through with them'.[3] Oratowa was a railway junction but a backwater compared with Pinsk, Minsk, and other Jewish centres in the Pale. And yet Eshkol recalled on another occasion: 'It was the beginning of the century—riots, pogroms. I myself received not once a severe blow with a wagon tongue.'[4] Moreover, his father was killed in that town in 1917 by followers of Petlura,

[1] Amos Eylon, 'Eshkol: Last of the First', *New Outlook* (Tel Aviv), vol. 12, no. 3 (105), March–April 1969, pp. 29–32.
[2] Terence Prittie, *Eshkol of Israel: The Man and the Nation*, Museum Press, London, 1969, p. 4.
[3] Marie Syrkin, *Golda Meir: Woman with a Cause*, G. P. Putnam's Sons, New York, 1963, p. 19.
[4] Eshkol obituary, 'Death of Eshkol at 73 Marks Shift from Old Leaders to the Palestine-Born', *New York Times*, 27 Feb. 1969, p. 32.

the Ukraine's most notorious anti-Semite of the day. Yet *pogroms* alone did not lead Eshkol to Palestine. Indeed, the vast majority of Russian Jews who migrated at the time, half a million or more, went to America.

Levi Shkolnick, as he was known until after Israel's independence, set out for Palestine early in 1914. This important *personal* decision was marked by caution and multiple influences, the twin characteristics of Eshkol's decisions throughout his *public* life. He began to think about *aliya* at the age of thirteen or fourteen; he acted five years later. Perhaps the normal hesitations were accentuated by the pull of an affluent home; in this aspect of his background Eshkol was not typical of his contemporaries. 'Our house was that of a big family, a big house of burnt bricks where grandfather and grandmother and grandsons and granddaughters all lived and all did very big business. They did everything—there is practically nothing in the world or in business that I dealt with in Israel that was strange to me in that house. They rented forests and flour mills, dealt with rivers and fishing, raised horses and cattle. What didn't they do? They even rented lands in the name of gentiles.'[1]

One of the positive influences on young Eshkol was socialism, notably the humanist strand as espoused by that unique association of Jewish workers in Poland, Lithuania, and Russia, the *Bund*. As he was to demonstrate over the decades in the socialist movement of the *Yishuv* and of Israel, Eshkol was attracted to its values and ideals, not to its theory and ideology. His view of socialism was derived from the *Ha-po'el Ha-tza'ir* leaders, 'who were my guides and mentors, and who developed important elements in the ideology of the Jewish workers—the principle of labor, labor settlement, Hebrew culture, a working nation, and a new society . . .'[2] Marxism and the class struggle were anathema to him.

A closely-related influence, with a direct thrust to Zion, was the philosophy of A. D. Gordon, who preached a return to the land as the key to normalcy for the Jewish People. 'We wanted to build Israel with our own hands', remarked Eshkol some months before his death in 1969. 'Our whole philosophy was contained in the phrase, "back to the soil".'[3] The ghetto—in his case the *shtetl*—provided a full Jewish life. And '*Yiddishkeit*' was embedded in Eshkol's character and personality. The Vilna experience was important, too, in directing him to *aliya*: there he joined the *Tse'ire Tzyon* youth group, an affiliate of *Ha-po'el Ha-tza'ir*, which was later to form part of the mainstream *Mapai* party.

The Zionist vision was another powerful inducement: 'In Jaffa [where he set foot in Palestine]', he told his biographer, 'I was born a second time.'[4] But unlike Ben Gurion and others who had received the call at an early age and could not be deflected, Eshkol admitted, with typical honesty: 'To tell the truth, I thought that after a year I would

[1] Ibid.   [2] Prittie, op. cit., p. 52.
[3] Ibid., p. 14.   [4] Ibid., p. 24.

return to Russia.'[1] Like most men of the Second *Aliya* he was also inspired by 'the light of the vision of the Prophets'—the belief in social justice and equality before God. Among individuals, 'a tremendous impression was made on me by Jabotinsky [the Revisionist leader]; what temperament, what speech, what Russian!'[2] But the decisive personal encounter was with Yosef Sprinzak. (He later served as the first Speaker of Israel's parliament.) Eshkol 'believed . . . that this meeting with Sprinzak [in Vilna] had removed all doubts from his mind'.[3] At last he yielded to the Zionist imperative.

During the pre-independence period Eshkol did not attain the first rank of *Yishuv* leaders, men like Arlosoroff,[4] Ben Gurion, Sharett, and Kaplan.[5] Yet he was active in many fields; and he revealed himself to be a hard-working, persistent, patient and modest man of organizing ability. He began as a labourer in Petah Tikva and in the vineyards of Rishon Le-tzyon. He served briefly in the Jewish Legion and helped to found Kibbutz Degania B soon after the First World War. He was an arms procurer for the Jewish underground as early as 1921, a founding member of the *Histadrut*, and a delegate to Zionist Congresses from the mid-twenties onwards. He headed the Jewish Agency's Settlement Department in Berlin from 1933 to 1936 and played a key role in the rescue of a segment of German Jewry. Thereafter he served as treasurer and member of the high command of *Haganah*. He was Secretary-General of the Tel Aviv Labour Council from 1944 to 1948. And when the state was born he was a key Ben Gurion aide as Director-General of the Defence Ministry. Throughout this thirty-five-year gestation period Eshkol displayed an abiding interest in the twin problems of water and agriculture.

His happiest and most productive role after independence was that of Head of the Jewish Agency's Land Settlement Department from 1949 to 1963 (and simultaneously, in 1951–2, Minister of Agriculture): in that dual capacity he directed the massive absorption of immigrants, almost 700,000, many of them to the land. From 1952 to 1963 he held the key portfolio of Finance and exercised ultimate authority over the economy as a whole: Ben Gurion gave him a free hand. Not without reason did many Israelis feel—Ben Gurion among them at the outset—that

---

[1] Eshkol obituary, *New York Times*, 27 Feb. 1969.
[2] Ibid.
[3] Prittie, op. cit., p. 13.
[4] Haim Arlosoroff, one of the most brilliant Labour Zionist leaders in the *Yishuv*, was, at the time of his mysterious assassination on the Tel Aviv seashore in 1933, the Secretary-General of *Mapai* and Head of the Political Department of the Jewish Agency. He was succeeded by Ben Gurion as leader of *Mapai* and by Sharett as Head of the Political Department.
[5] Eliezer Kaplan, who, as noted, came to Israel relatively late (in 1923 at the age of 32), was the dominant figure in the economic affairs of the *Yishuv* and the State from 1935 until his death in 1952.

Eshkol was well-prepared by experience to succeed BG as Prime Minister and Defence Minister in 1963.

(b) FROM CHARISMA TO COMPROMISE

Eshkol's indecisiveness during the agonizing weeks before the Six Day War cast a shadow over his record of achievement.[1] Yet time and reflection may confirm the assessment of Terence Prittie:[2]

The Jews, and the Israelis, are perfectionists. They recognized in Ben-Gurion a great man. . . . They saw in Eshkol an ordinary Jew, and they will surely come to recognize something symbolic in his achievement—which proved that to an ordinary Jew all things are possible. At the same time they have been very human in criticizing this 'ordinary' man. . . .

Eshkol played an epic role in the settlement of the land and in the supplying of the whole country with water. He helped to organize his nation's means of defense, its trade union machinery, and its principal political party. He planned the nation's economy over 12 of its first 15 crucial and formative years. A man who had never sought power, he became Prime Minister, and he led his country through its greatest crisis of all. Almost without intermission, he planned for the reunification of the Labor party, which had been the mainspring of Israel's political, social and economic development.

In character and personality Eshkol was very different from Ben Gurion and Sharett. He was much closer to the latter along the Courage–Caution spectrum. He possessed neither the intellectual talent nor the pretensions of his two predecessors as Prime Minister. He wrote very little, at any rate for publication.[3] He never articulated a vision of Israel's past and of the forces which led to independence. His interests were more mundane and practical. And although he came early to the land of Israel, he retained to the end his strong emotional links to Diaspora Jewry, unlike Ben Gurion and, until his later years, Sharett. He was, in fact, more at home in Yiddish than in Hebrew and was well known for his fund of Yiddish jokes and aphorisms, his sense of humour being a quality which neither Ben Gurion nor Sharett shared. Thus he always displayed a greater willingness to take into account the wishes and advice of the Zionist Movement and of world Jewry, as in his interpretation of the Ben Gurion–Blaustein 'agreement' of 1961.[4]

Eshkol was totally lacking in Ben Gurion's charisma and Sharett's diplomatic finesse. Rather he was a born committee-man, a careful,

[1] This will be amplified in the related volume on Israeli high-policy decisions.

[2] Op. cit., p. 349. A less informative work is Yosef Shapiro, *Levi Eshkol, A Biography*, Massada Ltd., Tel Aviv, 1969 (in Hebrew).

[3] Two collections of his speeches and essays were published: *B'ma'aleh Ha-derech* (On the Way), Ayanot Publishers, Tel Aviv, 1958; and *B'havlei Hitnahlut* (In the Pangs of Settlement), Am Oved, Tel Aviv, 1966. A useful collection of Eshkol's speeches as Prime Minister is to be found in Henry M. Christman, *The State Papers of Levi Eshkol*, Funk and Wagnalls, New York, 1969.

[4] See pp. 142–3 above.

determined planner with a special gift for getting on with people. Pragmatic and adaptable, he genuinely loved the soil and believed in the value of manual labour—but he did not venerate Spartan ideals for their own sake. His calm demeanour verged on the phlegmatic. Tireless in discussion, he won over his colleagues by solid and patient persuasion, not by force of personality or brilliant advocacy. He was a tough task-master, according to subordinates, but he worked as hard as they and displayed tremendous energy and durability in all spheres. He was a well-liked *haver*, down-to-earth, kind and tolerant. He had a common touch and never talked down to people.

Moderate in outlook, he was known for his skill at bargaining and conciliation. Typical was his conduct, on behalf of Ben Gurion, of the negotiations leading to a new coalition after the 1961 *Knesset* elections and those culminating in the reunification of the Labour Party. He was also the prototype of compromise, as revealed by his stance on the religious question during a heated parliamentary debate:[1]

The starting point is the will to build jointly a society based on mutual respect and mutual tolerance of people of different shades of opinion. We cannot ignore the uniqueness of the religion of the people of Israel as a national religion, just as we cannot overlook the fact that the majority of the people do not live their day-to-day lives according to the tenets of the *Halakha* [religious principles]. . . . It is the duty of the Government and of the Knesset to moderate carefully between the two extremes. . . .

Israel's 'heroic' phase was followed, of necessity, by one of consolidation in nation-building. As the successor to Ben Gurion, Eshkol adhered to type—the Shastri who followed Nehru, the Erhard after Adenauer and, in a different context, the Attlee after Churchill or the Pompidou after de Gaulle. And like some of these men his skills were not unimpressive. He was a better administrator and political manager than either BG or Sharett. He had an open mind, a proven ability to improvise, and a capacity to choose able men. Of his habit of consulting many and weighing carefully before deciding, one of his colleagues remarked in his favour: 'When Dayan is hesitating, his admirers say that he is thinking; but when Eshkol is thinking, his critics say that he is hesitating.'[2]

The fundamental difference in approach between Eshkol and Ben Gurion—*pragmatism* versus *dogma*—pervaded the gamut of foreign policy images. Underpinning this was a psychological pattern which may be termed 'BG contrariness': consciously or otherwise, Eshkol was aware that Ben Gurion's shadow hung over him, and some of his decisions seemed in part to be a reaction to this. Typical was his openly

[1] In reply to the *Knesset* debate on the formation of his first Government, 26 June 1963. Government Press Office, Jerusalem.

[2] Yigal Allon, the Deputy Prime Minister and a not disinterested spectator of the Eshkol–Dayan conflict, to Terence Prittie. Op. cit., p. 207.

expressed dislike of the Germans—whom BG appeared to be trying to rehabilitate—and his greater reliance on the United States for military and economic aid.

At one level it may seem contrived to attribute a coherent View of the World to Eshkol: there is no evidence that he thought carefully about Israel's external problems and goals before becoming Prime Minister, certainly not in his book, *B'Ma'aleh Ha-derekh*. And unlike Ben Gurion and Sharett, he depended on his technocratic aides for the drafting of speeches on foreign and security policy. An official who knew him well remarked after Eshkol's death that he never understood foreign policy: 'this was the greatest frustration of his public life'.[1] Nevertheless, Eshkol delivered many speeches and in so doing gave his assent to their content. In this *analytic and operational sense* he was the author of the images they conveyed. Their impact was blurred by the fact that he was a dismal speaker, unlike Sharett, the master of logical persuasion, and Ben Gurion, who was endowed with an inspirational rhetoric. Even his friendly biographer had to admit about Eshkol's speeches: 'there was nothing in them which needed to be forgotten, but seldom much which was remembered'.[2]

(c) PERCEPTION OF THE 'LARGER SPHERE'

Two phases are evident in Eshkol's foreign policy images during his tenure as Prime Minister: 1963–6 and thereafter. At the outset he declared: 'The new Government is a Government of continuity.'[3] Soon after, he defined his goals as the strengthening of *Tzahal* and of the political factors in support of Israel's sovereignty: 'This was the thinking that guided . . . Mr. Ben Gurion. . . . This Government is continuing and will continue to act in the same direction. . . . Another basic plank of our policy [is] peace.'[4] But these were mere verbal commitments to his predecessor.

Like all Israeli leaders, Eshkol perceived the reality of super-power and bloc conflict and the friendship of the United States for Israel. But whereas Ben Gurion viewed Moscow as rigidly hostile to Israel and Soviet Jewry—and was temperamentally incapable of a new approach—Eshkol perceived the need to re-examine policy periodically. Thus during his 1964 visit to Washington he adopted a conciliatory line towards the Soviet Union: 'My impression of Mr. Khrushchev's visit to Cairo is that he spoke about Israel in a much milder tone than before. I am inclined to believe that the Soviet Union is not interested in molest-

[1] Interview in Jerusalem, April 1966.
[2] Prittie, op. cit., p. 206.
[3] Government Press Office, *Press Bulletin*, 24 June 1963.
[4] Address to the opening of the 3rd session of the Fifth *Knesset*. Government Press Office, *Press Bulletin*, 21 Oct. 1963.

ing Israel.'[1] And in a speech to the Zionist Congress in January 1965 he remarked: 'We look forward to a change in [Moscow's attitude to Israel and Soviet Jewry]. I am confident that it will be brought about by the good sense of the Soviet people and Government and by the sensitivity of world public opinion.'[2] And again, in January 1966, he told the *Knesset*:[3]

I expressed the hope two years ago that, parallel with the improvement of our ties with the United States, France and Britain, there should also be more understanding between the Soviet Union and Israel. True, there has not been much progress in this direction, but we should not despair of the aim itself. . . .

And indeed reason dictates that there should be better understanding between Moscow and Jerusalem:

(a) Israel plays no part in what is called 'the Cold War'. . . .
(b) Israel supports the principle of abstention from the use of force for the solution of territorial disputes, as defined by the Soviet Union at the beginning of 1964. . . .
(c) On many occasions we have expressly emphasized that this principle should apply not only in the area of the Near East but also . . . in the whole world.

There were also acts to conform with this new image, notably the payment of $2 million compensation for Czarist Russian state property in Jerusalem. After the Six Day War, of course, Eshkol was denouncing Soviet repression of the Jewish minority in the USSR, her unqualified political support for the Arab states, and her massive supply of arms to Israel's enemies. But that was after the 'new look' had brought a response of unremitting hostility—an excellent example of the feedback effect of changes in the Operational Environment on Eshkol's images and policy.

The conciliatory line did not blur Eshkol's awareness of Israel's security problem in its global context. Thus to the Zionist Congress he declared with firmness:[4]

The problem of the country's security must—and does—take pride of place in our preoccupations. This is not the outcome of any ideological considerations; it is a matter of concrete necessity. Security is our first concern, and I may say that it has become, to a certain extent, a sacred value in its own right, because we are living in a situation that is determined by the declared desire of our enemies to wipe us off the face of the map. . . .

[1] As quoted in 'Eshkol's Statements on Foreign Policy', *New Outlook* (Tel Aviv), vol. 7, no. 6 (64), July–Aug. 1964, p. 57.
[2] Speech at the 26th Zionist Congress, in Jerusalem on 4 Jan. 1965, p. 7. Issued by the Government Press Office, Jerusalem.
[3] 'Statement by the Prime Minister, Mr. Levi Eshkol, in Presenting the Cabinet to the *Knesset*, 12 January 1966', p. 4. Issued by the Government Press Office, Jerusalem. This theme was reiterated in his address to the *Knesset* on 18 May 1966. Government Press Office, *Press Bulletin*.
[4] Speech to the 26th Zionist Congress, p. 2.

Israel's security front is also the front of Jewish survival the world over. It has two aspects, this problem of our security: what we call 'current security' and what is described as 'basic security'. From the point of view of current security, we are living in a period of relative—but not more than relative—quiet; it is not yet true, permanent and stable tranquillity. Behind the apparently tranquil borders . . . stand armed forces awaiting the hour of action. And it is not merely a question of potential danger, but of actual peril. . . .

And if we must beware of illusions over current security, we must be doubly on guard against complacency in the sphere of basic security. . . . The main centre of aggression [is] the Egyptian régime. . . .

In the context of security Eshkol, like Ben Gurion and Sharett, attached special importance to world Jewry. Relations of reciprocity 'exist—and must exist', he wrote in 1965; 'the two are linked and locked together'. He was a strong advocate of 'Israel centricity of Jewish peoplehood today' and rejected the 'Israel and Babylon' analogy of two parallel centres of Jewry, with US Jewry playing the Babylon role. At the same time, 'Israel cannot carry the burden unaided. . . . All the resources of our people are needed [for] Israel . . . as the heart of Jewry.'[1]

He shared the inherent Jewish distrust of *Goyim* and the feeling of total trust in his fellow Jews. He rejected the Ben Gurion view that 'everything depends on us', though he acknowledged that in the last analysis self-reliance is crucial. And he attached much more importance to diplomacy than did BG. Yet in the aftermath of the Six Day War he came close to formal acceptance of the 'two-camp thesis': 'During the days of preparedness and war we learned that, although we do not lack sympathy and support in the world, nevertheless we can rely first and foremost *only on our own strength and on the Jewish people*.'[2] This scepticism about the reliability of external forces, apart from Jewry, also found expression in his emphasis on self-sufficiency in arms. In 1968 he recollected:[3] 'I loved the land, and it was central to my philosophy of life. But when I became Minister of Finance [1952], it was at once clear to me that Israel's prosperity, security, and very existence depended on being given an industrial base. . . . We had to begin producing the weapons which we needed for our own defense, for we could not remain almost totally dependent on arms grudgingly allowed us by foreign governments.'

Of the United Nations Eshkol said relatively little. While he did not emulate Sharett's awe for the world body, neither did he share Ben Gurion's disdain for its role in the Arab–Israel conflict. As to the Third World, he was the only Israeli Prime Minister to visit Africa (in May–

---

[1] 'Israel and the Diaspora', State of Israel: *Government Year-Book 5725*, 1964/5, Jerusalem, pp. 7–12.

[2] 'Points from Address by Prime Minister Levi Eshkol at the Opening of the Winter Session of the *Knesset*, 30 Oct. 1967', p. 1. Government Press Office, Jerusalem.

[3] To Prittie. Op. cit., p. 181.

June 1966);[1] and while there, as well as in his assessment of his tour of seven new states, he indicated that Africa loomed large in his global image.[2]

Eshkol paid the necessary tribute to France, Israel's principal ally in the pre-1967 years. However, he perceived the United States as a more reliable and significant bastion than did Ben Gurion, Dayan, and Peres; this was due in part to the influence of his Foreign Minister, Golda Meir, supported by his Deputy, Abba Eban. And unlike Ben Gurion and Sharett, who did not act when the opportunities arose, he frequently expressed an interest in diplomatic relations with Peking, acknowledging China's significance in global politics.[3] All this was clearly indicated in an important address to the 10th Convention of *Mapai*, in February 1965.[4]

In his image of Germany, the most agonizing issue in Israel's foreign policy, Eshkol differed considerably from Ben Gurion: to BG Germany had changed; to Eshkol Germany was in the process of changing. Thus Ben Gurion declared as early as 1959: 'I say that Germany of today, the Germany of Adenauer and the Social Democrats, is not the Germany of Hitler. . . .'[5] And in 1960 he made the historic gesture of reconciliation by meeting Adenauer in New York, paying tribute to the German Chancellor as a wise and great man. As he remarked later, 'I felt [in 1960] and feel that he will be remembered in German and in European history as one of the great statesmen of our time.'[6] 'My view towards Germany', he remarked to the writer in 1966, 'is based upon the words of two Prophets, Jeremiah and Ezekiel. Their essence is, "don't hold a father responsible for the acts of his son or the son for the acts of his father".'[7] Yet for Ben Gurion the thrust to reconciliation lay in *realpolitik*:[8] 'Germany . . . is definitely a rising power. . . . To us, it cannot be unimportant whether West Germany is for or against Israel. . . . A hostile Germany might endanger the friendship with Israel of other peoples of western Europe, and could also have an undesirable influence on the United States. It is therefore doubly important for Israel to promote closer relations with Germany.'

[1] Mrs. Meir visited Africa four times (1958, 1959–60, 1962 and 1964), all during her tenure as Foreign Minister (1956–66).

[2] See 'Address by the Prime Minister, Mr. Levi Eshkol, on his Visit to Africa, in the *Knesset*, on 28 June 1966'. Government Press Office, *Press Bulletin*. This writer had the privilege of observing Eshkol's encounter with Africa as a guest on this tour.

[3] This will be explored in the related volume on high-policy decisions.

[4] See 'Points from Address by Prime Minister Levi Eshkol at the Tenth Convention of *Mapai*, the Israel Labour Party, Tel Aviv, February 16, 1965'. Government Press Office, *Press Bulletin*.

[5] 'Address by the Prime Minister, Mr. David Ben Gurion, in the *Knesset*, July 1, 1959', p. 14. Issued by the Government Press Office, Jerusalem.

[6] *Ben Gurion Looks Back . . .*, p. 170.

[7] Interview at Sde Boker, July 1966.

[8] *Ben Gurion Looks Back . . .*, p. 170.

Eshkol was not prepared to ease the German conscience with such finality. In the midst of the crisis which was to lead to diplomatic relations he told the *Mapai* Convention early in 1965:[1]

Our evaluation of the extent to which Germany has cast off her past is tested daily in the light of her deeds in the present. Jewish ethics does not believe in the principle, 'the fathers have eaten sour grapes and the teeth of the sons are set on edge'. But it is the sons themselves who are on trial, and in this respect we can only see an appalling moral weakness in the West German Government's surrender to Arab blackmail.

Nor was this a mere tactic to secure concessions: even after diplomatic relations had been established Eshkol repeated that the process of change was incomplete and that Germany had not yet fully expiated her heinous crimes. He made this point bluntly at a dinner for Adenauer in Jerusalem in 1966; the former Chancellor was perplexed and annoyed, for he had become accustomed to Ben Gurion's 'clean bill of health'.[2] In many statements Eshkol was to stress the theme '. . . understanding is growing and not diminishing. . . . We cannot relegate the darkness of the past to oblivion. Yet we must see the reality as it is, and be ready to recognize and correctly to evaluate *elements of progress*.'[3]

Eshkol, like all members of the decision-making Inner Circle, was acutely conscious of the link between global and Middle East politics. Thus to the *Knesset* he remarked in 1963: 'We are fully aware that inter-bloc tension has been one of the obstacles—though not the only one—to progress towards peace in our region.'[4] And with greater clarity about the multiple levels of international interaction, he remarked during the political struggle following the 1967 War:[5] 'The crisis in the Middle East is also due to the penetration of the influence of the Cold War into our area. Global international relations affect inter-Arab relations and the relations between Israel and the Arab States. This is the true situation: the crisis should not be blamed on the Arab–Israel dispute alone—it is much wider and more comprehensive.'

(d) SECOND *ALIYA* IMAGE OF 'THE ARABS'

In his image of 'the Arabs' Eshkol appeared to be deviating from Ben Gurion more markedly. (He did not, unlike BG or Sharett, articulate a view of 'the Middle East' as a region or an international system; implicitly, it was merely an extension of 'the Arabs'.) The changes were, in fact, those of style, tone, and nuance, but not less

[1] Op. cit., pp. 2–3.   [2] *Jerusalem Post*, 4 May 1966.
[3] Statement on Germany, published in *Ot* (Tel Aviv), Sept. 1966. Issued by the Government Press Office, Jerusalem.
[4] To the opening of the 3rd session of the Fifth *Knesset*, 21 Oct. 1963. Government Press Office, *Press Bulletin*.
[5] 'Reply by the Prime Minister, Mr. Levi Eshkol, to the Foreign Affairs Debate in the *Knesset*, 13 November 1967.' Government Press Office, *Press Bulletin*.

important for that. Eshkol portrayed a calmer and more confident attitude to Israel's security problem—not the grim and ominous picture of the Middle East which was typical of the Ben Gurion era. There was evident, too, more respect for the Arabs and their leaders, reflecting the Sharett (and Eban) perception of 'the Arabs'. This was illustrated in his reciprocal gesture, however muted, to President Bourguiba's call for a 'new look' at the Arab–Israel conflict:[1]

Israel's central aim in the Near East is peace. . . . There appear . . . some indications of a tendency which recognizes the need for coexistence and the senselessness and impossibility of solving disputes by means of war. An outstanding expression of this tendency has been given by Mr. Habib Bourguiba, President of Tunisia. . . . In rejecting these proposals . . . we do not belittle the importance of the principle of peaceful coexistence itself . . . the positive element in these declarations.

Sharett would have applauded these conciliatory gestures; he would have gone further. Yet Eshkol remained a prisoner of his own life experience; that is, he perceived 'the Arabs' through a Second *Aliya* lens. Life in the Pale had created a self-sufficient and internally tranquil existence—but it left the East European ghetto Jew isolated from the outer world. When he came to Palestine he was preoccupied with the building of Zion. And he lacked knowledge about 'the Arabs' as a people, culture, and society.

The impact of that environment on Second *Aliya* images was noted by an Israeli intellectual from an Arab land, Nissim Rejwan:[2]

. . . the most crucial and harmful [influence] has been that, in a very valid sense, *the Zionists managed to create Arabism and Arab nationalism in their own exclusivist image.* According to this image the Arabs were, *per se,* a self-contained 'nationality', an alien political and cultural entity standing in permanent and inevitable opposition to the Jews, who in turn constitute a separate, single 'nationality'.

Persuasive evidence is cited from Ben Gurion's remarks to George Antonius, the historian of the Arab nationalist movement, as early as 1936:[3]

As a point of departure the proposition must be accepted that the issue is not one between the Jews of Palestine and the Arabs of Palestine. . . . Instead, we must view *the Jews as one world entity* and *the Arabs as one world entity.* I truly believe that between the national aspirations of the Jewish people and the national aspirations of the Arab people . . . there is no inevitable contradiction.

---

[1] 'Statement . . . to the *Knesset,* 12 January 1966', p. 2. On other occasions there was a harsher tone, as in the more-publicized 'Israel's Peace Plan, A Statement by Mr. Levi Eshkol in the *Knesset,* 17 May 1965'. Israel Ministry for Foreign Affairs, Jerusalem.

[2] 'Israeli Attitudes to the Arab World', *New Outlook* (Tel Aviv), vol. 9, no. 5 (80), June 1966, pp. 25–6 (emphasis added).

[3] In *Ma'ariv* (Tel Aviv), 25 Feb. 1966, as quoted in 'Israeli Attitudes to the Arab World', p. 26.

Eshkol shared this perception of 'the Arabs' as a united 'world', though not through the rigid lens of Ben Gurion. Moreover, he continued to subscribe to the 'little notch' image of Israel and the Arab realm, though once more in a less harsh tone than BG:[1]

> I wonder whether your listeners are aware of the real dimensions of the problem. Israel has regained her independence in a *tiny patch* of 8,000 square miles, about the size of Wales. There are now a dozen Arab States, none of them independent before the end of the First World War, occupying territories covering a total of four and a half million square miles.
> Is there any sense in countries with such vast spaces . . . *to begrudge us this small corner* which is the basis for our independence?

By the autumn of 1966 Eshkol's image of 'the Arabs' had reverted to the Ben Gurion-type hard line under the impact of a change in the Operational Environment—the emergence of Arab guerrilla movements and mounting hostility from the Arab states. This is apparent in his opening address to the *Knesset* on 17 October 1966 and even more so in his reply to the foreign policy debate a month later, just after the retaliatory raid on El Samua: 'We do not undervalue the friendship, goodwill and assistance of friendly nations. . . . But we must always remind ourselves that the safeguarding of our security, the defence of our survival, the building of our road to a safer future—all these things must be done first of all by ourselves.'[2] So it remained, this image of the need to 'go it alone', until the Six Day War and the prolonged political struggle which followed.[3]

(e) MEIR: BACKGROUND OF ISRAEL'S LADY PRIME MINISTER

Formally, Levi Eshkol was the 'last of the first' to attain the summit of political power in Israel. But the Second *Aliya* was more than a wave of immigration in the years before the First World War. It was, as noted, a state of mind, a view of the world, and a set of values which embraced most Jewish pioneers before the rise of Nazi Germany. This included Golda Meir, the only woman in Israel's High Policy Élite of eighteen, and the only 'Anglo-Saxon', other than Abba Eban: she came to the Land of Israel in 1921—in the Third *Aliya*. Yet in all other respects she was more akin to the 'founding fathers'.

Only three years separate her from Eshkol, and four from Sharett: she was born in 1898, like them in the Ukraine (Kiev). When Golda Mahovitz was five the family moved to Pinsk in the Pale of Settlement,

---

[1] To correspondents in Tel Aviv, 26 July 1963 (emphasis added). Issued by the Government Press Office.

[2] 'Reply . . . to Proposals to Discuss the Security Situation in the *Knesset*, 15 November 1966'. Government Press Office, Jerusalem.

[3] Eshkol's perceptions during the period leading up to and following the Arab-Israel 'third round' will be discussed in that context, in the related volume.

and in 1906 they joined the exodus of Russian Jews to America. Her formative years, from the ages of eight to twenty-three, were spent in Milwaukee, with an important interval under the guidance of her elder sister, Shana, in Denver (1912–16): she ran away from home to assert her independence and there met her future husband, the shy, sensitive Morris Myerson.

Her East European phase provided Golda Meir with a negative inducement to Zion—the reality and persistent threat of *pogrom*. How deep was its impact is indicated by her remark many years later: 'If there is any logical explanation for the direction that my life has taken, it is the desire and determination to save Jewish children from a similar scene and from a similar experience [to that noted earlier].'[1] The positive motivation for *aliya* came from the American milieu. Caught up in the ferment of ideas towards the end of the First World War, she rejected all in favour of Jewish nationalism and became immersed in the socialist *Po'alei Tzyon*, the Jewish People's Relief for East European Jewry, the American Jewish Congress, and Yiddish-language folk schools. Her *aliya* in 1921 was a natural conclusion to this period of self-created *hakhshara* (preparation).

Golda Meir's life in Palestine was typical of the pioneering generation.[2] The Myersons—she retained the name until 1956—settled first in Kibbutz Merhavia in the Jezreel Valley, then briefly in Tel Aviv in 1923, and in Jerusalem a year later. She became Secretary of the *Mo'etzet Ha-po'alot* (Council of Working Women) in 1928, was a founding member of *Mapai* in 1929, and served for two years (1932–4) as emissary of the *Mo'etzet* to its sister movement in America, the Pioneer Women. She joined the Executive Council of the *Histadrut* upon her return and its powerful Secretariat a year later. In 1936 she began to organize its mutual aid services, especially its sick fund, *Kupat Holim*. During the war years she served on Palestine's War Economic Advisory Council. And in June 1946, when most of the *Yishuv*'s leaders were arrested by the British on 'black Saturday', Golda Meir became Acting Head of the Jewish Agency's Political Department. She negotiated with Jordan's King Abdullah twice, in November 1947 and early in May 1948, in a futile effort to persuade him not to join the Arab invasion. Between these quiet diplomatic missions, in January 1948, she raised $50 million for arms—a gargantuan sum at the time—in a triumphant personal appeal to American Jewry.

Throughout Israel's independence Golda Meir has been near or at

[1] As quoted in a cover story on Mrs. Meir, 'Middle East: The War and the Woman', in *Time* (New York), vol. 94, no. 12, 19 Sept. 1969, p. 30.

[2] The principal facts of her life are set out in 'an authorized biography' by Marie Syrkin, *Golda Meir: Woman with a Cause*, as well as in a biographical sketch, 'Golda Meir: The Greatest Challenge of a Crowded Career', *Jerusalem Post Weekly*, 17 March 1969. Her most insightful self-analysis of those life experiences is to be found in an interview with Kenneth Harris. *The Observer* (London), 17 Jan. 1971.

the centre of influence. As Israel's first Minister to the Soviet Union she provided the spark for Russian Jewry's massive demonstration of Jewish national consciousness, at Moscow's main synagogue on the High Holidays in 1948. She was a highly successful Minister of Labour from April 1949 to June 1956 and then succeeded Sharett as Foreign Minister—for almost a decade. A brief respite in 1966 was followed by two years as Secretary-General of *Mapai*; and then, after another withdrawal from office in 1968, she succeeded Eshkol as Prime Minister, in March 1969. 'The choice was not quite unanimous, and there were objections from several sides that the voting procedure was not satisfactory. . . . The decision had been made, as so often before, by the Party's top leadership.'[1] Yet she was the obvious successor to an 'old guard'-dominated Israel Labour Party. Within a few months she became the popular choice as well.

(f) INTUITION, DECISIVENESS, AND REALISM

Whereas Eshkol shared Sharett's penchant for caution, Golda Meir is in the Ben Gurion mould—quick, decisive, and a strong personality. In other traits she is more akin to Eshkol—simplicity, modesty, lack of intellectual sophistication, and earthiness. She possesses a 'fantastic intuitive sense', according to many aides, with a sure grasp of the essence of a policy issue. An emotional attitude is evident in some of her foreign policy postures, notably in her unbending refusal to be reconciled to the 'new' Germany: as Foreign Minister she disagreed sharply with Ben Gurion's 'realism' in this sphere, from the arms deals of 1957–8 through his advocacy of diplomatic relations. She was also unhappy with the decision to accept reparations in 1952 and steadfastly refused to ride in a German-made automobile. The widely publicized role of German scientists in Egypt in the early 1960s reinforced her attitude. In these matters she was closer to the unforgiving *Herut* than to Ben Gurion, her mentor for a long time. In more positive terms she was drawn by emotion to the plight of Africans struggling for dignity, autonomy, and welfare.

Some who worked with her in the Foreign Office remarked that Mrs. Meir acted on intuition, not on reason; further, that she had contempt for the expertise of professional diplomats. 'She doesn't read [memoranda]—and she doesn't write', said one frustrated Foreign Ministry intellectual. Indeed, whereas BG, Sharett, and Eban prepared their own speeches, Meir, like Eshkol and Sapir, had hers written by one or more staff members. Even members of her entourage noted that she read only 'the most necessary papers'. She enjoyed her years in the

---

[1] Lea Ben Dor, 'Why Choice Falls on Golda Meir', *Jerusalem Post Weekly*, 10 March 1969. This point was also made by the Hebrew-language press, notably *Ma'ariv* and *Yediot Aharonot* during the succession process following Eshkol's death.

Labour Ministry more than those in the Foreign Office 'because there you can get something done that people need and see the results'.[1] For the same reason her most ambitious—and successful—foreign policy initiative was the Israeli technical assistance programme in *Africa*. Her encounter with *Asia*, on the other hand, was less productive. By the admission of her admiring biographer, 'Golda was less successful in establishing warm personal ties with the statesmen of Asia.' And the reason given reveals much about her personality and character: 'While the basic human and political needs of the young African peoples appealed to her innate simplicity, the ancient, complex civilizations of Asia were harder to fathom. Subtlety and ambiguity were virtues which Mrs. Meir neither admired nor cultivated.'[2]

As politician and diplomat Mrs. Meir's strength lay in the realm of human relations. Her formal speeches at the UN and in the *Knesset* were uninspiring, as with Eshkol. She was at her best in extemporaneous remarks, especially with American Jews, to whom she spoke directly, from the heart, often bluntly but never with a patronizing air, and as one of them. 'She is always telling people,' remarked an aide, 'don't be so humble—you're not that great.'[3]

Her Jewish sense of humour, like that of Eshkol, is proverbial in Israel. Simha Dinitz, the Head of her Bureau at the Foreign Office from 1963 to 1965 and again when she became Prime Minister in 1969, recalled that, after a furious pace of work for two years, he suggested that she take a vacation. ' "Why?" she asked. "Do you think I'm tired?" "No," he replied, "but I am." "So take a vacation", she said.'[4] More than Eshkol, however, she was tough and determined—in spirit and action.

Selfless in service—'nothing was owing to me' as a public servant, was her abiding principle[5]—she has always been immovable on basic convictions: among her highest values are the natural right of Jews to an independent state and the welfare of Jews everywhere. As for Israel's security, she has been as rigid and unyielding as Ben Gurion. Not without reason did he reportedly refer to her as 'the best man I have in the Cabinet'. Most of her Arab adversaries would probably agree with the reported remark of a Jordanian Minister: 'Eshkol hated the hawks, but Golda flies in formation with them. She has always been hard as nails.'[6] Other characteristics were recalled by Dinitz when she became Prime Minister:

[1] Lea Ben Dor, op. cit.
[2] Syrkin, op. cit., pp. 296–7.
[3] Simha Dinitz, reported in 'A Tangy Flavor in Mrs. Meir's Views', *New York Times*, 18 March 1969.
[4] Ibid.
[5] To the press when she retired as Foreign Minister, as reported by Shalom Cohen, 'Mrs. Meir Looks Back . . .', *Jerusalem Post*, 16 Jan. 1966.
[6] As quoted in *Time*, op. cit., p. 26.

Golda has the strong qualities of a man and the extra qualities of a woman—intuition, sensitivity and humane feelings.

Since she's a Jewish mother and a Jewish grandmother, she superimposes family feeling on national destiny.

She is not a pacifist. . . . Golda would like to see a society at peace but she doesn't believe in the peace of the graveyard. She will not compromise on Jewish security and survival.

(g) IMAGE OF GLOBAL POLITICS

Golda Meir, like Eshkol, never attempted to conceptualize her View of the World: both probably regarded the exercise as without purpose. Yet she possesses more (commonsense) insight into the forces impinging on Israel's foreign policy than did Eshkol, perhaps no less than Ben Gurion and Sharett. She has a feel for friend and foe, apart from the obvious 'enemy', and an ability to influence the uncertain among men and nations.

The 'larger sphere' of global politics occupies a peripheral place in the articulated Meir image, judging from many of her speeches to the UN General Assembly.[1] Yet she was not unaware of super-power rivalry and its impact on the Middle East. In 1960 she observed that inter-bloc tension was of greater concern to Israel than to 'any other people'—because of Jewry's dispersion among the nations, the presence of large communities in both East and West, and because of Israel's precarious position; rivalry between the blocs, she noted, accentuates regional tensions, especially the Arab–Israel conflict. Yet even in that address to the *Knesset* she termed the Cold War a figure of speech; and the fear of a Third World War was exaggerated, for mutual deterrence is effective.[2]

Concern with the Soviet–American struggle for world hegemony was

[1] Her December 1956 address was understandably devoted primarily to the Suez-Sinai War and its causes (14 of 15 pages). But the same pattern is evident in 1957 (10 of 12 pages on 'the Arabs'), in 1958 (5 of 8 pages), and in 1959 (6 of 8 pages). In 1960, the 'Africa Year' at the UN, the phenomenal growth of new states there occupied more attention (6 of 10 pages). Thereafter the emphasis on 'the Arabs' was reasserted.

Strangely, there is greater recognition of the global dimension in her annual budget speeches to the *Knesset*. For example, half of her 1960 address dealt with 'the Arabs' and the rest with global and bilateral concerns—the Summit and Disarmament, the Common Market, the US, the UK and the Commonwealth, France, Western and Northern Europe, Cyprus, the Soviet Union and Eastern Europe, Africa, Asia, Latin America, International Co-operation and Aid, the Conference on the Law of the Sea, the UN, and Information. In 1961 there was even greater stress on issues and areas beyond the Middle East—indeed, more on Africa (10 of 36 pages) than on 'the Arabs' (9 pages). Relations with Asia were barely mentioned. This pattern of topic and content distribution continued to 1965. The texts of these speeches were issued by the Government of Israel Information Services.

[2] Issued by the Government Press Office, Jerusalem, Dec. 1960.

rarely expressed in the Meir utterances. And there is abundant evidence that she does not place a high value on the United Nations' role in the search for a viable Middle East settlement. Within months of assuming the foreign affairs portfolio she witnessed UN behaviour during the Sinai Campaign. As she recalled later, her 1 March 1957 speech to the Assembly announcing Israel's final withdrawal from Sharm-e-Sheikh was not one of her proudest moments. Moreover, her relations with Secretary-General Hammarskjöld were icy: she distrusted and disliked him. To her he symbolized the UN's indifference to Israel. And when the UN, ten years later, stood by helpless and seemingly little concerned during the grave crisis of May–June 1967, which she and most Israelis perceived as a direct threat to survival, she moved more and more towards BG's view of '*oom shmoom*'. The regularity with which the Security Council castigated Israel's reprisals in 1968 and 1969, with a conspicuously milder censure of Arab guerrilla raids across the border, only strengthened her image—of a weak and undisguisedly pro-Arab forum, with Secretary-General U Thant and the Security Council vying with each other for the role of principal Arab protector. Yet she never emulated Ben Gurion's utter disdain for diplomacy.

Like Eshkol's speeches, there is little worth remembering in the formal addresses of Golda Meir. Only on one aspect of the global setting —Africa—did she approach eloquence, on occasion: '. . . we all feel that we are in the presence of a revolutionary moment in human history', she began her speech to the fifteenth General Assembly in October 1960, when sixteen new states were admitted to the UN:[1]

You cannot expect the mother in an African village to be elated over the advance of medicine in the world when she sees her children suffering from trachoma, tuberculosis and malaria.

No people can build its future if it does not remember its past. But a people cannot live only by brooding over the past; it must invest all its energy and ability in the future.

The cry that goes out from the African and Asian continents today is: Share with us not only food, but also your knowledge of how to produce it.

She constantly sought to identify Israel with emergent Africa—their past colonial rule, their recent attainment of independence, and their future aspirations. As did Ben Gurion, she often referred to the gap between rich and poor states as 'the central problem of our generation'. Her genuine affection for Africans and empathy with their demands is doubted by none. Yet Golda Meir was no starry-eyed idealist about Africa, for an Israeli presence there meant 'jumping over the Arab

[1] Ibid. A collection of her earlier speeches is contained in Golda Meir, *This is Our Strength: Selected Papers*, New York, Macmillan, 1962.

fence'. 'Our aid to the new countries', she told the *Knesset* in 1960, 'is not a matter of philanthropy. We are no less in need of the fraternity and friendship of the new nations than they are our assistance.'[1] Similarly, in her budget speeches for 1960 and 1961 she concluded on a note of optimism, with Africa as the principal cause: 'Now [it is] possible to say that Israel has broken through the political siege . . . and out into the international scene' (1960); and 'the process [of breaking through the siege] has gone forward and become surer' (1961).[2] Nevertheless, she accepted Ben Gurion's dictum that, in terms of Israel's national interests, there is no substitute for the friendship of European and American states—for three reasons: they are the centres of Jewry; they are the centres of culture, science, and research; and they will remain for a long time the vital sources of arms which neither Afro-Asia nor Israel herself could (yet) provide.

As for Israel's ties with Diaspora Jewry, Golda Meir is much closer to Eshkol and Sharett than to Ben Gurion. At the same time she had, like Ben Gurion, a deep disdain for the Zionist organization. To many in Israel and abroad she is the supreme ambassador to world Jewry. And she openly subscribes to the dual function view of Israeli diplomacy: the Israeli Ambassador to the United States, she told an Israel Bond rally in 1959, 'is not merely Ambassador to Washington but also an ambassador to the Jewish people'.[3] She practised this doctrine constantly as Foreign Minister during her annual visits to the UN and again during her triumphant American tour as Prime Minister in September 1969. She did not openly proclaim her belief in the 'two-camp thesis'. But through word and deed she attached supreme importance to the bonds between Jewry and Israel in all spheres of public policy—financial and economic aid, pressure on friendly (and not so friendly) governments, immigration, the sense of solidarity, and in the last analysis the willingness to make the supreme sacrifice so that Israel might survive.

(h) IMAGE OF 'THE ARABS'—INTRANSIGENT ENEMY

Like Eshkol, Mrs. Meir has not perceived 'the Middle East' as a region of international politics, except in so far as it relates to 'the Arabs'. Like Ben Gurion, her image of 'the Arabs' derives principally from the Second *Aliya* prism and prolonged non-communication with the other Peoples of the region. Nowhere has her image of 'the Arabs' been more piercingly illuminated than in a *Knesset* debate on the Arab refugees in November 1961. There, in extemporaneous discussion, she spoke her mind with a degree of candour that is absent from her

[1] Speech to the *Knesset* on 24 Oct. 1960. Government Press Office, Jerusalem.
[2] Government Press Office, Jerusalem.
[3] *Jerusalem Post*, 5 May 1959.

formal speeches to the UN and Israel's parliament. As with Sharett's 1957 lecture on 'the two schools' in Israel's foreign policy, it merits careful attention.[1]

First came the nostalgic image of the War of Independence and the conciliatory offer on the refugee problem:

It is true that in 1949 we thought the war was over; the Arabs had tried to throw us into the sea and had failed; we should have to live in this region—and then we spoke of admitting not a hundred thousand refugees, but 'up to a hundred thousand'; and as is well known . . . not a single Arab leader rose up to say, 'aha, if you say that, let's sit down and make peace'.

As to the present and the future, and this is as accurate a portrait of Mrs. Meir's view of 'the Arabs' in 1970 as it was in 1961, when these remarks were made:

And since then we have said only one thing. We have said: we are ready to enter into negotiations with the Arab States on the refugee issue, we are ready to discuss things with them, *to negotiate on compensation*—and we have always said: *mutual compensation* . . . and if they want us to, we shall gladly help them also to settle the refugees in their countries. We've had experience in settling refugees.

How deep-rooted is the Meir image of Arab intransigence is evident in the following passage:

To this proposal, too, there has never been a favourable response. I have not yet found a single statesman who has paid a visit to the Arab States—and I include those who want to persuade us to make a 'gesture' . . . who came to us and was able to tell us that he had found someone who said: 'If Israel were to agree to take back such and such a number of refugees, I would make peace with her.'

To *Mapam* MK, Barzilai, she asserted her perception of the *link between the refugee problem and peace*:

The whole mistake is this . . . that you talk as if it were a refugee problem. There is a *peace problem* between the Arab States and Israel. When there is peace . . . then almost automatically the refugee problem will be solved. And if that is so, then there is no need for you to make a gesture and take back an agreed number. . . . Once they are reconciled to our existence and are ready to make peace with us . . . the refugee issue will not be a problem.

Mrs. Meir also invoked the kinship argument, the *image of a homogeneous 'Arab world'*:

Are they among foreigners, speaking a different language, professing a different faith? Will they change over to other customs and ways of life? . . . Is there not on both sides of the [Jordan River] line the same language, the same religion, the same way of life? There are large expanses of land, there is water, there is money.

[1] Government Press Office, Jerusalem (emphasis added).

Then came the renewed expression of *total mistrust of Arab intentions*, grounded in thirteen years of perceived reality:

They tried to destroy us, not to let us come into existence . . . by the weapon of military aggression, . . . economic boycott, . . . fedayin, . . . a political and diplomatic blockade—they have not succeeded. *One of the courses they hope to follow in order to destroy us is the refugee issue. This weapon is necessary to them.*

As for the Israeli view of the future, she added:

The declared stand of the Israel Government is not, 'No, not a single refugee', but *a solution of the refugee problem in the Arab States*. The State of *Israel cannot admit Arab refugees, and is not prepared to enter into any discussion on the basis of free choice*, for we cannot accept such a thing: we are a sovereign State. Nobody can choose to enter another State: the State has to authorize it.

At one point the symbol of the arch-enemy is invoked:

I promise you, that's what Shukairi will say in the [UN] Assembly. He will say it because they do not want a solution, and because the existence of the problem is necessary to them.

Rarely has the 'Ben Gurionist' image of 'the Arabs' among Israel's High Policy Élite been stated with such conviction. And this was in a period of relative tranquillity in the Arab–Israel conflict, almost at mid-point in time between the Sinai Campaign and the Six Day War.

Golda Meir's belief that direct negotiations are the *sine qua non* of a settlement is well expressed in a reported anecdote:[1]

She insists that Israel's problem is not territorial but rather that the enemy refuses to sit down and talk to us. Suppose we want to return the territory we have taken. 'To whom?' she would say. 'We can't send it to Nasser by parcel post.'

That her image of the road to peace has not changed over the years is underlined by the multitude of speeches made by her since becoming Prime Minister. One will suffice:[2]

I believe deeply and profoundly that peace will come, because the Arab States and Israel were fated to live side by side in this part of the world. The question remains, how many young men, Jews and Arabs, will have to pay with their lives for the *madness and irrationality of the Arab leaders*.

This was stated at an election rally towards the end of 1969, but there can be no doubt that it is an authentic expression of her view: it has been consistent over the years.

In the ultimate shaping of Israel's destiny and as to the role of the super powers and the Big Four in 'advising' the terms of a settlement in 1969–70, Golda Meir had indicated her commitment to 'realism' as early as 1961:[3]

---

[1] Dinitz, loc. cit.
[2] *Jerusalem Post*, 20 Oct. 1969 (emphasis added).
[3] *Knesset* debate, November 1961.

I don't know any country—and neither do you—that in vital questions affecting the essence of its existence and security will listen to what others tell it. . . . In the end, all the nations are equal in one thing, big nations and small alike . . . —the nation dwelling in its State is first of all responsible for its own security and existence. And *it sins if it listens to what others say when they tell it the contrary.* . . . In the end, only the Israeli nation will decide what is necessary to the State of Israel and its security. . . . *The Israel people will decide. And its decision is what settles the matter.*

Perceived external pressures, notably from the United States, may compel some adjustment in this doctrine; but the predisposition of Golda Meir is to view 'the Arabs' through the 'Ben Gurionist' lens and to respond with '*raison d'état*'.

(i) SAPIR: PRACTICAL MAN OF AFFAIRS

Pinhas Sapir does not fit the image of Israel's 'old guard'. There is, to begin with, an age gap of at least ten years (he was born in 1909, in Poland). Moreover, he arrived in Palestine rather late (1929), towards the end of the Fourth *Aliya*. Nor did he have the background of the typical Labour Zionist—the camaraderie of a youth movement, the commitment to socialist ideas, mystical attachment to the land, and communal or co-operative life in a *kibbutz* or *moshav*. He settled in the bourgeois village of Kfar Saba—as Secretary of the *Lishkat Ha'avodah* (Labour Bureau). But in his friendly attitude to private enterprise, which earned him the respect of bankers, industrialists, and business-men, he seemed much more the representative of General Zionism than of the Labour stream. Nevertheless, he is widely regarded by the Israeli public as a member of the *Mapai* 'old guard'.

Unlike Ben Gurion, Sharett, Eshkol, and Meir, and indeed most members of the High Policy Élite, Sapir was unknown in the years before independence. Thereafter his rise to influence was steady, especially in economic affairs. He was Director-General of the Defence Ministry from 1949 to 1953 and then of the Finance Ministry. In November 1955 he was elevated to the Cabinet as Minister of Commerce and Industry. Indeed, he owes his political career to Ben Gurion. When Eshkol succeeded to the prime ministership in June 1963, Sapir was given the Finance post as well, making him the economic czar over the public sector. He relinquished Commerce and Industry at the beginning of 1966 but remained the most powerful influence on economic policy. And in 1968 he yielded to pressure and succeeded Mrs. Meir in the powerful post of Secretary-General of *Mapai*—on the eve of the re-unification of the labour movement. By that time, in fact since 1963, he had become a valued member of the post-BG 'old guard', along with Eshkol, Meir, and Education Minister Aranne. (After the Seventh *Knesset* elections in October 1969, he re-entered the Government with greater influence than ever: he has been the undisputed ministerial decision-maker in economic policy, holding the double portfolio of Finance and of Commerce and Industry; and he remained the dominant figure in the Labour Alignment party machine.)

There is a consensus that Sapir is a 'human avalanche', a man of immense energy and tremendous stamina who works eighteen hours a day seven days a week throughout the year. He is adept at figures and, despite the lack of a formal education in economics, he has been a skilful manager of the nation's economy—though many felt he mismanaged the *mitun* (planned recession) of 1964–6. He is restless, impulsive, and informal. He is capable of outbursts of criticism, usually followed by apologies. Sapir lacks a sense of humour but he is known to be sentimental, goodhearted, and kind to people who work with him. He is tough with foes—and friends—in politics but has a strong sense of loyalty. He is free of any cultural or intellectual pretensions—his enemies call him boorish; and he admits, 'I enjoy a concert—when my wife takes me'. Yet he has displayed a genuine concern for education and culture in Israel: as Finance Minister he was generous in allocations; and a hobby has been to badger wealthy Jews in the Diaspora to make contributions for schools in the development towns; he has also shown a special interest in the universities of Tel Aviv and Beersheba.[1]

During his years as a civil servant, 1949–55, Sapir did not involve himself in policy decisions, even when he was Director-General of the Defence Ministry: he appears to have confined his attention to the administrative and financial aspects of the defence establishment, unlike his successor, Shimon Peres, who created a parallel Foreign Office from 1953 to 1963.[2] This non-involvement continued during the years when Sapir was a minister under Ben Gurion, 1955–63, partly because of his 'doveishness', which was not in accord with the policies of BG. He was not a member of the Ministerial Committee on (Foreign Policy and) Defence during that period. And as long as Ben Gurion was at the helm his influence in this sphere was nil.

Strangely enough, he did not join that vital committee even after Eshkol became Prime Minister and, as a result, acquired greater influence and responsibility as Minister of Finance, Commerce and Industry, from June 1963 to January 1966. (Eshkol, as Finance Minister, had been a member of that committee since its inception in 1953.) It was only the prodding of Eshkol and pressure within his own ministry that led him to accept membership of the much-enlarged (from 6 to 10) Ministerial Committee on Defence at the beginning of 1966, after the Sixth *Knesset* elections. Until then Sapir's only public intervention in foreign policy was over the ill-fated Lavon Affair; he strongly supported Eshkol against Ben Gurion, but even there his main concern was with domestic consequences, for party unity and national morale.

[1] This portrait is based upon interviews with colleagues and aides of Sapir.
[2] This will be elaborated in ch. 15 (c) ii below.

This is not to suggest that Sapir was without views on foreign and security policy; rather, that he did not express them in public until 1968–9. It was through quiet discussion with Prime Minister Eshkol from 1963 onwards that his perceptions were conveyed and his influence was felt. Colleagues and aides note that he has always been doveish, along with Education Minister Aranne and others. And he himself remarked in 1968: 'I do not accept the division of the Cabinet into hawks and doves. They even say I am a dove. I do not care what people call me. It does not mean anything.'[1] It is known that he questioned the wisdom of retaliation and the hard line from 1955 onwards. It is reported that he and Aranne, along with Eshkol, were the first ministers to press for Israel's withdrawal from the Gaza Strip and Sharm-e-Sheikh after the Sinai Campaign. He was known to have misgivings about the inevitability of massive allocations for defence. And towards the end of the 1950s Sapir was the only minister to oppose the expansion of research projects aimed at qualitative changes in Israel's long-term military capability.

The 'sudden' clash with Dayan over the future of 'the territories' merely carried Sapir's dissenting views into the public arena. These he played in low key during the first year after the 1967 War, partly because on this issue Eshkol was much closer to Dayan (Eshkol was much more hawkish on security policy than appeared, especially after that War), and Sapir was reluctant to appear in conflict with Eshkol. He was Chairman of the Ministerial Committee on the (Civil) Administration of the Territories but did not convene it often because of sharp differences with Dayan. It was only after he left his Cabinet post and became Secretary-General of *Mapai* (he remained a Minister without Portfolio) that he engaged in open debate.

(j) PARTNERSHIP WITH JEWRY

Sapir is aware of the global pre-eminence of the United States and the Soviet Union and the impact of their persistent rivalry on the Arab–Israel conflict. He was not an advocate of non-alignment and would have welcomed a more formal relationship with the US, which he perceives through a 'free world' lens and as a vital source of aid and support for a beleaguered Israel. In the debate over a primarily European (France–Germany) or American orientation, he supported Eshkol, Meir, and Eban on the latter as against Peres and Dayan. On the question of public pressure or quiet diplomacy to ease discrimination against Soviet Jewry, he supported Goldmann's low-posture policy. He does not appear to attach political significance to the Third World, though he has visited Africa on economic missions. And on the UN, as on most foreign policy issues, he follows Eban's lead.

[1] Interview with Mark Segal, *Jerusalem Post*, 22 Sept. 1968.

The one aspect of the global setting on which Sapir has strong, publicly aired views is Israel's links with world Jewry. He does not subscribe to the 'two-camp thesis' of BG. Rather, he shares Eban's concern about 'what the *Goyim* think' and rejects the idea of fortress Israel standing alone against the whole world: in the last analysis Israel must and should fight alone—if necessary—but not before exhausting all possibilities of securing external support. This, for example, was the rationale of Eban, Sapir, and the doveish half of the Cabinet in the May 1967 crisis.[1] At the same time he attached cardinal importance to world Jewry.

Over the years Sapir established strong personal ties with Jewish communities abroad, notably in the US, UK and France, as well as Latin America, as Israel's fund-raiser *par excellence*. In this respect his image is very close to that of Eshkol and Meir. Thus in 1964 he told a UJA Study Mission:[2]

If US Jewry fails to give us the requisite support for immigrant absorption, our basic economic progress may be considerably slowed down. . . . We have reached the [dangerous] situation [where a greater burden is falling on the Israeli tax-payer] while the participation of the Jewish people outside Israel is decreasing.

Paying tribute to world Jewry's aid, he referred to

the great help of the UJA, whose contributions in the spheres of immigration, agricultural settlement, Youth Aliya, and housing have often been decisive. . . . But this is far from sufficient. . . . There is a limit to what we can impose on the Israel citizen, just as there is a limit to the debts that the Jewish Agency and the Government can shoulder.

There is here an unmistakable image of genuine partnership, joint achievements, and shared responsibility in a spirit which was qualitatively different from that of BG.

Like most Israelis, Sapir was overwhelmed by world Jewry's response to the 1967 crisis. 'It is a revelation', he said upon returning to Israel from an emergency fund-raising campaign in June 1967. 'These people are not mere friends or even partners—they are our brothers.'[3] And in a similar vein he told the *Knesset*: '. . . we were shown conclusively that Diaspora Jewry—every sector and generation of it—lives by its link with Israel. . . . I feel sorry that the young Jews of Israel do not feel and do not always appreciate [this]. . . . Thus is carried on the 90-year chain of Jewish love [of the *Yishuv*] . . .'[4] Given his experience and his image of world Jewry's past role and future obligation, it was natural for Sapir to take the lead in organizing the Jerusalem Economic Conference in

---

[1] This will be elaborated in the analysis of the Six Day War decision, in the related volume.

[2] *Jerusalem Post*, 18 Oct. 1964.

[3] Ibid., 20 June 1967.

[4] Report to the *Knesset* on 19 June 1967, as translated. Ibid., 23 June 1967.

1968 to mobilize capital, skills, and manpower to expedite Israel's achievement of economic independence.

(k) DISSENT FROM A MODERATE

Sapir does not perceive 'the Middle East' as a distinctive 'region' or 'system', though he is conscious of the importance of economic ties with the 'periphery' countries, Iran and Ethiopia: like Eshkol and Meir, he does not think in intellectual terms. As for 'the Arabs', he shares the Second *Aliya* mentality of indifference and the failure, as Sharett remarked, to try to understand the other nation in Palestine. Yet in 1965 he welcomed Eshkol's 'winds of change' policy towards Israel's neighbours. In fact, he claimed that the new line was responsible for the Arab decisions not to carry out the threat to attack Israel over her National Water Carrier or the diversion of the Jordan headwaters.[1]

The Sapir–Dayan rift over 'the territories' burst upon an unsuspecting public in November 1968. There were undoubtedly personality and political rivalry dimensions to the feud. But the policy disagreement was no less genuine. It began with a mild reference to Dayan's policy as 'molly-coddling'.[2] Then, at the insistence of the press, Sapir stated his views more fully.[3] He strongly objected to integration of Arab residents of 'the territories' into Israel's economy—for demographic reasons; the addition of one million Arabs to the present 400,000 Israeli Arabs, with their higher birth rate, would soon transform Israel into a bi-national state. Asked what prompted his remarks, he declared that it was time the so-called doves spoke up lest all who disagreed with the hawks be considered traitors.

He favoured 'a treaty that would bring us true peace and secure borders without some of the million Arabs of the areas'. In the meanwhile, *Tzahal* 'will not (and should not) move from their present positions until peace is achieved'. Further, 'we all desire peace, and when the time comes for peace talks we will have to decide what price we are prepared to pay'.

By returning 'the territories', Sapir added, Israel would not be surrendering anything but would rather be 'freeing herself from a burden'. Israel, too, needs peace to reduce the gigantic defence burden, which she cannot bear for a long time, even with the help of world Jewry. Strangely, in the light of his disagreement with Ben Gurion on many issues, he approved BG's remark that there was a danger of manual labour in Israel being taken over by Arabs: 'What is at stake is the very existence of the State of Israel.'

[1] Public address in Haifa. Ibid., 27 June 1965.

[2] Before a student group in Beersheba. Ibid., 3 Nov. 1968.

[3] To the Vocal Newspaper at Beit Sokolow in Tel Aviv, on 8 November, and the *Kol Yisrael* Weekly Newsreel, on 9 November, as reported in *Jerusalem Post*, 10 Nov 1968 (emphasis added).

The danger of integrating the Arab masses into Israel, he concluded, is all-embracing—security, economic and political. And then came the Zionist credo: '*We always wanted a Jewish State, and we did not come back to the Land of Israel in order to work and shed our blood for a bi-national state.*'

Sapir reiterated these views frequently over the next few months and, in the process, clarified his grave concern. 'I believe that integration means converting Israel into an Arab State', he declared later in November; further, 'I claim that [Dayan's] plans for establishing facts will tie our hands once we reach the negotiating table.' He vigorously opposed the plan to establish four Jewish urban settlements near Arab centres on the West Bank, and he praised Eban's policies.[1] 'Maybe Dayan as a *sabra* has sentiments about Hebron', he remarked still later. 'I do not have any such sentiments . . .'—though he denied this report of his views in deference to the storm created by the religious parties.[2]

On one occasion Sapir asserted that Jerusalem, the Golan Heights, and the City of Gaza were not negotiable. 'I have doubts about all of the Gaza Strip. I would like it without the refugees.'[3] Later he moderated this: 'Apart from Jerusalem and the Golan Heights, we should leave all the options open, if we really want peace.'[4] And according to those who know him well, Sapir genuinely wants peace and thinks it is feasible, provided suitable concessions are made—by both sides.

The debate was suspended at the end of February 1969, with the death of Eshkol. It was resumed in the summer during the acrimonious debates within the enlarged Alignment (including *Mapam*) over the foreign policy and security planks in the platform for the impending elections to the Seventh *Knesset*. Eban was the most articulate exponent of the views noted here and clashed openly with Dayan. Sapir extended full support to Eban.[5]

Among the three high-policy decision-makers discussed here, Golda Meir is the most knowledgeable about foreign policy. She is also the most hawkish and rigid, while Sapir is doveish and flexible. Eshkol was much closer to Meir in his general View of the World. All three perceived the link with world Jewry in more generous terms of mutual bonds and *obligations* than does Ben Gurion; so too did Sharett. They also viewed America as the most important source of support. And, apart from Sharett, they failed to understand 'the Arabs'; it is doubtful that they ever tried. Sapir advocates a Sharett-type policy but it stems from concern—about a bi-national state—more than from a desire for reconciliation. Meir and, in a more moderate tone, Eshkol perceived

[1] *Jerusalem Post*, 24 Nov. 1968.   [2] Ibid., 1 and 2 Dec. 1968.
[3] Ibid., 1 Jan. 1969.   [4] Ibid., 11 May 1969.
[5] This clash will be explored in the related volume of this work.

all Arab leaders as Shukairies, following the Ben Gurion image until 1967, when their policies and his diverged. Meir and, in essence, Eshkol were as tough and uncompromising as their mentor had been during the preceding nineteen years. In short, there have been significant cleavages in image and policy among the five 'old guard' leaders.

CHAPTER 14

The Younger Men:
Allon, Dayan, Eban, Peres

Few societies in the contemporary world have produced a group of leaders comparable in stature to Israel's High Policy Élite. And it is doubtful whether any has a more talented second generation leadership than Allon, Dayan, Eban, and Peres, the four younger men in the decision-making Inner Circle. Yigal Allon was the most brilliant field commander in Israel's War of Independence before he was thirty. Moshe Dayan, less well known then, shares with China's Lin Piao and North Vietnam's Vo Nguyen Giap the halo of the most successful soldier since the Second World War. There is no more persuasive advocate in the world of diplomacy than Abba Eban, the voice of Israel at the United Nations and elsewhere since 1948, when he was thirty-three. And Shimon Peres, one of the outstanding Israeli technocrats, created a formidable bureaucratic-military establishment and laid the foundations for the alliance with France in the 1950s from the age of thirty.

At the beginning of Israel's third decade they were all prominent in public life: Allon as Deputy Prime Minister and widely perceived heir to the 'old guard'; Dayan as the charismatic Defence Minister; Eban as the eloquent Foreign Minister; and Peres, temporarily in eclipse, as a Deputy Secretary-General of the Israel Labour Party. (At the end of 1969 he joined the Cabinet.) There is an extraordinary similarity between Allon and Dayan in background, experience and skills. Dayan and Peres have been comrades in the security sphere and in politics for more than fifteen years and think alike on most policy matters—though Allon's outlook is not widely at variance on core issues. Eban is the most apart of the four and is regarded by all as the least typical of Israelis.

(a) BACKGROUND AND PERSONALITY

i. *The Sabra Leaders: Generals and Politicians*

Yigal Allon's family ties to the Land of Israel date back to medieval times on his mother's side, to Safed (Tsfat), one of the four holy cities of Judaism.[1] His father, Reuven Paicovitch, was brought to Palestine from Russia as a boy in the 1880s. Allon's grandparents were among the founders of Rosh Pina, the first Jewish settlement in the Galilee.

[1] The others are Jerusalem, Hebron, and Tiberias.

His parents helped to establish *Kfar Tabor* on the slopes of Mount Tabor in the Lower Galilee, where Yigal was born in October 1918. And he himself was a founder of *Kibbutz* Ginossar on the shores of the *Kinneret* (Sea of Galilee) in 1937. It has been his permanent home ever since.

Moshe Dayan, too, has a distinguished *sabra* background. His father, Shmuel Dayan, arrived from Russia in 1908, during the Second *Aliya*, and was a prominent figure in the mainstream of Labour Zionism until his death in 1968. His mother was a writer of distinction. Moshe was born in May 1915 in Degania, the first *kibbutz* in Palestine, which his parents helped to found in a desolate swampy area of the Jordan Valley. 'My first memory, as a child of five,' recalled the younger Dayan half a century later, 'was the day my father and I had to flee from our kibbutz, which the Arabs had set on fire. . . . And we went to the valley of Jezreel. . . .'[1] There his family founded the first *moshav* (co-operative farm settlement), Nahalal; and there Moshe Dayan spent his formative years.

This difference in background—*kibbutz* versus *moshav*—was not without significance in later years. But it was vastly outweighed until the mid-sixties by common experience. Both men were *sabras*, the only ones in the Inner Circle of decision-makers. Both grew up with plough and gun. Both received their early education in agriculture, Allon at the Kedourie Agricultural College, Mt. Tabor, Dayan in the high school of Nahalal. Allon went on to the Hebrew University and St. Antony's College, Oxford, in the 1950s and early 1960s, during the period between his two callings, the army and politics. Dayan, too, resumed his studies at an advanced age (42), attending the School of Law and Economics in Tel Aviv and the Hebrew University before entering the Government as Minister of Agriculture in 1959. Allon was to become Labour Minister two years later.

Their military careers, too, followed a strikingly similar path, beginning with the disturbances of 1936–9. Both men served in the Jewish Settlement Police and then in the *Haganah* Field Platoons. Both men came under the influence of Orde Wingate, who introduced novel tactics with his Special Night Squads. 'Every Israel soldier is a disciple of Wingate', said Dayan with characteristic directness on the eve of the Sinai Campaign; 'he gave us our technique.'[2] Allon was influenced even more by the equally legendary Yitzhak Sadeh, creator of the Field Platoons and, in 1941, of *Palmah*. He paid tribute to both:[3]

[1] Interview with Jacques Boetsch of *L'Express* (Paris) at Dayan's home in a Tel Aviv suburb, as translated in *The Montreal Star*, 26 May 1969.
[2] Reported by *Newsweek* (New York), 29 Oct. 1956, as quoted in *Jerusalem Post*, 25 Oct. 1956.
[3] 'The Making of Israel's Army', in Michael Howard (ed.), *The Theory and Practice of War*, Praeger, New York, 1965, p. 341.

The appearance of Wingate, with his extraordinary Zionist ardour inspired by the Bible, his unconventional military gifts and his outstanding courage, was an event of historic importance for the Haganah. . . . His Jewish counterpart and comrade in the illegal branch of the Haganah was Yitzhak Sadeh, a military genius of international calibre, one of the greatest commanders in Jewish history, the father of modern Jewish fighting, the teacher of most young Israeli commanders. He and Wingate together significantly modified the tactics of the Haganah.

(These comments also reveal much about the contrasting verbal styles of Dayan and Allon.) The two young *sabras* also commanded the Jewish units assisting the Australian–British invasion of Lebanon and Syria in 1941. Dayan, along with forty-two other *Haganah* men, had been released for this assignment after sixteen months of a five-year sentence in the forbidding Acre Prison. It was during that campaign that he lost his left eye and acquired his later widely known black eye-patch.

Allon was the most talented of Sadeh's young men, and he rose rapidly in *Palmah*: by 1945 he was commander of that élite commando force. And in the War of Independence he acquired heroic stature as commander of virtually all the major Israeli campaigns: in Upper Galilee, including Safed (Tsfat); on the Central Front (Lydda-Ramle and the Jerusalem Corridor); and finally the Southern Front where, in Operation *Ayin* in December–January 1948-9, he expelled the Egyptians from the Negev. Only political pressure from the UK—transmitted by the United States ambassador, McDonald—and the order of Ben Gurion at the end of 1948 prevented his conquest of the entire Sinai Peninsula.[1]

Dayan's record in the Arab–Israel 'first round' was much less distinguished; in fact, he served under Allon and Sadeh in the early campaigns (leading the capture of Lod and Ramle), before taking command of the Jerusalem front at the end of July 1948, after a much-criticized failure of *Aluf* (Brigadier-General) David Shaltiel to capture

---

[1] In the last week of December 1948 Israel moved to clear the Negev of remaining Egyptian troops and, in the course of the fighting, some *Tzahal* units crossed into Sinai. The UK issued an ultimatum to Israel to obey the Security Council Resolution of 29 December ordering a cease-fire and withdrawal to positions before the renewal of hostilities. McDonald delivered it to Sharett and then to Ben Gurion, who was in Tiberias. Lorch's account is brief and laconic: 'The Prime Minister assured him that Zahal was not invading Egypt . . . [and] had been instructed to withdraw. . . . Once the decision had been made . . . the forces of the southern front were ordered to withdraw from Sinai by January 2. This made the achievement of objectives in phase two of the operation more difficult, but not impossible. . . .' *The Edge of the Sword*, pp. 427–9. McDonald's account is more dramatic. First he saw Sharett but found his reply 'neither in itself satisfactory nor completely authoritative. I therefore told Sharett that I must see Ben Gurion as quickly as possible. I must have the definitive reply of the Prime Minister.' On New Year's Eve he rushed to Tiberias, a formidable distance of over one hundred miles in the midst of war, and there received Ben Gurion's assurance that Israeli troops were being withdrawn. McDonald, *My Mission in Israel 1948–1951*, Simon and Schuster, New York, 1951, pp. 114–21.

the Old City.[1] A biographer offered the following explanation for this lesser role in Dayan's otherwise dramatic leadership:[2]

Except on rare occasions, Dayan was never seen with the top brass of the Haganah. This was perhaps due to his having held himself aloof from political activities. . . . Dayan was not a kibbutz member, and did not see eye to eye with the Left-wing group which ran [!] the Palmach. Nor did he show any interest in being active in Mapai. . . . Thus it was that he lost his position in leadership and had to make way for men who had served during the war as officers in the British Army.

It was a disservice to Dayan, who amply displayed his military gifts during the next two decades.

Allon's active military career ended abruptly in 1950, when he left *Tzahal*. He had strenuously opposed the enforced integration of *Palmah* into the national army and was passed over in what many regarded as his pre-eminent claim to the post of Chief of Staff.[3] For a decade he was in the political wilderness, though he was a member of the *Knesset* from 1954 onwards and a leader of *Ahdut Ha'avodah*. He re-emerged as a national figure towards the end of 1961 as Minister of Labour when his party joined a new Ben Gurion-led coalition. In the 1967 crisis he was Eshkol's belated choice for the Defence Ministry—in a futile effort to keep Dayan out of this pivotal position; but the mass public along with opposition parties triumphed. Dayan acquired the reputation at home and abroad of Israel's pre-eminent military commander—as Chief of

[1] From the end of 1968 the rank equivalent of *Aluf* was Major-General.
The second truce in the 1948 War was to take effect at dawn on 17 July. Ben Gurion issued an order to the commander of the Etzioni Brigade to inform the Consular Committee in Jerusalem that he would cease fire in accord with the Security Council decision on condition that he was informed by midnight on the 16th that the Arabs, too, had accepted the decision and would cease fire at the same time. Yadin, the *Tzahal* Chief of Operations, then sent the following order to the brigade commander: 'Following the telegram of the Minister of Defence . . . concerning the truce, you are to decide what you will be able to carry out during this night. The evident possibilities: Sheikh Jarrah or a bridgehead in the Old City. In case only one possibility is feasible before the truce, you are to carry out Sheikh Jarrah.'
The brigade commander in Jerusalem decided to carry out Operation *Kedem*—the capture of the Old City, in a frontal attack, without prior encirclement. It failed, and at dawn all *Tzahal* forces returned to their bases. The Old City remained in Arab Legion hands. The truce went into effect on the evening of 18 July. Soon after, Shaltiel was replaced by Dayan as commander of the Jerusalem front. Lorch, op. cit., pp. 295–6. The controversy simmered and exploded periodically, with Ben Gurion blaming Shaltiel and Yadin, and the latter charging Ben Gurion with responsibility both as Defence Minister and for failing to order an assault on the Old City earlier. In this context the key point of controversy was Dayan, whom Ben Gurion praised to the extent of arguing that, had he been in command of *Tzahal*, 'the map of Israel would have been different'. *Ha'aretz* (Tel Aviv), 10 March 1964.
[2] N. Lau-Lavie, *Moshe Dayan: A Biography*, Vallentine, Mitchell & Co., London, 1968, p. 54.
[3] The unification of Israel's military and para-military forces was discussed in ch. 4 (*d*) above.

Staff, 1953–8, hero of the Sinai Campaign, and then as Minister of Defence during the Six Day War. He also became the most popular Israeli public figure, with a mass following, from 1967 onwards.[1]

Both men are endowed with impressive assets and qualities. They have deep roots in the society created by Jewish pioneers during the past ninety years. They are known for their personal courage, decisiveness, and inspirational leadership—on the battlefield and among their admirers generally. They are sensitive to the Middle East environment of Israel. In the view of many they understand the Arabs better than other members of the High Policy Élite. They have carefully-considered views on most aspects of public policy, notably on foreign and security matters. They have many years of experience in political life, including a decade or more in the *Knesset* and the Government. Both are highly intelligent and have faith in their own judgement of men and affairs. Of Dayan, Ben Gurion reportedly said in 1958: 'You have two diametrically opposed facets to your character—courage bordering upon the lunatic, offset and balanced by a profound tactical and strategic intelligence.'[2] The same assessment could be applied to Allon. And finally, there is a national consensus that they are the leading contenders for succession to the Second *Aliya* 'old guard'.

There are differences, however, between these leaders of Israel's *sabra* generation. Dayan is the pragmatist *par excellence*: his detractors accuse him of inconsistency, for he enunciates different policy positions from month to month, sometimes more frequently; this is especially true of pronouncements regarding 'the territories'—but Dayan defends this as a response to changing political circumstances. Allon retains an ideological commitment—to *kibbutz*-derived socialism, with a strong nationalist flavour. Both his views and his actions are marked by greater continuity and predictability. (This contrast is expressed in their party links, *Rafi* and *Ahdut Ha'avodah* respectively.) Dayan is more flamboyant in speech and manner. Allon gives the impression of greater prudence and caution. Dayan is direct, frank, easy in manner. Allon is more

[1] The most prominent Israeli agency engaged in public opinion polls, *Dahaf*, conducted five surveys in 1968 and 1969 based upon the following question: 'If the elections to the *Knesset* were to take place tomorrow, for whom would you vote?' The percentage results were as follows:

	May 1968	July 1968	December 1968	February 1969	April 1969
Eshkol or Dayan					
ESHKOL	31%	20%	20%	25%	
DAYAN	48%	51%	60%	61%	
Dayan or Allon					
DAYAN	62%	60%	no information	68%	52%
ALLON	21%	25%	,, ,,	22%	37%

Source: Made available by the *Dahaf* agency.

[2] As quoted in Lau-Lavie, op. cit., Introduction.

formal and appears to many persons more the intellectual. Dayan is unconventional in all things. At the same time he is more restless, obstinate, imperious, contemptuous, and unpredictable—in personality and political behaviour.

Dayan is a 'loner', fiercely independent in spirit, and an outspoken iconoclast: he arouses passionate devotion and intense hostility among Israelis. There is no one whom he admires, he declares candidly:[1]

'Not even Mr Ben Gurion?'

'Let me tell you something about Mr. Ben Gurion. He is probably the only person I admire. And finally no, not even him. I don't admire anyone. But I have a higher opinion of him than anyone else.'

Allon is much more the member of a team in cabinet and party. Moreover, he was for years a protégé of Yitzhak Tabenkin, the grand old man of the *Ha-Kibbutz Ha-me'uhad* movement, and of Yitzhak Sadeh, for both of whom he has often expressed admiration.

Sharett has been described as a Middle Easterner of the peaceful tribe, and Dayan, of the warring tribe. Allon is no less hawkish in policy but he has not acquired this extreme image. Dayan thinks aloud and is not averse to hesitation before making decisions. Thus, for example, he pondered a long time before joining *Rafi* in the 1965 *Mapai* split:[2]

I admit with pride that I hesitated before deciding to join Rafi. No, it wasn't just that I couldn't make up my mind. I hesitated and carefully weighed various things. If there had been more time, I would have continued to hesitate and weigh.

Allon has never admitted vacillation and, objectively, has been more decisive.

Dayan has, on occasion, engaged in revealing public self-analysis. To the charge of dilettantism he replied:

'It's not true. I'm very conservative. I've only concerned myself with two things in public life: agriculture and military affairs. And I've been concerned with these for a very long time, longer than anyone else in this country.

Dayan has written only one book, the widely known *Diary of the Sinai Campaign* (1965), but he has spoken out boldly on public issues with increasing frequency after the Six Day War.[3] 'I write very seldom,' he said with candour, 'and when I do, I write very slowly, because I want each word to mean exactly what I want to say. . . . And my hobby is

---

[1] *L'Express* interview, quoted op. cit.

[2] Interview with Moshe Kohn, 'Moshe Dayan: Why I Joined Rafi', *Jerusalem Post*, 10 Sept. 1965.

[3] A collection of his speeches and statements on security and foreign policy after that war was published as *Mappa Hadasha—Yehassim Aherim* (New Map—Other Relationships), Ma'ariv, Tel Aviv, 1969.

archaeology', he added.[1] Allon has written a penetrating analysis of the Arab–Israel conflict and of many aspects of Israeli society, *Curtain of Sand* (1960), an account of *Palmah*, and two volumes on the evolution of Israel's armed forces since the early days of the *Yishuv*.

On his Jewish identity Dayan remarked that Israel was founded more on the idea of a nation than on that of religion:

Yes, in our ancient history, at the time the Temple was being built by David and Saul, the Jews were not religious. . . .

I am not religious, I do not eat kosher, but I think I'm a good Jew because I speak the Jewish language, I fight for the Jewish state, I try to help Jews come here. . . .

I know my history and I want my children to be educated in this history. I want them to respect it, not from a religious point of view but for its philosophy of justice, mercy, the equality of peoples and the idea that God made man in his image.

Known for his courage, he described his sensations when he was buried in a landslide during an archaeological excavation:

I wasn't afraid, but I remember it because it was probably the only time I have really thought about death. . . . I tried to get out and found I couldn't. And then I saw the second part of the landslide coming and I told myself that this was it. I didn't think about anything else. . . . I lost consciousness. And the first thing I thought of when they got my head out was that it hadn't been my turn that time after all.

There is a direct and candid approach in these passages which endears Dayan to large masses of Israelis. Allon, too, possessed this quality in the past. But over the years he became more conventional—in the image of the party politician.

ii. The Non-Sabras: 'Bitzuist' and Advocate

Shimon Peres was the boy wonder of Israel's bureaucracy: at thirty he became Ben Gurion's principal aide in the Defence Ministry. Soon after, he forged the (unwritten) alliance with France and achieved secure access to modern weapons of high quality, both vital to Israel's survival in the 1950s.[2] According to Sharett, he was also responsible for persuading BG to seek entry into the European Common Market.[3] Certainly he played a key role in that initiative. He was, indeed, Israel's Adjunct Foreign Minister to the military establishments of western Europe, with powerful links as well to friendly new states in Africa and Asia.

Peres is not a *sabra* but his attachment to Zion dates from childhood: he was born in 1923 in the town of Volozin, White Russia. It was a

---

[1] *L'Express* interview, op. cit. The remaining extracts in this section are also taken from this interview.

[2] Peres' account of how this was done is contained in his *David's Sling*, ch. 3.

[3] Interview in Jerusalem, 8 July 1960.

unique environment, for all of the one thousand Jewish families spoke Hebrew as their mother tongue. Although initially drawn to the Left-socialist *Ha-shomer Ha-tza'ir*, he joined *Ha-no'ar Ha-oved*, the *Histadrut* youth movement, soon after his arrival in Palestine with his family at the age of ten. He attended high school in Tel Aviv and spent two formative years (15 to 17) at the Youth *Aliya* children's village of Ben Shemen, with a mixed group of Israeli and immigrant youngsters. Many years later, he described it as a romantic adventure, which encouraged both non-conformism and responsibility. 'I wouldn't say they were the happiest days of my life, because I'm always happy. But Ben Shemen gave us a rich, full world.'[1] After further training in *Kvutzat* Geva, he settled in *Kibbutz* Alumot until 1947. During that period he became National Secretary of *Ha-no'ar Ha-oved*, a role which he was to symbolize later in the 'young guard' of *Mapai*, along with Dayan.

Peres was released for work with *Haganah* HQ in 1947 and remained with the Defence establishment for eighteen years. He helped to create Israel's navy in 1949 and then headed the purchasing mission of the Defence Ministry in the United States. He became Deputy Director-General of the Ministry of Defence in 1952 and Director-General the following year. In 1959 he moved into the political arena: he entered the *Knesset*, along with Dayan, as spokesmen of *Mapai* youth, and was elevated to the post of Deputy Defence Minister. Thus, from the mid-fifties to 1965, when he resigned in the *Mapai* split, Peres was in the Inner Circle of the High Policy Élite.

With Ben Gurion's blessing and Dayan's hesitant approval, Peres created a new political party, *Rafi*, almost single-handed. The years 1965–8 were not quite a political wilderness for him, but the influence and glamour of the previous decade were increasingly removed from his grasp. He played a decisive role, along with Dayan, in bringing *Rafi* back into the Labour Zionist fold; indeed, he was the first advocate of complete merger, which was consummated in January 1968. Peres then became one of the two Deputy Secretaries-General of the Israel Labour Party (the other was from *Ahdut Ha'avodah*), at first under Mrs. Meir and then Sapir, with both of whom he had clashed openly over the years: their differences on policy were accentuated by a personality conflict and a thinly disguised struggle over the succession to Ben Gurion.[2] Just before the reunion of the three labour parties, during the 1967 crisis leading to the Six Day War, Peres was to play an important role in the pressure which created the National Unity Government, with Dayan as Minister of Defence.[3]

Shimon Peres is first and foremost a man of action, a '*bitzuist*', a

---

[1] Interview, in *Jerusalem Post*, 5 Nov. 1963.
[2] This will be elaborated in the following chapter.
[3] This role will be explored in the related volume on high-policy decisions.

brilliant executor of decisions. By temperament and behaviour he is a technocrat, who has long since abandoned ideology as a guide to policy. 'We are the Kennedy generation in Israel politics', he declared in New York in 1966. It 'is a generation of dialogue rather than rigid ideology. There is a widespread desire in Israel today to talk over anew principles and methods. . . .'[1]

Peres shares with Dayan a pragmatic approach to policy matters and a great respect for science and technology as the key to solving Israel's social and economic problems. He, too, is calm and cool in the face of crisis, ruthless in the pursuit of values—and he is more decisive He lacks Dayan's charisma with Israel's mass public; in fact, there is a tendency to mistrust his actions, so long associated with the secrecy of the security network. Yet he has a more systematic and orderly mind, with a penchant for original ideas. His speeches are lucid, calm, usually restrained, and persuasive.

Peres lacks the formal higher education of his peers. But this was compensated by a *guru*-disciple relationship with the legendary thinker of Labour Zionism, Berl Katznelson, to whom he attributes the greatest influence of his formative years. 'I see him as a mentor, as a teacher in the Indian tradition. . . . He had the most inquiring mind I have ever encountered . . . non-conformist, widely-read, erudite.'[2] Peres sat at his feet, weekly, for four years and acquired a feel for ideas. Indeed he has an intellectual flair, more impressive than that of Dayan and compara-ble in insight to Allon and Eban, though without the latter's literary elegance.

Abba Eban is the best-known Israeli in the chancelleries of the world and at the United Nations, where he commands respect as the con-summate advocate of a new state under permanent siege. To those who have heard his masterly flow of words he is the Churchill of contemp-orary diplomacy. Yet Eban's admirers and his supporters have remained mainly outside Israel, even after a decade of continuous exposure to the Israeli public (his critics say because of it)—as Minister without Portfolio (1959–60), Education Minister (1960–3), Deputy Prime Minis-ter (1963–6), and Foreign Minister since the beginning of 1966. To many he continues to be 'the outsider', out of tune with Israel's *sabra* generation, its concerns and aspirations, its behaviour, its approach to the issues of war and peace, its attitude to the rest of the world.

Of the four younger men in the decision-making Inner Circle, Eban is certainly the most distant in background and experience from the new Israeli society. Yet, like Peres—in an entirely different context—his Zionist roots are deep. Born in South Africa in January 1915 of Lithu-anian immigrants, he came to England as an infant. His grandfather was a 'fanatical Hebraist', and the young Aubrey was bilingual

---

[1] *Jerusalem Post*, 14 June 1966.
[2] To Mark Segal, *Jerusalem Post*, 31 July 1964.

(English-Hebrew) at the age of five. His mother was secretary to Zionist leader Nahum Sokolow, and Eban himself came to the attention of Weizmann—via Sharett and Katznelson—as a talented public speaker in the Zionist cause in the then hostile environment of England during the late 1930s. By then he was a Fellow of Pembroke College, Cambridge, after a brilliant academic record: he graduated from Cambridge in 1938 with First Class Honours in both Classics and Oriental Languages and Literature—Arabic, Hebrew, and Persian.

He worked briefly with Weizmann and Sharett at the London office of the Jewish Agency in 1939—in the preliminary negotiations for the creation of a Jewish Division in the British Army. He was a near-participant in the Dunkirk disaster: his boat crossing the Channel was met by British survivors from the German onslaught against France and the Low Countries in the spring of 1940. Thereafter his war service brought him increasingly into contact with the *Yishuv*. As Major Eban he was posted to Jerusalem in 1942, as Liaison Officer at Allied HQ, with the primary task of training Jewish volunteers for special missions in Palestine and behind the Nazi lines in Europe. Two years later he became Chief Instructor at the Middle East Arabic Centre in Jerusalem, established by the Allied command.

After demobilization in September 1946, and under the influence of the growing struggle of Palestine Jewry, he gave up his academic career and entered the Political Department of the Jewish Agency. He was thus the last of the High Policy Élite to settle in the Land of Israel, and the oldest (31). In the spring of 1948 he made his first appearance on the UN stage and pleaded the *Yishuv* cause with passion and conviction. Since then he has been the voice of Israel, from 1948 to 1959 as Permanent Representative to the United Nations and, simultaneously, from 1950 to 1959, as Ambassador to the United States. He resumed this role after the Sixth *Knesset* Elections, when he succeeded Golda Meir as Foreign Minister.

Eban had a unique status among Israel's envoys: it was probably higher than in his years as Minister and Deputy Prime Minister, from 1959 to 1966. Both Ben Gurion and Sharett had great faith in his capacity to explain Israel's actions, even when they aroused misgivings in Israel and abroad. A notable example was the Lake Kinneret raid in December 1955—when Ben Gurion reportedly punctured Eban's protest by telling him that, after he had listened to Eban's superb defence of the action, any doubts he might have had were removed.[1] On more than one occasion during the fifties Eban displayed the courage of his convictions by strongly opposing the BG–Dayan–Peres policy of retaliation. He also exerted influence on major policy issues, for example, the decision to press for a mutual defence agreement with the US

[1] Told to this writer by various persons in the Foreign Ministry and the Prime Minister's entourage at the time.

in 1954 and the decision to decline Communist China's offer of diplomatic relations early in 1955.[1] For the most part, however, he was the supreme diplomat, advocate, and implementer of policy arrived at by the Government of Israel.

While Dayan and Peres are perceived—at home and abroad[2]—as the hawks of Israel, Eban, along with Sapir, is viewed as the leading dove. In the broadest sense this is accurate, for Dayan and Peres are the proud continuators of the Ben Gurion path in foreign and security policy, while Eban is the practitioner, as well as the admirer, of Sharett's alternative approach, especially to relations with Israel's Arab neighbours. (This will become clear in the following analysis of their images.)

Eban's speeches are marked by an elegant style, which often obscures his ideas—in the *Knesset* as elsewhere. He is more formal than his peers in bearing, dress, manner, and speech. He is less quick to make decisions, more inclined to delay while the complex forces at work, both external and internal, and especially the former, unfold on the stage. As a diplomat, with a donnish air, he has a basic mistrust of 'the generals' and their '*bitzuist*' mentality, with the strong taint of chauvinism, total self-reliance, isolationism, and disdain for 'the world', an attitude so pronounced with Dayan and Peres. In this respect, as in others, Allon, though a general, has been closer in spirit to Eban since he entered the ranks of Government and the Ministerial Committee on Defence in 1961.

Eban's extraordinary appeal abroad, especially with Jewry and the intelligentsia, is not reciprocated among Israelis. There is, indeed, a greater tendency to depreciate his qualities than is evident among all other members of the decision-making Inner Circle: the 'alien' image runs deep.

Relationships among these four younger men are not easy to uncover. Dayan and Peres have been comrades for almost twenty years in government, party, and the Defence Establishment, and share a basic policy outlook. Yet Dayan, as noted, has no friends. Thus, while Peres served as Deputy Defence Minister to Ben Gurion and even Eshkol, it was *Rav-Aluf* (Major-, later Lieutenant-General) Zvi Zur, and not Peres, whom Dayan chose for this post in 1967; officially he is Assistant to the Minister of Defence.

Allon and Dayan have always displayed the mutual respect of outstanding military commanders: neither has ever been defeated in battle.

---

[1] To be elaborated in the related volume on high-policy decisions.

[2] See, for example, the *New York Times Magazine* article on Dayan, entitled, 'Hawk of Israel', by Curtis G. Pepper, 9 July 1967, and the lead question by Eric Rouleau, Middle East Editor of *Le Monde* (Paris) in an interview with Shimon Peres (28 Dec. 1968): 'You have the reputation of being, along with General Dayan, one of the leading "hawks" in Israel. Are you?'

Both are also conscious of their role as leaders of Israel's *sabra* generation and as rivals for the political succession to the ageing Second *Aliya* élite. Both have spoken publicly about each other with appreciation and, occasionally, with cordiality—never with a tone of harshness or abuse.[1] Dayan has not commented on Allon as often or recently. But he has never shown disdain, as he has for Eshkol, Sharett, and others. On the contrary, his rare references, for example on the Allon Plan for the West Bank, have not been unfriendly.

By contrast, Peres has not concealed his disagreements with Allon.[2] In part, this was a continuation of a party feud—*Rafi* versus *Ahdut Ha'-avodah*—and its corresponding clash in basic outlook on policy, pragmatism versus ideology. In part, it was personal. And Peres remembered that *Ahdut Ha'avodah* had prevented his entry into full membership of the Ministerial Committee on Foreign Affairs and Defence in 1960— because he was a mere Deputy Minister. In a similar vein, Eban and Dayan have displayed an increasingly hostile attitude towards each other's policies, reaching its peak in the debate over the Alignment's foreign policy and security planks in the election platform for 1969. Eban virtually called on Dayan to leave the party and rejected his 'oral interpretation' of the consensus on this crucial policy issue.[3] The conflict was resolved by two separate formulae in the platform—Dayan's 'strategic, security borders' in the security plank, and Eban's 'agreed, secure and recognized borders' in the foreign policy plank.[4]

Although Eban and Allon have policy differences, especially towards 'the territories', they display mutual respect. In 1965, when they served as joint chairmen of the then Alignment (*Mapai* and *Ahdut Ha'avodah*) Election Committee, Allon toasted their victory in the Sixth *Knesset* Elections as the only occasion on which Oxford and Cambridge graduates had combined to win an election in Israel! In the 1969 clash over the phrasing of the election platform, Eban declared that Allon shared his interpretation—and his assertion was not challenged.[5] The division among the younger leaders into two 'alliances' had tended to become polarized.

---

[1] For example, even with the public opinion polls showing a much larger support for Dayan as Prime Minister, on the eve of the 1969 elections, Allon remarked: 'We have many things in common, but there are also differences of opinion on important issues. Co-operation between us is not dependent on prior agreements over every issue. The relations between Dayan and myself are correct. Confronted with a common problem, there is full co-operation between us, both on the matter itself and at the human and collegial level. When we differ, we say what we think, and the Cabinet or party decides. The same applies when we agree. There is no need to pursue either individual pacts or "Jewish wars".' Interview with Ari Rath, *Jerusalem Post*, 24 Oct. 1969.
[2] Interviews in Israel in 1966.
[3] *Jerusalem Post*, 6 Aug. 1969.
[4] Ibid., 5 Aug. 1969.   [5] Ibid., 6 Aug. 1969.

(b) PERCEPTIONS OF THE GLOBAL SETTING

Israeli perceptions of international politics are dominated by Israel's struggle for survival and progress as an independent state. This is a natural focus for small and middle powers and especially for one whose existence since independence has been challenged by the reality of permanent war. It was true of Ben Gurion, notwithstanding his fascination for the sweep of history in the 'large sphere'. It was true of Sharett, the most cosmopolitan member of the Second *Aliya* leadership. It was (is) certainly true of Eshkol, Meir, and Sapir, whose View of the World rarely extended(s) beyond Israel and the Jewish People. And in large measure the four younger men in the Inner Circle display a preoccupation with the narrower realm of Israel's foreign policy.

This is not to suggest that Allon, Dayan, Eban, and Peres are unaware of global politics in their larger setting. On the contrary, all of them have articulated a view of the world which is not confined to 'the Middle East'. Among the four, Eban has been the most eloquent and has spoken most frequently about foreign affairs, as befits his preeminent role since 1948. At the other extreme is Dayan, who has been relatively uncommunicative about global political forces, except as they impinge on the Arab–Israel conflict; that is, a more insular view. Both Allon and Peres have been more outspoken on the broader international arena, Peres since 1957, Allon even earlier.

i. *Eban: A Diplomat's Perspective*

A careful reading of Eban's voluminous speeches during Israel's first decade reveals relatively little attention to the global system. Indeed, the Soviet Union is rarely mentioned, except in praise in the very early days (for her act of recognition and her support of Israel's entry into the UN) and in dismay in 1955–6 (for the total support given to the Arab states). The Third World, too, is conspicuously absent. The main themes were the Arab–Israel conflict, Israel and the Middle East, internal developments, and Israel's right to security. As for the global setting, the three main components were the United States, the UN, and Jewry.[1]

The special circumstances which created a transitory shared interest of the super powers in the Middle East during the late 1940s, to Israel's benefit, did not lead to Eban's expectation of long-term Soviet friendship. Nevertheless, as a faithful envoy he reflected the non-identification line at the UN until the Korean War. And in the autumn 1950 General Assembly he attempted the improbable role of honest broker in that

---

[1] Eban's speeches at the UN and in the United States were made available to the press and the public by the Israel Office of Information in New York. A selection of these is contained in his *Voice of Israel*, Horizon Press, New York, 1957 (1st ed.), and 1969 (2nd, enlarged, ed.). Subsequent citations refer to the 2nd ed.

conflict.[1] Throughout the early years, however, he perceived the United States as more important to Israel's survival. Thus it was Eban who took the lead in the quest for a closer attachment to Washington, from 1951 to 1955—through economic and military aid and a mutual assistance treaty. Typical was his remark in March 1955 that Israel's alleged isolation is false, that she has friendly relations with the majority of states and that, 'in this process of establishing relations . . . with other peoples, our strongest reliance has been upon friendship with the United States'.[2]

The theme of affinity between Israel and America recurs throughout his speeches, as illustrated by the following extracts:[3]

The American–Israel partnership owes more to historical affinities reaching back into the national experience of both peoples than to any transient conditions of political harmony or international expediency. . . .

The first element is the fact that both countries are built upon immigration. . . . The second common memory of both countries is of pioneering. . . . The most important element in our common tradition [is] democracy and the republicanism of both the United States and Israel. . . . Finally, we find an element of close affinity when we look at the culture and the science of our two countries. . . . (1953)

America has always acknowledged its debt to Israel's tradition for the truths of individual, social and international virtue on which its own Revolution was founded. In this decade, Israel's pioneering struggle has revived for many Americans the stirring memories of their own historic past. (1956)

It was natural for Eban as Ambassador to the United States to stress the 'common tradition' between Israel and America. But his behaviour indicated that his real image coincided with expressed views.

Until 1955 Eban and other Israeli decision-makers thought that they could ignore the Soviet Union as a vital factor in the Arab–Israeli conflict. The violent anti-Zionist and anti-Semitic character of Stalin's last years (the Slansky trial in Czechoslovakia, 1951–2, the Doctors' Plot, 1953, etc.) and the break in diplomatic relations, 1953, restored the historic Jewish image of a hostile Russia. Then came the massive Soviet-inspired Czech–Egyptian arms deal in the autumn of 1955 and the brutal Bulganin–Khrushchev threats of annihilation of Israel, during the Sinai Campaign. And while it was persistent American pressure that led to Israel's withdrawal from Gaza and Sharm-e-Sheikh in the spring of 1957, Eisenhower and Dulles made solemn pledges of support

[1] This point will be elaborated in the related volume on high-policy decisions.
[2] 'The Lofty Peak', speech before the Assembly of Jewish Organizations, Washington, 6 March 1955, *Voice of Israel*, p. 190.
[3] These are taken from *Voice of Israel*: 'The Common Tradition', to the Jewish Theological Seminary, New York, 11 Feb. 1953 (pp. 124, 125, 128, 130, 133); and to the America–Israel Society, Washington, 17 April 1956 (p. 13).

for Israel's right to free passage in the Tiran Straits—a diplomatic triumph in which Eban played the decisive role.[1]

During the next decade Soviet patronage of Israel's Arab enemies increased in intensity and scope, with military, economic, diplomatic, and propaganda aid on a massive scale.[2] Moscow's incitement of Syria and Egypt in the 1967 crisis leading to the Six Day War deepened Israeli mistrust of Soviet intentions. The US, by contrast, continued to appear as Israel's friend. And in the aftermath of that war she was the most helpful among the Big Four in the prolonged political struggle for a peace settlement. Washington also sold Israel vitally needed Phantom jet bombers to replace the embargoed French Mirage planes. This reality strengthened Eban's predisposition to perceive the super powers through a pronounced pro-American lens. For example, with an eye to undercutting the pro-Europe orientation of some colleagues, he remarked: 'There was a tendency in some quarters, until Mr. Eshkol's journey to Washington [May–June 1964], to underestimate the significance and potentialities of our interests in the United States'.[3]

Eban's image of the United Nations is in the Sharett tradition. He recognizes its limitations and shortcomings in the Arab–Israel conflict but also acknowledges its contribution to Israel's independence. And in the global system as a whole he perceives the UN as a stabilizing element of great value. Two illustrations of his articulated view may be noted. In a tenth anniversary address before the special assembly in San Francisco in 1955 he observed:[4]

The record is neither negligible nor unimpressive. Active hostilities in many parts of the world have been localized in scope and limited in duration. . . , in Kashmir and Indonesia, in Iran, in the Middle East, in the Balkans and Berlin and, above all, in Korea. . . . [Even in the absence of a major war between the super powers] we cannot lawfully deny the United Nations its due share of merit for this achievement. . . .

[Secondly] the United Nations may claim to have exceeded the expectations of its founders [in influencing] the golden age of national emancipation. . . .

[Thirdly] all [the specialized agencies] have helped to make the name of the United Nations in many lands a byword for fruitful and disinterested humanitarianism. . . .

This was a conventional but, on the whole, complimentary assessment of the UN role in world politics. On another occasion he remarked:[5]

[1] This point will be elaborated in the related volume on high-policy decisions.

[2] See Walter Laqueur, *The Struggle for the Middle East*, Routledge & Kegan Paul, London, 1969, for an analysis of Soviet policy in the region from 1958 to 1968.

[3] Interview with Francis Ofner, *The Jewish Chronicle*, London, 3 July 1964. Issued as a *Press Bulletin* by the Government Press Office, Jerusalem.

[4] 'Ten Years Ago We Were Not Here', to the United Nations Commemorative Assembly, San Francisco, 26 June 1955. *Voice of Israel*, pp. 206–15.

[5] To the Jerusalem Journalists' Association on 14 August 1963. *Weekly News Bulletin*, Jerusalem, 14–20 August 1963.

The main virtue of the UN is its universality. . . . Even when the Cold War was at its most tense, the UN served as a place where the two rival blocs could meet and maintain a dialogue. . . . The weak points are also well known. . . .

As to the State of Israel and the UN: here, too, the account is complex and not all on one side. The Organization played an important part in preparing political conditions towards the establishment of our State and in giving the decisive legal confirmation to its sovereign existence. . . . I do not forget, how could I, times of impotence, weakness and even indifference, but the Jewish people as a whole has not lost, in the final analysis, through the existence of the international organization. . . .

And while he had no illusions about the role of Secretary-General U Thant and the Security Council from May 1967 onwards, Eban continued to attach importance to the UN as the forum of world opinion. In that context, he shared Sharett's view of the need to seek external support and its impact on foreign policy, a position diametrically opposed to Ben Gurion's disdain for 'oum shmoum': 'The very exercise of seeking the support of world opinion imposes restraints of reason in the development of national policies, and operates against the formulation of national policies on the sole basis of egocentric emotion.'[1]

Eban's global image in the mid-1960s, just before and after he assumed office as Foreign Minister, was expressed most precisely in two speeches in Israel, one before the World Zionist Organization in January 1965, the other to the Knesset in March 1966. That image did not change in any essentials after the Six Day War.

The global setting, he told the Zionist convention, assumes greater importance for Israel because of her regional isolation. He stressed the friendship of the United States and Latin America, noting that there were no gaps of non-recognition. France he continued to perceive as the key to Israel's relations with Europe. As for Germany, 'the past affects the future; it cannot be allowed to dominate it exclusively'. There were, Eban declared, various credits for Israel in the existing global political environment: she has succeeded in preserving a local balance of security, thereby avoiding such crises as Vietnam, Cyprus, and the Congo: her basic objective—the preservation of sovereignty and integrity—is in harmony with broader international interests, for the Great Powers are committed to the territorial status quo in the international system; Israel possesses the intellectual and scientific power to compensate for demographic and spatial disadvantages; Arab fanaticism is against the spirit of tolerance in our age; and finally, distant friendships offset local enmities—and Israel is not cut off 'from our natural historical and geographic environment, which is the Mediterranean world'.

The paradox of the global setting, Eban observed, is that, while it is congenial to the universalist element in Israel's heritage, her numerical

[1] To the United Nations Commemorative Assembly. . . , Voice of Israel, p. 211.

disadvantage—13 states to 1—is most marked in that sphere. With pride and self-confidence he remarked that Israel's role in the developing world is 'widely respected—and full of honour. It is her principal vocation in international life. . . . May not Israel be a school, a laboratory, a pilot plant whose very compactness enables her to illustrate the diverse and developing processes at work in a struggling pioneer society . . .', for no state is more appraised, scrutinized, and inspected.[1]

In 1966 Eban defined Israel's concerns as 'those questions that affect mankind entirely', for 'Israel is no longer the newest, smallest, or poorest State in the world. . . . *We are somewhere in the middle of the scale.* . . .' He justified Israel's large number of diplomatic missions as 'an unavoidable reaction to the political assault which is mounted against us on a global scale and without respite. . . . The principle of "policy of presence" is forced upon us by a sheer reality. . . .' He tried to build upon the Tashkent precedent (in the Indo-Pakistani conflict) and called upon the Soviets to emulate that more even-handed role of mediation in the Middle East.[2] Soon after, Eban expressed the view that various principles of Israeli policy were akin to the declared policies of the USSR—'in favor of peaceful coexistence throughout the world and in the Middle East, of melting the cold war . . . of limiting the arms race [everywhere] . . . of the immediate liquidation of colonialism, [and] of respecting the territorial status quo . . .'. On the basis of this image he declared that Israel has no feeling of enmity towards the Soviet Union but he reflected the Israeli élite consensus that 'the change in the relations of the two countries must come from the Soviet Union's side'.[3]

Eban has often revealed an awareness of the vital links between the global and Middle East systems but never as acutely as in a 1966 interview:[4]

. . . it is impossible to isolate this region from the general international context. The influence of the powers can be felt here. . . . If the world map were composed only of Israel and the Arab countries the geo-political balance would not be in our favor. There would be a clear Arab superiority in all fields. However, *when we consider this region as a part of the world, the balance changes in our favor.* In the world context Jewish and international factors enter the picture, with the general effect of reinforcing the stability of our country's existence.

As for East Europe, he perceived, after discussions with Israeli envoys in that region, that 'though these states have a common social philosophy and co-operate on international policy, they are nevertheless seven

---

[1] The text was issued by the Government Press Office, Jerusalem.

[2] 'Extracts from the Budget Speech of the Minister for Foreign Affairs of Israel, Mr. Abba Eban, delivered in the *Knesset* on Wednesday, 23 March 1966.' Issued by the Government Press Office, Jerusalem (emphasis added).

[3] Interview with Amnon Kapeliuk in *Al Hamishmar* (Tel Aviv), as translated in *New Outlook* (Tel Aviv), vol. 9, no. 7 (82), Sept. 1966, pp. 11–21.

[4] Ibid., p. 13 (emphasis added).

individual sovereignties. This is especially the case with regard to Israel.'[1]

A notable lacuna in Eban's image of global politics is Asia: his view is concentrated on America and Europe, with a recognition that Israel's presence in Africa has diplomatic value. A rare occasion on which he spoke at length on Asia was his report to the *Knesset* in 1967, following a visit to five Asian states. There is little of substance, apart from an indication of Israel's primary goal: 'The progress of our relations with them is intrinsically important, not least as the point of departure for pursuing our attack on bastions of antagonism not yet breached.' He displayed cautious optimism—'I am convinced that, with a reasonable investment of manpower and resources, it is possible for Israel at once . . . to fortify its standing and positive presence in Eastern Asia and the Pacific Ocean. . . .' And he spoke of new plans. But they remain unfulfilled.[2]

Like his predecessors, Eban has always attached significance to Israel's links with Diaspora Jewry. Typical of his many remarks on this theme is the following: 'The union of spirit between Israel and the Jewish people everywhere is a fact of Middle Eastern, indeed, of universal history, no less pertinent than the more familiar calculations of oil and military strategy.'[3] There is no place in his image for the 'two-camp thesis', as his views on the UN and the global setting generally make clear. At the same time he concurs with Ben Gurion's sharp distinction between the foreign policy roles of Israel and the World Zionist movement: 'I do not, in all candour, believe that you can share our sovereign responsibility for the conduct of Israel's external relations.' Its function lay, rather, in implementation—in organizing 'Jewish solidarity and free world opinion in favour of Israel . . ., a political role of crucial importance'.[4]

ii. *Dayan: A Tzahal View of the Outer World*

Moshe Dayan's approach to decisions bears the imprint of his pre-eminent professional experience—the army:[5]

I believe in decisions, not majority opinions. A consensus is something neutral, which never really leads to a real decision. . . . A decision always implies risks and of course a lot of people don't like risks. Moreover, most of the time it's not a question of choosing between alternatives, but of inventing a new solution from scratch. It's very hard to get everyone to agree.

[1] Interview with Shalom Cohen, *Jerusalem Post*, 24 May 1966.

[2] 'Statement by the Minister for Foreign Affairs in the Knesset on 3 April 1967 on his Tour in Asia, Australia and New Zealand, and Israel's Relations with That Region.' Made available by the Ministry for Foreign Affairs, Jerusalem.

[3] Before the Assembly of Jewish Organizations. . . , *Voice of Israel*, p. 187.

[4] 'Israel in the Community of Nations', Address to the 26th World Zionist Congress, Jerusalem, 5 Jan. 1965, op. cit.

[5] *L'Express* interview, quoted op. cit.

As for the role of public opinion, 'it's not a way of making decisions but it's a way of expressing things'. And he added: 'But I don't think it can influence my party. Not in the right way, anyhow.' The quandaries and hesitations of Dayan as decision-maker were illuminated by his comment on the Six Day War:[1]

> In every situation one must decide. There are two sides to the matter and *things are never foreseeable*. You can never be sure that things you expect to happen will happen that way. *I at any rate am never sure.* . . . If you make a mistake, you make a mistake. But you have no choice. You must say yes or no, agreed or not agreed, do this or do that.

Dayan's utterances on international politics and foreign policy were rare until after his departure from *Tzahal* (1958) and relatively sparse until he became Defence Minister on the eve of the Six Day War. Since then he has become extraordinarily verbose—many think excessively so. Moreover, he has concentrated on the security aspect of Israel in her Middle East setting. Yet he was sensitive to the East–West global struggle and its impact on the Arab–Israel conflict. Two extracts from speeches he delivered in 1957 admirably portray this component of his overall image:

> We cannot rely on one bloc automatically coming to our aid if we are attacked at the instigation of the opposing bloc. We must realize that the struggle is for influence among the Arabs, not in Israel. If we have to stand up against one or more of the Arab states, supported in their attack by the Soviet Union, the United States will not necessarily help us. On the contrary the two blocs might compete in a shouting match against us.[2]

> The main political and military process, going on at the present in the Middle East arena, is the tightening of relations between the Soviet bloc and the Arab States. . . . For us, it means that the Arab states have involved the Soviet Union in their hostility to Israel. . . . This combination of Arab greed and Soviet eagerness to satisfy it makes for a particularly grave situation as far as we are concerned. . . .
> [While the super-power competition has split the Arab states], that interpower struggle for the Arab world increases the total means—largely military but also economic—that are being put at the disposal of the Arab states and also weakens the West's willingness to oppose the wishes dictated by their hostility to Israel. . . . The two blocs are outbidding each other in helpfulness [to the Arabs].[3]

The constancy of the Arab–Israel conflict and the links between the

---

[1] Interview with Shimon Kagan on *Kol Yisrael*, *Jerusalem Post Weekly*, 4 March 1968 (emphasis added).

[2] To an audience at Haifa May Cinema, speaking without notes. *Jerusalem Post*, 14 July 1957.

[3] Speech to the passing-out Third Class of the Command and Staff College in Israel. A partial text is in *Jerusalem Post*, 23 Aug. 1957, under the title, 'Concepts of Security'.

global and regional systems is evident in these passages, spoken in 1957 and still valid at the end of 1970.

During the 1961 election campaign—he was then a member of the Cabinet and its Ministerial Committee on Defence—Dayan rejected proposals that Israel adopt a neutralist foreign policy. Israel, he wrote in reply to *Mapam*'s Meir Ya'ari, must have a deterrent power 'that will once and for all disillusion the Arabs of any idea of the conquest and annihilation of Israel'; further, an announcement by a major power that it would come to Israel's assistance would probably be a decisive deterrent. Thus he was prepared to accept American military support under the Eisenhower Doctrine—or a Soviet undertaking to provide Red Army troops![1] As for Goldmann's proposal of a neutralist and neutralized Israel—an idea he repeated in his memoirs almost a decade later[2]—Dayan stated his view with typical candour:[3]

The present political situation in the Middle East is the result of a number oı political factors operating in many countries, and these factors are not subject to the vote of Israel's delegates at the U.N. Assembly; it is strange that Dr. Goldmann should suppose that it is in our power . . . to exert an influence on the U.S.S.R.'s domestic policy towards its Jewish communities . . . [by] a change in . . . our policy. . . .

I would prefer Israel to become a normal state . . . living at peace with its neighbours, maintaining an army so long as all the other states have armies, tied by formal and informal alliances with friendly states—than a sort of protectorate, the only state in the world whose arms are supervised and inspected, checked and balanced. . . .

[Finally,] I do not believe that today Israel is a 'party' to the cold war between West and East, and I do not believe that we should be a party to the political and military conflict between them. . . .

In 1966 he warned against seeking guarantees from foreign powers—which would make Israel a 'minor ward of guardians'. Israel, he said, should rely on *Tzahal*, not on guarantees.[4]

In one of many speeches delivered after the Six Day War Dayan offered a thoughtful perception of Soviet and American influence in the Arab–Israel conflict. He drew a comparison between what Moscow was able to achieve in 1956, with American acquiescence, and how ineffective their political efforts were in 1967. As to the future, the 'key to further belligerency or another round of war lay with Russia. The key to a political settlement lay with the United States.'[5]

[1] 'Guarantees of Security', *Jerusalem Post*, 12 May 1961.
[2] *The Autobiography of Nahum Goldmann: Sixty Years of Jewish Life*, New York, 1969, pp. 301 ff.
[3] 'No Simple Way to Peace: A Reply to Dr. Goldmann's New Orientation', in *Jerusalem Post*, 13 Aug. 1961.
[4] *Jerusalem Post*, 8 May 1966.
[5] To a Hebrew University student audience in Jerusalem in February 1968. *Jerusalem Post Weekly*, 12 Feb. 1968.

Dayan's image of the Jewish people and its relations with Israel appears to have undergone change over the years. Like many *sabras*, he tended to denigrate the behaviour of European Jewry during the Holocaust: the relative lack of struggle against Nazi oppression did not impress the young men and women who created a state against overwhelming odds. The revelations of the Eichmann trial, however, had a traumatic effect on Israeli youth and built a new sense of identity with Jews everywhere. Dayan was not unaffected. He was also influenced by the support of Jewry during the Sinai Campaign and, even more dramatically, during the 1967 crisis and after. Thus, when he was asked whether Israel, in her frontier policy, should pay attention to historical geography, he replied in the affirmative, with the following criteria: 'the Jewish people, the Bible—the book of the Jewish people, and the land—the land of the Jews'.[1]

In a revealing 1969 dialogue Dayan proclaimed his belief in nationalism, his desire to retain a Jewish state and, as noted, his identity as a Jew, as well as an Israeli, a member of the Jewish nation:[2]

I do believe strongly in nationalism, that each of us must learn his history and his language. We must have our own feast days and the Arabs must have their Ramadhan. . . . I want my children to go to a Jewish university. . . .

I don't want us to become a single nation (Arabs and Jews). I want to maintain a Jewish State and I don't want a mixed state. I want them as neighbours and I believe we can live together without hatred.

('Can you explain why you don't want a mixed state?')

Because the whole idea of a Jewish State is to give the Jews their own laws. You're not a Jew?

('Not that I know of.')

That's what I mean. A Jew is a very specific human being, not different from other people but he has his religion, his language, his history, his faith and his philosophy. And right now our problem is to preserve the union of our people. We have succeeded in preserving the Jewish nation for the last four thousand years because the Jews had to live in ghettos and suffered discrimination and persecution. Now they have won equality, and we could lose our identity in one generation. . . .

If the whole world becomes international, that's all right, but if everyone else continues to be themselves and we are the only ones to lose our identity, then I'd be very sad.

Dayan has rarely spoken in public about the United Nations. But from his actions as Chief of Staff and as Minister of Defence, and from his general View of the World, his disdain for the world organization may be deduced. In essence, he subscribes to Ben Gurion's extreme '*oum shmoum*' image and he has long expressed the need for self-reliance, as noted. He reasons that Israel's security requires an effective deterrent;

[1] In a radio interview, published in *Davar* (Tel Aviv), 28 May 1968.
[2] *L'Express* interview, op. cit.

that is, a level of military capability which can prevent war or, if it occurs, will ensure victory. In that task the UN role is marginal at most.

Over the years the Third World's importance in Dayan's image of global politics—as it pertains to Israel—has declined. He visited Africa in 1960 and 1963 and wrote a thoughtful series of impressions and analyses of new states in transition.[1] However, as with Ben Gurion, the critical test of significance for Dayan is ability to provide arms, and in that sense Euro-America has always been central to Israel's struggle against Arab hostility—and, therefore, to Dayan's foreign policy image.

In summary, Eban and Dayan both recognized the East–West Cold War as a phenomenon with spill-over effects on the Arab–Israel conflict, that is, the penetration of global rivalry into the Middle East system. Neither has displayed any expectation of Soviet friendship or even non-hostility. Both have revealed a greater affinity with 'the West'. The differences in this context are Eban's persistent stress on US aid, with Dayan inclined for a long time primarily to a Franco-German orientation; and secondly, Eban's greater emphasis on external forces, including the UN, and diplomacy in Israel's foreign policy, compared to Dayan's faith in self-reliance and, particularly, in *Tzahal*. In other terms, this is an outward versus an inward orientation. Both men perceived world Jewry as Israel's most reliable ally. Eban, however, fully rejects BG's 'two-camp thesis', while Dayan's view, in reply to a direct question, was more complex and ambivalent:[2]

When the words spoken by the *Goyim* are not backed by deeds, their weight is less than the deeds they do. And the words the Israelis speak are less important —much less—than their deeds.

But the trouble with the *Goyim* is that they not only speak but they also do. They do deeds and withhold acts—they give or do not give Phantoms. And, therefore, I do not under any circumstances denigrate the weight the *Goyim* carry in matters concerning us. My differentiation is not that everything we decide in the matter of Israel is important, and everything others say, that is, the *Goyim*, is not important.

The distinction between the *Goyim* and us is not the distinction between empty words and actions. In many things we are dependent upon them . . . and in many matters the words we speak remain floating in space like bubbles.

The distinction in essence is between words which are not backed by anything and policy which is accompanied by words, but also carries with it deed or forbearance or influence on deed . . . which may be determinist and fateful.

iii. Peres: A Technocrat's Image

'The question is whether we should view the world according to our prejudices or in terms of its objective reality, and try to obtain

---

[1] A series of six articles under the general title 'West African Diary' appeared in *Jerusalem Post*, 12, 19, 22, 26, and 29 Nov. and 3 Dec. 1963.

[2] To the Press Club at Beit Sokolow, Tel Aviv, on 27 December 1968. *New Map—Other Relationships*, pp. 66–7.

the maximum benefit from the political constellation that obtains in the world.'[1] Such is the 'realist' underpinning of Shimon Peres' View of the World. This reply to criticism of an invitation to West German Defence Minister Strauss to visit Israel in 1963 was amplified in another remark to the *Knesset*:[2]

Is Israel's enemy Germany or Egypt? . . . Germany—both Germanies—will take its place in the world without the Jewish factor being the main consideration. It will do so according to a logic independent of our attitude or opinion. We have to draw the inevitable conclusions. The past must not be forgotten, but neither must the future, which is the future of our existence. . . .

In order to obtain arms we need a conception; obsession will not avail.

The search for arms has, indeed, been at the core of Peres' policy orientation and its antecedent global image. This he enunciated with clarity and logic in the same *Knesset* debate, following the announcement of the formation of Eshkol's first government, in June 1963.

His point of departure was that 'the Middle East is a region suspended between two extremities: of turbulence and pre-war emotion, on the one side, and calm and indifference, on the other'. The deduction was that 'we have therefore no alternative but to build up a progressive, constant line of policy as a reply to the implacable Arab enmity; to their continually growing military might, and to the irresponsible and warlike outbreaks that still mark the Arab world'. Thus, 'we have to build up a deterrent force, both political and military. . . . We must deal with the problem of military balance. . . .'

There are, he went on, only three 'geographical locations' where modern weapons can be acquired: the Soviet Union, which withheld arms from Israel because of their bloc interests; the United States, whose modest sale of Hawk missiles reveals that 'their attitude is significant but not a permanent arrangement'. 'We are left with the European alternative—and this includes France's attitude.' This, in turn, is linked to the emerging unity of Europe. 'This is not a union for or against Israel. . . . However, . . . it will of necessity affect Israel's position, in practically all spheres, from the sale of oranges to the purchase of helicopters. . . . And if we are interested in Europe's attitude towards us, it is only reasonable that we should start now, today, to build up a political and security policy along similar lines to that of France.'

Finally, 'unfortunately, nothing can be taken for granted either in the political or the security field'.

All this led Peres to the following conclusion: 'The fact remains that

---

[1] To the *Knesset* in May 1963. *Weekly News Bulletin*, Jerusalem, 22–29 May 1963.

[2] In the course of an address outlining his views on defence and foreign policy, in June 1963. The full text appeared in translation in *New Outlook* (Tel Aviv), vol. 6, no. 7 (56), Sept. 1963, pp. 14–19.

we urgently need, and will need even more in the future, the help of a number of European states besides that of France. This is not a static need and to achieve it we have to work towards it. A political campaign —even a painful one—does not start off at the final large, established and exclusive terminus. It has to start at the beginning of the line, at those stations where the whole campaign is worked out and its line of action determined.' It was at that point that he taunted his critics: 'In order to obtain arms we need a conception; obsession will not avail.'

In policy terms this meant, for Peres, a new look at West Germany —ally of France, a major factor in the European community, and a source of modern weapons—and an attempt to seek entry into Europe via membership in the Common Market. These ideas he expounded from the late fifties on. The world has changed, he wrote in 1958: it has 'evolved beyond social patterns of the generation of early Zionists'; and Israel 'must look beyond the romantic ideas of her founding fathers'. There was a fourfold challenge to Israel's youth in the next decade: to build an adequate deterrent—and to achieve this Israel must join forces with other countries, for her security problems 'are likely to become increasingly international in scope'; to enter the European economic and political communities and to assist new African states; to plan more effectively, using modern science and technology; and to create new ideals for a new age.[1] The rationale for this guideline he stated in another article: 'In 1948 we fought to build a state; in 1959 we must fight to build a nation. The first goal was clear, but the present one is just as urgent and just as arduous.'[2]

Peres' View of the World and the policy concerns far transcend the 'search for arms perspective' in scope. In a more general analysis of Israel's foreign policy he perceived five relevant factors: her foes attack in word and deed; the Middle East is in flux and is an 'area of inter-power rivalry'; Israel does not belong to any bloc or military alliance; Israel is not just a state but is the only territorial basis of world Jewry; and, finally, 'our political system of permanent coalition influences policy-making'.[3] All these, taken together, he declared, play a crucial role in shaping Israel's foreign policy objectives.

Certain goals are common to all states, Peres noted: the will for peace, as expressed in the formation of the UN, the desire to avoid war, and the concern about filling the gap between rich and poor peoples; the penetration of other countries—ideological, political, and econo-mic; the mobilization of goodwill abroad—either as an accumulated reserve to be drawn on when needed or as support for limited goals or as a means of winning influence at home; and economic and social advance. For Israel security is the dominant objective: it 'overshadows

[1] 'The Next Ten Years', *Jerusalem Post*, 23 April 1958.
[2] 'Dead Symbols and Living Reality', *Jerusalem Post*, 21 Aug. 1959.
[3] This influence will be explored in ch. 16 (a) below.

and, unfortunately, often must overshadow all the others'. To those who rejected his 'realism' he said, 'you cannot break a siege by preaching'. And in the most general terms,

Relations do not arise on their own, but are made up of similarity of outlook and experience, political connections, and even personal connections. They do not develop by themselves and they do not remain forever. In some countries security relations do not necessarily run parallel to ordinary foreign relations and . . . we must take cognizance of the fact. . . . Security needs foreign relations for the establishment of military power, and its military power can in turn contribute to foreign relations.[1]

These ideas and others Peres elaborated in his book, *Ha-shlav Ha-ba* (The Next Stage).[2] Russia has changed, he wrote, and a break has occurred in 'the Communist Church', with revolutionary ardour moving to Peking. As for the United States and the Middle East, it is much more important for her to win Arab sympathy than to bring peace to the region. American friendship for Israel derives from the idealistic element in her politics, while the limits on friendship are the result of her global interests.

In the same public debate with Goldmann regarding neutralism, in which Dayan was engaged, Peres remarked that Israel *practises* 'real neutralism' and does not *talk* it: Israel is not tied to any bloc and does not have any foreign troops on her territory. Those who call themselves neutralists, he added, 'are usually neutral towards someone in particular'.[3] In private discussion his preference was emphatically stated: 'One cannot be neutral between right and wrong. Israel's place is with the free world.'[4] Yet in the aftermath of the Six Day War he advised Israel to state clearly that she is not playing any part in inter-bloc quarrels.[5]

Peres' dual perception of the UN is very similar to that of Ben Gurion. In the context of global politics, where two power blocs confront one another and frequently approach conflict, the United Nations, he remarked in 1960, performs two valuable functions: it cools tempers; and it provides a bridge between the protagonists. At the same time he criticized the UN and the then Secretary-General, Dag Hammarskjöld, for attempting to expand this role and 'build a house on a bridge', that is, for trying to create a super-state under UN control. In the Middle East setting he dismissed its contribution as marginal and negative.[6] He was more critical in his book: the UN's ability to contribute to peace and border tranquillity is illusory; further, it does not distinguish

---

[1] 'Many Roads Lead to Peace', *Jerusalem Post*, 31 July 1959.
[2] Am Ha-Sefer, Tel Aviv, 1965.   [3] *Jerusalem Post*, 5 Aug. 1961.
[4] Interview in Jerusalem, July 1960.
[5] To the Engineers' and Architects' Association in Tel Aviv. *Jerusalem Post Weekly*, 1 Jan. 1968.
[6] Interview in Jerusalem, July 1960.

between the aggressor and the victim of aggression; and it constitutes a political obstacle to Israel's quest for security.[1]

Peres is more aware than Eban and Dayan of the Third World—as a factor in global politics which impinges upon Israel's foreign and security policy. In this respect he shares Golda Meir's outlook; and, indeed, he was the principal architect of Israel's military aid policy to the new states from 1958 onwards. He described Israel's presence as 'our peaceful efforts in Africa to surround the belt of enmity with a belt of friendship in the new independent countries . . .'.[2]

Like all of his peers Peres attached cardinal importance to Israel's links with world Jewry, though he did not openly espouse Ben Gurion's 'two-camp thesis'. 'We are still a state that belongs to the Jewish people', he said, as Israel entered her third decade.[3]

For the ritual and procedure of diplomacy Peres showed utter disdain. For its substance—negotiations—he perceived a legitimate role within a narrow sphere: 'keep your powder dry and negotiate where possible but do not expect much' was his implied motto concerning armed force and diplomacy as instruments of foreign policy. Certainly, he declared, diplomats should be subordinate to defence experts in the formulation of high policy. These views he articulated during interviews in 1960 and again in 1966. On the latter occasion he also delineated the foreign policy solutions he would attempt in the next decade:[4]

1. To build a 'second Egypt' in Africa, that is, to help convert Ethiopia's economic and military strength into a counter-force to Egypt, thereby giving Africans another focus.
2. To bring Israel into the Common Market on a political rail, that is, to organize three countries to go into the Market together—Jordan, Lebanon and Israel—and thus to establish the basis of economic co-operation, the only type of co-operation that can precede peace.
3. To lay a new basis of France–Israel friendship; we must intensify scientific co-operation.
4. To widen our activities in Latin America and Asia. Africa has reached end point.
5. To build new links between Israel and world Jewry—with a reduced emphasis on money and more on intellect.
6. To bring China into the UN and secure recognition of China by all the Powers. This will make her more responsible and therefore reduce her hostility to Israel.
7. To bring about normalization of relations with North Africa.
8. To reduce our claims on the United States and strengthen our friendship—asking less and appreciating more.

[1] *Ha-shlav Ha-ba*, Part 1.
[2] 'Strategy, Security and Deterrents', *Jerusalem Post*, 19 April 1961.
[3] Interview with Mark Segal, *Jerusalem Post*, 22 Sept. 1968.
[4] Interview in Tel Aviv, June 1966.

With all these carefully thought-out programmes, Peres retains a mildly cynical image of how international politics are shaped: '. . . we tend to cling to the theory that international developments follow a logical line that is inexorable. However . . . I cannot but be struck by the fact that many of them were determined by blind chance.'[1]

These goals derived from his theoretical frame of reference on foreign policy, which Peres defined as 'sciopolitics'—to replace geopolitics: 'The size of a country is not its geography but its scientific and technological level. In geography there are maps; but in science there are frontiers, no maps.' At the same time he was pessimistic about the prospect for the achievement of these aims. 'Intelligence is very problematic and inadequate for decision-making', he remarked. First, 'the donors are so eager to get information that quantity is regarded as no less important than quality'. And secondly, 'the judgement of politicians is poor; they do not judge intelligence properly'. Finally, 'policy is an art that borders on suspicion'.

It was in that context that Peres explained why Israel should not be the first state to introduce nuclear weapons into the Middle East:

There must always be in the political judgement of Israel a historical sense—what will be said about us in 50 years. We have a double responsibility—self-defence of Israel and the self-respect of our generation. No responsible Israeli should forget this, though they are not equally important.

[Moreover,] Egypt may get the bomb, but then again she may not. Why precipitate this?

[Most important,] as long as suspicion that Israel has the bomb is a deterrent, why make a bomb? In our present situation [1966] suspicion is enough.

The nuclear policy of Israel is like a satellite in the sky. It must communicate without touching land.

His concluding remark, on leadership, revealed much about Peres' view of the world: 'Top leaders are not wiser than the second echelon —but they have more knowledge. The art of leadership is to do in a reasonable and acceptable way by a show of strength what is necessary.' (He cited the Cuba case, where 'Kennedy had knowledge that the Soviets would withdraw'.) 'This is not to downgrade the quality of judgement and courage of leadership. Great men like battle and like making decisions. But they are cautious. Those who avoid decisions are Kerenskys.'

iv. *Allon: Global Outlook of a Socialist–Zionist*

Yigal Allon's View of the World reveals the influence of the two main strands in his background: one is the blend of agrarian socialism and militant nationalism which characterizes the *Ha-Kibbutz Ha-me'uhad*

[1] *David's Sling*, p. 79.

movement; the other is his experience as *Palmah* commander during Israel's formative years, 1945–8. The result is an image with greater ideological content and flavour than that of his peers, tempered by a pragmatic, activist approach remarkably similar to that of Dayan and Peres, the '*bitzuists*'. Allon's outlook has also been affected by exposure to British higher education—a year at Oxford in 1960–1. This strengthened a natural propensity to intellectual thought and expression, which is reflected in the striking difference in tone and nuance from Dayan's statements on policy—and in the affinity to those of Eban, though without his verbal virtuosity.

The contrast with Dayan in this and other respects was finely drawn by one commentator as follows:[1]

Dayan is a quiet, moody man who expresses himself in brief, pithy statements that seem elaborately mysterious and codelike—a sort of shorthand that he challenges his listeners to decipher. In general, he says what he thinks, but it is not always a simple matter to understand fully what he has said.

Allon, by contrast, is outgoing and lucid. He expresses himself in detail and at length if he feels that is necessary. His highly structured outlines and handsomely presented policies repel some Israelis who find them more appropriate to British parliamentary procedure than to the earthier Israeli manner.

Whereas Allon tends to deal in programs and seems to enjoy the broad sweep of government, Dayan prefers to deal with specific problems and establish guidelines. Allon is an ideological Socialist. Dayan expresses no political philosophy. Allon is the team man and political idealist, Dayan the individual and technocrat.

Allon has always perceived the global struggle between East and West through the lens of non-alignment. In the early years he strongly supported the Ben Gurion–Sharett policy of 'non-identification', even while the dominant Left-socialist wing of *Mapam*, of which his *Ahdut Ha'avodah* was then a part, was committed to pro-Soviet 'neutralism'. With the re-emergence of virulent anti-Semitism and hostility to Israel in Eastern Europe during Stalin's last years, Allon led the move to separate from *Ha-shomer Ha-tza'ir*, which retained the *Mapam* name and the ideological link to 'the bastion of world socialism'. *Ahdut Ha'avodah* returned to its traditional middle position on the socialist spectrum of Israeli politics.

In foreign policy this meant equidistance from the super powers or 'genuine' non-alignment. And Allon was no less critical of the *Mapai*-dominated Government of Israel swing to the Right from 1951 to 1955, that is, the (Eban-supported) attempt to secure a US guarantee or military alliance. As he remarked in 1966, 'we wasted time and energy in trying to win membership in Western clubs. We failed and wasted our position with the East.' Further, in the perspective of time, 'my

[1] James Feron, 'Yigal Allon Has Supporters, Moshe Dayan Has Disciples', *New York Times Magazine*, 27 April 1969, p. 82. The article is on pp. 31, 82 ff.

belief in the wisdom of Israel's non-involvement [in the Cold War] proved to be correct'. He was one of the first on the Israeli Left to reject 'neutralism', Allon added. And he refuses to place foreign policy on a plane of moral commitment. 'You were committed to anti-Communism', he once told Ben Gurion; 'I am not committed to anti-Americanism.' More generally about BG, he remarked: 'Many dramatic quarrels could have been avoided had we not followed his prophetic zeal'.[1]

Allon had no illusions about Soviet hostility to Israel from 1955 onwards. At the same time he did not adopt a harsh anti-Soviet view in foreign policy and has never advocated formal alignment with the United States. In part this is a residue of his ideological antipathy to the excesses of American capitalist society and in part to his correct appreciation that such a policy would lead to rejection and humiliation. There is also the element of confidence in Israel's ability to triumph alone—'thanks to our efforts, the State of Israel today is unconquerable', he declared in the summer of 1969.[2] But perhaps the most important stimulus to continued non-alignment, in his view, is the welfare of Soviet Jewry: 'The second greatest foreign policy goal is the reunification of Israel with the Jewish community of Russia', he said in 1966.

He placed great emphasis on *aliya* from the USSR and offered an optimistic analysis of future Soviet policy. Jewry is the only abnormal *national* phenomenon in the Soviet Union, he said; and it is not the fault of the régime. They tried to solve an abnormal problem by abnormal means—assimilation—and it failed. A centralized system of government, he continued, cannot tolerate unsolved problems for long, especially a national problem and one that has international complications. There are precedents of Communist states allowing Jews as a national group to emigrate, with no upheavals; and they would not have occurred without Moscow's approval. If the Soviets do allow Jews out, they will rationalize it as a 'national right' to return to their historic homeland—and Gentiles in the USSR would fully accept this rationalization. Thus, he concluded, there must be a logical link between these expectations and Israel's policy towards the Soviet Union.[3]

Allon's concern about Soviet Jewry is part of his overall image of the importance of Jewry to Israel—a view shared by all his peers in the Inner Circle. On one occasion he noted with approval that Eshkol 'was always profoundly anxious lest the verdict of history should be . . . that our generation *created a state* but *lost a people*'. As often, he also invoked the solidarity theme and, without hesitation, acknowledged the role of Diaspora Jewry in Israel's progress: 'It can confront them [problems]

---

[1] Interview in Jerusalem, April 1966.
[2] 'Address by Mr. Yigal Allon, Acting Prime Minister and Minister of Immigrant Absorption, at the Human Needs Conference, Jerusalem, 16 June 1969', p. 15.
[3] Interview in Jerusalem, April 1966.

only thanks to the ideological and political solidarity, and the economic assistance, of the Jews in the Diaspora. It would be quite impossible to exaggerate [its] importance. . . .'[1]

Allon, like the other younger leaders, has a clear perception of the impact of the global struggle on the Middle East system. In an open letter to Nasser during a period of relative quiet, he wrote:[2]

This split between the nations of the Middle East is, as you know, being used by the big powers of both world blocs to penetrate our region. This, of course, endangers the independence of the new nations, including Egypt and Israel. It will, unless remedied, make these nations . . . increasingly dependent . . . on the policies of the great powers.

It was not that Allon anticipated direct Soviet military intervention in the Arab–Israel conflict. Indeed he was among the most ardent opponents of withdrawal in 1956, under Soviet threats of massive bombing.[3] And in 1967, he argued strongly against the likelihood of Soviet intervention—whereas Dayan had serious doubts.[4] Once again in 1969 Allon asserted his optimism on this vital issue and offered a plausible rationale for this perception:[5]

As long as the USSR fears that her military attack on Israel may bring her into conflict with other powers, she will hold back from taking this irresponsible step. The Soviet presence as it is today in the Mediterranean, in Egypt and in Syria, is adequate to ensure supervision over the regimes in the Arab countries and to cause anxiety to other Mediterranean states. It is not of a type which would permit direct military provocation of Israel. . . .

It is clear that, if the USSR meant to attack Israel, she would need a logistic layout completely different from the one she holds now and would need to send to the Middle East an army that does not fall short in size and power from that sent by the USA to South East Asia in the climax of the Vietnam War. [This] is on its own a great burden, but the matter becomes even more difficult when there is increasing unrest along the Sino-Soviet border on the one hand, and in the East Mediterranean, which is actually a closed lake from a strategic point of view and can become a strategic trap to Soviet forces which may enter it. . . . Keeping the status quo in the Middle East is in the interest of world peace. Therefore I doubt whether one need fear direct Soviet intervention in the Israel–Arab conflict.

The fact that the USSR intervened directly in Czechoslovakia and Hungary does not mean that she would behave in the same manner in Israel. For there, the countries belong to the Warsaw Pact. But I warn myself, despite my optimism in this matter, not to regard the USSR presence in the Middle East with ease. . . . [Yet] I continue to believe that, although in the war with the

---

[1] 'Address . . . at the Human Needs Conference. . .', pp. 2, 18–19.
[2] 'A Message to President Nasser', in *New Statesman*, (London), lviii, 1494, 31 Oct. 1959. Made available by Allon's office.
[3] Related to the author by officials and politicians, including Allon himself, in 1966.
[4] Related to the author by Israeli officials and politicians in 1968.
[5] Interview in *Ha'aretz* (Tel Aviv), 12 Sept. 1969.

Arab countries we remain alone on the battlefield, we will not remain alone if the USSR provokes war with us.

On the role of China he acknowledged, as few Israelis have done, 'the basic error which we made [in 1955], when China was more isolated and deemed important ties even with a small country such as Israel'. And he added: 'In the Middle East China represents an extreme and destructive factor, even more so than the USSR. Perhaps, when a positive change occurs in the relations between the USA and China, some sort of change will also occur in the Chinese attitude towards us.'[1]

Allon has displayed appreciation of the Third World as a global political force. The centre of his attention has been India, and he long nourished the hope that Nehru's socialism and commitment to democracy would overcome a misperceived 'national interest' in blind adherence to the Arab cause—but in vain. Nonetheless, he has remained faithful to the aim of Israel–India friendship as the anchor of Israel's Asian policy.[2] And, despite China's hostility, he has, as noted, consistently advocated Peking's admission to the UN. Africa has been more peripheral to his foreign policy image, except as part of the emerging world of new states with which Israel should be identified.

Despite this high value placed on Afro-Asia, Allon was an avid proponent of Israel's entry into the European Common Market. In a 1963 Chatham House lecture he called on the EEC to invite Israel and an Arab state to join the Market simultaneously; this was in accord with his view that a prerequisite to Middle East peace and regional co-operation is a common framework in which Israel and her neighbours can work together; the European Economic Community could provide an example.[3] (Peres echoed this view in 1966, as noted, and Eban did so in his address to the Council of Europe in September 1967.[4]) Allon also claimed that the possibility of Israel's integration into the Middle East has been verified 'by our success in Africa, which outlived coups d'état and other changes. It showed that Israel can be integrated with larger multi-national and multi-racial communities.'[5]

In the last analysis, however, Allon shares the Dayan–Peres view of self-reliance and the primacy of her strategic needs as the *sine qua non* of Israel's survival as an independent state. He does not dismiss the UN and public opinion; but neither does he attach Eban's importance to external perceptions and pressures. This part of his advocacy was most clearly enunciated in a 1969 analysis of Israel's defence forces:[6]

[1] Ibid.

[2] Allon's reflections on his 1959 visit to India are contained in his 'Meetings in India', *Mibbifnim* (From the Inside), Ein Harod, vol. 27, no. 4, Dec. 1965, pp. 355–71.

[3] 'The Arab–Israel Conflict: Some Suggested Solutions', *International Affairs*, London, vol. 40, April 1964, pp. 205–18.

[4] *Jerusalem Post*, 28 Sept. 1967.   [5] Interview in Jerusalem, April 1966.

[6] Draft Chapter VI ('Since June 1967') of a book on the development of Israel's military capability. Made available by Allon's office.

It may well be that Israel's desire to establish strategic borders different from the pre-1967 armistice demarcation lines will be misunderstood, and perhaps even opposed, by some members of the world body, including friendly ones. What is at stake, however, is Israel's security—that is, her very existence. It seems to me, therefore, that, while making every effort to explain her position and needs, Israel must not give way to international demands and pressures. . . .

If she is faced with the choice between withdrawal to the old armistice lines for the sake of short-term political gains and the establishment, even unilaterally, of new and secure borders at the cost of political complications, the second alternative should be preferred. The political difficulties, one may hope, will ultimately pass away, but only the capacity for self-defence will ensure Israel's survival. . . .

There is . . . no substitute for strategically defensible borders. . . . Defensible borders without peace are preferable to peace without defensible borders.

In this vein he castigated Soviet behaviour, using harsher and more colourful language than is his habit: 'Due to the Brezhnev Doctrine . . . the atheist marriage of the USSR with Muslim Syria and Egypt becomes a Catholic marriage which does not permit divorce.'[1] He also blamed the 'relative severity of the security situation' in 1969 on the Big Four meetings 'and the Arabs' desire to influence their discussions'. And he pressed for a tough Israeli response.[2]

Allon has also been one of the staunchest opponents of Israel's adherence to the nuclear non-proliferation treaty, without 'effective security arrangements'. 'And if pressure is exercised?', he was asked. 'When one speaks of security needs, I will not be a partner to surrender under any form of pressure.'[3]

It is difficult, indeed, to distinguish the foreign policy advocacy of Allon and Dayan, and for the most part of Peres as well, in the essential components of their image of the global setting. Eban stands apart from the two generals and the technocrat.

(c) IMAGES OF 'THE MIDDLE EAST' AND 'THE ARABS'

i. *Eban*

Among his peers in the Inner Circle Abba Eban has articulated the clearest image of 'the Middle East' as a region of international politics. There is, inevitably, an overlap with his view of 'the Arabs', but the analytic distinction is maintained; indeed it is central to his image of both—a geopolitical entity on the one hand, and a cultural, social, and psychological community, on the other.

[1] Among comments on foreign policy between 1967 and 1969. Made available by Allon's office.

[2] Interview with E. Agress, E. Ya'ari and T. Preuss in *Davar* (Tel Aviv), 22 April 1969.

[3] *Ha'aretz* interview, 12 Sept. 1969.

In a sweeping survey of the area and its people, caught up in 'the tide of nationalism', he declared in 1959:[1]

It is vital . . . to recall that the Middle East and the Arab world are not equivalent or identical terms.

The Middle East, as defined in the general practice of the United Nations, is inhabited by some 60 million Arabs, taking language as the broadest criterion, and by 75 million non-Arabs. There is a non-Arab Middle East extending from Turkey and Persia through Israel to Ethiopia; and if we extend the area to include Afghanistan and Pakistan, then the predominantly non-Arab character of the region becomes even more manifest. . . .

While full respect is due to the rights of Arab nations, it remains true that the Middle East has not been in the past, is not now and can never be in the future an exclusively Arab domain.

The inner, progressive truth about the Middle East is to be found not in the word 'unity' but in the greater words 'diversity' and 'tolerance'. . . . There is not one Arab nationalism alone. . . . There is not only Islam. . . . [Finally] the states of our region do not have the same points of emphasis in their international relations. . . .

This concept of a pluralist, multi-national and multi-cultural Middle East was to acquire the status of quasi-official Israeli doctrine, as noted earlier. But no one gave it such plausible exposition as Eban, the supreme advocate, in a myriad of speeches and essays over the years.[2]

In the context of international politics Eban perceived 'the Middle East' as a region of multiple conflict. Typical was his remark in 1963, with obvious allusion to Nasser's imagery of 'circles' of Egyptian influence:[3]

I believe that three circles of tension in our region are discernible: (a) tension between the world blocs; (b) tension between the rival and antagonistic Arab States; (c) tension between the Arab world and Israel.

These three circles are naturally interrelated, but each one has its own origins. Therefore, even if a considerable improvement takes place in relations between the two blocs, we will still have to face two other problems which influence the situation in our area: the great contention and strife within the Arab world, and the Israel–Arab conflict, which are not only results of inter-bloc tension.

On the critical question of Israel's proper place in 'the Middle East', Eban has been conspicuously assertive. Like most Israeli leaders he advocates a policy of co-operative coexistence. At the same time he rejected very early the claim 'that Israel's aspiration is for integration into the Middle East. . . . [Rather] I suggest that if Israel is now separa-

[1] *The Tide of Nationalism*, Horizon Press, New York, 1959, pp. 47–9.

[2] See for example his address to the 26th World Zionist Congress, op. cit., p. 3, and his 'Reality and Vision in the Middle East', in *Foreign Affairs* (New York), vol 43, no. 4, July 1965, pp. 632, 634–5.

[3] To the Jerusalem Journalists' Association. *Weekly News Bulletin*, Jerusalem, 14–20 Aug. 1963.

ted from the Arab Middle East, we owe that separation not only to the hostility of our neighbours but also to the nature of our own national movement.'[1] There is, he continued, little in 'the Middle East' to attract a renascent Israel—not its system of social exploitation or economic backwardness, nor its forms of political organization or its Arab culture. Rather, Israel desires to revive her Hebrew tradition, to maintain her links with Diaspora Jewry, to create a free society, and to build a modern economy. Eban further elaborated this point in his advocacy of an outward 'Mediterranean orientation':[2]

The most fruitful and natural regional concept is that of Mediterranean co-operation. . . . Three continents, Europe, Africa and Asia, look out upon it with all their diversity of fate and outlook. Five great civilizations were born here— Judaism, Christianity, Hellenism, Rome and Islam. It is a central compact world, congenial to the free interaction of commerce and ideas and alien to exclusiveness. . . . The issue is whether the Arab and Jewish nations, which have been primary agents in the Mediterranean adventure, can transcend their conflict in dedication to a new Mediterranean future, in concert with a rena-scent Europe and an emerging Africa.

When he became Foreign Minister, Eban stressed the 'natural right' theme: 'Israel is not an invader, an interloper, into the Middle East. Israel sprang from this region, and Israel is returning to it. . . .'[3] At the same time he reaffirmed his image of a pluralist Middle East: it was his authentic view, rooted in his studies of Oriental languages and literatures.

That knowledge also influenced his image of 'the Arabs'. In the midst of Israel's permanent war, Eban was capable of effusive tribute to Arab civilization:[5]

Its contours [the Arab heritage] are formed, its spirit expressed in a language of rich and potent variety. There is an Arabic literature of such versatility and range as to constitute a full humanistic education in itself. Apart from its contributions to the humane arts and to philosophy, the Arab mind has achieved radiant insight into the natural sciences. . . . [And while it] is not unreserved . . . this cultural unity exists.

Yet he also observed that 'factors of history, politics and law . . . create strong separatist impulses in the Arab world', that 'the economic factor reinforces this separation', and that political 'union has been the exception, not the rule'. And further, 'the liberated Arab peoples still live in a psychic world marked by three circles of tension: . . . in their relations with each other . . . with the Western world . . . and with

[1] 'Nationalism and Internationalism in the Middle East', Address to the Jewish Theological Seminary, New York, 29 Feb. 1952, in *Voice of Israel*, pp. 74–5.
[2] 'Reality and Vision. . .', op. cit., pp. 635–6.
[3] 'Extracts from the Budget Speech . . . 1966', p. 11.
[5] *The Tide of Nationalism*, pp. 23–4.

Israel'.[1] Nonetheless, he shared the predominant Zionist image of a homogeneous 'Arab nation' confronting a 'Jewish nation'.[2]

During another academic lecture in the fifties Eban declared that the Middle East crisis springs from imperfections in the Arab national movement: its lack of altruism; its obsession with the negative; its exclusive concentration on the political aspects of national freedom; the contrast between its political success and social irresponsibility; and its indifference to the wider interests of international order. By contrast, Israel could become 'a pilot plant which all Middle Eastern nations might emulate'.[3]

It is rare indeed to find Eban expressing a 'little notch' view of Israel and 'the Arabs'. On one such occasion he declared:[4]

We do not envy or begrudge the neighbouring people its huge inheritance. . . . [But] would it not have been an indelible disgrace to the human conscience if a world which had rightly liberated the Arab people in its continental Empire had not been able to carve out this tiny notch of territory to be the sanctuary of another people in the hour of its greatest woe?

No less striking—and rare among Israeli leaders—is the acknowledgement that

the Arab-Israel dialogue is not distorted on one side alone. Hostility usually evokes an attitude in its own image. The Israeli vision of Arab life and culture has been eroded by years of separation.

[Further,] Israel must try, above the conflict, to see her neighbor as she has been in her greater moments—the heir and author of a rich culture, the bearer of a tongue . . . without which a man is cut off from an inner comprehension of the Middle East.[5]

This theme was stated even more bluntly during an interview as Foreign Minister:[6]

Such kind of talk and thought [ideas like 'the Arabs only understand the language of force'] is fundamentally wrong. As Jews we must be sensitive to any national 'typology', to any attempt to give a whole people a negative appearance. It is our duty to educate the young generation towards an attitude of respect towards this region and its culture, languages and strivings for advancement. It is our duty to screen public speeches for insulting innuendoes and any derision of Arab culture.

[1] Ibid., pp. 31, 21, 19–20.
[2] Ibid., p. 18 ('the Arab nation'); 'The Outlook for Peace in the Middle East', Academy of Political Science, Columbia University, New York, 1957, p. 308 ('the liberated Arab nation'); 'Reality and Vision. . .', op. cit., p. 636 ('the Arab and Jewish nations').
[3] 'Nationalism and Internationalism in the Middle East', *Voice of Israel*, pp. 71–3.
[4] 'The Outlook for Peace in the Middle East', op. cit., p. 309.
[5] 'Reality and Vision. . .', op. cit., p. 634.
[6] 'An Interview with Mr. Eban', *New Outlook*, vol. 9, no. 7 (82), Sept. 1966, pp. 17–18.

No more forthright expression of the 'Weizmannist' approach is to be found among statements by Israeli leaders. This tone is also evident in Eban's formal addresses; for example, in his 1952 'Blueprint for Peace' speech to the General Assembly, the main proposals of which were repeated in his essay on 'Reality and Vision in the Middle East' thirteen years later: in sober words he dealt with what he termed the six major aspects of Israel–Arab relations—security, territorial, refugee, and economic questions, regional co-operation, and questions of diplomatic and juridical relations.[1]

All this did not prevent Eban from recognizing Arab goals *vis-à-vis* Israel: to prevent her physical existence; to reduce her territory; to flood her with hostile refugees; to uproot Jerusalem; to thwart the development of her diplomatic relations; to bar her from international organizations; to hinder her trade; to prevent her immigration projects; to discredit her, and to undermine her relations with the new states. Yet after almost two decades, he declared, the Arabs had suffered a 'total strategic defeat': 'not one of these aims has been attained; none of them is even remotely in sight'.[2] In 1965, too, he was able to exude optimism on the military balance: 'I would say that we are capable of thwarting and frustrating any attack upon us. But the military balance is not a static concept. It is moving all the time. We are caught up against our will in a constant escalation. . . .'[3]

Towards the end of 1969 he was even more sanguine. He discerned a world-wide 'apathy and passivity' about the Middle East, 'which rules out the chances of external intervention to do for the Arabs what they cannot do for themselves'. Furthermore, 'we have seen a convergence of American–Israel interests'. And changes in world politics diminish Arab influence on the Powers—the Middle East is no longer a strategic crossroads, he said; bases are no longer necessary in the space age; the oil market is dominated by buyers, not the Arab sellers; and the Suez Canal, closed for two years, is no longer indispensable.[4] And yet his persistent advocacy of keeping all options open to facilitate a negotiated settlement—against the growing mood of 'fortress Israel', most emphatically represented by Dayan and Peres—indicated that Eban remained committed to a 'Weizmannist' approach to 'the Arabs' in the post-Six-Day-War phase of Israel's foreign policy.

ii. *Dayan*

Moshe Dayan is first and foremost a soldier preoccupied with security. Unlike Eban he does not engage in formal conceptual analysis

[1] 'Peace in the Middle East', Israel Office of Information, New York, 1952. Reprinted as 'A Blueprint for Peace', *Voice of Israel*, pp. 93–122.
[2] 'Reality and Vision. . .', op. cit., p. 628.
[3] To W. Burdett in a broadcast on CBS, New York, 14 June 1965.
[4] To a United Jewish Appeal Study Mission, as reported in *Jerusalem Post*, 13 Oct. 1969.

of 'the Middle East', which is synonymous with 'the Arabs' in his image; and 'the Arabs' have been at the centre of his concern for decades. This is evident from a revealing and partly self-analytic reply to a question posed in 1969—'what is Israel's greatest problem?'[1]

Understanding the Middle East. Our greatest problem is to find out how to live with the Arabs. Because the fact is that we are trying to build a Jewish state here, and the Arabs consider us foreigners, invaders who are stealing their country. So, whether I'm a farmer, in uniform or Minister of Defence, I think about it continually. And as an individual, I like to try to understand them, not to know my enemy but to know my neighbors, and I really like them. I like simple men, whether they're Bedouins from the desert or peasants from the villages. And my main concern is not to impose upon them the fact that we have conquered their territory but to find a solution from both a political and human point of view. . . .

We shouldn't deny them any rights we want for ourselves. We must offer them terms that would suit our own people. . . .

I'm absolutely sure about this, I believe it possible for Jews and Arabs to live together without animosity. I'm absolutely convinced of this.

Within Israel, Dayan is reputed to have an uncanny insight into the Arab 'mind': 'he understands them—and they trust him' is a frequent remark among the attentive and mass publics. How then does Dayan perceive the Arab? One personal anecdote related by Dayan himself sharply distinguished his *sabra* perspective from that of the Second *Aliya* generation:[2]

When I was a child, I used to go with my late father for long walks around the Valley of Jezreel. We used to meet Arabs, and they, especially in the winter, covered their heads with their *kafiyas*, so that only their nose and eyes remained visible. My father, who was not born in the country—he came from Russia at the age of seventeen—used to say: 'Look, they have the look of murderers.' But these Arabs were not murderers, they were simple *fellahin*, and because it was cold and rainy they covered their heads with their *kafiya* and *agal* and of all their face you saw nothing but a nose and glistening eyes—which to me seemed dark and beautiful. My father, on the other hand, imagined that he saw through the *kafiya* the looks he recalled from his *shtetl* in Russia.

Yet this empathy could coexist in the same man with a severe indictment of 'illusionism' in Arab perceptions:[3]

[1] *L'Express* interview, op. cit.

[2] In a speech in Yafo (Jaffa), 14 Feb. 1969, as reported in an article by Shlomo Avineri, 'The Palestinians and Israel', in *Commentary* (New York), vol. 49, no. 6, June 1970, p. 31. Avineri also reported that 'Dayan once surprised a student audience in Tel Aviv when he told of his meeting with the young Palestinian poetess, Fadwa Toukan of Nablus. He then went on to recite a Hebrew translation of a very long, extremely moving, and outspokenly nationalistic poem of hers about Jerusalem called, 'My City, Occupied' (p. 42).

[3] Interview with Geulah Cohen, *Ma'ariv* (Tel Aviv), 1 Jan. 1968.

. . . They live in a world which is not truth and they do this almost like a man who needs hashish in order to feel himself present in the Garden of Eden. Reality is hell! The cure is therefore to swallow a lie-pill, which will give the sensation of Paradise. It often seems to me that all the Arabs—and on all levels —act as though under the influence of drugs. Yet illusion is worse than a lie. You make a lie consciously and you dominate it, while the illusion will finally dominate you.

. . . But they read these stories in order to encourage themselves. A 'Zadik' [wise man] will live in his belief, but because they are not 'Zadikim' they live in their illusions. . . .

The Arab mentality does not occupy my thoughts as a psychological problem; it explains to me why the Arabs do not want war. In fact, it would have been plausible that the morning after the Six Day War, when the Arabs discovered that we were sitting at the Jordan River and the Suez Canal, they would have gone towards a settlement. And here—a year has passed—and nothing. And not because reality does not weigh heavily upon them, but because their mentality stands as a barrier between them and reality and stops their eyes from seeing it as it really is. They prefer to ignore it, so long as their imagined concepts with which they live do not break down.

Nonetheless, Dayan is not prepared to accept the consequent pressure of friendly Powers, who argue that 'you are different, and from you one can demand consideration and concessions'. 'I know that there is an "Arab mentality". Every nation has its own mentality. But the Arab mentality is intelligent enough to know that ceasefire does not include the right to send Al-Fatah through the Jordanian lines. . . . Clear norms of what is allowed and what is forbidden between us and the Arabs must exist. An agreement must be an agreement, cease-fire—cease fire. . . .'[1]

Dayan's image of 'the Arabs' is inextricably linked with his perception of Israel's security needs. The most formal statement of his image of Israel's security problem was made in a *Foreign Affairs* article:[2]

First, as to its *uniqueness*:

There is no other state . . . whose very right to existence is so persistently challenged by all its contiguous neighbors. This is not the classic pattern of international conflict. . . .

Secondly, as to its *intensity*:

No state is as vulnerable as Israel in the configuration of its frontiers; none has such memories of recent aggression; none is beset by the nerve-wracking experience of hearing the renewal of aggression repeatedly threatened; none is assailed even now by every form of hostility short of regular warfare.

Thirdly, as to its *complexity*:

[1] Interview in *Yediot Aharonot* (Tel Aviv), 16 Aug. 1968.
[2] 'Israel's Border and Security Problems', *Foreign Affairs* (New York), vol. 33, no. 2, Jan. 1955, pp. 250–67.

Israel, while subjected to regional hostility, is not immune from any of the dangers which might ensue from a world conflict reaching into the Middle East. . . . [This] would face Israel with a double peril—attack by an invading Great Power and a simultaneous assault by neighboring Arab states.

Fourthly, as to Israel's *isolation*:

Moreover, Israel faces these manifold dangers with no sure prospect of assistance from any quarter. Israel is not integrated into any system of defense pacts or security guarantees. . . . Recourse to the United Nations Charter . . . is now a dubious safeguard. . . . Thus, not only does Israel face formidable dangers; she also faces them in unusual solitude.

There are three roads to progress, Dayan wrote: a negotiated transition from the armistice to permanent peace; revision of the Armistice Agreements; and demarcation of the border, the latter two being modest forms of relief. All three were rejected by the Arab states. 'Until then,' he concluded, 'the *Israel Defense Forces will face* a heavy task, and face *it virtually alone as the solitary effective means for safeguarding Israel's physical integrity.*'

This image of insecurity was almost universally shared in Israel: it remained unchanged until the Six Day War. Yet in 1966 Dayan advocated that those Arabs willing to serve in *Tzahal* should be enlisted: 'we cannot say to the Arabs we want you to be loyal citizens and at the same time hold them in suspicion'.[1] On the question of Israel's longterm relations with her neighbours, Dayan rejected Goldmann's proposal of 1961 that Israel integrate into an Arab-led Middle East Confederation. There is no evidence the Arabs want this, he wrote; there is no better reason for integration with the Arab states than with Turkey or Iran; and since Israel would retain her independence, a confederation would not serve any purpose.[2]

The victory of 1967 created a new perspective among Israel's decision-makers: for the first time the state possessed strategically advantageous frontiers—on the Golan Heights, at the Jordan River, and at the Suez Canal. Yet Dayan was quick to caution that, while they were ideal, apart from the border with Lebanon, they were not necessarily 'realistic'.[3] He also urged his countrymen to view the situation through an Arab lens:[4]

For example, the security enjoyed by the settlements of Upper Galilee . . . has been pointed out often, but how do the Syrians see this? Israeli armed forces are now an easy 60 kilometres from Damascus. . . . The Syrians are unlikely

---

[1] *Jerusalem Post*, 8 May 1966.

[2] 'No Simple Way to Peace: A Reply to Dr. Goldmann's New Orientation', in *Jerusalem Post*, 13 Aug. 1961.

[3] Interview with the editors of *Bamahane*, a *Tzahal* weekly. As reported in *Jerusalem Post Weekly*, 9 Oct. 1967.

[4] Address to the *Rafi* Convention in Jerusalem on 12 Dec. 1967. *Jerusalem Post Weekly*, 1 Jan. 1968.

to accept this as a basis for peace. . . . We shall have to be ready for a lengthy conflict.

For one of the effects of the War was to make the Arabs even less likely to come to terms with us than before. They see us now as even stronger, and as expansionists. The fact that we crushed the Arab armies in six days does not make it easier for their leaders to reconcile themselves to our existence. The way they see it is that, since the early days of Zionism, every crisis has led to an increase in our territory, and they fear further expansion.

In an equally unorthodox act, he said to captured Egyptian officers: 'You are returning to your country, and it would be well worth while if you should consider not only what you think but try and see things from our point of view.'[1] In that context he echoed Ben Gurion's view of the 'two worlds'—Jewish and Arab—and stated his long-term aim of genuine coexistence:

We regard ourselves as part of the Jewish world just as we consider the Arabs in our midst part of the Arab world. We do not seek to make them Jews— just as we do not wish to become Arabs. True we are a small people and may grow to five millions, but we can still live with you . . . without becoming part of you.

From that time onwards Dayan pressed for the establishment of 'new facts' and, increasingly, for the creation of a 'new map'. The rationale was realism. In essence, he argued as follows:

Israel will not withdraw from any of 'the territories' until a peace settlement is reached—'even the minimalists [Mapam and others] say that without peace we will not budge'.

Secondly, peace is not in sight. Israel should therefore put this enforced association to good use—for 'we are the Government in the territories. . . . This accords us rights and imposes obligations on us.' Thus an economic symbiosis should be created, as a basis for co-existence and co-operation.

More specifically, this means economic integration—the application of Israeli law and currency in 'the territories', the right of Arabs to work in Israel, the provision of essential services, and an 'open bridges' policy, that is, 'the right of free contact with the Arab states'. It also involves Israeli investment in the West Bank and Gaza.

But lest he be misunderstood, Dayan explicitly stated what should *not* be permitted: change of domicile, change of nationality, or change of status of 'the territories'. 'I must emphasize', he said, 'that [his proposed measures] do not mean annexation. . . . They will continue to be administered territories and will not become part of Israel.'

[1] As reported in *Jerusalem Post Weekly*, 22 Jan. 1968.

He also called for new settlements: 'we have to do our best to create a new reality, first of all in those places from which we do intend to withdraw. . . . We must set up outposts, create a new territorial map of the State of Israel. There is nothing holy about the map of 1948. . . . We must create facts, in order to build a new territorial map. . . . And we must lay the foundations for . . . coexistence.'[1]

It was this policy in 'the territories' that aroused the antagonism of Sapir and Eban.

As for Israel's strategic goals in the period of limited war, Dayan enunciated the following creed:[2]

Our strategy is to guard the [Suez] Canal line and not to march on Cairo; to defend the Jordan River line, but not to conquer Amman; not to go to Damascus or Beirut, but to mount retaliatory raids—in depth, breadth, and locations that are unexpected; to retaliate but to hit and return.

Thus did Dayan perceive 'the Arabs' and define Israel's proper policy in the third year of impasse following the 1967 War.

iii. *Peres*

If Eban may be described as a 'cosmopolitan' in foreign policy outlook, and Dayan a 'Middle Easterner', then Shimon Peres is preeminently a 'European' in his image. 'The Middle East', he remarked with disdain in 1960, 'is a creation of Western writers. We are not nearer Saudi Arabia or Iraq than Italy or Greece, certainly not culturally or even geographically.' The task, he said, is to 'de-Middle Easternize' Israel and to place her in her proper European context. Israel, he added, has virtually no contact with Arabs and should ignore them, concentrating rather on internal development and security.[3]

During the sixties Peres was to soften this extreme view—the total rejection of Israel's Middle East environment. But 'the Arabs' remained for him merely 'the enemy': unlike Dayan and Allon, he never displayed empathy for the Arabs as a people; nor did he, like all three of his peers, seek insight into the Arab mind. Indeed his image was permeated by 'Ben Gurionist' symbols only—Israel is in a permanent state of siege, Arab hostility is universal in time and space, 'the Arabs' understand only force, concessions would be fraught with disaster, etc. As in so many aspects of perception and advocacy, Peres was the most committed Ben Gurionist.

What are we to do, he asked in 1961, in the face of an enemy of great potential strength? His reply reveals the essence of Peres' approach to

---

[1] The post-1967 Dayan image and advocacy was most clearly articulated in an address to the National Students' Union Conference on 6 April 1969. The extracts are quoted from the text, in *Jerusalem Post Weekly*, 28 April 1969.

[2] Interview with Uri Dan, in *Ma'ariv* (Tel Aviv), 12 Sept. 1969.

[3] Interview in Jerusalem, July 1960.

'the Arabs': Israel must be ready to meet a military attack, for there is no alternative—no speeches, no acts, no slogans, no miracles; Israel must create a deterrent—psychological, political, and military—which is stronger than Arab power; Israel must prevent a defeat by political or other non-military methods, such as the proposed repatriation of half a million refugees; she must acquire modern weapons, both for war and as a deterrent, and she must build friendships with other states.[1]

Three years later Peres wrote: 'I do not anticipate peace agreements in the coming five to ten years. Peace is after all not an agreement but . . . a political relationship, competition without shooting. So our greatest problem is the avoidance of war.' Egypt, he continued, is the key to peace. And there are three stages to this cherished goal: to eliminate the threat to Israel's existence; to contain the menace to peace, and to build a 'Bailey bridge' towards normalization of relations with the Arabs. Israel, he noted, had passed the first stage, had created an effective deterrent, mainly with French aid, and had begun the third stage by strengthening relations with the periphery: 'Africa is becoming a Continent of Balance—at least as far as we are concerned.' And like Eban he called for a Mediterranean grouping, into a 'new community of understanding'.[2]

Peres' image of 'the Arabs' received its fullest expression in his book, *The Next Stage*: the tone throughout was that of the technocrat and planner viewing 'the enemy' and advocating a suitable response to the reality of conflict. The line of argument may be paraphrased schematically, as follows:

Israel accuses the Arabs not because of what happens on the borders but because they do nothing to prevent infiltration. Coercive action must be taken against them to demonstrate that this is the only alternative.

Israel must use force when there is no way to solve the problem peacefully.

Israel must be wary of excessive reliance on political means lest this lead to increasing foreign interference in her internal affairs.

There are two solutions to the problem of security—immediate peace and immediate war.

The threat of war may arise from three conditions: an attempt to change the geographical *status quo* by force; a sudden occurrence, for example, a major border attack; and foreign incitement to the Arabs to attack.

[1] 'Strategy, Security and Deterrents', *Jerusalem Post*, 19 April 1961.
[2] 'Power and Middle East Peace', *Jerusalem Post*, 28 Feb. 1964.

Strategies and tactics have changed in the Arab–Israel conflict; now the concept of bargaining from strength holds sway.

Egypt remains the strongest enemy, with the growth of both conventional and unconventional weapons.

While Israel has attained Jewish sovereignty, the goal of peace with the Arabs remained unfulfilled. There are three possible paths to peace: influencing external forces to intervene in some way in favour of peace; inducing the Arabs to accept negotiations or at least conversations about peace; and an Israeli effort to alter existing conditions.

Objectively viewed, no force in the world will be able to bring about a peace settlement, because of Arab obduracy.

There is a possibility that the Arabs will change but this is unlikely—for the Arab world is dictatorial and militaristic; its approach is always opportunistic.

Moreover, it has international support, even from those who oppose war, because of competition for influence in the Middle East.

Israel's policy must rest upon the development of her military capability.

Israel must meet force with counter-force.

The Sinai Campaign was a model of Israel's correct response to the persistent threat of Arab assaults.[1]

Peres' image of 'the Arabs' remained unchanged after the Six Day War. In a candid interview at the end of 1968 he remarked:

My group is convinced, by force of circumstances, that all the Arab 'doves' are in the occupied territories, while all the leaders of the Arab states, equally because of necessity, are all 'hawks'. . . .
    [Of the] three possible partners in any eventual settlement . . . the Jordan monarch is not free to negotiate . . . [and] the Egyptian President is as powerless as his Jordanian equivalent. . . .
    With the Palestinians . . . the question . . . is not so much a matter of territory, but of human relations. . . .
    Our main objective—I would say even the best bet—is to create the necessary atmosphere for the people to live together harmoniously, a coexistence which would lead directly to peace. We do not want to make them Israelis and we respect their national aspirations.

On the conditions of peace Peres was more explicit than other Israeli leaders:

[1] *Ha-shlav Ha-ba*, Part I.

We are ready to pay the highest price for peace. I can't tell you today what that price will be. . . . But it is certain that we will make sacrifices. . . . We are ready to hand over some of the territories. . . . It goes without saying that Jerusalem is not negotiable, that the Golan Heights are *essential to Israel's security*. As for the Jordan, as Mr. Eshkol said, no Arab army will have the right to cross that river. In Sinai the problem is basically Sharm-e-Sheikh. . . . Our best guarantee *would be* an Israeli presence.[1]

In the continuing internal debate over borders, 'the territories', and policy towards 'the Arabs' in general, Peres shared Dayan's advocacy in its entirety—'strategic, secure borders', the 'open bridges' policy, economic integration, and Jewish settlement in 'the territories'. This was evident during the bitter struggle over the foreign policy and security planks of the 1969 Alignment election platform. Peres and Dayan confronted Eban and Sapir, with Mrs. Meir attempting to reconcile the protagonists in the continuing conflict between Ben Gurionist and Sharettist perspectives on Israel and 'the Arabs'.[2]

iv. *Allon*

Like all members of the Inner Circle, Yigal Allon is primarily concerned with the Arab–Israel conflict; it could not be otherwise. Yet he also has a clear perception of 'the Middle East' as a distinctive entity in international politics. Thus, in his 1959 letter to Nasser he observed:

This region is normally regarded as an under-developed area. But . . . we have in this area enough natural wealth, oil and water, minerals and manpower, know-how and technological ability to make the Middle East the envy of other less-blessed regions. We stand at the crossroads of the world's great communications routes.

Then, like Goldmann and, on occasion, Ben Gurion, he advocated a *regional* solution to the problems afflicting all Middle East peoples:

From every point of view—economic and political, cultural and strategic—I believe that the ultimate solution for the entire region lies in the creation of a regional organisation, a Middle East commonwealth of sovereign nations, interdependent on each other for economic, political, cultural, scientific and defensive co-operation. This confederation would not only secure adequate national autonomy for all member states, but also ensure the presence of an efficient organisation to prevent conflict within the region and to establish it as a powerful instrument able to eradicate poverty, disease and illiteracy and to make a considerable contribution to the peace of the world.

[1] Interview with Eric Rouleau, *Le Monde* (Paris), 28 Dec. 1968, as translated in *New Middle East* (London), Feb. 1969, p. 62 (emphasis added). Peres' post-1968 image of 'the Arabs' and of the Middle East, as well as his policy prescriptions, were elaborated in his *David's Sling*, ch. 13–14.

[2] This debate was given widespread coverage in the Israeli press from July to October 1969.

And in his specific peace proposals he urged that 'all parties should insist that the Middle East be excluded from interference on the part of the world blocs . . .', that is, non-alignment.[1]

These views were reiterated frequently: to the author in 1960 and 1966;[2] during a public lecture at the Royal Institute of International Affairs in London in 1963;[3] and, most elaborately, as part of his overall image of the Arab–Israel conflict, in his *Curtain of Sand*. There he wrote:[4]

The division of the Middle East into spheres of influence between the West and the East, as was done in Europe at the end of World War II, in Korea or Indo-China, is not possible or desirable in the Middle East. It is impossible geographically because the American hold is stronger in the north, near the borders of the Soviet Union, while the psychological hold of the Soviet Union is towards the south, at the border of Africa. . . .

There are two discernible tendencies in Allon's articulated image of 'the Arabs': the first displays a conciliatory and co-operative approach, as in his letter to Nasser and the lecture at Chatham House; the second is much more hawkish in tone and substance, notably his book and an article in *Ot* in 1967. These will be the principal sources for the exposition of a vital strand in Allon's image.

In his 1959 letter to the Egyptian President he wrote:[5]

. . . if . . . you believe that Israel harbors expansionist aims, let me hasten to reassure you. I solemnly declare that no such intentions exist. . . . Israel does not constitute a menace to the Arab world. On the contrary, she is most anxious to be a friend and ally. . . . [Further,] the historic record, both of Moslem and Jew, as well as the similarity of our semitic languages, are evidence of the fact that Arabs and Jews may consider themselves not merely as neighbors but also as brethren.

And if the Arab states require a transition period from war to peace, he proposed an intermediate agreement such as a non-aggression pact. In that context he suggested an eight-point plan as a basis for discussion:

1. A condition sine qua non: the state of belligerency must be ended.
2. Cessation of all forms of war-mongering, including bellicose speeches, hate propaganda and military incursions. . . .
3. [As noted, non-alignment.]
4. Strategic and political arrangements . . . to prevent the possibility of sudden attack. . . .
5. . . . mixed observer units composed of Israelis and Arabs should be set up. . . . if desirable, accompanied by UN observers. . . .
6. Discussions on ways of solving the refugee problem . . . before a final peace settlement. . . .

[1] 'A Message to President Nasser', pp. 3, 4.
[2] Interviews in Jerusalem, Aug. 1960 and April 1966.
[3] 'The Arab–Israel Conflict—Some Suggested Solutions', *International Affairs*.
[4] *Masakh Shel Hol* (Curtain of Sand), Ha-Kibbutz Ha-me'uhad Publishing Co., Tel Aviv, 1960, p. 131.   [5] Op. cit., pp. 2, 4.

7. Initial, followed by regular contact [following the pattern of the US–China talks in Warsaw]. . . .
8. . . . common use of available communications. . . ; [for example, Israel would grant transit rights to Egypt and free dock facilities to Jordan and Syria, while Israel would receive land and sea links to Africa, Turkey and the Persian Gulf area.]

These points were reaffirmed in his book, and most of them were contained in his 1963 lecture as well, along with a proposed guarantee of existing Arab–Israel frontiers and large-scale economic development projects. He also offered Israeli compensation for Arab refugees and Israeli recognition of any non-hostile Arab union.

A harder line is evident in Allon's recollections about the War of Independence. 'We won the war but lost the peace', he said in 1960. Moreover, he had urged Ben Gurion not to stop fighting until a peace treaty was assured and not to accept an armistice agreement.[1] During the 1969 election campaign Allon revealed that he had refused to serve on the Israeli delegation to the Rhodes Conference twenty years earlier because he had been opposed to an armistice instead of peace.[2] And in 1956–7 he strongly urged Ben Gurion not to withdraw from Sinai and the Gaza Strip until further political gains were consolidated.[3]

Arab enmity was perceived as a constant in his *Curtain of Sand*, the result of diverse forces: xenophobia and religious fanaticism; the urge for revenge; inter-Arab competition for hegemony; domestic problems, requiring a diversionary external hate-object; and Great Power rivalry for influence in the Middle East. 'One cannot know if and when war will break out', wrote Allon. 'But two things are clear: first, the state of war is imposed upon us by the will and decision of the Arab leaders . . . ; secondly, the policy of the Arab leaders is to destroy Israel.' There were long-term factors conducive to peace, notably, the declining importance of Arab oil, the military balance between the super powers, leading to less pressure for spheres of influence, and the conflict between Egyptian ambition and the interests of other new states. In the immediate future, however, Israel must anticipate another Arab assault:

It is doubtful whether the boastfulness of Arab leaders allows them to give themselves a real account concerning the ratio of forces and their weak chances during an outright confrontation. . . . At any hour the Arabs see fit, either from the international point of view or due to their own illusions, they will try their luck again.

As with other components of his image of 'the Arabs', the similarity with Dayan is striking.

Allon defined the 1960 Arab–Israel relationship as one of limited

[1] Interview in Jerusalem, Aug. 1960.
[2] Reported in *Jerusalem Post*, 23 Oct. 1969.
[3] Interview in Jerusalem, Aug. 1960.

war and discerned four principal Arab tactics: ostracism, economic boycott, political offensive, and guerrilla warfare. Their interim objectives were to keep the Palestine problem in the international public view, to retain the initiative until the opportunity for revenge arose, to discourage foreign investment in Israel, and to demoralize Israeli border settlements.

In Allon's view, Israel's strategic position was less than ideal. For one thing, Egypt had a natural base of attack in the Sinai peninsula. Moreover, Jerusalem and most of central Israel were within artillery range from Jordan-controlled territory. And the Syrian army, encamped on the Golan Heights, threatened settlements in the Jordan Valley. Nor did Israel have any space for retreat. And the danger of being severed at the waist was ever-present. Finally, all of Israel was within a few minutes' bombing range of Arab airfields.

This pervasive insecurity led Allon to advocate an 'interceptive attack' as a necessary and legitimate form of defence:

As long as the Arab rulers refuse to make peace with Israel and continue to hope to overthrow her by economic blockade, or by direct military attack, the moral right and practical ability to carry out an interceptive counter-attack, whenever necessary, form the military guarantee for Israel's future existence. . . .

Sometimes it must precede ['Arab aggression'] by months, sometimes weeks and sometimes even a few days. . . . When there is no choice . . . by only a few hours, but precede it it must.

Allon urged maximum caution before recourse to 'active self-defence': he cited as *casus belli* a change in the *status quo* leading to the entry of non-Jordanian Arab troops into the West Bank, Syrian interference with Israeli development projects, the effective creation of a Palestine army, and Egypt's closure of the Tiran Straits—in short, any substantive change in the existing Arab–Israel balance of power. 'Nasser must know', he said to this writer in 1960, 'that, if he moves his troops through Sinai towards the Israel border, the Israel Army will intercept him. Israel will not act before the UAR or any Arab state begins to mobilize and concentrate on the border—but *it will intercept the Arabs before the attack begins*.' This indeed was the doctrine that guided *Tzahal*'s actions on 5 June 1967 after a massive Egyptian military concentration in Sinai and a closing of the Tiran Straits set in motion a third Arab attempt to destroy Israel.

Allon's advocacy extended to frontiers as well, for he wrote:[1] 'If the war breaks out again we must not repeat the historic mistake made in the War of Liberation and again in the Sinai Campaign. We cannot

---

[1] This analysis and the quoted passages are based upon *Masakh Shel Hol*, ch. 11 and the thought-provoking review of Allon's book by Simha Flapan—'The Theory of Interceptive War', *New Outlook* (Tel Aviv), vol. iii, no. 5 (27), April 1960, pp. 42–53. See also Y. Zofeh's reply, 'The Strategy of Defense', and Ze'ev Katz' rejoinder, 'There is an Alternative Strategy', ibid., vol. iv, no. 1 (32), Oct. 1960, pp. 46–53.

stop the war before we achieve full victory, the integrity of the country and a peace treaty which will guarantee normal relations between Israel and her neighbours. . . .'

In his 1967 perception (post-Six Day War), Allon reaffirmed the essentials of his image and advocacy as discussed in *Curtain of Sand*. Indeed he pressed for a hard line across the board. He asserted Israel's right to protect her Jordan water supply by military means. He warned against 'continued excessive Israeli restraint or passive defence only' lest an explosion ensue, and bluntly declared: 'let us beware of losing our offensive power by pinning down the whole army on defence duties. If we find ourselfed forced to act, we must be ready to act on the other side of the border as well, without letting the choice of targets and of methods become stereotyped.' He defended the El Samua raid of 1966 and noted a possible Arab miscalculation—like that which catalysed the Six Day War. He also showed foresight concerning a Palestine Arab national movement: Notwithstanding the fact that Palestine was long regarded as part of Syria, 'a national identity may develop as the result of new circumstances. . . . If, in addition, a leadership should arise which can point to military and political victories, a viable Palestine identity might be created.'[1]

After the 1967 War Allon's advocacy continued in the hawkish stream. He called for Jewish settlements in 'the territories', as did Dayan; yet he also urged self-rule for the Arabs 'which would not commit them to recognize the unity of Jerusalem or Israel's policies regarding the territories', a form of home rule.[2] 'If King Hussein's régime collapses,' he declared, 'Israel would be authorized to consider moving the cease-fire line eastwards, in keeping with its strategic needs.' As for Dayan's policy in 'the territories', he opposed the extension of Israeli law, towards the end of 1969, though admitting that he had favoured this step immediately after the war, and he also opposed economic integration—until a decision on the political future of 'the territories' was made; rather, he favoured 'economic engagement', that is, the gradual progress of shared basic plans. He also expressed doubts about continuing the 'open bridges' policy.[3]

The essentials of Allon's image and advocacy were virtually synonymous with those of Dayan. The 'Allon Plan' for paramilitary settlements on the hilly terrain overlooking the Jordan River was not qualitatively different from Dayan's proposal: both aimed at ensuring that the West Bank would be immune to Jordanian military

[1] 'The Last Stage of the War of Independence', *Ot* (Tel Aviv), Nos. 3–4, Nov. 1967, pp. 5–14. The *Ot* article was reproduced in summary, with extensive quotations, in 'A Strategy for Security', *Jerusalem Post*, 10 Feb. 1967.
[2] To the Israel Students' Union Conference, *Jerusalem Post*, 1 Oct. 1969 and again during the election campaign, ibid., 14 Oct. 1969. See also interview with Ari Rath, ibid., 24 Oct. 1969.
[3] Interview with Yair Kotler, *Ha'aretz* (Tel Aviv), 12 Sept. 1969.

penetration. Moreover, Allon also advocated drawing up a new map of Israel without further delay—indicating 'what we should keep for security and political reasons and what we should leave to others . . .'. And the guiding test should be Israel's security needs: 'we prefer secure borders that are not agreed to, to agreed borders which are not secure'.

Allon shared Eban's view that 'every possibility [of peace] must be explored according to changing circumstances' and acknowledged the difficulty facing the Arabs in making peace. Furthermore, 'my line is to meet with everyone, regardless of the outcome. Peace is not an exact science. . . .'[1] Yet this seemed like a *pro forma* gesture. The main thrust of Allon's advocacy *vis-à-vis* 'the Arabs', in 1969 as in the preceding twenty years, was hawkish, like that of Dayan and Peres. Only Eban spoke the genuine language of conciliation.

(d) INNER CIRCLE IMAGES: A COMPARISON

Before turning to the analysis of policy formulation it would be illuminating to place the subject of the three preceding chapters—the key images of Israel's decision-making Inner Circle—in an overall perspective. It will be seen that the images and advocacy of Ben Gurion and Sharett serve effectively to define the limits of the continuum of images and policy positions for the other seven Inner Circle members over six crucial areas during Israel's first twenty years.

Sharett rated the importance of *global system relations* far more highly than did BG. Both came to recognize the bipolarity of the international system and the penetration of the Middle East by the superpower struggle. Ben Gurion's early commitment to 'non-identification', dictated by a 'national interest' logic, quickly gave way to a marked pro-West inclination after the outbreak of the Korean War. Sharett's affinity for this policy was more ideologically grounded and gave way more slowly: he took care to leave the door open to a reconciliation with the Soviet Union.

Meir, Dayan, and Peres followed BG's precedent closely, relating to the global system principally from the standpoint of Israel's security needs. Eban and Sapir, like Sharett, were far more influenced by global system considerations, and counterposed a pro-American position to the Europe-oriented posture urged by Peres and, to a lesser extent, Dayan. Eshkol, like Meir and Sapir, lacked a detailed conceptualization of global system relations; but he tended towards Ben Gurion's position, while Allon's 'hawkishness'—that is, his affinity to Peres and Dayan—was somewhat tempered by his ideological commitment to non-alignment.

The view of the *United Nations*, its role in the creation of the State, and its ongoing importance in the Arab–Israel conflict were subjects of

[1] Rath interview, *Jerusalem Post*, 24 Oct. 1969.

extreme controversy. With rare moments of ambivalence, Ben Gurion dismissed the UN as of no consequence, insisting that Israel's birth and survival owed virtually nothing to any but the people of Israel: 'The State is the result of our daring.' His contempt was best captured in the phrase '*oum shmoum*'. Sharett strongly opposed this view, going so far as to assert that 'we owe our State to the United Nations'. Correspondingly, Sharett attached significant weight to the UN and to world opinion, while BG largely ignored them.

Once again Dayan, Peres, and (to a slightly lesser extent) Meir closely emulated Ben Gurion's outlook. Eban recognized the UN's shortcomings but insisted on its importance as well; Sapir followed his lead. Allon tended towards the BG pole on the grounds that no factor could supersede in importance the need for strategically defensible borders. Eshkol's (for the most part unarticulated) position was closer to dead centre between the two extreme approaches.

The area of *relations with the Third World* did not provide as clear a division among the nine. Ben Gurion smoothly integrated the notion of Israeli aid to Third World countries into his messianic perspective of Israel as a 'light unto the nations'. Sharett's high interest in good relations with the emerging states of Asia and Africa derived largely from his ideological preference for a policy of non-identification. He played the role of the architect, beginning the concrete formulation of policy guidelines for Israel's reach into the Third World. Both were also conscious of the political significance of these links in terms of improving Israel's international standing and 'leaping over the Arab fence'.

Meir, operating to a large extent on humanitarian grounds, served as the engineer, implementing Sharett's and other guidelines. She was successful in establishing the strong links that Israel in 1970 enjoyed with many African states, but was unable to accomplish the same in Asia. Eshkol demonstrated his awareness concretely with his African tour of 1966, while Allon vainly concentrated his efforts and concerns on wooing India. Eban and Sapir devoted relatively less attention to this area, while Dayan was oriented as usual to the priorities of security. Peres on the other hand was close to Golda Meir's concern and worked on military aid policy to Third World states.

All agreed that *relations with world Jewry* were crucial, that world Jewry was Israel's principal and only dependable ally, that the fate of Israel and world Jewry were profoundly interconnected, and that Israel must remain a Jewish state. Ben Gurion claimed responsibility for Jewry—'as we define it'—and split the world into two camps, Jewish and non-Jewish. Sharett gave far greater consideration to the needs and interests articulated by world Jewry and rejected the 'two-camp thesis'.

Dayan and Peres were closest to Ben Gurion, and Eban and Sapir to

Sharett in this area. Meir had a reputation as the supreme ambassador to world Jewry, and both she and Sapir served crucial fund-raising functions over the years. Eshkol also tended slightly towards Sharett's position but moved significantly towards Ben Gurion's 'two-camp thesis' after the experience of the Six Day War. Allon stood midway between the extremes; he was intensely preoccupied with the fate of Russian Jewry in particular.

The conception of the *Middle East system* held by Inner Circle members has analytical importance, as noted. In various writings Ben Gurion demonstrated his perception of the Middle East as a political system in itself with Core, Periphery, and Outer Ring components. He attached great importance to the development of the Shiloah 'Periphery doctrine' which conceptualized the Middle East as a multi-religious, ethnic, cultural, and national, rather than exclusively Arab or Islamic area. Eban elaborated this concept of a 'pluralist' Middle East. He advocated a policy of 'co-operative co-existence' for Israel but preferred an outward Mediterranean orientation to integration into the Middle East. Sharett perceived a system with a Core and Outer Ring, but focused his attention on the former. Allon's understanding of the system—*qua* system—was sophisticated and included suggestions for *regional* solutions to its problems and conflicts.

None of the others had a very clearly articulated image of the Middle East system. For Eshkol, Meir, and Dayan it did not have substantive meaning independent of their images of 'the Arabs'. Sapir was conscious of the economic relations with the 'Periphery' states of Iran and Ethiopia. Most extreme of all nine was Peres, whose overriding European orientation was expressed in his desire to 'de-Middle Easternize' Israel. (He was to moderate this position in the sixties.)

Most important were the images of '*the Arabs*' held by the Inner Circle. Ben Gurion had hoped for a harmony of interests but quickly became the classic 'Ben Gurionist'. This meant a view of 'the Arabs' as understanding nothing but force, as having a constant and implacable hatred of Israel, and as constituting a single, monolithic nation parallel and opposed to the Jewish nation. Interestingly, his resultant policy of reconciliation through toughness and retaliation gave way to a more conciliatory line after the 1967 War. Sharett on the other hand followed a 'Weizmannist' line throughout, arguing that the Arabs were not just enemies but *people* as well. This image was characterized by empathy and firmness—without rigidity.

Most 'Ben Gurionist' were Meir and Peres, who had little insight into the Arab world. Eban was the most consistent 'Weizmannist', with his tributes to Arab culture and civilization and occasional critique of Jewish insensitivity on this point. Sapir and Eshkol both had 'Second *Aliya*' perspectives; the former was 'doveish' out of a desire to preserve the Jewish character of the Israeli State, while the latter tended slightly to Sharett's pole (though the Six Day War redirected him significantly in the opposite direction). Allon's approach vacillates between the conciliatory and the hawkish, though he had thought through guidelines for gradual peace and integration further than any of the others. Dayan was at times capable of almost incredible sensitivity to and (apparent) sympathy for Arab perceptions, and at other times could criticize them with severity. Notwithstanding, security considerations were still uppermost for both Allon and Dayan.

The images held by Israel's Decision-Making Inner Circle may also be schematically represented by means of continua extending from the Sharett Caution Pole to the Ben Gurion Courage Pole. The most important in policy terms is that conveying their images of 'the Arabs', as follows:

FIGURE 4

CONTINUUM OF ISRAELI INNER CIRCLE IMAGES OF 'THE ARABS'

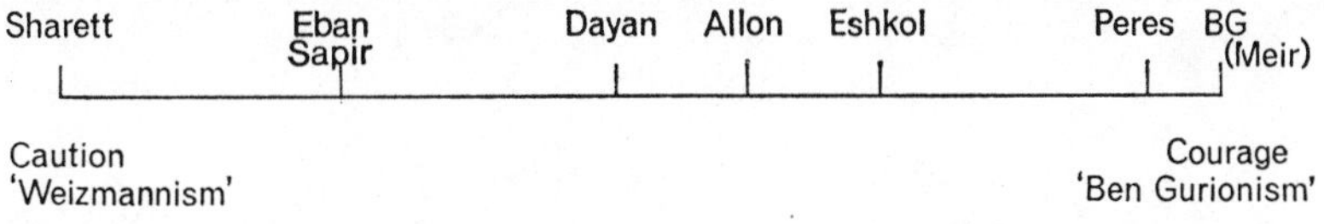

Sharett	Eban Sapir	Dayan	Allon	Eshkol	Peres	BG (Meir)

Caution	Courage
'Weizmannism'	'Ben Gurionism'

It should be stressed, however, that this representation is schematic and that the continuum construct exists at only the most general level. Significant cross-connections and overlappings emerge from a more rigorous analysis of images (see Appendix D). The younger Israeli decision-makers have absorbed the images of their elders, refined them, and transposed them from one level of the system to another. They see both their immediate environments and the world around them through a 'synthesized' and interlinked set of perceptions. The 'two-pole thesis' thus tends to become an over-simplified distortion of sophisticated and complex foreign policy images. Or, as Eban himself succinctly put it: 'There are hawks dressed in the feathers of doves and vice versa.'[1]

[1] In an interview with Eli Eyal on the *Galei Tzahal* (Army) radio station. Reprinted in *Bamahane* (Tel Aviv), 3 Feb. 1970.

PART III
PROCESS

CHAPTER 15

Formulation of High-Policy Decisions: I

The Operational Environment for Israel's foreign policy was analysed in Part I of this work, in accordance with our research framework. The Attitudinal Prism of the High Policy Élite and the core images held by its Inner Circle members were explored in Part II. There remains the discussion of the *process* of foreign policy—its forging and execution. This part will be divided into three: (1) the formulation of high-policy decisions (chapters 15 and 16); (2) an overview of the Foreign Service Technical Élite and the Parallel Technical Élite in other branches of the Government who implement these decisions (chapters 17 and 18); and (3) the instruments and techniques through which these policies are implemented, including both the Foreign Ministry and less conventional channels (chapters 19 and 20). We may begin with an attempt to define and apply general types of foreign policy decisions.

(a) TYPES OF DECISIONS

Foreign *Relations* have long been an object of historical inquiry. Foreign *Policy*, by contrast, has emerged only recently as a branch of social science. In the past fifteen years models, frameworks, approaches, theories, and hypotheses have proliferated. Yet it is a commentary on the state of the field that many books which are devoted to the analysis of foreign policy do not contain a single explicit reference to the meaning of *decision*, the motor force of state behaviour in international systems. The concept of decision is assumed but not defined; or it is used as a synonym for policy and is not regarded as essential to the inquiry.[1]

[1] A random check among books on foreign policy in English published between 1963 and 1969 reveals many to be devoid of any definition of a 'decision'. Some notable illustrations are as follows: J. E. Black and K. W. Thompson (eds.), *Foreign Policies in a World of Change*, New York, 1963 (with 24 specific country studies); R. C. Macridis (ed.), *Foreign Policy in World Politics* (3rd. ed.), New York, 1967 (with 10 specific country studies); M. C. Needler, *Understanding Foreign Policy*, New York, 1966; F. S. Northedge (ed.), *The Foreign Policies of the Powers*, London, 1968 (7 country studies); J. C. Plano and R. Olton, *The International Relations Dictionary*, New York, 1969 (the closest approximation is a reference to foreign policy); J. N. Rosenau (ed.), *Domestic Sources of Foreign Policy*, New York, 1967.

Among specific country studies that do not bother to define 'decision': Elie Abel, *The Missile Crisis*, New York, 1968; Alfred Grosser, *French Foreign Policy Under de Gaulle*, Boston, 1967; Karl Kaiser, *German Foreign Policy in Transition*, London, 1968.

See Appendix E for a survey of selected literature on foreign policy decisions.

It is important, therefore, to define and to classify foreign policy decisions: three universal indicators will be combined—a *time continuum*, a spectrum of *initiation–reaction*, and a *scale of importance*.

A foreign policy decision may be defined as the selection, among perceived alternatives, of one option leading to a course of action in the international system. A decision is made by an individual or individuals or a group authorized by the political system to act within a prescribed sphere of external behaviour.[1]

Foreign policy decisions occur at precise points in time; that is to say (in the Israeli system), the Foreign Minister or the Prime Minister or both, or the Cabinet or its Ministerial Committee on Defence, or on rare occasions the *Knesset*, or a Foreign Office committee or official(s) select option X at point Y in time, which leads to a course of action towards another state or states, an international organization, etc. The time span, however, between stimulus and decision, whether self- or externally-induced, and the selection of option X may extend from a day or less to many months (1—d days). And within the gestation period the number of pre-decisional stages may be one, a few, or many.

There is conspicuous variety, too, in the initiation–reaction mix. Virtually all decisions contain both types of stimuli, but the proportions vary from almost total initiative to almost total reaction. Furthermore, there appears to be *a meaningful correlation between these two spectra—time span and initiation–reaction—and the importance of foreign policy decisions*. As noted at the outset of this work, they may be scaled into three categories:

Strategic decisions may be defined as broad policy acts, measured by significance for the state's foreign policy system as a whole, duration of impact, and the presence of a subsidiary cluster of decisions. Those subsidiary clusters, to operationalize that policy act, constitute *Tactical* decisions. The continuous flow of foreign policy choices derived from Strategic and Tactical decisions may be designated *Implementing* decisions. In terms of measurable impact, Strategic decisions affect three or more components of the Operational Environment, including external and internal variables. Tactical decisions affect two components, and Implementing decisions usually no more than one.[2]

The evidence from Israeli foreign policy indicates that *Implementing* choices are characterized by *the highest proportion of reactive stimulus and the briefest time span* between inducement and decision. *Strategic* decisions reveal *much greater initiative and a much longer time span*. And *Tactical* decisions reveal *variety in both source of stimulus and time span*. This emerges from the graphical representation of selected Israeli decisions shown in Figs. 5–7.

[1] That process of selection may be rational or may be based upon 'non-logical' or personality stimuli. On this question see Sydney Verba, 'Assumptions of Rationality and Non-Rationality in Models of the International System', *World Politics*, xiv, 1, Oct. 1961, pp. 93–117.

[2] A somewhat similar fourfold typology of decisions, though not focusing on *foreign* policy, is to be found in David Braybrooke and Charles E. Lindblom, *A Strategy of Decision: Policy Evaluation as a Social Process*, The Free Press, New York, 1963, pp. 61–79.

FIGURE 5

IMPLEMENTING DECISIONS

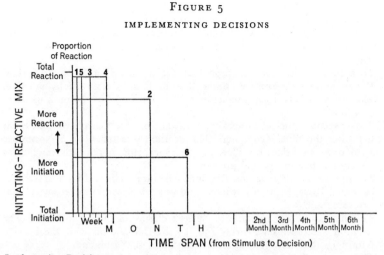

TIME SPAN (from Stimulus to Decision)

Implementing Decisions:

1. To send a complaint to the UN Security Council following a *Feda'iyun* raid.
2. To send a representative to a specific international conference.
3. To reply or not to reply to a letter to the editor of the *New York Times* critical of Israel—and if affirmative, in what form.
4. To criticize the Government of India for discourtesy to President Shazar while en route to Nepal for a state visit in 1966.
5. To protest or not to protest to the Government of Ghana for the expulsion of an Israeli diplomat from a social gathering during an OAU summit meeting in Accra in 1965.
6. To invite a foreign leader to visit Israel during a projected tour of Arab states.

FIGURE 6

TACTICAL DECISIONS

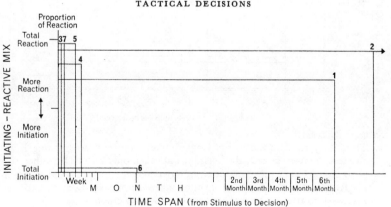

TIME SPAN (from Stimulus to Decision)

Tactical Decisions:

1. To decline an expression of interest from Communist China in diplomatic relations. The decision was taken by the Cabinet in April 1955, after six months of gestation. There was some Israeli initiative, but it was more reactive.

2. To accept the modified Johnson Plan for the distribution of the Jordan Waters among the riparian states. The decision, almost wholly reactive, was taken in July 1955 after almost 18 months of negotiation and lesser decisions.

3. To accept in principle Israel's withdrawal from the Gaza Strip and Sinai following the Sinai Campaign. The decision was taken on 8 November 1956, reversing a decision of less than 24 hours before not to withdraw; it was wholly reactive to external pressure.

4. To approve sanctions against Rhodesia when it proclaimed UDI in November 1965. It was primarily reactive and was taken within three days of that proclamation.

5. To delay a military response to Nasser's closure of the Tiran Straits. The decision was taken on 27 May 1967 by the Cabinet following the Foreign Minister's three-day visit to Paris, London, and Washington.

6. To integrate East Jerusalem into Jerusalem. The decision, entirely at Israel's initiative, was taken on 27 June 1967, a little more than two weeks after the Six Day War.

7. To reject United States proposals for a Jordan–Israel settlement, as announced by Secretary of State Rogers. The decision, entirely reactive, was taken by the Cabinet on 22 December 1969, within a day of their publication.

FIGURE 7

STRATEGIC DECISIONS

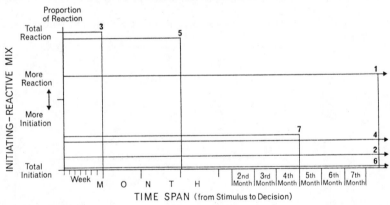

TIME SPAN (from Stimulus to Decision)

Strategic Decisions:

1. To make Jerusalem the seat of Government. Despite overwhelming Israeli public opinion in favour, the decision was taken only on 11 December 1949 —18 months after the declaration of independence. A UN General Assembly Resolution on the 9th, reaffirming a *corpus separatum* over the City, was necessary to trigger the more reactive-induced decision.

2. To seek reparations from Germany by direct negotiations. Six years passed after the first pre-decisional act in 1945; and the decision process took more than a year, culminating in approval by the *Knesset* Committee on Foreign Affairs and Security on 15 January 1952. The dire economic conditions shaped the decision.
3. To support United Nations actions in Korea. The decision, entirely reactive, was taken on 2 July 1950, seven days after the outbreak of war between North and South Korea.
4. To embark on the Sinai Campaign. It was in gestation for at least ten months, from January to October 1956 and, while reactive to *Feda'iyun* raids, was primarily an initiative of Israeli leaders.
5. To act on 5 June 1967. The decision took three weeks and was entirely a reaction to UAR actions from 14 May onwards.
6. To create an Israeli presence in Africa. An entirely Israeli initiative, though set against the stimulus of the Arab blockade, it took some years to crystallize.
7. To accept diplomatic relations with West Germany in May 1965, after four months of gestation.[1]

One Israeli academic, with experience in decision-making relating to military–security issues, described Israeli foreign policy since 1948 as comprising 'three or four decisions'. He meant initiated, Strategic decisions like the Sinai Campaign and the Six Day War. Lesser acts of selection among alternative options by decision-makers were dismissed as not worthy of being designated 'decisions': any reactive choices—and at the Tactical- or Implementing-level—are not, for Dr. Y. Harkabi, decisions.[2]

By contrast, Foreign Policy is here regarded as the totality of behaviour by a state in international systems: it includes all decisions—as defined earlier—whether the choices are made at the state's initiative or in response to external stimuli, or both; whether important or marginal; and whether made in an hour, a day, a week, a month. . . . Any choice of an option leading to action is a decision; and all of these decisions resulting in external behaviour constitute Foreign Policy.

It is not the purpose of this inquiry to explore *all* Israeli foreign policy decisions. We shall begin with a comparative analysis of *ministerial* roles and relationships—of Prime Minister–Defence Minister and Foreign Minister—during the period 1948–68, with a focus on the pairs of persons who held these posts. This will be followed by a probe into the relationships between the two crucial bureaucratic structures—Foreign Office and Defence Ministry—and, in that connection, the roles of the Defence Minister when he was not Prime Minister at the same time.

[1] The most important Strategic-level decisions (and some Tactical-level ones) will be analysed in a related volume on Israeli high-policy decisions.
[2] Interview in Tel Aviv, Oct. 1965.

In the next chapter attention will be concentrated on the roles of the Cabinet and its Ministerial Committee on Defence, on lesser structures, and on two high-policy decisions within the military–security issue-area of foreign policy—arms and Germany in 1957–8 and 1959, both of which led to the fall of the Israeli Government. In short, this and the following chapter will deal with the process relating to Strategic-level decisions.[1]

(b) PRIME MINISTER–DEFENCE MINISTER AND FOREIGN MINISTER: ROLES AND RELATIONSHIPS

In Part II of this book we explored the images held by Israeli high-policy decision-makers. Now we shall analyse the interacting behaviour of the High Policy Élite, especially of its Inner Circle. There were four pairs of persons at the summit of decision-making during Israel's first twenty years of independence: Ben Gurion as Prime Minister–Defence Minister had two Foreign Ministers, Sharett (1948–56) and Meir (1956–63); and Eshkol as Prime Minister–Defence Minister worked with Meir (1963–6) and Eban (1966–8).[2] Both Meir and Eban readily accepted the primacy of the Head of Government in the formulation of foreign policy, a striking feature of democratic states in the post-Second World War era;[3] Sharett as Foreign Minister did so in theory but less so in practice. This was not without consequence for decision-making. Nor was the diversity in *status-influence* among the four pairs.

The *Eshkol–Meir* relationship was the closest approximation to equals for, although the higher *authority* of the Prime Minister was acknowledged, they were of the same generation and rank of *Yishuv* and *Mapai* leaders, with many years of competent ministerial service and membership in all the key decision-making structures—Cabinet, Ministerial Committee on (Foreign Affairs and) Defence, *Sareinu* (Our Ministers), *Havereinu* (Our Comrades, that is, the senior leaders of *Mapai*), and the *Mapai* Leadership Bureau.

The greatest gap in status and influence was evident in the *Ben Gurion–Meir* period: as long as he was Prime Minister, BG was the towering political figure whose decisions, though challenged, were

[1] Types of Implementing decisions will be examined in ch. 20 below on the Foreign Ministry at Work.

[2] Sharett was also Prime Minister—but he was Foreign Minister at the same time. His key decision-making colleague in foreign and security policy from January 1954 to February 1955 was Defence Minister Lavon; that relationship will be examined in the following section.

The pair became a trio in 1967 with the appointment of Dayan as Defence Minister. And not infrequently there was an appearance of a disharmonious quartet, including Deputy Prime Minister Allon.

[3] Notable exceptions were Secretary of State Dulles under President Eisenhower (1953–9) and External Affairs Minister Pearson under Canadian Prime Minister St. Laurent (1948–57).

rarely set aside. The 'BG Complex' strengthened the institutional gap —much more for Meir than for Sharett.

The gap between *Eshkol and Eban* was also marked but for other reasons. Eban's superior knowledge and skill in foreign affairs was recognized and valued by the Prime Minister. But Eban was the supreme technician of the Gromyko–Couve de Murville–Rusk type, without an independent power base in the political system. Eshkol was Ben Gurion's (initially-chosen) successor and the senior leader of *Mapai*, the pre-eminent party within the Government coalition.

The *Ben Gurion–Sharett* relationship was the most complex—and significant—for decision-making. They were undoubtedly unequal in both status and influence. Yet Sharett was a political leader before independence, much more so than the other two Foreign Ministers, and he had a reputation as *the* foreign affairs expert of the *Yishuv*. His selection as Foreign Minister in 1948 was viewed as natural by the entire *Yishuv*. And he perceived his expertise as vastly superior to that of Ben Gurion, with a consequent 'right' to primacy in this sphere of public policy— though he understood and accepted the Prime Minister's ultimate *authority*. Not by accident was the Ben Gurion–Sharett relationship the most vibrant and tense, culminating in the rupture of 1956.

Measured along a simple ordinal scale, from greatest to least gap in status-influence, within the formulation pyramid, the ranking of Prime Minister -Foreign Minister relationship is:

1. Ben Gurion–Meir
2. Eshkol–Eban
3. Ben Gurion–Sharett
4. Eshkol–Meir

We may begin with the first in time and in impact upon Israel's foreign policy.

i. *Ben Gurion and Sharett*

Israel's charismatic leader had a clear and forceful image of the Prime Minister's proper role in the formulation of foreign policy. In his published oral memoirs he declared:[1]

I would say quite openly that an Israeli Prime Minister must also be his own Foreign Minister. Foreign affairs, like defence, is one of the key spheres of government, and, like defence, can be affected by a right or wrong decision at the lowest level, which is not the case with other ministries. . . . Because of this, I was naturally interested in all that went on in the Foreign Ministry. I would read all the important diplomatic cables each morning and would make whatever suggestions I thought fit. If foreign governments took any action or made statements or decided policy which affected Israel, I considered it my duty and my responsibility to *decide* on our reaction. Matters of vital issue

---

[1] Pearlman, *Ben Gurion Looks Back. . .* , pp. 127–8 (emphasis added to the word 'decide').

would of course come before the Cabinet for their decision. But I would make my position known between Cabinets. If it differed from that of the Foreign Minister, he could either accept my line or bring it before the Government. I agree that this may not have been always agreeable to Mr. Moshe Sharett. It would have been easier, I suppose, if I had interested myself as little in the day-to-day workings of his ministry as I did, say, in the Ministry of Works or the Postal Ministry. . . . Foreign affairs were different. I *did* want to know what was going on in every capital every day.

The nature of his relationship with Sharett in the policy process was stated at length by Ben Gurion to this writer with typical candour:[1]

I don't think every Prime Minister has to be Defence Minister as well.

I was always involved in Foreign Affairs. If there was a serious problem, the Foreign Minister and I would discuss it. Day-to-day issues I left to Sharett. I relied on him: he knew the details and he was honest. He always kept me informed. When there were differences of opinion, he accepted my view. Sometimes he opposed me in Cabinet discussion.

Until Sharett became Prime Minister he never made major decisions alone. After he became Prime Minister [and BG returned to the Cabinet as Defence Minister, in February 1955], I told him I would never act without his agreement.

If it was a matter of details, I accepted his view. If it was a question of principle, he accepted my views—though he may not have agreed. It was the same in the *Hanhalah* [in that context, the Jewish Agency Executive] before the State.

Sharett perceived his relationship with Ben Gurion in the policy process very differently. He had wide latitude and discretion in making (Tactical and Implementing) decisions, he remarked in 1960, four years after his resignation from the Government: 'Of course, I consulted the Prime Minister on basic [i.e. strategic] issues, by phone or in person.' Usually the matter was settled to their mutual satisfaction—and he modified or altered BG's view not infrequently during these discussions. In case of deadlock, and where Sharett felt strongly, he took the issue to the Cabinet. There the proposed action—retaliation—was sometimes overruled. 'Ben Gurion was not pleased on those occasions', when Sharett succeeding in mobilizing a doveish majority; while BG had said about these incidents, 'I didn't mind'.[2]

The question of timing was a frequent source of discord, continued Sharett, for Ben Gurion was indifferent to external consequences, while he, Sharett, was 'very concerned'. As an illustration of the Prime Minister's disdain for 'the external factor', Sharrett cited the *Kinneret* raid of December 1955, when he was negotiating with Secretary of State Dulles for United States arms. He had cabled Ben Gurion saying that a reply was promised within a few days. That same evening the Prime Minister sent a raiding party over the Syrian border: 'the negotiations went up in smoke'. Sharett brought this incident, which he described as

[1] Interview in Sde Boker, July 1966.   [2] Ibid.

'a dastardly act', to *Mapai*'s senior leadership group, its Political Committee; but the damage could not be undone.

It was in that context that Sharett assessed Ben Gurion's capability in foreign affairs:

> He lacks skill and subtlety. He does not think through all the consequences and implications of an act or statement. For example, his remark that 'Israel is part of Europe'—a brainwave of Shimon Peres—contradicts Israel's image as part of Asia and undermines her position in Afro-Asia.
>
> Ben Gurion relies on his own judgement much more than on any advisers. He is surrounded by little men unworthy of his trust.
>
> His mind is a powerful searchlight that is always focused on a specific object, with the result that the area surrounding it recedes even more into obscurity. He is interested in only a few broad themes and areas: the permanent irritant—Russia; the permanent challenge—America; the long-time friend—France. He is not, however, well-informed about foreign affairs generally.[1]

Ben Gurion was continuously involved in foreign policy but, by his own admission, with unequal emphasis on issue-areas: 'The things I thought about most concerned Security. Other areas of interest were Education, development of the Negev, and population dispersal. I didn't take a special interest in economic matters (and that included foreign economic issues). I left these to Eshkol and Kaplan. I never went to meetings of the Economic Committee of the Government.'[2] BG's involvement in the formulation of foreign policy can indeed best be portrayed in terms of a series of concentric circles (Fig. 8), stemming from the core of Security and the unshakeable conviction that foreign policy must be subordinate to security needs—certainly for Israel.

The innermost circle (1), where his interest was intense and permanent, comprises all issues concerning Israel's neighbours, that is, Borders, Armistice violations, Boycott, Refugees, UN discussions on the Palestine Question, the military and economic capability of Arab states, inter-Arab relations, contacts with Arab representatives, and, at decisive points, the Jordan Waters question. The second circle consists of all the larger political issues affecting relations with the Big Four: potential sources of arms and economic aid—the United States, France, Britain, and Germany—and the Soviet Union, because of Israel's commitment to three million Jews and Moscow's role as patron of the Arab states. Circle 3 comprises relations with the 'periphery states'—Turkey, Iran, Ethiopia, and Cyprus, those countries just beyond 'the Arab fence'—and the Horn of Africa. Those three circles must be set apart from all others in Ben Gurion's hierarchy of foreign policy interests; even among these one must distinguish between his obsession with 'the Arabs', his active involvement in the basic policy decisions with the four key states

---

[1] The Sharett assessment of Ben Gurion and their relationship as Prime Minister and Foreign Minister is based upon an interview in Jerusalem, July 1960.

[2] Interview in Sde Boker, July 1966.

FIGURE 8

BEN GURION'S FOREIGN POLICY CONCERNS

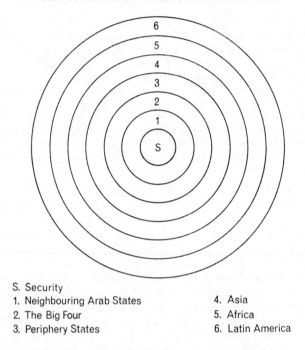

S. Security
1. Neighbouring Arab States
2. The Big Four
3. Periphery States

4. Asia
5. Africa
6. Latin America

for Israel's survival, and his more subdued but natural interest in the Periphery as a derivative of the first circle.

To these must be added any major issue concerning American Jewry, including relations with 'the Presidents' Club' (heads of major Jewish organizations in the US), Goldmann, the American Jewish Committee, and the leaders of religious groups. There was also for BG a set of circles of qualitatively lesser interest: Asia, partly due to his fascination for Oriental civilizations and Buddhism; then Africa, low on the scale despite its diplomatic importance to Israel and the challenge of under-development; and finally, Latin America.[1]

This geographically-based construct is enriched by evidence of the types of issues which engaged Ben Gurion's attention. Navon, his long-time Political Secretary, noted that

he did not interfere in day-to-day activities in foreign affairs, in appointments of Israel's envoys, except to the half dozen key posts and in special cases, or in most of Israel's votes at the UN. However, he was consulted regularly by the

[1] This construct is based upon insights gained from discussions in 1960 with members of Ben Gurion's staff, notably Navon, Peres, and Kollek.

Foreign Minister and gave his views. [More specifically] he would pen notes for Sharett—on documents or on scraps of paper—on anything to do with security, financial aid for Israel, all UN issues affecting Israel, Cold War issues on which Israel had to take a stand, American Jewry—the Presidents' Club, Goldmann, and the Rabbis.

In lesser matters he did not attempt to exercise a veto over the Foreign Ministry. But on major policy he reserved the final say—and he crushed all opposition to his views, as he did with Sharett. If there was quiet on the border, Ben Gurion would let Sharett go his own way; but if there was shooting, Ben Gurion would jump.[1]

Kollek expressed similar views from his experience as Director-General of the Prime Minister's Office from 1952 to 1965:[2]

It was not a case of Ben Gurion interfering in foreign policy. Rather, an informal pattern of frequent consultation developed with both Foreign Ministers [Sharett and Meir]. Consultation occurred on policy decisions, not on technical aspects of the conduct of foreign relations. But the line of division is very difficult to define: anything that is important. Ben Gurion did not insist on a veto over key issues: policy differences were thrashed out. But no major decision was taken without the Prime Minister's concurrence.

According to Yahil,[3]

he had an active interest in relations with Europe, but not in details; the question of what kind of association [with the Common Market] he left to the Foreign Minister and the economics Ministers. It was 'the larger political issues' concerning the United States, Russia, France, and Germany that interested him; also the Jordan Waters question at decisive points, in 1956 and 1961. For the rest, he allowed others to take the lead. [More generally,] Ben Gurion laid down the broad lines of policy but did not go into details, except in a few cases.

[As for Africa,] he encouraged Golda Meir's policy but he was not interested in details. But he was concerned with everything close to the Red Sea. He was also always interested in Burma and India, the first as an opening to Asia and because of Buddhism. Apart from these areas, he allowed the Foreign Minister and the Foreign Office free rein in foreign affairs.[4]

A succinct generalization embodying these themes about Ben Gurion's role in the decision process was suggested by Gazit, who was

---

[1] Interviews with Navon in Jerusalem, July 1960 and Dec. 1965.

[2] Interview in Jerusalem, Aug. 1960.

[3] Interview in Jerusalem, April 1966.

[4] An example of Ben Gurion's unorthodox foreign policy concerns was also cited by Yahil. During a mission to Germany in the spring of 1953 connected with the implementation of the Luxembourg Agreement on Reparations, the Berlin uprising occurred. A cable reached Yahil from the Director-General of the Foreign Office saying that the Prime Minister wanted him to proceed to Berlin and to prepare a report on the causes, process and consequences of the uprising. 'This was typical of Ben Gurion. He saw it as a possible turning point. But he was never interested in my experiences in Scandinavia [Yahil was Ambassador to Sweden from 1956 to 1959] apart from a briefing just before he went there on a visit.'

Foreign Minister Meir's Political Secretary from 1957 to 1960: 'Where Ben Gurion regarded the issue as important he made the final decisions —firmly. On everything else he was indifferent. He dominated, he overwhelmed, he overpowered—but he took no initiatives in foreign policy, even in issues he regarded as vital.' Apropos, 'during those three years he never asked Navon to call Mrs. Meir and suggest a policy line. He was the responsive agent to Foreign Office initiatives.'[1]

Ben Gurion's sources of information on foreign affairs were varied: cables from Israel's diplomatic missions, which he received three or four times a day and read, except for those on consular affairs; reports and letters from senior ambassadors, notably those in Washington, New York (UN), Paris, London, Rome, and perhaps one or two others; appreciation reports from the intelligence bureaux of the Army, the General Security Service, the Police, and the Foreign Office; occasional newspapers and journals, including the *Economist*, the *New Statesman*, *New York Times*, *The Times*, and the *Jewish Chronicle*; and face-to-face discussions with visitors from abroad, returning Israeli diplomats, Foreign Ministry officials, or anyone he cared to call.

Reference has already been made to Ben Gurion's pattern of decision-making in foreign policy. More schematically defined, his participation in the policy process was of four kinds:

1. Consultations with the Foreign Minister, usually two or three times a week.
2. Response to a Foreign Office initiative, that is, a request, usually conveyed through the Foreign Minister's Political Secretary, for the Prime Minister's views or directive on a specific matter.
3. Response to a particular Israeli action or a development abroad, derived from the cables; as noted, he would communicate his comments or suggestion for future conduct or policy through his Political Secretary to the Foreign Minister or some official in the Ministry.
4. The Prime Minister's own initiative. He wrote drafts of letters or messages to Heads of Government, if he saw fit. Navon invariably showed them to the Foreign Minister before they were dispatched— 'though Ben Gurion did not specifically request me [Navon] to do so, perhaps because he knew from experience that I would co-ordinate with the Foreign Minister'.

There were, of course, the institutional forums for discussion on foreign policy—the Cabinet, its Ministerial Committee on (Foreign Affairs and) Defence, *Sareinu*, and *Havereinu*. But the principal continuous link with the Foreign Office and, therefore, with day-to-day Implementing decisions was through the Political Secretaries of the Prime Minister and Foreign Minister. From 1952 to 1963 it was, essentially, Navon's telephone. Indeed this led one senior official in the Foreign Office to

[1] Interview in Jerusalem, Dec. 1965. Yahil's observations confirmed this view.

remark, in exasperation: 'Ben Gurion thinks that he and Navon can run the country.'[1]

Ben Gurion did not conceal his disdain for the ritual and formal aspects of diplomacy. Nor did he have great respect for the Foreign Service Technical Élite, with few exceptions. Their expertise was used to the minimum necessary for his knowledge about an important policy issue. As many remarked, BG rarely sought advice. To the extent that he did so, it came from a 'kitchen Cabinet' on defence policy. This comprised a few Cabinet colleagues, varying over time, *Mapai*'s defence specialists, a few senior civil servants from the Ministry of Defence, *Tzahal*'s Chief of Staff, Director of Intelligence and a few other officers, and the Head of the Security Service. According to one student of civil-military relations in Israel:[2]

Among those around Ben Gurion were Shaul Avigur, the. former Head of Haganah, Iser Arel [Harel], the Chief of Intelligence and Espionage, *Ha-Mosad* [not to be confused with *Tzahal*'s Intelligence Division, *Aman*], and other *ad hoc* 'security experts'. . . .

The group advised not only on questions of military strategy and doctrine but on foreign policy issues as well. This *ad hoc* cabinet . . . [which included Dayan and Peres] was vested with responsibility for making major decisions concerning Israel's security and the army's future. Cabinet ministers . . . were . . . expected to approve and defend these policies at home and abroad.

'Mr. Sharett was always correct in bringing matters to the Prime Minister for consultation': this was the assessment of the Director-General of the Prime Minister's Office for more than a decade.[3] Ben Gurion's Political Secretary for the same period remarked that Sharett's practice was not to consult the Prime Minister 'too often—only when he regarded it as a major issue'. When he did so it was through three media: his Political Secretary, who would contact his counterpart; writing to Ben Gurion; and meetings with him. Sharett, he continued, regarded the following issues as requiring consultation: any letter from a Prime Minister or Foreign Minister; all UN matters affecting Israel as well as controversial questions like the admission of Peking and *Apart-heid*—'they would go over the agenda together, after the Foreign Office had held preliminary discussions'; and any important problem posed by an Israeli diplomat. 'Sharett saw himself as the chief foreign policy-maker, not just as a technician. But he knew he had to go to the Prime Minister and get his approval on many matters.'[4]

These were all Tactical or Implementing decisions: Strategic-level

---

[1] Interview with Ya'acov Tsur, Acting Director-General of the Foreign Ministry, 1959–60, in Jerusalem, Aug. 1960.

[2] Amos Perlmutter, *Military and Politics in Israel*, Frank Cass & Co., London, 1969, p. 56.

[3] Interview with Kollek, Jerusalem, Aug. 1960.

[4] Interview with Navon, Tel Aviv, May 1966.

decisions were brought before the Cabinet at some stage in the policy process. Within the Foreign Ministry, Sharett's pattern of decision-making was akin to a university seminar, with participants persuading one another by rational discourse: the *Hanhalah*[1] was an active and vibrant discussion group during Sharett's period in office. His concept of *ee-hizdahut* (non-identification) was tested in this forum during the first year of independence. And it was there that Sharett's perception and advocacy on a myriad of issues were debated with his 'brains trust'—people like Eytan (Director-General throughout his tenure and beyond), Rosenne (Legal Adviser for all but one of the first twenty years), Shiloah (initiator of the Periphery Doctrine and, to many, the 'éminence grise' of the Ministry), Rafael, Kohn, and a few others. The 'Anglo-Saxon' group in the Foreign Office exerted predominant influence in the Sharett years, even more than later.[2]

Sharett was preoccupied with language: his critics termed it concern with style at the expense of substance. As one senior Ministry official remarked:[3]

> Like Eban, he loved language, was a master of language, and tended to yield to its symbolism. He tended to think formulas solve problems. [At the same time] Sharett always tried to apply analysis in preparing his case, though he didn't always succeed: he wanted his presentation to impress for its logic, as well as its language.

Another reported Sharett's initial reaction to King Abdullah's assassination and the likely succession of his son, Nayif: 'N*a*yif', he said, 'not Nay*i*f'.

In the final stage of decision-making within the Ministry, Sharett's habit was to consult an even smaller group than the *Hanhalah* or the full 'brains trust'. One participant, later a Director-General, recalled: 'Every Saturday evening he would call in three people—Eytan, Herzog and myself—and would go over the events of the week in preparation for his report to the Cabinet the next morning. He would tell us what he thought and would listen.'[4]

Sharett's failures in diplomacy were the result of vanity—both personal and (his perception of) national pride. A notable example was his emphasis on reciprocity, which delayed indefinitely an Israeli diplomatic mission in Delhi: the Government of India's attitude at the time of recognition in September 1950—it pleaded the inability to establish a legation in Israel immediately—was regarded as an affront, and it was rejected. Sharett's image of himself as Nehru's equal in foreign affairs

---

[1] The *Hanhalah* or Directorate of the Foreign Ministry comprises the Director-General, Assistant Directors-General, and Advisers—Legal and Political. It will be examined in ch. 20 below.

[2] To be discussed in ch. 17 below.

[3] Interview with Yahil, Jerusalem, July 1966.

[4] Interview with Rafael, Jerusalem, July 1960.

was not conducive to a more realistic long-term cost-benefit analysis.[1] He also misjudged the significance of Communist China and exaggerated the possible alienation of the United States when, by procrastination, he nullified a Peking initiative for diplomatic relations in 1955.[2] There were other errors too.

Sharett achieved much in the realm of diplomacy during the early years. More than any other individual, he secured the support of the United Nations, the super powers, and public opinion on three crucial occasions: the Partition Resolution of November 1947; recognition by Moscow and Washington in May 1948; and admission to the UN—while other states were still excluded—in May 1949. In essence, this assured Israel's legitimacy in the global system, thereby easing the task of *Tzahal* and the Prime Minister–Defence Minister. Sharett was also the principal architect of the Foreign Office. And through Non-Identification he was able to retain the continued support of America and the Soviet Union for a brief period—until the Korean War created the problem of necessary choice for the new state.

Despite these achievements, Sharett was compelled to resign as Foreign Minister in June 1956. It was the most important schism in terms of policy and process, for it symbolized the triumph of the 'Ben Gurionist' image and its derivatives—retaliation and rigidity: that image has enjoyed predominance in the High Policy Élite ever since. For this reason Sharett's departure from the Government merits careful attention.

Sharett's account was contained in a statement to the *Knesset* on 18 June, the day he resigned:[3] When Ben Gurion formed a new Government in August 1955, he asked to be excluded. 'I had well-founded reasons to fear that co-operation between my friend David Ben Gurion as Prime Minister and myself as Foreign Minister would not be successful this time.' The Prime Minister rejected his request, and 'I had to give way'.

Coming to the heart of the conflict, he remarked that during the past ten months 'co-operation between us was several times subjected to most uneasy tests [an implied reference to the *Kinneret* raid of December 1955, among others], which we managed to overcome by an effort to maintain a partnership. . . .

'But in recent weeks it has become clear to me that my resignation was unavoidable . . . not in connection with any pending political issue or with any current event or incident.' Rather, after a frank discussion with the Prime Minister on 3 June, 'I reached the absolute

---

[1] Related to the author by Foreign Ministry officials who observed this decision process.

[2] This important negative decision will be analysed in depth in the related volume on Strategic-level Israeli foreign policy decisions.

[3] The text is in *Jerusalem Post*, 19 June 1956.

conviction that it was impossible for me to remain in the Government of which he is the Head'. Sharett wanted to resign at once. Ben Gurion urged postponement. Four days later the Prime Minister conceded. A sharp debate was reported to have taken place in the Cabinet: Justice Minister Rosen of the Progressives (later, Independent Liberals) was understood to have called for the resignation of the entire Cabinet because of the importance of the Foreign Office; and *Mapam* and *Ha-po'el Ha-mizrahi* (later, National Religious Party) ministers reportedly objected to the manner in which Sharett's resignation had been decided—it was presented to the Cabinet as a *fait accompli*.[1]

Sharett's resignation was a *cause célèbre* and was treated as such, in the Israeli and foreign press and in the *Knesset*.[2] Ben Gurion denied that he had wanted to get rid of Sharett or had offered him the post of Secretary-General of *Mapai*; in fact, he had insisted, in August 1955, that Sharett join the Cabinet *because* of their differences. But later on, as the security position had become more acute, complete harmony was needed between the Foreign and Defence Ministers, as well as different leadership at the Foreign Office.

The timing of Ben Gurion's action appears, in retrospect, to have been linked to the Sinai Campaign, then in the planning stage: he was concerned lest Sharett jeopardize this crucial decision by mobilizing a slim Cabinet majority—just as he had succeeded in preventing some

[1] *Jerusalem Post*, 19 June 1956.

[2] *Ha'aretz* expressed the concern of many: the reason for the resignation was unclear, it remarked. Why did he have to resign and in what sphere could he not cooperate with the Prime Minister—if Ben Gurion declared that he would continue to follow the basic Government policy? The public was left in the dark about the circumstances and the implications of the resignation.

Ha-tzofeh wrote that a number of unsavoury things had come to the surface and urged that the matter be brought to the Cabinet for decision.

Herut called for the Government's resignation, adding that the new Foreign Minister, Mrs. Meir, represented the same school of thought as Sharett—'the extreme school of political defeatism'.

Lamerhav welcomed Sharett's departure. What Israel needs, it wrote, is not his caution but common sense combined with boldness and daring.

Al Hamishmar explained the resignation as due to a rift in policy, not just personal disagreement, and deplored the lack of Cabinet involvement.

Abroad, the *New York Times* and *New York Herald Tribune* interpreted the resignation as reflecting the growing strains of recent months and the attitude of the man in the street that Israel is being besieged and deserted by friends—and that it must exercise the right of active self-defence.

In the *Knesset*, a *Herut* motion calling for the entire Government to resign was defeated by 65 to 20, with 6 abstentions. A General Zionist motion of no-confidence had the same outcome. Argov of *Mapai*, Chairman of the *Knesset* Committee on Foreign Affairs and Security, termed Sharett's resignation an 'episode', a protest against the Great Powers for evasion of Israel's security needs. Hazan declared that his party, *Mapam*, received the news with sorrow and trepidation. And Harari of the Progressives criticized the lack of explanation to the House as 'an infringement of democracy'. All the editorials appeared on 19 June 1956.

retaliatory raids in 1955–6. Ben Gurion's account almost ten years later was mellowed in phrasing but essentially unchanged:[1]

Finally our ways parted, aided I confess by differences of personality which made working together difficult, though I had and have a high respect for his long and proud record of great service to the people and the country both before and after the establishment of the State. . . .

I put it to our party. I was prepared to go. The party decided to retain me, and Sharett resigned. It is unfortunate, but such things are inevitable in political life.

The decision was made by the forerunner of *Havereinu*, *Mapai*'s Political Committee. As Ben Gurion recalled later, he told his colleagues that either Sharett must go or he would resign. 'Aranne and Sapir went to Sharett and convinced him he must resign.'[2] And Mrs. Meir, speaking of this crisis in 1966, remarked: 'Sharett was wounded to the depth of his soul by his ouster from the Foreign Office. Ben Gurion said after Sharett's death,' she added with disdain, ' "I know it hurt Sharett; it hurt me too, but I had to weigh it against the security of the State".'[3]

The essence of the conflict, as expressed by the protagonists themselves, was confirmed by many colleagues and aides, who spoke frankly of this 'parting of the ways'. Navon summed up Ben Gurion's attitude to Sharett as follows:[4] 'He respected him as sincere, candid, a man of high moral scruples, brilliant, well-organized, and tidy in his thinking but lacking in *halutziut* [pioneering spirit], a vital quality for Ben Gurion. He consulted Sharett often, as his Foreign Minister, but the clash was deep—in temperament, character, political outlook and style.' Sharef added a time perspective: 'It was not a happy relationship. That was already evident in 1942 [when he came to work with both of them]. The unhappiness flowed from their basic differences over what was permissible, possible, and desirable. There were differences in temperament, philosophy—and irrational elements.'[5] And David Hacohen, who knew Sharett well, declared that it was Ben Gurion's role as Defence Minister, more than his position as Prime Minister, which was central to the friction: 'Ben Gurion insisted, and Sharett rejected the view, that Security must have priority over Foreign Affairs or, more correctly, that defence considerations must determine foreign policy.' In short, this was a clash of *institutional* interests. 'There were other sources of friction, however—personality, character, and basic approach to policy. Sharett did not accept the view that the threat or use of force was the way to solve problems. The clash was deep and complex.'[6] In Mrs. Meir's succinct summation, 'Ben Gurion as Prime Minister and

---

[1] *Ben Gurion Looks Back. . .* , p. 128.
[2] Interview in Sde Boker, July 1966.
[3] Interview in Tel Aviv, Aug. 1966.
[4] Interview in Jerusalem, Dec. 1965.
[5] Interview in Jerusalem, March 1966.
[6] Interview in Jerusalem, April 1966.

Sharett as Foreign Minister often disagreed. By 1956 co-operation between them was impossible.'[1]

The split occurred over two interrelated issues—the relationship between the Defence Ministry and the Foreign Office, and the activist versus diplomatic approach to the pursuit of Israel's external aims. The conflict may also be viewed in a framework of differentiation of function and time sequence. Ben Gurion was responsible for all policies directly related to the confrontation with Israel's Arab enemies. And Sharett had jurisdiction over Israel's normal diplomacy—relations with the UN and individual states, including the super powers. From 1949 to 1953 the emphasis was on the diplomatic field: thus Sharett played a prominent and highly-acclaimed role. As the security situation deteriorated, from 1954 onward, in the perception of BG, Dayan, and the *Tzahal* leadership generally, the clash between the two approaches increased in intensity. Stressing his diplomatic, moderate line, Sharett succeeded on at least four occasions in frustrating the BG–Dayan demand for retaliation. Concerned about the possible long-term implications for Security, Ben Gurion decided in 1956 that Sharett was a serious liability in the preservation of Israel's vital interests.

The depth and bitterness of the conflict is illuminated by a chance publication of Ben Gurion and Sharett memoirs concerning the first major retaliatory raid, on Kibya in October 1953. On the 18th, which Sharett referred to as 'a bitter, cursed day', Shapira asked at a Cabinet meeting if, as Foreign Minister, Sharett had been informed of the Kibya action in advance. Sharett's diary is dramatically revealing:[2]

I slipped a note to B-G asking if I could avoid giving an answer.

Earlier, B-G had noted that *he* had not been asked, since he had been on leave, but had added that if he had been asked whether to go ahead with it, he would have assented. This was a strange way of putting the facts: he was definitely asked, even if he had been ostensibly on leave. Not only had he given his opinion, but it was his opinion which had weighed the scales against mine.

In reply to Sharett's note, Ben Gurion asked if he (Sharett) had in fact known in advance.

This was also quite strange [Sharett continued], since Pinhas [Lavon, then Acting Defence Minister while BG was on leave] explicitly told him that I was against the action. I wrote him the facts.

Ben Gurion then replied [by note] that Lavon will shortly speak, and he will certainly put my opposition on record. But that was not to be the case. . . .

[1] Interview in Tel Aviv, July 1966.
[2] The following extracts were published by Sharett's son in *Ma'ariv* (Tel Aviv) and were reproduced in *Jerusalem Post* on 31 October 1965. Publication was sparked by a Ben Gurion memoir a few days earlier, in his series 'Things As They Really Were', *Yediot Aharonot* (Tel Aviv), 26 Oct. 1965, in which he had said that Sharett had known of plans for the action but had 'seen no reason to object'.

Soon after, Sharett wrote in his diary that he had told his wife he would have resigned 'rather than stand in front of a microphone and tell the people in Zion and the whole world some fictional account of something that really happened. But B-G himself conceived this version and initiated the broadcast certain of the justice and inner truth of what he was saying. . . .'

It was after Kibya that Sharett began taking Defence Ministry and/or *Tzahal* proposals of retaliation to the Cabinet. While Ben Gurion was in 'retirement'—and he was Prime Minister—he had his way on many occasions, though BG retained ultimate overall authority. After BG's return in February 1955, initially as Defence Minister only, the conflict became increasingly acute, with Sharett neutralizing BG's designs.[1] All this was accentuated by Ben Gurion's efforts to secure direct control over Armistice Affairs within the Defence Ministry. Sharett resisted and won, but in a formal sense only: violations of the Armistice were usually dealt with directly by Ben Gurion, using the expertise of the Foreign Office in this area as he saw fit. Sharett's resignation followed in due course.[2]

ii. *Ben Gurion and Meir*

The choice of Golda Meir to succeed Sharett in June 1956 reflected the victory of 'Ben Gurionism' and its policy consequence: the road to the Sinai Campaign was now open. Indeed the consensus then and later was that Ben Gurion wanted—and found—a Foreign Minister who would carry out his directives without dissent. This was assured for various reasons. First, Mrs. Meir, at the time, admired Ben Gurion as the 'Father of the Nation', who could do virtually no wrong. Moreover, as revealed by the analysis of élite images, she genuinely shared his image of 'the Arabs' and the need for a tough policy—retaliation—towards Israel's neighbours. And thirdly, she accepted the post with hesitation—some said, trepidation—because of lack of self-confidence.[3] She was simple in manner and tastes, not well-read or predisposed to read, and inexperienced in the intricacies of international politics. Sharett, by contrast, was polished, urbane, well-educated, widely read, a skilled professional for whom the post of Foreign Minister was natural, though he was much less decisive than she. Mrs. Meir was ill-prepared

[1] Ben Gurion revealed in 1970 that he had returned to the Government at the behest of *Tzahal* officers because 'we had serious problems with certain cadres in the Army. . . . I agreed on one condition: I would deal only with military affairs.' Thus, he had to report to Sharett, the Prime Minister, on defence matters—but Sharett was not obliged to reciprocate. Sharett and Nasser exchanged letters, added BG. 'But he [Sharett] didn't tell me about it officially.' Interview with Philippe Jean-Raymond, as cited in *Ha'aretz* (Tel Aviv), 12 Oct. 1970.

[2] The decision process on response to violations of the Armistice Agreements is examined in the next section of this chapter.

[3] Interviews with peers, aides and observers, in Israel during 1965–6.

for the world of diplomacy and knew it. As she herself remarked after leaving that portfolio ten years later, 'I wept to the *Haverim* not to impose the Foreign Minister's post on me.'[1]

The result was a fundamentally different role-relationship between the Prime Minister–Defence Minister and the Foreign Minister in the policy process. There was still another factor underlying the change— the leadership gap. Whereas Sharett had been prominent in the *Yishuv* since 1933, when he became Head of the Political Department of the Jewish Agency, and perhaps earlier, Mrs. Meir, as one of her peers remarked, 'was plucked out of a group by Ben Gurion in 1956 with the invitation, "come and succeed Moshe" '.[2] In short, she was more dependent on Ben Gurion than was Sharett. For while he respected BG's overall national leadership, Sharett did not feel, certainly not to the same extent, that he owed his position as Foreign Minister to Ben Gurion: they were less than equal in status but also less *un*equal.

Mrs. Meir's subordinate role in decision-making was further emphasized by the fact that, as her official biographer acknowledged in 1962—while she was still Foreign Minister: 'At no stage did Ben-Gurion relinquish the direction of foreign policy nor was he likely to do so whoever his foreign minister might be.'[3] The most conspicuous effect was greater harmony in the decision process. There was no longer any personal rivalry or basic differences on perceptions and policy. Mrs. Meir readily accepted the qualitative primacy of defence considerations and yielded to BG's prophetic wisdom in this sphere. This was apparent during the two major crises over arms and Germany in 1957–8 and 1959: she strongly opposed any relations with Germany; but there is no evidence that she challenged Ben Gurion in this matter, certainly not in the Cabinet discussions.[4]

This change was reflected in a different pattern of consultation: Sharett preferred to take disagreements to the Cabinet for decisions, while Meir settled her differences with Ben Gurion in private or in the pre-Cabinet *Sareinu* discussions. Such is the view of Navon and Kollek and Heads of the Foreign Minister's Bureau. Further, Meir exercised less discretion than did Sharett in Tactical and Implementing decisions; she tended to the safe side in deciding whether or not to bring a matter to the Prime Minister's attention. Thus consultations were more frequent, perhaps three or more unscheduled meetings weekly, as well as telephone conversations. Navon referred to the change as 'a breath of fresh air; the atmosphere was one of greater trust; and there was greater co-ordination of foreign and defence policy'.[5]

[1] Interview in Tel Aviv, Aug. 1966.
[2] Interview with David Hacohen, Jerusalem, April 1966.
[3] Syrkin, *Golda Meir*, p. 303.
[4] This will be documented in the analysis of these cases, in ch. 16 below.
[5] Interview in Jerusalem, Dec. 1965.

This was facilitated by the fact that Mrs. Meir never felt at ease in the protocol of diplomacy.[1] It was expressed, too, in a different approach to decision-making within the Foreign Office. Discussions at *Hanhalah* meetings were *ad hoc*, with very little preparation—'free-flowing and not focused', as one participant remarked. 'Mrs. Meir', said another, 'wanted to deal with the practical and operative end of policy, whereas Sharett always began with an analytic presentation. And unlike Sharett—or Eban—she did very little drafting.'[2] The basic contrast on the decision process was also stressed by Yahil, a former Director-General:[3]

Sharett created seminars. Discussions within the *Misrad* [Office] were lively and continuous. He would ask for position papers, and the pros and cons would be debated with intensity. Meetings under Sharett's leadership on positions to be taken at the UN were real university seminars.

Decisions under Mrs. Meir were much more pragmatic and less institutionalized. She had the great gift of spontaneously grasping the essentials of a problem. But there was very little policy planning in the long-run sense.

The 'absolute harmony' between Ben Gurion and Meir gave way within a year to friction. It was partly personal—the clash between Meir and Peres, then Director-General of the Defence Ministry—and partly institutional, that is, the jurisdictional conflict between the Foreign Office and the Defence Establishment. The core was Peres' alleged interference in foreign policy issues, especially over arms deals with Germany and France in the late 1950s.[4] As one senior official remarked, 'Ben Gurion didn't back him but he didn't block him either'.[5] Tension was heightened by the Lavon Affair, with Meir increasingly critical of Ben Gurion's obsessive behaviour. There was, too, a growing divergence in outlook, with Peres and Dayan urging a primary orientation to Europe, and especially France, while Meir inclined to view the United States as Israel's most reliable ally.

There is a consensus that the Foreign Office role in Strategic- and Tactical-level decision-making declined under Mrs. Meir. Sharett, surveying the change in 1960, remarked that the Foreign Ministry became 'a mere instrument of Ben Gurion. He alone makes major policy decisions; Golda merely executes them. She acts at the will of Ben Gurion; she does not take initiatives in foreign affairs.' The decision-making role of the Foreign Office since 1956, he concluded, was confined to minor technical matters.[6] A dozen senior Foreign Ministry

---

[1] Attested to by Mrs. Meir herself and by her biographer, Syrkin, op. cit., pp. 275 ff.
[2] Interviews with various participants in meetings of the Foreign Office *Hanhalah* while Mrs. Meir was Foreign Minister.
[3] Interview in Jerusalem, July 1966.
[4] This will be elaborated in the following section of this chapter.
[5] Interview with Ya'acov Herzog, Jerusalem, April 1966.
[6] Interview in Jerusalem, July 1960.

officials at the time agreed with this assessment.[1] They cited three illustrations of this reduced influence of the Foreign Minister and the Foreign
Office in decision-making:

1. Before 1956 the Prime Minister would never meet the UN Secretary-
   General or other high-level visitors alone; Foreign Minister Sharett
   was always present; and it was unthinkable to be otherwise. Thereafter, the Prime Minister met Hammarskjöld and others alone, with
   Foreign Minister Meir receiving a report of the discussion.
2. The Prime Minister would not make declarations on foreign policy
   without Sharett's approval of timing and content. And Ben Gurion
   rarely made such statements before 1956. Afterwards, he was much
   more active in articulating Israel's foreign policy, as well as formulating it.
3. Ben Gurion travelled abroad only once while Sharett was Foreign
   Minister (1951). This changed in 1960, with visits to Europe and
   America.

Mrs. Meir thought seriously of resigning after the 1959 *Knesset* elections but, as with Sharett in 1955, she was persuaded by Ben Gurion to
remain in office. Her major achievement as Foreign Minister was
Israel's conspicuous and successful 'presence' in Africa and the development of Israel's technical assistance programme in the Third World
generally. She acknowledged that the idea of an Africa policy was
elucidated in a paper by Sharett as early as 1955. But it was she who
gave it drive, purpose, and content.

iii. *Eshkol and Meir*

Eshkol's succession to Ben Gurion in June 1963 marked the great
divide in Israel's leadership: as noted earlier, it was a change from
charisma to competence, from vision to solidity. Nowhere was the contrast more striking than in their approach to decision-making, in foreign
as in domestic policy. The comparison may be portrayed in schematic
terms.

1. Ben Gurion's point of departure for decisions was a broad, abstract,
   theoretical world view. His approach to policy problems derived
   from the general frame of his outlook. Eshkol was an '*eesh meshek*', a
   practical man of affairs. His approach was pragmatic, dealing with
   each issue as it arose.
2. Eshkol detested dogma. Unlike Ben Gurion, his only dogma was
   anti-dogma.
3. Ben Gurion had *idées fixes*, an essentially closed mind with set views;
   and he was decisive. Eshkol had an open mind; he was flexible; and
   he appeared indecisive, because he took much longer to arrive at
   decisions. This explains the (erroneous) impression that Eshkol accepted the views of the last person with whom he spoke. Rather, he

---

[1] Interviews in Jerusalem, 1960, 1965–6, and 1968.

listened to all views and made decisions slowly. As Yahil put it, 'Ben Gurion would not discuss a matter about which he had not made up his mind. Eshkol crystallizes his thinking during the discussion. He needs people to stimulate his decision, to act as a catalyst to his thinking and discussion. This has advantages and disadvantages: decision-making under Eshkol is slower; it is also much more a collective decision.'[1]

4. Ben Gurion was a Leader; Eshkol was more akin to a Board Chairman. This, according to his admirers, had the merit of broad-based consultation. When Ben Gurion was right he was profoundly right and ahead of his people and his time; but when he was wrong he was seriously wrong. The consequence of Eshkol's decisions was less extreme.

In short, it was the difference between a charismatic and an 'ordinary' Prime Minister.

With the coming of Eshkol to the prime ministership, a new equilibrium emerged at the summit of foreign policy decision-making. As his Political Secretary remarked: 'Mrs. Meir is a party leader in her own right. She has strong views. And Eshkol had to consult her and convince her. Disagreements were common.'[2] The Director-General of the Prime Minister's Office at the time expressed similar views: 'Ben Gurion considered himself, and was considered, a towering figure—a man apart from his colleagues. Eshkol was more dependent on Mrs. Meir, for party reasons. Moreover, at the beginning he had no knowledge of, or pretensions about, foreign policy.'[3] Mrs. Meir's key aide in the Foreign Ministry spoke of 'great harmony; she brings before Eshkol all major foreign policy decisions discussed in the *Hanhalah* and, while he very seldom intervenes, she feels that the Prime Minister must have the ultimate decision.'[4]

Consultation was continuous: a regular one-hour weekly meeting between the Prime Minister and the Foreign Minister on Sunday at 4 p.m., with the PM's Political Secretary present; regular consultation between their Political Secretaries—'many times daily by telephone'—and between the Directors–General of the two ministries. As noted elsewhere, Eshkol activated the Ministerial Committee on Defence, still another forum for consultation. Mrs. Meir's pattern of consultation outside the Foreign Office extended beyond the regular and *ad hoc* sessions with the Prime Minister. There were frequent meetings with other ministers: for example, with the PM and the Minister for Religious Affairs (and the Chairman of the Jewish Agency) on matters affecting Jewry, and with the Ministers of Finance and of Commerce

---

[1] Interview in Jerusalem, July 1966.
[2] Interview with Aviad Yafeh, Tel Aviv, July 1966.
[3] Interview with Ya'acov Herzog, Jerusalem, April 1966.
[4] Interview with Simha Dinitz, Jerusalem, Dec. 1965.

and Industry on foreign economic policy issues. She was also a member of various Cabinet Committees—Defence, Common Market, Protocol, etc. And finally, the FM periodically consulted, i.e. reported to, the *Knesset* Committee on Foreign Affairs and Security.

The Prime Minister did not read Foreign Office cables except those concerned with his special interest—foreign economic policy: his Political Secretary read the important ones to him and provided a summary of others. Unlike Ben Gurion, Eshkol relied very heavily on his staff, notably Herzog and Yafeh, for information and advice about foreign affairs. Yet, ironically, Eshkol was more involved in foreign policy than was BG. 'On the one hand, Eshkol makes fewer decisions; on the other, his range of interests is broader. He does not have Ben Gurion's absolute concentration in a few areas.'[1] Thus, while Mrs. Meir had a more harmonious relationship with Eshkol, she had less freedom of action as Foreign Minister than with Ben Gurion. Relations with 'the Arabs' were at the core of Eshkol's interests, as with his predecessors, followed by the United States and France. He attached more importance than did BG to improved relations with the Soviet Union, and to Diaspora Jewry as well. Over the years he was involved in many Strategic-level decisions. He played a vital, sometimes decisive, role in the following: the Jordan Waters issue (in 1954-5, 1961, and 1966); the Common Market (1960 ff.); diplomatic relations with West Germany (1965); and the Six Day War (1967).[2]

iv. *Eshkol and Eban*

The departure of Mrs. Meir from the Foreign Office at the beginning of 1966 altered the role-relationship at the summit once more. Eban is much more the diplomat than the politician. He is, as noted, of the Rusk–Gromyko–Couve de Murville *genre*, the professional adviser to the Head of Government or Head of State in foreign affairs. Even more than Foreign Minister Meir with BG and Eshkol, he accepts the Prime Minister's higher authority in all policy. He has been the supreme advocate for Israel abroad and he has executed basic decisions. But with few exceptions (like the 'Middle East Tashkent' proposal soon after he assumed office) he did not initiate Strategic-level decisions. This had the advantage of harmony—the result of acquiescence—but the disadvantage of inadequate dialogue and dissent. Yet Eshkol greatly respected his knowledge, his vast experience in diplomacy, and his qualities: Eban filled a genuine void and thereby exerted influence, for Eshkol never felt at ease in this sphere.

One vital difference between Eban and Meir as Foreign Minister has been stressed. Mrs. Meir as a political leader in her own right could go

[1] Interview with Yahil, Jerusalem, July 1966.

[2] Most of these issues will be examined in a related volume on Israeli high-policy decisions.

her own way in a Cabinet discussion and attract colleagues to her views. Eban's influence-potential at that level of decision-making was more limited: he was more dependent on the Prime Minister. (This became more apparent after Mrs. Meir became Prime Minister in March 1969.) And, as was expected, he restored the intellectual tone of the Sharett era in discussion and debate, and the search for new paths in diplomacy.[1]

Some of Eban's attitudes to decision-making emerged in a 1970 interview:[2]

Q. You are faced, very often, with the need to make decisions. Do you have your own technique of decision-making?

A. We have a tradition of intuitive decisions, and many decisions concerning security matters are reached by the image of reality to which we wish to respond, I prefer using intuition combined with an attempt to analyse. Usually, the decisions which perhaps could be reflected upon later were those which were taken without an effort at analysis. What is analysis? In fact it is a notebook in which the positive and negative results of each side are listed. Generally it must obligate not only the Minister but his advisers as well. . . .

In my opinion, the diplomatic arm must be given an opportunity to present the government with a balanced picture. That is, if we do this, we should know the possibilities are such and such and the world political reaction will be so and so; this may or may not be influential in another area that perhaps the cabinet or the deciding committee would not even know about. It can be said that this suggestion is excellent from all points of view, but you should know that the day after tomorrow we are expecting . . . a decision to be taken on a major political matter or on a matter concerning arms . . . therefore it is preferable, in my opinion, to give some time between the discussion and the decision. I think there is much wisdom in the saying, 'to sleep on it', if circumstances permit.

Q. You talked about intuition and analysis. Would you not recommend—to yourself, the Prime Minister, the Government and all government bodies—to make use of the scientific side of decision-making?

A. Yes. This is what I meant when I said that one should engage in an exercise which includes all the given points and all possible results. We sometimes botched these steps. At times, perhaps, we were caught by surprise. Sometimes there were reactions which were not anticipated, and if there were a little more time they could have been taken into account. Whether one calls this an exercise or a war game, it is [nonetheless] a certain process in which people sit down and say: if this decision is taken, these are the likely consequences. The government could say that, in spite of the results of this exercise she will decide as she wishes. What is not to be permitted, in my opinion, is to decide without what is called in diplomacy 'consequences of an act'—a detailed knowledge of all the political outcomes.

Q. We do not use this method yet?

A. Not always.

[1] The decision-making process within the Israe lForeign Office will be examined at greater length in ch. 20 below.

[2] Interview with Eli Eyal on the *Galei Tzahal* (Army) radio station. Reprinted in *Bamahane* (Tel Aviv), 3 Feb. 1970.

(c) DEFENCE MINISTRY AND FOREIGN MINISTRY

The relationship between Prime Minister–Defence Minister and Foreign Minister in the formulation of Israeli high policy was defined as a changing equilibrium among four pairs of *individuals*:

from competition, friction and contrasting orientations (Ben Gurion–Sharett);
to acknowledged primacy of the Head of Government, harmony, and shared views of the world (Ben Gurion–Meir);
to greater influence of the Foreign Minister, along with more genuine harmony and common outlook (Eshkol–Meir);
to restoration of the influence gap between Prime Minister and Foreign Minister, modified by greater dependence on the acknowledged expertise of the latter (Eshkol–Eban).

That relationship had a deeper *institutional* base, namely, between the Defence Ministry and the Foreign Office. One reason was that, with two brief exceptions (1954–5 and 1967–8), the Prime Minister held the Defence portfolio as well—for eighteen of Israel's first twenty years. More fundamentally, the pervasive character of the Security problem since independence has compelled the meshing of the Defence and Foreign ministries in the policy process. Indeed, given its wide-ranging activities and responsibilities, the Defence Ministry has maintained a close relationship with all major branches of the bureaucracy:

with Foreign Affairs over all matters relating to Arab hostility and the impact of the conflict abroad;
with Finance, because of the very large share of the Budget allocated to Defence;
with Commerce and Industry regarding military imports, purchases and sales;
with Labour about the optimum use of manpower;
with Education concerning instructional programmes in *Tzahal* and *Gadna*; and
with Agriculture over the *Nahal* programme.

Thus, while Ben Gurion and others did not regard as imperative or inevitable the holding of the Defence portfolio by the Prime Minister, the Defence Ministry has always been the pivotal bureaucratic structure. And the Prime Minister is best equipped by his status and authority to co-ordinate the various liaison relationships spilling over from the needs of defence in a state under permanent siege.

While the intensity has varied over time, friction and rivalry between the two ministries has been permanent: everyone affirmed this reality about the key bureaucratic relationship in the policy process—during interviews in 1960, 1965–6, 1968, and 1969–70. Stated bluntly, the view of the Defence Establishment has been: 'They talk and we do things.' Among the Foreign Office professionals the attitude has been: 'They act as if nobody else exists—in the world or within Israel.'

i. Ben Gurion–Sharett–Lavon

The clash was not without traces of bitterness during the Ben Gurion–Sharett period, especially from 1953 to 1956. Three interrelated factors lay at its source: *individual, policy,* and *institutional.* Stated most generally, personality conflicts were enmeshed with different approaches to policy and with the struggle over who was to make decisions. From the earliest days *Tzahal* leaders, notably Dayan, had inculcated contempt for the Foreign Office in the Officer Corps: 'the cocktail-shmocktail boys' has always been thè symbol of that derision. And the attitude of Ben Gurion as Defence Minister was aptly paraphrased by aides and critics alike: 'We are not paying our diplomats to eat steaks and attend cocktail parties; it is their job to explain our actions. We do not act to save them embarrassment.' Underlying this view was Ben Gurion's conviction that all Israeli actions could be explained (away), provided they were successful.

Army and Defence officials persistently ridiculed Foreign Office methods and its alleged soft line and concern for 'the *Goyim*': in their preoccupation with foreign reaction, was the charge, they did not contribute to Israel's crucial foreign policy objective—security. The classic example of the contrast in role performance, and one often cited, was France in the mid-1950s: 'Israel's ambassador to Paris did not get a single revolver for Israel—all he did was to go to cocktail parties; but Peres and his men were able to deliver the goods.' To the Army the Foreign Office was saturated with 'Sharettism', the policy of caution and exaggerated concern with 'the external factor'. And it has always been a cardinal thesis of the Defence Establishment that, as long as Israel is in a state of siege the Defence Ministry must have primary responsibility for policy in the entire Security field—and that includes much of foreign policy. Foreign Office aides of Sharett were unanimous in declaring that he accepted this primacy in *general* but sought more effective co-ordination, a 'dovetailing of military and foreign policy'; to this the Army, the Defence Ministry, and BG were indifferent.

A major expression of that conflict in the early years was over decision-making control on Armistice Affairs. Ben Gurion perceived this solely as an extension of Israel's struggle for security against the persistent Arab assault. Sharett insisted that the Mixed Armistice Commissions with Egypt, Jordan, and Syria were Israel's only legitimate and regular avenue of contact with her neighbours, the most important aspect of her *foreign* affairs; and further, that the MAC and UNTSO were the institutional presence of the UN in the Arab–Israel conflict, once more, in the realm of foreign affairs. During the first five years decisions relating to Armistice violations were taken by the Defence Ministry with Foreign Office liaison. In 1954, as Prime Minister–Foreign Minister, Sharett succeeded in regaining formal control of this sphere: BG and the Army were agreeable because of the choice of a 'realist', Tekoah, one of the few professional diplomats whom they respected, to direct Armistice Affairs in the Foreign Ministry.

During the critical period of escalating Arab–Israeli tension preceding the Sinai Campaign—mid-1955 to October 1956—Ben Gurion engaged in a secret correspondence with UN Secretary-General Hammarskjöld. Information on Armistice Affairs came from Tekoah, and instructions to the Israeli UN Delegation from the Foreign Office Director-General, the Foreign Minister, or the Prime Minister, depending upon its urgency and significance as perceived by Ben Gurion. Then and later, decisions of major importance—retaliatory raids—were taken by the Defence Minister (sometimes in consultation with the Foreign Minister) and/or the Ministerial Committee on Defence and/or the Cabinet.

The decision process before the Sinai Campaign (1956) was described by one Director of Armistice Affairs, R. Kidron, as continuous consultation among five or six people—the Prime Minister, who was at the same time Minister of Defence, the Foreign Minister, the Chief of Staff, the Director-General of the Foreign Ministry, the Head of the Staff Duties Branch of the General Staff (who acted for the Chief of Staff in the latter's absence), and the Director of Armistice Affairs. The function of the General Staff Officer for Armistice Affairs was to provide the Director of Armistice Affairs with a constant flow of information, to transmit instructions and guidance to the Israeli Delegations to the Mixed Armistice Commissions, and to maintain contact with the United Nations Truce Supervision Organization on the technical-military, i.e. non-political, level. (Political liaison with UNTSO was the function of the Director of Armistice Affairs.) To facilitate liaison his office was located in the Armistice Affairs Department of the Ministry for Foreign Affairs.

Not all the above persons were concerned in every case. While a serous incident would inevitably involve Ministers directly, decisions were more frequently taken at the official level, the Ministers being informed through their Private Secretaries.

A typical case would begin with the receipt of reports of an incident at GHQ. In the context of the General Armistice Agreements these reports ran along two parallel channels: firstly, from the front line unit involved through the operations reporting system to the Head of the Staff Duties Branch and the Chief of Staff; secondly, from the Israel Delegation to the Mixed Armistice Commission concerned to the GSO, Armistice. The Chief of Staff would then report to the Prime Minister and Minister of Defence. The GSO, Armistice would inform the Director of Armistice Affairs in the Ministry for Foreign Affairs, who would in turn inform the Director-General of the Ministry for Foreign Affairs and the Minister for Foreign Affairs. At the same time the COS (or the Chief of Staff Duties Branch at GHQ) would get in direct contact with the Director of Armistice Affairs, or vice versa. The whole process of reporting and consultation was conducted by telephone and, in general, only a few minutes elapsed between the start of an incident and the decision how to react to it on the General Armistice Agreement level.

The basis of the system was speed and flexibility of communication, both up and down and laterally, the mutual trust and confidence of the persons involved at all levels, and a practical routine of co-operation. 'Things worked in a pragmatic way.'

FIGURE 9

DECISION-MAKING ON ARMISTICE VIOLATIONS

Prime Minister-
Defence Minister

Director,
Armistice Affairs

Foreign Minister
Director-General, FO

Chief of Staff
Head, Staff Duties Branch,
General Staff

Within the Foreign Office the Director of Armistice Affairs was responsible to the Director-General. From the outset he would report an incident to the Director-General or, in his absence, to the Foreign Minister. He would also contact the Defence Minister immediately through his Political or Military Secretary, and the *Ramatkal*—Chief of Staff—through his Military Assistant, a middle-ranking *Tzahal* officer who, since 1958, was the representative of the General Staff in the Foreign Office. The lines of communication were flexible, though these four components were almost always involved in the decision process.[1]

Sharef observed that institutional friction began with the coming of Lavon to the Defence Ministry (1954), for he tried to build it as a rival power base.[2] Evidence of the inter-personal tension has already been

[1] Based upon interview with M. R. Kidron in Jerusalem, June 1966 and correspondence, June 1970.
[2] Interview in Jerusalem, March 1966.

cited—the differing accounts of decision-making over the Kibya raid. Indeed Lavon's presence as Defence Minister exacerbated the tensions between Ben Gurion and Sharett. Further revelations point up the *institutional* dimension of the conflict.[1]

Ben Gurion wrote later that even Sharett, who 'was particularly sensitive to what the UN would say', had conceded that there are times when there is no alternative to using 'the two-edged sword' of retaliation raids; further, that Sharett had known of plans for the Kibya action but had 'seen no reason to object'. Sharett, who was Acting Prime Minister at the time, while BG was on leave in Sde Boker, wrote in his diary:

. . . today the Mixed Armistice Commission roundly condemned the killing [of a woman and two children in Yahud]. Even the Jordanian delegates voted in favour of the resolution. They took upon themselves to prevent such atrocities in the future. Under such circumstances, is it wise to retaliate?

I came to the conclusion that we are again confronted with a situation like that other time when I had a raid called off and in so doing broke off the vicious circle of bloody revenge for a fortnight or more. The Jordanians are shocked and certainly will do something. If we retaliate, we only make the marauder bands' job easier and give the authorities an excuse to do nothing. I called Lavon and told him what I thought. He said he would consult BG.

In the afternoon the UNTSO Chief of Staff sent a note to Lavon saying the Jordan Legion Commander offered to co-operate in finding the murderers. The *Tzahal* officer asked whether there was a change of plans. Lavon answered, 'No change'. Sharett then called Lavon into a private meeting and *tried to persuade him* to call off the raid (Sharett was then Acting Prime Minister, as well as Foreign Minister); Lavon informed him that BG had not accepted his objections. And power still lay with Ben Gurion, complicated by the presence of an Acting Defence Minister.

They disagreed about future decision-making as well. After Kibya, Sharett proposed, at first to Ben Gurion and then to *Sareinu*, that the Ministerial Committee on Foreign Affairs and Defence take responsibility for decisions on retaliation raids. BG opposed, arguing that this would ensure that no raids would take place. A compromise was reached: the Defence Minister and the Foreign Minister would make the decisions together; if the latter had any reservations, the Cabinet as a whole would deal with the matter. An Israeli student of civil-military relations wrote in this connection:[2] 'When Lavon succeeded Ben Gurion as Defence Minister and attempted to control strategic policy-making and also dominate tactical policy, wresting this power from Zahal's high command to himself, he upset the unofficial balance Ben Gurion had

---

[1] As reprinted in *Jerusalem Post*, 31 Oct. 1965.
[2] Perlmutter, op. cit., pp. 81–2. The general effect of the Lavon Affair on civil-military relations in Israel is explored ibid., ch. VII.

established in the Ministry on security matters, and thus Lavon stirred up a nest of hornets in the process'—in the relations between Defence Ministry and Foreign Office, it may be added.

ii. *Meir–Peres*

Friction between the two ministries in the Ben Gurion–Sharett era was essentially a spill-over from the competition between the two leaders and their policy differences. These two sources vanished with the resignation of Sharett. But the disquieting Lavon Affair did not. And other factors emerged in the next phase, with Meir and Peres as the *dramatis personae*. The conflict from 1957 to 1963 existed on four levels, intertwined and mutually aggravating.

There was, first, a deep clash of *personality*—between the sentimental, intuitive, and extroverted Mrs. Meir and the rational, intellectual, and secretive Shimon Peres. Foreign Minister Meir was almost 60 when the friction came into the open; Peres was not yet 35. Yet that *generation gap*, which many regarded as an independent variable, was related to the struggle between the 'old guard' (the *vatikim* or veterans) and the young men (the *tze'irim*) for control of *Mapai*: Mrs. Meir and Peres were performing crucial roles in this contest, still unresolved in 1970. As Ben Gurion moved towards the end of an illustrious career, that battle for control became accentuated by rivalry for the *inheritance of BG*, the 'Father of the Nation'.

The 'old guard'—Meir, Aranne, Eshkol, etc.—was not only old. It remained (emotionally) committed to socialism. And as the winds of change swept over Israel, they clung to their ideological roots. The young men—Dayan, Peres, etc.—were not only younger. They were technocrats, admirers of science and technology, disdainful of ideologies. They were (and are) pragmatic activists. They are, indeed, more genuine Ben Gurionists: he too had contempt for doctrine and wanted Israel to move from the Age of Ideology to the Nuclear Age or, more correctly, the Age of Scientific Excellence. To all these factors was added a renewed and more intense conflict over the appropriate *jurisdiction* of the Defence and Foreign ministries in the policy process.

Reflecting on this *cause célèbre* of Israeli politics after leaving the Foreign Office—but before she became Prime Minister—Mrs. Meir remarked:[1]

I don't think it is a matter of classification [the question of division of function], because in every Foreign Office Security is the main concern. In Israel, even more than in other states, Security is the principal objective.
There is no friction between the Foreign Office and the Defence Ministry in AIM. Rather, the friction was over METHODS—Peres' methods. The friction was man-made, not made by institutions. For example, in the French arms question, 1955–56, Peres simply refused to communicate with our Ambassador.

[1] Interview in Tel Aviv, Aug. 1966

There was no question on my part of belittling the French orientation. The
Great Powers do not compete on who is more friendly with Israel. Friendship
with France was perfectly compatible with America's friendship.
It was Sharett who broke the ice with France. Peres built on that. But I do
not want to minimize Peres' role or his achievements.[1]

Writing towards the end of the Ben Gurion era, Mrs. Meir's biographer
referred to:

a group of younger Mapai members [in the Defence Ministry] such as Moshe
Dayan and Shimon Peres, who sometimes arrogated authority. Delicate negotiations, properly belonging to the foreign ministry, were on occasion initiated
by representatives of the defense ministry without previous consultation with
the foreign minister.
[However, after her reappointment as Foreign Minister in 1961, claimed
Syrkin,] there was no longer any question of divided authority. Mrs. Meir held
the conduct of foreign affairs firmly in her hands. . . . The silent, not always
explicit, internal struggle was over. The crass exponents of *Realpolitik* among
some of the up-and-coming younger men of Mapai had learned how much
firm will remained in the 'ineffectual romanticism' of the older generation. . . .[2]

The cause of the jurisdictional conflict, according to Mrs. Meir's
advocate, was that 'lines of authority long blurred by the strong light
of Ben Gurion's paramount influence had to be demarcated'.[3] Navon
perceived the institutional struggle as focused on France and Germany:
'The Defence Ministry had representatives in both countries, among
others. Ya'acov Tsur, Ambassador to France, bitterly resented and
continuously protested to Mrs. Meir against the role of Peres in France
—including a proposed meeting with de Gaulle. Mrs. Meir supported
her envoy and protested to Ben Gurion.' He also noted the *clash between
the generations*—'Mrs. Meir, among others, deeply resented the aggressive
rivalry of Peres and Dayan in *Mapai*'—and the *personal* rivalry: 'Mrs.
Meir felt that these matters fell within her jurisdiction; and Peres, who
entered the *Knesset* in 1959, began to write and speak on matters of
foreign policy, appearing as a rival to Mrs. Meir, the Foreign Minister.'
At the core, in Navon's opinion, was the competition for influence
within *Mapai*: this provided the setting in which the conflict occurred
between bureaucratic structures.[4]
A veteran *Mapai* leader, David Hacohen, viewing the conflict 'from
the sidelines', also perceived multiple causes:[5]

[1] Later, while Prime Minister, she relegated the friction to marginalia: 'A few wires
got crossed between the two departments at a lower level, it is true. But that was soon
taken care of. As to this word 'clash', there was no, 'clash'. There never was any
division in policy. . . .' Interview with Kenneth Harris, *Observer* (London), 17 Jan.
1971. Her revised view is unconvincing.
[2] Syrkin, op. cit., pp. 303–4.
[3] Ibid., p. 304.
[4] Interview in Jerusalem, Dec. 1965.   [5] Interview in Jerusalem, April 1966.

Most important was Peres' entry into external affairs as a wildcatter, doing things and seeing people without keeping the Foreign Ministry informed and stealing their thunder. This happened frequently, beginning in 1959, involving Germany, France and the United States.

Mrs. Meir, and some ambassadors and senior Foreign Ministry officials, were angered at Peres' behaviour, performing feats which they could not, being received in high places—Couve de Murville, even Kennedy—without going through channels, achieving things on arms and contacts which Foreign Office people had to wait months for. Most of all, Mrs. Meir felt he was intruding into her sphere as Foreign Minister. She complained bitterly to Ben Gurion, who was Peres' protector.

While the clashes of personality and of the generations were present, as well as rivalry within *Mapai*, the core of the dispute was *status*—Peres was a junior minister—and *institutional interests*.

Peres spoke with candour in the midst of the conflict (1960).[1] His point of departure was the character of twentieth-century global politics —the artificiality of frontiers, the international dimension of most political acts and, especially, the links between military and political relations. One conclusion was that 'the conduct of foreign policy cannot be left to the Foreign Office alone'. Both the Foreign and Defence ministries have a role to play in close co-operation: 'This is true not only for Israel but perhaps more so than for other countries because of her special security problem.' Moreover, 'the Defence Ministry's approach differs from the Foreign Office in its preoccupation with security— access to arms and the conditions of survival. Friction is frequent over tactics and the techniques of executing policy. There must be a balance of risks and advantages. That friction is often exaggerated by personal rivalries, sensitivity, etc. The final decision in these matters is left to Ben Gurion—after conferences between the two ministries.'

His general formula for the division of function was as follows: 'In all spheres there should be co-operation. In two of them—security matters (access to arms) and relations with Israel's neighbours—the Defence Ministry should have primary responsibility, with the Foreign Office executing policy, in part. In three areas—Europe, America, Afro-Asia —the reverse should exist.'

This formula was changed somewhat—and expanded—by Peres after leaving the Defence Ministry (1966).[2] The senior partner in the division of responsibility was designated as follows:

Latin America, Russia and East Europe, Asia, Africa—the Foreign Office

West Europe and North America—'it depends on the issues':
    Economic matters, including the Common Market—the Foreign Office

[1] Interview in Jerusalem, Aug. 1960.
[2] Interview in Tel Aviv, June 1966.

Arms—Defence Ministry

(Apropos, 'the greatest problem for Israel in the last eighteen years has been the problem of securing arms—and in this the Defence Ministry must have control'.)

America—'the issues in order of importance':

American Jewry—the Foreign Office

Attitude of America to the Arab world and

An American Security Guarantee for Israel—Defence Ministry and Foreign Office together

Economic Aid—the Foreign Office

Arms—Defence Ministry

Miscellaneous—the two ministries together.

Friction between the two ministries over the years was readily acknowledged by Peres. His analysis of the reasons was trenchant:

1. The institutions were not developed in accordance with given plans. Jurisdiction was not decided 'before the father died and the children grew up'. All accepted Ben Gurion as the central figure—but were jealous of each other. The personality of Ben Gurion—it overshadowed all the others; they grew but they were overshadowed.
2. The lack of equilibrium between the two institutions in the national mind. The Army has the love and affection of the nation in much greater proportion—the army uniform has a much higher status than the ambassador's suit. The Army's status is somewhat reduced [1966] but it is still the most beloved institution.
3. Clash of personality.
4. Lack of national tradition in thinking on foreign affairs. Most parties have an ideological approach to foreign policy questions; the leaders are more interested in the internal aspects of party politics. Very few thought beyond that.
5. A natural institutional friction.
6. The Army contempt for the Foreign Office verbal approach to national problems.
7. Sharett was a Weizmannist.
8. The Foreign Office is the institution which represents national prudence; the Defence Ministry is the institution that represents national achievements. In Israel our achievements were so outstanding that it became the preferred guide to policy.

[Finally,] it is natural and essential for friction and disagreement to arise. The legitimate exercise of pressure by the two is necessary in policy-making. Why suppress disagreement? Accept it and reconcile it as much as possible. This is much healthier.

Of his specific clash with Mrs. Meir he perceived two causes: personal friction—'the difference between the generations, among others'; and her feeling that he had created a parallel Foreign Office. In his defence he remarked that all Defence ministries have their own networks and are deeply involved in foreign affairs, a natural extension from security affairs.

Senior Foreign Ministry officials agreed on the fact of friction but were less sanguine. One person termed consultation minimal—and friction maximal—during the Ben Gurion era. 'It was much worse when Sharett was Foreign Minister. The position improved under Mrs. Meir.' There was great friction abroad, too, especially between the Defence missions and embassies in Paris and London.[1] Many expressed this view. And, according to Gazit, while the Defence Establishment was involved in two general spheres of policy—Arab–Israel questions and sources of arms—it was guilty of 'illegitimate encroachment' in foreign affairs, especially in the 1950s, with its 'excessive' stress on deterrence and the need for arms.[2] Nevertheless, there were established institutional practices for consultation between the two ministries during the Ben Gurion era and beyond.

During Eshkol's tenure as Prime Minister–Defence Minister, the relationship with the Foreign Office in policy formulation was one of harmony, both with Meir and Eban as his Foreign Ministers. As Lourie remarked, 'decisions of importance were never taken without consultation—in contrast to Ben Gurion's habit of acting on his own'. Yahil, Yafeh and others concurred.[3]

The policy process became much more complex in the last eighteen months of Eshkol's prime ministership—with the return of Dayan to the centre of decision-making as Defence Minister. For the first time a tripartite *institutional* relationship existed—Prime Minister's Office, Foreign Ministry, and Defence Ministry. This was further complicated by the upsurge of Dayan's charismatic influence, the decline of Eshkol's prestige due to alleged weakness during the May–June 1967 crisis, and Foreign Minister Eban's lack of a political base in *Mapai* and in the country. The adverse effect on the formulation of foreign policy has already been alluded to and will be explored again in another context.[4] Suffice it to note the observations that

the . . . situation is to *some* extent reminiscent of 1954. The deep gulf between the Prime Minister and his Defence Minister has weakened the collective responsibility and the actions of both. . . . [And] as Defence Minister, Dayan

[1] Interview in Jerusalem, Oct. 1965.
[2] Interview in Jerusalem, March 1966.
[3] Ironically, too, that period 'was characterized by Zahal's most prosperous growth. David Ben Gurion and Moshe Dayan [Defence Minister from June 1967 onwards] were experts on military affairs and needs and while, on the whole, they satisfied the military, in several instances, they *overruled* the high command's requests for greater budgets. Levi Eshkol was no military expert and he depended on General Rabin (then Chief of Staff) for advice on Israel's military needs. . . . Eshkol, the Defence Minister, with full control over finances as well . . . failed to pull his weight against the aggrandizement of Zahal and complied with General Rabin's requests for expensive new weapons.' Perlmutter, op. cit., p. 106.
[4] In the analysis of the Six Day War decision, part of the related volume now in preparation on high-policy decisions since 1948.

perpetuates the patterns of civil-military relationships established by Ben Gurion over two decades ago. Like Ben Gurion, Dayan is at once an effective and domineering civilian administrator, and a superior military expert. Under him there has been a fusion and intimacy between civilian and military élites in the defence establishment. . . .[1]

And the clash between Defence Ministry and Foreign Office, symbolized by the personalities, images, and behaviour of Dayan and Eban, continued into 1970.

The extent of institutional competition or co-operation was not unrelated to the occupancy of ministerial posts. Tension was greatest in the 1954–6 period, at first within a complex triangular personal relationship—Sharett as PM and FM, Lavon as DM, and Ben Gurion as the ultimate wielder of decision-making power—and later with BG as Defence Minister and Sharett as Foreign Minister. Their two contrasting images of 'the Arabs', which extended to the Technical Élites of the Foreign Office and Defence Ministry, and their personality differences reached a point of irreconcilability under the impact of mounting Arab guerrilla attacks on Israel during the year before the Sinai Campaign. Harmony was at its peak in the 1965–7 period, with Eshkol as PM–DM and Meir as FM, followed by Eban. Ben Gurionist domination of the Defence Establishment passed with the departure of BG, Dayan, and Peres (1963–5). Yet there is no mechanical relationship of degree of harmony or tension between DM and FM (and their ministries) and the formulation process affecting Strategic-level decisions: for example, harmony in the autumn of 1956 led to decisive formulation (the Sinai Campaign); harmony between Prime Minister–Defence Minister and Foreign Minister in May 1967 did not. Other variables in the formulation process were no less important in determining the outcome.

[1] Perlmutter, op. cit., pp. 113–14.

CHAPTER 16

Formulation of High-Policy Decisions: II

(a) CABINET AND ITS DEFENCE COMMITTEE

Cabinet involvement in the foreign policy process was continuous and often intense. Thus Ben Gurion recalled: 'Foreign affairs were discussed almost every week in the Cabinet. It was the first and main topic: there was a report by the Foreign Minister followed by discussion. I cannot remember a single meeting at which foreign affairs were not discussed.'[1] The three Foreign Ministers and other Cabinet members concurred.[2] This practice had been institutionalized in the Jewish Agency Executive before independence.[3] It also derived from the authority vested in the Government to make foreign policy, as provided in the 1948 Law and Administration Ordinance and the Transition Law of 1949.[4] Moreover, every minister has had the right from the outset to request the Government Secretary to place a foreign policy issue on the agenda of a Cabinet meeting. It may also come before the Cabinet if the Prime Minister or the Foreign Minister considers Government approval of a proposed course of action necessary or desirable.

Cabinet emphasis on foreign policy was a logical consequence of permanent conflict. It was strengthened by the coalition character of Israeli Governments and the competing programmes of some coalition members.[5] This, in turn, gave rise to restraints and practices which enhanced the Cabinet as an organ of decision. First was a Government ruling in 1949 which prohibited individual acts by ministers in foreign affairs without prior Cabinet approval. This was designed to minimize the danger of divergent policies being pursued simultaneously—most dramatically displayed in the post-1967 advocacy of objectives and tactics by Allon, Dayan, Eban, Sapir, Begin *et al.* (Another reason for this intended restraint was that, as elsewhere, in fact more so, Israeli ministers regard themselves as foreign policy experts.)

A more important result of coalition government has been the practice of Cabinet voting. 'There is no other way to run a coalition', remarked a veteran civil servant.[6] Not all agreed. Ze'ev Sharef, Government Secretary throughout the Ben Gurion–Sharett phase, declared:

[1] Interview in Sde Boker, July 1966.
[2] Interviews in 1960 (Sharett) and in 1965–6, 1968, and 1969–70 (all others).
[3] Interview with Sharef, Jerusalem, March 1966.
[4] See pp. 126–7 above.
[5] As discussed in ch. 6 (a), in Appendix A and B, and in ch. 8 above.
[6] Interview in Jerusalem, July 1960.

'When they disagreed, each would place his own viewpoint before the Cabinet, and a vote would be taken. I disagreed vehemently with the procedure of voting in Cabinet and told both the Prime Minister and Foreign Minister.'[1] According to Cabinet rules, a vote must be taken if requested by any member—and it was often taken on controversial topics. The votes are registered in Government minutes. All ministers are bound by the majority decision: the principle of collective responsibility has been inscribed in all coalition agreements accompanying the formation of governments since the beginning of the State.[2] It was also explicitly mentioned in the draft *Basic Law on the Government* (1968): 'The Government is responsible to the Knesset on the basis of the principle of collective responsibility' (Article 4).[3]

While authority to make Strategic-level decisions in foreign policy has always rested with the Government, influence was not evenly distributed among its members, as noted.[4] The role of Cabinet, as distinct from individuals or groups within it, varied over time. In part, it depended on the presence or absence of a ministerial Committee dealing with foreign affairs and/or defence. These stages of Cabinet and Committee involvement in the decision process may be delineated as follows.

i. *Changing Roles*

1948–end of 1953: The Prime Minister–Defence Minister and the Foreign Minister constituted a duumvirate, as noted; that is, when they agreed, Cabinet approval was assured. Basic disagreements were rare during that period and were contained within the framework of their pre-Cabinet and inter-Cabinet-meeting discussions, oral and written. There was no Ministerial Committee at the time. And the Cabinet had virtually no influence on foreign or defence policy decisions. The consensus about this period was aptly summed up by Ben Gurion's Political Secretary for more than a decade: 'The Cabinet had the feeling that foreign policy was in good hands. They discussed these matters certainly, but when the Prime Minister and Foreign Minister agreed, they could get anything through the Cabinet.'[5] One further observation about Ben Gurion's behaviour during Cabinet discussions was that 'for many, many meetings he was just a neutral chairman; only when it was a matter close to his heart did he participate'.[6]

1954–mid-1956: The Cabinet emerged as an important decision-

---

[1] Interview in Jerusalem, March 1966.
[2] Interview with the then Secretary to the Government, Mrs. Y. Uzay, Jerusalem, April 1966.
[3] *Sefer Ha-Hukkim*, Jerusalem, 540, 21 Aug. 1968, p. 226.
[4] See pp. 211–21 above.
[5] Interview with Navon, Jerusalem, Dec. 1965.
[6] Interview with Sharef, Jerusalem, March 1966.

making organ in both foreign and defence policy, for various reasons. Throughout 1954 Ben Gurion was in 'retirement', and Sharett, then Prime Minister and Foreign Minister, brought all foreign policy issues of substance before the Cabinet. While security matters were under Lavon as Defence Minister, and Ben Gurion's influence was felt through Dayan as Chief of Staff and Peres as Director-General of Defence, Sharett was able, through Cabinet support, to withstand the pressure for retaliation; in the process, the Cabinet acquired influence over Strategic-level decisions.

Nor did this wane with the return of Ben Gurion in February 1955. By that time the basic clash between BG and Sharett over retaliation had come into the open; and Sharett appealed to the Cabinet over the head of the Prime Minister. Both men acknowledged this, as did other ministers; and sometimes the Prime Minister was overruled—by a narrow 7–6 majority, comprising two or three *Mapai* ministers and those from the NRP, then known as the *Mizrahi* and *Ha-po'el Ha-mizrahi*, and the Progressives or Independent Liberals. One such occasion was the BG–Dayan-sponsored proposal in October–December 1955 to occupy Sharm-e-Sheikh.[1] Another had been a Ben Gurion proposal during the 1948 War to take over an area near Hebron, when the Prime Minister declared in despair, 'generations will weep for the consequences of our mistake'.[2] A Cabinet colleague at the time recalled that incident many years later and added: 'It was clear to me that Ben Gurion was very doubtful of this operation—because he came to the Cabinet for approval.' Further, on the working of Cabinet, 'Ben Gurion was excellent in this. In all important questions he asked you to vote.'[3] Thus the Cabinet played a crucial role in decision-making, even though Sharett recalled later that he did not divulge everything about foreign policy' to his ministerial colleagues.[4]

The Ministerial Committee on Foreign Affairs and Defence existed during that second phase but it was utterly without influence, according to Eshkol, Meir, and Ben Gurion himself. 'I don't remember when it started to function', BG told this writer. 'I don't remember even sitting on this Committee [he didn't, except briefly in 1955]. For a long time it didn't exist. It was not important, because foreign affairs were discussed in the Cabinet.'[5] This was also true for security decisions by and large, because BG was always concerned lest *Tzahal* become a victim of political pressures—and 'the sons of all are in the army'. Navon exaggerated when he said 'there was not a single case concerning security which Ben Gurion did not bring to the Cabinet' and, further, that

---

[1] Dayan, *Diary of the Sinai Campaign*, pp. 12–15.
[2] Interview with Navon, Tel Aviv, May 1966.
[3] Interview with Pinhas Rosen, Jerusalem, Feb. 1971.
[4] Interview in Jerusalem, July 1960.
[5] Interview in Sde Boker, July 1966.

BG 'was scrupulous in letting the Cabinet decide'.[1] It was also an exaggeration to assert that the decision process in security matters was 'largely a one-man show; he behaved democratically, but his charisma and leadership generally carried the day'.[2] Closer to the truth is that security issues went to the *full* Cabinet, in so far as they were taken to the Government at all.

mid-1956–end of 1961: With the departure of Sharett in June 1956, Ben Gurion's dominance over security and foreign policy was unchallenged—as the decision to embark on the Sinai Campaign revealed.[3] And the Ministerial Committee on Foreign Affairs and Defence remained a nonentity. Yet Ben Gurion's prerogatives were severely tested in the two Cabinet crises over arms and Germany in 1957–8 and 1959 —to be explored shortly. The place of Cabinet in the decision process during that phase and even earlier was well portrayed by the Director-General of the Prime Minister's Office at the time, Teddy Kollek.[4] Cabinet meetings begin with a report on foreign affairs by the Foreign Minister; in her [Mrs. Meir's] absence, the Director-General of the Foreign Office or the Prime Minister reports. Thus major issues are placed before the Cabinet—at the regular weekly meeting on Sunday morning—'where a principle is involved, in the view of the Prime Minister and/or Foreign Minister; where no principle is at stake, according to them, they settle it between themselves'. An example of the former was the German arms deals; of the latter, the sale of two frigates to Ceylon: the Ceylonese were unwilling to take possession in Eilat— because of Arab pressure; thus the Foreign and Defence Ministers co-ordinated the transfer and informed the Cabinet of the transaction after the ships had sailed but before they had passed the Tiran Strait.

At the same time, 'the coalition character of the Government inhibits complete reports and full discussion'—for two reasons: 'because of concern that there might be leaks [as there was during one of the crises over German arms] and because a large part of Israeli foreign policy comes under the category "secret" and therefore does not go to the Cabinet, matters like contacts with the Arabs and relations with the "Periphery" states'. Yet 'the Prime Minister was certainly not given *carte blanche* to decide foreign policy before 1956 and, even since then, does not have full freedom of action.'

An almost identical assessment was provided by Navon.[5] And a Government Secretary noted that residual authority over matters to be placed before the Cabinet lay with the Prime Minister–Defence Minister; that is, the decision to seek—or to dispense with—Cabinet ap-

[1] Interview in Jerusalem, Dec. 1965.
[2] Interview with Ya'acov Herzog, Jerusalem, April 1966.
[3] This will be explored in a related volume on Israeli high-policy decisions.
[4] Interview in Jerusalem, July 1960.
[5] Interview in Jerusalem, July 1960.

proval on a security issue was at his discretion except for matters which are formally specified in law as falling within the jurisdiction of 'the Government'.[1] Indeed, the Defence Minister need not consult—let alone secure the approval of—his cabinet colleagues for such a major decision as mobilization of the reserves, though he must notify the *Knesset* Committee on Foreign Affairs and Security of this act within ten days; and that Committee may confirm or modify the order, withhold confirmation, or refer it to the plenary *Knesset*—but this is *legal authority* only.

1962–mid-1963: The arms deals with Germany caused great turmoil within the coalition Cabinets and led to the resignation of the seventh and eighth Governments, in December 1957 and July 1959, respectively: the controversy centred on control over security decisions; and Ben Gurion was accused of authoritarianism in this sphere. This dispute reached its zenith in 1961, when the Lavon Affair broke through the surface of Israeli politics. Ben Gurion resigned on 31 January, and the Cabinet crisis was not resolved until the formation of the tenth Government on 2 November. During the prolonged negotiations the lesser parties—*Ahdut Ha'avodah*, the Progressives, and *Mapam*—tried to wrest concessions from *Mapai*, notably the yielding of its monopoly over the 'big three' portfolios, Defence, Finance, and Foreign Affairs, and the introduction of institutional controls over military-security policy. Specifically, they urged that the Defence Ministry be accountable to a Cabinet Committee on Defence with full policy-making authority and, in the *Knesset*, to the existing Committee on Foreign Affairs and Security; and the latter was to be given broad investigative powers, including the right to subpoena any officer or official of the Defence Establishment, without seeking the Ministry's approval. Some, including Allon, also advocated the creation of a US-type National Security Council.

The outcome was a more modest innovation, the creation of a Ministerial Committee on Defence—as the price of *Ahdut Ha'avodah*'s return to the coalition: it came into existence on 2 November 1961 and consisted of Eshkol (Finance), Meir (Foreign Affairs), Dayan (Agriculture), Allon (Labour), and Shapira (Interior), under the chairmanship of Ben Gurion, Prime Minister and Defence Minister. The *Mapai* majority was overwhelming—four, with one each from *Ahdut Ha'avodah* and the NRP. Yet its powers were restricted to advice, because of BG's firm opposition to interference in the critical area of military-security matters and to the curtailment of the Cabinet's decision-making authority. Thus the Committee was granted the right to *request* information and, at its initiative or that of the Cabinet or the Prime Minister, to *discuss* all aspects of military affairs, from military planning and operations to arms purchases and weapons development. Its power to *investigate* was

[1] Interview with Mrs. Uzay, Jerusalem, April 1966.

limited to officers and Defence Ministry officials whom the Minister of Defence authorized to appear. And it was not given any policy-making authority. In short, Ben Gurion's paramountcy was barely dented, and the role of Cabinet slightly enhanced by its new—subordinate—pressure group.

mid-1963–1968: During Ben Gurion's last eighteen months in office the new Ministerial Committee on Defence was not encouraged—or even permitted—to become a major influence on decision-making, although its members were given full access to information in the security field and expressed views on a wide range of issues. The change came with Eshkol's succession in June 1963 and, especially, in January 1966, when the membership was increased from six to ten. As noted earlier, Eshkol himself termed it 'a miniature Cabinet' whose decisions, in effect, were final, 'like a War Cabinet'.[1] And Mrs. Meir referred to it as 'a powerful small Cabinet responsible for decisions on security'.[2] So it continued until the crisis of May–June 1967, when the Cabinet as a whole re-emerged as the principal decision-making organ on Strategic- and Tactical-level issues of foreign and security policy. Even before then, however, as Mrs. Meir remarked while still Foreign Minister, 'on basic issues the Cabinet makes decisions, for example, the votes on *apartheid*. And before every General Assembly there are at least two or three issues which the Cabinet has to decide.'[3]

These were *foreign policy* decisions. Indeed, one of the curious results of the enhancement of the Ministerial Committee on Defence under Eshkol was that, from mid-1963 to mid-1967 foreign policy issues received two hearings at the summit of Government, one in the Ministerial Committee and one in the Cabinet, while security matters were discussed once, in the Committee. With the further expansion of the Committee to 15 in May 1967, however, it became almost indistinguishable from the Cabinet of 22. And with a weaker Head of Government as a result of that crisis, along with a strong, competing Defence Minister, the Cabinet's decision-making power finally coincided with its authority. It continued in this role during the political struggle after the Six Day War.

Not all ministers were active in Cabinet discussions on foreign and security policy. Ben Gurion noted Barzilai and Bentov, the *Mapam* members; Carmel and Bar Yehuda from *Ahdut Ha'avodah*, 'Allon less so—he is ideologically more in tune with *Mapai*'; Shapira from the NRP; Rosen from the Progressives; and from *Mapai*, 'very few', Sharett, Dov Joseph, Meir, 'though not very much before she became Foreign Minister', and in later Cabinets, Eban.[4] Mrs. Meir singled out 'the *Mapam* people', 'the *Ahdut Ha'avodah* people', Aranne and Joseph from *Mapai*, 'and of course, Eban'.[1] And Eshkol referred to Meir, Eban, Galili, and Shapira.

The Cabinet is the final arbiter in Strategic-level decisions; that is, rivalries which are either personal or institutional, or both, are resolved at the Cabinet level. Indeed, Eshkol recalled: 'Sometimes discussion on foreign affairs goes on so long that other topics before the Cabinet do not get as much attention as necessary.'[2] On two such occasions disagreement rent the Government asunder. To these examples of decision-making we may now turn.[3]

(*b*) ARMS AND GERMANY: 1957-8 CRISIS

The first of Israel's Cabinet crises over foreign policy erupted in mid-December 1957: it lasted twenty-two days.[4] On the 16th the Government approved the dispatch of a high-level arms purchasing mission to Bonn, by a vote of 7 to 6, with two abstentions. *Ahdut Ha'avodah* ministers, the most vociferous among the opponents, called for a special Cabinet meeting to reconsider the decision and threatened to resign if it were implemented. The following morning that party's newspaper, *Lamerhav*, published details of the Cabinet debate and specified the breakdown of the vote: 7 (all *Mapai*) in favour, against 2 *Ahdut Ha'avodah*, 2 *Mapam*, 1 Progressive, and 1 *Ha-po'el Ha-mizrahi*. That evening, at a hastily-summoned session of the *Knesset* Committee on Foreign Affairs and Security, Ben Gurion cancelled the mission. It was a rare example of a newspaper causing a volte-face in Israel Government policy.

Further details were divulged rapidly. The Prime Minister told the *Knesset*, in reply to a question, that a party leader had been sent to West Germany in the first instance because of the absence of normal diplomatic relations (there was an Israel Reparations Mission in Cologne at the time); further, that Giora Josephthal, then Secretary-General of *Mapai*, had been selected because of his acquaintance with Adenauer —dating from the negotiations over German reparations in 1952. (Although their names were not divulged, he was to be followed by Dayan and Peres, then in Burma for celebrations on her tenth anniversary of independence.) The same day *Mapam* revealed that one of its ministers, Barzilai, had sought an extraordinary Cabinet meeting the day before and had been refused by one vote. The two smaller left-wing parties in the coalition were also reported to have made the cancellation

[1] Interview in Tel Aviv, Aug. 1966.   [2] Interview in Jerusalem, July 1966.

[3] They illuminate all three levels of the rivalry–co-operation nexus—inter-personal, inter-bureaucratic, and inter-party—which manifest themselves in the Cabinet, its Ministerial Committee on Defence, and on rare, dramatic occasions on the floor of the *Knesset* as well.

[4] This analysis is based upon the detailed daily reports in the Israeli press from 16 December 1957 to 8 January 1958, notably in *Ha'aretz*, *Jerusalem Post*, and *Ma'ariv*. For the background to Israeli-German arms links see Peres, *David's Sling*, pp. 66–74.

of the mission a condition of agreeing a new economic policy line with *Mapai*. There were no other publicly-known acts for a week. In the interval the Israeli press levelled charges and pronounced judgement.[1]

[1] The issue was first discussed on 18 December 1957 and ended on 8 January 1958. The crisis lasted 22 days, of which 19 were days on which newspapers appeared.

NAME	NO. OF EDITORIALS
Ha'aretz	9
Davar	7—least involvement (because pro-Government position)
Al Hamishmar	12
Lamerhav	15—extreme intensity
Ha-boker	11
Herut	9
Ha-tzofeh	9

The party newspapers revealed much about the images and objectives, as well as tactics, of the major participants.

Lamerhav defended its revelations and the actions of *Ahdut* ministers on a variety of grounds. It termed the cancellation of the mission 'an act of public responsibility', whatever the consequences (18 Dec.); it denounced as 'despicable' the 'contention that Ahdut Ha'avodah ministers committed a breach of faith and sabotaged the security of the State . . .' and termed the proposed mission 'not a security secret, but a political matter with grave consequences' (19th); *Ahdut* ministers knew their duties, it declared, but 'Ahdut Ha'avodah has no intention of waiving its elementary rights' (22nd); the intolerability of military relations with a pro-Western Germany was also cited— 'aggressive circles in various countries attach their hopes to Germany. What then has Israel to do with Germany?' (23rd); and the blame for the crisis was placed squarely on Ben Gurion (24th).

Al Hamishmar, speaking for *Mapam*, shared *Lamerhav*'s opposition to the mission but not the behaviour of *Ahdut Ha'avodah* ministers, and it stressed other factors, notably the value of non-alignment: it railed 'against the sterile pursuit of security guarantees from one of the rival power blocs in the world' and renewed its call 'for security guarantees from all the blocs' (18 December); it criticized the *Ahdut* ministers—they 'acted for tactical reasons out of narrow considerations' (19th) but termed *Mapai*'s 'political step . . . infinitely more serious'.

Davar, the *Histadrut* daily dominated by *Mapai*, focused exclusively on the issue of collective responsibility in its early editorials: 'A coalition Cabinet ceases to be a Cabinet as soon as one of its partners publishes details of the Cabinet's discussions for party political purposes. . .' (18 December); 'Therefore there is no room for forgiveness. Justice must take its course . . .' (22nd).

Herut assaulted Ben Gurion's 'dastardly' plan to establish military links with West Germany. Typical of its early editorials was the remark: 'In secrecy and stealth the leader of Mapai decided to send to Germany an official representative of the State. . . . This degradation of national honour . . .' (18 December); it also emphasized the split in labour ranks (19th), yet shared the *Ahdut* and *Mapai* view that this was a political issue, not a security matter (22nd).

The General Zionists' *Ha-boker* attacked the labour coalition and Government procedures but made no reference to the substance of the issue: 'It also appears that important political steps are taken without a decision by the Government' (19 December); further, 'A coalition party has disclosed a security secret. . . . These, then are the men to whom we entrust the security of our State' (20th).

Ha-tzofeh, the organ of *Ha-po'el Ha-mizrahi* and, later, of the National Religious Party, was the most moderate. It concentrated on the behaviour of *Ahdut* ministers and

The second phase of the crisis began on 24 December, when *Herut* MK Landau moved a Motion for the Agenda calling for a debate on 'Government Missions to Germany'.[1] Ben Gurion acknowledged that the purpose of the mission was to secure equipment 'vital for the security of the State, the security of immigration, and the security of our international trade'. He claimed that a new danger had arisen in the past year and that the only answer was equipment of the same type— 'a dimension which is not visible from land, sea or air'. And West Germany was now the only available source. He also reiterated his view favouring diplomatic relations and the need to deal with Germany, on grounds of realism: Germany was important in Europe, and Europe was vital to Israel. He would not hesitate to accept arms from any state and claimed that Israel's existence was in the balance: in that situation 'everything else becomes unimportant'. 'I stand before you unrepentant', he concluded. The Motion was defeated by 46 (*Mapai*, NRP and Progressives) to 14 (*Herut* and *Maki*), with 17 abstentions (*Ahdut Ha'avodah*, General Zionists, *Agudat Yisrael*, and *Po'alei Agudat Yisrael*). *Mapam* MKs conspicuously stayed off the floor of the *Knesset* until after the vote was taken. Thus the *Herut* motion split the coalition, whereas a similar *Maki* no-confidence motion a few days earlier had not.

Maki's Sneh moved to refer the issue to committee but was defeated 45 to 24: the party alignments were the same as on the Motion for the Agenda, except that the General Zionists supported the Sneh proposal, rather than abstaining. *Ahdut Ha'avodah* leader Galili, later a pillar in the Eshkol and Meir Cabinets, declared in an interview on the 25th that the issue for his party was whether or not there should be relations between *Tzahal* and the German Army: 'arms, yes, but relations, no' was its motto; the *Ahdut Ha'avodah* would oppose any 'orientation towards

---

called for the withdrawal of *Ahdut Ha'avodah* from the Government: 'It is inconceivable that political parties which make a mockery of the Government's resolutions . . . should continue to sit in the Cabinet' (18 December); and 'The Ministers of Ahdut Ha'avodah are notorious for their breaches of trust . . .' (19th).

Of the independents, the *Jerusalem Post* was very critical of the *Ahdut* ministers' action and termed it a delayed revenge for the disbandment of *Palmah* ten years earlier, and for their exclusion from military decisions (25 December).

Ha'aretz was the most sober in its assessment. It noted both emotional and political reasons for the opposition to Ben Gurion's plan and chided him for reawakening 'the German Complex'. At the same time, it criticized *Ahdut Ha'avodah*'s action, for it had long known of the Israel Government's efforts to seek guarantees and build closer relations with Nato countries: 'It has no right to remain in the coalition on the basis of the understanding to keep quiet as long as no Western partners were found and to sabotage the agreed policy as soon as there are good prospects for its implementation' (18 December); similar views were expressed on the 20th and 23rd.

[1] There are three possible responses to a Motion for the Agenda: it may be approved for discussion in the plenary *Knesset*; it may be passed to the relevant *Knesset* committee; or it may be deleted from the agenda.

Germany'. It was the kind of distinction common to Israel's sectarian politicians. The same day BG told the press that a different emissary had gone to Germany to complete the mission. He denied that any enslaving conditions had ever been laid down in Israel's arms purchases in the past. And he asserted that no one in the Cabinet had opposed the purpose of the mission.

All efforts to break the impasse failed. Ben Gurion rejected the dissident parties' claim to the right of their ministers to dissent from Cabinet decisions. And he proposed a Cabinet rule that a two-thirds majority could force the resignation of a minister, the essence of Eshkol's six-point compromise plan. Finally, after a week of further accusations and counter-charges, Ben Gurion resigned on the 31st: the issue, he wrote to the President, was violation of the cardinal principle of collective responsibility in the Government.

The coalition Government was revived on 6 January 1958 with the identical *Knesset* support: *Mapai* (40), NRP (11), *Ahdut Ha'avodah* (10), *Mapam* (9), and Progressives (5), a total of 75. It was approved on 17 January by 76 to 33. Yet, even after the 'new' Basic Principles for the eighth Government had been passed, Hazan for *Mapam* and Allon for *Ahdut Ha'avodah*, neither a minister, renewed before the *Knesset* their parties' opposition to relations with Germany.

Ha'aretz wrote that Israel's prestige and credibility had suffered from this Cabinet crisis (2 January); further, that press freedom was a victim of party conflict (7th); and finally, 'The new Government is no more united in regard to vital questions of foreign policy than its predecessor' (8th). This was dramatically confirmed during the second major Cabinet crisis over decision-making in foreign policy, eighteen months later. Indeed, the 1957–8 crisis was a relatively mild precursor of the struggle for control over decisions in the military-security sphere that shattered the successor coalition in July 1959. And that time it could not be revived without sharp animus.

(c) ARMS AND GERMANY: 1959 CRISIS

The second crisis over arms and Germany was shorter (14 days) but more intense than its predecessor.[1] Both were sparked by press reports. And the formal outcome was similar—Ben Gurion's resignation and the re-creation of the identical coalition in a 'new' Government. Yet the 1959 crisis revealed more dramatically how complex is the formulation of high policy; more specifically, the interplay of Cabinet, Ministry, Party and Personality in the cluster of decisions. Even less important

[1] The analysis of the 1959 crisis is based upon the extensive reports in the Israeli press from 25 June to 8 July, notably in *Ha'aretz*, *Jerusalem Post*, and *Ma'ariv*, along with texts of speeches made available by the Government Press Office, and interviews with some participants, including Ben Gurion.

variables were involved. All this was illuminated by the publication of secret documents during the crisis itself.

It began with a report on 24 June in *Der Spiegel* that the Federal German Republic had purchased mortar bombs worth £16 million from 'Soltam', a subsidiary of the *Histadrut*'s industrial empire, *Solel Boneh*. The next day Israel's Left- and Right-nationalists delivered scathing attacks on the arms deal. The results of *Der Spiegel*'s revelation and the assault by *Ahdut Ha'avodah* and *Herut* was another major political crisis.

The first stage was confused and confusing. The Leadership Bureau or Political Committee of almost all parties met during the three days 25–27 June (Thursday–Saturday) and stated an initial position. The *Ahdut* leaders unanimously reaffirmed the demand of their *guru*, Tabenkin, that the arms sale to West Germany be cancelled; and a party spokesman denied that there had been a Cabinet vote 'on this specific issue'; yet they favoured the coalition remaining intact. *Mapam*, too, expressed the hope that the coalition would continue. The progressives resolved 'to wait and see', while both *Herut* and the General Zionists criticized the decision, the former violently. Ben Gurion struck back and declared, in interviews with the *New York Times* and *Davar*, that *all* ministers knew about the contemplated transaction as early as December 1958—and *none* had opposed it. The relations between *Mapai* and *Ahdut Ha'-avodah* were now near breaking point—the latter being accused of using a security matter of supreme national importance for electioneering purposes: the Fourth *Knesset* Elections were due later in the year.

On Sunday, the 28th, the opposing positions were debated by Dayan and *Herut*'s Yohanan Bader over *Kol Yisrael*. The former Chief of Staff termed the arms sale 'significant for the future of the [Israel arms] industry'. Israel, he continued, could not afford to give up the slightest advantage. Furthermore, Germany would become strong with or without Israeli weapons—but would Israel? And finally, 'not all contacts with Germany are morally wrong; nor are all protests against such contacts morally right.' Bader invoked 'the voices of the Polish Jews who were slaughtered . . .'. That morning, too, the press devoted its editorials exclusively to the crisis.[1] Among the eight daily newspapers

[1] The second Cabinet crisis over Germany broke in the Press on 25 June 1959 and lasted to 8 July (14 days, with 12 press days).

NAME	NO. OF EDITORIALS	DATES	
		First	Last
Ha'aretz	7	26 June	7 July
Davar	5	26 June	8 July
Al Hamishmar	9	26 June	8 July
Lamerhav	7	25 June	17 July
Ha-boker	5	26 June	7 July
Herut	8	25 June	13 July
Ha-tzofeh	5	26 June	6 July

which were examined, only the *Jerusalem Post, Davar*, the *de facto Mapai* organ, and the General Zionists' *Ha-boker* supported the arms-for-Germany decision. The spokesmen for three members of the coalition Government were harshly critical—*Lamerhav, Al Hamishmar*, and *Ha-tzofeh*.

The Cabinet met on the 28th for four and a half hours and again on the 29th. At the first session *Ahdut* minister Bar Yehuda said that he could not recall Germany having been specifically mentioned at an earlier Cabinet meeting—and he might have misled his party unwittingly. (Indeed it was *Ahdut Ha'avodah* leaders Tabenkin and Galili, neither a Cabinet minister, who had taken the lead in demanding the cancellation of the agreement, claiming that *they* and *Ahdut Ha'avodah* as a party knew nothing of the deal. This intra-party lapse in communication was an additional variable in the crisis.) Ben Gurion replied by reading the protocol of the 14 December 1958 Cabinet meeting which clearly authorized the sale of arms to states to which the Foreign Ministry did not object; and Germany was specifically mentioned by BG. Moreover, all ministers were present. The same day, Sunday 28 June, Ben Gurion told *Mapai*'s Central Committee he would resign if the *Ahdut* and *Mapam* ministers did not withdraw their opposition to the agreement. The next stage was about to begin.

Ben Gurion's intense anger and sense of betrayal, along with the persistent assertion by the two Left parties' Cabinet ministers that they were not consulted *properly*, *both* gain credence from the secret documents pertaining to the decision itself.[1]

Cabinet minutes on the first discussion—and decision—relating to this issue make explicit, though passing, reference to Germany:

Meeting of the Cabinet on December 14, 1958. All members present.

SALE OF ARMS

Prime Minister: There is a law whose existence we have forgotten. . . . Now the Legal Adviser of the Ministry of Defence has found that according to para. 2 (*b*) of the Firearms Law, arms may be sold abroad only with the approval of the Government. It may, indeed, be possible to interpret the term 'firearms' in a more restricted or a wider sense. We have now received a larger order in dollars for mortar bombs in two sizes. The Legal Adviser to the Ministry of Defence has informed me that I must obtain the approval of the Government.
Mr. M. Bentov (Mapam): From whom is the order?
Prime Minister: From various countries in Europe.
Mr. P. Rosen (Progressives): All the same it is worth knowing which countries.
Prime Minister: To a number of countries—Holland, Germany, perhaps also [a third country]. I am asking for a general approval. . . .
Rosen: The intention was that there might be exports having a political significance.

[1] The texts, as authorized by the Cabinet at their 28 June meeting, were published in the press on 30 June.

Prime Minister: On several occasions there were orders in which the Foreign Ministry intervened and did not permit the sale. If there is no opposition, we have finished with this question.

Resolved: In accordance with para. 2 (*b*) of the Firearms Law 5709 (1949), to authorize the Ministry of Defence to sell arms to foreign countries in all cases in which the Ministry of Foreign Affairs has no objection.

At a Cabinet meeting on 18 January 1959 the Prime Minister noted that Government 'approval must be given for manufacture, and not only for sale, and we decided only on the sale'. Approval was given, without any further discussion. Then, on 29 March, an open clash occurred in the Cabinet, during the discussion of the Foreign Currency Budget for 1959/60. The Prime Minister reported: 'This year the Ministry of Defence will bring in — million dollars; an agreement has been signed with Western Germany.' Eshkol, then Finance Minister, interjected, 'I know that you are making me rich'. Barzilai of *Mapam* remarked: 'I have a question on this matter.' And then the conflict was bluntly stated:

Prime Minister: In which religious code of laws is it written that it is forbidden to sell arms to Germany?

Barzilai: It is not written in any religious code of laws, but I think that we should not sell arms to Germany.

Prime Minister: I do not think so.

Barzilai: I ask for a discussion on this.

Prime Minister: Good, next week. It is only to Western Germany that it is forbidden, or to Eastern Germany as well?

Barzilai: To Eastern Germany as well.

Prime Minister: Why did you travel to Eastern Germany? I refused to write a letter to a German Professor on a book of Spinoza, although he is a man of sterling character; I said that if he had been a Professor in Switzerland I should have written willingly.

Barzilai: In my opinion, it is possible and necessary to travel to every international gathering in Germany, Eastern and Western. Everyone goes; you [people] went to Western Germany before us.

Prime Minister: It is permissible to travel to Western Germany, but not to Eastern Germany. They have murdered and robbed and have not given back the loot. Western Germany at least wants to make reparations, but the others have murdered and also taken possession. There is a difference between Western and Eastern Germany.

Barzilai: Nevertheless, the sale of arms and travel are two different things.

Eshkol: We propose a foreign currency budget totaling — million dollars.

(The discussion on the Foreign Currency Budget continued and no one returned to the question of Germany. The discussion ended with a decision to approve the draft Foreign Currency Budget for 1959/60.)

Just after the Cabinet meeting on 29 March, the Secretary to the Government, Katriel Katz, wrote an Internal Memo to the Prime Minister concerning Barzilai's request for a 'special discussion' on the sale of arms to Germany: he recalled the 14 December debate and decision and sought Ben Gurion's 'special instruction' about placing the subject on the Cabinet agenda. Ben Gurion noted on this Memo: 'I did not subsequently consider it necessary to bring up this item for discussion unless Mr. Barzilai should demand it at a meeting of the Cabinet.'

Ahdut Ha'avodah entered the controversy two weeks later. On 14 April its two ministers, Bar Yehuda (Interior) and Carmel (Communications), sent a joint Secret-Personal letter to the Prime Minister–Defence Minister. They claimed that, during the discussion on the Foreign Currency Budget, on 29 March, 'The Government decided . . . to hold a discussion on this matter'. (There was, in fact, no *decision*; BG had merely replied to Barzilai's request for a discussion, 'Good, next week'.) They stated 'our unequivocal opinion, that we are absolutely opposed to the sale of arms to Germany . . . [and] express our hope that so long as the said discussion has not taken place in the Cabinet' the arms deal would not be implemented.

This letter did not reach Ben Gurion for fifteen days, an unusually lengthy delay even by Israel's postal delivery standards. He replied at once from Sde Boker that 'the Government's decision on the sale of arms . . . applies to all countries without exception. . . . For this reason, the matter does not require *further* discussion in the Cabinet. You have, however, the right to propose the *cancellation* of the decision, and until your proposal is adopted—if it is adopted—the decision remains in force, and the Ministry of Defence will act in accordance with it.' He concluded by referring to 'the absurdity of your proposal'.

Ben Gurion noted in his reply that the issue was not raised at a Cabinet meeting on 3 May 'although I proposed in my reply to Bar Yehuda and Carmel that they were entitled to propose a discussion with a view to the cancellation of the decision . . .'. He also referred to their errors: he had not made 'a statement on "the plans existing in the Ministry of Defence for the sale of arms to Western Germany" '; rather, that an agreement had been signed; furthermore, there was no Cabinet decision to hold a discussion.

The *Ahdut* ministers replied on 4 May: 'We do not recall an authoritative Government decision on the sale of arms to Germany by the Ministry of Defence without prior consultation with the Government. Even if we are shown that such a decision exists . . . we ask that this transaction should not be carried out before a discussion . . . has been held in the Cabinet.'

Ben Gurion's reply was blunt: 'The decision that you do not recall exists, and it states that arms may be sold to any country if the Foreign Ministry does not object. It does not say "if the Ministry of the Interior or the Ministry of Communications does not object". The Ministry of Defence has acted and will act according to this decision.' He also noted in his reply that six weeks then passed, with seven Cabinet meetings—and no one raised the question of arms for Germany or proposed a discussion.

The Cabinet approved the publication of these minutes and correspondence at their meeting on 28 June. It is clear that Ben Gurion's *legal* case is unassailable—a *decision* had been taken by the Government on 14 December 1958 and the arms agreement with Germany was therefore duly authorized. At the same time discussion was *pro forma*: the evidence demonstrates that a full and frank debate on the specific agreement with Germany or even the general issue of arms sales did not take place throughout the period of the controversy. Moreover, Ben Gurion certainly knew that both *Ahdut Ha'avodah* and *Mapam* were strongly opposed to an arms deal with Germany; after all, the previous Cabinet crisis was over this issue. It was also disingenuous for the Prime Minister to assert that they had not asked for a discussion: Barzilai had specifically done so on 29 March; and Ben Gurion had responded, 'Good, next week'. It was never held. And BG's own notes prove that he was doing everything possible to avoid it. The conclusion is unmistakable: the Left parties' representatives in the Cabinet were caught unawares, and Ben Gurion took advantage of their slow and inept response when the matter was first discussed in the Government.

Tension mounted swiftly after the publication of these documents, and for the next three days crisis pervaded the political system as a whole. On Monday, 29 June, *Maki* moved a no-confidence motion in the *Knesset*. Just minutes before the preliminary debate began, Ben Gurion walked out of a special Cabinet meeting, saying that he refused to sit at the same table with *Ahdut Ha'avodah* ministers until their party newspaper, *Lamerhav*, apologized for writing that he had distorted the facts of the arms transaction. While he was still there, a majority of *Mapai* ministers and Rosen voted to uphold the December 1958 decision and turned down proposals to cancel the sale. In Ben Gurion's absence, Rosen chaired the Cabinet session, which was devoted entirely to possible ways out of the impasse: BG sat next door and was kept informed by notes and visiting ministers! After a two-and-a-half-hour meeting, the Cabinet adjourned.

Mapai's supreme decision-making body, *Havereinu*, now entered the process: it met immediately after the Cabinet session and approved BG's proposal to hold a full-dress *Knesset* debate on the *Maki* motion— in order to force *Ahdut Ha'avodah* and *Mapam* to clarify their stand. It was noted that, if they spoke in Parliament against the sale, they would violate the coalition agreement that coalition MKs must get special Cabinet permission to oppose a Government decision publicly, in the *Knesset*.

The Cabinet met on the morning of 30 June, and Ben Gurion

reportedly said, 'This is the last regular meeting with them', referring to *Ahdut* ministers. With *Mapam* and *Ahdut Ha'avodah* members opposed, it voted that all ministers and coalition *Knesset* factions would be jointly responsible for the Cabinet decision of 14 December 1958. *Ahdut* ministers were singled out by BG for derision. Before the meeting he called all other members to his office for informal talks on the crisis; Barzilai refused to speak except in the full Cabinet. Moreover, the Prime Minister refused to sit together with *Ahdut* ministers, for *Lamerhav* had not yet apologized; he finally yielded to the persuasion of Eshkol and others. Rosen asked if he would agree to abstention by *Ahdut* and *Mapam* ministers in the *Knesset* votes; BG refused. (Barzilai and Carmel later accused *Mapai* ministers of violating an understanding reached at the 28 June Cabinet meeting that there would not be an open *Knesset* vote on the arms issue.)

The Cabinet adjourned at 10 a.m. on Tuesday the 30th. Then Ben Gurion presented a security review to a two-and-a-half-hour meeting of the *Knesset* Committee on Foreign Affairs and Security. That body, too, participated in the formulation of high policy when it passed a resolution recommending that the Government not cancel the arms deal: the vote was 9 (*Mapai*, General Zionists, and Progressives) to 6 (*Ahdut Ha'avodah*, *Mapam*, *Herut*, and NRP). The ministers present then left for a ten-minute Cabinet meeting, which decided to bring the *Knesset* Committee's resolution to the floor of Parliament—again over the objection of the Left parties' members. And the Government Secretary then told a press conference that, under Article 4 of the Coalition Agreement after the preceding Cabinet crisis, any minister who abstained without Cabinet approval 'must resign from the Government'.

The *Maki* no-confidence motion was defeated by 57 to 5, with 37 abstentions, comprising *Herut*, General Zionists, *Agudat Yisrael*, and *Po'alei Agudat Yisrael*. The debate, with more than twenty speakers, was almost a replica of the debate over Reparations at the beginning of 1952. Ben Gurion spoke at length on his motion presented the previous evening, 30 June: 'The *Knesset* opposes the cancellation of the sale of arms to the Federal German Republic.' It was approved on 1 July by 57 to 45, with 6 abstentions (*Mapai*, Progressives, and General Zionists in favour; *Ahdut Ha'avodah*, *Mapam*, NRP, *Herut*, and *Maki* opposed, and the two *Aguda* parties in abstention). Many years later, Ben Gurion referred to the unexpected support of the General Zionists: 'I was amazed because this had never happened in the State.'[1] It was, indeed, extraordinary—three parties within the coalition had voted against the Government, and its majority in the *Knesset* was achieved by the support of an opposition party!

Five other motions had been moved in the *Knesset*—by *Herut*, NRP, *Ahdut Ha'avodah*, *Mapam*, and *Maki*—all calling for the cancellation of

[1] Interview in *Sde Boker*, July 1966.

the arms deal. But the Speaker put the Government motion first and then ruled that there was no need to vote on the others. The arms sale had now been approved by the Cabinet, the *Knesset* Committee on Foreign Affairs and Security, and the *Knesset* itself. The Left coalition parties attempted to invoke a 1954 *Knesset* resolution opposing German rearmament, but the motion approved in July 1959 rendered it invalid. Yet the decision and its consequences had still not run their course.

The case of the critics within the coalition and their deeply felt resentment emerged during the 'great debate' in the *Knesset*.

Barzilai claimed that Ben Gurion had violated a Cabinet decision of March 1958—that every sale of arms to a foreign country must be approved by the Ministerial Committee on Foreign Affairs and Defence; and the Prime Minister admitted that no such transactions had been brought before the Committee between March and December 1958. Moreover, BG had not fulfilled his promise on 29 March to Barzilai to hold a Cabinet discussion 'next week'. He had not raised it afresh at the time, said Barzilai, because of an erroneous mobilization order on 1 April; he was certain the debate would be held after that matter was settled.

His *Mapam* colleague, Hanan Rubin, taunted the Government: 'Let them say when the agreement was made. It was made before December. What authority was there for it?'

Moshe Carmel, another of the protagonists, noted that *Ahdut Ha'avodah* views on arms for Germany were common knowledge—and they had never agreed to a sale of weapons, in the Cabinet or outside. He first learned of the *proposal* at the 29 March Cabinet discussion; and the Prime Minister's reply to Barzilai gave no indication that an *agreement* had been signed long before.

Both Carmel and Bar Yehuda then took the unusual step of saying to the *Knesset* that they 'announce, with a full sense of responsibility, that', at the initial, 14 December 1958, Cabinet meeting, 'we did not hear the word Germany when it was mentioned . . . by the Prime Minister. That is why we did not react.' Bar Yehuda added: 'Unfortunately we don't have a *Shin Bet*' (Israel's General Security Service, but in this context meaning a secret information service); it was not enough to be a Minister to get security information.

The crisis drifted during the next three days, 2, 3, 4 July, amidst reports of efforts to form a minority Government of *Mapai* and the Progressives, with the backing of General Zionists and *Agudat Yisrael* in the *Knesset*. Carmel and Bar Yehuda appealed to the *Ahdut Ha'avodah* Secretariat to allow them to resign—it refused. The climax of the crisis in decision-making was at hand.

At the Cabinet meeting of 5 July Ben Gurion announced that, if the four *Ahdut* and *Mapam* ministers did not resign by 6 p.m. he would resign. The Cabinet, too, demanded the resignation of Bar Yehuda, Carmel, Barzilai, and Bentov. They refused to do so. And so BG tendered his resignation that evening: his letter to the President of Israel saddled the two dissident coalition partners with total responsibility for the crisis and the outcome, but not everyone was convinced.

This indeed was the formal outcome of the 1959 crisis over the decision to sell arms to Germany. Elections were held in October, and the identical coalition was re-established, with Ben Gurion as Prime Minister–Defence Minister once more. There were other, long-term consequences of greater importance. Before summarizing them, we shall discuss two lesser structures involved in the formulation of Strategic-level decisions.

(d) OTHERS: *HAVEREINU* ET AL.

The German arms decisions also indicated a role for other structures, notably the *Knesset* Committee on Foreign Affairs and Security and *Havereinu*. The former passed a resolution opposing the cancellation of the arms deal—which was later presented as the Government Motion in the *Knesset*. And the latter supported Ben Gurion's strategy of compelling the Left dissidents to take a public stand by holding an open debate on the issue in Parliament, a rare occurrence in Israeli foreign and security policy. These were not inconsequential acts in the cluster of decisions and the process as a whole.

One of these structures has been explored elsewhere in this work, the *Knesset* Committees in the setting of Authorization of policy. It remains to assess their general role in the formulation of policy.

To the question, 'did the *Knesset* Committee exercise any influence on your thinking and decisions', Ben Gurion replied:[2]

Oh, yes. It was very important. There were two opposition groups—the Left on policy towards Russia, the Right on Israel's boundaries. Discussion was very serious. There was no demagoguery. It was very different from *Knesset* debates.

The most active participants were Bernstein [General Zionists], Harari [Progressives], Hazan [*Mapam*], Allon and Galili [*Ahdut Ha'avodah*]. There were none from the religious parties—Shapira being in the Cabinet; but Unna spoke.

Yet a distinction was drawn by BG between the Committee's influence on his *thinking* and on his *decisions*: on the latter it was marginal. Eshkol echoed this view: 'We look upon it as an important Committee. They [its members] demand their rights. It has representatives from the opposition parties too; that compels them to be listened to—and to be

---

[1] See ch. 6 (*d*).   [2] Interview in Sde Boker, July 1966.

responsible.'[1] And one of its most respected perennial members, Harari, who had referred to the *Knesset* Committee as 'the pulse of the Nation' in this sphere, declared that in some areas, including nuclear policy, 'it has more to say than the Government', especially under Eshkol.[2]

The consensus of members, observers, officials, and ministers is that the *Knesset* Committee was, for the most part, a consumer of information on foreign and security policy and only occasionally a decision-making organ. It is best described as an institutional pressure on policy within the formal framework of Israel's political system. That role was strengthened by its permissive links to parties and their leaders: this applied to the Cabinet as well. Ministers were forbidden to discuss security matters with others (as are members of the *Knesset* Committee) except with the leaders of their parties if they are not members of the Cabinet. Thus, Barzilai and Bentov of *Mapam* consulted party leaders Ya'ari and Hazan before indicating their view in the Cabinet on the proposed Sinai Campaign in 1956. Similarly, Justice Minister Rosen was accompanied by his party's foreign affairs expert, Harari, to Ben Gurion's home on 26 October 1956, for consultations on the Sinai decision. And later, under Eshkol, Independent Liberal Minister Kol told the Prime Minister he was sharing his knowledge on foreign and security matters with Rosen and Harari.[3] In this way, three political structures—Cabinet, *Knesset* Committee, and party leadership bureaus—have been intermeshed in the policy process.

The reality of *Havereinu* (Our Comrades) is beyond doubt; but its precise role in the policy process is difficult to assess. Ben Gurion had a clear recollection of this informal body, which comprised the *Mapai* ministers 'and a few others'—the Secretary-General of the party and the Secretary-General of the *Histadrut*. Were foreign affairs discussed? 'Oh yes, very often, especially when the issue was to lead to action, as with retaliation raids.' Although he had minutes of *Havereinu* meetings only since 1961 (BG was a meticulous diarist during the long years in power), they began 'before that, but long after independence'; it was in 1956, as others noted. To Ben Gurion, *Havereinu* and *Sareinu* (Our Ministers) were virtually the same, and *Sareinu* met every Thursday afternoon to synchronize views in order to avoid dissension within *Mapai* ranks at Cabinet meetings on the following Sunday. They discussed all major questions of foreign policy and defence, he added.[4]

Ben Gurion's Political Secretary, Navon, differentiated the two party organs and contributed further details about their composition, role, influence, and antecedents. '*Havereinu* is the most powerful decision-making organ within *Mapai*. Its basic membership was about ten [the head of *Mapai*'s *Knesset* faction was included]; but there was also a floating membership of up to ten persons, who were invited for special discussions, people like Sharett [when not in office], Avigur, branch leaders in Tel Aviv and Haifa, etc.' Navon agreed that, in its very function—to assure a *Mapai* consensus in a coalition Government—non-ministers were given access to Cabinet discussion; in fact, they helped to make Cabinet decisions—in advance, an intriguing variation on Cabinet practice. 'Defence was never discussed in that forum, and foreign affairs rarely.' (This apparent discrepancy is to be explained by Ben Gurion's assumed identity between *Havereinu* and *Sareinu*. Both the Prime Minister and his aide—and many others—stressed that foreign and security affairs were carefully discussed by the *Mapai* ministers before going to the Cabinet).[1]

It was in that context that Ben Gurion revealed his approach to decision-making. 'I had a *principle* that questions of *State* should be decided by the *Government*.' He cited two illustrations. After the first truce (June 1948), when Jordan destroyed the pumping station at Latrun, BG proposed a move on Jericho and an occupation of the Hebron pocket; he was defeated in the Cabinet by one vote. Secondly, when Egypt refused to allow the movement of food to Israeli troops in the Negev, in September 1948, the Prime Minister called in his three senior *Mapai* colleagues—Sharett, Kaplan, and Remez—and urged immediate action. The proposal was approved by the Government and led to the capture of Beersheba, followed by a deeper thrust to the south.[2]

Havereinu's antecedent in the policy process was the Political Committee of *Mapai*. According to Navon, it was a body of twenty-three, which existed in the early years, 'certainly from 1952 to 1956'. Although short-lived, this party organ was more important than *Havereinu* in this sphere. 'Foreign policy issues were debated there', said Navon. Ben Gurion concurred. And Sharett used to take his differences with BG to the Political Committee—which he took into his confidence 'up to a point'. Then, after his resignation, the Committee 'withered'. 'Since 1957', he remarked in enforced retirement three years later, 'Ben Gurion has had *carte blanche* in foreign policy; the party never debates these issues any longer.'[3] And the well-informed Sharef observed: 'The role of *Havereinu* was as much or as little as Ben Gurion wanted. He used it on matters which were unimportant to him.' Like everyone else, he noted that neither the *Mapai* Central Committee nor the Secretariat played a role in formulating foreign policy: 'They merely received information in this field.'[4]

Under Eshkol, various structures of decision-making were activated and/or enlarged. The Ministerial Committee on Defence was increased to ten at the beginning of 1966 and fifteen in June 1967, as noted. *Sareinu* comprised all ministers from the Alignment (12) and continued

[1] Interview in Jerusalem, Dec. 1965.   [2] Interview in Sde Boker, July 1966.
[3] Interview in Jerusalem, July 1960.   [4] Interview in Jerusalem, March 1966.

to meet every week before Cabinet sessions. *Havereinu*, too, was larger, with twenty-one—the twelve Alignment ministers, the Secretaries-General of the two parties and of the *Histadrut*, and half a dozen invitees. Because of its size, Eshkol formed an *Inner Committee of Havereinu*, a small group of *Mapai* and *Ahdut* leaders, varying from six to nine depending upon the issue, which met once or twice a week.[1] Thus, at the close of Israel's second decade there was a complex decision-making apparatus in foreign and security policy, with two informally linked hierarchies:

FIGURE 10

HIGH-POLICY DECISION-MAKING UNDER ESHKOL

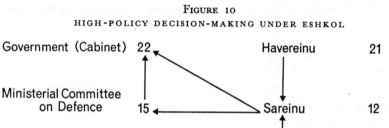

In reality, power lay with the Inner Committee of *Havereinu*, modified by non-Alignment members of the Ministerial Committee on Defence. When the Alignment leaders were agreed on a policy issue, approval was assured, for they commanded a majority in the Ministerial Committee and the Cabinet. But as the 1967 decision process revealed, and even more so the post-Six-Day-War disagreements, Alignment leaders and those in the reunited Labour Party were deeply divided on fundamental issues relating to Israel's foreign policy.

In summary, there is a *complex process of formulating high policy* in Israel, with multiple forces enmeshed in the struggle to influence and to make basic decisions on foreign and security policy: institutional (Cabinet, Ministerial Committee on Defence, *Knesset*, *Knesset* Committee on Foreign Affairs and Security, *Havereinu*, *Sareinu*, parties and the political committees); ideological; personal (Ben Gurion and the dissident Leftists); and the communications media (the publication of secret documents). The Foreign Office was inactive in the German arms cases, primarily because of the acquiescence of Foreign Minister Meir in the wisdom of Prime Minister Ben Gurion. And the Ministerial Committee on Defence was yet to emerge. But as other evidence suggests, both of these institutions participate in the decision-making process. The Cabinet is, however, the ultimate arena for Strategic-level decision-making in policy issues involving party, personal and institutional conflicts.

[1] Interview with Eshkol, Jerusalem, Aug. 1966.

CHAPTER 17

The Foreign Service Technical Élite

The Technical Élite in Israeli foreign policy comprises two groups:
(i) all persons who have occupied the post of Head of an operational
    Department or higher within the Ministry for Foreign Affairs, and
(ii) a Parallel Technical Élite in related branches of the civil and mili-
    tary bureaucracy.
The time period of this analysis, as with all other components of Israel's
foreign policy system, is 1948–68.[1]

Foreign Office senior personnel include the following categories:

Director-General
Deputy and Assistant Director-General
Adviser[2]
Head of Department[3]

Africa	International Organizations
Armistice Affairs	Latin America
Asia	Middle East
British Commonwealth	Research
Eastern Europe	United States
Economic	Western Europe
International Co-operation	

Head of the Foreign Minister's Bureau and Private Secretary to the
Minister

Head of Mission to

United States	Germany	Consulate-General,
United Nations	Italy	New York
France	Belgium[4]	
United Kingdom	Ethiopia[5]	
Soviet Union	Turkey[6]	

[1] The cut-off is the end of February 1968, just before a major reorganization took place in the Foreign Office.

[2] This excludes those who were given the title of Political Adviser or Adviser to the Foreign Minister without operational roles.

[3] Department names changed at various times. These were the names used for Ministry Departments before the reorganization of March 1968.

[4] Since 1960, when this post assumed importance because of negotiations and relations with the European Common Market.

[5] Since 1962, when the Israeli mission was changed from a Consulate-General to an Embassy.

[6] Until 1956, when the post was downgraded and headed by a Chargé d'Affaires.

The second-ranking official in missions to the US, UN, France, and the UK

The Parallel Technical Élite comprises the following:[1]

Chief of Staff
Director of *Ha-Mosad*[2]
Director of Military Intelligence[3]
Chief of General Staff Branch
Commerce and Industry Ministry
    Director-General
    Director of Foreign Trade
Defence Ministry
    Deputy Minister[4]
    Director-General
    Head, Department for International Co-operation
    Head of Defence Minister's Bureau[5]
    Military Attaché[6]
    Head of Purchasing Mission[7]
    Director of Defence Research
Finance Ministry
    Deputy Minister
    Director-General
    Director of Fuel Authority
Prime Minister's Office
    Director-General
    Political Secretary
    Military Secretary
Secretary to the Government

(a) PROFILE[8]

We may begin with the Foreign Service group. In the initial presentation (Table 27 and the accompanying analysis), the 87 persons are

[1] The following listing of categories, as with those in the Foreign Office, is not indicative of relative importance.

[2] From 1948 to 1968 there were three Directors of *Ha-Mosad* (The Institute), Israel's Special Intelligence Service.

[3] Known as *Aman* (*Agaf Modi'in*), the Intelligence branch of *Tzahal*.

[4] Also the Special Assistant to the Defence Minister, 1967–8, a *de facto* Deputy Defence Minister.

[5] Except when Dayan was Defence Minister, 1967 ff.

[6] To the United States throughout and, from 1953 to 1959, to France.

[7] To France—which covered all of Europe—from 1953 onwards. The Defence Ministry Purchasing Mission in the United States came under the jurisdiction of the Military Attaché in Washington.

[8] The data in this table and those which follow were derived from Curriculum Vitae-type dossiers made available by the Department of Personnel of the Israeli Ministry for Foreign Affairs. This co-operation, and the patient assistance of Mrs. M. Doryon, meticulous guardian of these files, is greatly appreciated.

undifferentiated as to Influence: an attempt to construct a Decision-Making Inner Circle for specific periods will be made later in the discussion. Throughout, the focus will be on life pattern and career.[1]

Table 27 specifies in detail the members of the Foreign Service Technical Élite from 1948 to 1968.

TABLE 27

MEMBERSHIP IN THE ISRAELI FOREIGN SERVICE TECHNICAL ÉLITE
1948–1968

Date of Entry, Duration, and Period in the Service

	Year of Entry into Technical Élite	Number of Years in Technical Élite	Number of Years in Foreign Service
Alon, M.	1960	5	17
Anug, Y.	1965	3	20
Arad, S.	1962	3	18
Arazi, T.	1961	1	20
Arnon, M.	1965	3	19
Arokh, A.	1963	5	18
Avidan, M.	1961	3	19
Avidar, Y.	1955	3	8
Avner, G.	1948	14[a]	20
Avriel, E.	1948	14[b]	14
Bar-Haim, S.	1966	2	8
Barromi, Y.	1962	6	17
Bartur, M.	1952	9	20
Ben-Dor, S.	1950	9	13
Ben-Horin, E.	1957	4	18
Bentsur, S.	1953	7	20
Biran, A.	1958	3	6

a. He began as Acting Head of an operational Department (Western Europe), not regarded here, normally, as a Technical Élite post. But as the first operative head of this Department—he was made Head thirteen months later—his membership in the Technical Élite is dated from his appointment as Acting Head.

b. He began his Foreign Office association as Minister to Czechoslovakia, not regarded here, normally, as a Technical Élite post. However, at that time, 1948, it was a vital diplomatic assignment because of Czechoslovakia's friendship for Israel, extending to substantial arms aid. Thus, in this case it is considered a Technical Élite post. This applies as well to his period as Ambassador to Ghana (1957–60). The 14 years do not include 2 years in the Parallel Technical Élite, one as Director-General of the Prime Minister's Office (1951–2), the other as Director-General of the Finance Ministry (1952–3). Nor does it include 2 years as Member of the *Knesset* (1955–7).

[1] Systematic studies of Foreign Service officers are virtually non-existent. An exception is R. Barry Farrell, *The Making of Canadian Foreign Policy*, Prentice-Hall of Canada, Toronto, 1969, ch. 4.

TABLE 27 (CONT.)

	Year of Entry into Technical Élite	Number of Years in	Number of Years in Foreign Service
Bitan, M.	1964	4	8
Chelouche, A.	1959	5	20
Comay, M.	1948	16	20
Dagan, A.	1960	2	18
Danin, E.	1948	20	20
Darom, A.	1949	8	17
Dinitz, S.	1963	3	10
Divon, S.	1949	11[c]	13
Doron, E.	1963	5	20
Eban, A.	1948	11[d]	11
Elath, E.	1948	11	13
Elizur, M.	1956	1	19
Elyashiv, S.	1948	7	7[e]
Erell, M.	1961	3	19
Eshel, A.	1955	8	19[f]
Evron, E.	1950	6[g]	12
Eylan, A.	1966	2	18
Eytan, W.	1948	20	20
Fischer, M.	1948	17	17[h]
Gazit, M.	1957	11	19
Goitein, D.	1952	1	4
Golan, D.	1964	2[i]	6
Gordon, Y.	1949	2	2[j]
Guriel, B.	1948	3	3[k]
Harel, A.	1959	3	6
Harman, A.	1953	12	16
Harman, Z.	1957	2	6

c. Similar to note a: he was Acting—and effective—Head of a Department (Middle East) for 3 years (1949–52); it was regarded by his peers as a Technical Élite post at the time.
d. He left the Foreign Service in 1959 and became a member of the High Policy Élite the following year.
e. This includes a brief period, less than a year, as Minister to Czechoslovakia and Hungary, regarded as a key assignment then. He died in 1955.
f. He died in 1968.
g. He was also a member of the Parallel Technical Élite for a year as Head of the Defence Minister's Bureau (1954–5).
h. He died in 1965.
i. He was also a member of the Parallel Technical Élite for 2 years (1966–8) as Director-General of the Commerce and Industry Ministry; in fact, he remained in that post until the end of 1969.
j. He left the Foreign Ministry after less than 2 years and served the UN Secretariat until his death in 1962.
k. He left the Foreign Ministry in 1951.

TABLE 27 (CONT.)

	Year of Entry into Technical Élite	Number of Years in Technical Élite	Number of Years in Foreign Service
Herzog, Y.	1948	14[l]	17
Hillel, S.	1963	5	9
Hyman, C.	1956	1	7
Kahane, S.	1953	3	18
Katz, K.	1951	7[m]	14
Kidron, A.	1959	4	15
Kidron, R.	1949	12	20
Kohn, L.	1948	13	13[n]
Leshem, M.	1965	3	19
Levavi, A.	1948	14[o]	20
Levin, D.	1953	7	20
Liveran, A.	1958	5	15
Lorch, N.	1960	3	13
Lourie, A.	1948	18	20
Lubrani, U.	1951	2[p]	7
Meron, G.	1948	4	4[q]
Meroz, Y.	1960	8	18
Michael, M.	1965	3	9
Miron, T.	1967	1	11
Najar, A.	1948	18	20
Palmon, Y.	1955	2	5
Pragai, M.	1948	4	20
Pratt, S.	1957	7	15
Rafael, G.	1948	13[r]	19
Raviv, M.	1966	2	9
Remez, A.	1960	8	8
Ron, E.	1966	2	10
Rosenne, S.	1948	20	20
Ruppin, E.	1964	1	14
Sasson, E.	1948	12	13

l. He was also a member of the Parallel Technical Élite for 3 years (1965–8) as Director-General of the Prime Minister's Office. He continues in that post as of the end of 1970.
m. He was also a member of the Parallel Technical Élite for 4 years (1958–62) as Secretary to the Government.
n. He died in 1961.
o. Similar to note a. He began as Acting Head and returned as Head of the same Department (Eastern Europe) after a post at a key mission within the same area (Moscow).
p. He was also a member of the Parallel Technical Élite for 2 years (1963–5) as Head of the Prime Minister's Bureau.
q. He left the Foreign Ministry in 1952.
r. This includes 5 years as Counsellor, Delegation to the UN, (1948–53), which was regarded by his peers as a Technical Élite post then.

TABLE 27 (CONT.)

	Year of Entry into Technical Élite	Number of Years in Technical Élite	Number of Years in Foreign Service
Sasson, M.	1966	1	17
Savir, L.	1965	3	20
Shek, Z.	1953	12	20
Shiloah, R.	1948	11	11[s]
Shimoni, E.	1966	2	2
Shimoni, Y.	1948	12[t]	20
Schneerson, M.	1955	5	19
Siddur, H.	1953	4	11
Tekoah, Y.	1954	12	20
Tov, M.	1948	7[u]	11
Tsur, Y.	1953	7	12
Yahil, H.	1959	5	14
Yuval, M.	1953	5	18

s. He died in 1959.
t. Similar to note a. He was Assistant Head, actually *de facto* Head while the Head (Middle East Department) was abroad in 1948–9; and he then became Head of another operational Department (Asia).
u. This includes 4 years as a member of the Delegation to the UN (1948–52); it was then a Technical Élite post, according to his peers. He left the Foreign Ministry in 1959 and returned in 1968.

The Year of Entry into the Technical Élite and the Number of Years within it were calculated rigorously from the data, based on the criterion of Technical Élite post as designated above. This created some methodological problems. For example, an influential member of the Technical Élite may have spent some years abroad, as head of a diplomatic mission not included in the eleven missions regarded as Technical Élite posts. While there he may have been consulted on issues beyond those affecting his particular state and may have exerted influence on general policy. However, those years were not included in the number of years of the person concerned in the Technical Élite—because of the danger of highly subjective judgement on 'influence'. This affects, in particular, Bartur, Comay, Herzog, Levavi, and Lourie: all but one had attained the rank of Assistant Director-General before proceeding to an 'excluded' post, and the one concerned had already held high office in the Ministry and abroad. Yet the states to which they were accredited during the 'excluded' years were regarded by consensus as outside the core group of eleven missions—seven throughout and four for certain periods.

There are also cases where the incumbent of a Technical Élite post has been less influential than the post itself: notable examples are some Consuls-General to New York, Ministers/Ambassadors to Moscow, and

Ministers to Italy in the early years. No attempt is made here, however, to rate the influence of holders of Technical Élite posts. There are also marked differences in importance of operational Departments within the decision-making and implementing process of the Foreign Ministry. However, all Heads of operational Departments have been included in this table of membership.

In addition to the 87 persons there were 10 others who held Technical Élite posts but who are not included in the analysis. One is Mrs. Meir, Minister to the Soviet Union for less than a year (1948–9): she has been examined in detail in the Inner Circle of the High Policy Élite. Eban, too, is a member of both élite groups; but he was an influential figure in the Technical Élite for eleven years (1948–59), in Washington and at the United Nations. He is therefore included in this analysis, as well as in the discussion of the High Policy Élite. There were 8 others.[1]

Within the Foreign Service Technical Élite there is a smaller group of important officials which may be termed the Formal Directorate.

TABLE 28

THE FORMAL DIRECTORATE OF ISRAEL'S FOREIGN OFFICE
1948–1968

Post	From original Technical Élite	Up through the ranks	Total
Director-General			5[a]
Deputy and Assistant Director-General	9	11	17 (20)[b]
Adviser	5	3	4 (8)[c]
Special Cases			2[d]
Total			28

a. One of the Directors-General, Ya'acov Tsur, held that post in an Acting capacity for a few months, in 1959–60. This was between the lengthy tenure of the first DG, Walter Eytan (1948–59) and Haim Yahil (1960–4). The others were Arye Levavi (1964–7) and Gideon Rafael (end 1967–   ).

[1] Three were persons who served in Technical Élite posts abroad—two in Rome at the outset of Israeli–Italian relations (S. Ginossar and M. Ishai) and one in Moscow in the early years (M. Namir, 1949–50). All came from outside the Foreign Service and did not continue in any branch of the bureaucracy. For one of them (Namir) this was a passing interlude in a lengthy political career. Thus they were not included in this analysis of the civil servant élite in Israeli foreign policy. One man served as Minister to London for less than a year and died in office (M. Eliash, 1949–50). Five were members of the Parallel Technical Élite for longer peiods than of the Foreign Service Technical Élite and will be treated in that context (H. Ben-David, A. Ben-Natan, T. Kollek, Y. Navon, Y. Rabin). One served as the second-ranking officer in the missions to Washington and London in the early years and has been omitted because of lack of data. There were also special cases, who have not been included in this analysis. Notable among them is Dr. Jacob Robinson, an American Jew of Lithuanian origin who played an important role as Legal Adviser to Israel's UN Delegation from 1948 until 1957.

b. Only one person has held the post of Deputy Director-General, Arthur Lourie, from 1966 onwards. Unlike many other Israeli ministries, the Foreign Office has not institutionalized this number two position in the hierarchy. In earlier years, however, there was a 'first among equals' in the group of Assistant Directors-General: he assumed the responsibility of the DG when the latter was absent or unavailable for a decision. Twenty persons held the post of Assistant Director-General (including Lourie, who was both Assistant and Deputy DG, but excluding all Assistant DGs in charge of Administration, except one who held a Technical Élite post as well—Bentsur): 3 of these later became DG. Nine of the 20 (or 7 of 18, excluding Levavi and Rafael, who later became DG) were members of the Technical Élite from the time they entered the Foreign Service; and all began their association with the Foreign Office in 1948. Of the other 11 (or 10, excluding Yahil, who later became Director-General), 4 entered the Technical Élite four years after joining the Service (Bartur, Bitan, A. Harman, and Hillel); 5 others entered the Technical Élite between six and eight years after joining the Service (Eshel and Tekoah—six, Ben-Horin and Bentsur—seven, and Gazit—eight); and one person, Chelouche, did so after eleven years in the Service.

Of the 20 persons at that rank 9 were original members of the Foreign Office-cum-Technical Élite. Two of those Double Originals served less than a year as Assistant DG, Elyashiv in 1955 (he died in office), and Avner in 1967–8 (he continues as Assistant DG in 1970). At the other extreme were 3 who served in this or an equivalent rank-and-role in three separate periods, from the early years to the close of the two decades of independence; Comay (1952–3, 1957–60, and from 1967 to 1970 as Ambassador-at-Large); Lourie (1953–7, 1965–6, and since 1966 as Deputy DG); and Levavi (1952–4, 1957–8, and 1960–4); thereafter, Levavi became DG. There were two other Assistant DGs in the fifties (Fischer, 1957–60, and Najar, 1957–8), and 2 in the sixties (Avriel, 1961–5, and Herzog, 1963–5).

Among the 10 Assistant DGs who came up through the ranks all but 3 attained that status in the closing years of the period under inquiry: Bitan, Eshel, Gazit, and Tekoah were appointed in the spring of 1966, soon after Eban became Foreign Minister, though the last two held an equivalent operational post as Adviser from 1965 onwards; Hillel was appointed in 1967, and Ben-Horin and Chelouche in 1968. Two others held that rank for extended periods in the earlier years, Bartur (1958–61) and Bentsur (1958–62), and Harman was Assistant DG in 1955–6.

c. There were 8 (operational) Advisers in the Foreign Office during the twenty-year period, 5 from the Double Original group and 3 who came up through the ranks. Two of the latter, as noted, held the post briefly before becoming Assistant DG (Gazit and Tekoah); one of the former became an Assistant DG (Herzog), and another became a DG (Rafael). A fifth attained that rank in 1967 (Miron). The other 3 were perennials, Shiloah, Kohn, and Rosenne, all starting in 1948: Shiloah until his death in 1959, apart from a period as Minister (No. 2) to the US; Kohn until his death in 1961; and Rosenne, Legal Adviser until 1967, when he became Deputy Permanent Representative to the UN.

d. There are two special cases: Eban, who never held a Formal Directorate post but was a *de facto* member during his eleven years in Washington and New York (the UN), and Danin, a permanent part-time Adviser on the Middle East.

Some analytic themes may be derived from these data. At first glance, the large membership of the Formal Directorate suggests marked mobility: 28 of the 87 persons in the Technical Élite, that is, one third, attained Directorate rank. This bare quantitative ratio, however, creates a distorted image of reality. Taking the period 1948–1966 there are 5 marginal members of the group: the Acting DG for a few months, Tsur; Elyashiv, who died after a few months as Assistant DG; Harman and Najar who held that post briefly before going to crucial assignments abroad (Washington and Brussels, respectively); and Bentsur, who was in charge of Administration. The last two years witnessed a sharp increase in the number of Assistant Directors-General: 8 persons who had never held that rank were appointed between 1966 and 1968. Thus for most of the period (eighteen years) the number of Formal Directorate members was really 15, not 28. These consisted of 3 Directors-General, 6 Advisers, 8 Assistant DGs, and 1 special case. (The discrepancy between 15 persons and 18 holders of FD posts is due to the fact that three persons, Levavi, Herzog and Rafael, held two such posts.) There were also other operationally influential persons among Department Heads and Heads of Missions abroad.

We turn now to some vital statistics about Israel's Foreign Service Technical Élite, beginning with their date of birth and time of arrival in Israel.

TABLE 29

FOREIGN SERVICE TECHNICAL ÉLITE 1948–1968

Date of Birth and Age upon Entry

Date of Birth	Number of Persons	Average Age of Entry into the Service	Average Age of Entry into Technical Élite	Formal Directorate Number of Persons	Average Age of Entry into Inner Circle
Pre-1900	3[a]	51·3	53·3	2	55
1901–1910	25	43·1	45·3	9	46·3
1911–1920	38	34·4	40·1	11	43·1
1921–1930	19	27·6	36·3	6	43·3
Post-1930	2[b]	28·0	33·0	—	—
Totals and Mean Averages	87	35·9	41·0	28	45·0

a. Among the 87 members of the Foreign Service Technical Élite only 2 were over 50 when they joined the Service. And only one of them was also in the Formal Directorate—Kohn. He was 54 when he became Political Adviser to the Foreign Minister, in 1948; but he had performed the same function for the *de facto* Foreign Minister of the *Yishuv*, Sharett, from 1934 to 1948, that is, since he was 40, in the Political Department of the Jewish Agency.

b. At the other extreme of the age spectrum, 2 members in the FSTE were born after 1930, both of them serving in Foreign Minister Eban's Bureau in the late 1960s (Raviv and E. Shimoni). If the outer limit is taken as 1926, there are only 2 other FSTE members, one a Head of Foreign Minister Meir's Bureau at the Foreign Office and, later, in the Prime Minister's Office (Dinitz), the other, the legal Adviser at the end of the two decades under inquiry (Miron).

All but 7 of the 87 persons were born between 1903 and 1926. Taking the data in Table 29, the bulk of the Foreign Service Technical Élite (63 of 87) and of the Formal Directorate (20 of 28) fall within the 1901–1920 period. Further, 2 of the Directors-General were from the 1901–10 decade (Eytan and Yahil), and 2 from the 1911–20 decade (Levavi and Rafael); only eight years separate their dates of birth (1905–13). Moreover, the Formal Directorate is almost equally divided between these two decades.

The average Age of Entry into the Service for the FSTE members born in these two decades is, in reality, lower than indicated above (43·1 and 34·4): many began their *de facto* diplomatic service with the Jewish Agency's Political Department. If their entry into the Foreign Service is dated to include the pre-State years the averages change to 40·0 and 32·3 years, respectively, for the members born in 1901–10 and 1911–20. Persons born in the 1901–10 decade moved quickly into Technical Élite posts: the 25 people in this group took an average of only 2·2 years from the time they entered the Service to reach a Technical Élite post. The 1911–20 group took almost three times as long to move into the TE—an average of 5·7 years for 38 persons. The 'younger men' took longer to enter Technical Élite posts, an average of 8·7 years for 19 persons.

The rapidity of movement of the 1901–10 group is explained in part by the fact that 11 of the 25 entered the Foreign Service in TE posts. Of the 38 persons in the 1911–20 group, 11 did so—but only 1 person in the 1921–30 group began at that high level. For the entire FSTE membership it took an average of 5·1 years from entry into the Service to a Technical Élite post.

Of the 19 persons in the 1921–30 group, 6 reached Formal Directorate rank: they include some of the brightest of the younger men (post-1920) in the Service. The proportion of FSTE persons born in each of the three decades who reached the Formal Directorate varied somewhat: 1901–10, 36 per cent; 1911–20, 28·9 per cent; and 1921–30, 31·6 per cent. However, the Average Age of Entry into the FD was almost identical for the three age groups: the discrepancy between the 1901–10 group and those of the following two decades disappears if one corrects for the *de facto* pre-State period in the Foreign Service.

Very few persons entered the Foreign Service Technical Élite below the age of 30: 2 in the 1911–20 age group, both at 29, and both of whom joined the Service in 1948 and assumed a TE post at once; and 3 in the 1921–30 age group, 2 of whom joined the Service in 1948 at the ages of 27 and 23, and the third in 1950 at 24. The other 82 persons were over 30 years of age.

The Average Age of Entry into the Service (35·9, really lower if the pre-State years in the Political Department are included), into the

Technical Élite (41), and into the Formal Directorate (43) are high, relative to the Parallel Technical Élite, as subsequent data will reveal.

TABLE 30

FOREIGN SERVICE TECHNICAL ÉLITE 1948–1968

Place of Birth

Country	Technical Élite	Formal Directorate
Germany	16	5
Russia	13	3
Israel	11	3
Poland	11	3
Czechoslovakia	5	2
South Africa	5	3
United Kingdom	5	2
Roumania	4	1
Argentina	2	
Austria	2	1
Iraq	2	1
Ireland	2	1
Latvia	2	
Syria	2	
Belgium	1	1
Egypt	1	1
Hungary	1	
Italy	1	
Turkey	1	1
Total	87	28

The place of birth of Israel's Foreign Service Technical Élite and Formal Directorate admirably reflects the 'ingathering of the exiles': no less than nineteen countries are represented in the former, and fourteen in the latter. Within the Technical Élite four countries of origin stand out: Germany, Russia, Israel, and Poland: together they account for 51 of the 87 persons. Nineteen others were born in Czechoslovakia, South Africa, England, and Roumania. Thus these eight countries account for 80 per cent of the TE members. The remaining 17 persons, or 20 per cent, are scattered among eleven states.

The heterogeneity is further reduced by an integration of places of origin along linguistic-cultural lines. Thus Czechoslovakia, Austria, and Hungary may be grouped with Germany as Central Europe. South Africa, the UK and Ireland may be similarly grouped. Latvia and the one case of Turkey may be added to Russia. One person, born by chance in Poland, belongs to Germany. And Iraq, Syria, and Egypt belong together. The revised Place of Birth map would be as follows:

Central Europe	25
Russia	16
Israel	11
Poland	10
Anglo-Saxon Lands	12
Arab Lands	5
Roumania	4
Other	4
Total	87

Thus Central Europe becomes more prominent, as does the Anglo-Saxon group of countries. Russia's representation is also increased. And the Arab states are seen to contribute 5 members to the FSTE. If Russia and Poland are grouped together as Eastern Europe, it would edge Central Europe, 26 to 25.

Within the Formal Directorate Germany stands out even more, with 5 of the 28 members. Russia, Israel, Poland, and South Africa each contributed 3 members; and Czechoslovakia and the United Kingdom 2 each. Thus these 7 countries account for 21 of 28 members, that is, 75 per cent of the Formal Directorate.

Applying the integration of places of origin, the revised data create the following distribution of the Formal Directorate:

Central Europe	9
Russia	4
Israel	3
Poland	2
Anglo-Saxon Lands	6
Arab Lands	2
Other (Belgium and Roumania)	2
Total	28

Two groups stand out—predominantly German-speaking Central Europe and the English-speaking lands: they account for more than half of the Formal Directorate and three of the four Directors-General. (The fourth, Levavi, received much of his higher education in Germany.) The United States is conspicuously absent from the 19 countries of birth of the 87 TE members. The domination of the Foreign Service Technical Élite and its higher sub-group will become sharper in the light of educational and linguistic data to follow.

Members of Israel's Foreign Service Technical Élite arrived not only from diverse lands but during half a dozen waves of immigration (*aliyot*) as well, as the following table indicates.

TABLE 31

FOREIGN SERVICE TECHNICAL ÉLITE 1948–1968

Arrival in Israel

	Number of Persons in Technical Élite	*Average Age of Arrival of TE Members*	*Number of Persons in Formal Directorate*	*Average Age of Arrival of FD Members*
Third *Aliya* (1919–23)	3	16·3	1	15
Fourth *Aliya* (1924–31)	11	20·1	2	25·5
Fifth *Aliya* (1932–8)	28	20·4	11	21·4
1939–1945	12	23·6	5	24·2
1946–May 1948	7	29·6	4	33·8
Post-Independence	12	34·3	2	34·5
Totals and Mean Averages	73*	23·9	25†	25·0

* 11 members of the Technical Élite were born in Israel and are therefore not included in this analysis; nor are 3 others, who arrived in the Fourth *Aliya* as infants, aged 1, 2, and 3.

† 3 of the 28 persons in the Formal Directorate were born in Israel: Chelouche, Danin, and Shiloah.

The vast majority of FSTE members, three-fourths, were under 30 when they arrived—some time between 1919 and 1945. Only 5 of the 73 persons were 40 or older when they reached Palestine–Israel; and 4 of these arrived after Independence. Similarly, of the 13 members who immigrated in their thirties all but 2 arrived after the Second World War. One fifth of the total, 15 persons, arrived as adolescents, in the age group 11–16. This included 5 of the 25 non-Israeli-born members of the Formal Directorate—Avner, Ben-Horin, Gazit, Hillel, and Miron. Thus 8 of the 28 FD members were either born in Israel or received much of their education in the *Yishuv*.

The largest number (28) arrived during the Fifth *Aliya* (1932–8), all but 6 during the early Nazi years, 1932–5. The Fifth *Aliya* contingent in the FSTE reflects almost the same proportion of the Fifth *Aliya* to the total immigration into Israel from 1919 to May 1948, 44 per cent of the Technical Élite and 44·6 per cent of total immigration. If the two 'old' immigrants of that *aliya*, 40 and 35, are excluded, the average age is below 20. The Fifth *Aliya* accounts for a disproportionately high share of the non-Israeli-born members of the Formal Directorate—44 per cent (11), compared to 38 per cent of the Foreign Service Technical Élite.

There is a steady rise in the Average Age of Arrival in the six *aliya* components of the FSTE, from 16·3 to 34·3. In the influential post-

Second-World-War group, 5 of the 7 persons were in their thirties when they arrived. All 5 of them came from English-speaking countries—the United Kingdom and South Africa. They included the first Director-General, Eytan, born in Germany but an Oxford don; a future Foreign Minister, Eban, a former Cambridge don; the long-time Legal Adviser to the Foreign Ministry, Rosenne; and two South African practising lawyers who held key posts in the Foreign Service, Lourie and Comay. With their superior command of English, the 'Anglo-Saxons' (with Herzog they were 6) held a pre-eminent position in the Foreign Service Technical Élite. They retained this status and influence even longer than Eytan's tenure as DG. In the larger post-Independence group of 12 only 1 was under 20 upon arrival in Israel and only 3 under 30; 4 persons were in their forties.

There is a qualitative difference in Age of Arrival between the Fifth *Aliya* and 1939–45 groups in the Formal Directorate on the one hand, and the post-Second-World-War group on the other. As noted, 5 of the 11 Fifth *Aliya* persons in the FD were adolescents upon arrival in Israel. Among the 1939–45 group of 5 FD members, 1 was in his late teens and 3 in their twenties; all 5 members of the post-Second-World-War group were in their thirties.

All of the six *aliya* components are represented in the Formal Directorate, but 3 groups stand out. The Fifth *Aliya* has the largest number of members (11). However, both the 1939–45 and 1946–8 groups have a higher proportion of their TE members in the Formal Directorate—41·7 per cent and 57·1 per cent respectively, compared to 39·3 per cent for the Fifth *Aliya*.

We turn now to the record of military service among the Foreign Service Technical Élite before Israel's independence (see Table 32). Almost 45 per cent of the Foreign Service Technical Élite (38 of 87) had some pre-State military service, equally divided between *Haganah* and the British Army. With few exceptions, *Haganah* service took place in the 1940s, during and after the Second World War. Thus service in *Haganah* and the British Army was competitive for most of the 38. Of the 19 persons who served in the British Army, 16 had prolonged Second World War service—at least 3 years, most of them 5 years: 3 were in the RAF, 3 in the British Army (UK), and 10 in the Jewish Brigade of British Middle East Forces.

More than forty per cent of the Formal Directorate (13 of 28) had some military service, divided between *Haganah* and the British Army. Of these, only 6 had considerable service, Eshel, Shiloah, and Shimoni in the former, Ben-Horin, Eban, and Rosenne in the latter. Comay and Fischer had as well, in other armies.

As a group the Foreign Service Technical Élite and its Formal Directorate had experienced substantial military service: an average of

TABLE 32

FOREIGN SERVICE TECHNICAL ÉLITE 1948–1968

Pre-State Military Service: Summary

	Number of Persons in Technical Élite	Number of Persons in Formal Directorate
Haganah	19*	6
British Army	19	4
Other	4	2
Total	42 (38)†	12

* Arazi, Avidan, Avidar, Meroz, Michael, Palmon, Shiloah, Y. Shimoni, and Tsur began their *Haganah* service before 1940—Arazi, Avidar, Shiloah, and Tsur in the late 1920s. Of the 4 men who served in both *Haganah* and the British Army, Guriel and Remez spent more time in the latter, Lorch and Meroz in the former. Among those who served elsewhere, Comay and R. Kidron were in the South African Army throughout the Second World War; Fischer was with the Free French Forces—he was later decorated; and Leshem fought in the Czech underground from 1942 to 1945.

† 4 served in both *Haganah* and the British Army, 2 mainly in *Haganah*, and 2 mainly in the British Army (during the Second World War). Almost all members of the FSTE were associated with *Haganah* in some form at some period. The above data and those contained in Appendix Table 19 are based upon the individual dossiers of Foreign Ministry personnel (many of which do not include participation in *Haganah*) and seem to refer to a more intensive or full-time service.

8·3 years in *Haganah* for 19 persons, 5·6 years if the exceptionally long service of Arazi, Avidar, Shimoni, and Tsur is set aside from the other 15 persons; and slightly less than 4 years for the 19 in the British Army. The 4 persons in other armies averaged 4·5 years of military service. For the group as a whole the average is 5·7 years of military service.

The education and language skills of Israel's Foreign Service Technical Élite reflect diversity and indicate qualifications of a high order (see Tables 33a and 33b).

The Foreign Service Technical Élite has an impressive group record in the field of higher education. All but 4 of the 87 members received some form of post-secondary education: 19 received a Bachelor's degree, 21 a professional degree, including 3 of the first group; and 24 received a postgraduate degree, including 12 persons who also had a Bachelor's or professional degree (and 1 who earned 2 postgraduate degrees).[1] Thus 49 FSTE members received a university degree—and 15 of them earned a second degree. There are also 29 persons who listed partial university studies in their Curriculum Vitae and 5 who attended only special courses beyond the secondary level—notably the Beth

[1] Of the 16 who earned two degrees, 8 were also members of the Formal Directorate: Chelouche, Comay, A. Harman, Herzog, Lourie, Najar, Rosenne, and Tekoah; 6 of these 8 were in the Anglo-Saxon group.

Higher Education, Degree, Institution, Year

University Studies Without Degree	Bachelor's Degree*	Professional Degree	Postgraduate Degree	Special Courses (Beyond Secondary School)
(29 members of the Technical Elite attended university but did not complete a degree; 5 of these attended two universities.	ARAD, New School for Social Research 1951	BARROMI, Dr. of Law, Rome 1945	AVNER, M.A. Oxford 1942	(12 members of the Technical Elite attended special post-secondary courses, 2 of them two such courses; 3 members received university degrees elsewhere and 4 others were also partial university students.)
	ARAZI, Licencié és Lettres, Sorbonne 1938	BEN-HORIN, LL.B. London 1950	BARROMI, M.A. Hebrew U. 1950	
	BEN-DOR, Liverpool 1931	CHELOUCHE, LL.B. Hebrew U. 1946	BIRAN, M.A. Johns Hopkins 1934	
	COMAY, Cape Town 1931	COMAY, LL.B. Cape Town 1931	PH.D. Johns Hopkins 1935	
13 others who listed partial university studies, one of them with two institutions and two with three universities in this category, completed a degree elsewhere, before or after these studies.)	DAROM, B.SC. Santiago 1929	DAGAN, Dr. of Law and Pol. Sc., Prague 1935	CHELOUCHE, Diploma en Sc. Pol., Paris 1953	
	DINITZ, B.S. Georgetown 1953	DAROM, LL.B. Santiago c. 1936	DINITZ, M.S. Georgetown 1958	
	ELATH, M.A. Georgetown U. 1930	ELYASHIV, Dr. of Law, Toulouse 1927	EBAN, M.A. Cambridge 1938	
	ESHEL, Berlin 1934	GOTTEIN, LL.B. London 1925	ELATH, M.A. American U., Beirut 1934	
	FISCHER, Licencié és Sciences Naturelles, Belgium 1928	GORDON, Licencié en Droit, Paris 1925	EYTAN, M.A. Oxford 1932	
	HARMAN, A., Oxford 1937	HAREL, M.D. Berlin 1937	GAZIT, M.A. Hebrew U. 1946	
	HARMAN, Z., B.SC. (EC.), LSE 1935	HARMAN, A., B.A. Law, Oxford 1937	GOLAN, M.A. Hebrew U. 1951	
	KIDRON, R., Stellenbosch 1936	HERZOG, Fischel Institute Rabbinic degree 1948	GORDON, Doctorat en Droit, Paris 1931	
	LORCH, Hebrew U. 1951	LL.B. Hebrew U. 1948	GURIEL, LL.M. Riga 1929	
	LUBRANI, London 1956	LIVERAN, LL.B. London 1941	HERZOG, PH.D. Ottawa 1963	
	MEROZ, London 1944	LOURIE, LL.B. Cape Town 1922	KOHN, LL.D. Heidelberg 1929	
	RAVIV, London 1961	MIRON, LL.B. Hebrew U. 1954	LEVAVI, M.A. Hebrew U. 1935	
	SHILOAH, Hebrew U. 1934	NAJAR, LL.B. French Law School in Cairo 1931	LEVIN, LL.D. Berlin 1934	
	SHIMONI, E., Johannesburg 1950	PRATT, LL.B. London 1934	LIVERAN, LL.M. London 1942	
	TSUR, Licencié, Sorbonne 1929	ROSENNE, LL.B. London 1940	LOURIE, M.A. Cambridge 1925	
		SCHNEERSON, LL.B. Hebrew U. 1937	MERON, Dr. Ec. Sc., Heidelberg 1926	
		TEKOAH, Licencié en Droit, L'Aurore U., Shanghai 1946	LL.D. Heidelberg 1929	
		TOV, M.D. Buenos Aires 1936	MIRON, S.J.D. Harvard 1957	
			NAJAR, M.JUR. Sorbonne 1933	
			ROSENNE, PH.D. Hebrew U. 1959	
			TEKOAH, M.A. Harvard 1948	
			YAHIL, PH.D. Vienna 1929	
	* B.A. unless otherwise indicated			
Total Number of man-courses 52	19	21	24	14

TABLE 33b

FOREIGN SERVICE TECHNICAL ÉLITE 1948–1968

Higher Education: Subjects of Study

	Number of Persons in Technical Élite	Number of Persons in Formal Directorate
Law	28	12
Economics	17	6
Political Science	17	6
History	12	2
Philosophy	4	2
Diplomacy and International Relations	14	3
Oriental Studies	10	3
Humanities	5	1
Other*	30	12
Total	132	47

* This includes Natural Science (3), Commerce (3), Medicine (3), Archaeology (3), Sociology (4), English Literature (2), Education (2), Classics (2), Journalism (2); and Art, Engineering, Modern Languages, Psychology, Philology, and Rabbinical Studies (1 each).

Hakerem Teachers' Seminary in Jerusalem and the Jewish Agency Public Service College (JAPSC), which existed for only two years, 1946–8.

Among the Formal Directorate of 28, 6 members received a Bachelor's degree, 10 received a professional degree, including 2 of the Bachelor group, and 13 received a postgraduate degree, including 6 who also had a Bachelor's or a professional degree. Thus 21 of the 28 Formal Directorate members received a university degree, and 8 of the 21 received a second degree. Of the 7 Formal Directorate persons without a university degree, 6 attended university for an average of two years—at Vienna, Prague, the London School of Economics, the Berlin *Hochschule* for Economics, Berlin University, Hebrew University, and the Trade and Industry Academy in Cluj, Roumania.

One branch of knowledge—Law—dominates the higher education of Israel's Foreign Service Technical Élite: of the 83 persons who attended university, 28 studied law; of the 49 persons who received a degree, 25, that is 50 per cent, received a law degree; and of the 15 members who hold a second university degree, 13 were trained in Law. By far the largest subject-group in the Formal Directorate, Law accounts for more than 40 per cent. This is twice as large as any other subject-group in the FD. The 12 FD members trained in Law are: Ben-Horin, Chelouche, Comay, Elyashiv, Harman, Herzog, Kohn, Lourie, Miron, Najar,

Rosenne, Tekoah. Yet it is noteworthy that none of the Directors-General received a degree in Law: Eytan studied Philology; Yahil, Political Science; Levavi, Philosophy, Physics and Mathematics; and Rafael studied Law.

The dominance of Law is accentuated by the fact that, while Economics was studied by 17 persons, few were thoroughly trained in that field. Indeed, of the 4 men who headed the Foreign Office Economic Department during the 20 years, only 1, Meron, had a degree in Economics. Political Science, too, is inflated in the data in Table 33b: those who studied this subject listed others as well.

No less than 23 different fields were listed by the 83 persons who attended university. Apart from Law and Economics and Political Science, only History, Diplomacy, and Oriental Studies claimed the attention of FSTE members—12, 14, and 10, respectively. And in the FD they were the subjects of study for 2, 3, and 3 persons, respectively. The crucial fact about the higher education of Israel's Foreign Service Technical Élite, as with other Foreign Services, is the pre-eminence of Law, with British universities and the Hebrew University of Jerusalem accounting for the bulk of legal degrees—9 in the UK and 4 in Israel.

Diplomats are expected to have a knowledge of languages. Yet it is doubtful that the linguistic skills of Israel's Foreign Service Technical Élite are excelled. No less than 20 languages are listed by the 87

TABLE 34a

FOREIGN SERVICE TECHNICAL ÉLITE 1948–1968

Language Skills

	Technical Élite Members	Formal Directorate Members
Hebrew	87	28
English	86	28
French	58	22
German	47	17
Arabic	17	5
Russian	14	4
Spanish	14	4
Italian	8	2
Czech	6	2
Polish	5	1
Other	13 (16)*	5 (8)†

* 13 members listed 16 'Other' language skills: Afrikaans (2), Chinese (1), Dutch (2), Hungarian (3), Lithuanian (1), Persian (1), Portuguese (1), Roumanian (3), Turkish (1), Ukrainian (1).

† 5 members listed 'Other' language skills: Afrikaans (1), Chinese (1), Dutch (1), Hungarian (1), Lithuanian (1), Persian (1), Roumanian (1).

TABLE 34b

FOREIGN SERVICE TECHNICAL ÉLITE 1948–1968

Number of Languages Spoken

	Technical Élite Members	Formal Directorate Members
Two	9	1
Three	18	5
Four	26	13
Five	24	4
Six	8	4
Seven	2	1
Total	87	28

members. They include all 5 official United Nations languages and all major tongues of Europe, North and South America, and the Middle East. The languages of Asia and Africa, however, are conspicuously absent, except for 1 person who speaks Chinese.

All 87 members know Hebrew, the official and working language of the Israel Foreign Service, though mastery of the language is uneven. This is also true for English. There is, obviously, an unequal command of English within a group with such diverse backgrounds. Yet all but one claim a working knowledge. And for no less than 10 Formal Directorate members, English is either the mother tongue (Comay, Eban, A. Harman, Herzog, Lourie, Rosenne) or the predominant language of higher education (Avner, Ben-Horin, Eytan, Tekoah). Indeed, skill in the principal language of diplomacy is one of the reasons for their initial entry and membership in the highest group of the Technical Élite.

Knowledge of French is not as general but is widespread nonetheless—58 of 87 members, including all but 6 in the Formal Directorate. For a state whose predominant language is neither of the principal languages of diplomacy, Israel is well served by her Foreign Service. Yet there is a qualitative difference between the place of English and French in Israel's FSTE. Compared with the 10 'Anglos', only 3 members of the Formal Directorate received their predominant higher education in French—Fischer, Najar, Tsur; and only for Fischer was it his mother tongue.

German is cited by fewer persons than French (47 to 58) but it ranks higher as a language skill for the group as a whole. Those who know German know it better than the comparable group in French—with very few exceptions. A striking indicator is that for 11 of the 17 German-knowing members of the Formal Directorate, German is either the mother tongue (Avner, Avriel, Bartur, Ben-Horin, Eshel, Eytan, Kohn,

Rafael, Yahib) or the predominant language of higher education (Bitan, Levavi). Thus German is a very close second to English among foreign language skills.

After these 4 languages there is a striking decline, though 3 others have a substantial number of speakers—Arabic, Russian, and Spanish. Arabic is known by 17 FSTE members, including 5 in the Formal Directorate; and Russian and Spanish are cited by almost as many in the FSTE—14—and are known by 4 FD members each.

For those 7 languages—English, French, German, Arabic, Russian, and Spanish, as well as Hebrew—the Israeli Foreign Service may be said to have ample skills in depth for diplomatic purposes. The only language deficiency in states where Israel has a resident mission is Japanese. The extent of language competence in the FSTE is evident in the data of Table 34b. Ninety per cent speak at least 3 languages; and this includes all but 1 member of the Formal Directorate. There is also an impressive number of speakers of 4 languages or more—almost 70 per cent of FSTE members and almost 80 per cent of the FD. And 5 languages are spoken by as many as 39 per cent of the FSTE, including almost one third of the Formal Directorate. Among the 5 Formal Directorate members who knew only 3 languages, French is the extra language for 4 of them, German for the other. The 4-language group is the Mean—with 13 FD members, slightly less than half of the total.[1]

Eban stands apart in a group of exceptional linguistic skills. While one other FSTE member speaks the same number of languages (7), Eban is a master linguist—in English, French, German, Spanish, Hebrew, Arabic, and Persian. Only Sharett, perhaps, was his equal—superior in some languages, inferior in others.

Technical Élite members displayed a variety of occupational interests before entry into the Foreign Service—in a few cases, concomitant with their diplomatic career (see Table 35).

Eleven persons engaged in university teaching, among them 5 Formal Directorate members. Eytan was a Lecturer in Philology at Queen's College, Oxford, from 1933 to 1946; Kohn was Associate Professor of International Relations at the Hebrew University from 1952 until his death in 1961—at the same time that he served as Political Adviser to the Foreign Minister; Lourie lectured in Law at Witwatersrand University in South Africa from 1928 to 1932; Gazit was a part-time lecturer

---

[1] They fall into three language patterns. For 6 persons the extra languages are German and French in that order (Avner, Avriel, Eytan, Kohn, Rafael, and Bartur); for all, German was the mother tongue. For 3 persons the extra languages are Arabic and French in that order (Danin, Hillel, and Shiloah); only for Hillel was Arabic the mother tongue. For 2 persons, Bitan and Yahil, both born in Czechoslovakia, the extra languages are German and Czech in that order. The 2 South African-born members of the group do not fit a pattern in this respect: Lourie's extra languages are French and German, and Comay's are Dutch and Afrikaans.

TABLE 35

FOREIGN SERVICE TECHNICAL ÉLITE 1948–1968

Other Occupations

Occupation	Technical Élite Members	Formal Directorate Members
Academic		
University	11	5
Other Teaching	5	1
Commercial	14	4
Legal	9	4
Journalism and		
Broadcasting	15	5
Kibbutz Membership	13	7
Knesset Membership	3	2
Labour Movement	8	4
Military	5	—
Organizational		
(Administrative)		
Work	6	3
Other Government		
Branches	21	5
Work for Other		
Governments	5	1
Miscellaneous	5	—

at the Hebrew University from 1946 to 1948; and Tekoah was a Teaching Assistant at Harvard in 1947–8. Among those who served briefly in the Foreign Service, Gordon was a Professor of Law at Fuad University in Cairo from 1935 to 1944; Meron was Lecturer in Economics at the Tel Aviv School of Law and Economics from 1949 to 1953, and earlier in the Mannheim *Hochschule* for Economics; and Biran became Director of the Government Department of Antiquities in 1961 when he left the Service; Eylan lectured in Russian studies at a Canadian university in 1947–8; and Darom was Lecturer in Law at the University of Santiago, Chile, from 1941 to 1948. Five Technical Élite members taught in primary, secondary, or adult schools—Darom in Chile, Shiloah in Baghdad, Y. Shimoni, Arokh, and Ben-Dor in Israel, the last at the élite Reali School in Haifa from 1932 to 1948.

No less than 14 persons had commercial experience, from small private firms (Chelouche) to banking (Meron), to *Histadrut* enterprises—Koor industries (Bitan, Remez) and *Solel Boneh* (Remez, Bentsur, and Evron). Another Formal Directorate member, Fischer, headed an agricultural development firm from 1930 to 1941.

Nine persons practised law, among them 4 FD members: Comay and

Lourie in South Africa, 1931–40 and 1927–33 respectively; Elyashiv in the Soviet Union from 1928 to 1934; and Najar in Cairo, 1933–47. In addition, Darom practised law in Chile from 1941 to 1948, Meron in Germany, 1932–3, and Pratt, Schneerson, and Goitein in Israel, between 1932 and 1953; the last became a Supreme Court Justice in 1953.

Journalism and Broadcasting occupied the attention of 15 TE members at some stage. A few were newspapermen abroad—Elath in Beirut from 1931 to 1934, Dagan and Leshem in Czechoslovakia, 1935–9 and 1948 respectively, and Eylan in London, 1939–41 and 1944–7. Some were transients—Levavi for *Davar* in 1936 and Shiloah for the *Palestine Post* in 1932–3. Some were associated with the Press longer—Arnon and Hyman with the *Palestine Post*, Goitein with the *Palestine Bulletin*, and Tsur with *Ha'olam* and *Ha'aretz*. One was a specialist on Arabic programmes for *Kol Yisrael*—Bar-Haim, as Head of Arabic Broadcasts from 1948 to 1960. Katz was Director of *Kol Yisrael* in 1946–7 and was *Tzahal* spokesman in 1948–9. And Yahil was Chairman of the Israel Broadcasting Authority from 1965 onwards, after completing a tour as Director-General of the Foreign Ministry.

Thirteen Technical Élite members belonged to a *kibbutz*, some for a year or two (Remez, Ruppin, E. Shimoni), some for 4 or 5 years (Eshel, Hillel, Y. Shimoni), Avidan and Rafael for 7 years, Bartur for 9 years, and the rest for a decade or more—Avriel since 1940, Bitan from 1939 to 1952, Levin from 1938 to 1952, and Yahil from 1929 to 1939. This included one fourth of the Formal Directorate (7 of 28) and 2 Directors-General, Rafael and Yahil.

Three persons were Members of the *Knesset*—Avriel from 1955 to 1957, between diplomatic assignments, and Hillel and Remez before entry into the Foreign Service, from 1953 to 1959 and 1956 to 1957 respectively. Hillel was later (1969) to join the Cabinet as Minister of Police.

The Labour Movement claimed the attention of 8 Technical Élite members, all but 1 before they joined the Foreign Service. Bitan and Evron held the important, quasi-diplomatic post of *Histadrut* Representative to the United States, 1952–5 and 1955–9 respectively. Among the other Formal Directorate members, Elyashiv was Secretary of the Tel Aviv Labour Council from 1934 to 1937 and a member of the *Histadrut* Executive (*Va'ad ha-po'el*) from 1937 to 1948, the last year as Director of a *Histadrut* School as well. Shiloah headed the Department of Arab Affairs of the *Histadrut* from 1933 to 1936. And Yahil held posts with the Haifa and Tel Aviv Labour Councils from 1939 to 1945, as well as a brief period, 1950–1, as Head of the *Histadrut* Immigration Department. Avidan, Doron, and Levin also devoted some years to the Labour Movement.

From the Military came 5 persons to the Foreign Service Technical Élite—Avidar, who had held command posts in *Tzahal*; Remez, the first OC, Israel Air Force, 1948–54; Harel, from the Army Medical Service; Lorch, who was Head of *Tzahal*'s Historical Section; and Michael, who had held senior army posts.

Six persons held high organizational or administrative posts, most of them after leaving the Foreign Service, and all in the educational–cultural field: Eban was President of the Weizmann Institute of Science from 1958 to 1968; Elath and Harman served in succession as President of the Hebrew University, from 1961 to 1967 and since 1967; Remez was Administrative Director of the Weizmann Institute in 1959–60; Yahil was Director of the Israel Foundation for Cultural Relations with World Jewry from 1964 to 1968; and Yuval was Assistant Director of the short-lived National Defence College from 1963 to 1965.

The largest number of FSTE members (21) held positions in other branches of the Israeli bureaucracy. The strongest link was with the Prime Minister's Office, in which 12 persons served. Avriel and Herzog were each Director-General, in 1951–2 and since 1965 respectively. Palmon, Divon, and Lubrani served in succession as Adviser on Arab Affairs to the Prime Minister, 1949–53, 1954–60, and 1960–3 (Lubrani had been Assistant Adviser on Arab Affairs from 1957 to 1960; he was also Assistant DG in the Prime Minister's Office in 1963 and Head of the Prime Minister's Bureau, 1963–5). Ben-Dor was Deputy Director-General of the Prime Minister's Office from 1963 to 1966. Others who served in that Ministry were Alon, Evron, Z. Harman, Hillel, A. Kidron, and Ruppin. Two men held key positions in economic ministries—Avriel as Director-General, Finance, in 1952–3 and Golan as DG, Commerce and Industry, from 1966 to 1969 (after various senior posts in Finance and the Bank of Israel). Ben-Dor, Golan, and Evron also served in the Defence Ministry, the last as Head of the Defence Minister's Bureau in 1954–5; Ben-Dor also served in the Ministry of Education and Culture.

Senior posts in other Government offices were held by the following: Avidar as DG, Labour Ministry, 1958–60, and Head of the Corporation Authority, Finance Ministry, 1966–8; Bar-Haim as Head, Department of Arabic Broadcasts, *Kol Yisrael*, 1948–60; A. Harman as Assistant Director, State of Israel Information Office, 1948–9; Herzog as Head, Department of Christian Affairs, Religious Affairs Ministry, 1948–54; Katz as Government Secretary, 1958–62, and Chairman of *Yad Vashem* since 1967. Eban was a special case, moving from the highest echelon of the Foreign Service to the Cabinet in 1959 and later, in 1966, to the post of Foreign Minister. Others who served in governmental branches outside the Foreign Service were Biran (District Commissioner in Jerusalem, 1949–55) and Meroz (Food Controller's Office).

A few FSTE members had worked for other Governments: Dagan for the Czech Government-in-Exile in London and then in Prague, from 1939 to 1949; Leshem also for the Czech Government, from 1945 to 1948; Darom as Director of Prisons in Chile from 1934 to 1939 and then as Legal Adviser to the Chile Ministry of Labour; Meron in the German Administrative and Legal Service; and A. Kidron, Meroz, and Shiloah briefly in the Mandatory Government.

Miscellaneous occupations included Evron (the Joint Distribution Committee), Z. Harman (social work in London and Jerusalem), and Tov (Head of a Buenos Aires Medical Centre, 1936–45).

Taken as a group, the Foreign Service Technical Élite has had vast experience, requiring a multiplicity of skills.

(b) DECISION-MAKING INNER CIRCLE

To dissect an inner decision-making group in foreign policy is a hazardous enterprise. There are no universal and precise criteria for measuring the influence of an individual who is consulted on a specific decision. Moreover, influence will vary with many changing conditions: time—viewed, in this inquiry, over a period of twenty years; type of issue or issue-area of policy; crisis, as compared with an initiated decision; the person who is Foreign Minister; the context of the decision-process; the relationship between Prime Minister and Foreign Minister and between the Foreign Office and Defence Ministry acting as bureaucratic pressures on policy; and many other variables relevant to decision-making, notably personnel, governmental structures, pressure groups, environmental stimuli, and perceptions—all interacting with one another. Thus any construct of a Decision-Making Inner Circle is subject to correction, with a high probability of error. It is at best an approximation, based upon shared insights from persons with lengthy membership in the Israeli Foreign Service and an analytic bent of mind. The construct is also subject to the vital *caveat* that very few Israeli decisions—even those of an implementing character—were made solely or primarily by the Foreign Ministry. Members of the Parallel Technical Élite played important roles in the day-to-day decision process, especially within the Military–Security and Economic–Developmental Issue-Areas but also in the primary area of Foreign Office concern, Political–Diplomatic issues.

With these constraints in mind we may proceed to an overview of the Decision-Making Inner Circle within Israel's Foreign Service from 1948 to 1968. Having examined the Formal Directorate of 28 and the larger Technical Élite of 87, we seek what one senior civil servant termed 'the real "in-group" close to the Minister, the people whom he consults on a wide range of issues'. Thus persons who are consulted on matters pertaining to their specific Department or area of jurisdiction—but nothing else—are not included in the Decision-Making Inner Circle: it is the broader consultation group which is so designated.

No attempt is made to scale the influence of members of this Inner

Circle—except to distinguish a Core Group of 'greater' influence from Others in the Circle. One object is to uncover the persons whom the different Foreign Ministers consulted during their tenure. Another is to determine whether there was a *continuing inner group* for the twenty-year period as a whole. Some of the persons were influential throughout, others for a more limited time when one Foreign Minister held office. Mrs. Meir's tenure for almost a decade is divided into two for convenience. The accompanying analysis will attempt to indicate more precisely roles and periods of influence.

Israel's first Foreign Minister, Sharett, held that portfolio for eight

TABLE 36

DECISION-MAKING INNER CIRCLE OF ISRAEL'S FOREIGN OFFICE
1948–1968

Foreign Minister	Core Group	Others	
Sharett	Eban	Avriel	Najar
1948–1956	Eytan	Comay	Navon
	Kohn	Danin	Rafael
	Shiloah	Elath	E. Sasson
		Evron	Shek
		Fischer	Tsur
		Herzog	
		Kollek	
		Lourie	
Meir	Eban	Avriel	
a. 1956–1960	Eytan	Comay	
	Fischer	Danin	
	Herzog	Gazit	
	Kohn	E. Sasson	
	Levavi	Tekoah	
	Najar		
	Shiloah		
b. 1961–1965	Avriel	Comay	
	Herzog	Danin	
	Levavi	Dinitz	
	Yahil	Gazit	
		Harman	
Eban	Bitan	Avner	
1966–1968	Comay	Chelouche	
	Lourie	Evron	
	Rafael	Gazit	
	Tekoah	Harman	
		Levavi	

years. During his tenure the number of persons consulted over a wide range of Foreign Office decisions was large—19. Yet this is deceptive: certain persons were in the Decision-Making Inner Circle very briefly; and the continuing Core Group was small. Four persons served as Sharett's principal advisers throughout the period 1948–56 and exerted the greatest overall influence on Foreign Office decisions among the Foreign Service Technical Élite: Eban, who held two strategic posts simultaneously, Ambassador to the US and Permanent Representative to the UN; Kohn as general Political Adviser; Shiloah as Adviser on the Middle East and, for part of the time, as Minister (No. 2) to Washington; and Eytan as Director-General of the Ministry.

To this compact group may be added a dozen others. Some had a special area of influence, though they were consulted more generally. And many were members of Sharett's Inner Circle for part of the time only, as indicated below:

Avriel	East Europe	1948–51
Comay	Commonwealth	1948–53
Danin	Arab Affairs	throughout
Elath	US and UK	throughout
Fischer	West Europe	throughout
Herzog	US	1954–6
Kollek	US	1948–52
Lourie	Commonwealth	1953–6
Najar	West Europe	1955–6
Rafael	UN	throughout
E. Sasson	Middle East	throughout
Tsur	France	1953–6

There were also three men who participated in the Inner Circle as Sharett's Private Secretary or Head of Bureau: Evron (1950–1), Navon (1951–2), and Shek (1953–6).

It is noteworthy that some members of Sharett's Inner Circle were abroad when they were consulted on a wide range of issues: from the Core Group, Eban throughout and Shiloah in the second phase (1953–1956); from the Others, Elath, Fischer, and Sasson for almost the entire period, Avriel, Kollek, and Rafael during the first phase (1948–53), and Tsur during the second. Thus 8 of the 16 members were 'in the field' all or part of the time they belonged to Sharett's Decision-Making Inner Circle.

If the Sharett period is divided into two, the Decision-Making Inner Circle consists of 12 persons until 1953 and 13 thereafter, excluding the men on his personal staff: 1948–53—the Core Group of 4 and Avriel, Comay, Danin, Elath, Fischer, Kollek, Rafael, and Sasson; 1953–6— the Core Group of 4 and Danin, Elath, Fischer, Sasson, Herzog, Lourie, Najar, Rafael, and Tsur.

During Mrs. Meir's early years as Foreign Minister the Core Group doubled. The original 4 (Eban, Eytan, Kohn, and Shiloah) retained major influence and their formal position (Shiloah returned from Washington in 1957 to the post of Adviser on Special Subjects). But the group was expanded to include Fischer, who assumed (formal) responsibility for Western Europe as Assistant Director-General, from 1957 to 1960; Herzog, who succeeded Shiloah in Washington in 1957 and continued his special role in Israel–US relations; Levavi, briefly as Assistant DG for Eastern Europe, 1957–8, though he had exerted influence in this region from the outset, and Najar, also briefly, in 1957–8.

Among the Others, Danin and Sasson continued to exert (lesser) influence on Arab and Middle East Affairs, and Comay returned from Canada to advise on the UK–Commonwealth area of policy. Yet there were additions to this group: Avriel, who returned to the Foreign Service to exert profound influence on Israel's Africa policy, among others, in Mrs. Meir's first phase, as Ambassador to Ghana; Gazit, as Political Secretary to an inexperienced Foreign Minister from 1957 to 1960; and Tekoah, as Director of Armistice Affairs from 1954 to 1958.

Only 3 among the 14 persons in the Decision-Making Inner Circle of the late 1950s (less than half as many as in the Sharett period) were abroad at the time of membership—Eban, Herzog, and Avriel. Others like Tekoah ceased to qualify when they were posted abroad, in his case to the UN, Brazil, and the Soviet Union from 1958 to 1965.

The Core Group was reduced from 8 to 4 in Mrs. Meir's second phase as Foreign Minister; death had removed Shiloah (1959) and Kohn (1961); Eban had moved to the High Policy Élite; and Eytan, Fischer, and Najar were abroad—influential in their specific areas (Paris, Rome, and Brussels–Common Market, respectively) but no longer Core Group members of the Inner Circle. Only Herzog and Levavi remained, the former in Ottawa, the latter returned from Belgrade. Two persons now entered the Core Group: Yahil as Director-General, recently returned from Sweden, and Avriel, back from Ghana, to direct Israel's expanding presence in Africa as Assistant Director-General.

Among the Others, Comay held the depreciated but still important post of Representative to the UN; Danin continued to advise on Arab affairs; Harman succeeded Eban in the perennially-significant Washington Embassy; and Gazit, as Minister to the US, continued to exercise influence as Shiloah and Herzog did before him. Finally, the Foreign Minister's Political Secretary from 1963 to 1965, Dinitz, participated in the decision process at the highest level within the Ministry.

During that period no less than 4 of the 9 Inner Circle members were 'in the field': Comay at the UN, Harman and Gazit in Washington, and Herzog in Ottawa; this was the highest proportion of all four periods. And if Eytan and Najar are included by virtue of the importance of their posts the ratio would rise to 6 of 11 Inner Circle Members.

There was a marked change in the Core Group with the coming of Eban to the Foreign Ministry at the beginning of 1966: none of the 4 members in the early 1960s remained in the group. Avriel was posted to Rome. Herzog moved to the Prime Minister's Office—a key Parallel Technical Élite post—as Director-General in 1965. Yahil had left the Foreign Service in 1964. And, while Levavi remained as DG of the Foreign Office for eighteen months, his influence was in decline. Comay and Lourie returned from the UN and London, respectively, to occupy key positions in Jerusalem. Tekoah, who had become an Adviser after concluding his Moscow assignment, entered the Core group in 1966. So too did Bitan, who took over Avriel's responsibilities for Africa and Herzog's role in relations with the US. And most influential in the Eban period was Rafael, at first as Ambassador-at-Large, a post which he exchanged with Comay in 1967. Then, at the end of that year, he succeeded Levavi as Director-General. Not one of these 5 persons had been in the Core Group of the Decision-Making Inner Circle, though they had been influential in the past.

Among the Others, apart from Levavi, Harman and Gazit continued to exert influence from the Washington Embassy; Gazit, when he returned in 1965, did so on the Middle East as Adviser and later as Assistant DG until 1967. Evron returned to the Inner Circle after fifteen years as Minister in Washington after Gazit. A newcomer was Chelouche, Assistant DG in charge of Economic Affairs but with wider concerns. And Avner returned to his initial regional special interest at the end of 1967, as Assistant DG in charge of Europe following a lengthy tour abroad.

Altogether 15 persons were in the Core Group at some time during the period 1948–68. There were 22 Others but 9 of them were members of the Core Group, too. Thus the Decision-Making Inner Circle comprised a total of 28 persons—6 in the Core Group alone, 13 Others, and 9 who were members of both categories. In broad terms there is a high coincidence between the composition of the Formal Directorate and the Decision-Making Inner Circle: 21 members of the latter were at some time in the Formal Directorate of 28—75 per cent.[1] Yet it is striking that 7 of 28 members of the Formal Directorate were not in the Decision-Making Inner Circle at any time. Moreover, the high (75 per cent) correlation of personnel does not extend to time spent in both

[1] Those who were not in the Formal Directorate are: Dinitz, Elath, Evron, Kollek, Navon, Sasson, and Shek. Four of the 7 were in the Inner Circle as Head of the Foreign Minister's Bureau or his Private Secretary (Dinitz, Evron, Navon, and Shek), though Evron re-entered later from Washington as well. Two men, Kollek and Navon, moved to key Parallel Technical Élite posts in the Prime Minister's Office. And Elath and Sasson held important posts abroad—Washington and London, and Ankara and Rome, respectively.

clubs.[1] Finally, in this context the correlation is deceptive because those FD members who were also in the 'real' Inner Circle were not in that group all the time they held a Formal Directorate post. Nor did their 'real' influence always correlate with their formal position in the hierarchy. The correlation is only a first approximation to overlapping membership in the Formal Directorate and the Decision-Making Inner Circle.

There is one further construct to delineate and explore—the Permanent In-Group. Although derived from the Core Group within the Decision-Making Inner Circle, as noted in Table 36, the two are not identical. The Core Group refers to individuals who are the principal advisers to a specific Foreign Minister during a particular period of time. Some may continue in that role when a new Foreign Minister comes into office—as did the original 4 (Eban, Eytan, Kohn, and Shiloah) in 1956 when Meir replaced Sharett. Yet those 4 were not in the Core Group in the early 1960s or thereafter. Some persons, as noted, may move from Core Group to Others or vice versa, as did Avriel, Comay, Herzog, Levavi, Lourie, Najar, and Tekoah. And there are Others who were in the Core Group briefly, like Bitan and Tekoah in the late 1960s. Not all Core Group members, however, are in the Permanent In-Group of the Decision-Making Inner Circle. The latter is a smaller, more closely-knit group of persons who constitute the continuing dominant figures in the Foreign Office over the period as a whole—though they may be more or less influential in the making of Foreign Office decisions at a point in time.

Of the 15 cumulative Core Group members in Israel's Foreign Service 11 may be designated as members of the Permanent In-Group. Bitan came late to the Foreign Service (1960) and was in the Decision-Making Inner Circle only in the last 2 years. Yahil was a member of the Core Group longer—4 years—but not before he became Director-General in 1960; and he was not identified by his peers as a Permanent In-Group member. Nor was Najar, despite his presence in the Foreign Service uninterruptedly since 1948, including senior positions—Brussels, Rome, Assistant DG—perhaps because he was 'in the field' 14 of the first 20 years. And Tekoah, despite his rapid rise in the Service, attained the highest level of influence in the Foreign Ministry only in the late 1960s.

The Permanent In-Group thus defined comprises the following— Avriel, Comay, Eban, Eytan, Fischer, Herzog, Kohn, Levavi, Lourie, Rafael, and Shiloah. They coalesce into 2 cultural-linguistic groups— Anglo-Saxon and German-educated Central European, the two dominant groups in the Foreign Service. A comparison in depth is offered in

---

[1] Apart from the 7 who were not in the FD, many were in the Inner Circle when they were not Formal Directorate members: Avriel, Fischer, Herzog, Najar, and Tsur in the Sharett period; Avriel, Gazit, and Tekoah in Meir's first phase; Comay, Gazit, and Harman in Meir's second phase; and Harman in the Eban phase.

Table 37 and the accompanying analysis. It must be emphasized once more that most Israeli foreign policy decisions, even of the implementing type, involved persons, pressure groups, and bureaucratic structures beyond the Foreign Office, often decisively.

The Israel Foreign Office Permanent In-Group from 1948 to 1968 comprised 11 persons, with 2 predominant cultural-linguistic-educational strands: Anglo-Saxon and Germanic (Central European). All In-Group members were Double Originals: that is, they joined the Service in 1948 and held Technical Élite posts at once. In fact, all but Herzog came to the Foreign Office from the Jewish Agency Political Department.

Continuity from the pre-State period was accentuated by the durability of the In-Group's association with the Foreign Service: 4 persons have been professional diplomats uninterruptedly since 1948, really 5, for Rafael should be included (all are still in the Service in 1970); 3 men were removed by death—Shiloah in 1959, Kohn in 1961, and Fischer in 1965; Herzog has been in the Parallel Technical Élite since 1965 in a key foreign policy post, Director-General of the Prime Minister's Office; so too was Avriel for part of the time he was not in the Foreign Service; and Eban retained a close association in the post-1959 period as a member of the High Policy Élite and, from 1966, as Foreign Minister. Thus they may be regarded as the *Permanent* In-Group, though other persons within the Decision-Making Inner Circle exerted as much or more influence on specific decisions or at certain stages of a decision process. The In-Group is a concept applied to the twenty-year period as a whole.

One member of the Anglo-Saxon group (Eytan) was born in Germany but he was educated at Oxford and was a don there for thirteen years before settling in Israel. Similarly, Levavi, though born in Russia, received much of his education in German; he writes most readily in German and is included in the Central European group. The terms 'Anglo-Saxon' and 'Germanic' are not rigidly derived from the formal data. Rather, they symbolize predominant influence on thought, manner of expression, and behaviour.

None of the 10 (Shiloah was a *sabra*) arrived in Palestine at the formative age of adolescence or earlier: Herzog was the youngest at 18. All the other Anglo-Saxons were over 30. All except Herzog had completed their basic university studies abroad. And all except Lourie had served in the British or Commonwealth armed forces during the Second World War. They were, in short, mature men when they settled in Israel, reflecting their Anglo-Saxon background in speech, manner, thought process, and behaviour. It remained conspicuously so throughout the twenty years and beyond. The Central European group, too, arrived after their studies in German-language universities, though

Name	*Years in Foreign Service*	*Date of Birth*	*Place of Birth*	*Arrival in Israel*	*Age on Arrival*
COMAY	20	1908	South Africa	1946	38
EBAN	11 (1948–59)	1915	South Africa	1946	31
EYTAN	20	1910	Germany	1946	36
HERZOG	17 (1948–65)	1921	Ireland	1939	18
LOURIE	20	1903	South Africa	1948	45
AVRIEL	14 (1948–51, 1957–68)	1917	Austria	1940	23
KOHN	13 (1948–61)	1894–1961	Germany	1934	40
LEVAVI	20	1912	Russia	1932	20
RAFAEL	19 (1948–64, 1965–8)	1913	Germany	1934	21
FISCHER	17 (1948–65)	1903–65	Belgium	1930	27
SHILOAH	11 (1948–59)	1909–59	Israel	—	—

In-Group

Years in Political Department	Military Service, Years	Higher Education: Degree, University, Field	Languages	Other Israel Government Posts
2	S. African Army 6	B.A. Cape Town LL.B. Cape Town LAW	4	—
3	British Army 6	M.A. Cambridge ORIENTAL STUDIES	7	Minister, 1959–
2	British Army 1	M.A. Oxford PHILOLOGY	4	—
—	Haganah 3	LL.B. Hebrew U. LAW PH.D. Ottawa LAW	3	Ministry of Religious Affairs 1948–54 DG, Prime Minister's Office 1965–
9	—	LL.B. Cape Town LAW M.A. Cambridge LAW	4	—
5	—	Vienna HISTORY	4	DG, PMO 1951–2 DG, Finance Ministry 1952–3 Member of *Knesset* 1955–7
14	—	LL.D. Heidelberg LAW	4	—
10	—	M.A. Hebrew U. PHIL. (Danzig, Heidelberg)	5	—
5	British Army 1	Berlin LAW + ECON.	4	—
1	Free French Army 4	B.A. NAT. SCI.	3	—
12	Haganah 7	B.A. Hebrew U. ORIENTAL STUDIES	4	—

Levavi was to complete his degree in Jerusalem. The Anglo-Saxons arrived late, in the 1946–8 period, except for Herzog (1939). All the Central European group (and Fischer), except Avriel, settled in Israel during the early 1930s. Apart from Kohn, they were much younger than the Anglo-Saxons when they arrived—in their early twenties. Yet they too retained the formative influence of their early years.

None was predominantly Israeli in culture and background. Nor was Fischer, the sole representative of French-language-and-culture within the Permanent In-Group. Only Shiloah was Israeli by birth, mother tongue, education—and even military service. Not by accident was he the leading specialist on the Arabs and the Middle East within the In-Group and the larger Decision-Making Inner Circle.

All members of the Permanent In-Group except Herzog served in the Political Department, but there is a marked difference in duration. Only Lourie among the Anglo-Saxons had more than 3 years service, while all in the Central European group had at least 5 years, with Kohn and Levavi a decade or more. In this respect Fischer was akin to the Anglo-Saxon group, and Shiloah, with 12 years service, the Central European group.

That contrast is related to their Military Service. All the Anglo-Saxons—except Lourie, who was in the Political Department at the time—had some army service in the Second World War. Two of them, Comay and Eban, were thus engaged for 6 years. Of the Central Europeans, however, only Rafael had any military service—and only for a year, in the British Army. Compared with the Foreign Service Technical Élite as a whole, with its near-equal participation in the British Army and *Haganah*, 4 of the 5 members of the Anglo-Saxon and Central European groups with military service were in the British (or other Commonwealth) Army; only Herzog spent some time in the *Yishuv* army; Shiloah did so earlier; and Fischer was in the Free French Forces.

There is a marked difference, too, between the predominant Foreign Service groups in the realm of higher education. Among the Central Europeans, Kohn had an LL.D. from Heidelberg, and Levavi an M.A. from the Hebrew University; but Avriel and Rafael had only two years of higher studies each, at Vienna and Berlin Universities. The Anglo-Saxons have a plethora of degrees: Eban and Eytan an M.A. from Cambridge and Oxford respectively; and the others two degrees each —all of them in Law. Fischer and Shiloah, too, were university graduates, with a B.A. in Natural Sciences and in Oriental Studies respectively. Most of the Permanent In-Group members have (or had) a knowledge of 4 languages—Hebrew, English, and many with French and German as well; only Eban and Shiloah knew Arabic. Fischer and Herzog, however, were confined to Hebrew, English, and French, while Eban commands 7 languages.

The predominance of two distinctive cultural-linguistic groups in the Diplomatic Establishment—Anglo Saxon and German-educated Central European—has been a cardinal feature of Israel's Foreign Service since 1948. Yet they are unequal in influence and they exhibit marked differences. The Anglo-Saxons are self-consciously Anglo-Saxon. The Central Europeans do not identify themselves with anything German —culture, language, society; on the contrary, that Germanic link is anathema. Moreover, English is a powerful and persistent bond among the Anglo-Saxons; German is not for the Central Europeans. The Anglo-Saxons often lapse into their mother tongue in private conversation and in small talk; the Central Europeans rarely do so. This linguistic attachment was accentuated by the fact that the Anglo-Saxons arrived in Israel later and were therefore not as completely merged into Hebrew and its culture. Beyond all this is a psychological advantage ascribed to the Anglo-Saxons. English is the principal language of contemporary diplomacy and they have a superior knowledge of the medium. Finally, and perhaps most important, the Central Europeans behave—or consciously try to behave—as Anglo-Saxons. It is the model to which Israeli Foreign Service members generally aspire. In that large sense, too, the Anglo-Saxons have dominated the Decision-Making Inner Circle, the Technical Élite, and the Foreign Service as a whole.

This pivotal fact contrasted sharply with the Parallel Technical Élite, especially the Defence Establishment. Indeed that was an accentuating source of friction between the Foreign and Defence Ministries throughout the period 1948–68. To the analysis of Israel's Parallel Technical Élite in foreign policy we may now turn.

CHAPTER 18

The Parallel Technical Élite

The Parallel Technical Élite in Israeli foreign policy comprises the following categories:
Chief of Staff
Director of *Ha-Mosad*
Director of Military Intelligence
Chief of General Staff Branch
Commerce and Industry Ministry
    Director-General
    Director of Foreign Trade
Defence Ministry
    Deputy Minister
    Director-General
    Director, Department for International Co-operation
    Head of Defence Minister's Bureau
    Military Attaché[1]
    Director of Purchasing Mission[2]
    Director of Defence Research
Finance Ministry
    Deputy Minister
    Director-General
    Director of Fuel Authority
Prime Minister's Office
    Director-General
    Political Secretary
    Military Secretary
Secretary to the Government

(a) PROFILE

The Parallel Technical Élite consists of 57 persons. In the initial presentation (Table 38) they are undifferentiated as to influence. Throughout, the focus will be on life pattern and career.

[1] To the United States throughout and to France from 1953 to 1959.
[2] In Western Europe.

TABLE 38

MEMBERSHIP IN THE ISRAELI PARALLEL TECHNICAL ÉLITE
1948–1968[1]

	Year of Entry into Parallel Technical Élite	Number of Years in Parallel Technical Élite
Amit, M.	1956	9
Argov, N.[a]	1948	10
Arnon, Y.	1955	13
Avigur, S.	1949	1
Bar-Lev, H.	1963	4
Be'eri, I.[b]	1948	2
Ben-Arzi, E.	1948	1
Ben-David, H.[c]	1958	5
Ben-Natan, A.[d]	1956	9
Bergman, D.	1952	14
Dayan, M.[e]	1953	5
Dinstein, Z.	1953	4
Dori, Y.	1948	2
Eskkol, L.	1948	1
Galili, I.[g]	1948	1
Geva, Y.	1967	1
Givli, B.	1950	4
Glikman, J.	1953	5
Harel, I.	1950	13
Harkabi, Y.	1955	4
Herzog, H.	1948	8
Horowitz, D.[h]	1948	20
Karni, N.	1965	3

a   He died in 1958.
b   He died in 1957.
c   He was also a member of the Foreign Service Technical Élite as Ambassador to
    Ethiopia, 1967–8. He died there in 1968.
d   He was also a member of the FSTE as Ambassador to West Germany from 1965
    to the beginning of 1970. (He continues to be in the FSTE as Ambassador to
    France.)
e   He was also a member of the High Policy Élite during that period (1953–8), from
    1959 to 1964 and again since 1967, as noted in ch. 10 above.
f   He was also a member of the HPE from 1951 until his death in 1969.
g   He was also a member of the HPE from 1966.
h   He was also a member of the HPE for 18 of the 20 years.

[1] Key: PTE   Parallel Technical Élite
       FSTE   Foreign Service Technical Élite
       HPE   High Policy Élite
Some persons continued to hold a PTE post beyond 1968. For example, Arnon re-
mained as DG, Finance Ministry, until the end of 1969, as Weizman did in the post of
Chief of the General Staff Branch. However, the calculation of 'Number of Years in
PTE' is based upon the period 1948–68 only. The 'Number of Years in PTE' may err
slightly: six months or more of any year in a PTE post is calculated as a full year.

TABLE 38 (CONT.)

	Year of Entry into	Number of Years in
		Parallel Technical Élite
Kashti, M.	1965	3
Kimche, S.	1962	4
Kollek, T.[i]	1952	13
Kosloff, Y.	1949	10
Laskov, H.	1955	4
Lifshitz, S.	1953	1
Limon, M.	1959	9
Lior, Y.	1965	3
Makleff, M.	1952	2
Nahmias, Y.	1953	4
Navon, Y.[j]	1952	11
Ne'eman, M.	1949	3
Nishri, E.	1956	3
Penn, I.	1959	3
Peres, S.[k]	1953	12
Prihar, Y.	1961	2
Rabin, Y.[l]	1960	7
Raviv, Y.	1967	1
Ron, R.	1964	2
Sapir, P.[m]	1949	6
Sharef, Z.[n]	1948	9
Shikler, Y.	1958	4
Shind, Z.	1952	1
Syrkin, S.	1953	2
Talbar, A.	1966	2
Tsour, M.	1955	13
Uzay, Y.	1962	6
Yadin, Y.[o]	1948	4
Yafeh, A.	1965	3
Yariv, A.	1957	8
Yisraeli, H.	1956	12
Weizman, E.	1966	2
Zorea, M.	1958	1
Zur, Z.	1959	5

i He was also a member of the FSTE from 1948 to 1950, as Head, US Department, Foreign Ministry.
j He was also a member of the FSTE from 1951 to 1952 as Private Secretary to the Foreign Minister.
k He was also a member of the HPE from 1955 to 1965.
l He was also a member of the HPE from 1964 to 1968.
m He was also a member of the HPE from 1955 to 1968 (and continues in that select group).
n He was also a member of the HPE from 1966 to 1968 (and continued in that group until the end of 1969).
o He was also a member of the HPE from 1948 to 1952.

There are 3 members of the PTE about whom sufficient information was unavailable: Y. Kedar, Y. Nisiahu, and K. Salmon, all from the Military Establishment. There are 6 others who were members of the two Technical Élites; they were analysed within the Foreign Service Technical Élite where they spent more of their time in the public service: J. Avidar, E. Avriel, D. Golan, Y. Herzog, K. Katz, and U. Lubrani. These 9 persons are not included in the total of 57 PTE members specified above.

Membership in the Parallel Technical Élite was distributed as follows during the period 1948–68:

Chief of Staff	8
Director of *Ha-Mosad*	3
Director of Military Intelligence	5
Chief of General Staff Branch	10
Commerce and Industry Ministry	7
Defence Ministry	27
Finance Ministry	6
Prime Minister's Office	8
Secretary to the Government	3
	77[1]

[1] The total of 77 posts includes 14 persons who held a second PTE position and 3 who held 3 PTE posts each:

Bar-Lev: Chief of General Staff Branch and Chief of Staff.
Ben-Natan: Director-General, Defence Ministry, and Chief, Military Purchasing Mission, Western Europe.
Dayan: Chief of General Staff Branch and Chief of Staff.
Herzog, H.: Director of Military Intelligence and Military Attaché to the United States.
Laskov: Chief of General Staff Branch and Chief of Staff.
Limon: Head, Department for International Co-operation, Defence Ministry, and Chief, Military Purchasing Mission, Western Europe. (He was also Navy Commander.)
Makleff: Chief of General Staff Branch and Chief of Staff.
Peres: Deputy Minister of Defence and Director-General, Defence Ministry.
Rabin: Chief of General Staff Branch and Chief of Staff.
Sapir: Director-General, Defence and Finance Ministries.
Sharef: Director-General, Prime Minister's Office, and Secretary to the Government.
Tsour: Director-General, Commerce and Industry Ministry, and Director of Foreign Trade.
Yadin: Chief of Operations and Chief of Staff.
Yariv: Director of Military Intelligence and Military Attaché to the United States.
Amit: Chief of General Staff Branch, Director of Military Intelligence, and Director of *Ha-Mosad*.
Dinstein: Deputy Minister of Defence and Finance, and Director of Foreign Trade.
Zur: Chief of General Staff Branch, Chief of Staff and Assistant to the Defence Minister

Thus there were 57 persons holding 77 PTE posts.

The average period of time spent in the Parallel Technical Élite was 5·6 years. Of the 57 members, 17 were marginal—9 with 1 year's service and 8 with 2 years or less. There were 11 long-term members, that is, each with 10 or more years in the PTE.[1] This group reveals a striking immobility in role: all but 2 of the 11 were in the same post throughout —and those 2 remained in the same Ministry. Only 2 of the 11 durable PTE members were professional military officers: Argov (Military Secretary to the Prime Minister) and Yisraeli (Head of the Defence Minister's Bureau). The long-term civilian members held a variety of administrative posts: DG, Finance; DG, Defence; DG, Commerce and Industry; DG, Prime Minister's Office; Director of Defence Research; Director of *Ha-Mosad*; Governor of the Bank of Israel; Director of Fuel Authority; Political Secretary to the Prime Minister; Deputy Minister of Defence; and Head, Defence Minister's Bureau. Thus the two crucial traits of the 11 are *fixity of individual role* and *diversity* of PTE *posts* held by them as a group.

The Defence Establishment (including Security) dominated the Parallel Technical Élite, accounting for almost three quarters of the posts—56 of 77. The two economic ministries—Finance, and Commerce and Industry—account for 13; and the Prime Minister's Office (excluding the Military Secretary) and the Government Secretary account for the remaining 7. The predominance of the military is evident in the fact that half of all PTE members (29 of 57) were in the professional military service, that is, they spent many years as high-ranking officers of *Tzahal*.

There is considerable *vertical* mobility within the Israeli decision-making élites concerned with foreign policy: 9 of the 18 High Policy Élite members were also in the PTE, some *successively* in time (Eshkol, Galili, Sapir, Sharef), and others *simultaneously* (Dayan, Horowitz, Peres, Rabin, and Yadin). They include 4 of the 9 HPE Inner Circle members (Dayan, Eshkol, Peres, Sapir). Among the 9 combined HPE-PTE members all but 2 were in the Defence Establishment.[2] There was also substantial *horizontal* mobility: 12 of the 57 PTE members had close links with the Foreign Office. To these may be added 8 other PTE members whose work was enmeshed with Israeli diplomats abroad— Military Attachés and Chiefs of Military Purchasing Missions. There was, in short, considerable lateral linkage between the two branches of the Foreign Policy Technical Élite.[3]

[1] The period of 10 or more years is widely used in the social sciences to designate 'long-term'. It may be noted that four other persons with 9 years in the PTE were very influential: Amit, Ben-Natan, Limon, and Sharef.

[2] Dayan, Rabin, and Yadin were 'professional' soldiers, the first two for most of their adult life. Eshkol, Galili, Peres, and Sapir held Defence Ministry administrative posts, either as Deputy Minister or Director-General or both. Only Horowitz and Sharef were 'civilians' (non-Defence Establishment) throughout, though Eshkol and Sapir fall into this type as well.

[3] Of the 5 joint members of the FSTE–PTE, all of whom were analysed within the

In the 1948–50 period there were 15 members of the Parallel Technical Élite: 6 were members for 3 years or less, 5 stayed on for 5 to 9 years, and 4 were long-term members (10 years or more).[1] As a whole the 1948–50 group remained prominent in public life: 5 were to serve in the High Policy Élite and others have been in parliament, public service enterprises, business, and universities.

There is no exact counterpart to the Formal Directorate of the Foreign Service Technical Élite, for the PTE is not a single-ministry, homogeneous group of persons. Nevertheless, there are comparable decision-making posts in the Parallel Technical Élite; these are designated in Table 39 as Formal Directorate-level (FD-level).

A majority of Formal Directorate-level members attained that rank from non-PTE posts. Leaving aside the 7 original (1948) FD-level members from the group of 29, only 4 held a PTE post before moving to the FD-level. All the other 18 moved to an FD-level post from outside the PTE as defined here. However, 4 persons, once at the Formal Directorate-level, moved laterally to another FD-level post:

Amit: from Director of Military Intelligence to Director of *Ha-Mosad*.

Peres: from Director-General, Defence Ministry to Deputy Minister of Defence.

Sapir: from Director-General, Defence Ministry to Director-General, Finance Ministry.

Zur: from an earlier role as Chief of Staff to Assistant to the Defence Minister, i.e. *de facto* Deputy Minister of Defence.

Occupants of the post of Deputy Minister of Defence stand apart from their peers at the FD-level: 3 of the 4 (other than the original member, Galili) came to this post from within the PTE. By contrast, 4 of the Directors-General, Defence Ministry (other than the original member) did not. Nor did the DG, Prime Minister's Office, the Government Secretary, and 1 of the Directors of *Ha-Mosad*.

The rate of change in occupancy of FD-level posts within the Parallel Technical Élite was very high at the outset, and in *Tzahal* throughout. There are also some durable members. Among the 8 original FD-level posts 4 changed hands after a year to eighteen months (Chief of Staff, Director of *Ha-Mosad*, Deputy Minister of Defence, and Director-General, Defence Ministry). The principle of rotation is rooted in *Tzahal*: the average tenure of Chiefs of Staff was slightly less than 3

Foreign Service Technical Élite, 2 held Formal Directorate-level posts in both Technical Élites: Avriel—Assistant DG in the Foreign Office, DG, Finance Ministry, DG, Prime Minister's Office; and Y. Herzog—Assistant DG in the Foreign Office and DG, Prime Minister's Office. A third held an FD-level post in the PTE—Katz, as Secretary to the Government.

[1] The long-term members held the following PTE posts uninterruptedly: Military Secretary to the PM, Director of *Ha-Mosad*, Governor of the Bank of Israel, and Director of the Fuel Authority.

TABLE 39

FORMAL DIRECTORATE-LEVEL OF ISRAEL'S PARALLEL
TECHNICAL ÉLITE 1948–1968

Post	Original PTE Members	Held Other PTE Posts	Did Not Hold Other PTE Posts	Total Number of Posts
Chief of Staff	1		7	8
Director of *Ha-Mosad*	1	1	1	3
Director of Military Intelligence	1	2	2	5
Defence Ministry				
Deputy Minister	1	3	1	5
Director-General	1	1	4	6
Finance Ministry				
Deputy Minister		1		1
Director-General	1	1	1	3
Prime Minister's Office				
Director-General	1		1	2
Secretary to the Government	1		1	2
	8[a](7)	9	18	35[b]

a   Sharef held the posts of DG, Prime Minister's Office, and Secretary to the
     Government simultaneously.
b   Six persons at the Formal Directorate-level of Israel's PTE from 1948 to 1968
     held 2 FD-level posts each:
     Amit: Director of Military Intelligence and Director of *Ha-Mosad*.
     Dinstein: Deputy Minister of Defence and Finance.
     Peres: Director-General, Defence Ministry, and Deputy Minister of Defence.
     Sapir: Director-General, Defence and Finance Ministries.
     Sharef: Director-General, Prime Minister's Office, and Secretary to the
                  Government.
     Zur: Chief of Staff and Assistant to the Defence Minister.
     Thus there were 29 persons at the Formal Directorate-level of the Parallel
     Technical Élite.

years (7 in almost 20 years). Dayan held this post for a shade more than
4 years, and Rabin 4 years; at the other extreme were Dori and Makleff,
about 1½ years each. Three of 5 Deputy Defence Ministers, too, held
that post very briefly—Galili, Avigur, and Dinstein, less than 2 years
each. The overall duration of occupancy of Formal Directorate-level
posts within the PTE was 6·2 years (9 posts over 20 years held by 29
persons). Six persons exceeded the overall average.[1]

[1] Durable occupants of FD-level posts in the PTE were the following:

Arnon as DG, Finance Ministry	1955–69	14 years
Ben-Natan as DG, Defence Ministry	1959–65	6 years
Harel as Director of *Ha-Mosad*	1950–63	13 years
Kollek as DG, Prime Minister's Office	1952–65	13 years

TABLE 40

PARALLEL TECHNICAL ÉLITE 1948–1968

Date of Birth and Age Upon Entry

Date of Birth	Number of Persons	Average Age of Entry into PTE	Formal Directorate-level Number of Persons	Average Age of Entry to FD-level
Pre-1900	6	52	4	50·5
1901–1910	8	44·8	4	43·0
1911–1920	18	38	13	38·6
1921–1930	25	37·1	8	37·4
Totals and Mean Averages	57	40	29	41·9

Among the 57 members of the PTE 6 were born before 1900: 3 of them (Dori, Eshkol, and Horowitz) were Double Originals, that is, they held Formal Directorate-level posts from the outset; and Eshkol and Horowitz also spent many years in the High Policy Élite. The average age of the 4 pre-1900 FD-level persons was 50·5 when they attained that rank. None was born after 1930. But the 1921–30 group accounts for almost 44 per cent of the total PTE. Yet, of these, only 32 per cent attained FD-level posts. They comprise 3 Chiefs of Staff (Bar-Lev, Rabin, and Zur), both Deputy Ministers of Defence (Dinstein and Peres), DG, Defence Ministry (Ben-Natan), and 2 Directors of Military Intelligence (Amit and Harkabi).

Almost one-third of the PTE members was born in the 1911–20 decade, and 13 of the 18 attained FD-level posts. They included 4 Chiefs of Staff (Dayan, Laskov, Makleff, and Yadin), a Deputy Minister of Defence (Galili), a Director of *Ha-Mosad* (Harel), 3 Directors of Military Intelligence (Givli, Herzog, and Yariv), 3 Directors-General (Arnon—Finance, Kollek—Prime Minister's Office, and Kashti—Defence), and 1 Secretary to the Government (Uzay).

It is a youthful group on the whole: 21 of the 29 Formal Directorate-level members were born after 1910, and their average age was 38 upon entry into FD-level posts. This was primarily due to *Tzahal*'s tradition of young Chiefs of Staff (an average age of 39·1 upon appointment to that post, 37·7 if the first Chief of Staff, Dori, is excluded). All Chiefs of Staff except Dori were born in the period 1915–24. The Directors-General, by contrast, are a much older group: 2 were born before

---

Peres as DG, Defence Ministry and Deputy Minister of Defence	1953–65	12 years
Sharef as Secretary to the Government	1948–57	9 years
Uzay as Secretary to the Government	1962–9	7 years

1900 (Eshkol and Horowitz) and 2 between 1906 and 1909 (Sharef and Sapir); these 4 DGs entered the High Policy Élite. Three others were born in the 1911–20 decade (Arnon, Kashti, and Kollek), and 3 in the 1921–6 period (Ben-Natan, Peres, and Tsour).

The proportion of PTE members who held FD-level posts was of a similar order for the first three age groups; it declined to a third in the 1921–30 decade. There was, however, a steady decline in average age of entry into FD-level posts for the four age groups—from 50·5 to 43·0 to 38·6 to 37·4—another indicator of the youthful composition of the Parallel Technical Élite (see Table 41).

The 'ingathering of the exiles' is less evident in the place of birth of Israel's PTE and its FD-level members than in Israel's population as a whole or the Foreign Service Technical Élite. Yet it is considerable: 12 countries for the PTE and 9 for its FD-level members. The concentration of place of origin among Israel's PTE members is even more striking when viewed along linguistic-cultural lines. Two areas stand out, but the order is reversed:

		PTE	*FD-level*
Eastern Europe		27	16
Poland	14	8	
Russia	7	4	
Latvia	4	2	
Bulgaria	1	1	
Lithuania	1	1	
Israel		16	9
Central Europe (Austria, Germany and Holland)		9	2
Other		5	2
Total		57	29

Thus Eastern Europe emerges as the principal reservoir of the Parallel Technical Élite, followed by Israel. Central Europe, so prominent in the place of birth of the Foreign Service Technical Élite, is a distant third. The Anglo-Saxon lands provided 1 PTE member only and the Arab lands none.

The same concentration is evident at the Formal Directorate-level: 9 from Israel, 8 from Poland, and 4 from Russia. The other 8 are scattered among 6 states. In the revised linguistic-cultural map the primacy of Eastern Europe is again clear, with 16; Israel follows with 9; together they account for more than 80 per cent of all FD-level members in the PTE. It is noteworthy that 56 per cent of the Israeli-born members attained FD-level posts, a much higher proportion than in the FSTE or

TABLE 41

PARALLEL TECHNICAL ÉLITE 1948–1968

Place of Birth

Country	Parallel Technical Élite	Formal Directorate-level
Israel	16	9
Poland	14	8
Russia	7	4
Austria	5	2
Latvia	4	2
Germany	3	
Roumania	2	
Yugoslavia	2	1
Bulgaria	1	1
Holland	1	1
Ireland	1	
Lithuania	1	1
Total	57	29

the HPE—or in Israel's political and party life as a whole. By contrast there are few Anglo-Saxons in the PTE and none from French-, Spanish-, and Arabic-speaking lands.

TABLE 42

PARALLEL TECHNICAL ÉLITE 1948–1968

Arrival in Israel

	Number of Persons in PTE	Average Age of Arrival of PTE Members	Number of Persons at FD-level	Average Age of Arrival of FD-level Members
Second *Aliya*	3	11·7	3	11·7
Third *Aliya*	3	17·7	2	21·5
Fourth *Aliya*	10	10·5	6	12
Fifth *Aliya*	19	17·3	7	17·6
1939–1945	3	20·7	1	14
1946–May 1948	–	–	–	–
Post Independence	3	28·3	1	35
Totals and Mean Averages	41*	16·3	20†	16·1

* 16 of the 57 PTE members were born in Israel and are therefore not included in this analysis.

† 9 of the 29 FD-level members were born in Israel: Amit, Dayan, Dinstein, Dori, Givli, Harkabi, Makleff, Rabin, and Yadin.

Only 4 of the 41 non-Israeli-born PTE members were over 30 when they arrived in Israel—and only one at the FD-level (Arnon, 35). In fact, the vast majority of the non-Israeli-born PTE members, 30 out of 40, were under 21 when they arrived. Almost half arrived in Israel either as infants or children (20 persons, from the ages of 2 to 10), or as adolescents (10 persons, from the ages of 11 to 16). The former included 2 Deputy Ministers of Defence (Galili and Peres) and 2 Chiefs of Staff (Laskov and Zur). The latter included 1 Deputy Minister of Defence (Avigur), 1 Chief of Staff (Bar-Lev), and 1 Director-General (Tsour).

If the group of infants and children are added to the Israeli-born, the number of predominantly Israeli-influenced members of the Parallel Technical Élite rises to 36 (out of 57); at the Formal Directorate-level it is 14 out of 29. If the adolescent group is added the comparable figures are 46 (out of 57) Israeli-educated PTE members and 17 of 29 at the FD-level, both markedly higher than in the Foreign Service Technical Élite and its Formal Directorate.

Among the Chiefs of Staff, 5 were born in Israel (Dayan, Dori, Makleff, Rabin, and Yadin); Zur arrived as an infant of 2, Laskov as a child of 6, and Bar-Lev as an adolescent at 14. Among the Directors of Army Intelligence 3 were born in Israel (Amit, Givli, and Harkabi); Yariv arrived at the age of 15, and H. Herzog at 17. Thus, the Israeli roots of *Tzahal*'s leadership are much deeper than for the Foreign Service leadership.

The largest number of PTE members by far (19) arrived during the Fifth *Aliya*, all but 3 during the early Nazi years, 1932–5. That *Aliya* accounts for almost half of the PTE members who were not born in Israel (19 out of 40) and slightly more than a third of the FD-level members who were born abroad (7 out of 20). The only other *Aliya* with more than 3 PTE members was the Fourth, with 10 persons. Although this was only slightly more than half the number of those who arrived in the Fifth *Aliya*, there are almost as many FD-level members— 6 (out of 10) compared with 7 (out of 19). All but 1 of the 6 persons who arrived during the Second or Third *Aliya* attained FD-level posts. Not a single person among the 41 non-Israeli-born PTE members arrived in Israel between 1940 and 1947.

For the 41 PTE members and the 20 FD-level members born abroad, the average age of arrival in Israel was barely beyond adolescence— 16·3 and 16·1, respectively: they are much lower than for the comparable members in the Foreign Service Technical Élite.

The record of pre-State military service is also very different (see Table 43).

Eighty per cent of PTE members had some pre-State military service. The ratio of *Haganah* to British Army was about 2·5:1. Eighteen began their *Haganah* service before 1940—2 of them in the late 1920s, 1 in the early 1930s, and the remaining 15 between 1936 and 1939.

TABLE 43

PARALLEL TECHNICAL ÉLITE 1948–1968

Pre-State Military Service

	Number of Persons in PTE	Number of Persons at Formal Directorate-level
Haganah	38	22
British Army (inc. Jewish Brigade)	15	5
Other	1	
Total	54* (46)	27† (24)

* 8 served in both *Haganah* and the British Army, 5 mainly in *Haganah*, 3 mainly in the British Army (during the Second World War).
See also †note to Table 32.
† 3 served in both the *Haganah* and the British Army, 2 of them mainly in the British Army, 1 in *Haganah*.

Of the 38 PTE members who served in *Haganah* no less than 21 had at least 8 years service, and 17 of them 10 years or more each. The *Haganah* group includes all the Chiefs of Staff except 1—Laskov. Also included are all 3 Directors of *Ha-Mosad*, all Directors of Military Intelligence except 1, and many Military Attachés.

The average period of service for the 15 PTE members in the British Army during the Second World War was 5 years. This group included 2 Chiefs of Staff (Laskov and Makleff), 3 Directors of Intelligence (Harkabi, H. Herzog, and Yariv), and the most senior Jewish officer from Palestine during the war (Lt.-Col. Ben-Arzi). It is noteworthy that 6 of the 8 Chiefs of Staff of *Tzahal* did not serve at all in the British Army.

Just as the Jewish Agency's Political Department was the personnel reservoir for the Foreign Service Technical Élite, the *Haganah* was the reservoir for the Parallel Technical Élite.[1]

The differences between the two Technical Élites extend to higher education as well (see Tables 44a and 44b).

Of Israel's 57 Parallel Technical Élite members, 44 received some form of post-secondary education. Nineteen received university degrees: 5 a Bachelor's degree (1 of them 2 such degrees), 7 a professional degree, and 8 a postgraduate degree; 2 persons earned 2 postgraduate degrees.[2] At the other extreme are 13 persons who did not receive any post-secondary education.

[1] The very high proportion with military service is partly explained by the composition of the PTE: the Chiefs of Staff, Directors of Military Intelligence, and many in the Defence Ministry have military service backgrounds. Yet the disparity with FSTE proportions—45 per cent with military service before Independence—is significant.
[2] The dates when degrees were awarded were not available in most cases.

21

Degree, Institution

University Studies without Degree	*Bachelor's Degree*	*Professional Degree*	*Postgraduate Degree*	*Special Courses*
(17 members of the PTE attended university but did not complete a degree; one of these attended 3 universities. 3 others who listed partial university studies, one of them with two institutions in this category, completed a degree elsewhere, before or after these studies.)	GEVA (Hebrew U.) KARNI (Columbia) KOSLOFF (Chicago) PENN (America U. of Beirut) TALBAR (LSE) (Hebrew U.)	BEN-ARZI I.E.G. (Faculté de Sciences) DINSTEIN LL.D. (Geneva) HERZOG, H. LL.B. (Cambridge) KIMCHE LL.B. (Hebrew U.) NE'EMAN LL.D. (Vienna U.) SYRKIN ENG. (Hanover) UZAY M.J. (Hebrew U.)	AMIT M.B.A. (Columbia) ARNON PH.D. (Amsterdam) BERGMAN PH.D. (Berlin) HARKABI M.A. (Hebrew U.); PH.D. (Hebrew U.) KOSLOFF M.A. (Chicago) LIFSHITZ PH.D. (Frankfurt) LIMON M.B.A. (Columbia) YADIN M.A. (Hebrew U.) PH.D. (Hebrew U.)	(3 members attended post-secondary special courses. In addition, 10 members of the PTE attended Military Staff Colleges.)
Total Number of man-courses 23	6	7	8	13 57

TABLE 44b

PARALLEL TECHNICAL ÉLITE 1948–1968

Higher Education: Subjects of Study

Subject	Number of Persons in PTE	Number of Persons at FD-level
Military Science	10	5
Law	6	3
Economics	7	2
Engineering	5	2
Political Science	5	1
International Relations	4	3
Business Administration	4	2
Others*	6	2
Unknown	4	2
Total	51†	22

* This includes Arabic Literature (2), Archaeology (1), Chemistry (1), Hebrew Literature (1), General Humanities (1), Philosophy (1), Sociology (1); some persons took 2 of these subjects.

† 2 PTE members are listed above under 3 subjects each, and 3 PTE members are listed above under 2 subjects each. Thus the total figure of 51 PTE members above refers to 44 persons. Similarly, 1 FD-level member is listed above under 3 subjects, and 1 FD-level member is listed under 2 subjects. Thus the total figure of 22 FD-level members refers to 17 persons.

Among the Formal Directorate-level members 1 received a Bachelor's Degree, 3 a professional degree, and 4 postgraduate degrees, 2 of them 2 degrees each (Harkabi and Yadin). Of the 21 persons at the FD-level without a university degree, 10 did not receive any post-secondary education; 7 attended university briefly—Columbia, Geneva, Ghent, Haifa Technion, Harvard, Oxford and Princeton, Sorbonne and Tel Aviv; and 4 attended Military Staff College.

No subject dominates the higher education of Israel's Parallel Technical Élite or its FD-level members—unlike the Foreign Service Technical Élite.

(b) COMPARISON: FSTE AND PTE

Israel's Foreign Service Technical Élite and her Parallel Technical Élite are not exactly comparable: the former is a homogeneous, single-ministry, long-term professional group; the latter is a heterogeneous, multiple-ministry group, though 'the Military' constitutes within the PTE the counterpart of 'the Diplomats' in the FSTE. This qualification must be borne in mind in the comparisons which follow.

i. *Membership* (Tables 27 and 38)

The FSTE consisted of 87 persons, the PTE of 57 persons, from 1948 to 1968. Different criteria were used in delineating the two groups: for the FSTE, all Heads of (operational) Departments and higher officials within the Foreign Office, along with Heads of 11 important Israeli missions abroad and the second-ranking person in 5 of these missions; for the PTE, higher-level officials are included, i.e. Deputy Ministers and Directors-General of certain ministries (Commerce and Industry, Defence, Finance, Prime Minister's Office), 3 key posts in *Tzahal* (Chief of Staff, Chief of General Staff Branch, and Director of Military Intelligence), Directors of *Ha-Mosad*, some Military Attachés and Chiefs of Defence Purchasing Missions, etc. The reason for the difference in criteria is the analytic focus of this inquiry—foreign policy; *a priori*, lower-level officials within the Foreign Ministry, such as Department Heads, are more directly involved in the foreign policy flow than their rank counterparts in other ministries and the Defence Establishment.

Average Period of Time in the Technical Élite: FSTE—9·5 years, PTE—5·6 years; Durables in the Technical Élite, that is, persons with 10 years or more membership: FSTE—24 (27·6 per cent of total); PTE—11 (19·3 per cent of total).

The Durables in both Technical Élites held a variety of posts. But whereas the 11 persons in the PTE performed the same type-role throughout their TE membership, 5 of the 24 FSTE Durables served in other components of the overall Technical Élite; for example, Avriel was Assistant DG, Foreign Office, DG, Finance Ministry, and DG, Prime Minister's Office. In short, there was greater diversity of role performance in the FSTE. There was, however, greater vertical mobility in the PTE: 9 of 18 High Policy Élite members served in the Parallel Technical Élite, only 1 in the Foreign Service Technical Élite.

ii. *Formal Directorate-level* (Tables 28 and 39)

Membership: FSTE 28, PTE 29.

Career Pattern: all 28 FSTE Formal Directorate members come from FSTE posts; only 4 at the PTE Formal Directorate-level came from PTE posts (Ben-Natan, Dinstein, H. Herzog, and Yariv).

Rate of Change in Occupancy of Formal Directorate-level posts: FSTE—28 persons held 11 posts over the twenty-year period; PTE—29 persons held 9 posts over the twenty-year period.

Occupancy of Director-General posts: there were 4 DGs in the Foreign Ministry, 4 in the Finance Ministry, and 4 in the Prime Minister's Office, with 1 long-term Director-General in each (Eytan, Arnon, and Kollek, respectively); and 6 DGs in the Defence Ministry, with 2 long-term (Peres and Ben-Natan).

Comparable Posts: there were 7 Chiefs of Staff to 1968 averaging slightly less than 3 years, none more than 4¼ years; and 3 Directors of *Ha-Mosad*, with 1 long-term.

iii. *Position Immediately Preceding Entry* (Appendix Tables 16 and 21)

Recruitment Reservoir: FSTE (and its FD)—Jewish Agency Political Department; PTE (and its FD level)—*Tzahal*. The proportion was comparable: approximately 60 per cent of the two Technical Élites came from the pre-eminent reservoir for each.

iv. *Date of Birth and Age Upon Entry into Technical Élite* (Tables 29 and 40)

A much higher proportion of PTE members was born before 1900—6 of 57, compared to 3 of 87 FSTE members. On the whole, however, the PTE is a much younger group. A larger proportion of the pre-1900-born PTE members reached higher posts—4 of 6 at the FD-level, and 2 of them in the HPE, compared to 2 of 3 FSTE members in the Formal Directorate, but none in the High Policy Élite.

Of the post-1930-born group in the Technical Élites, 2 were in the FSTE and none in the PTE.

Of the 1921–30-born group in the Technical Élite, a much higher proportion were in the PTE, 44 per cent compared to almost 22 per cent in the FSTE.

The 1911–20-born group is the highest-achieving in the PTE—13 (of 18) attained the FD-level—and in the FSTE as well, in absolute terms—11 (of 38); the proportion of PTE members to reach FD-level posts is almost 3 times as high as FSTE members from that age group.

The PTE is a younger group on the whole: more than a quarter (28·7 per cent) of the FSTE, but only 14·5 per cent of the PTE, was born in the 1901–10 period. Moreover, a large majority of FSTE members were born in the 1901–20 period (63 of 87, or 72·4 per cent), while a comparable majority of the PTE was born between 1911 and 1930 (43 of 57, or 75·4 per cent).

The 4 DGs in the FSTE assumed office at an average age of 49·5 (only 1, Eytan, was under 50—he was 38). Within the PTE, the 6 DGs, Defence Ministry, averaged 42 years, with Peres at 30 and Ben-Natan at 38 when they assumed office; the 4 DGs, Finance Ministry, averaged 42·8, with Avriel at 35 when he assumed office; the 4 DGs, Prime Minister's Office, averaged 40·5, with Avriel at 34; and the 8 Chiefs of Staff averaged 39·1, with 2 of them, Yadin and Makleff, at 32, when they assumed office. There is, then, a marked difference in the age of assumption of office as Director-General or its equivalent post in the two Technical Élites.

v. *Place of Birth* (Tables 30 and 41)

There is a conspicuous difference in the size of the Israeli-born component of the two Technical Élites and their Formal Directorate-levels:

FSTE—11 of 87, and 3 of 28; PTE—16 of 57, and 9 of 29, i.e. a ratio of more than 2:1 in the Technical Élite and of 3:1 at the FD-level in favour of the Parallel Technical Élite.

Eastern Europe and Central Europe are the most important linguistic-cultural sources for the FSTE, 26 and 25 respectively, followed by the Anglo-Saxon lands (12) and then Israel (11); the PTE is markedly different—Eastern Europe (27) and then Israel (16).

In terms of individual countries of birth, Germany stands first in the FSTE with 16 (of 87) and 5 (of 28) at the FD-level; in the PTE Israel stands first with 16 (of 57) and 9 (of 29) at the FD-level.

Another marked contrast relates to members whose mother tongue is English—very prominent in the FSTE (12 of 87, and 6 of 28 FD members), almost non-existent in the PTE—1 in each category. In short, German and English backgrounds are pre-eminent in the FSTE, while Eastern Europe and Israel are pre-eminent in the PTE. The pre-eminence of Israel is especially striking among 'the Military'.

vi. *Arrival in Israel* (Tables 31 and 42)

The proportion of PTE members born abroad is much smaller—41 of 57 (and 20 of 29 at the FD-level), compared to 76 of 87, and 25 of 28 at the FD-level for the FSTE.

The average age of arrival of PTE members is much lower—16·3 compared to 23·9 for FSTE members, and 16·1 to 25 for FD-level members. More PTE members arrived as youngsters—10 before the age of 10 and 10 from 11 to 16 years of age, i.e. 20 of 41, compared to 3 infants and 15 adolescents, i.e. 18 of 76 foreign-born FSTE members.

In both Technical Élites the Fifth *Aliya*, especially 1932–5, was the largest arrival period (28 of 76 in the FSTE, and 19 of 40 in the PTE); at the Formal Directorate-level, too, the Fifth *Aliya* stands first, 11 of 25 and 7 of 29, respectively. Very few of the PTE members arrived after the onset of the Second World War, only 3 of 40 (all in 1939), while 19 of 87 FSTE members did so.

vii. *Pre-State Military Service* (Tables 32 and 43)

There is a qualitative difference in the proportion of Technical Élite members with military service—46 of 57 in the PTE, 38 of 87 in the FSTE; at the Formal Directorate-level the gap is also great—24 of 29 in the PTE, 13 of 28 in the FSTE.

Haganah was the principal reservoir for the PTE, a counterpart role to the Jewish Agency's Political Department for the FSTE; more emphatically so—38 of the 57 PTE members came from *Haganah*, 26 of the 87 FSTE members from the Political Department. There is, too, a contrasting importance in the two military services: participation in *Haganah* was, proportionately, much higher in the PTE (83 to 33 per cent) and in the FSTE it was much higher in the British Army (49 to 30 per cent). The contrast is not without significance, perceived and real, for behavioural predispositions of Foreign Ministry officials on the one hand and of those in PTE posts, especially 'the Military', on the other.

viii. *Education* (Tables 33 and 44, and Appendix Tables 20 and 23)

The PTE has a much lower proportion of members with an advanced education than the FSTE:

	FSTE	PTE
number of persons with higher education	83 of 87	44 of 57
number of persons with degrees	49 of 87	20 of 57
number of FD persons with degrees	21 of 28	8 of 29

The United States was more prominent in the education of the PTE— 9 of 42, compared to 8 of 82 in the FSTE.

Both groups are highly concentrated by country of higher education and by university: FSTE—Israel and the UK (Hebrew University and University of London); PTE—Israel (Hebrew University). Law was the pre-eminent subject of study in the FSTE—28 of 82, and 12 of 28 Formal Directorate members. In the PTE no such concentration exists, other than on military science.

ix. *Other Occupations* (Table 35 and Appendix Table 24)

There is less variety in the occupations cited by PTE members: pre-university teaching, journalism and broadcasting, and pre-State service in other governments are noted by FSTE members but not by anyone in the PTE. There are many more Academics in the FSTE— 16 to 3, or in proportional terms, 18·4 per cent of the FSTE members, and 5·3 per cent of PTE members.

Involvement in Commerce was approximately of the same order— 14 of 87 in the FSTE, 9 of 57 in the PTE.

Whereas only 3 persons in the FSTE (among them, 2 FD members) became members of parliament, no less than 10 of 57 PTE members, all of them at FD-level, became MKs up to 1968. More generally, members of the PTE were much more involved in politics. Notable among these were Dayan, Dinstein, Harel, H. Herzog, Peres, Sapir, Sharef, and Zur. Moreover, PTE members were far more actively involved in *Mapai* and in domestic politics.

The starkest contrast relates to a military career: 5 FSTE members served in *Tzahal* for substantial periods before moving to the Foreign Office; 28 of the PTE were permanent or long-term army officers.

Almost one-quarter of FSTE members (21 of 87, among them 5 of 28 FD members) served in government posts other than the Foreign Ministry. The number cited for PTE in this regard (31) is not comparable for it includes all government posts held by them, including their core PTE post.

A sharing of responsibility for foreign policy between the Foreign Office and the Defence Ministry is not unique to Israel: from super powers like the United States and the Soviet Union, through great, middle and small powers, this dual structural involvement is apparent with greater or lesser degree of conflict and co-operation and with different proportions of influence. Yet in few if any states (certainly not in pluralist competitive political systems) is the role of 'the Military' so vital and legitimately recognized as such.[1] This results from the essence of Israel's core problem—survival in the face of permanent threats of annihilation by her neighbours, causing a higher proportion than elsewhere of the ablest young men to choose a military career.

The perception of the threat by the two Technical Élites is not always identical. Where they differ is in the perception of the outer world and of the kinds of response which are required by Israel. And those perceptions are shaped by the contrasting life experiences of their members, viewed in collective terms. The Foreign Service Technical Élite is more outer-directed, the Parallel Technical Élite is inner-directed.

The FSTE has a much higher proportion of foreign-born, foreign-educated members, with greater external influence upon their thought and behaviour, upon their assessment of alternative courses of action, and upon their scale of values in foreign policy decisions. The PTE has deeper roots in Israel—with a higher proportion of Israeli-born and Israeli-educated members, acculturated through Israel's supreme nation-building institutions, *Haganah* and *Tzahal*.

[1] One indication of this is the emphasis of several parties on military expertise as a quality of leadership, partly in order to secure public support in election contests.

CHAPTER 19

Implementation: Some Auxiliary Methods

There are many techniques available to states in implementing Strategic-level decisions. The principal one is the Foreign Office. Yet other ministries have been involved in this process: the Defence Ministry (and *Tzahal*), in the Military-Security issue-area, through Military Attachés and Purchasing Missions, and, of course, through military actions on the borders, all this reflecting broad foreign policy objectives; and in the Economic-Developmental issue-area, Finance, and Industry and Commerce, through Economics Ministers and Commercial Attachés in many embassies, through fiscal and trade policies, and through measures to attract foreign investment, Bond sales, etc. One may add the ministries of Religious Affairs and of the Interior, which impinge on the vexed Jerusalem issue and which affect Israel's image abroad.[1] The working of the Foreign Ministry will be dissected in the following chapter. Here we shall examine some of the less traditional instruments of implementation: Heads of State and Government; *Kol Yisrael* (Arabic) Broadcasts; the *Histadrut*; and Jewry.

(a) HEADS OF STATE AND GOVERNMENT

The foreign policy of Israel, as of other states, is carried out by various persons acting through a diversity of institutions and employing different methods. At the most formal level are official tours by the President, which symbolize Israel and her aspirations. Dr. Weizmann, the first Head of State (1948–52), was too ill during his last years to travel extensively: he made only one visit, to the United States and the United Nations in April 1949, a gesture to the Power and the world body which had assisted the birth of the new state. President Ben Zvi held office much longer, from 1952 to 1963, but he made only three formal visits abroad—to Belgium and Holland in July 1958, to Burma in October 1959, and to four new African states in July 1962; the last two reflected Israel's presence among the new nations and the importance she attached to the Third World.

President Shazar has been more active since he assumed office in 1963—but four of his seven journeys overseas to the end of 1970 were to represent Israel at the funeral of famed public figures—Kennedy,

[1] The implementing role of other ministries will be analysed in some case studies o high-policy decisions in a later volume.

Churchill, Eisenhower, and de Gaulle. One of his tours, to Nepal in March 1966, was to arouse further Israeli resentment at the Government of India's unconcealed eagerness to curry favour with the Arab states wherever possible: in this case it was by discourtesy to the Head of a recognized state pausing on Indian soil en route to a mutually friendly state for an official visit. Israel's ties with Nepal were strengthened. And Shazar was also successful in symbolizing the bonds between the Jewish State and the Jewish People during his tours of Chile, Uruguay, Brazil, and the United States in June 1966, and of Canada in May 1967, on the eve of the Six Day War. In all these instances, discussions with foreign Heads of State took place, but the implementing role of Israel's Presidents has been essentially one of presence and goodwill.[1]

The Prime Minister, too, has carried out policy during visits to foreign lands—indeed in a much more substantive manner. Ben Gurion went abroad only once in the first twelve years of independence—to the United States in the spring of 1951; but it was of lasting significance, for he launched the first State of Israel Bonds drive which, over the years, has raised more than a billion dollars to sustain and expand the Israeli economy. There was a marked change in 1960: BG travelled extensively during the last phase of his tenure as Head of Government.

There was the historic meeting with Adenauer in New York, in March, symbol of a willingness to embark upon a path of reconciliation with the most horrendous of Jewry's oppressors—in a long history of oppression. More tangibly, Ben Gurion established the basis for assured long-term West German economic aid after Reparations came to an end (anticipated for 1965).[2] In June 1960 he visited two of Israel's most steadfast friends, Holland and Belgium. He also met de Gaulle, when Franco-Israeli friendship was still firm—and made it firmer. He returned to France the following May, as part of a tour of North Atlantic states, including Canada, the UK, and the US. Most important, he strengthened the ties with the recently-elected President Kennedy—who felt, and expressed, a genuine debt to American Jewry, in *his* image indissolubly linked with Israel.[3] In December 1961 Ben Gurion indulged an old, special friendship for Burma and U Nu, and his fascination for Buddhism, by making a pilgrimage to Burma, including a much-publicized few days of meditation. And finally, in August 1962, he toured northern Europe, symbolizing Israel's affection and reciprocal friendship for the peoples of Scandinavia.

Eshkol was no less active as a Prime Minister implementing foreign policy. In May–June 1964, a year after he assumed office, he visited the United States and established warm personal ties with President John-

---

[1] Details of overseas tours by the Presidents of Israel were provided by the Office of the President, Jerusalem.

[2] This point will be elaborated in the related volume on Israeli high-policy decisions.

[3] Interview with Yitzhak Navon, Jerusalem, Dec. 1965.

son. The following month he went to Paris for talks with de Gaulle—who continued to term Israel, publicly, 'friend and ally'. In March–April 1965 he visited England, and in May–June 1966 he made a highly-successful goodwill tour of seven African States—Senegal, Ivory Coast, Liberia, Congo (Kinshasa), Malagasy, Uganda, and Kenya. Finally, and most important, Eshkol held further talks with Johnson in January 1968, which resulted in the sale of valuable US arms to Israel, including Phantom and Skyhawk planes. Prime Minister Meir's visit to the United States in September 1969 was also directed to military (and economic) aid, notably the request to purchase an additional 50 Phantoms and 80 Skyhawks. She also paid a formal visit to the United Nations in October 1970 on the occasion of the twenty-fifth anniversary of the world body.

Israeli Heads of Government help to implement foreign policy in other ways as well. One is through discussions with a steady flow of influential visitors—statesmen, legislators, leaders of industry and labour, journalists, intellectuals, etc. A notable example was the Ben Gurion–Hammarskjöld talks in 1955–6 about freedom of passage through the Suez Canal. A related technique is confidential correspondence, mostly with other Heads of Government. Little has been published thus far; but that which has, for example the Ben Gurion–Eisenhower letters, in 1956–7 during and after the Sinai Campaign, has far-reaching significance.[1] And senior officials in the Prime Minister's Office under all four Israeli Heads of Government confirmed that this form of diplomacy at the summit was not an uncommon practice.[2] The most widespread method of prime ministerial implementation of policy, however, is oral communication: speeches and statements before the *Knesset* or meetings of political parties; addresses to Zionist and other congresses in Israel; interviews with foreign and Israeli correspondents; press conferences, and extemporaneous remarks. Taken together, these represent a major, continuing—and often decisive—role in the carrying out of foreign policy.

There are also *sub rosa* contacts between Israel and her neighbours, sometimes involving direct emissaries of the Heads of Government. At the lowest level are quiet meetings between Israeli intelligence personnel and Arabs from many strata of society, mostly outside the arena of conflict, and some arranged through the good offices of third parties. These are, naturally, unreported; and they cannot be measured in frequency or intensity—certainly not by an outsider. From time to time

[1] Part of the correspondence appears in Ben Gurion's 'Israel's Security and Her International Position', pp. 35–6, 37, 45–7, and 52. Some of these letters and others were published in the Eisenhower memoirs of that period, *The White House Years: Waging Peace 1956–1961*, Heinemann, London, 1966, pp. 184, 186, 187, 189, and 684–5.

[2] Interviews with Heads of the Prime Minister's Bureau under Ben Gurion, Sharett, Eshkol, and Meir, in Israel, 1960, 1965–6, 1968, and 1970.

news of abortive mediation efforts comes to the surface, as with Ben Gurion's revelation in 1965, already noted, of four attempts he made to establish contact with Nasser, and a British MP's disclosure that, in 1954, he had served as Sharett's emissary to the Egyptian President.[1] There was also a direct Israeli initiative in 1954, involving Shiloah and E. Sasson of the Foreign Office, and an informal approach to Nasser by Prime Minister Dom Mintoff of Malta early in 1956.[2] There were others. And in 1968–70 there were several reports (denied) of secret meetings of Foreign Minister Eban and Deputy Premier Allon with King Hussein in London and elsewhere.[3]

(b) KOL YISRAEL (ARABIC) BROADCASTS[4]

The Voice of Israel performs two functions in Israel's Foreign Policy System: the first, communicating images of the Operational Environment to Israel's decision-makers, has already been discussed. The second is directed to implementing Israel's foreign policy by means of foreign-language broadcasts in a dozen languages. Notable are Russian, French, English and, especially, Arabic programmes. The last merit special attention, for they are one of the few effective ways of breaking the barrier of non-relations with her neighbours.

[1] See ch. 11, note 2 on p. 283 above for the Ben Gurion revelation. Maurice Orbach brought a message from Nasser to 'my brother Sharett', saying he wanted peace. He saw Nasser secretly several times and claimed to have worked out with Ali Sabry a peace and coexistence formula involving the cessation of hostile propaganda, free passage for non-Israeli shipping to and from Israel through the Canal, Israeli technological aid for industrial developments in Egypt, termination of border incidents, less harsh treatment for spies, and high-level contacts to implement the agreement. This was all denied by the Egyptian Embassy in London. Jerusalem Post, 1 Aug. 1965. According to Israeli circles, Orbach merely tried to ameliorate the human aspects of the trials of Jews in Egypt (in 1954) and never discussed important political issues with Egyptian leaders. Ha'aretz, 30 July 1965. Sharett denied some of Orbach's allegations, saying that Orbach's memory had misled him on several details. Ma'ariv, 27 Dec. 1964, as recalled in Ha'aretz, 30 July 1965, and by Jon Kimche in an article in Ma'ariv, 10 May 1970. Orbach insisted, after the Egyptian and Israeli denials, that his talks with Nasser in 1954 were at Nasser's invitation. Jerusalem Post, 8 Aug. 1965.

[2] As reported, respectively, in Ma'ariv and in Yediot Aharonot (Tel Aviv), 4 Aug. 1961, and by Uri Dan, in an interview with Mintoff, in Ma'ariv, 25 May 1961. These were reproduced in 'On Peace and Negotiations', New Outlook (Tel Aviv), vol. 6, no. 1 (50), Jan. 1963, pp. 49–51.

[3] Deputy Premier Allon met Hussein three times in September 1968; Foreign Minister Eban was present at one session. Eban also reportedly met Hussein in October 1968 and/or January 1969. Eric Rouleau in Le Monde (Paris), 6–7 July 1968. Both Governments denied that meetings had taken place. This writer accepts Rouleau's view. Later reports indicated that about ten meetings were held between Hussein and Israeli leaders, most of them with Allon. Time (New York), vol. 96, no. 21, 23 Nov. 1970; Le Nouvel Observateur (Paris), no. 315, 23 Nov. 1970.

[4] Since the autumn of 1969 it has been known as Shiddurei Yisrael (Israel Broadcasts).

The origins of *Kol Yisrael*'s Arabic broadcasts were modest. In 1946 *Haganah* built a mobile, weak radio transmitter capable of reaching people in Palestine: there were brief irregular broadcasts—fifteen minutes every four or five days—designed to convince the Palestine Arabs that the Jews were there to stay and that the State of Israel would be established. In December 1947, just after the UN Partition Resolution was passed, the Jewish Agency's Political Department decided to publish an Arabic supplement to the daily *Palestine* (later, *Jerusalem*) *Post*. All was in process when the *Post* building was blown up. As a substitute medium of communication the Political Department decided to introduce a regular daily half-hour broadcast in Arabic: its content was divided between news and a news commentary on one or two important developments of the day.

That formative phase was followed by a period of minimal attention to a vital link with the Arabs. *Kol Yisrael* was established as the State Radio in 1948. From 1948 to 1957 the daily time allotted to Arabic broadcasts was only between forty-five minutes and an hour; to the initial half hour in the evening was added fifteen minutes, later increased to half an hour—in the afternoon, when few Arabs listen to the radio. The reasons for Israeli indifference were threefold: psychological, namely, the lack of conscious awareness by Israeli high-policy decision-makers of their Middle East environment and Israel's place within the region; secondly, perception of political constraints, that is, the belief that little could be accomplished, and so why bother; and thirdly, economic-technological—the shortage of funds and the absence of a transmitter capable of reaching far beyond Palestine.

The third phase, from 1957 on, witnessed a qualitative change in this instrument of foreign policy. The construction of a new, powerful transmitter made this possible. But the catalyst was continuous pressure for expanded facilities by a small group who realized its importance, notably Danin, Adviser to the Foreign Minister on the Middle East, Navon, Political Secretary to Prime Minister Ben Gurion, E. Sasson, who was deeply involved in the project from the outset as Head of the Foreign Office Middle East Department (1948–9) and a respected adviser on the Arabs, and Bar-Haim, Head of the Arab Department of *Kol Yisrael*. All attempts until 1957 failed. Finally they were able to convince Kollek, Director-General of the Prime Minister's Office, who was in charge of broadcasting.

The programme was increased to $5\frac{1}{2}$ hours a day, and in 1960 to $7\frac{1}{2}$ hours. It was planned and supervised by a Committee on Arabic Broadcasts, which came into being in 1958, comprising Danin, Navon, Bar-Haim, and the then Assistant Head of the Foreign Office Middle East Department, M. Sasson. Although lacking a statutory role, the Committee exercised effective control over policy. And from a half-dozen professionals the staff grew to 20, with 50 other technicians, and administrative personnel—a total of about 130 in 1966. That rapid growth was made possible by a reservoir of skilled Iraqi Jews and the influx of Egyptian Jews after the Sinai Campaign.[1]

The basic aim of the expanded programme, as always, has been 'to persuade the Arabs that Israel is here to stay'.[2] Its guiding principle has been to tell the 'whole truth' about the Arab world and about Israel, 'to provoke listeners but never to insult them or their leaders, Arab culture, or Arab traditions'. Yet there was a conspicuous gap between principle and practice, according to some Israelis capable of assessing its content. The operational technique was described as follows:

> to play up everything that indicates Israel is firmly established and is recognized by the world—from international sports meetings in Israel, the completion of new roads, schools, and settlements, and the continuous arrival of immigrants, to friendly greetings from statesmen and the press: the theme of Israel's growing links with states and peoples everywhere is emphasized constantly;
>
> to stress that Israel wishes to live at peace with her neighbours;
>
> to note the possibility of advantageous mutual co-operation;
>
> to insist that Israel is not 'imperialist'—by asserting that it was Arab hostility from the outset which forced Israel to seek assistance and support outside the Middle East; in short, to propound the thesis that the Arabs are primarily responsible for Israel's ties with the West—because Israel is not prepared to commit national suicide;
>
> and to declare that Israel will not yield concessions or territory by force.

Table 45 indicates the daily programmes offered by the *Kol Yisrael* Department of Arabic Broadcasts between 1960 and 1967. Altogether there were almost 43 hours each week—with slightly more than 7 hours a day on Sunday and Wednesday, 6 hours on Friday, and between 5 and 6 hours daily on all the other days. There was a very wide range of subject-matter, no less than 31 separate programmes—with an average of 24 a day throughout the week. Of these, 3 accounted for large blocs of time: News, with 41 broadcasts—6 a day, except for 5 on Friday, involving one-fourth of the allotted time; and Arabic songs and music, with 47 broadcasts combined, using about one-third of the total time.

There was a massive expansion of Arab-language broadcasts after

---

[1] This account is based upon an interview with Bar-Haim who in 1960 moved to the Foreign Ministry's Middle East Department.

[2] This phrase was used by both Navon and Danin in interviews in Jerusalem, in July 1960 and April 1966 respectively. The following analysis is based upon the interviews with Navon, Danin, and Bar-Haim.

the Six Day War—to 16¼ hours a day 7 days a week, that is, 114 hours a week or almost three times as much as the pre-1967 War period (and sixteen times the volume of Arabic broadcasts before the Sinai Campaign of 1956). This included 15 news bulletins a day, all but 2 of 15 minutes each and totalling 3½ hours of news a day (3 hours on Friday) or 24 hours a week: before that war there were 10 hours of news weekly.[1] Belatedly—after each war—Israeli decision-makers came to appreciate the significance of this technique of implementing their foreign policy decisions.

The size of the audience and the impact of these broadcasts are impossible to measure precisely.[2] Navon speculated in 1960: '*Kol Yisrael* Arab broadcasts are heard by as many radios as there are sets in the neighbouring Arab countries. Moreover, they are believed by many as the most truthful in the region.' Danin referred to the audience in 1966 as 'a very large community of regular listeners all over the Arab world'. Furthermore, *Kol Yisrael* ranked second to the BBC in the size of its Middle East audience; and, said Danin, it has the reputation of being the most accurate news source. In that connection, he remarked that visiting American diplomat Robert Murphy told Israelis in 1958 that Lebanese cabinet meetings paused when Israeli newscasts began: 'Let's find out what's happening in Lebanon.'

Various means are available to evaluate audience receptiveness and the general impact of Israel's Arabic broadcasts: intelligence reports; comments by tourists and diplomats in Arab states who later visit Israel; open replies to some of these broadcasts in the Arab press and radio; reference to them by Arab leaders in their speeches, especially Nasser, who reportedly perused the daily monitor of *Kol Yisrael* Arabic broadcasts; remarks by Arabs in conversation with Israelis abroad; and letters from Arabs to *Kol Yisrael*.

It is 'highly probable' that the image of a permanent Israel, the main aim of these broadcasts, has been implanted in the minds of a large number of Arabs. But they have certainly not succeeded in persuading the Arab leadership to accept Israel and the idea of peaceful coexistence. In 1960 Navon made the following perceptive comment: 'The Arabs have a genuine feeling of pain at defeat in war and the loss of Palestine. There is also hatred and fear of Israel. A slow, long-term process of psychological change will have to occur—on both sides, for both are ignorant of each other—before mutual understanding is possible. [How much more true this is after the 1967 War!] The Arab broadcasts contribute to that process.'

[1] Calculated from data provided by the Department of Arabic Broadcasts, *Kol Yisrael*, Jerusalem.
[2] By contrast, as noted in ch. 9 above, the size of audience within Israel has been assessed in several careful surveys by the Central Bureau of Statistics, conducted in co-operation with the Israel Broadcasting Authority.

PROGRAMMES	SUNDAY		MONDAY		TUESDAY	
	Min/ Day	*Fre- quency*	*Min/ Day*	*Fre- quency*	*Min/ Day*	*Fre- quency*
The News	90	6	90	6	90	6
Koran	20	2	20	2	20	2
Morning Thoughts	13	1	13	1	13	1
Songs (Arabic)	70	5	105	5	55	4
Commentary	25	2	10	1	25	2
Selections from Newspaper Articles	10	1	10	1	18	1
Talk to Refugees	15	1				
Greetings from Israeli Arabs to Relatives Abroad	10	1	10	1	10	1
Truth and Lies			20	1		
The Middle East This Week			15	1		
Poet's Corner	20	1				
Play						
Short Story						
The East in the Eyes of the World	15	1				
Selections from the Israeli Press	15	1	15	1	15	1
Selections from the Arab Press						
Farmers' Corner	10	1			10	1
Talk by M. Tantawi (Egyptian Dialect)	15	1				
Women's Corner	30	1				
Sports Corner					20	1
Weekly Review						
Courtroom Cases	30	1				
Strange Stories			15	1		
Talk by 'Son of Mesopotamia' (Iraqi)					15	1
The Wednesday Club						
Listeners' Letters						
Around the World						
Music	45	3	15	1	60	3
Religious Programme (Acco)						
The Arts						
Survey of 1965						
Total	433	29	338	22	351	24

Source: Derived from material made available by the Department of Arabic Broadcasts, *Kol Yisrael*, Jerusalem.

WEDNESDAY Min/Day	Fre-quency	THURSDAY Min/Day	Fre-quency	FRIDAY Min/Day	Fre-quency	SATURDAY Min/Day	Fre-quency	TOTAL Fre-quency	Hours	Min-utes
90	6	90	6	90	6	65	5	41	10	5
20	2	20	2	10	1	20	2	13	2	10
13	1	13	1	13	1	13	1	7	1	31
55	4	40	3	35	4	40	3	28	6	40
10	1	25	2	10	1	10	1	10	1	55
10	1	10	1	8	1			6	1	6
								1		15
10	1	10	1	10	1	10	1	7	1	10
		20	1	20	1			3	1	
				repeat						
								1		15
								1		20
20	1							1		20
15	1					30	1	2		45
								1		15
15	1	15	1	15	1	15	1	7	1	45
15	1			15	1			2		30
		10	1					3		30
								1		15
								1		30
								1		20
20	1							1		20
								1		30
								1		15
15	1							2		30
repeat										
15	1	15	1					2		30
		repeat								
20	1							1		20
		15	1					1		15
80	4	65	3	30	1	110	4	19	6	45
				20	1			1		20
				30	1			1		30
				60	1			1		60
423	28	348	23	366	23	313	20	169	42	57

(c) HISTADRUT

In the course of a Budget speech to the *Knesset*, Foreign Minister Meir observed that the Foreign Office receives assistance from many sources in carrying out its technical assistance programmes: various ministries; the Jewish Agency Settlement Department; the *Histadrut*; universities; health organizations; co-operative settlements; and public and private industry.[1] Suffice it here to note briefly the wider role of Israel's all-encompassing trade union movement, the *Histadrut*.

One of its central bureaucratic structures is concerned with foreign policy—the International Department. It has an informal liaison with the Foreign Office, but there is no formal machinery for consultation. The key operational link is with the Ministry's Department of International Co-operation. Upon request, from new states wishing to learn from Israel's rich experience in this field, the *Histadrut* has supplied trade union advisers; and its affiliated enterprises have furnished assistance in various fields, first in Burma, then in Ghana, and from 1960 onwards throughout the Third World.[2] The *Histadrut* also created, in 1960, the widely-respected Afro-Asian Institute for Labour Studies and Co-operation.

The goals of the Institute are self-defined as follows: 'To train manpower for the Labour and Co-operative Movements in Africa and Asia in order to enable each movement to integrate more effectively in the general process of social programs and development of its own country. . . .' Its study programme, following the *Histadrut* model, combines theory and practice, in trade union, co-operative and management activities. The guiding spirit throughout has been Akiva Eger, the Institute's Director, whose philosophy is that 'it is the mission of the labor movement to integrate the whole of a developing nation into a co-operative way of life'. Described as 'probably Israel's best-equipped training center for foreigners', with a permanent professional staff of twelve, the Institute has trained more than 1,000 students from abroad in the *Histadrut* image.[3]

The second form of implementation activity derives from the *Histadrut*'s association with labour organizations around the world. During any crisis, indeed on any substantive foreign policy issue affecting Israel, the *Histadrut* calls upon fraternal bodies to rally to the Israeli cause.

---

[1] Budget Speech to the *Knesset* on 23 May 1960. Issued by the Government Press Office, Jerusalem.

[2] For a brief account of these *Histadrut* activities see Leopold Laufer, *Israel and the Developing Countries: New Approach to Cooperation*, Twentieth Century Fund, New York, 1967, pp. 22–4, 131–3. For the earlier period see the author's *New States of Asia*, Oxford University Press, London, 1963, ch. 5, and Mordechai E. Kreinin, *Israel and Africa—A Study in Technical Cooperation*, Praeger, New York, 1964, esp. pp. 13ff. and 126–32.

[3] The quotations are taken from Laufer, op. cit., p. 159; the Institute is examined on pp. 159–62.

Noteworthy are the American AFL-CIO, with a record of unqualified support during the two decades under inquiry; the ICFTU, the umbrella organization of social-democratic trade unions; and its constituent members in France, Germany, the UK, Holland, Belgium, and Northern Europe.

A few examples of a general practice may be noted. The *Histadrut* rallied its trade union comrades to press for free passage of Israeli ships and cargoes through the Suez Canal, especially between 1956 and 1967, by enlisting the active support of the International Transport Workers Federation. It created a storm of indignation over the emotion-laden issue of German scientists in Egypt, in 1963–4, and the German Government's planned Statute of Limitations on the trial of war criminals. And throughout the 1960s it stimulated international trade union pressure in support of Israel's request for associate membership in the European Common Market—or, at least, a preferential tariff agreement. (Agreements of the latter type were concluded in 1964, 1967, and 1970.)

This has been a continuing activity. And, while its effectiveness cannot be measured precisely, the *Histadrut* has demonstrated an ability to convey Israel's foreign policy demands to the highly-organized world of international labour. Moreover, through that movement, at conferences, by means of telegrams, letters and resolutions, it has affected the behaviour of states where the national trade union organization is strong, articulate, and committed to Israel's survival and welfare.[1]

(*d*) JEWRY

Jewish communities all over the world have played a significant role in assisting the attainment of Israel's foreign policy goals. This is true of Jewry in the US, France, the UK, Canada, and Latin America. Owing to the size and wealth of American Jewry (and the position of the United States as a world power) its role has been of exceptional importance.

i. *Reality*

The vehemence of US Jewry's support of Israel was reflected in the mass demonstrations held during President Pompidou's visit to the United States in February 1970. The protest was directed against France's pro-Arab policy, which had recently been accentuated by her agreement to sell more than 100 Mirage jet planes to Libya, a self-declared ally of Israel's most formidable adversary, Egypt. In the event,

[1] Based upon an interview with Ze'ev Levin, long associated with the *Histadrut*'s external activities, later, Israel's Consul-General (and Ambassador) to Cyprus, and thereafter, Ambassador to Kenya.

French policy was not moved. Indeed the French Head of State reportedly attacked Israel as 'a racial and religious state'.[1] And President Nixon 'decided to hold in abeyance for now a decision with respect to Israel's request for additional aircraft'.[2]

That was not the first time Diaspora Jews had expressed their solidarity with Israel. And even though the effort failed, the intensity of their demonstrations brought into sharp relief the issue of the 'proper' relationship between Jews and the Jewish State. Critics ranged from anti-Semitic adherents of the infamous Protocols of the Elders of Zion—who perceived this as part of a vast, continuing Jewish conspiracy 'to rule the world'—through the vociferously anti-Zionist American Council of Judaism and its Arab allies, to those like René Massigli, former Secretary-General of the French Foreign Ministry, who raised the sinful spectre of 'double loyalty'.[3] Defenders of the demonstrations emphasized the open, pluralist character of the American political system. Dissent and peaceful protest, they noted, were enshrined as legitimate—in fact, high-value—activities of individuals and groups in American society. Many asserted, too, the natural right of Jews to view Israel as their second home—or original homeland—and to use their influence to assist Israel in her struggle for survival. Thus Canada's Prime Minister, Pierre Elliott Trudeau, declared before a *B'nai B'rith* audience:[4]

An inextinguishable memory and the hope for a new beginning formed a personal bond that held together the Jews of the Diaspora, in the very image of that Jerusalem, of which . . . all the parts are as one. . . .

Indeed the new roots that Jewry has established there, as in ancient times, continue to inspire and to unite the members of the Diaspora, and Jews throughout the world have come to regard Israel as a spiritual home.

It is an enrichment for the Jews of Canada, as for their fellow citizens of English, French or Irish origin, to have a mother country to which they are bound by close and ancient ties of kinship.

It is a well-known fact that the voting behaviour of American Jews is influenced by the attitudes of candidates towards Israel and the Arab–Israel conflict. In this sense they have served as an interest group advocate for Israel, trying to secure the election of pro-Israeli members of Congress. Yet, as Safran emphasizes, Jews are not the first ethnic group to act in this manner. The Irish in the United States opposed Jay's Treaty with England in 1794 and played a key role in defeating a proposed fisheries treaty with Canada in 1888. Dutch Americans

[1] *Jerusalem Post*, 2 March 1970, based upon agency reports from Chicago and New York.

[2] From the text of Rogers' statement on 23 March 1970. *Jerusalem Post*, 24 March 1970.

[3] *Le Monde* (Paris), 26 Feb. 1970.

[4] From the text, reproduced in the *Montreal Star*, 14 Feb. 1970.

pressed for US involvement in the Boer War. American Catholics pressed strenuously for intervention on the side of Franco's insurgents in the Spanish Civil War. And Polish Americans urged US hostility to the Communist régime in Warsaw after the Second World War. In short, the behaviour of American Jews is another illustration of ethno-religious politics in the pluralistic American polity.[1]

Some have argued that the difference in *degree* of advocacy by American Jewry on Israel's behalf constitutes a difference in *kind*. But that is merely judgement based upon bias—upon a predisposition to exaggerate the *foreign policy* influence of six million American Jews. This dimension of influence is indeed exaggerated, for there are strong countervailing pressures at work—US oil interests acting as a powerful lobby on Middle East policy, a traditionally pro-Arab group of Foreign Service professionals in the State Department, known as the 'Arabists', and others. Certainly the Nixon decision of early 1970 challenges the difference of degree/difference in kind hypothesis, for it was made in the face of massive pressure, including a condemnation of the Rogers Proposals as 'endangering the security of Israel and imperilling the cause of a just and lasting peace in the Middle East', by a special National Emergency Conference on Peace in the Middle East, sponsored by the 'Presidents' Club'.[2]

Many civil servants, too, have commented on the role of Jews as a pressure group in support of Israeli policy. Thus Eytan wrote in his account of *The First Ten Years*:[3]

[American Jews] are a political factor whose influence may vary but is always felt. . . . American Jews have never hesitated, as American citizens, to bring their weight to bear in the cause of Israel, though it is hard to say how often, if ever, it has been decisive. Anything they do, they must do of their own free will. Israel cannot employ, command or incite them, though she can, and does, keep them informed of her policies and needs.

For Herzog, Israeli decision-makers perceived 'a metaphysical source, a natural assumed link, a belief that they are part of us'; and he acknowledged that Jews abroad have played a valuable role in Israel's pursuit of foreign policy goals.[4]

Another Assistant DG drew a distinction between the relative importance of American Jewry as a pressure group for Israel in the 1948–53 period and in the 1960s: 'In the early days, when Israel was weak, the American Jewish factor provided important leverage in Washington and was necessary—to compensate for Israel's weak power position; as time went on, however, its role became less vital.' He also

---

[1] *The United States and Israel*, pp. 276–80. A more elaborate treatment of this subject is found in Lawrence H. Fuchs (ed.), *American Ethnic Politics*, Harper & Row (Torchbooks), New York, 1968.
[2] *Jerusalem Post*, 28 Jan. 1970.   [3] p. 201.
[4] Interview in Jerusalem, March 1966.

dismissed the value of American Jewry in securing military aid: 'One doesn't get arms by publicly pressing for them—as Sharett discovered during his disastrous talks with the Big Four Foreign Ministers in Geneva in 1955.'[1] The 1970 case—with Jewish public pressure and Nixon's negative reply—seems to support this thesis.

ii. *Independence and After*

The classic example of Jewry's role as a pro-Israeli pressure group relates to US behaviour on the issue of independence: it was the first and most significant foreign policy decision of the Jewish state. The memoirs—of both Americans and Israelis—are revealing on this process of implementing policy for a state in the making.

Among American officials concerned with 'The Palestine Question', Secretary of Defence Forrestal, who opposed an independent Israel, was one of the most critical. In his diary entry of 1 December 1947, just after the historic Partition Resolution of the UN General Assembly, he wrote:[2]

. . . Lovett [Under-Secretary of State] reported [during a Cabinet lunch] on the result of the United Nations action on Palestine over the week end. He said he had never in his life been subject to as much pressure as he had been in the three days beginning Thursday morning and ending Saturday night. . . .

I said I thought the decision was fraught with great danger for the future security of this country.

President Truman was extraordinarily blunt about the pressure of American Jewry. In November 1947 Weizmann denied the charge of American Jewish pressure. Truman wrote:[3]

Unfortunately Dr. Weizmann was correct only to the extent that his immediate associates were concerned. The facts were that not only were there pressure movements around the United Nations unlike anything that had been seen there before but that the White House, too, was subjected to a constant barrage. I do not think I ever had as much pressure and propaganda aimed at the White House as I had in this instance. . .

Referring to the tense days of the spring of 1948, Truman recalled:[4]

The Jewish pressure on the White House did not diminish in the days following the partition vote in the United Nations. Individuals and groups asked me,

---

[1] Interview with Mordekhai Gazit, Jerusalem, April 1966. For a comprehensive scholarly analysis of the American Zionist movement as a political interest group, advocating the cause of the *Yishuv* and, later, a Jewish state, see Samuel Halperin, *The Political World of American Zionism*, Wayne State University Press, Detroit, 1961, ch. 2, 9, 12. This study, however, concludes with the establishment of Israel; indeed only a few pages are devoted to the post-1945 period. Thus it sheds no light on the role of Jewry in implementing the foreign policy of the new state.

[2] Walter Millis (ed.), *The Forrestal Diaries*, Viking Press, New York, 1951, p. 346.

[3] Harry S. Truman, *Years of Trial and Hope* (vol. 2 of Memoirs), Doubleday, New York, 1956, p. 158. See also pp. 140, 153.   [4] Ibid., p. 160.

usually in rather quarrelsome and emotional ways, to stop the Arabs, to keep the British from supporting the Arabs, to furnish American soldiers, to do this, that, and the other. I think I can say that I kept my faith in the rightness of my policy in spite of some of the Jews . . . , I mean, of course, the extreme Zionists.

Truman then related the Eddie Jacobson episode. His old friend and business associate from Kansas City pleaded with him to see Weizmann at a time when the US Government appeared to be withdrawing its support for partition in favour of a State Department-inspired proposal of Trusteeship over Palestine. Truman finally yielded and met the Zionist leader on 18 March 1948. The President was persuaded to remain staunch to his commitment to a Jewish state, though not without contrary pressure. Indeed, despite his scathing criticism, Truman was genuinely sympathetic to the Jewish plight and its national aspirations, as is evident from other parts of his memoirs.[1]

Weizmann made only an oblique reference to the role of Jewry in that crucial period: 'American Jews who until recently were remote from the Zionist movement took a keen interest in the United Nations discussion and helped us in the work' (Proskauer of the American Jewish Committee, Baruch, Herbert Swope, Warburg, and Henry Morgenthau, Jr.), apart, of course, from Abba Hillel Silver, the US Zionist leader who, along with Sharett, conducted 'the official pleading of our cause before the United Nations . . . with great skill and energy'.[2]

Nahum Goldmann was more direct. Recalling the autumn 1947

[1] 'The fate of the Jewish victims of Hitlerism was a matter of deep personal concern to me', he began his account of the Jewish–Arab struggle for Palestine from 1945 to 1948. As for the Balfour Declaration, 'this promise, I felt, should be kept, just as all promises made by responsible, civilized governments should be kept'. He was also critical of his technical advisers in the autumn of 1945: 'The State Department continued to be more concerned about the Arab reaction than the sufferings of the Jews.' When, on 15 May 1948, he accorded recognition to Israel, Lovett reportedly said to him, 'They [the State Department career men] almost put it over on you.' It is, in fact, clear from his memoirs that, for Truman, the humanitarian rescue of a people in distress was his guiding motive. Ibid., pp. 132, 140, 165.

This is emphasized as well by Dean Acheson in his memoirs: 'From many years of talk with him I know that this represented a deep conviction—[that] the Balfour Declaration seemed to him "to go hand in hand with the noble policies of Woodrow Wilson, especially the principle of self-determination"—in large part implanted by his close friend . . . Eddie Jacobson. . . .' Indeed, Acheson, who 'did not share the President's views on the Palestine solution to the pressing and desperate plight of great numbers of displaced Jews in Eastern Europe . . .', went out of his way to dismiss the Attlee-Bevin charge that Truman was 'inspired by domestic political opportunism'. 'This was not true despite the confirming observations of some of his associates, such as Bob Hannegan, Jim Forrestal, and James Byrnes, collected by Mr. Attlee in his memoirs. Mr. Truman held deep-seated convictions on many subjects. . . .' *Present at the Creation*, Norton, New York, 1969, p. 169.

[2] Chaim Weizmann, *Trial and Error*, Harper & Bros., New York, 1949, p. 457. American Jewish leader Dr. Israel Goldstein, World Chairman of *Keren Ha-yesod*, added a brief memoir on US Jewry's aid in the political struggle for independence. *Jerusalem Post* (Special Independence Day Supplement), 10 May 1970.

struggle at the UN over the Partition Resolution he wrote: 'In the intervening days (Thanksgiving Day, the 27th of November, and the next two days) we campaigned frantically. President Truman himself lent a hand by conferring with various delegates. All the good will we could count on was mobilized to secure the votes of a few undecided delegations.'[1]

Ze'ev Sharef, an Israeli chronicler of that momentous period, also acknowledged the implementing role of American Jewry: 'It is true that pressure was brought to bear by the American Jewish community upon him [Truman] and upon the Democratic Party, and the wishes and aspirations of that community were frequently drawn to his attention.'[2] Moreover, he reconstructed in great detail the Eddie Jacobson role as link between Truman and Weizmann in March 1948.[3]

The influential American Jewish Committee (AJC), which opposed an independent Jewish state until August 1946, also confirmed this pressure-group role. In its proud record of advocacy on behalf of Israel it noted that in 1947 it established a close working relationship with the Jewish Agency at the UN and helped to interpret the Agency's views to the US Government, it submitted a brief to UNSCOP urging partition as the only solution, and it telegraphed Secretary of State Marshall, urging support for the majority UNSCOP proposal of partition; in 1948 it urged Truman to lift the arms embargo, expressed 'keen regret' at the US Government's espousal of Trusteeship, and asked the US to press for firm action by the Security Council to 'put an end to the invasion of Palestine—summarily'.[4]

The role of advocate for Israeli foreign policy goals was performed in America by other groups as well. The most powerful instrument was the

---

[1] Referring to 1946, he wrote: '... influence had to be brought to bear on the American government....' At some length he narrated his own role in discussions with a Cabinet committee of three appointed by Truman to deal with the Palestine problem—State (Under-Secretary Acheson), Treasury (Snyder), and War (Patterson): 'My principal task was to secure the support of these three cabinet ministers for partition.... I ... managed in three long, exhaustive conversations to convince Acheson....' And finally, Truman's Adviser, Niles, informed him that the President had accepted *his* partition plan—on 9 August 1946! *The Autobiography of Nahum Goldmann*, pp. 224, 233, 245.

Once more the American sources differ. Neither the Truman nor the Acheson memoirs makes any reference to Goldmann's talks with the Cabinet committee of three, especially with Acheson. What Goldmann refers to as 'those few days in Washington, momentous ones for our foreign policy, [which] were thus crowned with success', made no impact on Acheson or Truman—or on Weizmann, or on anyone else who wrote memoirs of that period.

[2] *Three Days*, p. 36.

[3] Ibid., pp. 230–44, 'Dr. Weizmann Seeks Recognition of the State'. This is an intriguing and informative account of Weizmann's vital diplomatic role in the crucial last months before statehood, especially in persuading Truman to retain his commitment to Partition and Independence.

[4] *In Vigilant Brotherhood*, pp. 27–30.

Conference of Presidents of Major Jewish Organizations, founded in 1955 and comprising all important Zionist and other Jewish organizations, other than the AJC. The 'Presidents' Club' was involved in the whole gamut of US-Israel relations—arms for Israel, the denial of arms to Arab states, a guarantee of Israel's security, economic aid, the muting of US Government reaction to Israel's policy of retaliation, etc.: 'all through the years the State Department's pro-Arab policy was hindered by Jewish organizations making their views known and their influence felt'.[1]

Jewish pressure on behalf of Israel continued through the years, often through quiet diplomacy, with the link between input (pressure) and outcome (US policy) somewhat blurred. Some highlights of the AJC catalogue of its record of support illuminate this role.[2]

Recognition: In September 1948, Blaustein discussed *de jure* recognition with Truman; it was granted on 31 January 1949.

In October the AJC expressed its strong opposition to US official circles favouring the Bernadotte Plan, which would have detached the Negev from Israel, ostensibly in exchange for Western Galilee. Truman was not taken in: 'I did not like this change', he wrote in his memoirs. 'It looked to me like a fast reshuffle.'[3]

Economic Aid: In September 1948, Blaustein urged Truman to make a large loan; an Export-Import Bank loan of $100 million was granted in the spring of 1949.

In the autumn of 1950 he pressed for a further loan to assist the absorption of immigrants; a loan of $35 million came in January 1951.

There were further contacts in 1950, 1951, 1952, and 1953; two substantial grants-in-aid were made in June 1951 and June 1952, for $63·5 million and $70 million respectively.

It may be exaggerated to suggest, as the AJC account does, that its advocacy was wholly or even primarily responsible for the benefits that accrued to Israel. Yet that role was a lubricant in the process. And the AJC performed an implementing function in other fields as well: pressure for Great Power public support for existing frontiers—which found expression in the Tripartite Declaration of 1950; unsuccessful efforts to persuade the US to sell arms to Israel—all through the 1950s; public pressure on Adenauer in 1958 to eradicate UAR subversive interference in the prosecution of war criminals, and attempts, in 1963, to persuade the West German Government to act on the issue of German scientists in Egypt; and pressure on the US Government in 1957

[1] Interview with Goldmann, Jerusalem, June 1966.
[2] *In Vigilant Brotherhood*.   [3] Op. cit., p. 166.

and 1960, without success, to use its influence to secure free passage for Israeli ships through the Suez Canal.

Perhaps the most significant instance of a successful implementation role by Jews in Israeli foreign policy—after 1947–8—was that of Goldmann in the negotiations leading to the Reparations Agreement of 1952. While it was not the one-man achievement suggested by his memoirs, he was the central figure, especially in moments of crisis, when decisions by the German Chancellor were necessary. Formally, the Jewish Claims Conference, of which Goldmann was President, conducted the negotiations jointly with a Government of Israel Delegation.[1]

Less dramatic was the extent and outcome of Jewish pressure during the period of political struggle following the Sinai Campaign. The AJC presented a three-point peace programme to Dulles on 3 November 1956: the US should call upon the UN to require the Arabs to enter direct negotiations with Israel for a peace settlement; a refusal to negotiate should be branded as incompatible with the UN Charter; and the US, among others, should guarantee the treaties so reached.[2] Goldmann claimed, in retrospect, that American Jewish pressure, along with the support of friendly non-Jewish groups, was primarily responsible for blunting the threat of US sanctions and for securing US acceptance of Israeli 'assumptions' as a pre-condition to withdrawal in the spring of 1957. Pressure, he added, took the form of letters to Congressmen, protests, meetings, demonstrations, etc. And, while the Israeli Embassy knew of their plans, 'the tactics were our own'.[3] Referring to the mid-July 1956 period, just before Nasser's nationalization of the Canal, a member of Eisenhower's entourage wrote: 'Congress [was] under continual pressure from Israel's lobbies. . . . It was extremely doubtful if the President could have obtained Congressional approval of the grants and loans to the Egyptians at that point. . . .'[4]

There are countless other illustrations of American Jewry's implementing role in Israeli foreign policy—by the Presidents' Club and its constituent members, the AJC, etc. Thus, at the time of the Beirut airport raid in December 1968, both the Zionist Organization of America and the American Jewish Congress sharply criticized the State Department's protest to Israel: 'not one human life was lost' in the reprisal raid, whereas no United States Government action was taken in the face of 'terrorism and murder' against the El Al plane in Athens. They were joined in this protest by the New York Board of Rabbis.[5]

[1] Goldmann's highly personalized account, which depreciates the roles of all others, s to be found in his *Autobiography*, ch. 22. This important issue will be explored in depth in the related volume on Israeli high-policy decisions.

[2] *In Vigilant Brotherhood*.

[3] Interview in Jerusalem, May 1966.

[4] Sherman Adams, *First Hand Report*, Hutchinson, London, 1962, p. 198.

[5] *New York Times*, 30 Dec. 1968.

(In 1969, and again in 1970, during the quest for more Phantoms and Skyhawks and other military aid, American Jewry succeeded in getting hundreds of Congressmen to sign petitions urging the US Government to sell arms to Israel.)

Like its predecessors, the Nixon Administration was sensitive to Jewish opinion—despite the decision in March 1970 to defer the sale of planes. Thus a *New York Times* review of Middle East lobbies in the US disclosed that, some days before the official announcement, a copy of the official statement turning down the Israeli request was delivered to Max Fisher, a leader of the United Jewish Appeal: his mission was to explain the disappointing decision to Israel's friends. Indeed, there seemed to be a feeling among American Jews at the time that their ability to influence US policy in a pro-Israel direction was clearly and sharply declining under the Nixon Administration.

More generally, the *Times* reported that the Administration and many politicians believed Israel had effective control over some American Zionists.[1] The evidence was very thin. Closer to the truth is the proposition that American Jews *know* what Israel's basic foreign policy aims are, *feel* a deep community of interests with Israel, and *act* independently to further these objectives—without any qualms of 'double loyalty', for they see no conflict of interests between the United States and Israel. There is no control and no need for control. It is autonomous behaviour by sophisticated groups of American Zionists. The same is true of Jews elsewhere, with a difference in effectiveness. In Latin America, such a role was spasmodic—and less essential. In France it was not necessary from 1954 to 1967—and impossible thereafter. And British Jewry is articulate but less influential in UK politics, though it has often advocated pro-Israeli policies, especially through the Labour Party.

iii *Legitimacy*

The legitimacy of American Jewish pressure on the US Government to adopt policies favourable to Israel is openly asserted by Israelis and American Jews alike. Some proclaim it with passion, for example, Rabbi Abba Hillel Silver, one of the most eloquent of American Zionists. On the assumption that 'the most effective representation in a democracy is through organized public opinion', Silver declared:

If our cause is just, let the American people speak up—its ministers and educators, its writers and journalists, its leaders of capital and labour, its State Legislators, its Congressmen and Senators. . . . Let them make known their will to our Government and to our Chief Executive. . . . Let us rally all men of good will everywhere in the world. . . . Let a mighty chorus of voices rise to the ears of the men whom destiny has chosen for great decisions. . . .[2]

[1] As reported in an INA dispatch to the *Jerusalem Post*, 7 April 1970.
[2] Address before the American Zionist Policy Committee, 21 March 1945, as reprinted in Silver's *Vision and Victory*, New York, 1949, p. 83.

Among Israelis the *right* of Jews everywhere to support the Jewish state actively—with financial aid, political influence, and immigrants— is a self-evident proposition. Indeed to most it is an *obligation* flowing from the unity of the Jewish People, rooted in history, culture, religion, tradition, and memory, mostly of anguish. The Israeli sense of isolation, heightened over the years by a siege mentality and periodic disappointments from assumed Great Power friends, found increasing expression in the 'two-camp thesis' of Ben Gurion. 'We are a people that dwells alone', wrote Israel's commanding figure, soon after the Sinai Campaign. 'The only loyal ally we have is the Jewish people.'[1] And in 1962 he declared that, while Israel is an end in itself, she is also a means—to the full redemption of Jewry. In that context, Israel's 'only "ally" is the Diaspora. . . . This partnership is not laid down in any covenant signed and sealed; it is written in Jewish history, in the heart of every Jew loyal to his people.'[2]

About the influence of Jews abroad Peres remarked: 'World Jewry is a legend, and you cannot kill a legend. Talking to European leaders, one sees the importance they attach to world Jewry.' As for Israel's proper behaviour, 'one should exercise economy in using Diaspora Jewry to assist Israel's foreign policy—because this would place Jews in an awkward position, and they can do less than State of Israel representatives'. 'We were', he added, 'eager to win the support of the Presidents' Club, not as a condition to our action but because we wanted them to understand our plans.'[3]

Dov Joseph, who held many portfolios in the Government of Israel between 1949 and 1965, cited as a model the behaviour of British Jews in 1946–7: they openly opposed the British Government's repressive acts in Palestine and its refusal to support Jewish statehood. 'Where Jews feel their Government's actions and policy towards Israel are wrong, they should protest. This does not mean *a priori* attachment to, and defence of, Israel's behaviour. It means only *a priori* sympathy for Israel.' In general, he continued, Latin American Jewry displayed the model attitude of Jews to Israel and to their own country. 'They have no difficulty in feeling loyalty to Argentina, for example, as citizens [a legal status], and at the same time as members of the Jewish nation [a cultural entity].' And, as Tsur and others had noted, 'Latin American Governments accept this dual identification'.[4]

One Assistant DG in the Foreign Office remarked that he had told a visiting Jewish member of Congress—in the presence of a US Embassy

[1] 'Israel and the Diaspora', in State of Israel, *Government Year-Book 5718*, 1957–8, Jerusalem, p. 32.
[2] 'Achievements and Tasks of Our Generation', in State of Israel, *Government Year-Book 5722*, 1961–2, Jerusalem, p. lxxi.
[3] Interview in Tel Aviv, May 1966.
[4] Interviews in Jerusalem, Aug. 1960.

officer: 'The two pillars of Israel's security are the Israel Defence Forces and American Jewry.' Further, 'both the United States Government and the country at large accept the role of American Jewry as a legitimate lobby. The Government receives delegations frequently and sometimes calls them in. If it did not, public opinion would assert itself. Yet in 95 per cent of the issues Israel does not involve American Jews.'[1] Another Assistant DG distinguished the existence of the Jewish factor from its use by Israel: 'A sophisticated Israeli diplomacy would recognize that the Jewish factor is a given in American politics. All American politicians know it and take it into consideration. To flaunt it constantly and bluntly is heavy-handed and likely to boomerang. Just as an army does not assert its heavy firepower for every skirmish, so too Israel must not overextend this asset in its armoury.'[2]

It remains to make the central point that what has here been designated an implementing role in terms of Israeli foreign policy is a natural and completely legitimate function of interest groups within their own political system. As for the Government of Israel part of the equation, all states seek allies, whether they be sovereign entities or socio-economic, cultural, or ethnic groups. And such an implementing role is an inherent part of the deeply penetrated political systems of the contemporary world. Those who raise the spectre of double loyalty distort or fail to understand the realities of the political process in foreign policy.

As for the legitimacy of Jewry's role, the most candid and persuasive rationale was provided by an Assistant DG of the Israeli Foreign Office —to a visiting State Department official. 'The Almighty placed massive oil deposits under Arab soil, and the Arab states have exploited this good fortune for political ends during the past half-century. It is our good fortune that God placed five million Jews in America. And we have no less a right to benefit from their influence with the US Government to help us survive and to prosper.'[3]

[1] Interview with Moshe Bitan, Jerusalem, April 1966.
[2] Interview with Gazit, Jerusalem, April 1966.
[3] Interview in Jerusalem, Aug. 1960.

CHAPTER 20

The Foreign Ministry at Work

(a) ORIGINS

The *Misrad Ha-hutz* (Foreign Office) emerged as a natural continuation of the Jewish Agency's Political Department, which 'had been a Foreign Ministry in all but name and external authority'.[1] And as the analysis of the Technical Élite revealed, the Israeli Foreign Service has been dominated by the men of the Political Department. Indeed their influence was pervasive in moulding behaviour within the Ministry: the Decision-Making Inner Circle in the early years, remarked one knowing official, 'were members of an established club with a highly-developed *esprit de corps*; they had known each other for years and had an easy informal relationship; this contributed to close co-operation and rapid decisions'.[2]

The initial structure of the ministry can be traced to 15 October 1947, when the Jewish Agency appointed a high-level committee to plan the administrative organization of the new state in the making. Sub-committees were formed to design each ministry, with Eytan, then Principal of the Agency's Public Service College (JAPSC), the 'school for diplomats', as a one-man committee to plan the Foreign Office.[3]

The 'Outline Plan for a Foreign Office and Foreign Service of the Jewish State' was presented to the parent committee on 9 January 1948; and the second (final) draft was submitted at the end of January —ready to be activated on Independence Day. Its basic assumption— in fact, the very first remark—was 'that we should not spend more money on a Foreign Office than is absolutely necessary. At the same time, even a Foreign Office and Foreign Service run on modest lines must cost a good deal of money.' The British influence, which is evident throughout, extended even to idiosyncratic expression: 'It will there-

[1] Eytan, *The First Ten Years*, p. 208.
[2] Interview with H. Radai, Jerusalem, March 1966.
[3] Eytan's memoir, p. 209. Ze'ev Sharef, in one of the most detailed primary sources on the events leading to statehood, offers a similar account of the plan for the Foreign Office but attributes it to a number of persons: 'The plan for the Ministry for Foreign Affairs was drawn up by a group of members of the Political Department of the Jewish Agency Executive, and it was the same group which later built up the Foreign Ministry.' *Three Days*, pp. 53–4. Radai referred to an informal committee of three—Eytan, Levavi and himself—who met between January and May 1948 to discuss the structure of the Foreign Office and Foreign Service. Interview noted above. But these discussions came after the Plan had been drafted and accepted; that is, they concerned its implementation. Eytan himself acknowledged the role of students of the JAPSC in preparing the Plan, by providing helpful research. Most persons interviewed over the years accepted Eytan's version of a one-man committee.

fore be better to make reasonable financial allowance from the start than to risk spoiling the ship for a hap'orth of tar!'[1]

Eytan proposed an administrative structure of seven geographic Departments—Middle Eastern, Western European, Eastern European, North American, Latin American, British Empire, and Asian and African—and six functional Departments—United Nations. Consular, Economic, Legal, Information, and Training and Research. These were to operate under the supervision of a Director-General. There was also provision for a Secretary-General, in charge of Establishment and general administrative services, Finance, Registry, and Protocol—with the further authority 'to act as his deputy' in the absence of the DG. (This became a point of tension in the early years and led to the resignation of the only person who held the post of Secretary-General, in 1953; apparently, he interpreted his authority literally and attempted to extend his role of deputy to policy matters as well; thereafter, the status of the administrative head of the ministry was reduced to that of one of a number of Assistant Directors-General.) Hebrew was designated the working as well as the official language, 'subject to any special exigencies of the service'; and the DG was to standardize Hebrew equivalents for expressions in diplomatic practice. That task, Eytan wrote later, 'was accomplished, almost singlehanded, by the Foreign Minister himself'.[2] He also envisaged the appointment at a later stage of three Deputy DGs, to be responsible for the geographic, functional, and administrative Divisions.

The diplomatic and consular services were to be integrated into 'the Foreign Service' whose personnel 'shall be interchangeable with that of the Foreign Office'. The highest rank in the Service was to be Minister in charge of a Legation, that is, Envoy Extraordinary and Minister Plenipotentiary. And to begin with, three categories of missions were to be established within six months after independence:

A. Legations in London, Moscow, Washington, and Paris
   Passport Control Offices at Hanover, Munich, Vienna, Berlin, and Bucharest ('immediately')
B. Consulates-General in Shanghai, Prague, Ankara, and Teheran
   Consulates in Warsaw and Rome
   Passport Control Offices at Aden and Budapest ('as soon as possible')
C. Consulates-General in Stockholm and Rio de Janeiro
   Consulates in Bombay, Brussels, Johannesburg, Montreal (or Ottawa), and Melbourne (or Sydney)
   Passport Control Offices at Algiers and Sofia ('before six months have passed')

[1] This extract and the account of the 'Outline Plan' which follows are taken from the final draft, made available through the Foreign Ministry, Jerusalem. The Plan is carefully summarized, with extensive verbatim extracts, in *The First Ten Years*, ch. 10, 'The Foreign Service'. [2] Ibid., pp. 208–9.

(There were some deviations in practice: the Consulate-General in Stockholm and the Consulate in Rome were established earlier than planned; Hanover was dropped, etc.)

It was a well-conceived distribution of posts and a rather elaborate Establishment for a small new state. Yet it was justified, Eytan wrote in retrospect, by Israel's world-wide interests and needs. More specifically, Israel is surrounded by enemies—and seeks friends everywhere; she is the object of boycott—and seeks economic ties wherever possible; she is constantly preoccupied with United Nations debates—and needs political support; and Israel's bonds with the Diaspora mean universal interests and ties.

The 'Outline Plan' laid down a meticulous rank and linkage system: Ministers = Director-General, and Consul-General = Head of Department; Ministers to be responsible to the Foreign Minister through the DG, and Consuls-General and Consuls to the DG—through the head of the relevant geographic Department, for political matters; to the head of the Consular Department for visas, protection of citizens, etc.; to the head of the Economic Department for trade and other economic matters; to the head of the Information Department for information, press, propaganda and cultural matters; and to the Secretary-General for administrative, financial, and communications matters.

The timetable for implementation of the Plan was no less precise: the DG was to be appointed by 1 February 1948, the Secretary-General ten days later, and other senior officers by 15 March; representatives were to be dispatched in the second half of March to negotiate recognition with foreign governments; and 'the whole machinery to be at immediate notice [on] "Z" day—15th May (say)', with seventy-two persons, including thirty-eight officers, to be at their desks and forty others ready to leave for posts abroad, including four Ministers, four Counsellors and four First Secretaries. Certainly the author of the Plan could not be faulted for lack of attention to detail.

The proposed budget was very small—a maximum of £P (Palestine pounds) 400,000, then worth $2 million, half of which was for salaries and allowances. It was smaller than, but obviously derived from comparison with, the Foreign Office–Foreign Service budgets of Egypt, Iraq, and Lebanon.[1] The Plan also provided for liaison between the Foreign Office and related branches of the bureaucracy—the Economic Department with the Trade and Industry Ministry, the Information Department with 'all other Ministries and other relevant organizations', the Legal Division with the Justice Ministry, and the Secretary-General, in financial matters, with the Finance Ministry. A

[1] As noted in the 'Outline Plan', they were:
Egypt (1945) £P436,700
Iraq (1945 budget) £P386,000
Lebanon (1948 estimates) £P383,000

security screening of all employees was proposed. And as befits the Oxford don, the author added: 'Probably the single most important piece of equipment for the Foreign Office is a library': various categories of books were specified.[1]

The dictates of war modified the timetable of the 'Outline Plan', a well-conceived framework of the British type. Thus on Independence Day, 14 May 1948, two persons started work with the Foreign Minister in Tel Aviv's *Hakirya*, the provisional seat of Government: the others were caught in the siege of Jerusalem. Eytan went down to Tel Aviv during the first Truce—12 June—and, a few days later, asked Foreign Minister Sharett who was to be Director-General: 'why, I thought you would be', was the reported reply. Eytan served as DG for the next eleven years, as long as all his successors combined until mid-1970.

The staff grew from two to a hundred within a month. Everything had to be organized simultaneously and with very little experience, for, while the Jewish Agency's Political Department eased the initial personnel problem, new procedures had to be mastered. The first act of the Ministry was to inform the Governments of the world that Israel had been established as a state and to submit requests for recognition.[2] (The first to comply was the US and then the USSR, Guatemala, Poland, Uruguay, Czechoslovakia, South Africa, Yugoslavia, Hungary, Roumania, Finland, and Costa Rica.) No one knew how to draft a letter of credence, with the result, a celebrated case, that, when Avriel presented his letter as newly-appointed Minister to Prague, the Czech Government returned it, saying that Israel's envoy was recognized but suggesting that the letter be redrafted in a customary manner 'as per the attached specimen'.[3]

There were other minor deviations from the Plan: the introduction of embassy-level missions as early as 1949, in response to US initiative, a practice that had become almost universal in Israel's diplomatic representation abroad by 1965; the change in location of a few Passport Control Offices, as noted; and the rapid closure of some of these posts as soon as most of the immigrants were on their way to Israel. Yet the basic structure of the Foreign Office and its underlying ideas derived from the 'Outline Plan'.

[1] The consensus among Foreign Office personnel and librarians interviewed was that newspapers and periodicals are in much greater demand than books: the *New York Herald Tribune*, *The Times*, and *Le Monde* are in constant use; *The Economist*, *Observer*, the *New Statesman*, and *Time* are widely read. Academic journals are used infrequently, except for specialized legal materials. *Foreign Affairs* is read by some. About 90 per cent of all foreign-language materials used are in English.

[2] When Gideon Rafael, later a DG, took the cables seeking recognition to the Tel Aviv Post Office on 14 May for urgent dispatch, he was told in no uncertain terms by the clerk on duty that they had to be paid for. He returned to the Ministry for the required funds, and the cables were duly sent!

[3] Shabtai Rosenne, in a lecture on the Foreign Ministry at the Middle East College of Public Administration, as reported in *Jerusalem Post*, 16 May 1949.

(b) STRUCTURE

The organizational framework of Israel's Ministry for Foreign Affairs in 1949 incorporated most of Eytan's proposals, as evident in Figure 11: a Director-General with authority and responsibility for the work of the entire Ministry; a Secretary-General supervising the administrative sphere; and groups of geographic and functional Departments. There are some differences, however: the addition of (personal) advisers to the Foreign *Minister* (there were 3 in 1949, Kohn, Shiloah, and Danin), as well as a Legal Adviser to the Foreign *Ministry* (Head of the Legal Department, Rosenne); the elevation of Research to the status of an *Agaf* (a Division); the addition of Departments—Cultural, and Foreign Visitors; and some changes in nomenclature—International Organizations instead of the UN, United States instead of North American, British Commonwealth instead of British Empire, and Asia, which was not established until November 1949, instead of Asian and African. In its essentials, however, the Eytan scheme was accepted.

There were various organizational changes in the Foreign Office during the first twenty years. Armistice Affairs was added in 1951—until then it was under the direct jurisdiction of the Defence Ministry. Asia was enlarged to include Africa in 1957, and Asia–Africa was split into two Departments in 1960. Among the functional Departments, Research was reduced in status in 1952. Political and Economic Planning was added at the beginning of 1960, essentially to combat the Arab boycott. International Co-operation was added in 1959–60, initially as a Section, then as a Department. A stillborn Middle East *Agaf* was created in 1966. And Armistice Affairs was disbanded after the 1967 War, symbol of the replacement of the 1949 Armistice Agreements by a Cease-Fire in a new context.

The rank of Assistant DG was introduced in 1952 (Comay and Levavi were the first) and they increased in number over the years. The post of Secretary-General was abolished in 1953, his functions being assumed by an Assistant DG in charge of Administration. In 1966 a Deputy DG was appointed (Lourie), though the function of acting for the DG in his absence existed as early as 1952.[1] And the post of Ambassador-at-Large was introduced in 1966.

The most far-reaching *formal* reorganization of the Ministry occurred in March 1968. Notable structural changes are evident in Figure 12:

---

[1] The authority to act in the name of the Director-General during the latter's absence was held successively by the following:

Michael Comay	1 April 1952–7 July 1953
Arthur Lourie	22 June 1953–6 September 1957
Michael Comay	1 July 1957–27 March 1960
Arye Levavi	7 August 1960–14 October 1964
Arthur Lourie	11 July 1965–31 March 1966

Lourie was appointed Deputy Director-General on 1 April 1966.

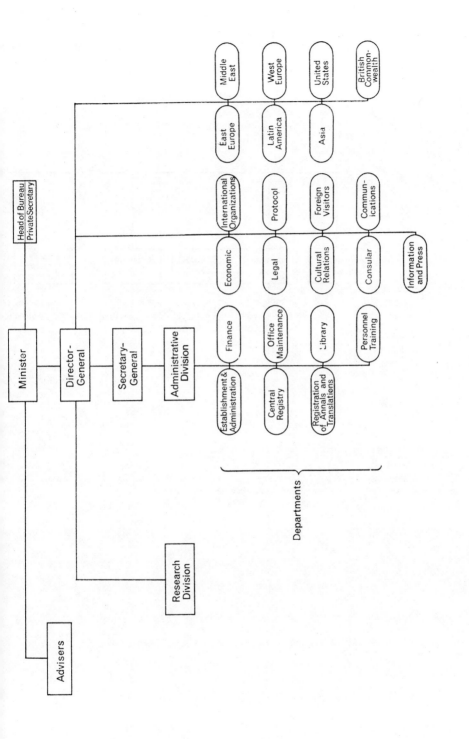

Figure 12. Structure of t

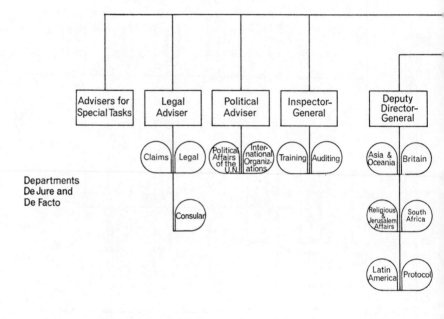

Departments
De Jure and
De Facto

Source: Based upon a Memorandum from the Director-General's Bureau,
Ministry for Foreign Affairs, Jerusalem, 1 March 1968.

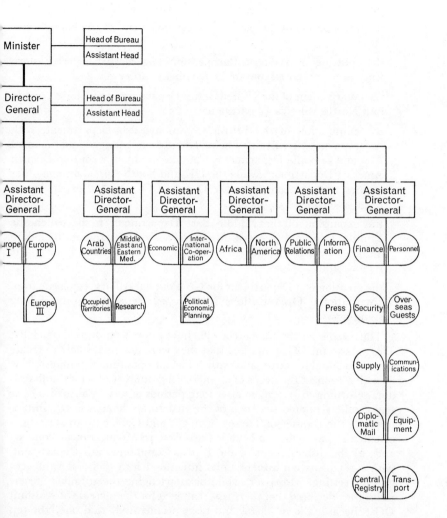

the proliferation of Assistant DGs, to the largest number in the Ministry's history—seven, including the Deputy DG, supervising administrative, functional, and geographic Departments;

the introduction of the post of Inspector-General of the Foreign Service;

the splitting of Western Europe into two Departments (Eastern Europe had been a separate Department earlier);

the enlargement of the United States Department to include Canada in a North America Department;

the elimination of the British Commonwealth Department, with Australia and New Zealand being added to an enlarged and renamed Asia and Oceania Department (Canada, as noted, went to the North America Department, while the UK and South Africa, among other regions, were placed under the Deputy DG, who had expert knowledge about these countries);

the expansion of the Middle East Department, to be called the Middle East and Eastern Mediterranean Department, including Turkey, Cyprus, Greece, and Iran, as well as the Arab states of the region; and

the creation of a Department for UN Political Affairs—separate from International Organizations (the *de facto* separation was of long standing).

The reasons for the changes of 1968 have not been indicated officially. Three Assistant DGs remarked that they were designed solely to create posts of a suitable status, and with sufficient operational responsibility, formally, to meet the needs of an increasing number of senior ambassadors returning to Jerusalem after long periods of service abroad. Other senior officials noted that two of the structural changes were substantive: (1) the transfer of Turkey, Cyprus, and Greece, from a Europe-oriented Department to a Middle East–Eastern Mediterranean context; and (2) the disbandment of the British Commonwealth Department, with most of its constituent units integrated into their relevant geographic setting. Moreover, while acknowledging the stimulus of new posts, they declared that there was real need for the increase of Assistant DGs: 'Because the problems and tasks proliferated,' said one, 'the top of the pyramid had to expand as well; the past two years have proved the wisdom of the reorganization.'[1]

The functions of the Foreign Ministry are clearly defined in its annual *Skira* or Report:[2]

[1] Interviews in Jerusalem, Jan. 1970.

[2] Ministry for Foreign Affairs, *Skira* (Report): *Appendix to the Foreign Minister's Speech on the Budget of the Ministry for 1966–67*, Jerusalem, p. 1. Later *Skirot* have a slightly different wording of the Ministry's functions.

to maintain the official ties of the State of Israel with the rest of the world. This function is expressed:

in the presentation of State matters before governments of the nations of the world and before international organizations;

in constantly informing the governments, organizations, and peoples of the whole world about Israel's attitudes and problems;

in the development of cultural relations with governments and nations;

in the reinforcement of economic and trade relations with states;

in the extension of cooperation to developing nations;

in the safeguarding of the rights of Israeli citizens abroad and in the provision of consular services for citizens of other countries;

in addition to this the Foreign Office is involved in strengthening the relations between the State of Israel and the Jewish communities abroad and their essential interests.

The functions listed above are executed by the Foreign Office through two principal arms: the Head Office in Jerusalem and the legations abroad.

(c) RECRUITMENT

'The Foreign Office is faced with special manpower problems', remarked the Assistant DG (Administration) in his 1966–7 Survey.

The turnover is large; the requirements of service in Israel and abroad and the wide framework of duties, necessitate much flexibility in the employment of manpower. With this in mind . . . a special system was devised for the manpower structure . . . [with] special principles. . . .
1. Division of workers into three separate sections: the political section, the foreign administrative section, and the administrative section (domestic);
2. Establishment of global standards in the political and foreign administrative sections, in contrast to the more functional standards accepted in other ministries. . . .
3. Establishment of personal *dragim* [diplomatic ranks] in addition to the wage grades. . . .
4. Correspondence between the *dragim* and the tasks assigned to the workers. . . .
5. Setting of definite time periods for the advancement of workers through the ranks. . . .[1]

The personnel problem at the outset was eased by the flow of twenty-four senior members of the Political Department to the Foreign Ministry —sufficient to provide a skeletal staff for all geographic departments and the directorate of the new ministry. But this source was quickly exhausted. Recruitment by recommendation was the norm until 1953, for a large number of middle- and senior-level posts had to be filled

[1] Ibid., p. 39.

quickly—a problem which confronted the Foreign Service in many new states.[1] Preference was initially given to two groups: to Anglo-Saxons, partly because of the need for English, partly because the selection process was in the hands of Anglo-Saxons; and to East Europeans, who had multiple language skills. By 1951–2 the latter were no longer in demand, for the Soviet bloc turned against Israel and relations were minimal thereafter. It was an unsatisfactory method, Eytan acknowledged; but it produced fewer misfits than expected, in his judgement, and many of those were dismissed.[2] This assessment was not widely shared by his colleagues, however. Indeed, half a dozen other leading members of the Technical Élite bemoaned the personnel legacy of those years. 'The Ministry is full of dead wood' was the common thread of their criticism.[3] And, while widespread incompetence in a Foreign Office, especially in the middle ranks, is not unique to Israel, the political cost is rather greater than for most small states, because of the extraordinary importance of foreign relations to a state under permanent threat of extinction.

The rank structure of the Foreign Office–Foreign Service was 15 to 1 in ascending order until 1 April 1964; thereafter it became 1 to 20. Ranks 15 to 8 (until 1964) and 1 to 12 (afterwards) were administrative staff recruited through the Labour Exchanges and the Civil Service Commission. Examinations for technical and linguistic competence are held for candidate secretaries, and a security check is mandatory for all, with appointments on a trial basis for six to twelve months. Recruitment into the diplomatic grades was conducted by a Foreign Office Selection Board of senior officials until 1959, though examinations, annually since 1953 except for one year, were held as the first stage of recruitment. These were open, de facto, to university graduates, from 22 to 30, with a knowledge of Hebrew and either English or French. The opportunities for bias were less than in the pre-1953 method of 'recommendation', but they continued to exist and, as elsewhere, to be practised.[4]

The system of recruitment changed in 1959 with the enactment of the Civil Service (Appointments) Law: public announcements of vacancies in the Foreign Office became mandatory for diplomatic grades, as did annual examinations by the Civil Service Commission, with the Foreign Ministry participating and with follow-up interviews for the top 20–30 candidates. It 'ratified the principle, already decided upon formally by administrative decision, that in accepting employees into the rank of civil servants, the "merit system" must be adhered to. . . . Only

---

[1] For example, research into the Indian Foreign Service and its recruitment patterns revealed this to be an acute problem, a point to be elaborated in a later study of India's foreign policy.

[2] Op. cit., p. 215.

[3] Interviews in Jerusalem, summer 1960 and 1965–6.

[4] Interviews with Foreign Service officers, Jerusalem, 1960, 1965–6, 1968, 1970.

in exceptional cases is the "merit system" disregarded.'[1] In the first batch (1960), 17 persons were selected from 220 applicants; they were placed in a reserve, to be called as vacancies arose.

The grade-rank structure of the Foreign Service may be designated as follows:

Until 1 April 1964		*After 1 April 1964*	
Grade (*Darga*)	Rank (*Dereg*)	Grade (*Darga*)	Rank (*Dereg*)
7–6	Third Secretary	13	Trainee
6–5	Second Secretary	14–15	Third Secretary
5–4	First Secretary	15–16	First Secretary
4–3	Counsellor	16–18	Counsellor
3–2	Minister	17–19	Minister
1	Ambassador	19–20	Ambassador
		20	Director-General

The minimal mandatory period at each diplomatic rank (*dereg*) has been in dispute between the Foreign Office and the Civil Service Commission for many years. Formally, it remains 2 years for a Trainee, 6 years for a Third or Second Secretary, 5 years for a First Secretary, and 6 years for a Counsellor, that is, 19 years as a minimum before appointment as Head of a diplomatic mission. There have been many exceptions in the early years. And even later these rules were not rigidly applied.

Promotions and postings, in fact all appointments, are made by the Ministry's *Va'adat Minuyim*, the Appointments Committee. Two officials have always been members—the Director-General and the Assistant DG (Administration); there have usually been more. When Eytan was DG (1948–59), the Committee was a well-established body which met regularly: the DG was first among equals. Under Yahil (1960–4) it continued as an active and well-represented body, including Assistant DGs and Head of Personnel; it met once or twice a month. Under Levavi, however, the Committee atrophied (1964–7), as did other consultative agencies within the Foreign Office: it met very infrequently and was virtually de-institutionalized, with decisions concentrated in the hands of the DG and the Assistant DG in charge of Administration. Indeed, whenever the latter has been an assertive personality, for example, Radai, who was Secretary-General from 1948 to 1953, and Nitzan, Assistant DG (Administration) from 1961 to 1968, he exercised enormous influence over the whole area of appointments, promotions, and postings.

In reality, the appointment procedure has always been divided between two committees. As of 1968, the one concerned with 'senior' personnel (Department Heads and higher in Jerusalem and all heads o. mission) consisted of the FM, DG, Deputy DG, Assistant DG (Administration), and the Inspector-General. Formally, heads of mission and

[1] State of Israel, Civil Service Commission, *Twenty Years of Service*, Jerusalem, 1968, p. 18.

the DG are appointed by the Government upon the recommendation of the FM. In fact, the FM has *carte blanche* in selecting his Director-General. The maximum period of service at any post is normally 5 years, but there have been notable exceptions: Eban at the UN (11 years) and in Washington (9 years); Elath in London (9 years); Comay at the UN (7 years); Eytan in Paris (more than 10 years); and Najar in Brussels (8 years). The *Va'adat Minuyim* for junior ranks (up to and including Counsellors and Deputy Department Heads) consists of the DG, Deputy DG, Assistant DG (Administration), the Inspector-General, and two others, namely the Head of Personnel and a representative of the Ministry staff appointed by the DG.

A focus of influence and controversy, the Appointment Committees underwent their greatest transformation under Rafael (1967–   ). The selection process became more centralized and increasingly the monopoly of the DG and his administrative aides.

These recruitment procedures produced a 'professional' Foreign Service of varying quality. Eytan's sanguine view has been noted, along with the reservations of others. Sharett informed the *Knesset* in 1955 that three qualifications were stressed: deep roots in the country; knowledge of foreign languages and ability to deal with people; and loyalty to Israel. And with typical intellectual honesty he added: 'this latter quality obtains among our present staff, though not all may always measure up entirely to the other requirements'.[1] Whether or not the situation was 'tragic', as some declared, the 1960s appear to have witnessed a decline in the attractiveness of the Foreign Service—due to higher salaries in comparable fields, the improvement of living conditions in Israel, the availability of foreign travel in other occupations, and the presence of genuine hardship posts in the Service, especially with regard to the education of children. Thus, while it remains true that there has never been a shortage of applicants, the quality has not been consistently high.[2]

Morale within the Foreign Service has been adversely affected by the fundamental gap between the values of a society under siege and the *raison d'être* of diplomacy. The Israeli public has always displayed a heroic image of *Tzahal*, with admiration for its qualities of courage and sacrifice, and for the achievement of dramatic victories, often in the face of superior Arab military capability. Israel's diplomats, by contrast, are viewed as formalistic, as specialists in accommodation to external pressures, as practitioners of caution and compromise. These are not qualities which create deference in a society under threat and high tension. As one senior member of the Foreign Service wrote: 'The pride that existed at the beginning has been replaced by indifference

---

[1] As reported in *Jerusalem Post*, 1 March 1955.
[2] A widely-shared view among outstanding veteran Foreign Service officers, as co veyed in interviews, 1960, 1965–6, 1968, and 1970, in Jerusalem.

. . . towards diplomacy.' And among the causes, 'the Israeli places a higher value on tasks which have the character of pioneering'. Moreover, 'the Israeli remembers the whole shameful history of the Jewish people's pleading with superior authority; and he forgets that sometimes we succeeded (as in the Mandate period) in negotiating on equal terms.'[1]

Ben Gurion's domination over defence *and foreign* policy for fifteen years also left its mark. *Tzahal* was favoured, and the Foreign Service was denigrated, in the hierarchy of institutions regarded as necessary to the attainment of Israel's basic goals. Nor did that primacy of popular affection and governmental preference change in the post-BG years: it has been difficult for diplomacy to thrive in a setting of pervasive conflict; and the cumulative effect on Israel's diplomats has been visible despondency.

The second source of demoralization has been pressure by political parties and other ministries to place their members in the Foreign Service. Party influence is strong in Israel's Civil Service generally, but much less in the Foreign Office than in other ministries—except Defence. There was never more than a handful of senior members of the Service who belonged to *Mapai*, wrote Eytan in 1958; and they attained their position by merit. Every effort was made to keep party pressures out, but it became 'increasingly difficult to resist'. Only 10 per cent of the heads of mission in 1958 were party nominees, he added, apart from a 'fair number' of other non-career persons chosen because of special qualifications. This referred mainly to ex-Army officers, who are most evident in Israel's burgeoning diplomatic presence in Africa.[2] While precise data on 'outsiders' are unavailable, many professional members of the Service disputed Eytan's claim that there were too few to affect morale. Indeed in 1962 the rumblings of discontent, especially in the middle echelon, came to the surface, with demands for preferential treatment for insiders by the *Va'adat Minuyim*.[3]

Party pressure came mainly from the religious groups. As early as 1954 the Foreign Minister was asked in the *Knesset* whether it was true that religious Jews had been purged from, or denied entry into, the Service. Sharett replied to Yitzhak Raphael that this notion existed only in his imagination and that a substantial number of religious Israelis served in missions abroad. Not only was there no discrimination, he remarked, but where there were two candidates for the Foreign Service of otherwise equal qualifications, a religious and traditional background was considered in a person's favour.[4]

---

[1] R. Yogev (a pseudonym), 'Lie, Truth and "Dugri" [Frankly]', *Ma'ariv* (Tel Aviv), 13 Aug. 1965.

[2] The appointment of General Yitzhak Rabin as Ambassador to Washington in 1968 drew attention to the retired Army officers' role in the diplomatic service of Israel.

[3] Interviews with Foreign Service officers, Jerusalem, 1965–6.

[4] As reported in *Jerusalem Post*, 25 Nov. 1954.

(*d*) GROWTH

The expansion of Israel's diplomatic representation has been striking, especially in the first decade, as evidenced in the following data.

TABLE 46

GROWTH AND GEOGRAPHIC DISTRIBUTION OF ISRAELI
DIPLOMATIC AND CONSULAR MISSIONS

Place	1949	1950	1954	1959	1965	1967	1968
Africa	1	1	2	8	27	29	29
North America	4	3	5	7	11	13	13
Latin America	2	8	13	22	14	15	16
Australia & New Zealand	1	2	2	2	2	2	2
Western Europe	9	11	19	21	21	21	23
Eastern Europe	6	6	7	7	7	7	1
Asia	–	1	5	7	8	9	9
Other	–	5	6	6	–	–	–
Total	23	37	59	80	90	96	93

1950 figures: There were 15 ministers and 1 ambassador (to the US and the UN). Africa refers to South Africa. Western Europe includes one mission to the UK. In addition, there were 7 *Aliya* (Immigration) officers—in Aden, China, Denmark, Kenya, Libya, Sweden, and Tunisia—and 8 honorary Liaison Officers in Latin American states. 'Other' refers to 1 mission in Greece, 2 in Turkey, and 2 to the UN, 1 in New York and 1 in Geneva.

1954 figures: Israel was represented in 48 countries: diplomatic missions in 37 (5 embassies—US, USSR, UK, France, and Canada; 31 legations; and 1 diplomatic representation, in Greece) and consular offices in another 11 countries. With 2 missions to the UN, this totals 50. The discrepancy is due to the presence of more than one consulate-general or consulate in one country. Africa includes 1 mission to South Africa. Western Europe includes 2 missions in the UK. And Other refers to 1 mission to Cyprus, 1 to Greece, 2 to Turkey, and 2 to the UN.

1959 figures: The number of countries in which Israel was represented rose to 55. The biggest change, however, was in the level of representation—from 5 to 22 embassies, and from 31 to 15 legations. Counting non-resident diplomatic missions, there were 24 embassies, 30 legations, and 1 diplomatic representation. There were also 2 missions to the UN. The remainder were consular offices. Africa includes 2 missions in South Africa. Western Europe includes 1 mission in the UK and 1 in Gibraltar. 'Other' refers to 1 mission to Cyprus, 1 to Greece, 2 in Turkey, and 2 to the UN.

1967 figures: This was the peak year in Israel's representation—96 missions in 78 states. They were divided as follows: 65 embassies, 9 legations, 3 other types of diplomatic representation, 14 consulates-general and 5 consulates. The major change since 1959 was the dramatic increase in Africa, already evident in 1965 and even earlier. There was also an increase in representation in North America and, from 1959, a decline in Latin America. (By 1965 the 'Other' category had been absorbed by the specific geographic categories.)

1968 figures: The one notable change in Israeli representation is in Eastern Europe—all Communist bloc states except Roumania broke off diplomatic relations during the Six Day War. The 93 missions (including 23 non-resident) were divided as follows: 64 embassies, 5 legations, 3 other types of diplomatic representation, 17 consulates-general and 4 consulates—in 73 states.

The measure of Israel's expanding diplomatic presence is illuminated by a comparison of the 1949 and 1968 figures—from 23 to 93 missions. The most spectacular growth was in Africa, almost entirely a colonial world in 1949, with one conspicuous decline— Eastern Europe.

The data have been taken from the Government of Israel *Year-Books* and, for the 1960s, from the annual *Report* of the Foreign Ministry.

A study of foreign ministry field staffs of independent states in 1963–4 indicates a median of 102 foreign service officers distributed over 25 overseas missions. Chadwick Alger and Steven J. Brams, 'Patterns of Representation in National Capitals and Intergovernmental Organizations', *World Politics*, xix, 4, 1967, p. 651.

The growth of Israel's representation is very impressive, given the relentless efforts of the Arab states to isolate, malign, and destroy her. If attention is confined to *diplomatic presence*, the trend remains unchanged: 16 missions in 1950, 37 in 1954, 55 in 1959, and 77 in 1967. The number of missions, however, has not been accompanied by a proportionate growth in the number of employees. This imposed a steadily increasing burden of work on Foreign Service officers in the field. Thus, in 1968 only 8 of 93 missions had a staff of 10 or more; 12 missions were staffed by 1 person only, and another 49 missions by 2 or 3 persons. In short, almost two-thirds of all Israeli missions were conducted by 3 or fewer persons. And approximately 40 per cent of all Israelis 'in the field' serve in places where the climate, education, and health conditions are regarded as a hardship. Finally, in this context, the distribution of Israelis serving abroad does not correspond with the distribution of missions. The notable disproportions are Africa (1968—31·5 per cent of missions and 19·5 per cent of employees) and Western Europe, with a reverse position (1968—25·0 per cent of missions and 39·1 per cent of employees). North America shows a higher proportion of staff to missions (20·4 per cent to 13·0 per cent), and Latin America reveals the opposite (12·3 per cent to 17·4 per cent).[1]

The growth of Israel's Foreign Service is also evident in employment and budget data. At the end of 1959 there were 377 employees,

[1] The data in this paragraph and the two that follow are taken from the annua Foreign Ministry *Reports*, as follows:
growth in number of missions and employees, *Report, 1966–7*, p. 32.
missions according to number of workers, *Report, 1968–9*, p. 43.
the 40 per cent distribution in hardship posts, *Report, 1966–7*, p. 33.
geographic distribution of persons and missions, *Report, 1968–9*, p. 42.
number and breakdown of employees: for 1959, the *Government Year-Book, 1959–60*.
for 1964, *Report, 1966–7*, p. 32.
for 1968, *Report, 1968–9*, p. 46.
age distribution, *Report, 1968–9*, p. 50.
budget data, *Report, 1966–7*, p. 57, and *Report, 1968–9*, p. 60.

including all administrative personnel; five years later the staff had more than doubled—to 833—a further reflection of Israel's presence in Africa after 1960. Of these less than half—401—were in the Political Section, and that included persons in clerical as well as in diplomatic grades. By 1968 the comparable figures were 873 and 561; of the latter more than two-thirds were in the field. By that time, too, it was no longer a young Service: only 7 per cent of the Political Section were under 30; 44 per cent were in the 40–50 age group; and 70 per cent were over 40.

There is no more striking indicator of growth than the Foreign Ministry budget. The first year, it was less than £11 million; the budget for the 21st year was £172 million. Periodic devaluation explains the rise in part, especially in 1954–5, 1962–3, and 1968–9. General expansion of the number of missions abroad, the size of staff, etc., also accounts for the steady rise. About half the budget is for salaries. Two-thirds of the total is spent in foreign exchange. Yet the overall figure is modest, given the number of missions Israel maintains and the importance of her diplomatic presence throughout the world.

(e) PROCESS

Foreign policy decisions were classified earlier into three broad types: Strategic, Tactical, and Implementing.[1] Viewed in that perspective, the Israeli Foreign Office is concerned primarily with the last, that is, with external behaviour which attempts to operationalize Strategic- and Tactical-level decisions. Those decisions are generally made by higher authority—by the Prime Minister alone or the Prime Minister and Foreign Minister in close consultation, or the PM, FM and Defence Minister, and one or two others acting as an inner Cabinet, or by the Ministerial Committee on Defence, or by the entire Government. Their choice among available options is often influenced by advice offered or solicited from one or more members of the Decision-Making Inner Circle of the Technical Élite. But the *raison d'être* of the Foreign Ministry is to assist those with political authority to attain high-policy objectives—through the day-to-day conduct of relations with other states and with international organizations. And those relations impose a continuous challenge to make the correct Implementing decisions.

That role is not unique to the Foreign Office of Israel: all Foreign Ministries perform the function of implementation of high-policy decisions. Yet it is accentuated by the tradition of *Rikuz*—centralization or concentration at the top. Rooted in the *Yishuv*, it continued automatically after independence; and since 1948 it has pervaded the entire political system, especially parties and the civil service. Within the Foreign Office, as will be indicated later, it has been conspicuous. The

[1] See ch. 15 (a) above.

acute and persistent threat to Israel's survival has legitimized, rationalized and entrenched *Rikuz* as the core of the decision-making pattern. An array of decisions is made day by day in the Foreign Ministry; indeed, hour by hour. Formally, they are processed through a Policy Machine which comprises various layers of authority and responsibility: Foreign Minister; Director-General; Assistant Director-General; Heads of Department, and others. How authentic the Policy Machine is in practice is subject to speculation—and widespread scepticism, to be noted below. Nevertheless, the Machine can be defined precisely and analysed in terms of process.

There are seven major sources of the decisions which are taken in the Foreign Office: the Minister; the Director-General; Assistant Directors-General; Advisers; Heads of Department; envoys; and Heads of the Bureaux of the Minister and the Director-General. Yet origin of the decision flow is not always—in fact, often is not—identical with the ultimate decision-maker(s). (Throughout the following analysis we shall use abbreviations—FM, DG, Assistant DG, HD, for Heads of Department, and HB, for Head of Bureau, either of the Foreign Minister or the Director-General.)[1]

i. *Foreign Minister*

There are three sub-types of decision flow emanating from the FM.

(1) *Decisions Originating from and Determined by the Minister.* The process usually begins with his (or her) remarks on an incoming cable or an oral comment to the HB. An instruction to act is indicated and is sent to the Head of Department concerned or the relevant Assistant DG or the DG, either directly or, more likely, through the Head of the Minister's Bureau (HB). The latter will, in any event, convey the Minister's decision to those persons who are not expected to act directly upon the FM's instruction.

The decision may be appealed by any person so informed, more likely by the DG or Assistant DG but in the earlier years by the

[1] The primary source for the following analysis of the decision-making process in Israel's Foreign Office is interviews with Foreign Service officers in Jerusalem in 1960, 1965–6, 1968, and 1969–70. With some persons there were as many as a dozen interviews over the years, only rarely less than an hour each. They include:
all 3 Foreign Ministers of Israel
4 of the 5 Directors-General since independence
the 1 Deputy Director-General
12 persons who held the rank of Assistant Director-General
3 persons who held the rank of Adviser
20 persons who held the post of Department Head
15 persons who held a post as Head of Mission
4 persons who served as Head of the Foreign Minister's Bureau
2 persons who served as Head of the Director-General's Bureau
A number of these persons served at various levels of the hierarchy and offered insights from various vantage points. They are counted above at each level that they served.

Department Head as well. Dissent may be channelled directly to the FM; but if it emanates from the HD it probably goes, indirectly, through the Assistant DG or DG or the HB.

The Minister may overrule the dissent immediately or call for a consultation with the DG, the appropriate Assistant DG, and the Department Head(s) concerned; there the decision will be reconsidered and either confirmed or altered. The decision as to whether the FM will overrule dissent or call for a 'consultation' will depend on his style of decision-making and on his perception of three variables: the urgency of action, the importance of the issue, and the intensity of dissent. His image will be 'a sense of the situation' or qualitative judgement, not quantitatively measurable.

(2) *Decisions Originating from but not Determined by the Minister*. The process is set in motion by his remarks, either penned on an incoming cable or conveyed orally to his HB or others. The operational act is to call for a 'consultation'. Who will be invited is entirely at the FM's discretion: normally, he will summon the DG, and the relevant Assistant DG and HD. The kind of meeting may vary—from a formal *Hanhalah* (Directorate) to an informal two-minute exchange of views with interested persons. The choice of type of meeting depends upon his image of urgency and his assessment of the importance of the decision.

(3) *Pre-Decisional Opinions by the Minister*. The flow starts with a remark by the FM, expressing disagreement with, or a judgement about, the report of a Head of Mission. The comment may be sent to the DG, an Assistant DG, or the pertinent HD—or to all three persons. It is conveyed, usually by the Minister's HB, as 'Opinion', in contrast to instructions, which are sent 'for Action'. But the FM's remarks often induce an interaction of thought and articulated responses, orally or in writing, that ultimately influence decisions.

Three Assistant DGs with many years in the Service declared that FM decisions of the first sub-type were very rare, and of the second only slightly less so. One commented: 'Sorry to disappoint you; there is no system as to the kind of decision the Minister will make; it is purely accidental. He may pick a memo or a cable out of a tray. It may come to him by accident. He may not know what is going on. The communication network is not effective.'

(4) There are also *decisions taken by the Foreign Minister in direct contact with 'outsiders'* (persons outside the Ministry or even the Government as a whole); for example, the Foreign Minister of another state. These are later communicated, for information purposes, to officials in the Foreign Ministry.

(5) And another forum through which the FM makes decisions is *public statements* at home and abroad—of all kinds—for they commit

him, the Ministry, and the Government as a whole: they create precedents, sometimes with far-reaching foreign policy consequences.

There were, all agreed, striking differences in the attitude and behaviour of Israel's Foreign Ministers regarding the decision-making process within the Ministry. Three indicators were used for comparison:

(1) *Degree of Concentration of Decision-Making Authority.* Sharett was the most centralizing FM—as might be expected of the creator of the Foreign Office; indeed, he made the most minute decisions throughout his tenure. Meir was second in this respect, and Eban last, though all tended to monopolize decisions on issues of special interest to them.

(2) *Range of Interests.* Sharett ranked first among his peers in this too: he displayed the widest range and the deepest involvement in detail. Meir was second in both respects, while Eban has confined his interest to a few major issues—the US, Big Four and Big Two Talks, Information, Jerusalem, etc.

(3) *Consultation.* Sharett held the most frequent group meetings, Eban the least. Sharett respected intellectuals and listened to the views of Ministry officials—'he wanted to know what others thought'. Eban is the most self-assured, while Meir depended heavily on the knowledge of her Foreign Office aides, especially in the early years.

Many described Eban as a loner, who is preoccupied with what *he* is thinking and doing, everything else being unimportant. This led to demoralization, said some. 'He doesn't need or want meetings. His DG imposes some on him, because he thinks it good for morale among officials and good for Eban—a feedback of reaction and ideas.' Another described him as 'completely self-sufficient, reminiscent of Ben Gurion on a larger stage. He doesn't need advice, except on purely technical matters, like GATT, the Common Market, or international law on civil aviation. He holds consultations, but they are *pro forma*; they are usually monologues. He informs but rarely listens or takes advice—except from his DG, whose fertile mind he respects, and for whom he feels the bond of friendship.'

Meir was more dependent than either Sharett or Eban. 'But on major political decisions she relied on instinct.' 'She had a certain distrust of over-educated intellectuals', said another; 'especially those of the Western type', said another. 'Never have we returned to the Sharett practice,' bemoaned another official '—a real testing of ideas with high level discussion, which Sharett needed.' One person with experience under all three FMs remarked: 'Sharett had an insatiable curiosity; Eban's curiosity is more selective; and Mrs. Meir had opinions.'

'Sharett knew everybody in the *Misrad* (Office)', recalled a veteran '—name, face, family details. He was interested in the welfare of each.

He treated members of the Foreign Office as one large family—his official family. Not so Mrs. Meir. True, the *Misrad* has grown in personnel, but her contact and consultation was limited to the DG, some Assistant DGs, some Department Heads, and the Head of her Bureau—people who could provide her with information.' Eban's consultation network has been even more sparse—his DG and those having technical expertise.

ii. *Director-General*

The same sub-types of decision process which flow from the Minister's action are also evident in the DG pattern. He may originate and determine a decision by noting an instruction on an incoming cable. This will be channelled to the relevant HD and/or Assistant DG, either directly or through his Head of Bureau. Dissent may feed back to the DG from either the HD or Assistant DG or both, either directly or, frequently, through the HB. The DG may overrule immediately or, very rarely, yield to the dissent. He may also call for a 'consultation' with the officials concerned and, on that basis, reaffirm, modify, or set aside his initial decision. But it is he who decides.

The DG may also originate a decision—but not determine it—by noting a wish for consultation about a specific issue. The discussion may be brief or prolonged. It may be held immediately or may be delayed to a regular meeting of the *Hanhalah*. And it may be formal or informal. Whatever its character, this kind of decision emerges from the group. Like the FM, too, the DG may express an opinion on a cable or a report from an Israeli envoy, or on some other document, which may ultimately lead to—and influence—a Ministry decision. There is still another decision flow in which the DG is a central figure: an Israeli envoy may seek his instructions or approval for a course of action, either directly or through the relevant HD. The DG will determine the decision, usually after consultation.

In summary, the DG initiates and decides an issue, seeks a consultation (from which a decision flows), expresses an opinion (which may lead to a decision), or responds to an envoy's query with a decision. He may also, like the FM, commit the Foreign Office, other ministries, or the Government, by statements made to the press, on radio and television, during official visits abroad, etc. One Head of a Director-General's Bureau estimated that, in his experience, 80 per cent of all decisions flowing from the DG were reactive, and 20 per cent were initiating; the latter were more important. Two other Bureau Heads concurred. All agreed, too, that decisions initiated and determined by the DG occur much more frequently than those by the FM. This is especially true of Rafael, DG since the end of 1967: 'It occurs all the time with Rafael—on anything, from *hasbarah* (information) to political action.' That kind of decision was also taken by Levavi (1964–7), though less frequently, and much less by Eytan (1948–59) and Yahil (1960–4).

As with the Foreign Ministers, there are differences in the attitude and behaviour of the DGs with respect to the decision process. There is an absolute consensus among Foreign Service veterans that Rafael stands apart in the extent of *concentration of decisions* in his own hands: Yahil was at the other end of the spectrum, with Levavi and Eytan in between, but the gap between Rafael and all the others was very striking. All possess a wide *range of interests*. Eytan, Yahil, and Levavi are highly-educated intellectuals, trained in philology, the social sciences and philosophy and the natural sciences, respectively. Rafael is credited by most of his peers with one of the most fertile minds in the Foreign Service.

The DGs were not cast in the same mould with respect to *techniques of work and consultation*. Eytan was the most systematic. He read everything and, in the British Foreign Office tradition, he noted his instructions and views with care. All the others did much of their decision-making orally—in face-to-face discussions or through Israel's favourite means of contact, the telephone. Rafael involves himself in almost all decisions of substance, with a disconcerting tendency to usurp the decision-making role of senior colleagues. Levavi transferred much of the preliminary sifting of materials to his Bureau: its task was to prepare a précis of all incoming paper. Yet as he himself remarked, he read all important cables (about 200 a day) and left no decisions of substance to his aides. Despite this relief from minutiae, he added, the volume of paper was much larger than that of his predecessors. So it was. And for Rafael it is even more demanding: the burden of responsibility has increased steadily.

Eytan was the prototype of the British Permanent Under-Secretary. He was not politically conscious and did not insist on making all decisions himself. The other DGs were more politically aware. Eytan put a high value on consultation—regular, institutionalized patterns of decision-making. Yahil, too, relied on the continuous exchange of ideas, but mostly through oral communication and a method less institutionalized than Eytan's. Levavi's pattern of consultation was the most *ad hoc*, operating on the 'principle' of 'consultation when necessary, with those most directly concerned'. Rafael restored the institutional fabric (to be analysed later), which had atrophied under Levavi, but his zest for centralization reduced the operational significance of consultation by committee. In human relations, according to Foreign Service veterans, Eytan was the most interested in the persons who served at home and abroad—as was Sharett among the Foreign Ministers.

iii. *Assistant Director-General*

The role of Assistant DG is 'difficult to define precisely', remarked a person who had held that post at different times during more than twenty years in the Service. He may originate a decision by noting on a cable or may initiate consultation—below, with the HD and/or above, with the DG—which might produce a decision. He may express a pre-decision opinion, with potential effects on future decisions. And he may respond to HD suggestions, easing the upward flow to DG and, some-times, FM, as well as to instructions, proposals, or opinions from above. In short, he may—and does—engage in all types of decision process noted earlier, except one: unlike the FM and DG, he does not normally determine decisions alone—though there have been notable exceptions.

One view was that the primary function of an Assistant DG is super-vision, not initiation—but with a role in many decisions involving consultation near the summit of the Ministry. A more general—and assertive—view was that an Assistant DG 'initiates anything that strikes him as having to do with policy', with some acting as *de facto* DGs in their own spheres, especially those in charge of Economics and Africa.

In the hierarchy of status and responsibility, the Assistant DG must forge viable relations with the HD below him and the DG above. 'His relationship to the Head of a Department under his supervision will vary, depending upon his bent, personality, and assertiveness.' Some Assistant DGs were proponents and practitioners of active, continuous consultation, a sharing of responsibility for decisions. Others were in-clined to concentrate the decision-making function in their own hands. One noted his pattern as 'several meetings daily', by telephone or brief face-to-face contact, with the Head of a Department under his jurisdiction in which he had special knowledge, and 'two or three times weekly' with an HD whose area was rather remote from his experience. All Assistant DGs interviewed concurred that consultation was not institutionalized—but that contact was frequent. One, for example, noted 'three or four times daily' with the HD of an exceedingly active and vital Department, 'three or four times weekly' with the HD of a less sensitive and less controversial Department. All observed that the ini-tiative for consultation was shared in roughly equal measure between themselves and their HDs. Moreover, while an HD was allowed to take an issue directly to the DG, he would rarely do so without first con-sulting his Assistant DG—perhaps because of the knowledge that, in any event, the DG would consult the Assistant DG concerned.

In six years as Assistant DG, recalled one person, he had overruled an HD decision two or three times. As to the demarcation of responsi-bility, the line is unclear but mutually understood—by most. 'No one ever told me how to operate', said one Assistant DG who also headed two departments during twenty years of experience. 'There are no directives as to how to behave and what decisions to take. There are no procedures laid down. At all levels', he added, 'the outer limits of per-missible decisions are self-determined—by tact, experience, tradition, and knowledge of the system.' All other Assistant DGs with whom this was explored, in fact all other Foreign Service officers interviewed, echoed this generalization in similar words.

In the upward relationship—Assistant DG to DG—there are five variables impinging upon a decision process. One is the character of the DG, especially his attitude to the delegation of decision-making authority. Another is the subject-matter of the decision—its importance and urgency as perceived by the DG. A third is the character of the Assistant DG, whether he tends to be assertive and decisive or passive and cautious. A fourth is the Assistant DG's sense of the situation, namely, his view as to whether or not the issue falls within his jurisdiction. 'I will never decide on my own if it is a really important question', said one Assistant DG who was highly respected and could have exercised final discretion in his own sphere if he so wished. Other Assistant DGs tried wherever possible to decide on their own.

The relationship between the DG and the Assistant DG, that is, the personal equation, is the last but often the most important variable. Under a centralizing, dynamic and self-confident Director-General like Rafael, the Assistant DGs have tended to be denigrated in the decision process. Under a systematic DG who believes in the virtues of regular and continuous consultation, like Eytan, or a DG who welcomes initiative and is not predisposed to monopolize decision-making, like Yahil and Eytan, the Assistant DGs thrived, with corresponding high morale. And even under Levavi, though to a lesser extent, the Assistant DGs played an important role—despite his dislike of formal consultation procedures.

The post of Assistant DG, according to some Foreign Service veterans, originated as a salary-status device in the early 1950s: 'You must always remember that people in the Ministry are always on the margin of funds.' Another reason has been the constant pressure of Israeli diplomats to get home—'perhaps a unique situation in Foreign Services'. 'This is the positive aspect of their Zionism, a desire to live in Israel and to ensure their children's growth in a homeland and Hebrew education.' Thus more jobs have been needed at the senior level.

Some officials, including incumbent Assistant DGs, regarded the post as unnecessary for efficient decision-making: 'If you have good Department Heads you don't need Assistant DGs, especially if there is a strong Head of the DG's Bureau.' Moreover, 'the Assistant DG tends to depreciate the role of Department Head.' All the same, 'since things are concentrated at the top, and the DG can't do everything by himself, there is a need for an echelon to whom he can delegate some of the work.' This ambivalent assessment was in sharp contrast to the positive view of another Assistant DG. 'It is a necessary level in the decision-making hierarchy for the following reasons: (a) Department Heads have little influence; without the intervention of the Assistant DG in the upward flow, their proposals would have no influence; (b) many proposals by Department Heads are not "well-cooked"; they need the advice and, sometimes, the revision of persons with wider experience; and (c) many "important decisions" get made at the Assistant Director-General levels.' As evidence, he noted that 95 per cent of Israel's decisions regarding her diplomats' words and deeds in Africa were made by him as Assistant DG and that 50–60 per cent of day-to-day decisions regarding policy towards the US were made by the Assistant DG in charge of North America; key decisions in this realm, of course, were made by higher authority, he acknowledged. In other areas the assessment was less sanguine. 'Much depends upon the personality of the two men', was the consensus theme.

iv. *Adviser*

The post of Adviser has existed in the Foreign Office from the outset; but most persons at that rank played a consultative rather than operational role. The Legal Adviser (Rosenne, 1948–67, and Miron, thereafter) was an exception: he directed the Legal Division comprising one or more Departments. Gazit and Tekoah as Advisers in 1965–6, and Comay as Political Adviser, 1967–70, also had operational functions— equal to those of an Assistant DG; in fact, Comay ranked immediately after the Deputy DG. All the others, however, including some with great influence, had an ill-defined place in the formal Establishment.

There were three notable Advisers to the Foreign *Minister*, as distinct from the Ministry: Leo Kohn, Political Adviser from 1948 until his death in 1961, the elegant draftsman and man of ideas; Reuven Shiloah, Adviser on Special Matters from 1948 to 1953 and Political Adviser from 1957 to his death in 1959, a policy innovator with unusual insight on the Middle East and liaison with defence and intelligence agencies; and Ezra Danin, whose knowledge of the Arabs has made him a valued Adviser on the Middle East since 1948. None had jurisdiction over specified Departments or topics; but all had direct and continuous access to the FM and the DG. Indeed, Kohn and Shiloah are universally regarded as members of the Foreign Service Decision-Making Inner Circle and of the Permanent In-Group. In a narrower sphere, Ya'acov Herzog was an influential Adviser on Jerusalem from 1948 to 1957, for most of that time a senior official in the Ministry of Religious Affairs.

The first Adviser to create an operational sphere of jurisdiction was Rafael, who replaced Shiloah in 1953—as Adviser on Middle East and UN Political Affairs: during the next four years he was in direct control of these two vital areas of policy. But it was not until the appointment of Gazit and Tekoah as Advisers in 1965 that the status-role problem surrounding this post came to a head. They were *de facto* Assistant DGs without the rank—or formal authority. As Levavi, then DG, explained it: 'There is no rational basis for this innovation. It does not derive from the earlier post of Political Adviser. It involves the functions of Assistant DG, without his authority.' The rationalizing distinction was that Assistant DGs were in charge of Departments, while the two Advisers supervised Topics. In a sense this was true: Tekoah had jurisdiction over UN and international organization matters generally—as Rafael had had a decade earlier; but Gazit was to direct Departments dealing with the Middle East—the Middle East itself, Political and Economic Planning, and Research. It was less than satisfactory because of the blurred lines of authority.

The real reason for the 'compromise' was internal personnel tensions—rivalry and jealousy, accentuated by their relative youth, 43 and 40. Both men, along with four others, were promoted to Assistant DG the following year, thereby eliminating the unreal distinction: they continued to perform the same function. The rank óf Political Adviser (and Ambassador-at-Large) was bestowed on Comay at the end of his tour of duty as Permanent Representative to the UN, in 1967: in functional terms, he and Tekoah had exchanged posts, at the two ends of the decision-implementing process. Thus, where Advisers were given specific areas of responsibility, their role in the decision flow was indistinguishable from that of Assistant DGs—except for Kohn and Shiloah, who were *sui generis*.

v. *Head of Department*

The status and influence of HDs in the Foreign Ministry has varied over the years. In the Sharett-Eytan period (1948–56) it was high: most Department Heads were from the Political Department Double Originals; there were fewer Assistant DGs—none until 1952, only three thereafter, until 1957; all HDs attended the *Yeshivat Boker* (Morning Meeting) by right; and the DG was not possessive in his attitude to control over decisions. During much of Meir's tenure as FM, however, there was a steady decline, primarily because of a marked centralizing thrust among Assistant DGs in the late 1950s and early 1960s. As one HD remarked bitterly at the time, 'we are junior officials, without any authority to make decisions'. Others concurred. The proliferation of Assistant DGs in 1966–7 further complicated the pattern of authority. But by 1970 there appeared to be a reverse trend: as Foreign Service veterans, including Heads of Mission, returned to the home office, where there was little room at the top, even senior officers had to be content with an HD position.

The role of a Department Head in the decision process is shaped by most of the variables noted in the discussion of Assistant DGs, especially his character and personality, the relationship with his immediate superior, and the type of issue. There is clearly an inverse correlation between the importance of the decision and the autonomy of the HD; more precise measurement is very difficult. And what is 'important', said all interviewed HDs, depends entirely on one's discretion, based upon experience, knowledge, and sense of the situation. 'What I consider to be important I take up with my superiors', said one, reflecting the general attitude. Another remarked: 'If there is no instruction from higher authority, it is my decision; I can stick my neck out.' And a third indicated that he had never been asked, 'why didn't you consult X?' or told, 'you had no right to make that decision yourself'.

While their discretion is self-determined, the consensus was that most HDs tend to exercise it with caution. They may be said to originate a vast number of decision flows; but most are determined jointly with their immediate superior, with 'important' issues being brought to the attention of the DG, and 'exceptional' cases to the FM as well. HDs also originate—and determine—routine instructions to envoys in their area. And thirdly, there are lateral decisions, taken together by two or more Department Heads, for example an economic-political decision not involving a change in policy. As a general rule, the moment a 'real problem' arises in Israel's relations with another state or an international organization, HDs feel the need to consult upwards. And, in fact, the pattern of continuous consultation between HD and Assistant DG is rooted in the Ministry. With few exceptions, the Department Head is an aide to the Assistant DG, with wide latitude of discretion.

An 'exceptional' case involved the buzzing of a plane carrying Indian Prime Minister Nehru through Israeli air space en route to Gaza, in 1960. At the outset the HD, Asia, wanted to give wide and official publicity to one point, namely, that the Israeli Government had not known Nehru was in the plane. Too many elements were involved, however, for him to make the decision himself. The DG, too, was unable to decide; and so the issue went to the FM who, in turn, took it to the PM. At that moment Ben Gurion was involved in urgent correspondence with the UN Secretary-General: he decided to wait, and the opportunity for a clarifying statement passed. About two weeks later, in reply to a question in Parliament, Nehru said that he 'assumed' the Government of Israel was aware he was in the plane. The HD then acted swiftly: he renewed his initial proposal—directly to the FM, through a telephone conversation with the Head of her Bureau. Approval was given immediately and the statement was published, thereby reducing the diplomatic fall-out of an unintentional incident. It illustrated well the decision process in a sensitive issue, along with the limits —and the permissible initiative—of the HD's role in decision-making.

vi. *Head of Mission*

Of an Israeli Head of Mission, as perhaps of most envoys of all states, it was aptly said: 'The ambassador makes more decisions of less consequence than any other level in the Service.' There were notable exceptions, especially the original group of Israeli diplomats—Eban in

Washington and at the UN, Elath in London, Fischer in Paris, Avriel in Eastern Europe, and Sasson in Ankara. All were well-known and fully-trusted members of the Decision-Making Inner Circle. Their cables and reports certainly had great influence on the perceptions and decisions of the FM (Sharett), the DG (Eytan), and very likely, through them, on the Government. This changed later, as the number of envoys increased greatly. But the original Political Department group stayed abroad a long time (Eban and Elath until 1959, Fischer until 1957, Avriel, off-and-on, until 1960, and Sasson until 1961); and they continued to influence decisions extending far beyond their posts.

The Israeli envoy's influence depends partly on his status within the Service. It depends, too, on the importance of his state to the makers of high policy. A third variable is his reputation for knowledge and judgement. And a fourth, as with all levels in the hierarchy, is his character. Some envoys act timidly, following instructions from the home office rigidly and never daring to take initiatives. Others try to assert autonomy and solve problems in the field on their own—how to run their mission, what to say to the Foreign Office and other ministries with which they have contact, what kind of information programme to use in their setting, and the wide range of challenges confronting any envoy. Some press proposals on the FM or DG, others consume directives. Some send a barrage of cables and reports to Jerusalem, others keep these to a minimum. These communications are the largest single source of decision-flows in the Ministry. And the envoy's portrait of reality shapes the perception of decision-makers at home. It is the latter's instructions, requests for further information, or expressions of opinion —by the FM, DG, Assistant DG, and/or the HD—which constitute the next stage in the flow. And since the vast majority of decisions are reactive, the envoy's stimulus is a vital element in the process.

How vital that stimulus can be, and the Israeli diplomat's potential influence, are evident in the pattern of decision-making on UN issues. This was especially true of the Sharett period, when UN policy was made in the Foreign Ministry. Later, FM Meir brought many *Hanhalah* recommendations to the Cabinet, adding an important restraint on the autonomy of the Permanent Representative. Other factors (to be noted) depreciated his role in the 1960s. Yet the nature of the process left ample discretion.

The Permanent Representative has traditionally come to Jerusalem in the late summer for consultations on the Provisional Agenda of the General Assembly. The 'annual conference', involving the FM, DG, relevant HDs, and the *Hanhalah*, lasts from three or four days to a week. 'They did not decide in great detail', remarked one veteran participant; 'they were not very efficient meetings.' No one dissented from this view. Most of the time is devoted to the perennial Arab Refugee issue and the techniques best suited to withstand the certain Arab—

Soviet bloc assault on Israel at the forthcoming Assembly. Little time is left to discuss other issues except those of special concern to Israel. The result, according to those interviewed, has been a significant transfer of decision-making authority to the UN Delegation—over all but core issues; and on those the policy line is clear from past decisions.

'Unless judged important by the Delegation, votes were decided in New York', remarked one person who had served for years as Deputy Permanent Representative. And, while the Israeli mission was better briefed and instructed than most, it had a large area of discretion. In practice, decision-making was distributed as follows (at least until 1959): the General Assembly's First Committee and the Special Political Committee—the FM and Eban; the Second, Third, Fourth, and Fifth Committees—the Deputy Permanent Representative; and the Sixth Committee—the legal experts, Drs. Robinson and Rosenne. And, since little time was available at the daily morning session during the Assembly to consider economic and social issues, Israeli members of the relevant committees had considerable discretion.

The wide latitude enjoyed by the Delegation lasted until 1959. Three factors had been responsible for that status: the special authority of Eban; delays in communication, which limited control by Jerusalem; and the importance of Latin America to the outcome of Assembly votes—with Israel's resources marshalled in New York as a special group in the Delegation headed by Moshe Tov. All this changed in 1960: the lesser stature of Eban's successor, Comay; improved communications with the home office; and, most important, the Africa explosion in the world body. Post-1960 Africa was to the UN what Latin America had been before—approximately one third of the total membership. But there was one vital difference: Israel's expertise on Latin America and her communications network were centred in New York; by contrast, Israel's expertise on Africa was centred in Jerusalem, under the direction of Assistant DG Ehud Avriel, along with direct communication facilities to African Governments. All this permitted—and induced—greater direct control by the Foreign Ministry over Israel's UN activities. Finally, the increasing complexity of the Assembly, with 120 delegations or more, created greater dependence on the resources of the home office.

Despite this declining autonomy, the Delegation continued to influence decisions at home. UN affairs in Jerusalem had always been under the control of a senior Foreign Service Officer—Rafael from 1953 to 1957, then Comay until 1960, and after a lapse Herzog, Tekoah, and, from 1967 to 1970, Comay again. Many confirmed that the UN network was autonomous: Tekoah noted that he sent an average of thirty-five cables daily during the Assembly, without consulting anyone except as he saw fit; and in 1970 it was agreed that Comay had *carte blanche* in this sphere. Thus, as a senior member of the Service explained, while policy lines are laid down in Jerusalem, the Delegate to the UN contributes to decisions in two ways: during the annual consultation in Jerusalem and in the regular dialogue from New York; and secondly, through the exercise of judgement and discretion when unexpected situations arise. Decisions, concluded Lourie, emerge from the continuous exchange between the Delegation and Jerusalem—though the Ministry has the primary role in making broad policy. No other Head of Mission has the influence of the Permanent Representative to the UN, but Ambassadors to the US and France have been influential at different times and on different issues. Certainly the Israeli Head of Mission is not a mere 'messenger boy' carrying directives from home.

vii. *Bureaux of Foreign Minister and Director-General*

The Foreign Ministry's decision-making process has been profoundly affected by two lateral (and, formally, subordinate) structures—the Minister's *Lishka* or Bureau and the Director-General's *Lishka*. They existed from the outset, but their influence varied with FMs, DGs, and Heads of Bureau.

Sharett had two principal assistants—a Political Secretary and a Head of the Minister's Bureau (or Private Secretary). The two posts were merged in 1957, in what one incumbent termed 'a massive dual function'.[1] They were separated once more in 1966 by Eban (and reunited by him in 1970). From 1948 to 1953 the Political Secretary was more influential: the first three to hold this position—Evron, Navon, and Lubrani—moved on to key assignments in the Technical Élite.[2] Thereafter, the post of Political Secretary atrophied, and it ceased to exist in 1956. A group of bright Foreign Service officers served as Head of Bureau from 1953 to 1966—Shek, Elizur, Gazit, Meroz, and Dinitz.[3] When the post was divided again, its (really, their) influence declined markedly.

---

[1] Simha Dinitz, Head of Bureau under Meir, from June 1963 to January 1966.

[2] Ephraim Evron (1948–51) was Head of the Defence Minister's Bureau during Lavon's controversial tenure, in 1954–5, and in the sixties was Minister (No. 2) to London and Minister (No. 2) to Washington. (In 1968 he was, briefly, Ambassador to Sweden and then Ambassador to Canada.)

Yitzhak Navon (1951–2) became Ben Gurion's devoted Political Secretary (Head of Bureau) and held that key post from 1952 to 1963. (He then became a member of the *Knesset* and, later, one of its Deputy Speakers.)

Uri Lubrani (1952–3) was Head of the Prime Minister's Bureau from 1963 to 1965 and Ambassador to Ethiopia from 1968 onwards. Moreover, for six years he held key posts in the Prime Minister's Office (though not regarded as Technical Élite posts in foreign policy): 1957–60, as Assistant Adviser on Arab Affairs, and 1960–3, as Adviser on Arab Affairs.

[3] Ze'ev Shek (1953–6) was Minister (No. 2) to Paris from 1960 to 1963 and then Head of the Western Europe Department during the crucial period 1963–7. (Thereafter he served as Ambassador to Austria.)

Michael Elizur (1956–7) became Head of the North American Department in 1968

The principal task of the Head of Bureau (HB) has been the sifting and co-ordination of materials that are directed to the FM. There are four major sources:

(1) letters and reports from field missions, sent directly to the FM or indirectly through the geographic departments;
(2) memoranda, notes, and oral communication from the DG, Assistant DGs, and HDs, seeking consultation with the Minister, approval of a course of action, opinion on a proposal, or expressing dissent over some instruction;
(3) cables from Israel's envoys: in 1966 there was an estimated average of a hundred incoming and a hundred outgoing substantive cables a day. Incoming 'technical' cables are allocated by the Director of Communications, a decision-making function with occasional political consequences.[1] The Assistant HB sifts the incoming 'operational' cables and removes the less important ones for his attention. Of the remaining eighty, the HB decides which to send (or show) to the FM, which to tell him (her) about by brief oral summary, and which to send to the relevant HD for further details, for clarification, or for action; some are dealt with directly by the HB, especially when the policy line is clear; and
(4) intelligence and appreciation reports.

The function of the Political Secretary or, later, the HB acting in that capacity, was to provide research assistance, mainly to deal with questions in the *Knesset*, and for the drafting of speeches, especially for FM Meir: Sharett and Eban prepared most of their own speeches. The

---

after serving as Assistant Head of the Western Europe Department (1964–5) and of the Asia Department (1965–7).

Mordekhai Gazit (1957–60) was Minister (No. 2) to Washington from 1960 to 1965, and then Adviser (1965–6) and Assistant Director-General (1966–7) in charge of the Middle East, and later (1970) Assistant DG in charge of North America.

Yohanan Meroz (1960–3) was Minister (No. 2) to Paris from 1963 to 1968 and then became Head of the Europe 1 Department.

Simha Dinitz (1963–6) was Minister (No. 2) to Rome from 1966 to 1968 (and then Minister (Information) to Washington from 1968 to 1969, when he returned to serve as Head of the Prime Minister's Bureau for Mrs. Meir).

[1] For example, the 'Accra incident': in 1965, Israel's Ambassador to Ghana sought instructions about attending an OAU function to which all envoys resident in Ghana were invited. The cable was considered not urgent and did not reach the Africa Department until the following morning—after the event. The Ambassador decided to attend and was asked to leave by the host Government—under pressure from the UAR delegation. The Israeli press reacted with anger to this incident on 26 October 1965. For example, *Ha-boker* referred to it as 'unprecedented in the relations between friendly countries. . . . Israel has no choice but to recall her Ambassador'; *Ha-tzofeh* termed it 'rude insolence'; *Herut* called it an insult; and even the communist *Kol Ha'am* termed it 'worthy of condemnation'.

two important annual addresses are the Budget speech to the *Knesset* and the General Policy speech before the UN General Assembly. The process of preparation offers insight into decision-making, especially the role of the HB. The FM discussed the speech with him and indicated the points she wished to include. He prepared a first draft, on which she made amendments. He then prepared a second draft, which went before the *Hanhalah* for discussion and possible revision. The HB then prepared the third and final draft. The process was similar in the case of the UN speech, with senior members of the UN Delegation performing the same role as the *Hanhalah* on the Budget speech.

One of Meir's Bureau Heads, Dinitz, noted that the distribution of materials depended on her schedule of meetings. Travel abroad and election campaigns were other important variables, for cables drawn to her attention would be kept to a minimum; many were summarized. More generally, the pressure on an FM's time—for whatever reason—affected the quantity and flow of information going to the Minister and thus affected the decision process. Meir as FM read about sixty incoming and ten outgoing cables daily, leaving wide discretion to her HB—and decision-making authority to her DG. However, by noting many incoming cables, she influenced decisions conveyed in the reverse flow. And her Political Secretary was present to ensure that her instructions were carried out. Indeed, his major role was to lubricate the communications machine, by allocating the daily input of demands for action or opinion to the relevant officials and supervising the responsive follow-through. The importance of that function and of the HB to the Minister, especially in the Meir era, was confirmed by others.

The parallel body, the Director-General's Bureau, had a lower status and less influence throughout the period under inquiry: until 1959 it was headed by a Principal Assistant; and none of the HBs held a Technical Élite post until 1968. 'The *Lishka* upstairs [where the FM's suite is located] was always strong', said one Assistant DG; 'most of the time it was weak downstairs [the DG's suite].'[1] The bulk of the time of the Director-General's HB is devoted to processing cables: under Levavi there was an average of 150 incoming and 150 outgoing cables a day. All go first to the Assistant HB for a preliminary sifting: very rarely was there an error of consequence, said one Bureau Head, though he acknowledged this to be a decision-making act. The second stage is handled by the HB, who decides to whom cables should be sent. All code cables go to the FM, the DG, the Deputy DG, and the two Bureau

---

[1] The influence of the latter changed drastically in 1969 because of a confluence of circumstances: a weak FM Bureau; a DG involved in all aspects of the Ministry's work, including minutiae, who realized the need to elevate the post; an FM prepared to leave most of the internal Ministry activities to his DG; and the appointment of an able official to the post, who had the confidence of the senior echelon in the *Misrad*.

Heads; most—but not all—are sent to the Assistant DGs (for whom this partial limitation has been a source of resentment). And some are sent to the Department Heads.

Levavi used to receive about 100 incoming cables daily, in three or four batches. He would note instructions or communicate his views orally, along one of four paths: arrange a consultation with the FM or some official(s), in the Ministry or, sometimes, with persons in related ministries; issue instructions for action; send a cable to X; or 'let's wait and see'. A similar process applied to outgoing cables, which in theory the DG (or, in fact, his Bureau Head) had to approve, with the HB deciding which ones to show the DG. This pattern was common to all, but the degree of DG reliance on his *Lishka* varied. 'Levavi liked to deal with material which had been processed by his *Lishka* or a Department before it came to him.' The others read everything.

As with his counterpart upstairs, the Head of the DG's Bureau deals with few cables directly: 'on perhaps ten or fifteen a day I may initiate action', said one person in this post. More often, he proposes action to the DG. Other cables he passes on 'for information', but as they are of 'no consequence' he does not follow them up. And a fourth group of cables are sent to Department Heads 'for action'; often the HB suggests a meeting or makes a substantive proposal in that regard. More generally, his functions were well summarized by one Bureau Head as follows: to co-ordinate actions arising from cables; to follow through actions required by Ministry personnel; to co-ordinate activities of the Foreign Office with the Security Establishment; and crisis management, for example, mobilizing response to the hijacking of an El Al airliner to Algeria in July 1968 or the Swissair disaster in February 1970.

The influence of the two Bureau Heads lies—negatively—in their control over the distribution of cables, and—positively—in their crucial role of brokers: they transmit proposals, ideas, and requests from Assistant DGs and HDs to the DG and the FM. 'The *Lishka* puts things to the Minister on our behalf', said one Assistant DG. 'The DG's *Lishka* oils the machinery of the *Misrad*', said another. And one Department Head remarked: 'The Department Director can exclude from consultation persons who he knows or thinks will oppose his proposal—by proceeding through the Political Secretary [that is, the HB] of the Director-General or the Minister.' Indeed, all welcomed strong Bureau Heads as 'constructive collusion' in getting decisions processed to the top. 'They lubricate the flow of demands and decisions', noted an Assistant DG, '—both laterally and vertically.'

The relationship between the two Bureaux does not appear to have been dominated by friction. Initiative for action can, and does, come from either. Co-ordination is maintained by constant telephone communication. The FM's Bureau is concerned with higher-level linkages—with the PM, Defence Minister, Cabinet, etc., while the DG's Bureau maintains close liaison with counterparts in the PM's Office, the Defence Ministry, the *Lishka* of the Chief of Staff, etc. It has proved to be a viable sharing of functions.

viii. *Consultation*

The patterns of consultation within the Foreign Office have varied over the years, in the degree of institutionalization, the frequency of meetings, and their substantive role. The decisive variable has been the attitude to decision-making held by the DG in office. One important committee, the *Va'adat Minuyim*, has already been discussed. There were two others: the *Yeshivat Boker* (Morning Meeting), sometimes called the *Segel*, literally, the Corps, referring to its composition; and the *Hanhalah* (Directorate), also known by some as the Policy Committee.

Both these organs of consultation flourished under Eytan, DG from 1948 to 1959. The *Yeshivat Boker* met daily from 7.45 to about 8.45 under his chairmanship to discuss developments of the previous twenty-four hours and the problems arising therefrom. All Heads of (operational) Departments were invited, along with Advisers and Assistant DGs. The Ministry was then a relatively compact community, and such a broad-based committee was not too large for meaningful deliberations. It began, according to some original members, because many HDs felt they were inadequately informed and were not involved in the decision process: Eytan introduced the *Yeshivat Boker* to give his colleagues a sense of participation. Some criticized it as a 'talkfest', but many more recalled it with affection as a morale booster and a stimulus to thought. 'Department Directors felt they knew what was going on and that they were a part of it', said one veteran; half a dozen others concurred.

Eytan also had a daily meeting of his 'cabinet' or Policy Committee, later to be known as the *Hanhalah*. At that time it comprised the Political Advisers—Kohn and Shiloah—the Secretary-General, and, from 1952 onwards, the Assistant DGs and other operational Advisers, like Rafael, along with *ad hoc* invitations to HDs most directly concerned. The FM often attended. The Policy Committee took decisions. The *Yeshivat Boker* was not an operational body *per se*, but if a consensus was reached it influenced decisions. There were as well *ad hoc* meetings required in the hourly flow of Foreign Office business. But it was the two institutionalized committees of the Ministry which provided ample regular consultation among the members of the *Segel*—Department Heads and higher. The Policy Committee met less frequently in the later Eytan years.

The *Yeshivat Boker* continued during Yahil's tenure as DG, from 1960 to 1964, but with less vigour, esprit, and influence. For one thing, it met two or three times weekly, rather than daily. Moreover, while its formal composition remained the same, the growth of the Ministry had increased the size of the *Segel*. Indeed it became steadily larger, because prestige demands led to the invitation of many Heads of non-operational administrative departments. 'It ceased to have meaning', was the consensus among participants. At the same time the Policy Committee was reinvigorated, for Yahil was an admirer of collegial decision-making. Under him the Directorate included all Assistant DGs and Advisers, with *ad hoc* invitations to relevant HDs. Mrs. Meir recalled it as having met 'at least weekly', and she attended regularly.

A fundamental change in patterns of consultation occurred when Levavi was DG, from 1964 to 1967. The *Yeshivat Boker* became a weekly meeting and was reduced to an information forum, with lectures or reports by returning diplomats, other Government officials, and visitors. Many senior members of the Ministry, including the DG, ceased to attend regularly. More important, the Directorate ceased to exist— *de facto*—because Levavi was a firm believer in individual decision-making. There were frequent meetings, perhaps two or three times weekly, to decide on a specific issue. Attendance varied, depending upon the topic. Critics affirmed two other variables affecting attendance— caprice and availability: 'the right person might not be a favourite of the Director-General or might just not be around', remarked one Assistant DG.

Ad hoc meetings of the senior staff were also held at the initiative of the FM—irregularly, but on average once a fortnight. A few specific problems were discussed at each meeting, with decisions being issued in the form of a 'Protocol' and a 'Directive' prepared by the Bureau Head. Meir also called in Department Heads for information sessions, with the ubiquitous HB in attendance: he prepared a *Sikkum* or summary, and if a decision was reached, a 'Directive' for 'Action' as well. Yet there were gaps in the decision flow. FM decisions were sometimes made in the presence of the HD, without the DG—and, more often, the reverse. Moreover, as some HDs of the Meir era recalled, 'we are obliged to report to the Foreign Minister, but she is not obliged to report to us'. That responsibility lay with her HB. More than occasionally, however, they remained in the dark about discussions between the FM and an important visitor from their region.

The *Yeshivat Boker* formally ceased to exist under Rafael, DG since the end of 1967. The *Hanhalah*, however, was revived and reinstitutionalized as a weekly meeting, on Wednesdays, from 10 to 11. Its core membership is the DG, Assistant DGs, Advisers, and the two Bureau Heads. The relevant HDs are invited *ad hoc*. 'Today', remarked one member in 1970, 'the *Hanhalah* is mainly a consumer of information— largely because of the personality of the Director-General and because of its composition. There are some meetings at which crucial decisions are taken, but for the most part it is a sounding board.' Another observed: 'It is a forum for discussion and information. It creates a mood of consensus. It decides very rarely—but it gives people satisfaction. Its purpose is the same as the original *Yeshivat Boker*—to bring more people into the picture of what is going on beyond their sphere.' Rafael as DG also has bi-monthly meetings with HDs, a pale reflection of the *Yeshivat Boker* and the most striking commentary on the consultation mechanisms within the Ministry. There are also, of course, informal meetings, to deal with urgent problems.

In summary, the changing patterns of consultation may be schematized as follows:

DG	Yeshivat Boker	Hanhalah	'Ad hoc' Meetings
Eytan	daily (substantive)	daily	occasional
Yahil	2 or 3 weekly (substantive)	weekly	occasional
Levavi	weekly (informational)	irregular (bi-weekly)	frequent
Rafael	————	weekly	frequent

Many senior Foreign Service officers criticized these patterns of consultation, and 'the absence of a Policy Machine'. The division of responsibility has always been blurred, remarked many, with resultant tensions and inefficiency. Neither Sharett nor Meir was interested in rationalizing the decision process, it was noted. And an effort in 1959 to create a special inquiry committee foundered on traditional mistrust of precise organization and planning of foreign policy. 'The Machine exists formally', observed an Assistant DG, 'with a clear hierarchy. But that formal chain of decision is often cut through by side influences. And really major decisions start much higher up. Many do not even come before the *Hanhalah* for discussion or information, let alone for decision.' Further, 'there is a widespread feeling in the *Misrad* that there is much talk—of no consequence. And often, the orderly process of decision-making is interrupted by a direct approach of an Adviser or Assistant Director-General to the Director-General or the Minister.'

Another veteran remarked of the Policy Machine: 'In theory it exists—the DG, Assistant DGs, Department Directors; each is a policy-making machine in himself. Beyond that the Machine and the process are diffused. They are not well defined.' And still another remarked, cynically: 'There is no correlation between what is discussed and what is decided.' 'Anything that goes beyond routine is decided by the DG or higher, usually by him,' said one senior official dejectedly, in 1970, 'except technical matters—like the Common Market. The tradition is such that people at the level of Department Director don't take responsibility or initiative, for it would be resented higher up in the hierarchy. The principle of *Rikuz* [Centralization] is entrenched in the

Ministry.' This fixed pattern of centralized decision-making stands in sharp contrast, and reveals non-adaptation, to the increasing complexity of foreign policy issues resulting from changes in the operational environment since Israel's independence.

As for policy planning, a few bemoaned its absence. 'Thinking, except in the context of a specific problem, is frowned upon', said one Assistant DG. And Levavi, while DG, acknowledged that he was sceptical about the utility of policy planning, especially in the Foreign Office of a small state. 'The problem is that, beyond a certain point, contingency planning for a pygmy like Israel serves no purpose. There is thinking about broad policy lines, but on an *ad hoc* basis. Dealing with a specific problem stimulates "planning", but it is neither continuous, integrated nor systematic. [Moreover,] very few memoranda are written, because of the informality and ready access of officials to one another.' And, as for the type of decisions, said Levavi, no attempt has been made to classify them. Sophisticated discretion was the basis of deciding which decisions a DG should bring to the Minister, which to pass on to Department Heads, and which to make himself.

Centralization of decision-making within the Ministry is assured by the procedure for dispatch of cables. All drafts of outgoing cables are sent to the DG's Bureau: they are scrutinized by its Head and are initialled by the DG or his aide before being sent. The author may be called in to revise the draft. If the issue is vital, and the DG is absent, an attempt will be made to secure his approval by telephone. If the cable is delayable, it will await his return. And if the cable is urgent, and the Deputy DG is available, he is authorized to approve. In reality, the Head of the DG's Bureau performs the control function most of the time. Less important technical cables are dispatched without the approval of the Director-General or his HB.

Incipient planning was present in the 1950s through Kohn and Shiloah, the Political Advisers. But it was not policy planning as generally understood. They did not produce proposals based upon long, sustained, and careful study of a single problem. In fact, remarked some senior officials, the memoranda they wrote were not, in essence, different from those which Department Heads should write.

Suggestions for the establishment of a Policy Planning Board were rejected by Foreign Minister Eban, too, on the grounds that precedents had not been successful elsewhere; further, that persons on such a Board, divorced from day-to-day decisions, produce excessively theoretical designs. Yet in 1966–7 Eban instituted a General Review of Israel's Foreign Policy, including: the international aspects of the Arab–Israeli dispute, notably at the UN, and what should be done; the place of Israel in regional organizations; Israel's position *vis-à-vis* China's representation at the UN; arms control in the Middle East; Vietnam; African issues at the UN, etc.

According to Rafael, who was in direct charge of the Review, this was the first time in eighteen years that systematic planning on basic and current issues had taken place. This seems unduly optimistic, however, in the perspective of 1970. If anything developed from the Review, it has not been easily discerned. Rather, the prevalent view in the Ministry was well expressed in the remark, 'sometimes decisions emerge, sometimes they get made. Perhaps only with a Minister can it be said that an individual makes a decision.' Moreover, if categorization is sought, there are three types of decision:

whatever is in the frame of a clear line of policy is made by the Department Head;

decisions which elaborate upon or go beyond a policy line are made by the Director-General in consultation with the relevant Assistant Director-General;

decisions of decisive importance involving a new line or a marked break in policy are made by the Foreign Minister, in response to initiatives from the DG, the Assistant DG, rarely from the Department Director, or by the Minister himself.

Yet these are decisions within the permissible limits of policy made by the Foreign Office. Strategic-level and most Tactical-level decisions are made by higher authority, with the Foreign Minister participating. The typology noted above refers to Implementing decisions, as construed in this analysis, and on occasion to the higher, Tactical level.[1]

---

[1] The classification of decisions employed above is not intended to suggest iron-clad boundaries between the different levels within the Foreign Office, for it is recognized that there is much spill-over in decision-making functions.

CONCLUSIONS

Israel's Foreign Policy System:
The First Twenty Years

Our inquiry into Israel's foreign policy draws to a close. The time-space dimensions have been broad—a new state within global and regional systems of international politics during the first twenty years of independence. An attempt has also been made to uncover the forces affecting choice among policy options. Yet those forces are not entirely amenable to analysis, partly because of limits on free access to data. And even where information is available there is a formidable problem of integrating facts to explain past decisions and to permit propositions about probable future behaviour. To overcome that problem and to bring the myriad data into a semblance of order a new research design has been applied. It is well to restate the essentials of that analytical framework and the postulates underlying the approach.

Foreign Policy has been defined as a system of action. Its outputs or decisions, which constitute state behaviour, are the product of inter-action among inputs or pressures within and between two Environments—Operational (or real) and Psychological (or perceived). A major task in foreign policy analysis is to dissect both of these Settings, to explore their component parts, and to discover their points of convergence and divergence. The first Environment—Operational—indicates the boundaries of the possible in foreign policy choice and action; the second—Psychological—reveals the desirable in the minds of decision-makers.

A basic postulate of our inquiry is that policy choices and the consequences of decisions will be unsuccessful to the extent that the two Environments are not congruent. Thus it is necessary to examine with care the Operational and Psychological Environments. It is also essential to designate the high-policy or Strategic-level decision-makers, whose Attitudinal Prism and specific images provide the key to understanding the motor force of state behaviour—the Psychological Environment.

The Environment (both Eo and Eps) has been differentiated into two broad categories, External and Internal, each with five components. The external setting comprises: the Global System (G); the Subordinate System (S); Other Subordinate Systems that may impinge upon a state's behaviour (SO); bilateral relations with dominant powers in the International System (DB), and specific bilateral relations with any other actor in a system (B). The internal components of the Environment have been designated as Military Capability (M), Economic Capability (E), Political Structure (PS), Interest Groups (IG), and Competing Élites (CE). All of the internal variables and three of those in the external setting have been analysed in detail for the period 1948–68; Other Subordinate Systems were not sufficiently relevant to an overall inquiry into Israel's Foreign Policy System (they will be for some Strategic-level decisions to be examined in a later volume); the same applies to bilateral relations with states other than the super powers.

The analysis proceeded from the Operational Environment for Israel's foreign policy to the Communication Network through which reality is transmitted to the decision-makers. This led to a political-biographical dissection of Israel's High Policy Élite and its Inner Circle, that is, those who are authorized by the political system to make Strategic-level decisions. The lens through which information about the Operational Environment is filtered by decision-makers (or anyone) was then examined, along with the content of their View of the World. Perceptions of the internal setting were given less attention, for they were not key catalysts to policy choices. The flow from Operational Environment to Psychological Environment then led to an inquiry into the processes of Formulation and Implementation in Israel's Foreign Policy System. Three levels of decision were differentiated—Strategic, Tactical, and Implementing—with the focus on the first: the process pertaining to Israeli High Policy was examined during the twenty years after independence.

What were the major findings of the inquiry into Israel's Foreign Policy System? These may best be summarized within the categories of the Research Design, beginning with the Operational Environment.

Global System: The Global System of international politics experienced persistent change in its structural and textural features during the period under investigation. Three phases were discerned: tight bipolarity from 1948 to 1956; loose bipolarity from 1956 to 1962; and polycentrism thereafter. The principal actors throughout were the United States and the Soviet Union, the super powers, pursuing their objectives through various instruments and institutions—political, economic, psychological and ideological, and military, within the UN, as well as through regional organizations and blocs—sometimes with greater reliance on coercion, at other times using less overt pressures.

For Israel, as for all states, those goals and methods impinged on vital interests. A few illustrations will suffice:

support by the super powers was decisive in securing approval of the UN Partition Resolution in November 1947 and Israel's admission to the UN in May 1949;

Soviet bloc military aid to Israel was vital during the 1948 War of Independence;

massive Soviet bloc arms to Egypt in 1955–6 created the conditions of insecurity which culminated in the Sinai Campaign, and the combined pressure of Washington and Moscow compelled Israel's withdrawal from the Gaza Strip and Sinai in March 1957;

Soviet military and political backing—and serious miscalculations—contributed significantly to the outbreak of the Six Day War; and

once more, in 1969–70, actions and inactions by the super powers were crucial to a new and intense phase of Arab–Israeli confrontation.

All this and more demonstrates a persistent trait of the Operational Environment for Israel's foreign policy, namely, the irresistible penetration of the Middle East Subordinate System by the dominant powers of the Global System. Never was the significance of this pressure from the Environment so manifest as at the time of writing (December 1970).

The universal organization within the Global System has also been omnipresent in Israel's external setting. The UN was witness—some would say midwife—to the birth of a modern Jewish State. It succeeded in terminating the first round of Arab–Israeli warfare and assisted the process of negotiations leading to the Armistice Agreements of 1949. The system of Mixed Armistice Commissions and the Chief of Staff of UNTSO eased border tension from time to time. The UNEF helped to keep the antagonists apart from 1957 to 1967, when an impetuous Secretary-General displayed remarkably inept judgement and thereby contributed to the array of miscalculations culminating in the Six Day War. And since that time much of the diplomatic conflict arising out of that war, involving super powers, great powers, middle powers, and the parties themselves, has centred on the UN-sanctioned Cease-Fire and the Security Council Resolution of 22 November 1967. Thus the United Nations was a persistent source of penetration into the Arab–Israel conflict. But unlike the US and the USSR, its influence on Israeli foreign policy decisions was marginal, except in 1948–9.

Most other features of the Global System from 1948 to 1968 were irrelevant to Israel's foreign policy. Indeed, viewing the period as a whole, only two were crucial to the setting for Israeli decisions. One was penetration of the region and the conflict by the super powers and the UN. The other was a steadily rising level of destructive technology, whose increasingly costly and sophisticated weapons were sought and acquired by Israel and the Arab States.

Subordinate System: Viewed as part of Israel's external Environment, the Middle East Subordinate System comprised three concentric circles of states: a Core of Israel and her five immediate Arab neighbours; a Periphery of eight actors, including four non-Arab states— Cyprus, Ethiopia, Iran, and Turkey; and an Outer Ring of six others extending from the Maghreb to South Yemen. Some members moved from one to another category during the twenty years; some entered the system very late; but the Core group remained constant. Conflict was permanent, with three nodal points in the system's level of violence —1948, 1955–6, and 1967.

There were two features of the Middle East system, one pervasive and the other durable, which made it a crucial component of Israel's foreign policy setting: Arab hostility extending to continuous threats of annihilation; and deep penetration by a super power with massive military aid to her avowed enemies. Other relevant features of the system were: the escalating level of weaponry, imposing vast expenditures upon Israel; tendencies towards political, economic and, especially, military integration among the Arab states, posing grave dangers to Israel's security; political instability within many of those states, with spillover effects on the great unifier—war against Israel; and the status of the Middle East as a zone of open competition between the super powers and their blocs, with penetration reaching its zenith in the third phase, after the 1967 War. As noted, no other subordinate system was important throughout the period, though Western Europe became increasingly so as a source of military and diplomatic support for Israel, with Common Market affiliation a major goal of foreign policy in the 1960s.

Military Capability: There was a marked Arab superiority in all the tangible indices of military capability—before the 1967 War: geography; military-age manpower; financial resources available for defence; and weapons. That Israel triumphed in three rounds of warfare was due to certain countervailing assets: an accurate early warning system; an effective intelligence network; the strategy of offensive–defence or interceptive warfare; interior lines of communication as compensation for a tiny land base; and the lack of contiguity between Egypt and those states comprising the Arab Eastern Front.

As for the Arab numerical advantage in potential military manpower, Israel has always displayed a mobilization capability of a qualitatively higher order. Moreover, *Tzahal* is characterized by superior training, a psychology of sacrifice and victory, and more creative leadership. Israel has also compensated for smaller financial resources by more effective use, by nation-wide sacrifices in the form of steep taxation, and by sustained aid from world Jewry. And finally Israel had (and continues to have) the supreme asset of overwhelming consciousness by the total population of '*ein breirah*' (no alternative); for the price of defeat is almost universally believed in Israel to be extinction. In short, the fact of Arab superiority in the material indicators of military power has, through the perception of Israeli decision-makers, induced a permanent search for arms; indeed it has been one of the most significant inputs into Israel's Foreign Policy System. Stated differently, much of Israel's behaviour in the external world has been a response to that military imbalance. It continues to be so in 1971.

Economic Capability: In the early years Israel's economy was precarious. Much of the time, too, it has been heavily dependent upon foreign aid—for labour, capital investment, raw materials, and technological progress. That component of the Operational Environment stimulated two major decisions in Israeli foreign policy—to seek and accept German Reparations (1950–2) and to continue the effort to attain associate membership in the European Common Market. Moreover, the need for a sound and expanding economic base from which to be able to wage war has been a powerful inducement to rapid economic growth; and Israel achieved one of the most rapid and sustained growth rates in the world. The outcome by 1968 was an impressive lead over all individual Arab States and over the four eastern Arab Core members—Jordan, Lebanon, Syria, and Iraq—combined.

As the Arab–Israel conflict entered the third decade of protracted war, Israel possessed a superior economic capacity both to sustain foreign policy goals and to support military power, partly because of a more highly developed industrial structure and partly because of greater independence from politically conditioned foreign aid. More generally, her Survival Potential seems beyond doubt—unless a super power intervenes with *massive direct* military force—for Israel is superior to her Arab enemies in all four basic components: Armed Forces, Economic Capacity, Administrative Competence, and, most important, the Will to Survive.

Political Structure: Israel has a complex political structure—her party and electoral systems, the institutions which make and apply rules, and the constitutional legacy for authorizing decisions. One aspect of the structure, coalition government, has been influenced by foreign policy—through the principle of complementarity in policy priorities: *Mapai*'s high priority in foreign policy has, from the outset, been traded off against the NRP's high priority in marriage, divorce, Jewishness, and related matters. Yet foreign policy has never been a major obstacle to coalition-building, as revealed by the reconstitution of the cabinet—with the Left dissenters—after the crises over German arms in 1957 and 1958–9. Nor has foreign policy been decisive in Israel's general elections.

The reverse flow of influence—from political structure to foreign policy—has been more significant, with the coalition character of Israeli government acting as the environmental input into the Foreign Policy System. Sharett mobilized support from lesser coalition parties to thwart some proposed retaliation raids in the 1953–5 period; and the Left coalition members hampered Ben Gurion's German policy in the late 1950s. Process, too, was affected, for the fact of coalition government led to concealment of sensitive issues from the cabinet. At the same time other elements of the political structure have been, at most, of peripheral relevance: neither debates in the *Knesset* and its Foreign Affairs and Security Committee nor elections have significantly changed foreign policy decisions.

Interest Groups and Competing Élites: An array of Israeli interest groups generates and transmits demands on foreign policy to those who make decisions. The most influential is also the most secretive, namely the Defence Establishment, including the higher officer corps. Pressure has been continuous to acquire more and better-quality weapons for *Tzahal*. Moreover, they have attempted, with less success, to shape Strategic-level, that is, high-policy decisions in times of crisis; for example, pressure against withdrawal from Gaza and Sinai in 1957 and efforts to induce a more rapid military response to Nasser's challenge in May 1967.

Diaspora Jewry has been an advocate as well, but only marginally so within Israel's Foreign Policy System: there its more important function has been to assist in the implementation of Israeli decisions by pressing its own governments for material and diplomatic support for Israel. Diaspora Jewry's best-known figure, Nahum Goldmann, has frequently advocated dissenting views—on approaches to the Soviet Union, on terms for a peace settlement, etc.—but with little discernible effect on Israel's foreign policy decisions; a notable exception was German Reparations, which Goldmann, along with many others, urged the Government of Israel to seek and accept. The Israeli Foreign Ministry Establishment has also acted as an interest group, pressing their views on a wide range of issues, sometimes with success though not always with wisdom; for example, in opposition to acceptance of diplomatic relations with Peking in 1955 and in their belated recognition of the need for a firm Israeli position on South Africa's *Apartheid* policy.

Associational interest groups have had virtually no influence on decisions, though the Land of Israel Movement has been an intangible constraint on Israeli decision-makers' freedom of action since the 1967 War concerning the terms of a peace settlement. And while Israeli academics and commentators have become increasingly vocal in criticism of Israel's policy towards her Arab neighbours, their impact on decisions has not been evident.

Israel's competing political parties fall into three broad types—the Ideological Left, with *Mapam* as the prototype; the Nationalist Right, epitomized by *Herut*; and the Pragmatists, best exemplified by *Rafi*. But there are more parties competing with *Mapai* for power than there are alternative foreign policy orientations. Their policy towards 'the Arabs' provides an index of their competing advocacy. *Mapam* moved from a posture in favour of a bi-national state (before 1948) to a policy of concessions, conciliation, compromise and co-operation, and then, after 1967, to a call for a confederation with Jordan. *Maki*, further to the Left and traditionally anti-Zionist, has pressed since the late 1950s for recognition of the national rights of both Jews and Arabs in Palestine. *Ahdut Ha'avodah* and *Herut* were the most militant and non-compromising towards 'the Arabs', the first deriving from *kibbutz* activism, the second from Revisionist ideology. Both the General Zionists and the Progressives (Independent Liberals) have been close to the *Mapai* Arab line, though the former, later known as the Liberals, moved towards the harsher *Herut* stance when they joined to form *Gahal* in 1965. Certainly the advocates on the Left have never induced change in Israel's *Mapai*-dominated official policy towards the Arab states. The Centre and religious parties were in basic agreement with *Mapai*. Rather, it was *Ahdut Ha'avodah* and, since 1967, *Herut*, which acted as serious restraints on change and moderation in the most vital area of foreign policy. Indeed, along with the hawkish wing of *Mapai*, they paralysed the decision process in the 'wall-to-wall' coalition government on the most burning issue of the state.

Communication Network: For Israel's decision-makers the most important media of communicating information about the Operational Environment are intelligence briefings, cables, newspaper news, and radio. The first are crucial for Defence personnel and the High Policy Élite; the second are the most important for Foreign Ministry officials. And press and radio news constitute the indispensable sources of daily, even hourly, information on Israel's external setting.

The principal finding of our analysis is that, contrary to general belief, press and radio news are complementary, not competitive, sources of information. Persons who rely on *Ha'aretz* alone or even *Ha'aretz* and *Ma'ariv* together receive a limited image-forming supply of factual news. Any other permutation involving the two leading daily Israel newspapers and *Kol Yisrael*'s almost hourly news bulletins have the same effect. Only a combination of all three sources provides an adequate information base. Cable and intelligence reports, and a selection of foreign newspapers, provide a necessary supplement to decision-makers.

High Policy Élite: Who made the Strategic-level decisions in Israel's foreign policy during the period 1948–68? The High Policy Élite (to be differentiated from the Technical Élites, which implement those decisions) was found to be a small, relatively homogeneous group of eighteen persons. Two-thirds were born in the Czarist realm of western Russia and territory later restored as Poland, half of them before 1900. Those who arrived in Palestine during the Second *Aliya* (1904–14) were predominant in the HPE throughout the first twenty years of independence, and the Second *Aliya mentality* even more so. Only four were *sabras*—Allon, Dayan, Rabin, and Yadin—who all made their mark in *Tzahal* and were influential in the Military-Security issue-area of foreign policy.

Within the High Policy Élite there was an Inner Circle of nine persons who, at different times, played decisive roles in the shaping of Strategic-level decisions: Ben Gurion and Sharett, who functioned as a duumvirate in the first phase, 1948–56; Eshkol and Sapir in the Economic issue-area most of the time, with the former first among equals in foreign policy as a whole from 1963 to 1969; Meir, the only woman in the group, from 1956 onwards, especially in the Political-Diplomatic realm; Dayan, Peres, and Allon in military matters, the first two throughout the post-Sinai-Campaign Ben Gurion era and Dayan both earlier and later as well, Allon from the early 1960s onwards; and Eban as Foreign Minister since the beginning of 1966. In reality the Inner Circle consisted of two groups separated by age, background, and outlook: an 'old guard' of East European pioneers from the Second *Aliya*, with an ideological blend of Zionism and humanist socialism; and a 'young guard' of *sabras* or near-*sabras*, pragmatists and technocrats.

Attitudinal Prism: Another basic postulate of our approach is that foreign policy choices derive from images of the Environment held by a core group of decision-makers. The lens through which members of the Inner Circle filter information has been designated as the Attitudinal Prism. And the Prism is shaped by interacting forces within society— the political culture, the historical legacy, and the personality traits of decision-makers.

For Israel's Inner Circle the dominant strand of the political culture is its Jewishness. Indeed the fact and consciousness of being Jewish creates a unique prism:

the notion of Jewry as a world People of which Israel is an integral part;

the idea of Israel as the bastion of world Jewry, with concomitant rights and obligations;

the memory of Israel's link with Jewish antiquity;

the assertion of Israel's legitimate role as successor to the collective and individual interests of those who survived the Holocaust;

the expectation that world Jewry will assist in the resettlement of part of the Jewish People in its Homeland; and

the 'two-camp thesis', which perceived Jewry as the only certain and reliable ally of Israel.

These themes were manifested in decision-makers' reflections on basic foreign policy issues of which four were noted: the *Apartheid* question at the UN; the problem of Soviet Jewry; the Swastika-daubing incidents of 1959; and the Eichmann case. Jewishness was the dominant input from the two Environments in shaping those decisions.

Another dimension of Jewishness in Israel's foreign policy was the sense of messianic mission, most emphatically expressed in Ben Gurion's 'light to the nations' concept: decisions on Africa revealed this input role most clearly. Other strands of Israel's political culture with an effect on foreign policy were the East European roots of members of the High Policy Élite and their socialist ideology. Thus the values of nineteenth-century socialist idealism provided a major thrust for Israel's policy towards the Third World. They were also instrumental in Israel's rejection of diplomatic ties with Spain's Fascist régime. There were other illustrations of this link.

As for historical legacy, the Jewish presence in the Holy Land and the expectation through the ages of a Return was the primary image of Israel's decision-makers, leading to the proclamation of independence, the first and most important foreign policy decision. Perceptions and the choice of policy after 1948 were also affected by more recent historical experience—the British Mandate. The need to reconcile the interests of Israel and world Jewry dates from that period, as does the friction between the protagonists of diplomacy (caution) and activism in Israeli foreign policy.

The content of decisions was also influenced by the personality predispositions of high-policy decision-makers, especially the dichotomy between extremism and compromise, between rigidity and flexibility. Ben Gurion and Dayan stood at one end of this personality spectrum, Sharett and Eban at the other. Meir, Allon, and Peres, and to a lesser extent Eshkol, fell into this firmer and tougher school, Sapir into the softer line. There was also a contrast between 'men of words' and 'men of deeds', though some of the latter (Ben Gurion, Allon, Peres) were also talented in the use of words. Finally, there was the formidable 'BG Complex', from which all Israeli decision-makers suffered until Ben Gurion's resignation in 1963—and many even later. 'What will the Old Man say?' was a crucial question before any decision of consequence.

Beyond all this was the early life experience of Israel's first generation of political leaders—before they returned to Zion. The Second *Aliya* mentality was a key element in the Inner Circle's Attitudinal Prism.

Life in the Pale had created a self-sufficient and internally tranquil existence but it left the East European ghetto Jew isolated from and impervious to developments outside his exclusivist society. When he came to Palestine he was preoccupied with the rebuilding of Zion. He lacked knowledge about 'the Arabs' and was, on the whole, indifferent to them as a people, culture, and society. Ben Gurion and others among the founding fathers conjured in their minds a historic, inevitable confrontation between two world entities, one Arab, the other Jewish. And that distorting lens of a tightly knit, united, homogeneous 'Arab world' contributed to the sharpening of the cleavage. More generally, Israel's Second *Aliya* leaders, with the notable exception of Sharett, never understood 'the Arabs' and hardly tried to do so.

Élite Images: All of these prismatic elements were reflected in the Views of the World expressed by Israel's most influential foreign policy decision-makers. This is evident in the detailed comparison of Inner Circle images at the end of Part II of this book. It is sufficient here to recapitulate the main findings.

(1) The perceptions of Ben Gurion and Sharett defined the two extremes of the continua for all other members of the Inner Circle during the period 1948–68—*the pole of Courage versus the pole of Caution.*

(2) The points of divergence in the Ben Gurion and Sharett images of the *global system* had more policy significance than their shared themes. While both recognized its bipolarity and the pivotal role of super-power conflict, as well as advocating non-identification in the early years and then closer ties with the West after the outbreak of the Korean War, Ben Gurion's view was more 'inner-directed', Sharett's more 'outer-directed'; that is, Sharett attached much more importance to external words and deeds than did BG. Meir, Dayan, and Peres followed Ben Gurion's lead in relating global system developments solely to narrow-gauge Israeli security interests. Eban was in the Sharett stream in this as in most respects. Allon's image of the super powers was tempered by his ideological predisposition in favour of non-alignment.

(3) Ben Gurion denigrated the *role of the UN* in world politics and dismissed its contribution to the creation of Israel as fiction. So too did Dayan, Peres, and, to a slightly lesser extent, Meir and Allon. By contrast, Sharett and Eban magnified the UN's significance in the Arab–Israel conflict and more generally in international relations.

(4) Ben Gurion perceived the *Third World* in terms of the historic movement of anti-colonialism, of which Israel was a part, and defined Israel's proper relations with the New States as acting out the 'light to the nations' mission. Both he and Sharett recognized the Third World's political-diplomatic importance for Israel; and Meir added a humanitarian dimension in her image of Africa and related

advocacy. To other Inner Circle members the Third World was peripheral, apart from Allon's special interest in India.

(5) There was a total consensus that *world Jewry* is vital to Israel—and vice versa. But while Ben Gurion made a rigid distinction between 'the two camps'—Israel and Jewry, and others—and asserted Israel's primacy as bastion of the Jewish People, Sharett perceived with more empathy Diaspora Jewry's interests and needs, and he was more tolerant and trustful of the *goyim*. Certainly until the late 1960s Dayan and Peres accepted the Ben Gurion conceptions in this regard, while Eban and Sapir shared the Sharett image and advocacy. Eshkol moved closer to BG's 'two-camp thesis' after the 1967 War. And Meir and Allon showed greater respect for Diaspora Jewry's autonomous rights and significant contribution to Israel's progress.

(6) Ben Gurion, Sharett, Eban, and Allon had a conceptual image of '*the Middle East*' as a system or region of inter-state politics. Other Inner Circle members identified it totally with 'the Arabs'.

(7) It is in that component of their perceptions that the contrast be-tween Ben Gurion and Sharett—and their followers—is greatest. Ben Gurion viewed '*the Arabs*' as implacable enemies and advocated the permanent application of force until they accepted Israel's right to exist, *force majeure*. Sharett, the supreme Weizmannist in foreign policy, perceived 'the Arabs' as people, not just as enemy, and urged flexibility and the rational search for reconciliation by compromise. Meir is the most extreme Ben Gurionist, even more than her mentor who, after the Six Day War, moved closer to Sharett's image and policy line in this core issue. Peres, too, is close to the pre-1967 Ben Gurion image, while Eban is the leading exponent of Weizmannism in the Israeli Inner Circle. Sapir follows Eban's lead. Dayan combines Ben Gurionism with sensitivity to Arab fears and aspirations. And Allon displays Ben Gurionist harshness along with an awareness of the need for conciliation.

More generally, the continuum of two poles—Courage and Caution or Ben Gurionism and Weizmannism—is accurate only in a general sense. Inner Circle images are sophisticated and complex, with much overlapping and convergence in their Views of the World, both at the global and Middle East–Arab levels.

Formulation: From a survey of the literature on foreign policy analysis it was discovered that the concept of decision is assumed by many but explored by few; more often it is used as a synonym for policy. And where decisions are analysed there is great variety of approach. It became necessary, therefore, to provide an explicit universally-valid definition of 'decision' and to classify types of foreign policy decisions. Three indi-cators were combined—a time continuum, a spectrum of initiation-reaction, and a scale of importance. A *foreign policy decision* was thus defined as *the selection, among perceived alternatives, of one option leading to a course of action in the international system.* Decisions are made by individuals or a group authorized by the political system to act within a designated area of external relations.

Foreign policy decisions occur at precise points in time; but the time span between stimulus and choice of an option may extend from a day to some months. Moreover, the proportion of initiation and reaction varies markedly. Yet time span, initiation-reaction mix, and the importance of the decision are interlinked and give rise to a,threefold typology of decisions: *Strategic* decisions are defined as broad policy acts, measured by significance for a state's foreign policy system as a whole, the duration of impact, and the presence of a subsidiary cluster of decisions. *Tactical* decisions are those which operationalize a broad policy act. And *Implementing* decisions are the continuous day-to-day flow of choices deriving from higher-level core decisions. The evidence from Israeli policy indicated that Implementing decisions have the highest proportion of reactive stimulus and the briefest time span between inducement and choice. Strategic decisions showed much greater initiative and a much longer time span. And Tactical decisions were characterized by variety in source of stimulus and in time span.

The analysis of key structures and persons in the decision-making process relating to Israeli high policy indicated the following findings:

(1) Among the four pairs of persons at the summit of decision-making, the Eshkol-Meir relationship (1963-6) was the closest approximation to equal; the greatest gap in status and influence was evident in the Ben Gurion-Meir period (1956-63); the gap was also wide between Eshkol and Eban (1966-9) but for other reasons; and the most complex—and significant—relationship was that between Ben Gurion and Sharett (1948-56).

(2) There was persistent tension and frequent conflict between the branches of government most directly concerned with foreign and security policy—the Foreign Office and the Defence Ministry. At its source lay three interrelated factors—individual, policy, and institutional: that is, personality clashes were linked to contrasting images and advocacy, and the struggle for control over high-policy decisions. The conflict reached its zenith in the period 1957-63, with Meir and Peres as the antagonists. But it was much more complex then, operating on four mutually-aggravating levels: personality; generation gap; jurisdiction (between the ministries); and rivalry for the inheritance of Ben Gurion.

(3) The Cabinet's involvement in foreign policy was continuous and often intense, a logical consequence of permanent conflict with Israel's neighbours. From 1948 to the end of 1953 high policy was in the hands of a Ben Gurion-Sharett duumvirate, as noted; the Cabinet acquiesced. From 1954 to mid-1956 the Cabinet was influential

because of BG's 'retirement' and Sharett's practice of bringing all foreign policy issues of substance before the Government as a whole. Ben Gurion's dominance was reasserted in 1956 and continued until his last resignation in June 1963. A new Ministerial Committee on Defence became important under Eshkol. Then, in the May 1967 crisis, the full Cabinet re-emerged as the operative organ of high-policy decision.

(4) The analysis of Israel's decisions on arms and Germany (1957 and 1958–9) confirmed the presence of many structures in the formulation of Strategic-level decisions. Most important were the Cabinet, the Defence Ministry, party committees, the Press, and ultimately the *Knesset*. There was also a role for less well-known structures, notably the *Knesset* Foreign Affairs and Security Committee and *Havereinu*, an informal *Mapai* leadership group.

Implementation: Like all states Israel uses various methods to implement foreign policy decisions: Heads of State and Government; the *Histadrut*; *Kol Yisrael*'s Arabic broadcasts; and Jewish communities in the Diaspora. The bulk of day-to-day decisions are made by the Foreign Ministry and the Foreign Service Technical Élite. A complex decision-making process involves half a dozen layers within the bureaucracy—in ascending order, from Department Head to Assistant Director-General to Director-General to the Foreign Minister, with Bureau Heads to the FM and DG and Heads of Mission occupying lateral but important roles.

The Foreign Service Technical Élite comprised 87 persons from 1948 to 1968. It was found to be an 'outer-directed', predominantly foreign-born and foreign-educated group, whose leadership arrived in Palestine late (post-1945), whose apprenticeship was spent mainly in the Jewish Agency's Political Department, and who received a more advanced university education than their peers in other branches of the bureaucracy.

The Parallel Technical Élite comprised 57 persons during the first twenty years. It was, by contrast, 'inner-directed', with a larger proportion of Israeli-born members, many more than in the FSTE who arrived in Palestine as infants or adolescents, with a higher component of the Israeli-educated, and with a large majority acculturated through the key nation-building institutions, *Haganah* and *Tzahal*. This accounted, in part, for the different attitudes to foreign policy issues and for the persistent friction between the two Technical Élites. In the public image of Israel the performance of the Foreign Ministry was conspicuously less successful than the Defence Establishment in the pursuit of core objectives.

Our inquiry revealed that Israeli decision-makers perceived certain constraints on their foreign policy options. These may be summarized in terms of the key components of a Foreign Policy System as defined at the outset of this book.

(1) Israel is a self-conscious Jewish state whose historical legacy and *raison d'être* link her indissolubly to Jewish communities everywhere. (Global)

(2) Israel is dependent upon one or more super and great power(s) for military and economic assistance and diplomatic support. (Global, Military Capability, Economic Capability)

(3) The combined voting strength of the Arab, Soviet, and non-aligned groups at the UN has made a pro-Israel resolution in the General Assembly or the Security Council impossible since the early 1960s. (Global)

(4) Israel is totally isolated within the Core of the Middle East system and is confronted with a permanent challenge to her security; that condition, and her geographic position, have imposed a persistent quest for military aid. (Subordinate, Military Capability)

(5) Israel is vastly outnumbered by the Arab states, thereby creating a continuous demand for immigrants to augment her military and economic manpower. (Subordinate, Military Capability, Economic Capability)

(6) Coalition government is a fixed element of Israel's political system, causing restraints on foreign policy choices. (Political Structure)

(7) '*Ein breirah*' (no alternative) is the lynchpin of Israel's political thought and behaviour. (Psychological Environment)

(8) Historical legacy and Arab enmity have created the necessity for activism and militancy in Israeli behaviour. (Process)

Some of these perceptions (1, 7, 8) are articles of faith for Israel's decision-makers. Others are rooted in the Operational Environment. Indeed, viewed in the perspective of two decades, the Israeli Inner Circle has correctly perceived:

the manifest *threat* posed by the Arab states—its intensity, gravity, and pervasiveness;

Israel's *isolation* in the Middle East Core and, increasingly since the 1967 War, in the global system;

her *dependence* on uncertain external sources for decisive military assistance; and

the absence of '*breirah*'—an alternative—to self-defence against the threat of extinction.

These and other characteristics of the Environment indicate a high degree of congruence between image and reality *for the period as a whole*.

Israel's images and policy on the core issue of 'the Arabs' since 1948 suggest a general proposition about long-term state behaviour: *the Psychological Environment of a decision-making group in foreign policy is in large measure a product or mirror of the Operational Environment.* If reality is harsh, rigid, and forbidding over a prolonged period, perception of reality will be harsh, rigid, and forbidding. This, in turn, imposes severe constraints on the creativity-potential of decision-makers. And their images feed back into the Operational Environment to create further rigidity—in a continuous interaction. *The result is that conflict resolution becomes increasingly improbable.*

Two other propositions follow from this thesis. *Change in either Environment becomes difficult to generate, let alone sustain.* And, most important, *change is possible only by a qualitative jump within one or other of the Environments.* In the context of the Arab–Israel conflict this must emerge within decision-makers' perceptions, for basic change is improbable in the Operational Environment—in the short run. This need not and almost certainly would not occur simultaneously in the View of the World held by the decision-makers of Israel, Egypt, the United States, the Soviet Union, and the Palestinian Arabs; the images of other participants, such as France and the UK, are peripheral in the power and alignment patterns of the third decade of protracted conflict. Change in one actor's images could stimulate a general process of readjustment.

What, then, are the prospects for change in the perceptions underlying Israel's foreign policy? They must be judged remote, given two major findings of our inquiry—*stability of image patterns* and *minimal circulation in the decision-making élites.* Yet to note these and the mutually-negative impact of the two Environments in Israel's foreign policy does not absolve the decision-makers from failure to innovate: the domestic environment was no less harsh and forbidding, especially in the early years; but they innovated with remarkable success in the absorption of immigrants, nation-building, technology, and strategy, as well as the mobilization of men and resources for economic development. Not without reason has Israel been acclaimed—or decried—as a 'miracle in the desert'.

The analyst, too, bears a responsibility—beyond the description, explanation, and prediction of state behaviour: it is to lay bare his evaluation of the record, in this case of Israel's performance in the vital field of foreign policy. There have been notable achievements and notable failures. And the latter, in this writer's judgement, are too important to be explained solely in terms of the deterministic interaction of the two Environments; for decisions are made by men, not by environments.

The assessment which follows is based upon a prolonged search for the truth about Israel's foreign policy, extending from 1960 to 1970. Some of the findings are set out in the foregoing pages; others will be contained in a companion volume of studies of high-policy decisions since 1948: to make Jerusalem the capital of Israel; to seek and accept reparations from Germany; to support UN actions on the Korean War and to decline an offer of diplomatic relations with Communist China; to participate in a plan for the sharing of Jordan Waters; to launch the Sinai Campaign; to seek entry into the European Common Market; to establish diplomatic relations with West Germany; to assert Israel's right to free passage through the Tiran Straits, leading to the Six Day War; and to respond to the American peace initiative of 1970. The observations that follow are based upon the evidence uncovered and upon a dual postulate: that rigorous analysis must precede the making of value judgements; and equally, that the results of scholarly inquiry compel assessment of the record.

There were six major achievements of Israeli foreign policy during the period under investigation:

instant recognition and support by the super powers during the critical formative phase, 1948–9;

early admission to the United Nations, that is, legitimacy, at a time when many states, old and new, were excluded;

diplomatic relations with the vast majority of states;

a positive image and established presence in post-colonial Africa;

crucial military and diplomatic support from France in the form of a *de facto* alliance from 1955 to 1966; and

massive US economic and military assistance, the latter especially after the 1967 War.

These were not inconsiderable attainments. Yet there were countervailing failures in the first four issue-areas. And there was another, for which there was no counterpart—the still-elusive goal of peace. To these we may now turn, with tentative hypotheses on the causes of error.

Israel's independence was facilitated by a rare display of US-USSR 'co-operation' in the early years of post-Second World War international politics—with diplomatic recognition, political support, and, in the case of the Soviet bloc, military aid. Indeed, no other new state was created under such auspicious political circumstances. Yet within two years that unique power asset had been dissipated. To some extent this was due to forces beyond the control of Israel—increasingly tight bi-polarity in the global system and the pressure to 'stand up and be counted' with the outbreak of the Korean War. But in no small measure it may be attributed to policy choices flowing from élite images and mistaken calculations.

Like many other states who perceived a precedent for their own security, Israel supported the Security Council resolutions on Korea in June–July 1950. But the effusive declarations of affinity for the 'free world' by Sharett and Eban during the General Assembly debates in 1950 and 1951 went far beyond what was necessary for a new, small member of the UN. In perspective, this was not mere rhetoric but a conscious act in an unremitting quest for a US guarantee or treaty of alliance. That goal dominated Israeli foreign policy from 1951 to 1955 and has been pursued with varying degrees of intensity since then. It remains elusive, for the United States has persistently refused to make *formal* public commitments tantamount to a security *guarantee*. Even direct *military* aid was denied to Israel until the early 1960s.

The foreign policy costs were substantial. One was Israel's gradual isolation from the Third World of Non-Alignment, a point to be elaborated later. More important, in the perspective of 1970, a pro-American posture on Korea marked the beginning of alienation from the other super power. There was ample provocation in the excesses of Stalin's last years. But anti-Semitism was not unique to the Soviet Union. And the Holocaust did not prevent Israel's acceptance of reparations from *Germany*—a decision justified in terms of national interest. Those who rationalize Israel's early disenchantment with the Soviets note that Moscow was unresponsive to an Israeli request for economic aid in 1950. Yet they must know that the Soviet Union did not provide foreign aid to *any* state outside the Communist bloc until 1956. Nor is there evidence that identification with the West—in spirit, values, ideas, and institutions—produced ample compensatory assets to offset the discarding of support or at least non-hostility by a super power. It has been argued that subsequent Soviet policy on the Arab–Israel conflict makes this critique 'academic'. This is specious *ex post facto* reasoning. And the error is compounded by the complacent view, widely shared among Israeli decision-makers, that whatever Israel does is irrelevant to the decisions of 'hostile forces'. To assert this may be self-satisfying, but it is contradicted by the evidence: great significance is attached to Israel's behaviour by other international actors, including the super powers, especially since the Six Day War but earlier as well.

Israel's policy towards the super powers can be explained only in part by misjudgement of national interests. A deeper cause is to be found in the decision-makers' View of the World. The High Policy Élite was, throughout, dominated by *Mapai*, whose leaders were nurtured in the anti-Communism of Social Democratic and Zionist ideology: they were, as noted, the children of the first (1905) Russian Revolution. Persistent Soviet hostility to Jewish nationalism from 1917 onwards deepened the mistrust. And, while Communist bloc support in the 1947–9 period was welcomed, it was viewed as a temporary deviation from an ideological norm. This was correct; but foreign policy decisions are often the product of expediency; and this does not preclude the pursuit of long-term goals on the basis of a coincidence of interests. Israel did not make a sustained effort in this direction. Indeed, the refusal of economic aid in 1950 was perceived as confirmation of the expected reversion to Soviet hostility. And, over the years, the treatment of Soviet Jewry was portrayed by Israeli leaders as comparable with the German slaughter of European Jewry. This is not to ignore the undisguised anti-Israeli policy of the Soviet Union or her maltreatment of Soviet Jews. It is, rather, to assert that inter-state relations, even those between a super power and a small power, are the result of *interaction*— of articulated images, of postures, and of decisions. Stated differently, Israel's decision-makers felt a much greater affinity with the West and acted accordingly at the earliest opportunity. Their View of the World, buttressed by a questionable calculus of security, led them, in this writer's judgement, to discard a valuable power asset.

Another asset that was allowed to erode was the United Nations. The 1960s witnessed Israel's increasing isolation within the universal organization, expressed by condemnatory resolutions in the Security Council and the General Assembly. While the political arithmetic of the UN became more and more loaded against her, Israel reacted with a Fortress Israel mentality, rather than trying to counter the trend. One reason for this predicament was her conscious choice of identification with the West: as the world body became transformed into a numerically preponderant Afro-Asian club, Israel's failure to align with the non-aligned ensured her isolation.

The problem had deeper roots—in the ambivalent perceptions of the UN among Israel's decision-makers. The dominant image was expressed in Ben Gurion's derogatory '*oum shmoum*'. This shortsightedness demands criticism because, for all its failings, the UN was an element of support in Israel's quest for legitimacy and acceptance. And, whether its role was maximal, as with Sharett, or minimal, as with Ben Gurion, the United Nations' contribution to Israel's independence cannot be dismissed. Israeli critics claim, and rightly so, that the world organization has proved to be incapable of preventing war—in the Middle East as elsewhere—or of guaranteeing Israel's security; further, that it is more often critical of Israel's behaviour, and harshly so, than of her adversaries'. Yet to denigrate the UN role to the extent that Israeli decision-makers have done is no less an error of judgement than was Stalin's disdainful reference to the influence of the Catholic Church, 'how many divisions does the Pope have?' Once more, a power asset was allowed to become a power liability, the process eased in part by a depreciation of the UN role in Israel's independence, a narrow-gauge calculus of security, and an image of impotence and hostility towards the Jewish state.

The record of Israel's diplomatic links is impressive, with virtually total presence in North and South America, Western Europe, Africa, and, until 1967, Eastern Europe. Yet there remain striking lacunae, especially in Asia. Some are Muslim states, like Afghanistan, Pakistan, Malaysia, and Indonesia. The view that these are beyond the pale, as 'natural allies' of the Arab states, is not confirmed by Israel's ability to sustain relations with other Muslim states like Turkey, Iran, and Nigeria. It is argued, persuasively, that the Arab–Muslim alliance could not be breached in South and South-East Asia. But with regard to the world's two most populous states, Israeli policy was unimaginative.

Whether, in fact, a full-fledged diplomatic mission would have been accepted by India soon after her recognition of Israel in September 1950 remains obscure; but it is clear that Sharett's insistence on the 'principle' of reciprocity made it easier for the obstructionists in Delhi to triumph. (Thereafter, the Government of India rejected all approaches for normalization with what many Israeli decision-makers believe to be dishonest behaviour.) More inept was the rejection of an approach from Peking early in 1955 to establish formal ties.

The consequences of the China decision are difficult to measure. Its defenders resort once more to *ex post facto* reasoning: China's subsequent pro-Arab policy would have nullified an Israeli presence in Peking. Perhaps, but perhaps not. There were no Sino-Arab links at the time. The incident occurred on the eve of Bandung. Relations with China might well have had a spill-over effect on India's attitude to Israel, for that was the period of Sino-Indian friendship. It might have led to Israel's invitation to the first Afro-Asian Conference. And that in turn would have eased Israel's acceptance into the Third World— without adversely affecting her friendly ties with the West. Whatever might have been was aborted by Israel's lack of foresight, and in the approach to India by a stolid formalism. Both were 'missed opportunities', and the China decision a policy failure of the first order.

The direct cause of Israel's negative decision on China was misperception—of the probable US attitude and the accompanying price in economic and military aid. (In fact, high officials in the American Administration explicitly disclaimed disfavour or resort to sanctions if Israel were to accept the Chinese approach.) What, then, accounts for that error in judgement? Partly it was the prevalent policy line: Israeli decision-makers were anxious to avoid any act which might undermine the goal of an American security guarantee. Partly it was unfamiliarity with Asia in general and China in particular: Sharett, Eban, and others who made that decision were Europeans by background, education, outlook, and affinity; the world east of Iran, certainly its importance in international politics, seemed beyond their comprehension. And this handicap was even more conspicuous within the Foreign Service. All this suggests a third source of misassessment, with wider implications—decision-makers' images of Non-Alignment. Israel has never been formally aligned. She is, in fact, one of the few states which do not belong to a pact, bloc, alliance, or regional organization. Nor does she have a security guarantee by a super power. She does not even have a community of culture or language. She is, in truth, alone. Thus Israel's policy-makers may be credited with a unique achievement—all the disadvantages of non-alignment and none of the benefits of alignment! Israel is excluded from the non-aligned group at the UN and elsewhere; at the same time she is denied membership in any Western alliance.

It had not always been so. From 1948 to 1950 Israel followed the path of Non-Identification, one of the Basic Principles of the first coalition Government. Thereafter, as noted, she moved towards a *de facto* alignment with the West: that shift was catalysed by the need for arms and economic aid, rationalized by a perception of renewed Soviet hostility, and eased by indifference to the Third World. The last merits attention, particularly because it is rarely noted in analyses of Israeli foreign policy, by practitioners and scholars alike.

In terms of the social forces which have shaped contemporary world politics, Israel is the territorial expression of the Jewish national liberation movement. Yet that term is studiously avoided in the speeches and writings of her leaders, as well as in the state's propaganda materials. Nor is this mere semantic nuance or oversight. Rather it symbolizes the unwillingness of Israel's decision-makers to identify their struggle with the anti-colonial revolt. Either they did not understand or were reluctant to acknowledge the fundamental truth that Israel's independence is part of a global movement of national liberation in the era of European imperial decline. It was not by accident that independence came in 1948, during the tidal wave of British withdrawal from the 'crown jewel' of empire, India. Yet Israelis sought deeper meaning for the 'miracle' of rebirth in the historical and theological roots of the Jewish People. It was a false dichotomy: those roots had been present for millennia, but they required an environment in which national independence could be asserted.

The policy consequence was isolation from the emerging Third World in Asia. Israel rarely acted to strengthen that natural link and found herself increasingly excluded from the growing multi-national force of Non-Alignment. Only later was there a positive response to the second wave of anti-colonialism, in Africa from the late 1950s on. But by then the image of a Western Israel had been fully formed. All that was required was exploitation of that image by the Arabs and their Soviet patron. There are some who term this analysis 'academic' on the grounds that membership in the non-aligned club would be insignificant compared to military and economic aid. But this too is a specious claim:

the evidence demonstrates that Non-Alignment is not an obstacle to assistance from the super powers; if anything, it leads to more aid! Once more a power asset was wasted, for Israel possessed the conditions of Non-Alignment *par excellence*.

It would be inaccurate to make Israel and her foreign policy primarily responsible for the protracted war with her Arab neighbours. There can be no doubt, in this writer's judgement, that the absence of peace is overwhelmingly the result of Arab intransigence; more specifically the refusal to recognize the legitimacy, legality, and permanence of Israel. The relevant question in this context is whether Israeli policy contributed to an easing of that psychological block. The evidence points strongly to a negative reply. It is this shortcoming which causes the most disquiet, for relations with the Arabs constitute the core issue-area of Israeli foreign policy.

Courage and imagination are qualities correctly attributed to the people of Israel. The odds in favour of survival against overwhelming Arab numbers were remote—certainly in 1948. And the need to be ready for an assault at any time was met by a 'garrison democracy', in which individual freedom flourished along with social cohesion, economic development, and political stability. But these qualities are not readily discerned in the struggle for peace.

There can be no doubt that Israel as a nation passionately desires peace and accommodation, and, even more, reconciliation and co-operation with her Arab neighbours: anyone who has lived in Israel is persuaded of the genuineness of this objective. Yet those who make and enunciate her foreign policy have not shown originality in moving beyond declarations of intent to concrete proposals for peace. To say, as Prime Ministers Ben Gurion and Meir repeated constantly, that they were prepared to go anywhere at any time to negotiate peace with the Arab states is a reasonable posture in a normal conflict. It is not sufficiently innovative, however, to meet the needs of the special conflict relationship in which Israel finds herself. Even within Israel the murmurs of discontent began to be heard in the spring of 1970, especially among students and university teachers.

At no time has the paucity of imagination been so striking as in the period since the Six Day War. (One other illustration of stagnancy is apt, however: in 1952 Eban delivered a major policy speech before the UN General Assembly, entitled 'Blueprint for Peace'; the main themes were reaffirmed as a 'new approach' by Eshkol thirteen years later!) The grand gesture to break the total impasse in the summer of 1967 was not forthcoming, perhaps because it was not politically feasible in the euphoria of total victory. And during the next three years Israeli decision-makers evinced a commitment to certain verbal formulae, notably 'direct negotiations' and 'redeployment of forces', though never, under pain of ostracism from the Establishment, the word 'withdrawal'. It was a curious lapse from logic and consistency, for Israel had accepted, from the outset, the November 1967 Security Council Resolution, which explicitly referred to 'withdrawal from territories occupied [in the June War]'. Indeed this tactic created the (erroneous) impression that Israel's emphasis on method was a ploy to delay negotiations, which inevitably would involve withdrawal. What made the tactic even more incomprehensible was the fact that, then, a clear majority—in the Government and in the country—were willing to make substantial territorial concessions as part of a *genuine peace* settlement.

Ironically, it was Ben Gurion, the only high-policy decision-maker with historical vision, who publicly advocated withdrawal, as early as June 1967 and consistently thereafter, from all occupied territories except Jerusalem and the Golan Heights. But that display of imagination occurred after he had resigned from the summit of power. His successors followed the path of Ben Gurionism, not the views of Ben Gurion in his twilight years. Nor has there been evidence of imaginative formulae to deal with complex specific issues—apart from Dayan's 'open bridges' policy regarding the West Bank. The axiomatic theme of a united Jerusalem as the capital of Israel does not absolve decision-makers from the responsibility to acknowledge the legitimate Arab interest in a 'presence' in Jerusalem. The same is true for Sharm-e-Sheikh, Gaza, and the Golan Heights. Legitimate Israeli security-needs dictate that they not be returned to Egyptian and Syrian control—but is that necessarily synonymous with the perpetuation of unilateral Israeli control?

The bankruptcy of that 'policy' was revealed in August 1970, when Israel accepted the US (Rogers) 'peace initiative': in so doing she abandoned the commitment to 'direct negotiations', broke the spell surrounding the word 'withdrawal', and reaffirmed her acceptance of the November 1967 Security Council Resolution. Here was a striking instance in which policy-makers allowed a situation to develop where external pressure—from the United States—was able to determine an Israeli Strategic-level decision. Moreover, Israel was more isolated diplomatically than ever before in her history.

Israelis tend to dismiss this isolation as of no consequence and to blame it on mendacity in a world of anti-Semitism—a logical corollary of the 'two-camp' thesis. It is true that, in the last analysis, Israel's ability to survive and prosper will depend on self-help, that is, on the strength of *Tzahal* and the morale of her people, though military capability is still dependent on external aid. It is also true that persecution and anti-Semitism have been central to Jewish history. But that reality does not relieve—or excuse—the analyst and the policy-maker from asking whether Israel's behaviour did or did not contribute to this diplomatic dead end.

Decision-makers do not appear to have posed this question: this is one conclusion to be reached from our inquiry. They have thereby failed to perform a vital task of leadership—self-analysis free of clichés. Convinced, rather, that Israel's responsibility for her isolation is marginal, indeed that it is external to her control, she has been niggardly with funds and manpower in the struggle for men's minds. Since the Third World and the New Left hate Israel or do not understand the Arab–Israel conflict, the argument seems to be, why bother to combat it. And whatever image-building is attempted, it lacks the innovative brilliance of the Military in Israel. It is shaped by Western-oriented leaders and intellectuals to satisfy the Establishments of Western states —few of which require persuasion of the legitimacy of Israel's vital interests; the rest of the world is ignored.

The most fundamental explanation for these attitudes is to be found in the pervasive élite images of global and regional politics in the period following the 1967 War:

(a) misperception of US aims, purposes, and policy, and the concomitant failure to adjust to the reality of 'even-handedness';

(b) continued denigration of the UN, compounded by growing antipathy;

(c) an even sharper polarization of external forces in terms of the 'two-camp' thesis;

(d) the hegemony of the 'Security Complex', which pervades all foreign policy decisions of substance, even when 'security' is marginal or irrelevant to the issue; and

(e) an inflexible adherence to the Ben Gurionist image of 'the Arabs' as Israel's implacable enemies, 'who understand only the language of force'.

That image of 'the Arabs' contained a large element of truth; but it suffered from constancy in a world of change. That is to say, the reality of Arab hostility, whose existence has been too flagrant to require further proof, was compounded by an Israeli policy response which did not appear to recognize change: in the balance of military power and, therefore, the doubtful wisdom of behaving—always—as if Israel were the weaker party in the conflict; in the political system of Egypt created by the coming to power of Nasser, and the possibility, never fully exploited, of achieving accommodation of vital interests; in the character of 'Palestine', that is, the emergence of a genuine Palestine Arab nationalist movement, especially after the Six Day War (indeed, one of the by-products of that traumatic event); and in the character of political forces in the Arab–Israel confrontation, that is, the fact that whatever arrangements may be reached with Egypt, Jordan, and even Syria and

Iraq, Palestine Arab nationalism will have to be recognized, and Israel and Arab Palestine will have to live side by side as independent states in the historic boundaries of Eretz Yisrael, that is, post-1967 Israel and Jordan.

What has been absent in Israeli decision-makers' images of the Arab–Israel conflict has been the kind of historical vision that made the Sate of Israel become a reality; only in the case of Ben Gurion has that vision, at times, been extended to coexistence and accommodation with 'the Arabs'. Even the proponents of Caution have not displayed imaginative ideas in an attempt to achieve the goal they recognize to be an historic necessity. Most of the responsibility lies with the immature character of Arab nationalism, its self-delusions, and its inability to recognize the legitimacy of a Jewish national liberation movement in the Jewish People's historic homeland. Yet Arab attempts to destroy Israel—at birth and continuously since then—have stimulated innovative and imaginative responses in the realms of defence and nation-building. There has not been a commensurate response in foreign policy —either in the Middle East or global systems in which Israel is an active participant. The upshot was that, at the end of 1970, Israel was in a condition of near-total dependence on the United States.

In summary, during her first two decades Israel made massive progress in military and economic capability, both absolutely and relative to the combined strength of her Arab adversaries. Moreover, she mastered the problems of nation-building and attained impressive social cohesion. Throughout, her political system has been an island of democracy in a sea of authoritarianism. And few societies have attained her level of humanism, social equality, individual freedom, and popular control over the fate of the nation. But those achievements have not been matched in the sphere of foreign policy. The supreme goal of peace has been thwarted mainly by Arab intransigence and, increasingly, Soviet hostility. In part, too, the failure lies in the basic foreign policy decisions which Israel made in response to her leaders' perceptions of their environment. The qualitative jump in the Psychological Environment remains an historic task unfulfilled.

APPENDICES AND APPENDIX TABLES

BALANCE OF PAYMENTS ON CURRENT ACCOUNT: 1949–1968
(millions of dollars)

	Credit	Debit	Net Credit
1949	43	263	– 220
1950	45·8	327·6	– 281·8
1951	66·6	426·1	– 359·5
1952	86·4	393·2	– 306·8
1953	102·3	365·2	– 262·9
1954	135·2	373·2	– 238·0
1955	143·9	426·6	– 282·7
1956	177·9	534·5	– 356·6
1957	222·0	557·2	– 335·2
1958	216·9	550·9	– 334·0
1959	265·7	581·1	– 315·4
1960	336·3	668·5	– 332·2
1961	397·9	847·3	– 449·4
1962	471·8	951·3	– 479·5
1963	576·8	1,018·8	– 442·0
1964	619·2	1,184·0	– 564·8
1965	710·7	1,223·8	– 513·2
1966	832·2	1,272·5	– 440·3
1967	908·4	1,439·9	– 531·5
1968	1,146·8	1,865·0	– 718·2

(The estimated deficit for 1969 was between $900 million and $1 billion, and for 1970 more than $1,200 million.)

Sources: The figures for 1949–59 are taken from Halevi and Klinov-Malul, *The Economic Development of Israel*, Table 50, p. 141; these in turn are derived from various primary sources. The figures for 1961 and 1962 are taken from CBS, *SAI 1967*, no. 18, Table H/1, p. 193; and those for 1960 and 1963–8 from ibid., 1970, no. 21, Table G/1, p. 193. In the above figures exports were recorded as f.o.b., imports as c.i.f., for 1949–57. Both were recorded as f.o.b. since 1958.

APPENDIX TABLE 2

THE GEOGRAPHIC PATTERN OF MERCHANDISE TRADE:
IMPORTS 1949–1965 (per cent)

	US and Canada	Latin America	UK	Western Europe	Eastern Europe	Asia, Africa and Oceania	Total
1949	35·7	8·3	9·5	25·5	9·5	11·5	100
1950	42·4	7·3	9·1	24·6	5·8	10·8	100
1951	38·0	4·0	10·9	32·0	3·1	12·0	100
1952	45·3	2·8	8·7	31·1	1·7	10·4	100
1953	39·7	3·2	12·2	37·6	0·9	6·4	100
1954	34·0	2·2	10·9	45·8	2·8	4·3	100
1955	33·8	1·9	11·6	45·0	2·0	5·7	100
1956	37·1	2·7	11·2	43·0	1·2	4·8	100
1957	30·8	2·3	13·4	46·0	2·3	5·2	100
1958	33·9	3·2	13·2	42·7	2·1	4·9	100
1959	33·5	1·8	12·6	44·1	1·6	6·4	100
1960	33·2	0·7	12·9	46·0	0·8	6·4	100
1961	33·0	0·6	14·5	45·8	1·1	5·0	100
1962	37·2	1·4	17·2	37·7	1·4	5·1	100
1963	31·4	1·2	21·7	38·1	1·6	6·0	100
1964	28·1	1·4	20·4	42·6	2·2	5·3	100
1965	28·3	2·0	21·4	39·2	2·1	7·0	100

Source: Halevi and Klinov-Malul, op. cit., Appendix Table 6, pp. 290–1. The figures were derived from M. Michaely, *Foreign Trade and Capital Imports in Israel*, Am Oved, Tel Aviv, 1963 (in Hebrew), p. 84 (for 1949–53) and CBS, *SAI*, various issues (for 1954–65).

APPENDIX TABLE 3

THE GEOGRAPHIC PATTERN OF MERCHANDISE TRADE:
EXPORTS 1949–1965 (per cent)

	US and Canada	Latin America	UK	Western Europe	Eastern Europe	Asia, Africa and Oceania	Total
1949	17·0	0·4	53·7	21·5	6·0	1·4	100
1950	25·1	0·3	31·3	30·5	10·7	2·1	100
1951	24·9	0·9	32·8	34·5	4·6	2·3	100
1952	28·1	0·7	29·2	33·9	6·1	2·0	100
1953	23·6	0·5	26·1	44·3	3·5	2·0	100
1954	18·2	1·3	23·0	49·0	5·2	3·3	100
1955	20·0	1·3	20·9	49·1	3·9	4·8	100
1956	19·6	0·5	22·3	45·4	4·6	7·6	100
1957	15·9	0·6	20·6	51·7	3·6	7·6	100
1958	15·7	0·8	21·8	47·6	5·1	9·0	100
1959	17·3	1·6	19·6	46·3	4·8	10·4	100
1960	15·3	1·7	17·2	51·1	1·9	12·8	100
1961	17·7	1·1	14·9	48·7	2·7	14·9	100
1962	17·9	1·0	14·2	50·3	3·0	13·6	100
1963	15·4	1·0	14·1	53·0	2·8	13·7	100
1964	16·7	1·7	12·7	49·0	4·0	15·9	100
1965	16·4	1·4	12·1	48·9	3·9	17·3	100

Source: As for Appendix Table 2.

Appendix Table 4

PRINCIPAL SOURCES OF UNILATERAL TRANSFERS AND LONG-TERM CAPITAL: 1949–1965
($ million)

	Unilateral transfers			Long-term capital		Total unilateral transfers and long-term capital		
	World Jewry (1)	US Government[a] (2)	German Government (3)	World Jewry[b] (4)	US Government[c] (5)	World Jewry (1)+(4) (6)	US Government (2)+(5) (7)	German Government[d] (8)
1949	118·0	—	—	25·0	18·0	143·0	18·0	—
1950	90·0	—	—	21·0	44·4	111·0	44·4	—
1951	123·0	14·0	—	97·0	27·7	220·0	41·7	—
1952	104·8	86·0	—	81·4	27·5	186·2	113·5	—
1953	84·6	46·9	40·9	65·4	4·4	150·0	51·3	40·9
1954	133·2	38·6	88·4	57·1	1·8	190·3	40·4	88·4
1955	83·2	20·5	106·3	48·0	23·3	131·2	43·8	106·3
1956	128·4	6·8	104·9	65·0	30·5	193·4	37·3	104·9
1957	98·0	24·1	122·9	63·7	9·0	161·7	33·1	122·9
1958	111·8	16·4	135·1	47·5	12·8	159·3	29·2	135·1
1959	104·1	9·5	137·1	60·7	19·7	164·8	29·2	137·1
1960	123·5	13·9	173·5	81·7	21·1	205·2	35·0	173·5
1961	137·0	10·4	198·8	92·3	21·6	229·3	32·0	198·8
1962	141·8	8·0	180·9	122·6	31·1	264·4	39·1	180·9
1963	173·2	5·9	167·4	175·6	31·8	348·8	37·7	167·4
1964	191·8	8·2	151·1	170·4[e]	42·1	362·2	50·3	151·1
1965	206·3	4·7	129·4	131·3[e]	51·8	337·6	56·5	129·4
Total 1949–65	2,152·7	313·9	1,736·7	1,405·7	418·6	3,558·4	732·5	1,736·7

a Grants and technical assistance.　b Some of the net private foreign investment included here is undoubtedly from non-Jews.
c All loans from US Government agencies, including Export-Import Bank.　d Unilateral transfers only, since there are no repayments

APPENDIX TABLE 5

UNILATERAL TRANSFERS AND LONG-TERM CAPITAL AS
PERCENTAGE OF IMPORT SURPLUS

	World Jewry	US Government	German Government
1949	65·0	8·2	—
1950	39·4	15·7	—
1951	61·2	11·6	—
1952	60·7	37·0	—
1953	57·0	19·5	15·6
1954	80·0	17·0	37·1
1955	46·4	15·5	37·6
1956	54·2	10·5	29·4
1957	48·2	9·9	36·7
1958	47·7	8·7	40·5
1959	52·2	9·3	43·5
1960	61·0	10·4	51·5
1961	53·1	7·4	46·1
1962	58·2	8·6	39·8
1963	86·3	9·3	41·4
1964	63·6	8·8	26·6
1965	64·8	10·9	24·8
Average 1949–65	59·2	12·2	28·9

Source: Based upon Halevi and Klinov-Malul, op. cit., Table 59, p. 158.

APPENDIX A

Foreign Policy in Government Programmes

The articulated content of coalition programmes provides another index of the interrelationship between Israel's political structure and her foreign policy. Some quantitative data are set out in the following table. They reveal that:

(1) the number of topics dealt with was relatively unchanged, with an average of eleven;
(2) the articulation of 'basic principles' became increasingly voluble from the Third *Knesset* onwards;
(3) this elaboration of aims extended to foreign policy as well;
(4) foreign policy ranked high in the volume of words, with an average of fourth, but was never the highest (it ranked second in 1959 and shared second place with 'Education and Science' in 1966); and that
(5) in all six Government Programmes economic topics were the most voluminous by far; in 1949 and 1951 they accounted for half the total number of words, and in 1955 and 1966 almost 30 per cent.

A simple frequency count provides some insight but this must be supplemented by a more evaluative content analysis: by rank of foreign policy in the list of principles; the tone and stress of delineation; and changes through time.[1]

The Government Programme approved by the First *Knesset* in March 1949 contained a succinct statement of five principles of foreign policy:

1. 'Loyalty to the principles of the United Nations Charter and friendship with all freedom-loving states, and in particular with the United States and the Soviet Union.'
2. 'A striving towards a Jewish-Arab covenant within the framework of the United Nations Organization.'
3. 'Support for every measure to strengthen peace, ensure the rights of man and the equality of peoples the world over, and strengthen the authority and competence of the United Nations Organization.'
4. 'Assurance of the right of exit from every country to Jews who wish to return and make their home in their historic homeland.'
5. 'Effective safeguarding of the independence and full sovereignty of the State of Israel.'

---

[1] The direct quotations and the data on which the following analysis is based are taken from the *Basic Principles of Government Programmes*, as reproduced in the *Government Year Books* indicated in the sources to the following table.

FOREIGN POLICY IN THE 'BASIC PRINCIPLES OF THE GOVERNMENT PROGRAMME'

Knesset	Date of Approval	Total Number of Chapter Topics	Total Number of Points	Foreign Policy and Security		
				No. of Chapters / No. of Topics	No. of Points	Rank in Volume of Words
1st	9 March 1949	10	39	2 (1 each)	5 (For. Pol.), 1 (Sec.)	4[a]
2nd	8 October 1951	b	27	b	1 (For. Pol.), 1 (Sec.)	5[c]
3rd	3 November 1955	14	54	1 (combined)	6	5[d]
4th	16 December 1959	12	83	1 (combined)	10	2[e]
5th*	2 November 1961	12	83	1 (combined)	10	2[e]
6th	12 January 1966	10	86	1 (combined)	13	2[f]

Sources: State of Israel: *Government Year Books* 5711 (1950–1), pp. 50–6;
5714 (1953), pp. 47–9 (Hebrew version);
5717 (1956), pp. 25–31;
5721 (1960), pp. 3–6 (Hebrew version);
5726 (1965–6) special supplement, pp. 1–8.

Divrei Ha-Knesset vol. 32, p. 204, Jerusalem, 1961;
Government Year Book

* Prime Minister Ben Gurion informed the *Knesset* that the preceding 'Basic Principles . . .' had been adopted by the new Government in full.

a (1949) 'Development' was the most voluminous chapter by far; then came 'Education', 'Labour', and 'Foreign Policy' and 'Security' combined. All but three chapters contained 1 point: 'Development' (21), 'Immigration' (6), and 'Foreign Policy' (5).

b (1951) Not numerically specified.

c (1951) Economic topics accounted for more than half the total volume of words, as well as 14 of the 27 points; education matters followed, and then, tied for third in volume, came 'Basic Laws' and 'Fair Employment'; a shade lower, and also tied in volume, were 'Foreign Policy and Security', taken together, and 'Laws Concerning Civil Servants'.

d (1955) 'Economic Policy' was the most voluminous chapter by far; then came 'Moral Rectitude and Widespread Voluntary Activity'; then, bunched together in volume, came 'Integration of Jewish Communities from Abroad', 'Settlement of the Country', and 'Security, Peace and Foreign Policy'.

e (1959, 1961) Only 'Economic Policy', with 20 points, exceeded 'Foreign Policy' (10 points) in volume of words.

f (1966) 'Economic and Social Life' is the most voluminous (2+ of 7½ pages), followed by 'Education and Science' and 'Foreign Policy', each a little more than 1 page.

The 1949 foreign policy values, in order of occurrence, are as follows:

1. United Nations
2. Friendship with US and USSR } equal
3. Peace with Arab Neighbours
4. Global Peace
5. Rights of Man } equal
6. Equality of Peoples
7. Right of Jews to Migrate to Israel
8. Independence and Sovereignty

In evaluative terms the most striking feature of this statement is the pre-eminence accorded the UN, a symbol, undoubtedly, of its role in the creation of Israel. The universal body is noted four times in five brief points, with intense expressions of friendship—'loyalty to the principles of the United Nations Charter', a Jewish-Arab covenant 'within the [UN] framework', and 'support for every measure . . . to strengthen [its] authority'; the UN is also listed first among the values. Israel's initial policy of Non-Identification is reflected in the equal value of friendship for the super powers. Peace with the Arabs is a major aim and value. And the *raison d'être* of the state is reflected in the affirmation of the right of Jews anywhere to migrate to Israel.

The foreign policy section in the second Government Programme, approved in October 1951, was also very brief:

The Government will promote relations of friendship and mutual aid with every peace-loving country, without inquiring into its internal régime; it will devote itself to the preservation of peace in the world and to the strengthening of the authority of the United Nations to this end; it will strive for permanent peace with the neighbouring countries and for cooperation with them in the development of the Middle East; it will stand guard over the sovereignty of the State of Israel in external affairs, its freedom within, and its international tranquillity; and it will look to the right of the Jews in all countries to emigrate to Israel and to share in the up-building of the Land. The Government will promote trade relations with all countries on equal terms.

There were only two changes in the content of foreign policy values, but the order of occurrence differed somewhat:

1. Friendship with all Peace-Loving States
2. Global Peace
3. United Nations Authority } equal
4. Peace with Arab Neighbours
5. Sovereignty
6. Internal Freedom } equal
7. Right of Jews to Migrate to Israel
8. Trade with all Countries

The 'Rights of Man' and 'Equality of Peoples' have been replaced by 'Internal Freedom' and 'Trade with all Countries'. In evaluative terms there are two noteworthy changes from 1949 to 1951. First is the marked reduction in weight and tone of reference to the UN. It is noted only once—and as an instrumental value, that is, 'strengthening of the authority of the United Nations to this end' (world peace). And while peace with Israel's neighbours is reaffirmed, it is no longer specified 'within the framework of the United Nations': the disenchantment with the universal organization had begun. Secondly, the super powers are not mentioned by name. Non-Identification had fallen victim to the Korean War, as expressed in the replacement phrase, 'friendship with every peace-loving country'. As for order of occurrence, the most conspicuous change is the reference to sovereignty—from eighth to fifth position in the list.

In the third set of Basic Principles of Government Programme, approved by the *Knesset* in November 1955, foreign and security policy were combined as one of fourteen chapters. The tone and stress are much more nationalist throughout. This is evident, initially, in the order of appearance of values:

1. Increased Military Preparedness
2. Protection of Frontier Settlements ⎫
3. Relaxation of Border Tension and Peace ⎬ equal
   with Arab Neighbours ⎭
4. Friendship with all Peace-Loving States ⎫
5. Friendship with Asian Peoples ⎬ equal
6. Friendship with States with Jewish Communities ⎭
7. Right of Jews to Migrate to Israel
8. Reduction of International Tension
9. Sovereignty, Territorial Integrity, Independence ⎫ equal
10. Democracy ⎭

The qualitative change is more sharply reflected in the choice of words. Thus the first point, referring to military preparedness, reads:

The Government will persist in determined efforts to increase our military preparedness and improve the organization, equipment, training and morale of the Israel Defence Forces. . . .

The second point acknowledges the obligation to

continue meticulously to observe the Armistice Agreements . . . ; at the same time it [Israel] will insist on observance of the Agreements by our neighbours.

Most striking are the explicit bases of Israel's relations with states in the global system:

(a) The requirements of Israel's security, of peace in the world as a whole and particularly in the Middle East;

(b) The requirements of Israel's security, immigration, development and economic independence;

(c) The position and the needs of the Jewish people dispersed all over the world;

(d) Fidelity to international cooperation and the principles of the United Nations Charter.

This is the only reference to the UN in the entire document. Finally, there is great stress on national interests, unequivocally expressed:

In all its foreign relations it is incumbent upon the Government of Israel to maintain its full sovereignty, territorial integrity, independence and democratic régime. . . .

The foreign policy provisions of the coalition programme approved in December 1959 reveal a change from nationalist to internationalist values, though the former are reaffirmed. The shift in stress is indicated by the order of listing of values—after the *Knesset* election following the Sinai Campagn:
  1. General and Complete Disarmament and Global Peace
  2. Peace (Non-Aggression Pacts) with Arab Neighbours
  3. General and Complete Disarmament (regional, Middle East)
  4. International Co-operation in accord with UN Principles
  5. Friendship with all Peace-Loving States
  6. Friendship with Asian and African Nations
  7. Right of Jews to Assist and to Migrate to Israel
  8. 'Ingathering of the Exiles'
  9. Sovereignty, Territorial Integrity, Independence ⎫ equal
 10. Democracy ⎭

The prominence given to disarmament is noteworthy, and the 1959 Basic Principles were the first to incorporate this value as such. There is also an expression of flexibility regarding the goal of peace with Israel's neighbours—the first reference to non-aggression pacts as desirable interim arrangements. The most persuasive evidence of the shift in tone, however, is the fact that the first six values are internationalist in character—disarmament, peace, and friendship. The approaching explosion of independence in Africa is acknowledged. And two basic points, relating to the foundations of Israel's foreign relations, were taken *in toto* from the previous programme. There is, finally, a pointed reference to Soviet Jewry, which now assumed new importance as a source of immigrants:

The Government will make every effort to achieve support for the 'ingathering of the exiles' and for securing permission to migrate from the lands in which immigration is not yet free.

The Basic Principles approved in January 1966 were the most voluble of all six Government Programmes under analysis; this is evident in the foreign policy section as well. The list of values contained many from earlier statements, along with a few innovations. There were two conspicuous clusters:

1. Sovereignty, Territorial Integrity, Independence
2. State Welfare and Security
3. Internal Freedom
4. Enhanced International Status for Israel

} equal

5. Global Peace and General and Total Disarmament
6. Elimination of Aggression and Belligerency
7. Relaxation of Tension between States and Blocs
8. Eradication of Racial and Religious Discrimination
9. Completion of the Liberation of all Colonial Peoples
10. International Co-operation
11. Development of Under-Developed Areas

} equal

12. Peace and Co-operation with Arab Neighbours (Peace Treaties or Non-Aggression Pacts)
13. General and Complete Disarmament (regional, Middle East)
14. Right of Jews to Assist and to Migrate to Israel
15. Friendship for all Peace-Loving States
16. Elimination of Anti-Semitism
17. Strengthened United Nations

National interests are accorded the highest rank. Global peace and disarmament are reaffirmed but *after* the first cluster of nationalist values. Moreover, 'Foreign policy will be designed to safeguard' the latter, while 'The Government will support every step likely to advance peace. . . .' The second cluster is more in the nature of elaborations of the value of global peace, especially 6 and 7, but the reference to racial discrimination and independence for all nations, clearly alluding to South African *Apartheid* and the African independence movements, are not found in the programmes of the 1950s. Values 12–15 and 17 were long-established, but Israel went on record unequivocally as intending to act on behalf of world Jewry, when anti-Semitism was involved:

The Government will be alert to every manifestation of the danger of anti-Semitism and the revival of Nazism in any country in the world. It will demand that Nazi criminals be brought to trial and punished. . . .

Finally, the demotion of the UN value from the peak of 1949 to the trough of 1966 is striking. It appears as the last in a lengthy list of values. And earlier it is mentioned in a blunt instrumental tone:

. . . the Government will endeavour . . . to obtain aid from . . . the United Nations against the Arab countries' policy of hostility, and to secure assistance for Israel's security.

A content analysis of articulated government programmes is one but by no means the most important technique of exploring a foreign policy system. In this inquiry it has revealed the changing foreign policy value hierarchies of Israel's coalition régimes: internationalist values were pre-eminent in the Government Programmes for 1949, 1951, and 1959; nationalist values were dominant in 1955, 1961, and 1966.

APPENDIX B

Party Leaders' Statements on Foreign Policy in Election Campaigns

A survey of reported campaign speeches in three Israeli elections (1959, 1961, 1965) reveals that few persons spoke on foreign policy and security, and that even for the party leaders with a special interest in this issue area foreign policy was a small part of the campaign oratory. The more important reported speeches may be summarized as follows:

Fourth Election 1959

Yigal *Allon* and Moshe *Carmel* (*Ahdut Ha'avodah*) urged an activist posture to overcome the Suez Canal boycott and Nasser's threat to block the Straits of Tiran.

Moshe *Dayan* (*Mapai*) attacked the *Mapam* attitude to the Sinai Campaign—'*Mapai* feels that, if necessary, force will be used'; he welcomed closer French-Arab ties, acclaimed French help to Israel, and renewed Israel's desire for peaceful co-operation with the Arabs—joint exploitation of natural resources, a joint port of Akaba and Eilat, joint potash works, and joint exploitation of water and electric power with Jordan and Syria.

Shimon *Peres* (*Mapai*) attacked *Mapam* for advocating peace with the Arabs on any conditions.

Golda *Meir* (*Mapai*) asserted that the struggle for free passage in the Suez Canal would continue.

Hanan *Rubin* and Ya'acov *Hazan* (*Mapam*) advocated a conciliatory line towards peace with the Arabs, including concessions on the refugee problem.

Arye *Ben-Eliezer* (*Herut*) declared, 'there will be no peace with the Arabs as long as the Ben Gurion Government is in power'.

Menahem *Begin* (*Herut*) proposed a Franco-Israel Friendship Treaty and criticized the recent sale of arms to Germany.

Yosef *Burg* (NRP) claimed that *Mapai* was split on foreign and security policy—Sharett and Eban versus Dayan.

Fifth Election 1961

In so far as foreign policy was discussed, it focused on the dual proposals of non-alignment in the Cold War and Israel's integration in a

Middle East confederation, introduced by Nahum *Goldmann*, President of the World Zionist Organization, towards the end of the election campaign. Campaigning for the newly-united Liberal Party (General Zionists and Progressives), Goldmann attacked 'the prevalent attitude of wait-and-see, don't-do-anything, of staying put, of being afraid to try anything new'; and he merged his proposals as follows: 'our orientation towards the Western bloc is making it even more difficult for Israel to integrate into the region', though he acknowledged that the Arabs 'are not prepared now to make peace'. (*Jerusalem Post*, 4 August 1961.) Even before that, however, the Arab refugee issue was debated, in the light of *Mapam*'s proposal for substantial repatriation.

Pinhas *Sapir* (*Mapai*) countered, 'by allowing 300,000 Arabs back into Israel we would in effect be permitting a full-scale invasion of an enemy without the use of artillery or tanks'.

Levi *Eshkol*, Giora *Josephthal*, and *Dayan* (all *Mapai*) also adopted a hard line against repatriation—'a political not a resettlement issue', said Dayan, but he offered compensation even before a peace treaty.

Golda *Meir* (*Mapai*) rejected the *Mapam-Ahdut Ha'avodah* proposals for neutralism—'a responsible Government cannot be neutral towards one of the major world powers which, each week, supplies arms to our neighbours . . . [for use] against Israel'.

The most vociferous criticism of Goldmann's proposals came from *Mapai* and *Herut*.

Ben Gurion lashed out at 'the important visitor from New York', ridiculed the idea of integrating with the Arab world, and accused Goldmann of 'knowingly misleading the public'.

Meir termed the idea 'not only illogical but impractical'.

Abba *Eban* chided Goldmann for making a vague proposal 'and then rushing for the exit'.

Peres was blunter: 'we reject this camouflaged neutralism of kowtowing to the stronger power'; Israel, he added, practises genuine neutralism—it is not a member of a bloc and has no foreign troops on its soil.

Dayan declared that neutralism would not impress the Soviets; it would only help cut off the means for Israel's progress and security; he also published a rejoinder, 'No Simple Way to Peace'.

For *Herut*, *Begin* declared that a policy of neutralism was worthless under the existing conditions of siege; further, that Goldmann spoke 'the language of the *Golah*'; and

Yohanan *Bader* dismissed the proposals as 'totally unrealistic', an amalgam of ideas taken from Semitic Action (*Kena'anim*), *Maki*, *Mapam*, and the Magnes group (favouring a bi-national state); the return of Arab refugees would be dangerous too.

Sixth Election 1965

Dayan was the *enfant terrible* of this election campaign, with his provocative line on Israel's Arabs and the publication of his book, *The Sinai Campaign*. Ben Gurion was not far behind, with disclosures of sensitive security matters. France was a major focus of attention; and personal criticism was sharper.

Dayan (for *Rafi* this time) urged Israeli Arabs to maintain (cultural) contact with other Arabs; to the charge that this was dangerous for security, he said, 'A distinction should be made between advising Israeli Arabs to integrate and to assimilate, for the latter is unnecessary and unlikely to succeed; I advise the Israeli Arabs to act as I would act if I were an Israeli Arab; they must be loyal to the State and its laws but should remain a separate entity.'

Eshkol (*Mapai*) called Dayan's speech 'an extreme in irresponsibility'; but the issue did not persist.

Ben Gurion (*Rafi*) denied his involvement in the Kibya raid (October 1953), attributing it to his *bête noire*, Lavon; the son of the late Prime Minister–Foreign Minister, Sharett, published an extract from his father's diary disputing this.

David *Hacohen* (*Mapai*) declared that Ben Gurion, as Prime Minister, had often submitted to United States pressure.

Meir (*Mapai*) was the most scathing on the publication of Dayan's *Sinai Diary*: 'public discussion . . . only poisons the atmosphere; [the book was] dripping poison on the open wounds in the hearts of bereaved parents' by suggesting that certain operations in the Sinai Campaign were unnecessary.

Herut tried to exploit the visit of Field-Marshal Amer to Paris in October 1965.

Ben-Eliezer made a dramatic flight to Paris 'to protect Israel's interests'; he criticized the Foreign Ministry line that French ties with Cairo were good for Israel and charged lack of initiative by the Government.

Dayan (*Rafi*), by contrast, welcomed ties between Israel's friends (France) and the Arabs, in the hope of a feedback effect on the Arabs conducive to peace.

Ben Gurion (*Rafi*) expressed confidence in de Gaulle's unwavering friendship for Israel; but

Peres (*Rafi*) called for new policies towards France 'because the previous one has reached a stage of inertia'.

On a more personal note, *Degani* (*Rafi*) called for a new Foreign Minister, 'a real personality . . . who will not be afraid to lay down a truly dynamic policy'; and

Eban (*Mapai*) caustically dismissed the *Gahal* platform as 'a strange blend of *Herut*'s irresponsibility and the General Zionists' timidity.

It contained so many platitudes and clichés I did not think it was real.'

There were undoubtedly other speeches echoing these themes, some unreported, some reported in media not consulted for this survey. Apart from 1955, however, and to a lesser extent 1965, foreign policy topics comprised a small portion of the total volume of campaign oratory. Their influence on the outcome was uneven in the six contests. Yet all coalitions have displayed deference to this area of public policy.

Source: Jerusalem Post and *Ha'aretz* files for October 1959, July–August 1961, and October 1965. The survey did not cover the full election campaign periods.

APPENDIX TABLE 7

DAILY AVERAGE OF TELEGRAM TRAFFIC (FOREIGN MINISTRY)

| | Number of Telegrams | | | |
	1963–4	1964–5	1965–6	1966–7
Incoming Telegrams	130	159	155	151
Outgoing Telegrams	133	163	175	164
Total	263	322	330	315
	Number of Words Daily			
	1963–4	1964–5	1965–6	1966–7
Incoming Telegrams	7,800	9,672	9,025	9,051
Outgoing Telegrams	8,400	9,517	11,804	9,626
Total	16,200	18,189	20,829	18,677

OPEN AND CONFIDENTIAL TELEGRAMS (percentage)

| | Outgoing Telegrams | | | Incoming Telegrams | | |
	1963–4	1964–5	1965–6	1963–4	1964–5	1965–6
Open	43·5	30·0	44·7	35·0	26·0	43·7
Confidential	56·5	70·0	55·3	65·0	74·0	56·3
Total	100·0	100·0	100·0	100·0	100·0	100·0

The daily flow of cable traffic increased by 20 per cent from 1963–4 to 1964–5 in both the number of telegrams and the volume of words and then remained stable during the next three years. The distribution of outgoing telegrams shows a striking increase in the confidential stream in 1964–5, from 56·5 per cent to 70 per cent, and then a return to 55·3 per cent. The 1964–5 distribution of incoming cables was even more sharply skewed—26 per cent (open) and 74 per cent (confidential). And the larger proportion of 'confidential' telegrams throughout symbolizes Israel's intense security consciousness. The data on telegram traffic into and out of the Israel Foreign Office are derived from the annual *Skira* (Report), Ministry for Foreign Affairs: *Appendix to the Foreign Minister's Speech on the Budget of the Ministry*:

for 1963–4 *Report 1965–66*, p. 56;
for 1964–5 *Report 1966–67*, p. 62;
for 1965–6 *Report 1967–68*, pp. 76–7;
for 1966–7 *Report 1968–69*, pp. 67–8.

Ministers of the Governments of Israel
May 1948–May 1968[1]

ALLON, Yigal	born 1918, Israel Labour, November 1961–January 1968 Deputy Prime Minister and Immigrant Absorption, January 1968–	Ahdut Ha'avodah
ALMOGI, Yoseph Aaron	born 1910, Poland Without Portfolio, November 1961–September 1962 Development and Housing, September 1962–May 1965 Labour, January 1968–	Mapai Rafi
ARANNE, Zalman	1899–1970, Russia Without Portfolio, January 1954–June 1955 Transport, June–November 1955 Education and Culture, November 1955–May 1960 and June 1963–	Mapai
BAR YEHUDA, Yisrael	1895–1965, Russia Interior, November 1955–December 1959 Transport, May 1962–May 1965	Ahdut Ha'avodah
BARZILAI, Yisrael	1913–1970, Poland Health, November 1955–November 1961 and January 1966– (Also Posts, November 1958–December 1959)	Mapam
BEGIN, Menahem	born 1913, Poland Without Portfolio, June 1967–	Herut Gahal

[1] An open-ended date indicates that, as of May 1968, the minister held the specified portfolio. There were many changes after the Seventh *Knesset* Elections in October 1969 and again in 1970.

BEN AHARON, Yitzhak	born 1906, Roumania Transport, December 1959–May 1962	Ahdut Ha'avodah
BEN GURION, David	born 1886, Poland Prime Minister and Defence Minister, May 1948–January 1954 Defence Minister, February–November 1955 Prime Minister and Defence Minister, November 1955–June 1963	Mapai Rafi
BENTOV, Mordekhai	born 1900, Poland Labour and Construction, May 1948–March 1949 Development, November 1955–November 1961 Housing, January 1966–	Mapam
BERNSTEIN, Peretz	1890–1971, Germany Commerce, Industry and Supply, May 1948–March 1949 Commerce and Industry, December 1952–June 1953	General Zionist
BURG, S. YOSEPH	born 1909, Germany Health, October 1951–December 1925 Posts, December 1952–June 1958 Social Welfare, December 1959–	Ha-po'el Ha-mizrahi (NRP)
CARMEL, Moshe	born 1911, Poland Transport, November 1955–December 1959 and May 1965–	Ahdut Ha'avodah
COHN, Haim	born 1911, Germany Justice, June–December 1952	non-party
DAYAN, Moshe	born 1915, Israel Agriculture, December 1959–November 1964 Defence, June 1967–	Mapai Rafi
DINUR, Ben-Zion	born 1884, Russia Education and Culture, October 1951–November 1955	Mapai
EBAN, Abba	born 1915, South Africa Without Portfolio, December 1959–August 1960 Education and Culture, August 1960–June 1963	Mapai

	Deputy Prime Minister, June 1963–January 1966	
	Foreign Affairs, January 1966–	
Eshkol, Levi	1895–1969, Russia	Mapai
	Agriculture and Development, October 1951–June 1952	
	Finance, June 1952–June 1963	
	Prime Minister and Defence Minister, June 1963–June 1967	
	Prime Minister, June 1967–	
Galili, Yisrael	born 1911, Poland	Ahdut
	Without Portfolio, January 1966–	Ha'avodah
Geri, Jack Myer	born 1901, Lithuania	non-party
	Commerce and Industry, November 1950–October 1951	
Govrin, Akiva	born 1902, Russia	Mapai
	Without Portfolio, December 1963–December 1964	
	Tourism, December 1964–January 1966	
Gruenbaum, Yitzhak	1879–1970, Poland	General
	Interior, May 1948–March 1949	Zionist
Gvati, Haim	born 1901, Poland	Mapai
	Agriculture, November 1964–	
Joseph, Dov	born 1899, Canada	Mapai
	Supply, Rationing and Agriculture, March 1949–November 1950	
	Transport, November 1950–October 1951	
	Commerce and Industry and Justice, October 1951–December 1952	
	Without Portfolio, December 1952–June 1953	
	Development, June 1953–November 1955	
	(Also Health, June–November 1955)	
	Justice, November 1961–January 1966	
Josephthal, Giora	1912–1962, Germany	Mapai
	Labour, December 1959–November 1961	
	Development and Housing, November 1961–August 1962	

KAPLAN, Eliezer	1891–1952, Poland Finance, May 1948–June 1952 (Also Commerce and Industry, March 1949–November 1950) Deputy Prime Minister, June–July 1952	Mapai
KOL, Moshe	born 1911, Poland Development and Tourism, January 1966–	Progressive (Independent Liberal)
LAVON, Pinhas	born 1904, Poland Agriculture, November 1950–October 1951 Without Portfolio, August 1952–January 1954 Defence, January 1954–February 1955	Mapai
LEVIN, Rabbi Yitzhak Meir	born 1894, Poland Welfare, May 1948–September 1952	Agudat Yisrael
LUZ, Kadish	born 1895, Russia Agriculture, November 1955–December 1959	Mapai
MAIMON, Rabbi Yehuda Leib	1875–1962, Russia Religious Affairs and War Veterans, May 1948–October 1951	Mizrahi (NRP)
MEIR, Golda	born 1898, Russia Labour and National Insurance, March 1949–June 1956 Foreign Affairs, June 1956–January 1966	Mapai
MINTZ, Benyamin	1903–1961, Poland Posts, July 1960–May 1961	Po'alei Agudat Yisrael
NAFTALI, Peretz	1888–1961, Germany Without Portfolio, October 1951–June 1952 Agriculture, June 1952–November 1955 (Also Commerce and Industry, June–November 1955) Without Portfolio, November 1955–January 1959	Mapai

NAMIR, Mordekhai	born 1897, Russia Labour, June 1956–December 1959	Mapai
NUROCK, Rabbi Mordekhai	1884–1963, Latvia Posts, November–December 1952	Mizrahi (NRP)
PINHAS, David Zvi	1895–1952, Hungary Transport, October 1951–August 1952	Mizrahi (NRP)
REMEZ, David	1886–1951, Russia Transport and Communications, May 1948–November 1950 Education and Culture, November 1950–May 1951	Mapai
ROKAH, Yisrael	1896–1959, Israel Interior, December 1952–June 1955	General Zionist
ROSEN, Pinhas	born 1887, Germany Justice, May 1948–October 1951 and December 1952–November 1961	Progressive (Independent Liberal)
SAPHIR, Yoseph	born 1902, Israel Transport, December 1952–June 1955 Without Portfolio, June 1967–	General Zionist Gahal
SAPIR, Pinhas	born 1909, Poland Commerce and Industry, November 1955–May 1965 Finance, June 1963–January 1968 Without Portfolio, January 1968–	Mapai
SASSON, Eliahu	born 1902, Syria Posts, November 1961–January 1967 Police, January 1967–	Mapai
SERLIN, Yoseph	born 1906, Poland Health, September 1953–June 1955	General Zionist
SHAPIRA, Haim Moshe	1902–1970, Poland Immigration and Health, May 1948–October 1951 Religious Affairs, October 1951–June 1958	Ha-po'el Ha-mizrahi (NRP)

	(Also Interior, March 1949–December 1952 and June–November 1955)	
	(Also Welfare, December 1952–June 1958)	
	Interior, December 1959–	
	(Also Health, November 1961–January 1966)	
SHAPIRO, Ya'acov Shimshon	born 1902, Russia Justice, January 1966–	Mapai
SHAREF, Ze'ev	born 1906, Roumania Commerce and Industry, November 1966– (Also Finance, January 1968–)	Mapai
SHARETT, Moshe	1894–1965, Russia Foreign Affairs, May 1948–January 1954 Prime Minister and Foreign Affairs, January 1954–November 1955 Foreign Affairs, November 1955–June 1956	Mapai
SHAZAR, Zalman	born 1889, Russia Education and Culture, March 1949–November 1950	Mapai
SHITREET, Behor Shalom	1895–1967, Israel Police, May 1948–January 1967	Sepharadim Mapai
TOLEDANO, Rabbi Ya'acov Moshe	1880–1965, Israel Religious Affairs, November 1958–October 1960	non-party
WARHAFTIG, Zerah	born 1906, Poland Religious Affairs, November 1961–	Ha-po'el Ha-mizrahi (NRP)
YESHAIAHU, (Sharabi) Yisrael	born 1910, Yemen Posts, January 1967–	Mapai
ZADOK, Haim Yoseph	born 1913, Poland Commerce and Industry, May 1965–November 1966 (Also Development, May 1965–January 1966)	Mapai
ZISLING, Aaron	1901–1965, Russia Agriculture, May 1948–March 1949	Ahdut Ha'avodah

APPENDIX D

Content Analysis of Élite Images:
Israeli Decision-Makers[1]

SECTION I

FREQUENCY COUNT

Introductory Note on Methodology

The following tables are based upon an analysis of fifteen thousand words each of five foreign policy decision-makers: David BEN GURION, Moshe DAYAN, Abba EBAN, Golda MEIR, and Moshe SHARETT. The source material was foreign policy speeches delivered over a twenty-year period to a variety of audiences, both domestic and international. Speeches dealing with foreign policy were collected and a random sample was then selected for analysis.

The length of speeches varied among the five decision-makers. In an effort to provide maximum depth the units of analysis were not reduced initially to comparable length. After the raw frequency totals were computed, however, the results were weighted according to the length of the particular unit compared to the average length of all the units analysed for all decision-makers. It is this adjusted frequency count which appears in the tabular analysis.

After the material was sampled, it was coded for analysis. The basic rule of content analysis was used—no sentence can be left in a compounded form. Generally, each unit-statement will contain one subject, one verb, and one object. If, for example, a unit-statement should contain two objects, the statement is broken down and coded as two separate assertions.

In this study, coding was done by two judges. After several trial runs, standard tests of reliability were used to check consistency of category definition and coding. The level of intercoder reliability ranged from ·75 to ·83 which is considered acceptable.

The frequencies of occurrence were then totalled across units and are presented in tabular form. The degree of salience of individual components of the decision-maker's image is derived from the patterns of occurrence. Interpretation of the results of frequency analysis must

[1] This content analysis was a joint enterprise of Prof. Janice Stein, a McGill colleague and the author.

be made with care. Underlying frequency analysis is the assumption that important information is communicated; further, that the more important information is communicated more frequently. Simple frequency analysis, however, provides us with no insight into sources' attitudes toward material being communicated nor the way in which components are associated. Despite these limitations, however, frequency analysis has proved to be an extremely reliable guide in isolating the important components of a decision-maker's image.

Analysis of Appendix Table 8

Global System

Ben Gurion and Sharett: A Comparison

1. Sharett revealed an *overwhelming focus* on *one component* of the global system; Ben Gurion did not. Sharett revealed a *preoccupation with the United Nations*; Ben Gurion accorded it considerable attention—but *less than three other components* of the system, 'New Nations, Third World . . .', the US, and the USSR.
2. The *primary object* of attention for Ben Gurion was the *Third World*; Sharett was oblivious of this component.[1]
3. *Both* men manifested *relatively equal awareness* of the two *Super Powers*.
4. Sharett was *oblivious* to the factor of *Technology and Nuclear Weapons*; Ben Gurion was *not*.
5. *Both* men were *conscious* of the *Cold War*, but it was not central to their image. For Ben Gurion it was the second lowest in the frequency scale of six components coded, ranking with Technology and Atomic Weapons (and both are *qualitatively less than all other components*). For Sharett the 'Cold War' was the *lowest of* the four *components* he mentioned.

Ben Gurion's references to the global system reveal a primary but not overwhelming focus on the *Third World*; relatively equal attention to the *Super Powers* and the *United Nations*; and equal but qualitatively less attention to the *Cold War* and the factor of *Technology*.

Sharett's references to the Global System reveal an overwhelming focus on the *United Nations*; almost equal attention to the *Super Powers*; and total lack of attention to the *Third World* and *Technology*.

Dayan and Eban: A Comparison

1. Eban revealed an *overwhelming focus* on two components; Dayan's references *were more evenly distributed* among four. The *primary object*

[1] All Sharett's speeches were drawn from the 1950s, his active period as Foreign Minister and Prime Minister. At this time, only a small proportion of Third World states had achieved independence.

DECISION-MAKERS' IMAGES OF THE GLOBAL SYSTEM

Decision-Maker	Cold War (Struggle between two blocs)	United States	Soviet Union	United Nations	New Nations, Third World, Asia and Africa	Technology and Atomic Weapons	Totals
Ben Gurion	14	37	34	29	46	13	173
Sharett	8	15	13	41	0	0	77
Meir	17	9	6	77	57	33	199
Dayan	12	26	16	37	0	3	94
Eban	4	13	53	90	21	19	200

of attention for Eban—and Dayan—was the *United Nations*; with Eban it verged on the predominant.

2. Eban devoted *much more attention* to the *USSR* than to the US, Dayan the *reverse*, but the gap in attention is much greater in Eban's speeches (53–13 compared to 26–16).

3. The *Cold War* was virtually ignored by Eban; Dayan accorded it relatively more attention (2% to 8% of the total references to the Global System, respectively).

4. Eban manifested *much greater awareness* of the *Third World* and *Technology and Atomic Weapons* than did Dayan; in fact, there was not a single Dayan reference to the Third World.

5. Dayan's references exhibit a *predominant cluster of attention*—the Super Powers and the Cold War.

Dayan's references to the Global System reveal a primary focus on the *United Nations*; a predominant cluster of attention—the *Super Powers* with emphasis on the US and the *Cold War*; a total unawareness of the *Third World*; and only marginal attention to *Technology*.

Eban's references to the Global System reveal a near-predominant focus on the *United Nations*; conspicuously greater attention to the *USSR* than to the *US*: this reflects his preoccupation with a major threat to Israel's security; almost total indifference to the *Cold War*; and a consciousness of the *Third World* and *Technology* much greater than that of the Cold War.

Ben Gurion, Sharett, Meir, Dayan, Eban: A Comparison

1. The *United Nations* was the *most frequently mentioned* component in the coded speeches of *all decision-makers except Ben Gurion*. Relative to their total references to the global system, Sharett revealed an overwhelming focus on the UN (53%), followed by Eban (45%), Dayan (39%+), Meir (39%), with a sharp drop to Ben Gurion (17%). A careful reading of many speeches indicates that with Sharett and Eban it was *respectful and positive* on the whole; with Dayan and Meir it was *critical* and, not infrequently, *disdainful* as well—and *even more so with Ben Gurion*.

2. At *the other extreme* is the *Third World*, which was *totally ignored* in the coded speeches of Dayan and Sharett. In proportional terms Meir gave it the most attention (28·5% of all her references to the Global System),[1] followed by Ben Gurion (26·5%) and Eban (10%). However, in terms of the distribution of references among the six components of the Global System which were coded, the *Third World ranked first* in Ben Gurion's speeches, second with Meir (after the United Nations), and a distant third with Eban (after the United Nations and the Soviet Union). (This evidence, which identifies

[1] This undoubtedly reflects Meir's heavy involvement in the Africa programme.

Meir and Ben Gurion as *the most conscious of the Third World*, among the decision-makers coded, accords with non-quantitative evidence based upon a wider reading of speeches by members of Israel's Inner Circle.)

3. There is a *wide range of emphasis* in the attention accorded the *Super Powers*: the number of times mentioned; taken together as a proportion of all references; the distribution between them; and the attention to the closely related component, Cold War. In *combined proportional terms*, the ranking is Dayan (44·5% of all references to the Global System), Sharett and Ben Gurion (36·5%), Eban (33%), with a sharp drop to Meir (7·5%). In the more important *distribution of attention between the Super Powers*, Eban was the *only one* of the five decision-makers to mention the *Soviet Union more frequently*. Moreover, the gap in frequency of references was greatest with Eban (53–13). It was least with Sharett, the initiator of the policy of non-identification (15–13), and Ben Gurion (37–34). Dayan's spread was wider (26–16), but much less than Eban. Meir mentioned the *Cold War most frequently* (17), a striking contrast with her inattention to the US and the USSR individually and combined; she was followed closely by Ben Gurion and Dayan, then Sharett, and, conspicuously last, Eban. In proportional terms the ranking changes: Dayan (almost 13%), Sharett (10%), Meir (8·5%), Ben Gurion (8%), and Eban (2%). Perhaps most striking in this context is the *comparatively little attention* accorded *by all five decision-makers* to the Cold War aspect of the Global System.

4. Of the five decision-makers, Meir paid greatest attention to *Technology* (17%), followed by Eban (10%) and Ben Gurion (8%). Dayan and Sharett were almost totally indifferent to this component (3% and 0% respectively).

5. Among the five decision-makers, Ben Gurion manifested the *most even and widespread distribution* of references to components of the *Global System*: there were two clusters (US, USSR, and UN, 37, 34, and 29 respectively, and Cold War and Technology, 14 and 13), while the highest frequency, the Third World, was 46. Eban was at the *other extreme*: distribution was wide but sharply uneven (90 for the United Nations, with a sharp drop to the Soviet Union, 53, and again a sharp drop, to the Third World and to Technology, 21 and 19). *So, too, with* Sharett, from 41 for the United Nations to 15 and 13 for the Super Powers, and then 8 for Cold War. Meir's *frequency distribution is more even*, from 77 (United Nations) to 57 (Third World), 33 (Technology), 17 (Cold War), etc. Dayan's *distribution*, too, is *more akin to* Ben Gurion's in this respect, from 37 (United Nations) to 26 (US), to 16 (USSR), etc.

Thus, the pattern of emphasis among the five Israeli decision-makers differed sharply. Ben Gurion, the architect of Israel's foreign policy, revealed an appreciation of all the components of the Global System. His heavy emphasis on the Third World is no doubt a reflection of his missionary vision of Israel as 'a light unto the nations'. Sharett, at the other extreme, also concentrated heavily on the United Nations, but paid relatively equal attention to both Super Powers while underplaying the cold war aspect of the Global System. This pattern of emphasis reflects Sharett's role as the originator of Israel's policy of non-identification.

Dayan emphasized the United Nations and the United States; Eban paid more attention to the United Nations and the Soviet Union. This divergence in emphasis is partially explained by Dayan's largely internal role and Eban's largely external role. Eban's heavy emphasis on the USSR is a function of its increasing importance as a security threat. Finally, Meir's heavy emphasis on the Third World reflects her pioneering role in the development of Israel's policy in Africa.

Analysis of Appendix Table 9

Subordinate System

Ben Gurion and Sharett: A Comparison

1. Sharett was oblivious to *inter-Arab relations* in the coded speeches, while Ben Gurion barely noted this component (6 of 129 references).
2. Ben Gurion almost totally ignored *super-power penetration of the Arab 'system'*. Sharett mentioned this 18 times, that is, 12% of all his references to the Subordinate System; and he emphasized Soviet penetration twice as often as that from the US.
3. The contrast was most marked with regard to the *linkage between the Global and Subordinate Systems*: Ben Gurion referred to it only twice, Sharett 31 times, 21% of all his references in this context. Moreover, Sharett emphasized Global System penetration of the Middle East, with little attention to the reverse flow.
4. Taking the *combined data* on *inter-system linkages*, Sharett displayed a much more acute perception of this phenomenon; he referred to this 49 times (33% of all his references to the Subordinate System), while Ben Gurion noted it only 4 times out of 133 references.

Dayan and Eban: A Comparison

1. Both Dayan and Eban were virtually oblivious to *inter-Arab relations* in their coded image of the Subordinate System: Dayan mentioned it once, and Eban 3 times.
2. Dayan accorded much greater recognition to *super-power penetration of the Arab 'system'* than did Eban (25–9 references, and, in proportional terms, 8·5% of all his references to the Subordinate System,

DECISION-MAKERS' IMAGES OF THE SUBORDINATE SYSTEM

Decision-Maker	Whole Sub-ordinate Sys-tem: Middl East, Neare East, 'The Arabs'	The Arabs: Inter-Arab conflict	Sub-Total: Sub-System and the Arabs	Penetration of Arab sys-tem by USA	Penetration of Arab sys-tem by USSR	Sub-System penetrating Global Sys-tem	Global Sys-tem penetra-ting Sub-System	Sub-Totals: Links Be-tween Global and Sub-System	Totals
Ben Gurion	123	6	129	0	2	0	2	4	133
Sharett	100	0	100	6	12	5	26	49	149
Meir	157	0	157	0	3	36	46	85	242
Dayan	213	1	214	14	11	26	28	79	293
Eban	183	3	186	0	9	2	1	12	198

to 4·5% for Eban). Furthermore, while all of Eban's references were to Soviet penetration, Dayan mentioned US penetration more frequently (14–11).

3. The contrast is noteworthy with regard to the *linkage between the Global and Subordinate Systems*: Eban referred to this only 3 times (though there is ample evidence from other speeches that he is acutely aware of this facet), while Dayan mentioned it 54 times (18% of all his references). No less striking, Dayan's references were al-almost equally divided between the two sources of penetration.

4. The *combined data* on *inter-system linkages* indicate a fundamental contrast in their images as coded: Dayan referred to this 79 times (27% of all his references to the Subordinate System), while Eban mentioned this only 12 times (6% of all his references).

Ben Gurion, Sharett, Meir, Dayan, Eban: A Comparison

1. One noteworthy feature of the data is the *paucity of attention* given to *inter-Arab relations* by all five Israeli decision-makers. Sharett and Meir did not mention this aspect of the Middle East Subordinate System, in 149 and 242 references, respectively. Dayan referred to it only once, Eban 3 times, and Ben Gurion 6 times, among 293, 198, and 133 references, respectively. In short, developments within the 'Arab world' that do not impinge on Israel were regarded as irrele-vant and were *excluded from the Israeli decision-makers' articulated images of 'the Arabs'*.

2. The Israeli decision-makers accorded *slightly more attention to super-power penetration of the Arab 'system'*. Ben Gurion, Meir, and Eban made no reference to US penetration, while Sharett mentioned it 6 times; only Dayan gave this component more than passing recognition (14). All but Dayan noted Soviet penetration more frequently than inter-vention from the United States: Eban (9–0); Meir (3–0); Ben Gurion (2–0); and Sharett (12–6). Dayan noted Soviet penetration 11 times, three less than American penetration.

3. The *linkage between the Global and Subordinate Systems* was given *much greater attention* by three of the Israeli decision-makers. Meir men-tioned this link 82 times, one-third of all her references to the Middle East Subordinate System; Sharett noted it 31 times (21%), and Dayan 54 times (18%). Only Ben Gurion and Eban ignored this component, referring to it 2 and 3 times, respectively. Sharett perceived Global System penetration of the Middle East Subor-dinate System but very little of the reverse flow (26–5 references). It is noteworthy that Meir and Dayan mentioned penetration *from* the Subordinate System frequently, in fact, almost equally with the more readily accepted flow from the Global System, 36 to 46 references by Meir, 26 to 28 by Dayan.

4. The *combined data* on *inter-system linkages* reveal even *sharper contrasts*: Meir, Dayan, and Sharett accorded this substantial attention, 85, 79, and 49 references, respectively; in proportional terms, this is 35%, 27%, and 33%, respectively, of all their references to the Middle East Subordinate System.

In summary, Israeli decision-makers paid almost no attention to inter-Arab conflict. As noted, developments within the 'Arab world' that do not impinge on Israel were regarded as irrelevant and were excluded from decision-makers' articulated images of 'the Arabs'. Three decision-makers, however—Meir, Dayan, and Sharett—were sharply aware of inter-system linkages; these are crucial to Israel's security problem.

Analysis of Appendix Table 10

Near Neighbours

Ben Gurion and Sharett: A Comparison

1. Among Israel's Near Neighbours, *Egypt* was the *overwhelming focus of attention* in the coded images of both Ben Gurion and Sharett (56·5% of all Ben Gurion's references in this context, and almost 60% of Sharett's references to Near Neighbours). When the references to Egypt's President Nasser are added, the proportions become 64% and 61%, respectively.
2. Among the *other Arab states* of the Near East core there was *relatively equal attention* on the part of Ben Gurion; Sharett *concentrated on Jordan* (7 references) with only 2 each to the other states.
3. *Individual Arab leaders* were accorded *little attention*; only Nasser and Hussein were mentioned, 6 times by Ben Gurion (all to Nasser), and twice by Sharett (1 to each). Thus the *Arab states*, not Arab leaders, *were objects of perception by Israel's pre-eminent decision-makers in the formative years.*
4. *Iraq* received the *lowest frequency* from *both* men—but in Sharett's references this rank was shared with Syria and Lebanon.

Dayan and Eban: A Comparison

1. *Egypt* was Eban's *primary*—but not overwhelming—*focus of attention* among the Near Neighbours (56, or 38·6%, of all his references in this sphere); for Dayan, references to *Jordan exceeded Egypt* in his coded speeches—slightly (50–42). When the references to Nasser are added to Eban's references to Egypt, its predominance in his image is accentuated (79, or 54·5% of all his references); for Dayan, Jordan's first rank is strengthened when his references to the two Arab leaders are added (53–43).

DECISION-MAKERS' IMAGES OF NEAR NEIGHBOURS

Decision-Maker	Egypt	Jordan	Syria	Lebanon	Iraq	Sub-Total	Nasser	Hussein	Totals
Ben Gurion	43	7	9	7	4	70	6	0	76
Sharett	19	6	2	2	2	31	1	1	33
Meir	26	25	11	1	11	74	27	35	136
Dayan	42	50	8	5	10	115	1	3	119
Eban	56	20	31	7	6	120	23	2	145

2. Eban's *references* to Israel's Near Neighbours were *more evenly distributed* (Egypt—56, Syria—31, and Jordan—20); Dayan's attention was *concentrated on Jordan* (50) and *Egypt* (42); together, they accounted for 77% of all his references to Near Neighbours.

3. *Syria* was mentioned *frequently* by Eban (31); in fact, it ranked second in his image of Near Neighbours; by contrast, Dayan noted Syria only 8 times.

4. *Lebanon* received the *lowest frequency* from *both* men.

5. Eban accorded *very striking attention* to one Arab leader, Nasser (23 references—more than any Arab *state* except Egypt and Syria); Dayan barely mentioned Hussein and Nasser.

Ben Gurion, Sharett, Meir, Dayan, Eban: A Comparison

1. Among Israel's Near Neighbours, *Egypt* was the *primary object of attention* in the coded images of three decision-makers—Sharett, Ben Gurion, and Eban. In *proportional terms*, Sharett *ranks first* with almost 60% of all Near Neighbour references to Egypt (61% including references to Nasser); Ben Gurion's focus on Egypt was even *more concentrated* if Nasser references are included (64%). These are followed by Eban (38·6%, rising to 54·5%), Dayan (35%, rising to 36%), and Meir (19%, rising to 39%) with the inclusion of references to Nasser.

2. Two decision-makers accorded *considerable attention to* Nasser—Meir and Eban; in fact, Meir's references to Egypt's President exceeded her references to Egypt. By contrast, Dayan and Sharett mentioned Nasser only once, and Ben Gurion did so 6 times.

3. Only Meir gave more than passing attention to King Hussein, but in her case it was a *very high frequency*, higher than her references to Nasser (35–27) and higher than for either Jordan (25) or Egypt (26).

4. Taken together, Meir's references to Hussein and Nasser (62) account for 45·5% of all her references to Israel's Near Neighbours. This reveals *a highly personalized image of 'the Arabs'*. By contrast, the proportion of references to Arab leaders to all their Near Neighbours' references was 3% for Dayan, 6% for Sharett, and 7% for Ben Gurion; only with Eban was it somewhat higher, 17%, all indicating a *more collective image of 'the Arabs'*.

5. In terms of *distribution of references*, Sharett's and Ben Gurion's coded images are the *most concentrated*—on Egypt alone; Meir and Dayan focused on *two states*—Jordan and Egypt, in that order, though the difference is slight (60–53 for Meir, including references to Nasser, and 53–43 for Dayan); Eban accorded considerable attention to *three states*—Egypt, Syria, and Jordan.

6. In terms of *combined frequency*, for all five decision-makers, *Egypt* was a

clear first—186 and 58 for Nasser; Jordan was second, with 108 and 41 for Hussein; Syria followed with 61; the others were marginal.

7. *Jordan* was *second* to Egypt in the *Israeli decision-makers' coded images*: for Dayan and Meir it ranked first among the Near Neighbours, and for Sharett it was second in frequency.

8. *Syria* received *substantial attention* from Eban *only* (31 references, and second to Egypt in his coded image); with all other decision-makers Syria ranked a distant second (Ben Gurion) or third (Meir, tied with Iraq, and Sharett, tied with Lebanon and Iraq) or fourth (Dayan).

9. *Lebanon* was *marginal* in the coded Israeli images, especially for Meir, Sharett, and Dayan; among none did it rank higher than a distant third in frequency (Ben Gurion). *Iraq*, too, was *marginal*, except for Dayan (10 references).

In summary, Egypt and Jordan emerge as the primary foci of attention by Israeli decision-makers. Generally, the Arab states, not Arab leaders, were the objects of perception by Israel's pre-eminent decision-makers. Their view of their Near Neighbours, with the exception of Meir, was not personalized: it was rather political–institutional.

Analysis of Appendix Table 11

Symbols

Ben Gurion and Sharett: A Comparison

1. The *only symbol* to which Sharett *accorded significantly greater attention* than Ben Gurion is *Peace* (76–31). The gap is accentuated by a *proportional comparison*: peace was the focus of 30% of Sharett's Symbolic statements and only 10% of Ben Gurion's statements, that is, a ratio of 3:1.

2. *Equal or near-equal frequency* is apparent in their references to War/Conflict, Sovereignty/Nationhood, Liquidation/Genocide, and Democracy. In *proportional terms*, Sharett gave *slightly more attention* to all but the Sovereignty symbol among the group.

3. In most of the *crucial nationalist indicators*, Ben Gurion's references *exceeded* those of Sharett:

Aggression	(11%–8%)
Freedom/Independence	(16%–6%)
Security/Self-Defence	(16%–6%)
Struggle/Survival	(8%–3%)
Tradition/History	(7%–5%)

The *qualitatively greater Ben Gurion emphasis* in this sphere is evident from a comparison of *their combined frequency count* for these Symbols, along with War/Conflict and Sovereignty/Nationhood: in *proportional*

DECISION-MAKERS' IMAGES OF SYMBOLS

Decision-Makers	Peace	War, Conflict	Aggression	Freedom, Independence	Security, Self-Defence	Sovereignty, Nationhood	Struggle, Survival	Tradition, History	Liquidation, Disappearance, Genocide	Equality	Disarmament	Socialism	Economic Development	Co-operation	Democracy	Totals
Ben Gurion	31	25	35	51	52	20	25	23	10	7	0	1	31	5	13	329
Sharett	76	25	20	15	15	15	7	13	18	2	4	3	18	6	16	253
Meir	91	27	35	28	2	10	13	33	18	4	12	0	27	20	0	320
Dayan	62	45	43	10	18	6	6	4	27	1	0	0	7	5	0	234
Eban	41	47	45	21	40	41	30	3	14	4	3	0	33	12	0	334

terms, these comprised 70% of all Ben Gurion Symbolic references and only 30% for Sharett.

4. There was a *striking paucity of attention* by both men to Socialism, Equality, Disarmament, and Co-operation.

Dayan and Eban: A Comparison

1. In *simple frequency count,* Dayan's references *exceeded* those of Eban for two Symbols, *Peace* (62–41) and Liquidation/Genocide (27–14). *Dayan's greater focus on Peace is accentuated* by a *proportional comparison*: 27% to 12% of all Dayan and Eban references to Symbols.

2. Eban's references to *most crucial nationalist indicators exceeded* those of Dayan, though the gap narrows, and in one case is reversed, by a *proportional comparison*:

	Percentage of Total References
Aggression	13·5–18
Freedom/Independence	6 – 4
Security/Self-Defence	12 – 7·7
Sovereignty/Nationhood	12 – 2·6
Struggle/Survival	9 – 2·6

A comparison of *their combined frequency count* for these nationalist Symbols, along with War/Conflict and Tradition/History, reveals the following: in *proportional* terms, these comprised 68% of all Eban Symbol references and 52% for Dayan.

3. There was a *striking paucity of attention* by both men to Socialism, Democracy (not a single reference to either), Equality, Disarmament, and Tradition/History, with slightly more references to Co-operation.

Ben Gurion, Sharett, Meir, Dayan, Eban: A Comparison

1. Sharett ranks first in the proportion of references to Peace (30% of all references to Symbols). He is followed by Meir (28·4%), Dayan (27%), Eban (12%), and Ben Gurion (10%).

2. A *proportional comparison* of the *crucial nationalist indicators* reveals the following ranking:

Rank	*Percentage of Total Symbolic References*
Ben Gurion	70
Eban	68
Dayan	52
Meir	46
Sharett	30

3. There are certain *striking Meir disparities* within these nationalist Symbols:

(a) her references to *War/Conflict*, though almost identical to those of Ben Gurion in absolute and relative terms, are *qualitatively less than* those of Eban and Dayan, viewed as a percentage of total references to Symbols;

(b) she made *only 2 references* to *Security/Self-Defence*, much lower than anyone else;

(c) her frequency counts for *Sovereignty/Nationhood* and *Struggle/Survival* are much lower than for Eban and Ben Gurion; and

(d) her references to *Tradition/History* (10% of her Symbolic references) are *qualitatively higher than* those of *all* her colleagues; only Ben Gurion approached this emphasis.

4. *All but* Dayan accorded *Economic Development moderate attention*—from 7% to 10% of all their references to Symbols; Dayan barely noted it (7 times).

5. There is a *noteworthy paucity of attention* by all five or most of the five decision-makers with regard to

Socialism (Meir, Dayan, and Eban did not mention it, and Ben Gurion did so only once);

Equality (none mentioned it more than 4 times, except Ben Gurion—7); and

Disarmament (Ben Gurion and Dayan did not refer to it once, while Eban did so only 3 times, and Sharett 4 times).

Moreover, *Democracy* was not mentioned by three persons—Meir, Dayan, and Eban; and *Co-operation* was barely noted by Ben Gurion, Sharett, and Dayan.

In summary, four of the five Israeli decision-makers devoted more than half their symbolic references to nationalist symbols.[1] They paid correspondingly little attention to such symbols as socialism, democracy, and equality. Their emphasis on nationalist and conflict symbols reflects their overwhelming preoccupation with Israel's struggle for security and survival.

Frequency Count: General

Ben Gurion, Sharett, Meir, Dayan, Eban: A Comparison

1. Ben Gurion made a *total* of 431 coded references: half were directed to the Global System, 31% to the Subordinate System, and 19% to Israel's Near Neighbours; that is, there was an *equal division* between 'the larger' and 'the smaller sphere'.

2. Sharett's coded references were fewer—278: 34% were focused on the Global System, 54% on the Subordinate System, and 12% on Israel's Near Neighbours.

[1] Sharett is the exception,

3. Meir made 581 references, of which 35% were directed to Global System components, 41% to the Subordinate System, and 24% to Near Neighbours; that is *two-thirds* of her references were to '*the smaller sphere*'.

4. Dayan made 520 references, of which only 21% were to the Global System; the balance, almost four-fifths, were to the Middle East *Subordinate System* (55%) and *Near Neighbours* (24%).

5. Eban's coded references were 571: of these, 40% concerned the Global System, 35% the Subordinate System, and 25% Near Neighbours.

In short, Dayan manifested the *greatest attention* to the Middle East System and Israel's neighbours (79%), followed by Sharett (66%), Meir (65%), Eban (60%), and Ben Gurion (50%). All of Israel's foreign-policy-makers devoted at least half their attention to Israel's immediate environment. Once again, this reflects their preoccupation with Israel's struggle with her neighbours. It is this struggle which shapes Israeli decision-makers' view of the 'larger sphere'.

SECTION 2

ADVOCACY STATEMENTS

Introductory Note on Methodology

The following table is based on the analysis of advocacy statements found in the sampled speeches of the five foreign policy decision-makers. An advocacy statement is defined as one which advocates or urges a course of action or policy for Israel. Such a statement usually contains the verb 'must' or 'should'. For example, Ben Gurion remarked, 'The State must bend its stoutest efforts to maintaining military security.'

The initial categories for classification of these statements were numerous. Preliminary coding of advocacy statements revealed, however, that about 90% fell into nine categories—three at each level. At the Unit level, advocacy statements dealt with General Security of the State, that is, those statements advocating a task for Israel alone; Economic Development; and Democracy.

At the Subordinate System level, advocacy comprised Buberism, that is, reconciliation through compromise; Ben Gurionism, that is, reconciliation resulting from superior strength: this leads logically to a policy of retaliation; and Weizmannism, that is, reconciliation through rational search for moderate solutions: this leads to a policy of lowering the general level of tension by constructive acts.

Finally, at the Global System level, advocacy statements dealt with the global system generally, the United Nations, and world Jewry.

These are the nine categories used in Appendix Table 12. In addition, Ben Gurion and Dayan made some advocacy statements at the Global System level concerning Alignment and Non-Alignment, which are grouped under the category, Other.

The coding was done by two judges at two separate levels. First, all advocacy statements were extracted from the speeches. At this time, statistical tests of reliability were run and proved satisfactory. Then the statements were masked and coded into the nine categories. Again, checks on reliability proved satisfactory. Finally, the totals within each category were adjusted to the average number of words for each decision-maker. It is these adjusted totals which appear in the cells of Appendix Table 12.

APPENDIX TABLE 12

ADVOCACY STATEMENTS BY ISRAELI DECISION-MAKERS

	Ben Gurion	Sharett	Meir	Dayan	Eban
UNIT					
General Security	30	9	0	40	1
Economic Development	20	2	8	0	0
Democracy	3	0	1	0	0
UNIT SUB-TOTAL	53	11	9	40	1
SUBORDINATE					
'Buberism'	1	0	0	0	0
'Ben Gurionism'	2	2	0	4	5
'Weizmannism'	16	8	13	10	9
SUBORDINATE SYSTEM SUB-TOTAL	19	10	13	14	14
GLOBAL SYSTEM					
General Global	8	2	13*	0	3
United Nations	1	2	1	0	7
World Jewry	8	1	1	0	0
Other	14†	0	0	2‡	0
GLOBAL SYSTEM SUB-TOTAL	31	5	15	2	10
TOTAL	103	26	37	56	25

* All but three of these statements related to 'developing states'; two advocated disarmament, and one, peaceful coexistence.

† Non-alignment with Super Powers (3); alignment with the United States (2); alignment with Europe (2); and alliance with Asia and Africa (7).

‡ Non-alignment with Super Powers.

Examples of Advocacy Statements

BEN GURION
Unit Advocacy:
General Security of the State
We must be prepared for a protracted spell of peacelessness.
We must stand guard with increased military capacity.

Economic Development
We must constantly expand our exports.
We must make our economy more efficient.

Democracy
The State must bend its stoutest efforts to safeguard democratic
    freedom at home.

Subordinate System Advocacy:
Buberism
In the Middle East, Israel's endeavours must be moral.

Ben Gurionism
We must break through the wall of hatred erected by our neighbours.

Weizmannism
A Jewish-Arab alliance is a historic necessity for both sides.
Israel should agree to the neutralization of the entire Middle East
    area.

Global System Advocacy:
General Global
On the world scene, Israel's endeavours must be moral.
Israel must not disregard the battle of Titans.

United Nations
Israel must not confine itself to the ambit of the United Nations.

World Jewry
Israel must not support any aggressive design against any countries
    where Jews live.

SHARETT
Unit Advocacy:
General Security of the State
Israel's paramount need at this hour is additional arms.
As a state surrounded on all its land borders by hostile forces,
    Israel's primary preoccupation must be her security.

Economic Development
Development must be defended at all costs.

Subordinate System Advocacy:
Ben Gurionism
In this sphere there must be no withdrawal, since the very existence
of its people is at stake.

Weizmannism
Without diminishing the importance of considerations of day-to-day
security, we must always bring the question of peace into our
overall calculations.

Global System Advocacy:
General Global
It must be clear that Israel's place in the regional family cannot be
the only factor determining her international position.

United Nations
We must pursue steadfastly the earliest possible settlement of these
issues through the good offices of the United Nations.

World Jewry
We must not divest ourselves of our universal Jewish associations.

DAYAN
Unit Advocacy:
General Security of the State
We must create a new territorial map of the State of Israel.
We must set up military bases that will provide for security within
the new map.

Subordinate System Advocacy:
Ben Gurionism
We should not enable Arabs to transfer their domicile from Gaza to
Israel.
We must insist upon direct negotiation.

Weizmannism
We should not try to compel the Arabs to accept our nationality.
We must allow the Arabs contact with Jordan.

EBAN
Unit Advocacy:
General Security of the State
If the arms race is joined, we must not lose it.

Subordinate System Advocacy:
Ben Gurionism
It is in the regional interest that Arab and Jewish populations should
be integrated in environments akin to them in ethnic affinity.

Weizmannism

We must now transcend our conflicts in dedication to a new Mediterranean future.

It would be useful to conclude agreements committing both parties to policies of pacific settlement.

Global System Advocacy:

General Global

Our tormented region must be removed from the scope of global rivalries.

United Nations

The interests of the United Nations would be best served by participation of the Central People's Government of China.

MEIR

Unit Advocacy:

Economic Development

We must go more deeply into our desert with irrigation.

We must develop quickly.

Democracy

We must follow the system of true reporting, even if we have to make depressing announcements.

Subordinate System Advocacy:

Weizmannism

Agreements must include undertakings to refrain from all hostile acts of a military character.

There must be complete disarmament of Israel and the Arabs under mutual inspection.

Global System Advocacy:

General Global

Israel is committed to a policy of disarmament.

The Governments of developing states should regard the futherance of technology as a major object of their national policies.

World Jewry

The doors of Israel must remain open forever to any Jew who wishes to come to its shores.

Analysis of Appendix Table 12

Advocacy Statements by Israeli Decision-Makers

Ben Gurion, Sharett, Meir, Dayan, Eban: A Comparison

1. In the coded materials Ben Gurion made by far the *largest number of advocacy statements* (103); he was followed by Dayan (slightly

more than half as many), then Meir, and Sharett and Eban (both, one fourth as many such statements as Ben Gurion).

2. In terms of *distribution of advocacy statements*, Dayan directed an *extraordinarily high proportion* of his statements to the *Unit (Israel) level* (71%); he was followed by Ben Gurion (51%), Sharett (42%), and then, a sharp drop, to Meir (25%) and Eban (4%). Stated in other terms, Dayan and Ben Gurion accorded the *greatest attention to Israel*: it was the centre of their advocacy.

3. Dayan's statements at the *Unit level* were devoted *exclusively* to *Israel's Security*; Sharett's many fewer statements were *predominantly* focused on *Security* (9 of 11). Ben Gurion made more such statements than did Sharett, but these comprised a smaller proportion of his Unit-level statements (56·5%). Eban made only one statement directly relating to Security, and Meir none.

4. One of the *most noteworthy* results of this Content Analysis is the *heavy emphasis* placed *on Economic Development—especially by Ben Gurion* (20) and Meir (8, all but one of her statements at that level). In fact, advocacy relating to Economic Development constituted 37·5% as many statements as those directed to Security, and more than a fourth of all coded advocacy statements relating to the Unit level. Thus this evidence suggests that *Israeli decision-makers perceive a very close link between the Military-Security and Economic-Developmental issue areas of foreign policy.*

5. *Democracy* was *barely mentioned* in these statements—and only by Ben Gurion and Meir.

6. The *almost complete absence* of 'Buberist' advocacy is striking—only 1 of 70 statements at the Subordinate System level.

7. The coded data indicate *more statements of the 'Weizmannist' than the 'Ben Gurionist' type*. This is especially so with Meir (13–0), Ben Gurion (16–2), and Sharett (8–2). (Other evidence reveals a much more pronounced 'Ben Gurionist' image for Ben Gurion and Meir—and much less than these materials indicate for Eban. One probable reason for the discrepancy is that 'Ben Gurionist'-type images are usually definitions of Arab intentions, as perceived by Israeli decision-makers, *not direct statements* of advocacy.)

8. Eban made many more advocacy statements at the Subordinate System level than at the Unit level; Sharett's statements were almost equally divided; and the distribution of Ben Gurion's and Dayan's statements was almost 3:1 in favour of the Unit level.

9. If the *statements at the Unit and Subordinate System levels* are *combined*— there is much overlapping at these levels, especially for Israeli decision-makers operating in a permanent-conflict regional system —Dayan emerges as the *most preoccupied with the 'smaller sphere' of foreign policy* (54 of 56 statements). All the other decision-makers made more advocacy statements directed to that level than to the

'larger sphere'—the Global System—but the proportions varied: Sharett, *surprisingly*, ranked next to Dayan (81% of all his statements; he was followed by Ben Gurion (70%), though he made a substantial number of advocacy statements at the Global level, in fact, many more than at the Subordinate System level; then came Eban (60%), and Meir (59%).

10. At the *Global System* level Meir's advocacy statements were *most sharply skewed* (13 of 15); Sharett's few statements were evenly divided; and Ben Gurion directed an equal number of statements to the General Global and World Jewry categories, along with a larger number, almost half of his Global System statements, to Non-alignment and Alignment for Israel.

11. Only Eban accorded *primary attention* in his Global System advocacy to the *United Nations* (7 of 10 statements).

In an attempt to discern patterns of association among Israeli decision-makers, their advocacy statements were submitted to correlation analysis. The Spearman (rho) correlation was used. Appendix Table 13 presents the results of this analysis.

APPENDIX TABLE 13

CORRELATION OF ADVOCACY STATEMENTS

	Sharett	Eban	Dayan	Ben Gurion	Meir
Sharett	—	·69	·81	·65	·25
Eban	·69	—	·60	·008	·32
Dayan	·81	·60	—	·56	·004
Ben Gurion	·65	·008	·56	—	·36
Meir	·25	·32	·004	·36	—

The results of Appendix Table 13 confirm the generally expected patterns of association among Israeli decision-makers, with one startling exception. The distance between Ben Gurion, for example, and Eban is expected. Eban devoted the greatest attention to the 'larger sphere' while Ben Gurion was preoccupied with the 'smaller sphere'. Both represent opposite ends of the spectrum in both the form and content of their advocacy. The proximity of Eban to Sharett is likewise expected; Eban is generally accepted as the heir to the Sharett legacy.

The distance of Golda Meir from the other four decision-makers is somewhat surprising. She is significantly associated with no other foreign policy-maker. Her independence of any specific set of orientations to foreign policy and from any group of decision-makers is confirmed by these data.

The unexpected correlation which emerged from these data is the strong association between Dayan and Sharett, and the emergence of a cluster which groups Dayan with Sharett and Eban. At first glance, this seems to contradict initial expectations about Dayan. Several alternative explanations of this correlation can be offered. First, this strong correlation could be the result of a sample error; alternatively, the correlation may be partly a function of role. Dayan as Defence Minister speaks almost exclusively to a domestic audience and therefore finds it unnecessary constantly to reiterate the source and scope of the threat to Israel's security. Rather, he stresses constructive solutions to the dilemma confronting Israel.

It can also be suggested that Dayan has taken Sharett's global images and transposed them on to the 'smaller sphere'. Dayan emerged as the foreign policy decision-maker most preoccupied with the Middle East. In this context, he shares with Sharett such goals as integration, peace, and co-operative living as peoples, not enemies. He is a revised and refined adaptation of Sharett to the Middle East.

In conclusion, the generally simplistic interpretation and labelling of Israeli foreign policy decision-makers is a gross injustice. At a very general level, there are two poles of foreign policy images and interpretation—represented by the Caution and the Courage School. As more sophisticated sets of images are constructed, however, which examine the three levels of foreign policy images, significant cross-connections and overlappings emerge. The present generation of Israeli decision-makers, represented by the Younger Men, has absorbed the images of past leaders, transposed these images from one level of the system to another and has refined their images. They see their immediate environment and the world around them through more sophisticated and interlinked sets of perceptions which synthesize the memory of the past and the challenge of the present. The two younger men—Eban, the Foreign Minister, and Dayan, the Defence Minister—are each closely associated with the other. Despite their differing legacies from past experiences and training, they represent not the extremes of the spectrum but rather a refined and sophisticated version of the two poles.

As Eban, known throughout the world as Israel's most prominent 'dove', remarked in a Hebrew-language interview, 'When some future historian compares my votes with so-called "hawk" votes, he will be perhaps very surprised. In Israel, there are "hawks" dressed in the feathers of "doves" and vice-versa.'[1]

[1] *Bamahane,* 3 Feb. 1970. Interview with Abba Eban by Eli Eyal.

APPENDIX E

Survey of Selected Literature on Foreign Policy Decisions

Among those studies which explore 'decisions' there is considerable variety in definition:

SNYDER, BRUCK and SAPIN, pioneers in the systematic analysis of foreign policy, devote much space to decision-making, decision-makers, decisional units, decision-making approach, decisional system, and definition of the situation—the intellectual process of decision; but the concept of 'decision' is not examined as such. Its meaning is contained within a definition of 'decision-making', as follows:

Decision-making is a process which results in the selection from a socially-defined, limited number of problematical, alternative projects (both objectives and techniques) of one project intended to bring about the particular future state of affairs envisaged by the decision-makers.

Thus a 'decision' is 'the selection . . . of [goals and instruments to achieve a desirable] future state of affairs'.[1]

SAPIN, in a later book entitled *The Making of United States Foreign Policy*, writes: 'This study is focused on the formulation and administration of United States foreign policy. . . . Attention will be directed to major foreign policy decision-making. . . .' A 'decision' is not defined.[2]

Snyder's most prominent student, GLENN PAIGE, noted in his study of *The Korean Decision*, 'the first attempt to apply the Snyder, Bruck, and Sapin framework explicitly in empirical research', that 'the decision-making frame of reference originally did not specify a typology of decisions'. Nor does he fill this lacuna; he merely terms the Korean decision 'a crisis decision'. He follows HERMANN's[3] definition of a *crisis* as 'a situation that (1) threatened high priority goals of the decisional unit, (2) restricted the amount of time in which a response could be made, and (3) was unexpected or unanticipated by the members of the decision making unit' and he concludes: 'A crisis decision is thus taken to

---

[1] Richard C. Snyder, H. W. Bruck, Burton Sapin (eds.), *Foreign Policy Decision-Making*, The Free Press, New York, 1962, pp. 14–185. The extract is from p. 90.

[2] Frederick A. Praeger for the Brookings Institution, New York, 1966, p. 2.

[3] Charles F. Hermann, *Crises in Foreign Policy-Making: A Simulation of International Politics*, China Lake, California, 1965, p. 29, as cited by Paige, p. 276. For an elaboration of Hermann's concept of crisis see his *Crises in Foreign Policy: A Simulation Analysis*, Bobbs-Merrill, Indianapolis, 1969, Ch. 2.

be a response to a high threat to values, either immediate or long range, where there is little time for decision under conditions of surprise.' The time span for the Korean study was six days, 24–30 June 1950.[1]

The STANFORD GROUP have produced valuable studies of crisis decisions as well, using the quantitative technique of content analysis. Notable are the crisis period leading to the outbreak of the First World War, from 27 June to 4 August 1914, and the Cuban missile crisis decision, October 1962. But these are confined to one type of decision—made under stress—and the concept of 'decision' is not carefully defined.[2]

[1] *The Korean Decision*, The Free Press, New York, 1968, pp. 5, 275, 276.

[2] Publications of the Stanford Group on decision-making include the following:

Dina A. Zinnes, Robert C. North, and Howard E. Koch, Jr., 'Capability, Threat and the Outbreak of War', in James N. Rosenau (ed.), *International Politics and Foreign Policy*, Free Press of Glencoe, 1961, pp. 469–82.

Dina A. Zinnes, 'Hostility in International Decision-Making', *The Journal of Conflict Resolution*, vi, 3, Sept. 1962, pp. 236–43.

M. George Zaninovich, 'Pattern Analysis of Variables Within the International System: The Sino-Soviet Example', ibid., pp. 253–68.

Ole R. Holsti, 'The Belief System and National Images: A Case Study', ibid., pp. 244–252.

Robert C. North, Richard A. Brody, Ole R. Holsti, 'Some Empirical Data on the Conflict Spiral', *Peace Research Society (International) Papers*, vol. 1 (1964), pp. 1–14.

Ole R. Holsti, Richard A. Brody, Robert C. North, 'Measuring Affect and Action in International Reaction Models: Empirical Materials from the 1962 Cuban Crisis', *The Journal of Peace Research*, 1964, pp. 170–90.

Ole R. Holsti, 'East-West Conflict and Sino-Soviet Relations', *The Journal of Applied Behavioral Science*, vol. 1, 1965, pp. 115–30.

Ole R. Holsti, 'The 1914 Case', *American Political Science Review*, lix, June 1965, pp. 365–378.

Ole R. Holsti and Robert C. North, 'The History of Human Conflict', in Elton B. McNeil (ed.), *The Nature of Human Conflict*, Prentice Hall, Englewood Cliffs, New Jersey, 1965, pp. 155–71.

Ole R. Holsti and Robert C. North, 'Comparative Data from Content Analysis: Perceptions of Hostility and Economic Variables in the 1914 Crisis', in Richard L. Merritt and Stein Rokkan (eds.), *Comparing Nations: The Use of Quantitative Data in Cross-National Research*, Yale University Press, New Haven, 1966, pp. 169–90.

Dina A. Zinnes, 'A Comparison of Hostile Behavior of Decision-Makers in Simulate and Historical Data', *World Politics*, xviii, 3, April 1966, pp. 474–502.

Robert C. North, 'Perception and Action in the 1914 Crisis', *Journal of International Affairs*, xxii, 1, 1967, pp. 103–22.

Charles F. Hermann and M. G. Hermann, 'An Attempt to Simulate the Outbreak of World War I', *American Political Science Review*, lxi, June 1967, pp. 400–16.

Ole R. Holsti, 'Cognitive Dynamics and Images of the Enemy: Dulles and Russia', ch. II in David J. Finlay, Ole R. Holsti, and Richard Fagen, *Enemies in Politics*, Rand McNally and Co., Chicago, 1967.

Dina A. Zinnes, 'The Expression and Perception of Hostility in Prewar Crisis: 1914', in David Singer (ed.), *Quantitative International Politics: Insights and Evidence*, The Free Press, New York, 1968, pp. 85–119.

Ole R. Holsti, Robert C. North, and Richard A. Brody, 'Perception and Action in the 1914 Crisis', ibid., pp. 123–58.

For a challenging critique of the Stanford studies see Robert Jervis, 'The Costs of the Quantitative Study of International Relations', in Klaus Knorr and James N.

JAMES A. ROBINSON, another Snyder colleague, notes the interrelationship of 'influence', 'power', 'policy', and 'decision'. More specifically,

'Policy' refers to goals of any social system, the means chosen to effectuate those goals, and the consequences of the means. . . . 'Power' designates participation in the making of policies involving sanctions, and it is such policies that are usually designated by the term 'decision'.

He goes on to distinguish 'policy' from 'decision' and notes 'the decision paradox', 'that is, having a decision without actually deciding'. More precisely, the situation is one of having a policy without a decision by the unit under analysis.[1] Yet the concept of 'decision' as 'policies involving sanctions' is not elaborated into a general typology.[2]

GEORGE MODELSKI, in his original and rigorous *A Theory of Foreign Policy*, does not use the term 'decision' but he refers to 'the actions toward the outside world in which the policy-maker himself engages on his community's behalf', and these he designates 'his "output" '—that is, decisions.[3]

JOSEPH H. DE RIVERA, in a lengthy analysis of 'The Individual's Decision', writes: 'It is not at all clear what a decision is', yet he answers his own doubt by adding: 'ultimately a course of action must be selected and acted upon'.[4]

PHILIP M. BURGESS explores 'the relation of elite images to foreign policy choice situations' and 'foreign policy outcomes', both synonyms for decisions. But no further elaboration is offered.[5]

One scholar, who has been an active participant in the making of United States foreign policy, ROGER HILSMAN, writes: 'The business of Washington is making decisions that move a nation. . . . What is decided is policy.' He cautions, however:

We assume that what we call the 'decisions' of government are in fact decisions—discrete acts, with recognizable beginnings and sharp, decisive endings.

Rosenau (eds.), *Contending Approaches to International Politics*, Princeton University Press, Princeton, N.J., 1969, ch. 10; for a persuasive reply see Robert C. North, 'Research Pluralism and the International Elephant', ibid., ch. 11.

[1] In this connection Robinson cites Warner R. Schilling, 'The H-Bomb Decision: How to Decide Without Actually Choosing', *Political Science Quarterly*, lxxvi, 1961, pp. 24–46.

[2] *Congress and Foreign Policy-Making*, The Dorsey Press, Homewood, Illinois (rev. ed.), 1967, pp. 2–3 and fn. 8, p. 3. See also James A. Robinson and Richard C. Snyder, 'Decision-Making in International Politics', in Herbert C. Kelman (ed.), *International Behavior*, Holt, Rinehart and Winston, New York, 1966, pp. 435–63.

[3] Princeton Studies in World Politics, no. 2, Frederick A. Praeger for the Princeton Center of International Studies, New York, 1962, p. 5.

[4] *The Psychological Dimension of Foreign Policy*, Charles E. Merrill, Columbus, Ohio, 1968, p. 105.

[5] *Elite Images and Foreign Policy Outcomes: A Study of Norway*, Ohio State University Press, Columbus, Ohio, 1969, p. 4.

We like to think of policy as rationalized, in the economist's sense of the word, with each step leading logically and economically to the next. We want to be able to find out who makes decisions, to feel that they are the proper, official, and authorized persons. . . .

The reality, of course, is quite different. Put dramatically, it could be argued that few, if any, of the decisions of government are either decisive or final. Very often policy is the sum of a congeries of separate or only vaguely related actions.[1]

This may be true of the United States—during a specified time period, 1961–3; but that hardly merits such a sweeping generalization. Nor is it clear whether this chaotic process applies to all decisions or merely 'the really big decisions'. And, in any event, the task of the scholar is to reconstruct rationally and systematically what appears to the practitioner sheer disorder and chance.

A similar view to that of Hilsman was expressed by an Israeli counterpart, also a member of the foreign policy Technical Élite:[2]

Policy is not made by one decision—but may be made by one explosion. It is an empirical process, tested here and there, checked, discussed, developed in the course of many decisions. It is never made in an *a priori*, analytical way. No one really knows in the end who actually produced the policy. Policy evolves; it is not made. Only those who implement it can really claim it as their own.

Policy, then, is the sum of many decisions. But, while the concluding remark may satisfy the professional's need for self-esteem in the formulation process, it is utterly inaccurate for anything but day-to-day Implementing Decisions, as distinct from high policy—which has never been made in the Israeli Foreign Office, a point already discussed

KENNETH BOULDING, as noted, was very precise: 'A decision involves the selection of the most preferred position in a contemplated field of choice. Both the field of choice and the ordering of this field . . . lie in the image of the decision-maker.'[3]

Still another attempt at precise definition is made by JOSEPH FRANKEL:[4] 'Foreign Policy consists of decisions and actions which involve to some appreciable extent relations between one state and others.' He rejects the classification of decisions as a sub-category of actions, for example in T. Parsons and E. A. Shils, eds., *Toward a General Theory of Action*, 1951, pp. 4–8, and continues:

an important distinction between decisions and actions lies in their spheres of operation: decisions take place in the decision-maker's mind whereas actions

[1] *To Move a Nation*, Doubleday & Co., New York, 1967, pp. 4–5.
[2] Gideon Rafael, then a Political Adviser to the Foreign Minister and, from late 1967, Director-General of the Ministry for Foreign Affairs. Interview in Jerusalem Aug. 1966.
[3] 'National Images and International Systems', *The Journal of Conflict Resolution*, iii, 2, June 1959, pp. 120–1.
[4] *The Making of Foreign Policy*, Oxford University Press, London, 1963, p. 1 (emphasis added).

take place in his environment. By *decision-making* then, is understood an act of determining in one's own mind a course of action, following a more or less deliberate consideration of alternatives; and by *decision* is understood *that which is thus determined*. By *action* is understood *a thing done*, a deed, or the process of acting or doing.

The distinction which Frankel draws between decision-making and decision, on the one hand, and between decision and action, on the other, is an excellent starting point for the analysis of foreign policy decisions. But, like other scholars who attempt to define a 'decision', he does not probe further and distinguish types of decision: they remain an undifferentiated mass—in his case, courses of action determined in the minds of decision-makers. This blur is even more striking in the extracts from the practitioners. And even insightful studies of specific decisions, such as Japan's decision to surrender in August 1945,[1] and China's decision to enter the Korean War in October 1950,[2] do not go beyond fascinating historical reconstruction and plausible analytic speculation, respectively: they do not provide a framework for analysing other decisions.

[1] Robert J. C. Butow, *Japan's Decision to Surrender*, Stanford University Press, Stanford, California, and Oxford University Press, London, 1954.

[2] Allen S. Whiting, *China Crosses the Yalu*, The Macmillan Company, New York, 1960; reissued Stanford University Press, Stanford, California, and Oxford University Press, London, 1968.

Foreign Service Technical Élite: Supplementary Data

Research into Israel's Foreign Service Technical Élite uncovered further data which add to the understanding of its origins, composition, education, and other occupational activities of its members. The following analysis, which incorporates these supplementary findings, is designed as an extension of the political-biographical exploration of the FSTE provided in chapter 17.

Where did the members of the Foreign Service Technical Élite come from, in terms of bureaucratic, professional, or entrepreneurial posts held before they entered the Technical Élite? This is the first theme of the supplementary analysis.

APPENDIX TABLE 14

THE ISRAELI FOREIGN SERVICE TECHNICAL ÉLITE
1948–1968

Time Pattern of Entry

Membership from Date of Entry Into Foreign Service	*Up Through The Ranks*	*Years in Foreign Service Before Appointment to Technical Élite Post*		
		1–5	*6–10*	*More than 10*
30	57	24	19	14

1. Of the 30 persons who held Technical Élite (TE) posts when they entered the Foreign Service, 24 joined the Foreign Ministry when it was formed in 1948. Among the other 6, two entered the Service in 1949 and one in 1950, the first directly from *Tzahal*, the second from overseas, and the third via a Technical Élite-level post in the Education Ministry. A fourth entered the Foreign Service Technical Élite in 1955 as Ambassador to Moscow, coming from a command post in *Tzahal*, a fifth in 1960 from a senior administrative post in the Weizmann Institute, and a sixth in 1966, as Head of Bureau for the new Foreign Minister, Eban. Thus, apart from those who manned Technical Élite posts when the Foreign Ministry was established

(24) and those who joined the Ministry in lesser-rank positions in 1948 and moved up later (11), there were only 6 who entered the Service at a high level. The conclusion is unmistakable: *parallel or lateral entry into the Foreign Service Technical Élite was rare in Israel.*

2. Among the 24 Double Originals, that is, persons who joined the Foreign Service in 1948 and were in the Technical Élite at the outset, 16 became members of the Formal Directorate (FD) of that TE: this comprised Directors-General (DG), Deputy and Assistant DGs, and (operational) Advisers—and special cases like Eban. Thus more than half the total membership of that Formal Directorate from 1948 to 1968 (28) came from the Double Original group. If one takes the 18-year period, May 1948–February 1966—before the inflationary spiral in Assistant DG appointments—and excludes the marginal Formal Directorate members (as explained in Table 28), the proportion is even higher: 13 of the 14 active Formal Directorate members date from the 1948 Double Original group.[1]

3. Among the 57 Technical Élite members who came Up Through The Ranks, the largest group (24) attained a TE post in 5 years or less; 19 persons took 6 to 10 years, and 14 more than 10 years from the time they entered the Foreign Service. This indicates *considerable upward mobility to the Technical Élite level.* There was much less into the Formal Directorate or the Decision-Making Inner Circle.

4. The rapid-advance group (1–5 years) includes 6 of the 12 persons who rose from the ranks to the Formal Directorate: 4 of them took 4 years to enter the Technical Élite (Bartur, Bitan, A. Harman, and Hillel); and 2 took 5 years (Bentsur and Tsur). *Most of these men also moved quickly from Technical Élite post to the Formal Directorate.*[2] This sector of the Up Through The Ranks group includes a

---

[1] Of the 16 Double Originals who were also in the Formal Directorate at some time, 8 were members of the Foreign Service throughout the 20 years: Avner, Comay, Eytan, Levavi, Lourie, Najar, Rafael (with a brief leave), and Rosenne. Four died in office: Elyashiv (1955), Shiloah (1959), Kohn (1961), and Fischer (1965). Avriel left the Service in 1968. Danin was a special case—Adviser on the Middle East as a part-time employee of the Foreign Office. Eban moved to the High Policy Élite; and Y. Herzog was seconded to the Prime Minister's Office in 1965. Thus apart from Nature's toll this was a remarkably durable group.

Three of the 24 Double Originals in the FSTE left the Service in 1951–2—Guriel, Meron, and Gordon, Heads of the Research, Economic, and International Organizations Departments, respectively.

[2] Bartur, 6 years, from 1952, as Head of the Economic Department, to 1958, when he became Assistant Director-General in charge of Economic issues; Bitan, 2 years, from Head of the United States Department in 1964 to Assistant in charge of North America and Africa, in 1966; Harman, from Consul-General in New York in 1953 to Assistant DG two years later; Hillel, simultaneously, as Assistant DG in charge of Africa, in 1967; Bentsur, from Head of East Europe in 1953 to Assistant DG in 1958; and Tsur, in 1959, as Acting Director-General, after 6 years in a key ambassadorial post, Paris.

relatively large number of 'drop-outs' or transients in the Foreign Service, 7 of 24.[1]

5. Almost half the number of persons who rose from the ranks to the Formal Directorate (5 of 12) came from the 6–10-year gestation period before entering the Technical Élite: Eshel and Tekoah (6); Ben-Horin (7); Gazit (8); and Yahil (9). With one exception, how-ever (Yahil, who entered the Technical Élite and Formal Directorate simultaneously in 1959), they took much longer to move from the TE to the Formal Directorate than did the preceding group.[2] Unlike the rapid-advance group, there was only one transient. Five persons from this middle-advance group joined the Foreign Office late— from 1957 onwards: Michael and Ron; from lengthy periods of service in *Tzahal*; Bar-Haim from *Kol Yisrael*; and Miron and Raviv directly from their university studies. All 5 remained continuously in the Foreign Service from their date of entry. All others in this group are long-time members of the Service—at least 15 years. In short, *the middle-advance group was a more stable component of* the Foreign Service.

6. Among the slow-advance group (14), only 1 entered the Formal Directorate—Chelouche, in 1968, 9 years after he attained a Technical Élite post which, in turn, was 11 years after he joined the Foreign Service. This group is *an even more stable component* of the Foreign Service: all served 17 years or more, except one with 14 years (and 6 in related branches of the Government).

7. A comparison of the upward flow from Technical Élite to Formal Directorate by groups reveals that 16 of the 24 Double Originals, that is, 66·7 per cent of the 1948 TE members, entered the higher level of the Service (really 16 of 21 because 3 of the Double Originals dropped out of the Service very early, thus 76 per cent), while 12 of 63, that is, below 20 per cent of all others did so. Taking the group that rose through the ranks, it is 20 of 57, or 35 per cent. The differ-ence, not unnatural, is marked. Viewing this over time, 11 of the 16

[1] Biran, who returned to archaeology after 3 years in Los Angeles and 3 years as Head of Armistice Affairs; Golan, who moved back and forth between economic ministries and the Foreign Office, before becoming Director-General of the Com-merce and Industry Ministry; Harel, who served for 3 years in Bucharest and then 3 years as Ambassador to Moscow, leaving the Service thereafter; Mrs. Z. Harman, the only woman to attain TE rank, as Head of the International Organizations Depart-ment, who moved on to social welfare activities but remained associated with the Foreign Service (her husband was Ambassador to the United States from 1959–68); Goitein, who was Head of Mission to South Africa for 3 years and then Minister (No. 2) to Washington; Lubrani, who spent as much time in the Prime Minister's Office as in the Foreign Office; and Palmon, who left the Foreign Service in 1959 and had spent more time as Adviser on Arab Affairs to the Prime Minister than in the Foreign Office.

[2] Gazit took 8 years, Ben-Horin and Tekoah 11 years, and Eshel 12 years. In two of these cases, it should be noted, much of that period was spent at key foreign posts: Gazit, 5 years in Washington, and Tekoah, 5 years at the UN and in Moscow.

Double Originals who were also members of the Formal Directorate attained that rank by 1953; 1 was Assistant DG briefly in 1955, 2 others became Assistant DGs in the late fifties, 1 in 1961, and 1 in 1967. Among the 12 who came Up Through The Ranks, 1 attained that rank briefly in 1955, 2 in 1958, and 2 in 1959; the other 7 entered the Formal Directorate in the period 1965–8.

8. Among the 57 persons who entered the Technical Élite from the ranks it took an average of 7·6 years from their date of entry into the Foreign Service. If the 8 transients are excluded from the calculation the average is 8·3 years for 49 persons.[1]

APPENDIX TABLE 15

FOREIGN SERVICE TECNHICAL ÉLITE 1948–1968

Average Period by Time in the Service

Years in the Foreign Service	Number of Persons	Average Number of Years in TE	Corrected Average Number of Years in TE
20	21	11·0	11·0
15–19	27	6·0	6·7
10–14	18	7·3	11·8
Less than 10	21	3·2	10·4
Totals and Mean Averages	87	6·8	9·5

1. Only 3 of the 21 perennials in the Foreign Service held Technical Élite posts throughout the period. Another 2 were TE members for 18 years, 1 for 16 years, 2 for 14 years, and 4 for 12 years each. At the other extreme to these 12 veterans were 5 others, each with 5 years or less in the Technical Élite.[2]

2. Members of the 15–19-year group may be regarded as veterans: all but 4 had entered the Foreign Service by 1951, and those 4 by 1953.[3]

[1] The comparable figures for each sub-group are as follows:

1–5 years	24 persons	average time to enter TE	3·5 years
6–10 years	19 persons	average time to enter TE	7·7 years
more than 10 years	14 persons	average time to enter TE	14·1 years

[2] The average of 11 years' membership in the Technical Élite for the 21 perennials in the Foreign Service was derived as follows: the 21 20-year veterans could have been TE members 20 years each—an overall Total Number of Years in the TE of 420 years; the actual Total Number was 232 years; thus the real average was 11 years.

[3] Their total number of years in the Technical Élite was 161, leading to a simple average of 6·0 years per person. However, the total number of potential years in the TE for the 27 was not 540 years, but the cumulation of individual periods in the Foreign Service from the time of entry for each, which is 478 years. Therefore the corrected average is $\frac{161}{478} \times 20$, namely, 6·7 years.

Thus, the 27 should be added to the 21 perennials. And to them should be added 9 persons from the 10–14-year group who were crucial in the formative years: some died, like Shiloah and Kohn; others left, like Eban; others reached Director-General status.[1]

3. For the 18 persons in the 10–14-year Foreign Service group the simple average membership in the Technical Élite is 7·3 years. Corrected along the lines of potential TE membership, the average is 11·8 years—the highest group average in the entire FSTE. The change from simple to corrected average is even more marked among the 21 persons who spent less than 10 years in the Foreign Service: it rises from 3·2 to 10·4 years. And for the entire group of 87 persons the corrected average membership is 9·5 years—of a theoretically possible 20 years, *another sign of durability*.

APPENDIX TABLE 16

FOREIGN SERVICE TECHNICAL ÉLITE 1948–1968

Position Immediately Preceding Entry into Foreign Service

Political Department of		
Jewish Agency		18
in Palestine	10	
Abroad	8	
Haganah and *Tzahal*		4
Education		5
Other		3
UN	1	
Banking	1	
Other Ministry	1	
Total		30

* Virtually all of the 18 were also associated with the *Haganah*.

1. The Jewish Agency's Political Department was the Foreign Office of the *Yishuv* from 1931 to 1948, perhaps even earlier. Its role as the personnel reservoir of Israel's Foreign Ministry in the formative stage is confirmed by the above data. In most cases *the change was merely one of form*, a natural move from a post in a *de facto* Foreign Office to a *de jure* one. This is evident from the roles played by many members of the Political Department immediately before and after independence:

[1] The cumulative potential Number of Years in the Technical Élite for those 57 veterans is 1,012: the actual number was 488. Thus the corrected average membership in the TE for the enlarged group of 57 veterans in the Foreign Service is $\frac{488}{1,012} \times 20$, namely, 9·7 years.

Avriel   Aliya 'B' (illegal immigration of Jews to Palestine from
                1939 to May 1948) and arms procurement, to Minister
                to Czechoslovakia.
Comay   Commonwealth Section of Political Department, to
                Head, British Commonwealth Department.
Danin   Adviser on Middle East Affairs—unchanged.
Eban   Jewish Agency Representative to the UN—unchanged,
                and then Israel's first Permanent Representative to the
                UN.
Elath   Director, Jewish Agency Office in Washington, to
                Special Representative and then Ambassador to the
                United States.
Eytan   Principal, Jewish Agency Public Service College, to
                Director-General.
Fischer   Political Secretary, Jewish Agency Office in Paris, to
                Diplomatic Representative and then Minister to
                France.
Kohn   Political Secretary, Jewish Agency Office in Jerusalem,
                to Political Adviser to the Foreign Minister.
Levavi   Eastern Europe Section of Political Department (and
                Vice Principal, JAPSC) to Acting Director, Eastern
                Europe Department.
Lourie   Director, UN Office of the Jewish Agency, New York,
                to Consul-General to New York and Deputy Head, UN
                Delegation.
Najar   Director of Information, Jewish Agency Office in Paris,
                to Counsellor, Legation to France.
Rafael   Counsellor, Jewish Agency Delegation to the UN, to
                Counsellor, UN Delegation.
Rosenne   Legal section of Political Department, to Legal
                Adviser, Foreign Ministry.
Sasson, E.   Head, Arab Section, Political Department, to Head,
                Middle East Department.
Shiloah   Adviser on Middle East Affairs, to Political Adviser on
                Special Matters.
Shimoni, Y.   Secretary, Arab Section, and Head, Middle East Re-
                search Section, Political Department, to Assistant Head,
                Middle East Department.
Tov   Jewish Agency Office in Washington (dealing with
                Latin American Affairs), to UN Delegation and then
                Head, Latin America Department.

Among the 18 members of the Technical Élite from the beginning
who came directly from the Jewish Agency's Political Department,
14 were also in the Formal Directorate; in fact, 10 of the first 11

members of the Formal Directorate (1948–53) came from the Political Department. To cap *this structural and personnel merger,* Sharett, Head of the Political Department from 1933 to 1948, became the first Foreign Minister of Israel.

2. The remaining 12 TE members from their date of entry into the Service fall into two groups: those who joined the Foreign Office in 1948, and those who came later. Three of the 6 Double Originals who were not from the Political Department left the Service in the early years as noted: Gordon, Guriel, and Meron. One of the others, Y. Herzog, later became a member of the Formal Directorate.[1] The post-1948 group of TE members from their date of entry into the Foreign Service joined the Ministry between 1949 and 1966.[2]

3. *The Political Department's dominance was virtually total* in so far as Technical Élite *personnel* are concerned. Its impact on the Foreign Ministry at Work was also profound, as noted in chapter 20.

---

[1] The others were Pragai, a student at the JAPSC who became Private Secretary to the Foreign Minister (he did not remain in the TE thereafter); and Elyashiv, who moved from Director of the *Histadrut* School to head the Eastern Europe Department; he was also in the Formal Directorate briefly in 1955.

[2] Divon came to the Foreign Office in 1949 from *Tzahal* and was Acting Head of the Middle East Department for 3 years; Darom, the only person among the early TE group to come directly from abroad (he was a lawyer and Law Lecturer in Chile), was one of the Foreign Office experts on Latin America; Ben-Dor came to his FSTE post from the Ministry of Education and Culture in 1950; Avidar was an *Aluf* (Brigadier-General) when he was appointed to head the Moscow Embassy in 1955; Remez, another recruit from *Tzahal*—he was a prime mover in the creation of the Israel Air Force—came directly from the Weizmann Institute, where he was Administrative Director, to head the new Department of International Co-operation in 1960; and E. Shimoni was Head of the Deputy Prime Minister's Bureau when he accompanied Eban to the Foreign Office in the same post, in 1966. None of these persons served in the Formal Directorate during the first twenty years.

TECHNICAL ÉLITE MEMBERS FROM THE RANKS

Position Immediately Preceding Entry Into Technical Élite

Ambassador	Minister	Chargé d'Affaires	Counsellor	First Secretary	Consul-General	Consul	Department	Other
ANUG (Uruguay)	GOITEIN (S. Africa)	ALLON (Ankara)	DAGAN (Burma)	GAZIT (UK)	BIRAN (Los Angeles)	ARAD (New York)	ARAZI (Head, Public Relations)	ELIZUR (Press Officer)
ARNON (Ghana)	HAREL (Roumania)	LORCH (Colombo)	ERELL (US)	KIDRON, A. (UK)	ESHEL (Vienna)	YUVAL (Nicosia)	AVIDAN (Acting Dir., Latin America)	GOLAN (Asst. Controller, Foreign Exchange)
AROKH (Sweden)	HYMAN (S. Africa)	SASSON, M. (Ankara)	HARMAN, A. (New York)		PRATT (Chicago)		BAR-HAIM (Asst. Dir, Middle East)	HARMAN, Z. (Head, Technical Aid Bureau, Prime Minister's Office)
BITAN (Sweden)	TSUR (Uruguay, Argentina et al.)	SHEK (Prague)	LIVERAN (United Nations)				BARROMI (Asst. Dir., West Europe)	KATZ (Adviser on Special Subjects)
DORON (Chile & Ecuador)			MIRON (United Nations)				BARTUR (Asst. Dir., Economic)	MEROZ (Asst. Head, Reparations Mission to Cologne)
EYLAN (Kenya)			SCHNEERSON (Brazil)				BEN-HORIN (Asst. Dir, Asia and	
HILLEL (Ivory Coast et al.)								
LESHEM (Congo-Kinshasa)								
MICHAEL (Uganda et al.)								
RON (Ivory Coast et al.)								

RUPPIN (Malagasy)
YAHIL (Sweden, Norway, Denmark)

Africa)
BENTSUR (Acting Dir., East Europe)
CHELOUCHE (Asst. Dir., Economic)
DINITZ (Head, DG Bureau)
EVRON (Principal Asst., US)
KAHANE (Asst., Latin America)
KIDRON, R. (Head, Research Section, Research)
LEVIN (Asst. Dir., Asia)
LUBRANI (Principal Asst., Middle East)
SIDOR (Asst. Dir., Research)

PALMON (Adviser on Arab Affairs, Prime Minister's Office)
RAVIV (Asst., Foreign Minister's Bureau)
SAVIR (Asst. Head, Reparations Mission to Cologne)
TEKOAH (Deputy Legal Adviser)

1. The pattern of entry into the Technical Élite from the ranks reveals *great diversity—horizontally and vertically*. Among the 57 TE members who did not begin their Foreign Service career in a Technical Élite post, all but 3 rose directly from within the service; and those 3 had had previous assignments in the Service: Golan as Commercial Attaché in Ankara and Economic Counsellor in Manila, Z. Harman with the UN Delegation, and Palmon, who was in the Ministry's Political Department during the first year.

2. More than half the group assumed a TE post at the conclusion of a foreign assignment (35), while 19 entered the Technical Élite from within the home office.

3. There was great variety of ranks at the 'take-off' point into the Technical Élite: 16 heads of Mission (Ambassadors and Ministers)— 20, including Chargés d'Affaires; 6 Counsellors; 2 First Secretaries; 3 Consuls-General, and 2 Consuls; and within the home office, 1 Department Head, 2 Acting Heads, 7 Assistant Heads, 1 Bureau Head, Principal Assistants and even Assistants. There were sundry other 'take-off' posts such as Press Officer, Deputy Legal Adviser, and Assistant Head of a quasi-diplomatic Reparations Mission to Cologne.

   Among the Heads of Mission 4 were serving in Europe—by chance, 3 of them in Sweden; 7 were in Africa, 3 in Latin America, and 2 in South Africa. The Chargés d'Affaires who moved into the Technical Élite added the Middle East (Turkey, 2), Asia (Ceylon), and Europe (Czechoslovakia) to the variety. Two of the 6 Counsellors who moved directly to a Technical Élite post served on Israel's UN Delegation, 2 in the United States, 1 in Burma and 1 in Brazil. Both men who rose directly from First Secretary to the TE served in the London Embassy. Taking the 5 Consuls-General and Consuls together, 3 served in the US, 1 in Vienna, and 1 in Nicosia immediately before entry into the Technical Élite.

4. Within the Ministry (home office) many Departments were represented at the 'take-off' point of entry: 2 each from Latin America, Middle East, Economic, Research, and Asia (and Africa), and 1 each from Western Europe, Eastern Europe, United States, Director-General's Bureau, and Public Relations. To this variety may be added Press Office, Foreign Minister's Bureau, Office of the Adviser on Special Subjects, and the Legal Adviser's Office. In rank they ranged from a Head, through Acting Head, Assistant Head, Principal Assistant, to Assistant. Thus there was *no rigid pattern of promotion* directly into the Technical Élite—*either from preferred Departments or from points in the scale of rank and function*: they ranged from Ambassador to Assistant, and from Middle East Department to Public Relations.

5. As noted earlier, 12 of the 57 TE members who rose from the ranks later entered the Formal Directorate. In terms of their functional

and rank point of entry into the Technical Élite, 4 were Heads of Mission (2 became DG), 1 was a Counsellor, 1 First Secretary, 1 Consul-General, 4 Department Assistants or Acting Heads, and 1 Deputy Legal Adviser. Here, too, *diversity was the norm.*

APPENDIX TABLE 18

FOREIGN SERVICE TECHNICAL ÉLITE 1948–1968

	TECHNICAL ÉLITE		*FORMAL DIRECTORATE*	
	Number of Persons	*Average Number of Years*	*Number of Persons*	*Average Number of Years*
(a) Zionist Activity: Political Department				
1–2 years	8	1·6	5	1·6
3–6 years	7	4·1	5	4·4
7–10 years	6	9·0	2	9·5
More than 10 years	5	13·4	3	12·7
Totals and Mean Averages	26	6·3	15	5·8
(b) Other Zionist Activity				
1–2 years	12	1·6	5	1·8
3–6 years	19	4·2	9	4·3
7–10 years	3	7·7	1	7·0
More than 10 years	4	16·0	2	20·0
Totals and Mean Averages	38	4·9	17	5·6
(c) Combined Zionist Activity				
1–2 years	10	1·7	3	2·0
3–6 years	22	4·5	11	4·8
7–10 years	7	8·1	2	7·0
More than 10 years	12	14·5	7	13·7
Totals and Mean Averages	51	6·8	23	7·3

1. Zionist Activity has been divided into two categories for this analysis—the Jewish Agency's Political Department (the precursors of the Foreign Service, as noted), and Other.[1] The latter includes a wide variety of activities for the Jewish National Movement: organizing Youth Aliya in the 1930s; directing offices of the Jewish National

[1] The distinction between Political Department and Other does not imply differentiation in terms of importance; rather, it permits analysis of continuity from the pre-State Foreign Service to that after independence.

Fund; Aliya 'B' during and immediately after the Second World War; directing *He-halutz* (pioneer) training of youth in preparation for *aliya*; missions abroad for the Movement; press and information work; representation of the Jewish Agency in key cities; organizational work—executive membership of Zionist Organizations, etc.; direction of Zionist youth movements; teaching; research and documentation, etc.

2. Reference was made earlier to the continuity from the Political Department to the Foreign Service—with a formal change in the position held by 17 persons. The above data supplement this basic theme about the personnel of the Foreign Service by exploring the time spent in the Foreign Service of the *Yishuv*. Almost one-third of all Technical Élite members from 1948 to 1968 served in the Jewish Agency's Political Department, 26 of 87 persons. This includes more than half the total membership of the Formal Directorate over the twenty-year period, 15 of 28 persons. Nor was this pre-State Technical Élite activity a transient or marginal phenomenon: 18 of the 26 were in the Political Department at least 3 years, 11 of these at least 7 years, and 5 persons more than 10 years. Viewed in terms of the Formal Directorate, 10 persons—of a total of 28 during the period 1948–68—spent at least 3 years in the TE of the Jewish Agency's Foreign Service, 15 of them at least 7 years, and 3 more than a decade. For 11 FSTE members and 5 FD members the average period of such activity before 1948 exceeded a decade.

3. A larger number of FSTE members participated in other forms of Zionist activity: almost a third spent a year or two in these activities—and the vast majority 6 years or less. The overall average was 4·9 years compared with 6·3 years in the Political Department. In reality the difference is much greater, for 'Other' includes a variety of activities, lacking the homogeneous and continuous participation in one vital area of the Jewish nation's struggle for independence. Among the Formal Directorate members, only 3 of 17 spent more than 6 years in other Zionist Activities.

4. There were 4 persons with very extensive activities (more than 10 years) outside the Political Department: Tsur (27 years, all with the Jewish National Fund); A. Harman (13 years, mostly with the British Zionist Federation); Doron (13 years, mostly as Director of the Youth Department, *Keren Hayesod*); and E. Shimoni (11 years, mostly with the South African Zionist and *Po'alei Tziyon* organizations). Within the Political Department, the 11-years-plus group comprised: Elath, later Ambassador to the US and the UK; Kohn, Political Adviser to the Foreign Minister for 13 years after independence; E. Sasson, later Minister to Turkey and Italy; Shiloah, later Adviser on the Middle East and Special Matters; and Danin, later Adviser on the Middle East. How *extensively involved in*

Zionist activity was the post-independence Foreign Service Technical Élite is indicated by the following: no less than 51 of the 87 persons had engaged in formal, institutional Zionist activity; and 41 of
them spent at least 3 years in this public service. In the case of 12
persons the average was almost 15 years. To those noted above must
be added: Levavi (12 years, almost all in the Political Department),
Lourie (15 years, many of them with the London and New York
offices of the Political Department), and Yuval (13 years, mainly
with departments of the Jewish Agency in Jerusalem).

5. All but 5 members of the Formal Directorate had participated in
some form of Zionist activity. Half of the 23 persons averaged about
5 years of service, while 7 persons averaged almost 14 years: these
were Harman, Kohn, Levavi, Lourie, Shiloah, Tsur, and Danin.

APPENDIX TABLE 19

FOREIGN SERVICE TECHNICAL ÉLITE 1948–1968

Pre-State Military Service (Years in Brackets)

Haganah		British Army (Second World War) (including Jewish Brigade)		Other
Arazi	(19)	Arad	(4)	Comay (6) (South African
Avidan	(7)	Arokh	(4)	Army)
Avidar	(21)	Barromi	(5)	Fischer (4) (Free French
Chelouche	(2)	Ben-Horin	(5)	Forces)
Divon	(7)	Eban	(7)	Kidron (5) (South African
Eshel	(4)	Evron	(5)	Army)
Guriel	(3)	Eytan	(1)	Leshem (3) (Czech Under-
Hillel	(7)	Guriel	(5)	ground)
Herzog	(3)	Harel	(4)	
Lorch	(3)	Kahane	(3)	
Lubrani	(6)	Lorch	(2)	
Meron	(3)	Meroz	(1)	
Meroz	(10)	Pragai	(5)	
Michael	(11)	Remez	(5)	
Palmon	(9)	Ron	(5)	
Remez	(2)	Rosenne	(6)	
Shiloah	(7)	Rupin	(5)	
Shimoni	(12)	Savir	(5)	
Tsur	(21)	Schneerson	(4)	
Total*				
(Persons)	19		19	4

* See Note to Table 32.

FOREIGN SERVICE TECHNICAL ÉLITE 1948–1968

Higher Education: By Country and University

Country	University Studies Without Degrees	Bachelor's Degree	Professional Degree	Postgraduate Degree	Special Courses	Total
ISRAEL	(17) 15 Hebrew U. 1 Technion 1 Tel Aviv School of Law & Ec.	(3) Hebrew U.	(4) Hebrew U.	(5) Hebrew U.	(9) 5 JAPSC 4 Beth Hakerem Teachers' Seminary	38
ARGENTINA			(1) Buenos Aires			1
AUSTRIA	(2) Vienna			(1) Vienna		3
BELGIUM		(1) Louvain				1
CANADA				(1) Ottawa		1
CZECHOSLOVAKIA	(4) 3 Prague 1 German U., Prague		(1) Prague			5
CHILE		(1) Santiago	(1) Santiago			2
CHINA			(1) L'Aurore, Shanghai			1
EGYPT			(1) French Law School, Cairo			1
FRANCE	(4) 2 Paris 1 Paris Art Academy 1 Grenoble	(2) Sorbonne	(2) 1 Paris 1 Toulouse	(3) Paris		11
GERMANY	(9) 3 Berlin 1 Cologne 1 Freiburg 1 Frankfurt	(1) Berlin	(1) Berlin	(3) 2 Heidelberg 1 Berlin		14

	(52)	(21)	(20)	(23)	(14)	Total
	1 Hamburg 1 Heidelberg 1 Merburg					
ITALY	(2) 1 Florence 1 Rome		(1) Rome			3
LATVIA				(1) Riga		1
LEBANON				(1) American U., Beirut		1
POLAND	(3) 1 Cracow 1 Danzig 1 Warsaw					3
ROUMANIA	(1) Cluj U.				(1) Cluj Trade & Industry Academy	2
RUSSIA	(1) Kiev					1
SOUTH AFRICA		(4) 2 Cape Town 1 Stellenbosch 1 Johannesburg	(1) Cape Town			5
SWITZERLAND	(3) Basle				(1) Graduate Institute, Geneva	4
UNITED KINGDOM	(4) 3 London 1 LSE	(7) 1 LSE 1 Liverpool 3 London 1 Cambridge 1 Oxford	(6) 5 London 1 Oxford	(4) 1 Cambridge 1 London 2 Oxford		21
UNITED STATES	(2) 1 Cincinnati 1 Harvard	(2) 1 Georgetown 1 New School for Social Research		(4) 1 Georgetown 2 Harvard 1 Johns Hopkins	(3) 2 Harvard Business School 1 Woodrow Wilson School, Princeton	11
TOTAL	52	21	20	23	14	130

1. The overall total of 130 university or special courses attended comprises 45 persons who attended one institution of higher learning, 31 who attended two institutions, 5 three institutions, and 2 persons four universities.

2. The *countries of higher education reflect in part the dispersion of world Jewry*: the Foreign Service Technical Élite studied in no less than 21 countries. Yet one population centre of world Jewry, Russia, is barely represented; and the other, the United States, is grossly underrepresented. More precisely, one person received his higher education in Russia, and 8 members, in part, in the United States. Of those 8, only 5 received degrees from American universities, and 3 from institutions of the first rank, 2 from Harvard and 1 from Johns Hopkins, all postgraduate degrees. Only 1 person with a US university degree, Tekoah, and another, with a Canadian university postgraduate degree acquired in mid-career, Y. Herzog, represented North American higher education in the Formal Directorate.

3. In reality the higher education of Israel's Foreign Service Technical Élite was *highly concentrated by country, by university, and by field of study*. Two countries stand out from the data—Israel and the United Kingdom. Germany, France, and the US follow as a group, with South Africa as a special case. The other 15 countries are marginal— with no more than a single university degree earned in each of 12 of them, and none in the other 3 countries.

4. The data on higher education in Israel may create a misleading impression of primacy among the Foreign Service Technical Élite: of the total, 17 units refer to partial university studies, and 9 others to special post-secondary courses; that is, almost 70 per cent were not completed university degree programmes.[1] Altogether 12 Technical Élite members received Israeli degrees, all at the Hebrew University.[2]

In summary: 31 members of the Foreign Service Technical Élite were exposed to higher education in Israel: 13 had partial university studies, 12 received a degree, and 6 took special courses but did not receive a university degree. About 25 received their basic higher

[1] Of the 17 with partial university studies in Israel, one, Ben-Horin, later completed a law degree at London University; another, R. Kidron, a B.A. at Stellenbosch University in South Africa; and a third, Meroz, a B.A. at London University. Of the 9 who attended the JAPSC or the Beth Hakerem Teachers Seminary, Gazit had received an M.A. at the Hebrew University before attending the JAPSC. Shiloah and Biran were at the Teachers Seminary in the late 1920s before completing, respectively, a B.A. at the Hebrew University and an M.A. and Ph.D. at Johns Hopkins.

[2] Three earned a B.A. (Elath, Lorch, Shiloah), 4 an LL.B. (Chelouche, Herzog, Miron, Schneerson), and 5 postgraduate degrees (Barromi, Gazit, Golan and Levavi an M.A., and Rosenne a Ph.D.); of these Barromi and Rosenne received their basic university education elsewhere, at Rome and London University, respectively. Four persons received higher degrees elsewhere after their studies in Jerusalem—Elath in Beirut, Chelouche in Paris, Herzog in Ottawa, and Miron at Harvard.

education in Israel. Among the Formal Directorate of 28, 6 persons received a university degree in Israel.[1]

5. The UK stands second to Israel in the higher education of the FSTE—21 to 38 course programmes. However, 17 of the 21 UK units represent completed degrees, i.e. 80 per cent, compared with 30 per cent of those in Israel.[2]

   The importance of British higher education is evident in the data on the Formal Directorate: 7 members (1 more than with the Israeli degrees) were educated at London, Oxford, or Cambridge: Avner, Ben-Horin, Eban, Eytan, A. Harman, Lourie, and Rosenne.

6. South Africa contributed 5 degrees to 4 members of the Technical Élite, including 2 persons—Comay and Lourie—in the Formal Directorate.

7. German higher education has the third highest numerical component—but only 5 of the 14 represent degrees.[3] The picture changes drastically if all partial university studies in Germany and Austria are included: 14 members of the FSTE received some higher education there, among them 7 members of the Formal Directorate—Avriel, Bartur, Eshel, Kohn, Levavi, Rafael, and Yahil.

8 France accounted for more university degrees than Germany—7 to 5 (or 6, including Austria).[4] Belgium (Fischer) and the French Law School in Cairo (Najar) may be added, making 9 degrees. Altogether 11 members of the FSTE received their higher education in French, in whole or in part, 12 if Tekoah's French law degree from Shanghai is included. Three persons with degrees from France were in the Formal Directorate: Tsur, Chelouche, and Najar; Fischer may be added.

9. Members of Israel's Foreign Service Technical Élite studied at 50 institutions of higher learning. Yet only half a dozen merit attention in this context:

[1] Shiloah a B.A., Chelouche and Herzog each an LL.B., Gazit and Levavi an M.A., and Rosenne a Ph.D. Two of them, Shiloah and Gazit, received their entire higher education in Israel, Chelouche predominantly so, and Herzog his rabbinical and legal studies. Levavi spent two years at Danzig and Heidelberg before completing his M.A. in Jerusalem; and Rosenne did his first degree (Law) in London.

[2] Six of the 17 were Bachelor's degrees: Ben-Dor, A. Harman, Z. Harman, Lubrani, Meroz, and Raviv; the first 3 were British by background, the other 3 came to the UK from Israel for their university studies. Six persons took professional degrees in England, all in Law: Ben-Horin, Goitein, A. Harman, Liveran, Pratt, and Rosenne. And 5 persons received postgraduate degrees: Avner, Eban, Eytan and Lourie an M.A., and Liveran an LL.M.

[3] 1 B.A. (Eshel), 1 M.D. (Harel), and 3 LL.D.s (Kohn, Levin, Meron). Austria adds 1 postgraduate degree (Yahil, Ph.D.).

[4] This comprised 2 Bachelor's degrees (Arazi and Tsur), 2 professional degrees, both Law (Elyashiv and Gordon), and 3 postgraduate degrees (Chelouche, Gordon, Najar).

Hebrew University	27 persons	including	12 degrees
London University (inc. LSE)	18 (20) persons	,,	9 (10) degrees
Sorbonne	7 persons	,,	4 degrees
Oxford	3 persons	,,	4 degrees
Berlin	4 persons	,,	3 degrees
Cape Town	2 persons	,,	3 degrees

The pre-eminence of the Hebrew University and London University is clear for the Technical Élite as a whole. The distribution is less skewed for degrees of the Formal Directorate members: Hebrew University (5); Oxford (3); Cambridge, Cape Town, London, and Sorbonne (2 each); Berlin, French Law School in Cairo, Harvard, Heidelberg, L'Aurore University in Shanghai, Ottawa, Toulouse, and Vienna (1 each).

Parallel Technical Élite:
Supplementary Data

Research into Israel's Parallel Technical Élite uncovered further data which add to the understanding of its origins, composition, education, and other occupational activities of its members. The following analysis, which incorporates these supplementary findings, is designed as an extension of the political–biographical exploration of the PTE provided in chapter 18.

Where did the members of the Parallel Technical Élite come from, in terms of bureaucratic, professional, or entrepreneurial posts held before they entered the Technical Élite? This is the first theme of the supplementary analysis.

APPENDIX TABLE 21

PARALLEL TECHNICAL ÉLITE 1948–1968

Position Immediately Preceding First Entry

		Into PTE	Into FD-level Posts
Army:		33	21
Tzahal	25		
Haganah	8		
Government Bureaucracy		17	6
Other:		7	
Jewish Agency	2		2
Academic	2		
Business	2		
Professional	1		
		57	29

1. The Israel Defence Forces have served as the personnel reservoir of the Parallel Technical Élite concerned with foreign policy. No less than 33 of its 57 members (almost 60 per cent) entered PTE posts directly from *Tzahal* or *Haganah*—almost exactly the same proportion of Foreign Service Technical Élite members furnished by the Jewish Agency's Political Department. This included 5 of the 7 original FD-level members—Dori as Chief of Staff, Be'eri as Director of (the

predecessor of) *Ha-Mosad*, H. Herzog as Director of Military Intelligence, Galili as Deputy Minister of Defence, and Eshkol as Director-General, Defence Ministry.

2. *Haganah* or *Tzahal* provided the Parallel Technical Élite with all Chiefs of Staff, all Directors of *Ha-Mosad*, all Deputy Ministers of Defence, all DGs, Defence Ministry except 1, the 1 Deputy Minister of Finance, 1 of the 3 DGs, Finance Ministry, all Directors of Military Intelligence, all Chiefs of the General Staff Branch, and all Military Attachés.

3. The only other substantial source of PTE (and FD-level) members was the government bureaucracy. Among those who entered a PTE post from the civil service were:

Arnon	Director of the Economic Planning Authority
Kollek	Minister (No. 2) to the US
Nahmias	Deputy Inspector-General of Police
Navon	Private Secretary to the Foreign Minister
Shind	Ministry of Commerce and Industry—Controller
Tsour, M.	Ministry of Finance
Yafeh	Foreign Office Information Department.

4. The Army's predominance is once more confirmed by the data on FD-level members: 21 of the 29 persons who rose to FD-level posts come from *Tzahal* or *Haganah*; the civil service accounts for 6 members; and the Jewish Agency's Political Department provided Horowitz and Sharef—both of whom were also members of the High Policy Élite.

APPENDIX TABLE 22

PARALLEL TECHNICAL ÉLITE 1948–1968

Zionist Activity: Jewish Agency and Other*

	Number of Persons in The PTE	Average Number of Years in The PTE	Number of Persons at The FD Level	Average Number of Years at The FD Level
1–2 years	3	2	2	2
3–6 years	3	4	3	4
7–10 years	1	7	1	7
Over 10 years	3	15	3	15
Totals and averages	10	7	9	7·6

* Other—Zionist youth groups, Zionist federations in the Diaspora.
Note: The data in this table are, at best, an approximation. For many PTE members this aspect of the biographical material is sparse and unreliable.

1. The most striking feature of the data in Appendix Table 22 is the paucity of participation by PTE members in Zionist organizational activity: about 10 of 55 persons were involved in this field of public service. The only PTE members with more than a decade of Zionist service were: Avigur, with more than 20 years in the organizational service of the Movement, most of it in building *Haganah*; Horowitz, Director of the Jewish Agency's Economic Department from 1935 to 1948; and Uzay, in the Agency's Political Department. Others in the Political Department were Dinstein, Kollek, and Sharef.

2. The principal reason for this marginal role in the Jewish Agency and related activities is the participation of most PTE members in the *Haganah* or in the British Army, almost all in the Jewish Brigade, or in both during the Second World War. And most of the PTE members were too young to have been active in Zionist activities before 1939.

3. It is noteworthy that 9 of the 10 PTE persons who were involved in Zionist Organizational activity reached FD-level posts.

PARALLEL TECHNICAL ÉLITE 1948–1968

Higher Education by Country and University

Country	University Studies Without Degree	Bachelor's	Professional	Postgraduate	Special Courses	Total
ISRAEL	(11) 5 Tel Aviv 4 Hebrew U. 2 Technion	(3) Hebrew U.	(2) Hebrew U.	(2) Hebrew U.		18
UNITED KINGDOM	(3) 1 London U. 1 LSE 1 Oxford	(1) LSE	(1) Cambridge		(9) Military Staff Colleges	14
UNITED STATES	(3) 1 Harvard 2 Columbia	(2) 1 Chicago 1 Columbia		(3) 2 Columbia 1 Chicago	(3) 1 Princeton 1 Harvard 1 Washington	11
FRANCE	(2) 1 Grenoble 1 Sorbonne		(1) Faculté de Science			4
GERMANY			(1) Hanover	(2) 1 Berlin 1 Frankfurt	(1) Military Staff College	3
SWITZERLAND	(1) Geneva		(1) Geneva			2
AUSTRIA			(1) Vienna			1
BELGIUM	(1) Ghent					1
HOLLAND				(1) Amsterdam		1
IRELAND	(1) Wesley					1
LEBANON		(1) Beirut				1
Total number of man-courses	22	7	7	8	13	57

1. Members of the Parallel Technical Élite studied in 11 countries. Three stand out from the data—Israel, the UK, and the US. The other 8 countries are marginal, with no more than a single university degree earned in 5 of them, and none in 2 of them.

2. While 16 persons were exposed to higher education in Israel, only 5 received a degree, all at the Hebrew University. Of the 11 with partial university studies in Israel, 2 received degrees elsewhere. Among the Formal Directorate-level members, 4 received their degrees at the Hebrew University. The UK stands second in the total number of PTE members who received a higher education— but 9 went to Military Staff Colleges and only 2 received British university degrees. Nine persons studied in the United States and 5 degrees were received, 3 from Columbia and 2 from Chicago. For the rest, 3 degrees were earned in Germany and 1 each in Austria, France, Holland, Lebanon, and Switzerland.

3. Members of Israel's Parallel Technical Élite studied at 24 institutions of higher learning, including Military Staff Colleges, yet only the Hebrew University stands out: 7 persons received a degree there. The only other university where more than one person received a degree is Columbia (3 persons).

APPENDIX TABLE 24

PARALLEL TECHNICAL ÉLITE 1948–1968

Other Occupations

Occupation	Parallel Technical Élite Members	Formal Directorate-Level Members
Academic	3	2
Commercial	9	3
Legal	2	0
Kibbutz Membership	7	5
Knesset Membership	10	10
Military	28	13
University Administration	2	2
Government Bureaucracy	31	19

1. Members of the Parallel Technical Élite manifested a variety of occupational backgrounds and interests. There were few Academics—only Bergman, Harkabi, and Yadin. All are on the faculty of the Hebrew University after leaving the PTE (Bergman was also a Professor at the Weizmann Institute of Science for many years)—in Organic Chemistry, International Relations and Middle Eastern Studies, and Archaeology, respectively.

2. Nine persons were engaged in Commerce at some stage, including 3 FD-level members of the PTE: Arnon managed a diamond-polishing firm before assuming his long-term post as Director-General, Finance Ministry; Givli filled a senior position in the Shemen Oil complex; and H. Herzog with the Wolfson Industries in Israel after leaving *Tzahal*. Other PTE members involved in Commerce have been Glikman, Kosloff, Lifshitz, Ne'eman, Prihar, and Ron.

3. Only 2 persons have been practising lawyers, Kimche and Ne'eman.

4. There are 7 *kibbutz* members within the Parallel Technical Élite, 6 of them at the Formal Directorate level. Argov belonged to *Ein Gev* from 1937 onwards. Avigur has been a member of *Kvutzat Kinneret* since 1918. Ben-Natan was a '*kibbutznik*' from 1938 to 1944 in *Medorot Zeraim*. Eshkol was a founder and continuous member of *Degania Bet* from 1920 until his death in 1969. Galili continued to make his home in *Na'an* after becoming a minister in 1966. Peres was a member of *Alumot* from 1943 to 1947. And Sharef belonged to *Shfayim* from 1929 to 1935. In most cases, however, *kibbutz* membership became formal only. While the *kibbutz* remained their home to some extent, membership was qualified in vital matters, such as equality, the eschewal of private property, etc.

5. Ten persons were members of the *Knesset* until 1968—and all 10 have occupied FD-level posts: Avigur, Dinstein, Eshkol, Sapir, and Sharef from *Mapai*, Dayan, Harel, Navon, and Peres from *Rafi*, and Galili from *Ahdut Ha'avodah*.

6. The largest occupational group by far are 'professional' members of *Tzahal*: they comprise half of the PTE and of its FD-level members —28 of 57 and 13 of 29. 'The Military' include the 8 Chiefs of Staff, the 5 Directors of Military Intelligence (i.e. the 13 FD-level members), 8 Military Attachés, 2 Directors of Military Purchasing Missions, 3 Military Secretries to the Prime Minister, a Miliatary Secretary to the Defence Minister, and a Head of the International Co-operation Department within the Defence Ministry.

7. Two men held university administrative posts—Dori as President of the Haifa Technion for many years, and Sharef as Administrative Director of the Weizmann Institute.

8. The greatest variety of occupational posts is evident within the Government bureaucracy—no less than 31 persons in the PTE, including 19 FD-level members. Many of these are also High Policy Élite members—Dayan, Eshkol, Galili, Horowitz, Peres, Rabin, Sapir, and Sharef. Among the others are: Ben-Natan, Kollek, Nahmias, Navon, and Yafeh in the Foreign Service; and Arnon, Ben-Arzi, Makleff, Kashti, Laskov, Shind, M. Tsour, and Zur in public service corporations like *El Al*, *Mekorot*, the Port Authority, the Dead Sea Works, and Zim Navigation Company.

SELECT BIBLIOGRAPHY

A. PRIMARY SOURCES

    (i) OFFICIAL RECORDS AND REPORTS
    (ii) OTHER WRITTEN SOURCES
    (iii) SELECT LIST OF PERSONS INTERVIEWED

B. BOOKS AND PAMPHLETS

C. ARTICLES

D. JOURNALS, NEWSPAPERS AND PERIODICALS

Select Bibliography

A. PRIMARY SOURCES

(i) OFFICIAL RECORDS AND REPORTS

Government of Israel, Ministry for Foreign Affairs, *Budget Speech of the Foreign Minister to the Knesset* . . . , Jerusalem (annual)
— *Skira* (Report): *Appendix to the Foreign Minister's Speech on the Budget of the Ministry for* . . . , Jerusalem (annual)
— *United Nations General Assembly and Security Council Resolutions on Palestine 1947–1961*, Jerusalem (n.d.)
State of Israel, Central Bureau of Statistics, *Radio Listening and Television Watching January 1969* (Special Series, no. 292), Jerusalem, 1969
— *Statistical Abstract of Israel*, Jerusalem (annual)
State of Israel, Civil Service Commission, *Twenty Years of Service*, Jerusalem, 1968
State of Israel, *Divrei Ha-Knesset* (Official Records of the *Knesset*, in Hebrew), Government Printer, Jerusalem 1949–68
State of Israel, *Government Year-Book* (annually since 1949)
— 'The Presidency in the First Decade of the State of Israel', *Government Year-Book 5719*, 1958/9, Jerusalem, 1958
State of Israel, Government Press Office, *Newspapers and Periodicals Appearing in Israel 1969–1970*, Jerusalem, 1970
— *Press Bulletin* (daily), Jerusalem
State of Israel, *Records of the Provisional State Council*, Tel Aviv, 1948–9 (in Hebrew)
State of Israel, *Sefer Ha-Hukkim* (Laws of the State of Israel), Jerusalem
State of Israel, *Taknon Ha-Knesset* (Regulations of the *Knesset*), Jerusalem, November 1965
United Nations, Statistical Office, *Demographic Year-Book*, New York, 1949
— *Statistical Yearbook*, 1953 and 1966, New York
United Nations, *Yearbook of National Accounts Statistics, 1962 and 1966*, New York
— *Who's Who, Israel* (annual), Tel Aviv

(ii) OTHER WRITTEN SOURCES

Allon, Y., 'A Message to President Nasser', *New Statesman* (London), lviii, 1494, 31 Oct. 1959
— *Masakh Shel Hol* (Curtain of Sand), (Tel Aviv, 1960)

Allon Y., 'The Arab-Israel Conflict: Some Suggested Solutions', *International Affairs* (London), 40, April 1964

— 'The Making of Israel's Army: The Development of Military Conceptions of Liberation and Defence', in Howard, M. (ed.), *The Theory and Practice of War: Essays Presented to B. H. Liddell Hart on His Seventieth Birthday* (New York, 1965)

— *The Campaigns of the Palmah* (Tel Aviv, 1965), in Hebrew

— 'Meetings in India', *Mebifnim* (From the Inside), Ein Harod, 27, 4, December 1965, pp. 355–71

— 'Active Defence—A Guarantee for Our Existence', *Molad* (Tel Aviv), 1 (24), 2 (212), July–August, 1967 (in Hebrew)

— 'The Present Security Situation in a Strategic Mirror', *Ot* (Tel Aviv), 1, 2, Winter 1967 (in Hebrew)

— 'The Last Stage of the War of Independence', *Ot* (Tel Aviv), 3–4, November 1967 (in Hebrew)

— *The Making of Israel's Army* (London, 1970)

— *Shield of David* (Jerusalem, 1970)

— Interviews in the Israeli Press 1965–70

Ben Gurion, D., *Rebirth and Destiny of Israel* (New York, 1954)

— *In the Battle* (Tel Aviv, 1955), in Hebrew

— *Medinat Yisrael Ha-Mehudeshet* (The State of Israel Reborn), 2 vols. (Tel Aviv, 1969)

— 'Israel Among the Nations', State of Israel, *Government Year-Book 5713*, 1952/3, Jerusalem

— 'Israel and the Diaspora', State of Israel, *Government Year-Book 5718*, 1957/8, Jerusalem

— 'Israel's Security and Her International Position Before and After the Sinai Campaign', State of Israel, *Government Year-Book 5720*, 1959/1960, Jerusalem

— 'Towards a New World', State of Israel, *Government Year-Book 5721*, 1960/1, Jerusalem

— 'Achievements and Tasks of Our Generation', State of Israel, *Government Year-Book 5722*, 1961/2, Jerusalem

— 'The Vision of Isiah for Our Time', *New York Times Magazine*, vi, 20 May 1962

— 'On Peace and Negotiations', *New Outlook* (Tel Aviv), 6, 1 (50), January 1963

— 'Science and Ethics', *Brandeis University Publications*, 1, 1, 9 March 1960

— 'Why Adolf Eichmann Must be Tried in Israel', Government Press Office, Jerusalem, June 1960

— Interviews in Israeli and World Press 1948–68

— Memoirs in *Davar* (Tel Aviv)

    'The Campaign for the Negev' (26 February 1965)

    'The Problem of Authority over Palmah' (2 April 1965)

'The Government Crisis After the Altalena' (16 April 1965)

'From Underground Organization to Regular Army' (9 July 1965)

'Discussion with the Commanders of Palmah' (16 July 1965)

'Debate on the Dissident Organizations in Jerusalem' (30 July 1965)

'The Plot to Destroy Jerusalem Through Thirst was Eliminated' (6 August 1965)

'Birth Pangs of Coalition' (24 December 1965)

'*Tzahal*—Educator and Integrator of the Nation' (28 January 1966)

'USSR Broke Diplomatic Relations with Israel' (25 March 1966)

'Exchange of Messages with the two Great Powers' (5 August 1966)

Christman, H. M., *The State Papers of Levi Eshkol* (New York, 1969)

Dayan, M., *Diary of the Sinai Campaign* (London, 1966)

— *Mappa Hadasha—Yehassim Aherim* (New Map—Other Relationships) (Tel Aviv, 1969)

— 'Israel's Border Problems', *Foreign Affairs* (New York), 33, 2, January 1955

— 'Concepts of Security', *Jerusalem Post*, 23 August 1957

— 'Guarantees of Security', *Jerusalem Post*, 12 May 1961

— 'No Simple Way to Peace: A Reply to Dr. Goldmann's New Orientation', *Jerusalem Post*, 13 August 1961

— 'West African Diary', *Jerusalem Post*, 12, 19, 22, 26, and 29 November and 3 December 1963

— 'Why I Joined Rafi', interview, *Jerusalem Post*, 10 September 1965

— [Boetsch, J.] Interview with Dayan, in *L'Express* (Paris), reported in *The Montreal Star*, 26 May 1969

— Interviews in Israeli and World Press 1967–70

Eban, A., *Voice of Israel* (New York, 1957, 2nd ed. 1969)

— *The Tide of Nationalism* (New York, 1959)

— *My People: Story of the Jews* (New York, 1968)

— 'Israel in the Community of Nations' (Address to the 26th World Zionist Congress, Jerusalem, 5 January 1965)

— 'Reality and Vision in the Middle East', *Foreign Affairs* (New York), 43, 4, July 1965

— 'Moshe Sharett's Life Was Like the National Saga Itself', *Jerusalem Post*, 8 July 1965

Eban, A., Interviews in Israeli and World Press 1966–70

Election Programmes of political parties for *Knesset* elections in 1949, 1951, 1955, 1959, 1961, 1965, 1969: *Agudat Yisrael*; *Ahdut Ha'avodah*; *Gahal*; General Zionists; *Herut*; Independent Liberals; *Maki*; *Mapai*; *Mapam*; National Religious Party (*Mafdal*); *Po'alei Agudat Yisrael*; *Rafi*; *Rakah*; *Sepharadim*

Eshkol, L., *B'ma'aleh Ha-derech* (On the Way), (Tel Aviv, 1958)

— *B'havlei Hitnahlut* (In the Pangs of Settlement), (Tel Aviv, 1966)

Eshkol, 'Eshkol Statements on Foreign Policy', *New Outlook* (Tel Aviv), 7, 6 (64), July-August 1964
— 'Israel and the Diaspora', State of Israel, *Government Year-Book 5725, 1964–5,* Jerusalem
— 'Points from Address by Prime Minister Levi Eshkol at the Tenth Convention of *Mapai*, the Israel Labour Party, Tel Aviv, Feb. 16, 1965', Government Press Office, Jerusalem
— Interviews in Israeli and World Press 1963–9
'Death of Eshkol at 73 Marks Shift from Old Leaders to the Palestine-Born', *New York Times*, 27 February 1969
Eytan, W., *The First Ten Years: A Diplomatic History of Israel* (New York, 1958)
Meir, G., *This is Our Strength; Selected Papers* (New York, 1962)
Pearlman, M., *Ben Gurion Looks Back in Talks with Moshe Pearlman* (London, 1965)
Peres, S., *Ha-Shlav Ha-Ba* (The Next Stage), (Tel Aviv, 1965)
— *David's Sling* (London, 1970)
— 'The Next Ten Years', *Jerusalem Post*, 23 April 1958
— 'Many Roads Lead to Peace', *Jerusalem Post*, 31 July 1959
— 'Dead Symbols and Living Reality' in *Jerusalem Post*, 21 August 1959
— 'Strategy, Security and Deterrents' in *Jerusalem Post*, 9 April 1961
— 'Power and Middle East Peace', *Jerusalem Post*, 28 February 1964
— 'Outlines for an Israeli Foreign Policy', *New Outlook* (Tel Aviv), 6, 7 (56), September 1963
— Interviews in Israeli and World Press 1967–70
Ramati, S., *Israel Defence Forces* (Jerusalem, 1958, 5th rev. ed., 1969), Israel Today, no. 4
Sharef, Z., *Three Days* (London, 1962)
Sharett, M., *Israel in a World of Transition* (Jerusalem, 1956), speeches
— *Besha'ar Ha'umot* (At the Gate of the Nations), (Tel Aviv, 1958), speeches
— *Mashot B'Asya* (Roaming Over Asia), (Tel Aviv, 1958)
— 'Statement ... before the General Assembly of the United Nations, Sept. 27, 1950', Government Press Office, Jerusalem
— 'Israel and the Near East' (Address to the World Affairs Council of Philadelphia, 19 June 1952), Government Press Office, Jerusalem
— 'Israel and the Middle East' (Address before the National Press Club, Washington, 10 April 1953), Government Press Office, Jerusalem
— 'On Peace and Negotiations', *New Outlook* (Tel Aviv), 6, 1 (50), January 1963
— 'Foreign Policy and Security—A Symposium', *Ot* (Tel Aviv), i, 1 September 1966
— 'Israel and the Arabs—War and Peace', in *Ot* (Tel Aviv), I, September 1966, as translated in *Jerusalem Post*, 18 October 1966

— [Lachower, S. (ed.)] *The Writings of Moshe Sharett, A Bibliography 1920-65* (Jerusalem, 1965), in Hebrew

(iii) SELECT LIST OF PERSONS INTERVIEWED[1]

AKZIN, Benyamin	Professor of Political Science and Constitutional Law, The Hebrew University
ALLON, Yigal	*Ahdut Ha'avodah* leader; Cabinet Minister 1961– ; Deputy Prime Minister 1968–
ALMOG, Shmuel	Director-General, *Kol Yisrael*
AMIR, Shimon	Head, Director-General's Bureau, Foreign Ministry
ANUG, Yeshayahu	Assistant Head, Western Europe Department, Foreign Ministry
ARGOV, Meir	Chairman, *Knesset* Foreign Affairs and Security Committee
ARGOV, Shlomo	Assistant Head, US Department, Foreign Ministry
AROKH, Arye	Head, Department of International Organizations, Foreign Ministry
AVNER, Gershon	Assistant Director-General, Foreign Ministry
AVNERI, Uri	Member of *Knesset* (MK), leader of *Ha'olam Hazeh* faction
AVRIEL, Ehud	Assistant Director-General, Foreign Ministry
AYNOR, Hanan	Head, Africa Department, Foreign Ministry
BAR-HAIM, Shaul	Head, Middle East Department, Foreign Ministry
BAR-ON, Hanan	Head, Director-General's Bureau, Foreign Ministry
BARTUR, Moshe	Permanent Representative to UN office, Geneva
BEN-DOR, Mrs. Lea	Deputy Editor, *Jerusalem Post*
BEN GURION, David	Prime Minister and Defence Minister 1948–53, 1955–63
BEN-HORIN, Elyashiv	Head, Asia Department, Foreign Ministry
BERGER, Herzl	Chairman, *Knesset* Foreign Affairs and Security Committee
BITAN, Moshe	Assistant Director-General, Foreign Ministry
COMAY, Michael	Permanent Representative to the UN
DANIN, Ezra	Adviser to the Foreign Minister
DAROM, Avraham	Head, Latin America Department, Foreign Ministry

[1] In the case of Civil Servants, the position noted is that held at the time of the interview. Where more than one interview took place, over a period of time, the position indicated was that held when the last of a series of interviews, some of them extending between 1960 and 1970, occurred.

DAYAN, Moshe — Cabinet Minister 1959–64; Defence Minister 1967–

DINITZ, Simha — Head, Foreign Minister Meir's Bureau

DIVON, Shmuel — Assistant Head, Middle East Department, Foreign Ministry

EBAN, Abba — Cabinet Minister 1959– ; Foreign Minister 1966–

ELATH, Eliyahu — Political Adviser to the Foreign Minister

ELIACHAR, Elie — President, Council of the Sepharadi Community, Jerusalem

ERELL, Moshe — Chargé d'Affaires, Nepal

ESHKOL, Levi — Cabinet Minister 1951–69; Prime Minister and Minister of Defence 1963–7; Prime Minister 1967–9

EYTAN, Walter — Director-General, Foreign Ministry

GAZIT, Mordekhai — Assistant Director-General, Foreign Ministry

GOLAN, David — Head, Department of International Co-operation, Foreign Ministry

GOLAN, Yitzhak — Department of News and Current Events, *Kol Yisrael*

GOLDMANN, Nahum — Former President, World Zionist Organization; President, World Jewish Congress

GORDON, Amos — Director, News and Current Events, *Kol Yisrael*

GUTMANN, Emanuel — Senior Lecturer in Political Science, The Hebrew University

HACOHEN, David — Chairman, *Knesset* Foreign Affairs and Security Committee

HARARI, Ishar — MK, Independent Liberal Party

HARKABI, Yehoshafat — *Aluf*, Director of Strategic Studies, Ministry of Defence

HAZAN, Ya'acov — MK, *Mapam* leader

HERZOG, Ya'acov — Director-General, Prime Minister's Office

HOROWITZ, David — Governor, Bank of Israel

KADDAR, Mrs. Lou — Private Secretary to Foreign Minister Meir

KARNI, Nahman — Head, Department of International Co-operation, Ministry of Defence

KIDRON, R. Mordekhai — Director of Armistice Affairs

KOLLEK, Teddy — Director-General, Prime Minister's Office

KOHN, Leo — Adviser to the Foreign Minister

LANDAU, Haim — MK, *Herut*

LESHEM, Moshe — Head, Africa Department, Foreign Ministry

LEVAVI, Arye — Director-General, Foreign Ministry

LEVIN, Ze'ev — Deputy Head, International Department, *Histadrut*

LEWIN, Daniel   Head, Asia Department, Foreign Ministry
LIOR, Yisrael   Military Secretary to Prime Minister Eshkol
LORCH, Netanel   Head, Africa Department, Foreign Ministry
LOURIE, Arthur   Deputy Director-General, Foreign Ministry
LURIE, Ted   Editor, *Jerusalem Post*
MEIR, Mrs. Golda   Cabinet Minister 1949–66; Foreign Minister 1956–66; Prime Minister 1969–
MERIDOR, Ya'acov   MK, *Herut*
MEDZINI, Meron   Lecturer in Political Science, Tel Aviv University; Director, Government Press Office in Jerusalem
MICHAEL, Michael   Head, Research Department, Foreign Ministry
NAVON, Yitzhak   Head, Prime Minister Ben Gurion's Bureau, 1952–63; MK 1963–
NEVO, Yosef   *Aluf Mishne* (res.), *Tzahal*; military affairs commentator
NITZAN, Ya'acov   Assistant Director-General, Foreign Ministry
OREN, Nissan   Lecturer in International Relations, The Hebrew University
PATINKIN, Don   Professor of Economics, The Hebrew University
PELED, Elad   *Aluf (res.)*, *Tzahal*; Director, National Defence College
PERES, Shimon   Deputy Minister of Defence 1959–65, Cabinet Minister 1969–
PRATT, Simha   Head, British Commonwealth Department, Foreign Ministry
RADAI, Haim   Secretary-General, Foreign Ministry
RAFAEL, Gideon   Director-General, Foreign Ministry
RAVIV, Moshe   Political Secretary to Foreign Minister Eban
RIMALT, Elimeleh   MK, General Zionist (Liberal) Party leader
RIVLIN, David   Head, Foreign Minister Eban's Bureau
ROSEN, Pinhas   Minister of Justice 1948–51, 1952–61
ROSENNE, Shabtai   Legal Adviser, Foreign Ministry
RUBIN, Hanan   MK, *Mapam*
SAPHIR, Yoseph   MK, General Zionist (Liberal) Party leader
SCHIFF, Ze'ev   Journalist, *Ha'aretz*
SCHWEITZER, A.   Journalist, *Ha'aretz*
SHAREF, Ze'ev   Cabinet Minister 1966–
SHARETT, Moshe   Foreign Minister 1948–56; Prime Minister 1953–5
SHAPIRA, Haim Moshe   Cabinet Minister 1948–70
SHEK, Ze'ev   Head, West Europe Department, Foreign Ministry
SHERESHEVSKY, S.   Editor of *Ner*, organ of *Ihud*

SHIMONI, Emanuel	Head, Foreign Minister Eban's Bureau
SHIMONI, Ya'acov	Assistant Director-General, Foreign Ministry
SHINNAR, Felix	Head, Reparations Mission to West Germany
SNEH, Moshe	MK; Israel Communist Party leader
TEKOAH, Yoseph	Adviser to the Foreign Ministry
TSUR, Ya'acov	Acting Director-General, Foreign Ministry; Chairman, Jewish National Fund
UZAY, Ya'el	Secretary to the Government
WALLENSTEIN, Arye	Journalist, Reuters (Israel)
YAFEH, Aviad	Head, Prime Minister Eshkol's Bureau
YAHIL, Haim	Director-General, Foreign Ministry
YUVAL, Moshe	Head, Department of Information

B. BOOKS AND PAMPHLETS

Acheson, D., *Present at the Creation* (New York, 1969)

Adams, S., *First Hand Report* (London, 1962)

Almond, G. A., & Coleman, J. (eds.), *The Politics of the Developing Areas* (Princeton, 1960)

Almond, G. A., & Powell, G. B., *Comparative Politics: A Developmental Approach* (Boston, 1966)

American Jewish Committee, *In Vigilant Brotherhood* (New York, 1965)

Avneri, U., *War or Peace in the Semitic Region* (Tel Aviv, 1947), in Hebrew

— *Total War* (Tel Aviv, 1947), in Hebrew

— *Israel Without Zionists: A Plea for Peace in the Middle East* (New York, 1968)

Baer, G., *Population and Society in the Arab East* (London, 1964)

Baker, H. E., *The Legal System of Israel* (Jerusalem, 1968)

Banai, Y., *Unknown Soldiers* (Tel Aviv, 1958), in Hebrew

Baron, S. W., *A Social and Religious History of the Jews*, 3 vols. (New York, 1937)

Bar-Zohar, M., *Suez: Ultra-Secret* (Paris, 1964)

— *Ben Gurion: The Armed Prophet* (Englewood Cliffs, N.J., 1968)

Bauer, Y., *From Diplomacy to Resistance* (Philadelphia, 1970)

Begin, M., *The Revolt: Story of the Irgun* (Tel Aviv, 1964)

Black, J. E., and Thompson, K. W. (eds.), *Foreign Policies in a World of Change* (New York, 1963)

Braybrooke, D., and Lindblom, C. E., *A Strategy of Decision: Policy Evaluation as a Social Process* (New York, 1963)

Brecher, M., *The New States of Asia* (London, 1963)

— *India and World Politics* (London, 1968)

Buber, M., *Te'uda V'ye'ud* (Testimony and Destiny), II, *People and World* (Jerusalem, 1967)

Burgess, P. M., *Elite Images and Foreign Policy Outcomes: A Study of Norway* (Columbus, Ohio, 1969)

Cohen, Bernard C., *The Press and Foreign Policy* (Princeton, N.J., and London, 1963)

Creamer, D., *Israel's National Income 1950–54* (Jerusalem, 1957)

De Rivera, J. H., *The Psychological Dimension of Foreign Policy* (Columbus, Ohio, 1968)

Dinour, B., *et al.* (eds.), *History of the Haganah*, 2 vols. (Tel Aviv, 1956), in Hebrew

Easton, D., *A Framework for Political Analysis* (Englewood Cliffs, N.J., 1965)

Eisenhower, D., *The White House Years: Waging Peace 1956–1961* (London, 1966)

Eisenstadt, S. N., *Israeli Society* (London, 1967)

Eliav, A. L., *Between Hammer and Sickle* (New York, 1969)

Farrell, R. B. (ed.), *Approaches to Comparative and International Politics* (Evanston, Ill., 1966)

— *The Making of Canadian Foreign Policy* (Toronto, 1969)

Fein, L. J., *Politics in Israel* (Boston, 1967)

Finlay, D. J., Holsti, O. R., Fagen, R. R., *Enemies in Politics* (Chicago, 1967)

Fox, A. B., *The Power of Small States* (Chicago, 1959)

Frankel, J., *The Making of Foreign Policy* (London, 1963)

Friedmann-Yellin, N., & Eldad, Y., *The History of Lehi* (Tel Aviv, 1962), in Hebrew

Fuchs, L. H. (ed.), *American Ethnic Politics* (New York, 1968)

Goldmann, N., *Sixty Years of Jewish Life* (New York, 1969)

Graetz, H., *History of the Jews*, 6 vols. (Philadelphia, 1891–8)

Grosser, A., *French Foreign Policy Under de Gaulle* (Boston, 1967)

Halevi, N., & Klinov-Malul, R., *The Economic Development of Israel* (New York, 1968)

Halperin, S., *The Political World of American Zionism* (Detroit, 1961)

Halpern, B., *The Idea of the Jewish State* (Cambridge, Mass., 1961)

Hanoch, G., *Income Differentials in Israel* (Jerusalem, 1961)

Harkabi, Y., *The Arab Position [Stand] in the Israel-Arab Conflict* (Tel Aviv, 1968), in Hebrew

Hattis, S. L., *The Bi-National Idea in Palestine During Mandatory Times* (Haifa, 1970)

Henriques, R., *One Hundred Hours to Suez* (London, 1957)

Hermann, C. F., *Crises in Foreign Policy: A Simulation Analysis* (Indianapolis and New York, 1969)

Herz, J., *International Politics in the Atomic Age* (New York, 1959)

Hilsman, R., *To Move a Nation* (New York, 1967)

Horowitz, D., *State in the Making* (New York, 1953)

— *The Israel Economy* (Tel Aviv, 1954), in Hebrew

Horowitz, D., *The Economics of Israel* (London, 1967)

Hurewitz, J. C., *Middle East Politics: The Military Dimension* (New York, 1969)

— (ed.), *Diplomacy in the Near and Middle East: Vol. 2. A Documentary Record 1914–1956* (Princeton, 1956)

— (ed.), *Soviet-American Rivalry in the Middle East* (New York, 1969)

Institute for Strategic Studies, *The Military Balance* (London, annual, 1963–70)

Israel Defence Forces (Historical Branch), *The History of the War of Liberation* (Tel Aviv, 1959), in Hebrew

Janowsky, O., *Foundations of Israel: Emergence of a Welfare State* (Princeton, 1959)

Kaiser, K., *German Foreign Policy in Transition* (London, 1968)

Kaplan, M., *System and Process in International Politics* (New York, 1957)

Kimche, J. and D., *A Clash of Destinies* (New York, 1960)

Kishon, E., *Unfair to Goliath* (New York, 1969)

— and Gardosh, K. (Dosh), *So Sorry We Won* (Tel Aviv, 1968)

Knorr, K., *The War Potential of Nations* (Princeton, 1956)

— *Military Power and Potential* (Lexington, Mass., 1970)

Kochan, L. (ed.), *The Jews in Soviet Russia Since 1917* (London, 1970)

Kraines, O., *Government and Politics in Israel* (Boston, 1961)

Kreinin, M. E., *Israel and Africa—A Study in Technical Cooperation* (New York, 1964)

Kurzman, D., *Genesis 1948: The First Arab-Israeli War* (Cleveland and New York, 1970)

Lachover, Shmuel (ed.), *Writings of David Ben Gurion: Bibilography, 1910–1959* (Tel Aviv, 1960), in Hebrew

Laqueur, W. Z., *Communism and Nationalism in the Middle East* (New York, 1956)

— *The Struggle for the Middle East* (London, 1969)

Lau-Lavie, N., *Moshe Dayan: A Biography* (London, 1968)

Laufer, L., *Israel and the Developing Countries: New Approach to Cooperation* (New York, 1967)

Lerner, D., *The Passing of Traditional Society* (New York, 1958)

Lorch, N., *The Edge of the Sword: Israel's War of Independence 1947–1949* (New York, 1961)

Macdonald, R. W., *The League of Arab States* (Princeton, 1965)

McDonald, J. G., *My Mission in Israel 1948–1951* (New York, 1951)

Macridis, R. C. (ed.), *Foreign Policy in World Politics* (3rd ed., New York, 1967)

Merrill, J. C., *The Elite Press* (New York, 1968)

Michaely, M., *Foreign Trade and Capital Imports in Israel* (Tel Aviv, 1963), in Hebrew

Mikunis, S., *In the Storm of the Times* (Tel Aviv, 1969), in Hebrew

Millis, S. W. (ed.), *The Forrestal Diaries* (New York, 1951)

Modelski, G., *A Theory of Foreign Policy* (New York, 1962)

Morgenthau, H. J., *In Defence of the National Interest* (New York, 1951)

— *Politics Among Nations* (New York, 1948, 4th ed. 1967)

Nirenstein, A. (ed.), *A Tower from the Enemy* (New York, 1959)

Niv, D., *Battle for Freedom: The Irgun Tzva'i Le'umi*, 3 vols. (Tel Aviv, 1963–7), in Hebrew

North, R. C., Holsti, O. R., Zaninovich, M. G., Zinnes, D. A., *Content Analysis: A Handbook with Applications for the Study of International Crisis* (Evanston, Ill., 1963)

Northedge, F. S. (ed.), *The Foreign Policies of the Powers* (London, 1968)

Nunberg, R., *The Fighting Jew* (New York, 1945)

O'Ballance, E., *The Arab-Israeli War 1948* (New York, 1957)

— *The Sinai Campaign 1956* (London, 1959)

Paige, G. D., *The Korean Decision* (New York, 1968)

Paltiel, K. Z., *The Progressive Party: A Study of a Small Party in Israel* (Jerusalem, 1964), unpublished Ph.D. thesis

Patinkin, D., *The Israel Economy: The First Decade* (Jerusalem, 1960)

Perlmutter, A., *Military and Politics in Israel* (London, 1969)

Plano, J. C., and Olton, R., *The International Relations Dictionary* (New York, 1969)

Polk, W. R., *The United States and the Arab World*, rev. ed. (Cambridge, Mass., and London, 1969)

Prittie. T., *Eshkol: The Man and the Nation* (New York, London, Tel Aviv, 1969)

Rackman, E., *Israel's Emerging Constitution 1948–1951* (New York, 1955) 1961, 2nd ed., 1969)

Ratosh, Y., *Shalom Ivri* (Pax Hebraica), (Tel Aviv, 1967)

Report of a Study Group of the Hebrew University, *Israel and the United Nations* (New York, 1956)

Ringelblum, E., *Notes from the Warsaw Ghetto* (New York, 1958)

Robertson, I., *Crisis: The Inside Story of the Suez Conspiracy* (New York, 1965)

Robinson, J. A., *Congress and Foreign Policy-Making* (rev. ed., Homewood, Ill., 1967)

Rosecrance, R. N., *Action and Reaction in World Politics* (Boston, 1963)

Rosenau, J. N. (ed.), *International Politics and Foreign Policy* (New York, 1961, 2nd ed., 1969)

— (ed.), *Domestic Sources of Foreign Policy* (New York, 1967)

Rosenberg, M. J., et. al., *Attitude Organization and Change* (New Haven, 1960)

Rosenne, S., *Israel's Armistice Agreements with the Arab States: A Juridical Interpretation* (Tel Aviv, 1951)

Sachar, A. L., *A History of the Jews* (New York, 1953)

Safran, N., *The United States and Israel* (Cambridge, Mass., 1963)

Safran, *From War to War: The Arab-Israel Confrontation 1948–1967* (New York, 1969)

Sapin, B., *The Making of United States Foreign Policy* (New York, 1966)

Schwartz, S. M., *Jews in the Soviet Union* (Syracuse, 1951)

Seligman, L. G., *Leadership in a New Nation* (New York, 1964)

Shapiro, Y., *Levi Eshkol, A Biography* (Tel Aviv, 1969), in Hebrew

Silver, A. H., *Vision and Victory* (New York, 1949)

Snyder, R. C., Bruck, H. W., Sapin, B. (eds.), *Foreign Policy Decision-Making* (New York, 1962)

Syrkin, M., *Golda Meir: Woman with a Cause* (New York, 1963)

Teller, J., *The Kremlin, the Jews and the Middle East* (New York, 1957)

Truman, H. S., *Years of Trial and Hope* (New York, 1956)

Vital, D., *The Inequality of States* (Oxford, 1967)

Weizmann, C., *Trial and Error* (New York, 1949)

Whiting, A. S., *China Crosses the Yalu* (Stanford and London, 1968)

Wiesel, E., *The Jews of Silence* (New York, 1966)

Yadin, Y., *Masada* (New York, 1966)

Zerubavel, G. (ed.), *The Book of Palmah*, 2 vols. (Tel Aviv, 1955), in Hebrew

Zidon, A., *Knesset: The Parliament of Israel* (New York, 1968)

— *Israel and the United Nations* (New York, 1956)

C. ARTICLES

'Army', 'War', *The Jewish Encyclopedia*, vols. ii & xii (New York and London, 1902)

'War', *The Universal Jewish Encyclopedia*, vol. 10 (New York, 1943)

'Jews in Armed Forces', in Roth, C. (ed.), *The Standard Jewish Encyclopedia* (New York, 1959)

'Death of Eshkol at 73 Marks Shift from Old Leaders to the Palestine-Born', *New York Times*, 27 February 1969

'Defenders of the Middle East' (series of 6 articles), *The Economist* (London), vols. 158, 159, 24 June–22 July 1950

'Middle East: The War and the Woman', *Time* (New York), 94, 12, 19 September 1969

Akzin, B., 'The Role of Parties in Israeli Democracy', *Journal of Politics*, 17, 4, November 1955

— 'The Knesset', *International Social Science Journal*, 13, 4, 1961

Alexander L. M., 'The Arab-Israeli Boundary Problem', *World Politics*, vi, 3, April 1954

Alger, C., and Brams, S. J., 'Patterns of Representation in National Capitals and Intergovernmental Organizations', *World Politics*, xix, 4, 1967

Alter, R., 'Zionism for the 70's', *Commentary* (New York), 49, 2, February 1970

Antonovsky, A., 'Classification of Forms, Political Ideologies and the Man in the Street', *The Public Opinion Quarterly*, xxx, 1966

Arian, A., 'Voting and Ideology in Israel', *Midwest Journal of Political Science*, x, 1966

Avineri, S., 'The Palestinians and Israel', *Commentary* (New York), 49, 6, June 1970

Avneri, U., 'Unofficial and Unrepresentative but . . . ' *New Middle East* (London), 12, September 1969

Banks, M., 'Systems Analysis and the Study of Regions', *International Studies Quarterly*, 13, 4, December 1969

Begin, M., 'Conceptions and Problems of Foreign Policy', *Ha'Uma* (Tel Aviv), March 1966

Ben-Dor, L., 'Why Choice Falls on Golda Meir', *Jerusalem Post Weekly*, 10 March 1969

Binder, L., 'The Middle East as a Subordinate International System', *World Politics*, x, 3, April 1958

Bloomfield, L. P., and Leiss, A. C., 'Arms Transfers and Arms Control', in Hurewitz, J. C. (ed.), *Soviet–American Rivalry in the Middle East* (New York, 1969)

Boulding, K., 'National Images and International Systems', *The Journal of Conflict Resolution*, iii, 2, June 1959

Bowman, L. W., 'The Subordinate State System of Southern Africa', *International Studies Quarterly*, 12, 3, September 1968

Brecher, M., 'International Relations and Asian Studies: The Subordinate State System of Southern Asia', *World Politics*, xv, 2, January 1963

— 'Elite Images and Foreign Policy Choices: Krishna Menon's View of the World', *Pacific Affairs*, xl, 1 & 2, Spring and Summer 1967

— 'The Middle East Subordinate System and its Impact on Israel's Foreign Policy', *International Studies Quarterly*, xiii, 2, June 1969

Brecher, M., Steinberg, B., Stein, J., 'A Framework for Research on Foreign Policy Behavior', *The Journal of Conflict Resolution*, xiii, 1, March 1969

Cantori, L. J., and Spiegel, S. L., 'International Regions: A Comparative Approach to Five Subordinate Systems', *International Studies Quarterly*, xiii, 4, December 1969

Cohen, Bernard C., 'Mass Communication and Foreign Policy', in Rosenau, J. N. (ed.), *Domestic Sources of Foreign Policy*, New York, 1967

Cohen, S., 'Mrs. Meir Looks Back . . .', *Jerusalem Post*, 16 January 1966

Decalo, S., 'Messianic Influences in Israeli Foreign Policy', *Occasional Papers in Political Science*, 2, University of Rhode Island, 1967

Deutsch, K. W., and Singer, J. D., 'Multipolar Power Systems and International Stability', *World Politics*, xvi, 3, April 1964

Dinitz, S., 'A Tangy Flavor in Mrs. Meir's Views', *New York Times*, 18 March 1969

Easton, D., 'An Approach to the Analysis of Political Systems', *World Politics*, ix, 3, April 1957

Eilon, A., 'Eshkol: Last of the First', *New Outlook* (Tel Aviv), 12, 3 (105), March–April 1969

Eliachar, Elie, 'Israeli Jews and Palestinian Arabs: Key to Arab-Jewish Coexistence', Council of the Sepharadi Community, Jerusalem, 1970

Etzioni, A., 'Alternative Ways to Democracy: The Example of Israel', *Political Science Quarterly*, 74, 2, 1959

Feron, J., 'Yigal Allon Has Supporters, Moshe Dayan Has Disciples', *New York Times Magazine*, 27 April 1969

Flapan, S., 'The Theory of Interceptive War', *New Outlook* (Tel Aviv), 3, 5 (27), April 1960

— 'The Utter Necessity of Peace', ibid., 6, 3 (52), March–April 1963

— 'Beginnings that Bore Fruit', ibid.

— 'Wonderful Logic—All Wrong', ibid., 6, 7 (56), September 1963

Galtung, J., and Ruge, M. H., 'The Structure of Foreign News: The Presentation of the Congo, Cuba, and Cyprus Cases in Four Norwegian Newspapers', *Journal of Peace Research*, 2, 1, 1965

Goldmann, N., 'Military Strength is not Enough', *New Outlook* (Tel Aviv), 6, 5 (54), June 1963

— 'The Greatness of Moshe Sharett', *Jerusalem Post*, 24 June 1966

— 'The Future of Israel', *Foreign Affairs* (New York), 48, 3, April 1970

— 'The Failure of Israeli Foreign Policy' and 'Israeli Foreign Policy, Part II: What Can Be Done', *New Outlook*, 13, 5 (115), June 1970, and 13, 6 (116), July–August 1970

Goodland, T. M., 'A Mathematical Presentation of Israel's Political Parties', *British Journal of Sociology*, 8, September 1957

Gutmann, E., 'Citizen Participation in Political Life: Israel', *International Social Science Journal*, 12, 1, 1960

— 'Some Observations on Politics and Parties in Israel', *India Quarterly*, 17, 1, January–March 1961

— 'Israel', *Journal of Politics*, 25, 3, August 1963

Guttmann, L., 'Whither Israel's Political Parties?', *Jewish Frontier*, 28, 12, December 1961

Haikal, M. H., 'The Political Solution and Armed Conflict', *Al-Ahram* (Cairo), reprod. in *New Outlook* (Tel Aviv), 10, 8 (92), November 1967

Halpern, B., 'The Role of the Military in Israel', in Johnson, J. J. (ed.), *The Role of the Military in Underdeveloped Countries* (Princeton, 1962)

Hellman, D. C., 'The Emergence of an East Asian International Subsystem', *International Studies Quarterly*, 13, 4, December 1969

Herz, J., 'The Territorial State Revisited: Reflections on the Future of the Nation–State', *Polity*, i, 1, 1968

Hodgkin, T., 'The New West Africa State System', *The University of Toronto Quarterly*, xxxi, October 1961

Hoffmann, S., 'Discord in Community: The North Atlantic Area as a Partial International System', *International Organization*, xvii, 3, Summer 1963

Holsti, O. R., 'The Belief System and National Images: A Case Study', *The Journal of Conflict Resolution*, vi, 3, September 1962

— 'The 1914 Case', *American Political Science Review*, lix, June 1965

— 'Cognitive Dynamics and Images of the Enemy: Dulles and Russia', in Finlay, D. J., Holsti, O. R., and Fagen, R. R., *Enemies in Politics* (Chicago, 1967)

Howard, M., and Hunter, R., 'Israel and the Arab World: The Crisis of 1967', *Adelphi Papers* no. 41, The Institute for Strategic Studies (London), October 1967

Israeli Socialist Organization (Matzpen), 'A Collection of Political Statements 1967–1969', Tel Aviv, n.d.

Jervis, R., 'Hypotheses on Misperception', *World Politics*, xx, 3, April 1968

— 'The Costs of the Quantitative Study of International Relations', in Klaus Knorr and James N. Rosenau (eds.), *Contending Approaches to International Politics* (Princeton, 1969)

Kaiser, K., 'The Interaction of Regional Subsystems: Some Preliminary Notes on Recurrent Patterns and the Role of Superpowers', *World Politics*, xxi, 1, October 1968

Kaplan, M. A., 'Some Problems of International Systems Research', *International Political Communities: An Anthology* (New York, 1966)

Kemp, G., 'Strategy and Arms Levels 1945–1967' in Hurewitz, J. C. (ed.), *Soviet–American Rivalry in the Middle East* (New York, 1969)

Kissinger, H. A., 'Domestic Structure and Foreign Policy' in *Conditions of World Order, Daedalus*, xcv, Spring 1966

Klementynowski, L., 'Five Years of New Outlook', *New Outlook* (Tel Aviv), 6, 2 (51), February 1963

Kohn, L., 'The Constituent Assembly of Israel', *Israel and the Middle East*, 1, January 1949

Krivine, D., 'The Jewish Partnership in Israel's Industry', *Jerusalem Post*, 24 October 1969

Lavon, P., 'A Chosen People and a Normal Society', *New Outlook* (Tel Aviv), 5, 2 (42), February 1962

Livneh, E., 'You Can't Sit Down with the Man Who Wants to Kill You', *Jerusalem Post Weekly*, 1 July 1968

Louvish, M., 'Radio News Bulletins Faulty', *Jerusalem Post*, 12 September 1969

McClelland, Charles A., and Ancoli, Anne, 'An Interaction Survey of the Middle East', University of Southern California, Los Angeles, March 1970 (mimeo.)

Modelski, G., 'International Relations and Area Studies: The Case of South East Asia', *International Relations*, ii, April 1961

North, R. C., 'Research Pluralism and the International Elephant', in Klaus Knorr and James N. Rosenau (eds.), *Contending Approaches to International Politics* (Princeton, 1969)

O'Ballance, E., 'The Army of Israel', *Journal of the Royal United Service Institution*, ciii, 1958

Pepper, C. G., 'Hawk of Israel', *New York Times Magazine*, 9 July 1967

Peretz, M., 'The "Compass" Astray', *New Outlook* (Tel Aviv), 12, 8 (108), November 1969

Perlmutter, A., 'The Israel Army in Politics: The Persistence of the Civilian over the Military', *World Politics*, xx, 4, July 1968

Rabin, Y., 'Why We Won the War', *Jerusalem Post Weekly*, 9 October 1967

Rejwan, N., 'Israeli Attitudes to the Arab World', *New Outlook* (Tel Aviv), 9, 5 (80), June 1966

Robinson, J. A., Hermann, C. F., and Hermann, M. G., 'Search Under Crisis in Political Gaming and Simulation', in Pruitt, D. G., and Snyder, R. C. (eds.), *Theory and Research on the Causes of War*, Englewood Cliffs, New Jersey, 1969

Robinson, J. A., and Snyder, R. C., 'Decision-Making in International Politics, in Herbert C. Kelman (ed.), *International Behavior* (New York, 1966)

Rosecrance, R. N., 'Bipolarity, Multipolarity, and the Future', *The Journal of Conflict Resolution*, x, 3, September 1966

Rosenau, J. N., 'Pre-Theories and Theories of Foreign Policy', in Farrell, R. B. (ed.), *Approaches to Comparative and International Politics* (Evanston, Ill., 1966)

— 'Foreign Policy as an Issue-Area', in Rosenau, J. N. (ed.), *Domestic Sources of Foreign Policy* (New York, 1967)

Rosenne, S., 'Basic Elements of Israel's Foreign Policy', *India Quarterly* (Delhi), xvii, 4, October–December 1961

Sager, S., 'The Birth of Parliament in Jerusalem', *Jerusalem Post*, 25 October 1970

Sasson, E., 'The (Occupied) Territories in Exchange for a Genuine Peace', *Ha'aretz*, 26 April 1970

Seliger, M., 'Positions and Dispositions in Israeli Politics', *Government and Opposition*, 3, 4, Autumn 1968

Shazar, Z., 'A Tribute to Ben Gurion on his 70th Birthday', *Davar* (Tel Aviv), 21 October 1956, reprinted in *Jerusalem Post*, 30 September 1966

Shefer, E., 'Israel, The Economic Power of the Middle East', *Yediot Aharonot* (Tel Aviv), 27 February 1970

Shereshevsky, S., 'Peace—Without a Peace Treaty', *New Outlook* (Tel Aviv), 4, 7 (38), July 1961

Sprout, H. and M., 'Environmental Factors in the Study of International Politics', in Rosenau, J. N. (ed.), *International Politics and Foreign Policy* (rev. ed., New York, 1961)

Stock, E., 'Immigration as a Factor in Foreign Policy in the 1950s' (Jerusalem, 1969), unpublished paper

Verba, S., 'Assumptions of Rationality and Non-Rationality in Models of the International System', *World Politics*, xiv, i, October 1961

Waltz, K. N., 'The Stability of a Bipolar World', *Daedelus*, xciii, Summer 1964

Yogev, R. (a pseudonym), 'Lie, Truth and "Dugri" [Frankly]', *Ma'ariv* (Tel Aviv), 13 August 1965

Zartman, W., 'Africa as a Subordinate State System in International Relations', *International Organization*, xxi, 3, 1967

Zinnes, D. A., 'A Comparison of Hostile Behavior of Decision-Makers in Simulate and Historical Data', *World Politics*, xviii, 3, April 1966

— 'The Expression and Perception of Hostility in Prewar Crisis: 1914', in Singer, J. D. (ed.), *Quantitative International Politics: Insights and Evidence* (New York, 1968)

D. JOURNALS, NEWSPAPERS AND PERIODICALS

Adelphi Papers	(London)	monthly
Al Hamishmar	(Tel Aviv)	daily, Hebrew
Ba-mahaneh	(Tel Aviv)	weekly
Bema'arakha	(Jerusalem)	bi-monthly
Commentary	(New York)	monthly
Davar	(Tel Aviv)	daily, Hebrew
Economist	(London)	weekly
Foreign Affairs	(New York)	quarterly
Ha'aretz	(Tel Aviv)	daily, Hebrew
India Quarterly	(New Delhi)	
International Social Science Journal	(Paris)	quarterly
International Studies Quarterly	(Denver)	
Israel Digest	(New York)	fortnightly
Israel's Oriental Problem	(Jerusalem)	monthly
Jerusalem Post	(Jerusalem)	daily
Jewish Chronicle	(London)	weekly
Jewish Frontier	(New York)	monthly
Journal of Conflict Resolution	(Ann Arbor, Michigan)	quarterly
Journal of Politics	(South Bend, Indiana)	quarterly
L'Express	(Paris)	weekly

Le Monde	(Paris)	daily
Ma'ariv	(Tel Aviv)	daily, Hebrew
Mabbat Hadash	(Tel Aviv)	weekly, Hebrew
Midwest Journal of Political Science	(Detroit)	quarterly
Montreal Star	(Montreal)	daily
Ner	(Jerusalem)	monthly, Hebrew
New Middle East	(London)	monthly
New Outlook	(Tel Aviv)	monthly
New York Times	(New York)	daily
New York Times Magazine	(New York)	weekly
Newsweek	(New York)	weekly
Ot	(Tel Aviv)	quarterly, Hebrew
Pacific Affairs	(New York, later Vancouver)	quarterly
Political Science Quarterly	(New York)	
Public Opinion Quarterly	(Princeton)	
Siah	(Tel Aviv)	irregular
The Military Balance	(London)	annual
Time	(New York)	weekly
Weekly News Bulletin	(Jerusalem)	
World Politics	(Princeton)	quarterly
Yediot Aharonot	(Tel Aviv)	daily, Hebrew

Glossary

Agaf Modi'in	Intelligence Branch of the Israel Defence Forces (IDF)
Agudah	see *Agudat Yisrael*
Agudat Yisrael	ultra-orthodox, anti-Zionist movement; its branch in Israel is a political party
Ahdut Ha'avodah	Unity of Labour Party; formed as a coalition of *Po'alei Zion* (*Tziyon*) and other minor Socialist-Zionist parties in *Eretz Yisrael* in 1919. Merged with *Ha-po'el Ha-tza'ir* in 1929/30 to form the *Mapai* party. Faction B, which split from *Mapai* in 1942, assumed the old name *Ahdut Ha'avodah*. In 1954, when it split from *Mapam*, this group assumed the name *Ha-Tenu'ah Le'Ahdut Ha'avodah* (The Movement for the Unity of Labour)
Al-Ahram	Arabic for 'The Pyramids', semi-official Cairo daily newspaper
Al-Fatah	Inverted initials of (Arabic) 'Movement for the Liberation of Palestine'; also Arabic for 'The Conquest', the largest Palestinian guerrilla organization, founded in 1965, based mainly in Jordan
Al Hamishmar	'On Guard', daily newspaper of *Mapam*
Aliya (pl. *Aliyot*)	immigration
Aliya 'B' (*Beth*)	illegal immigration of Jews to Palestine from 1939 to May 1948
Aliya Hadasha	New Immigration, a political and social group representing Central European immigrants to Palestine mainly from Germany in the 1930s
Altalena	arms ship of *Etzel* (IZL), brought to Israel in June 1948; it was shelled by IDF owing to IZL's defiance of Government orders to all underground movements to merge into Israeli army and deliver to it all arms
Aluffim (sing. *aluf*)	Generals; includes ranks from Brigadier-General (*Tat-Aluf*) to Lieutenant-General (*Rav-Aluf*)
Aman	abbr. for *Agaf Modi'in*
Am Oved	Working People, large publishing house associated with the *Histadrut*

Am Yisrael	People of Israel
Anaf Tafkidim Me'uhadim	Special Tasks (Intelligence) Branch of the Police
Assefat Ha-Nivharim	House (Assembly) of Representatives of the pre-1948 *Yishuv*
Atam	abbr. for *Anaf Tafkidim Me'uhadim*
Ba-mahaneh	'In Camp', weekly of IDF
Bilu, in colloquial Hebrew also *Biluim*	first small group from Eastern Europe to renew Jewish immigration to Palestine, in 1880s
Bitzu'ist	equivalent of technocrat, pragmatist in colloquial Hebrew
B'nei Brith	'Sons of the Covenant', an international Jewish fraternal organization
Darga	level or grade of salary
Davar	'Word', daily newspaper of the *Histadrut*
Dereg	rank
Divrei Ha-Knesset	official records of the *Knesset*
Ee-hizdahut	Non-Identification, Hebrew Israeli term for Non-Alignment
Ein breirah	no alternative
Eretz Yisrael	Land of Israel, Palestine
Etzel	abbr. for *Irgun Tzva'i Le'umi* (also IZL); see *Irgun Tzva'i Le'umi*
Feda'iyun or *Feda'iyia*	Arabic for 'self-sacrificer for cause', i.e. command of suicide-squad; first organized by Egyptian army in 1955, later used for all Arab guerillas
Gadna	para-military or pre-military youth organization, organized initially by *Haganah*
Gahal	abbr. for *Gush Herut Liberali*, *Herut*-Liberal bloc, formed by merger of *Herut* and Liberal (formerly General Zionist) parties in 1965
Gahal	abbr. for *Giyyus Hutz La'aretz*; see there
Galei Tzahal	'Waves of *Tzahal*', Army Broadcasting Service
Galut	exile
Goyim	Nations, colloquially used for nations other than Jewish and individual non-Jews
Giyyus Hutz La'aretz	Overseas Recruitment project enlisting Jews from abroad, prospective immigrants
Ha'aretz	'The Land', influential independent daily newspaper
Ha-boker	'The Morning', daily newspaper of Liberal Party, defunct since 1969
Hakhshara	preparation, period of agricultural training prior to immigration and settlement in *kibbutz*

Hadassah	Women's Zionist Organization of America, active in social and medical work, e.g. building hospitals in Israel; also name of major Jerusalem hospital
Haganah	Defence, principal underground military self-defence organization of Palestine Jews, founded in 1921
Ha-Kibbutz Ha'artzi	The National Kibbutz; *kibbutz* movement of *Ha-shomer Ha-tza'ir*, established in 1927
Ha-Kibbutz Ha-me'uhad	The United Kibbutz; *kibbutz* movement—officially non-party, *de facto* mainly of *Ahdut Ha'avodah*, established in 1927; also a publishing house
Hakirya	the quarter housing government offices
Halakha	religious law
Halutziut	pioneering
Ha-modi'a	'The Informer', daily newspaper of *Agudat Yisrael*
Ha-Mosad	The Institute, which deals with all Israeli intelligence activities abroad
Hanhalah	Directorate
Ha-no'ar Ha-oved	Working Youth, the *Histadrut* organization of young workers
Ha'olam Hazeh	small Left-wing party which grew out of weekly magazine of same name
Ha'oved Ha-tziyoni	The Zionist Labourer, workers' organization of General Zionist Party
Ha-po'el Ha-mizrahi	workers' branch of *Mizrahi* Party; separate political party in Israel
Ha-po'el Ha-tza'ir	The Young Labourer, a Zionist-Socialist (non-Marxist) party, founded in 1905; merged with *Ahdut Ha'avodah* in 1929/30 to form *Mapai*; also a weekly by the same name, defunct since 1970
Ha-shomer Ha-tsa'ir	The Young Guard, a Zionist Left-Socialist movement, which established *Ha-Kibbutz Ha'-artzi* and became from 1948 onwards the basis of *Mapam*
Ha-tenu'ah Lema'an Eretz Yisrael Ha-shlemah	Land of Israel Movement, which arose after 1967 War, advocating Jewish rule over the entire territory included in Mandatory Palestine
Ha-tzofeh	'The Scout', daily newspaper of National Religious Party
Ha-Va'ad Ha-Le'umi	The National Council, the elected body representing the Jews of Palestine during the British Mandate

Haver (pl. *haverim*)	comrade, common term used in Israeli socialist movements
Havereinu	'Our Comrades', referring to *Mapai* leadership group, including party's members of the Cabinet and others; supreme informal decision-making group
Havlagah	self-restraint, policy of static defence and abstention from retaliation, referring initially to the 1936–9 disturbances; more generally, advocated by moderate elements in *Yishuv* and *Haganah*
Hasbarah	Information (–Service)
Ha-yom	'Today', daily newspaper of *Gahal*, defunct since 1970
Heder	literally, room, traditional religious primary school
Heker	research; Research Department of Foreign Office
Herut	Freedom Party, formed by Revisionists as legal successor to *Etzel* in 1948; merged with Liberal Party in 1965 to form *Gahal*
Him	abbr. for *Heyl Mishmar*, Guards, organization of older soldiers of *Haganah*, used for defensive missions
Hish	abbr. for *Heyl Sadeh*, Field Troops, the active reserves of *Haganah*
Histadrut	literally, organization; The General Federation of Jewish Labour in *Eretz Yisrael*, founded in 1920
Ihud	Union; a small group of intellectuals who, prior to the establishment of Israel, advocated a bi-national state and Arab-Jewish understanding as the solution to the struggle over Palestine
Irgun Tzva'i Le'umi	National Military Organization, an underground force under Revisionist command, which seceded from *Haganah* in 1938 over the question of the use of extremist methods
IZL	abbr. for *Irgun Tzva'i Le'umi*
Kashrut	Orthodox dietary laws
Kena'anim	The Canaanites, a small group which propounds the generally unaccepted concept of a new Hebrew Nation that should sever links with Jews outside Israel and merge into a Semitic Middle East Federation

Kibbutz (pl. *kibbutzim*)	a collective or communal settlement based primarily on agriculture, in recent years diversifying into industry as well
Kibbutz Galuyot	'Ingathering of the Exiles', the immigration and absorption of Diaspora Jews and their merger into one nation
Kinneret	a lake in north-eastern Israel, Sea of Galilee or Lake Tiberius
Knesset	the Israeli Parliament
Kol Ha'am	'Voice of the People', daily newspaper of the Israel Communist Party (*Maki*)
Kol Yisrael	Voice of Israel, the Israeli Broadcasting Service until 1969, when the name was changed to *Shiddurei Yisrael*, Israel Broadcasts
Kupat Holim	Sick Fund, the medical aid organization of the *Histadrut*
Lamerhav	'Into the Open', daily newspaper of *Ahdut Ha'avodah*
Lehi or *LHI*	abbr. for *Lohamey Herut Yisrael*, Fighters for the Freedom of Israel, an underground Revisionist movement which advocated and practised individual terrorism; founded in 1940 by Avraham Stern (thus also known as Stern Group), it was dissolved in 1951
Lishka	Bureau
Lishkat Ha'avodah	Labour Exchange
Ma'arakh	The Alignment, an electoral alliance formed by *Mapai* and *Ahdut Ha'avodah* in 1965 on eve of Sixth Elections; similar Alignment, in 1969, of Israel Labour Party and *Mapam* on eve of Seventh Elections
Ma'ariv	'Evening News', independent newspaper with widest circulation in Israel
Mabbat Hadash	'New Look', the weekly of *Rafi*, defunct since 1968
Mahal	abbr. for *Midnadvei Hutz La'aretz* (volunteers from abroad) 1948
Maki	abbr. for *Miflaga Kommunistit Yisraelit*, the Israel Communist Party
Mapai	abbr. for *Mifleget Po'alei Eretz Yisrael*, the (social-democratic) Israel Workers Party, largest party in Israel since its foundation; formed in 1929/30 by a union of *Ha-po'el Ha-tza'ir* and *Ahdut Ha'avodah;* it merged with a revived *Ahdut Ha'avodah* and *Rafi* to form the Israel Labour Party in 1968

Mapainik	colloquial, member of *Mapai*
Mapam	abbr. for *Mifleget Po'alim Me'uhedet*, the (Zionist-Marxist) United Workers Party, formed in 1948 by a union of *Ha-shomer Ha-tza'ir* and *Ahdut Ha'avodah*; the latter split off in 1954; *Mapam* joined an Alignment with the Israel Labour Party in 1969
Massada	see *Metzada*; also publishing house
Matzpen	'Compass', organ of the Israeli Socialist Organization, a small revolutionary group which advocates the de-Zionization of Israel and her integration into a socialist Middle East
Metzada	the last stronghold of the Jewish revolt against the Roman Empire in the first century A.D., symbol of resistance and the struggle for independence
Misrad	office
Misrad Ha-hutz	Foreign Office
Mitnadvei Hutz La'aretz	abbr. *Mahal*; volunteers from abroad in 1948 War
Mitun	turning down, recession (economic), usually referring to Israel's economic policy 1964–7
Mizrahi	Orthodox group within the Zionist Movement; in Israel it is the larger of two components of the National Religious Party (NRP or *Mafdal*)
Mo'etzet Ha-po'alot	Council of Working Women, affiliated to the *Histadrut*
Moshav (pl. *moshavim*)	co-operative settlement of smallholders
Nahal	abbr. for *No'ar Halutzi Lohem*, Fighting Pioneering Youth, *Tzahal*'s military-agricultural pioneer unit, established in 1949; used to form and maintain agricultural border settlements, as part of military service
Ner	'Candle', organ of *Ihud*
Olim (sing. *oleh*)	immigrants
Ot	'Letter', journal of the Alignment, founded in 1966, ceased publication in 1967
Oum	abbr. for *Oumot Me'uhadot*
Oumot Me'uhadot	United Nations
Palmah	abbr. for *Plugot Mahatz*, literally, striking platoons or shock troops; the élite unit of *Haganah* and its only formation permanently mobilized, *Palmah* was founded in 1941 and dissolved in 1949 when it was merged into *Tzahal*

Plugot Mahatz	full name of *Palmah*
Po'alei Agudat Yisrael	the religious party representing ultra-orthodox workers
Po'alei Zion (Tzyon)	Workers of Zion, the first Zionist-Socialist party in the Diaspora; Marxist in orientation; its Palestinian branch was formed in 1906 and merged with other small parties to create *Ahdut Ha'avodah* in 1919
Pogrom	massacre, usually referring to periodic raiding, looting, and massacre of Jews in Eastern Europe
Rafi	abbr. for *Reshimat Po'alei Yisrael*, the Israel Workers' List, a *Mapai* splinter group formed by Ben Gurion and Peres in 1965; it merged with *Mapai* and *Ahdut Ha'avodah* in 1968 to form the Israel Labour Party
Rakah	abbr. for *Reshima Kommunistit Hadasha*, New Communist List, anti-Zionist party which split from *Maki* in 1965; Moscow-oriented, it is composed mainly of Arabs
Rama	abbr. for *Rosh Mifkada Artzi*, the (political) Head of National Command of the *Haganah*
Ramatkal	abbr. for *Rosh Ha-Mateh Ha-klali*, Chief of the General Staff of *Haganah* and, since 1948, of *Tzahal*; Commander-in-Chief of the Israel Defence Forces
Rikuz	centralization, concentration
Sabra	literally, prickly pear; name used for Israelis born in Israel
Sareinu	'Our Ministers', referring to *Mapai* Cabinet Ministers
Sefer Ha-Hukkim	Book of Laws, the official collection of laws enacted by the *Knesset*
Segel	staff
Shabat	Sabbath
Shalom Ivri	'Pax Hebraica', Hebrew Peace, short-lived minuscule Israeli pressure group advocating integration of Israel into the Semitic world
She'arim	'Gates', daily newspaper of *Po'alei Agudat Yisrael*
Sherut Bitahon (Klali)	the (General) Security Service, responsible for all counter-intelligence within Israel
Shiddurei Yisrael	Israel Broadcasts; successor name to *Kol Yisrael* since 1969
Shin Bet	abbr. for *Sherut Bitahon*
Shtetl	(Yiddish) small Jewish town or village in Eastern Europe

Siah   abbr. for *Smol Israeli Hadash*, the Israeli New
                                Left, a small group formed at the end of 1967;
                                it advocates two independent states in historic
                                Palestine, one Jewish, one Arab
Sikkum   summary; (Foreign Office) summaries of top-
                                level discussions
Solel Boneh   large, *Histadrut*-owned contracting, construc-
                                tion, and industrial complex
Taknon Ha-Knesset   the *Knesset* rules of procedure
Torah   The Law, usually referring to Pentateuch
Tzahal   abbr. for *Tzva Ha-Haganah Le-Yisrael*, the
                                Defence Forces of Israel or Israel Defence
                                Forces; established under the Defence Service
                                Act of 1949
Tze'irim   the young ones
Va'ad Le'umi   see *Ha-Va'ad Ha-Le'umi*
Va'adat Minuyim   Appointments Committee (o. the Foreign
                                Office)
Vatikim   literally, veterans; used to designate 'old-
                                timers', for example in an occupation, long-
                                established settlers, etc.
Yediot   short for *Yediot Aharonot*, in common usage
Yediot Aharonot   'Latest News', independent, daily evening
                                newspaper
Yeshivat Boker   Morning Meeting, held during the first decade
                                of the Foreign Office
Yishuv   literally, Community, refers to Palestine
                                Jewry during the British Mandate 1920–48

Abbreviations

AFP	Agence France Presse
AID	Agency for International Development
AJC	American Jewish Committee
AP	Associated Press
BG	David Ben Gurion
CENTO	Central Treaty Organization (formerly the Baghdad Pact)
COS	Chief of Staff, Duties Branch, at GHQ
CPP	Communist Party of Palestine
DLF	Development Loan Fund
EEC	European Economic Community
FAO	Food and Agriculture Organization
GATT	General Agreement on Tariffs and Trade
GHQ	General Headquarters
GNP	Gross National Product
GSO	General Staff Officer
IBRD	International Bank for Reconstruction and Development (World Bank)
IDF	Israel Defence Forces
ILO	International Labour Organization
IMF	International Monetary Fund
INA	International News Agency
JAPSC	Jewish Agency Public Service College
JDC	Joint Distribution Committee
JTA	Jewish Telegraph Agency
MAC	Mixed Armistice Commission
MEDO	Middle East Defence Organization
MK	Member of the *Knesset*
NATO	North Atlantic Treaty Organization
NRP	National Religious Party
OAS	Organization of American States
OAU	Organization of African Unity
OECD	Organization for Economic Co-operation and Development
OEEC	Organization for European Economic Co-operation
ONUC	Organisation des Nations Unies au Congo
PAGY	*Po'alei Agudat Yisrael*
PLO	Palestine Liberation Organization
PR	Proportional Representation
SEATO	South-East Asia Treaty Organization

UJA	United Jewish Appeal
UN	United Nations
UNCTAD	United Nations Conference on Trade and Development
UNEDO	United Nations Economic Development Organization
UNEF	United Nations Emergency Force
UNSCOP	United Nations Special Committee on Palestine
UNTSO	United Nations Truce Supervisory Organization
UP	United Press
WZO	World Zionist Organisation
ZOA	Zionist Organization of America

NAME INDEX

SUBJECT INDEX